Psychology

PRINCIPLES IN PRACTICE

SPENCER A. RATHUS

HOLT, RINEHART AND WINSTON

Harcourt Brace & Company

Austin • New York • Orlando • Atlanta • San Francisco • Boston • Dallas • Toronto • London

STAFF CREDITS

Executive Editor
Sue Miller

Managing Editor
Jim Eckel

Project Editor
Nicole Sherbert

Art, Design and Photo
Richard Metzger
Art Director

Robin Bouvette
Designer

Sally Bess
Jennifer Dix
Sonya Mendeke
Design Team

Peggy Cooper
Photo Research Manager

Lisa Hastay
Elinor Strot
Photo Research Team

Sam Dudgeon
Staff Photographer

Victoria Smith
Photography Specialist

Greg Geisler
Image Services Director

Debra Schorn
Design File Management Administrator

Jane Dixon
Linda Wilbourn
Image Services Staff

Production
Gene Rumann
Production Manager

Belinda Barboza
Adrian Bardin
Kim Anderson
Shirley Cantrell
Media Production Team

Multimedia
Armin Gutzmer
Manager of Training and Technical Support

Cathy Kuhles
Technical Assistant

Editorial Permissions
Lee Noble
Permissions Editor

Editorial Development
Visual Education Corporation

For acknowledgments, see page 584, which is an extension of the copyright page.

Printed in the United States of America

ISBN 0-03-015449-9

12 13 032 05 04 03

Teacher Consultant

Jim Matiya
Carl Sandburg High School
Orland Park, IL

Academic and Teacher Reviewers

Lydia Fitzgerald
Faribault High School
Faribault, MN

Dale Kinney
Ralston Senior High School
Ralston, NE

Dr. Aida Hurtado
University of California,
Santa Cruz
Social Psychology

Dr. Michela Gallagher
University of North Carolina,
Chapel Hill
Experimental/Biological and
Cognitive Psychology

Dr. Keith D. White
University of Florida
Biological Psychology

Dr. David Cohen
University of Texas, Austin
Clinical Psychology

Dr. Terry Davidson
Purdue University
Behavioral Neuroscience

Dr. Jeremiah Faries
Northwestern University
Cognitive Psychology

Dr. Arthur Staats
University of Hawaii
Cognitive Psychology,
Intelligence

Dr. Julie Hubbard
University of Delaware
Child Clinical Psychology

Dr. Anne C. Fletcher
University of North Carolina at
Greensboro
Developmental Psychology,
Adolescence

Dr. Thomas Bradbury
University of California,
Los Angeles
Developmental Psychology

Dr. Daniel N. McIntosh
University of Denver
Social Psychology

Calvin P. Garbin, Ph.D.
University of Nebraska
Quantitative and Research
Methods

Dr. Nancy Russo
Arizona State University
Social Psychology, Gender

Dr. Kevin Williams
State University of New York,
Albany
Behavioral Psychology

Dr. Timothy Anderson
Vanderbilt University
Abnormal Psychology

Dr. Bertram Malle
University of Oregon
Social Psychology

Contents

Contents   **v**

FEATURES ■ **Case Studies and Other True Stories**

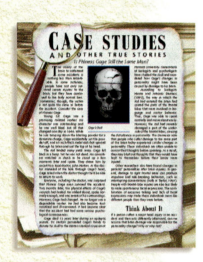

■ Exploring Diversity

■ Psychology in the World Today

■ Readings in Psychology

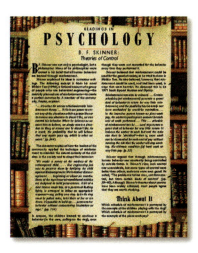

REFERENCE ■ Charts and Graphs

SKILLS HANDBOOK

The study of psychology involves more than simply memorizing a series of names and terms. You will need to develop a variety of critical thinking skills to fully grasp the range of concepts and methods used in the study of psychology. As your study skills improve, your understanding of the science of psychology will improve as well. The lessons included in this Skills Handbook will equip you to improve your study methods, build your vocabulary, and sharpen your research and writing abilities. The final section will help you to understand and navigate the Internet and the World Wide Web.

1 Identifying the Main Idea

The ability to identify and understand the main idea is crucial to understanding any complex subject. This is particularly true of the study of psychology because the significant theories and methods may sometimes get lost among numerous detailed examples.

TRUTH OR fiction?

Read the following statements about psychology. Do you think they are true or false? You will learn whether each statement is true or false as you read the chapter.

- Psychologists never guess about the answers to the questions they ask.
- You have to do a study more than once to be sure its results are valid.
- Asking the students in your psychology class for their opinions on a topic is a good way to figure out how people in the larger community feel about that topic.
- Some psychological studies take years or even decades to complete.
- Taking a pill that does not contain any medicine might have the same effects as taking one that does.
- Psychologists sometimes have to deceive participants in a study.

TRUTH OR fiction REVISITED

It is not true that psychologists never guess about the answers to the questions they ask. After psychologists ask a research question, they form a hypothesis, or an educated guess, about the answer. Psychologists do have reasons for their hypotheses, however, and once they have formed their hypotheses, they test them.

Psychology: Principles in Practice is designed to help you focus on the main ideas in psychology. The "Truth or Fiction?" statements that introduce each chapter—accompanied with the "Truth or Fiction revisited" statements throughout the chapter—are intended to guide your reading. The "Thinking About Psychology" questions that close each section are intended to help you gauge whether or not you have grasped the main ideas of the section. You will still need to focus your reading, however. Applying these basic guidelines will help you identify the main ideas in whatever subject you read.

How to Identify the Main Idea

1. **Read introductory material.** Read the title and the introduction, if there is one. They often indicate the main ideas to be covered.

2. **Have questions in mind.** As you read, formulate questions about the subject that you think may be answered by the material. Having such questions in mind will help you focus your reading.

3. **Note the outline of ideas.** Pay attention to any headings or subheadings. They will provide a basic outline of the major ideas. You may also want to write down this outline and use it to guide your reading.

4. **Distinguish supporting details.** As you read, distinguish sentences providing supporting details from the general statements they support. A series of examples may lead to a conclusion that restates or reinforces a main idea.

2 Identifying Cause and Effect

Identifying and understanding cause-and-effect relationships is one essential concept in the study of psychology. It is necessary to investigate not only what caused a certain behavior or feeling to occur, but also what emotions, thoughts, and behaviors may happen as a result. To help determine the answers, psychologists ask such questions as: What is the individual's or group's background? Is this an isolated incident or does the behavior indicate a pattern? What external events may contribute to this type of feeling or pattern of behavior? Could biological processes be involved in producing this type of behavior?

How to Identify Cause and Effect

1. **Look for clues.** Certain words and phrases are immediate clues to the existence of a cause-and-effect relationship. Examples of such clue words and phrases are listed here.
2. **Identify the relationship.** Read carefully to identify how concepts are related. Writers do not always clearly state the link between cause and effect.
3. **Check for complex connections.** Beyond the immediate cause-and-effect relationship, check for other, more complex connections. Note, for instance, whether (1) there were additional causes of a given effect, (2) a cause had multiple effects, and (3) these effects themselves caused further events.

CLUE WORDS AND PHRASES

CAUSE	EFFECT
as a result of	aftermath
because	as a consequence
brought about	depended on
inspired	gave rise to
led to	originated from
produced	outcome
provoked	outgrowth
spurred	proceeded from
the reason	resulting in

Applying Your Skill

Review the first example in the diagram below, taken from the case study on page 65. The diagram demonstrates an important cause-and-effect relationship.

In some instances, an effect may also become a cause. The second example below, taken from page 425, demonstrates this concept.

Practicing Your Skill

From your knowledge of psychology, choose a sequence of feelings, thoughts, and behaviors that may share a cause-and-effect relationship. Draw a simple cause-and-effect chart showing the relationship between these feelings, thoughts, and behaviors. Then write a paragraph that explains the connections.

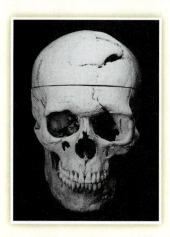

Cause: Phineas Gage experiences severe physical trauma to the underside of the frontal lobes of his cerebral cortex.

Effect: Gage's personality changes. He becomes ill-mannered, foul-mouthed, and undependable.

Cause: A person experiences a very depressing situation.

Effect/Cause: The depressing situation may reduce the activity of noradrenaline in the brain.

Effect: The chemical changes in the brain may worsen the depression.

3 Studying Primary and Secondary Sources

There are many sources of firsthand psychological information, including self-reports, recorded and videotaped interviews, diaries, letters, photographs, laboratory data, and other documented research results. These are examples of *primary sources*. Primary sources are considered valuable tools for studying psychology because they offer a close-up view of clinical experiences and research results.

Secondary sources are descriptions or interpretations of events written after the events have occurred by persons who did not participate in the actual events. Textbooks, such as *Psychology: Principles in Practice*, biographies, encyclopedias, and other reference works are examples of secondary sources. Writers of secondary sources have the advantage of knowing what theories and research results were later proved or disproved. They are in a position to provide a broader perspective than that available to one person at a specific time.

How to Study Primary and Secondary Sources

1. **Study the material carefully.** Consider the nature of the material. Is it anecdotal (telling a story) or scientific? Is the information presented verbally or visually? Is the material upon which the conclusion was made based on firsthand information or on the accounts of others? Note the main ideas and supporting details. They are often important clues about the source of the material.
2. **Consider the audience.** Ask yourself: For whom was this information meant originally? For example, a case history that was written for and published in a professional journal would probably differ in style and perhaps also in content from a case history relayed orally by a professor during a class lecture.
3. **Check for bias.** Watch for words or phrases that signal the author's one-sided view of a person, event, or concept.
4. **When possible, compare sources.** Study more than one source on a topic, if available. Comparing sources gives you a more complete, balanced account of a subject.

Practicing Your Skill

1. What distinguishes secondary sources from primary sources?
2. What advantage do secondary sources have over primary sources?
3. Why is it important to consider the origin of a source?

4 Building Vocabulary

The study of psychology may challenge your reading comprehension. As you read *Psychology: Principles in Practice* you will encounter new and unfamiliar words. With regular effort, however, you can master these new terms and turn the study of psychology into an opportunity to enlarge and improve your vocabulary. The steps listed below will help you accomplish this.

How to Build Vocabulary

1. **Identify unusual words.** As you read the chapters, list any words that you cannot immediately define or pronounce.
2. **Study context clues.** Study the sentence and paragraph in which you find the new term. The setting in which the word appears, or the *context*, may give you clues to the word's meaning by providing examples or definitions of more familiar words that have the same meanings.
3. **Use the dictionary.** Use a dictionary to learn how to say the words on your list and to look up their exact definitions.
4. **Review new vocabulary.** Be on the lookout for ways to use the new words in homework assignments, classroom discussions, or in ordinary conversation. The best way to master a new word is to use it.

Practicing Your Skill

1. Define *context*. How can a word's context provide clues to its meaning?
2. As you read the rest of this Skills Handbook, list any unusual or unfamiliar words that you encounter. Write down what you think each word means, then check your guesses against the dictionary's definition or the Glossary in the back of the book.

5 Creating an Outline

An outline is a tool for organizing information. It is a logical summary that presents the main points of what you plan to communicate. Creating an outline is an important part of writing a paper. An outline enables you to highlight the main ideas you intend to express in your paper and list the supporting details you want to cover. An outline is only a skeletal structure for the final piece of writing. However, the writing process itself becomes much easier when the outline on which an essay is based is thorough and well organized.

How to Create an Outline

1. **Order your material.** Decide what specific information you want to emphasize. Then order or classify your research material with that focus in mind. Determine what information belongs in the introduction, what should be in the body of your paper, and what to reserve for the conclusion.

2. **Identify main ideas.** After organizing your material, identify the main ideas you plan to highlight in each section. These topics will be the main headings of your outline.

3. **List supporting details.** Determine the important details or facts that support each main idea. Rank and list them as subheadings, using additional levels of subheadings as necessary. Subheadings must come in pairs, at the least. That is, no *As* without *Bs*, no *1s* without *2s*, and so forth.

4. **Put your outline to use.** Structure your essay or report according to your outline. Each main heading, for instance, might form the basis of a topic sentence to begin a paragraph. Subheadings would then make up the content of the paragraph. In a longer paper, each subheading might be the main idea of a paragraph.

Practicing Your Skill

Read Section 1 in Chapter 3. Create an outline to organize the complex biological concepts described in the section. Then use the outline to write a brief essay about the structure and functions of the nervous system.

Using PQ4R

I. What is classical conditioning?
   A. Who is Ivan Pavlov?
   B. What do US, UR, CR, and CS mean?
   C. How is adaptation to the environment related to conditioning?
      1. What is a taste aversion?
      2. What is extinction?
      3. What is spontaneous recovery?
      4. How do generalization and discrimination relate to classical conditioning?
   D. What are some applications of classical conditioning?
      1. What are flooding and systematic desensitization?
      2. What is counterconditioning?
      3. How does the bell-and-pad method for bed-wetting work?

6 Conducting Library Research

To complete research papers or special projects related to the field of psychology, you may need to use resources other than this textbook. Conducting thorough research generally requires using the resources available in a library.

Finding Information

To locate a particular book in a library, you need to know how libraries organize their materials. Books of fiction are alphabetized according to the last name of the author. To classify nonfiction and reference books, libraries use the Dewey decimal system and the Library of Congress system. Both systems assign each book a *call number* that tells you its classification.

To find the book's call number, look in the library's *card catalog.* The catalog lists books by author, by title, and by subject. Finding a particular book is simple if you know the author's name or the book's title. If you do not have this information, however, or if you just want to find some books about a general subject, you can look up that subject heading. Some libraries have computerized card catalogs, which can make searching for specific information even easier.

Librarians can help you become familiar with using the card catalog and can direct you to a book's location within the library. They can also suggest additional resources.

Using Resources

In a library's reference section, you will find encyclopedias, indexes to magazines and newspapers, specialized dictionaries, atlases, and abstracts. Early in your research, encyclopedias will often be an effective resource. Encyclopedias include articles explaining basic psychological concepts and methods; historical information; biographical sketches of important figures in the field of psychology; and cross-references to articles in such related fields as medicine, biology, anthropology, and sociology.

Libraries also house specialized dictionaries of psychological terms and concepts. These dictionaries define and describe the more important terms, movements, people, and theories you may wish to include in your research.

Periodical indexes can also be extremely useful. They are especially helpful if you are looking for relevant, up-to-date articles containing facts and statistics about a particular subject. *The Readers' Guide to Periodical Literature*, which lists articles published in magazines, can be extremely useful. Additionally, *the New York Times Index* catalogs all news stories published in the *the New York Times*, the U.S. daily newspaper with perhaps the most extensive coverage of current events and issues.

Practicing Your Skill

1. How are books of fiction classified? In what two ways do libraries classify nonfiction and reference books?
2. What kinds of references contain information about terms used in psychology?
3. Where would you look to find recent coverage of a controversial new theory?

7 *Writing About Psychology*

Psychology: Principles in Practice provides you with numerous writing opportunities. Chapter and unit reviews contain writing exercises that give you the chance to focus your writing on a particular aspect of psychology.

How to Write with a Purpose

Always keep your basic purpose for writing in mind. This purpose may be to analyze, to evaluate, to synthesize, to inform, to persuade, or to hypothesize. Your purpose will determine the most appropriate approach to take.

Every purpose for writing suggests its own form, tone, and content. The point of view you adopt will shape what you write, as will your intended audience.

Each writing opportunity provided in this textbook will have specific directions about what and how to write. Regardless of your subject matter, you should follow certain basic steps in the writing process. The following guidelines can help you plan and improve your writing.

How to Write a Paper

1. **Identify your purpose in writing.** Read the directions carefully to identify the purpose for your writing. Keep that purpose in mind as you plan and write your paper.
2. **Consider your audience.** When writing for a specific audience, choose the tone and style that will best communicate your message.
3. **Create an outline.** Think and plan before you begin writing your first draft. Organize themes, main ideas, and supporting details into an outline.
4. **Collect information.** Conduct research, if necessary. Your writing will be more effective if you have many details at hand.
5. **Write a first draft.** Remember to use your outline as a guide when you attempt the first draft. Each paragraph should express a single main idea, or a set of related ideas, with details for support. Be careful to clearly demonstrate the relationships between ideas, and to use proper transitions—sentences that build connections between paragraphs.

6. **Review and edit.** Revise and reorganize your draft as needed to make your points clearly. Improve your sentences by varying their length and structure, by omitting clichés and substituting more precise language, and by adding appropriate adjectives and adverbs. Then check for correct spelling, punctuation, and grammar.

7. **Write your final version.** Prepare a neat, clean final version. Appearance is important; while it may not affect the quality of your writing itself, it can affect the way your effort is perceived.

Practicing Your Skill

1. What factor, more than any other, should affect how and what you write? Why?

2. Why is it important to consider the audience for whom you are writing?

3. What steps should you take to edit a first draft? Why is this important?

8 *Using the Internet*

The Internet is a vast, world-wide collection of computers linked by telephone lines that convey and receive data. Millions of information sources are found on the Internet, in no order and with no one person or organization in control of the content. Government agencies, universities, libraries, non-profit and for-profit organizations, businesses, and individuals put the information "out there" for anyone's use—usually for free.

Data on almost every conceivable subject is available to anyone who has access to a computer, an Internet provider—that is, a service company that can hook up the computer to the system—a telephone jack, and a modem. A *modem* is an internal or external device connected to your computer that enables your computer to transmit and receive information electronically via telephone lines.

The World Wide Web

Several attempts have been made to organize the vast amounts of varied information available on the Internet. One such effort is the World Wide Web. The Web was designed to make all on-line information part of one matrix of interconnected documents and services. Almost every resource available on the Internet can be accessed via the World Wide Web.

Information on the Web is organized according to category and is stored in a particular, unique location. The location is known as an address, or *URL*—short for Universal Resource Locator—on the Internet. Software programs such as Netscape or Mosaic, called *Web browsers*, enable a computer to locate addresses and to search subject categories anywhere on the Internet, including the World Wide Web.

Web Pages

Web URLs share certain basic characteristics because all Web documents are created using the same computer language, HyperText Markup Language, or HTML. A Web URL always begins with the four letters *http*, which simply states that the address was created in HTML. Your Web browser can go directly to any URL that you type into its locator box.

All Internet addresses indicate the *domain*, or the nature of the information's source. These sources are indicated by suffixes on the address. The suffixes include the following: *gov* for government agencies; *com* for a business or commercial enterprises; *org* for nonprofit organizations; and *edu* for educational institutions.

Your browser is like a taxi that does not recognize landmarks, but finds its way only by specific addresses. If you know the address you need, getting there is a snap. Just be sure to type the address exactly as you have seen it, including strange-looking symbols, spaces, and upper- and lower-case letters. Give it an incorrect address—even a "dot" out of place—and you will receive a message on your screen saying "Cannot retrieve."

But where will your browser take you?

To a Web *homepage,* the opening page of a Web document. Think of it as a table of contents. Web pages contain underlined or highlighted words and images called *hyperlinks.* Clicking on a hyperlink will take you to a related or "linked" Web page, either within this site or in another location on the Internet. Hyperlinks function in a nonlinear fashion. By clicking on hyperlinks, you can "surf the Net," traveling to a seemingly unlimited number of Web sites.

Navigating the Web

You can navigate your way around the Web in three ways:

- by clicking on the hyperlinks that interest you, and exploring the Web. This is commonly referred to as "browsing."
- by using search tools, primarily keyword searches, that identify your subject category.
- by commanding the browser to go directly to a specific Internet resource that may be in another collection of organized data.

It is important to write down any potential sources of information in a log. This will enable you to easily find the URL again and command your browser to take you there.

The best way to familiarize yourself with the intuitive nature of the Internet is to spend some time exploring the Web—clicking on hyperlinks, and finding your way back again. If your time on the Internet is limited, however, and you need to conduct research on a specific topic, you will need to focus your search.

A broad search will give you a sense of just how many documents are related to your subject, but it will not tell you whether these documents will be useful or relevant to your particular research project. A search of the key term *psychology*, for example, yields over 60,000 relevant documents. Rather than scanning an overwhelming amount of data, you can limit your initial search by these two methods:

- Lists of lists, or *menus.* Use a keyword search (or the URL, if you have it) to go directly to an on-line reference library, such as the Library of Congress, which lists Web sites by subject and gives their URLs.
- Clearinghouse lists. These are roughly equivalent to on-line encyclopedias merged with directories.

A Trial Run

Let's say you want to research a paper on the following topic: "The Effect of Weather on People's Moods." A hunch told you that the rainy day was putting you and your friends in bad moods. The following steps provide an example of how you might successfully navigate the Web and complete your research.

1. Decide on your topic: moods and weather.
2. Determine your research needs. Gather no more and no less information than is necessary to complete your project.
3. Create a list of possible keywords, for example, climate, rain, depression, happiness, and even rainy-weather cities, such as Seattle and London.

You may find a promising Web site containing hyperlinks that lead you to a Web page in the "health" category. Here you may find a description of "seasonal affective disorder." This sounds like your topic, only it is more about seasons (winter) than rain. Still, it's too close to ignore. So you can go "surfing."

Clicking on one hyperlink may not reveal anything relevant. Another hyperlink on the next "page," however, may tell you about light therapy treatment, and refer you to a hospital research program using light therapy in London.

At this point, you may need to stop and evaluate your approach. Ask yourself: Am I now on a fascinating but completely irrelevant side alley? If you answer yes, which, at some point in time, will happen, you will need to reassess your topic.

Ask yourself whether your topic has changed, and if so, do you want to get it back on your original track or follow this somewhat different and, it seems, more focused direction? Often, the process of researching reveals that a selected topic was too vague at the start.

Sometimes, however, you do not have the option of altering or narrowing your topic, either because it was assigned or because you committed yourself to it. What can you do? Don't get frustrated, there are still several options.

- Try other approaches. University psychology departments, research facilities, and professional psychological associations worldwide usually have Web sites.
- Try using another Web browser. All software packages are not identical. Some are more powerful than others and will retrieve more data, or more specific data.

Above all, be patient with yourself. You are developing a new and complex skill. It takes practice, experience, and faith in your own intuition to develop truly efficient on-line research skills.

UNIT 1

INTRODUCTION TO
PSYCHOLOGY

CHAPTERS

1 *What Is Psychology?*

2 *Psychological Methods*

WHAT IS PSYCHOLOGY?

Chapter 1

Objectives

1 Identify the goals of psychology, and explain how psychology is a science.

2 Describe the work done by psychologists according to their areas of specialization.

3 Explain the historical background of the study of psychology.

4 Describe the six main contemporary perspectives in psychology.

A DAY IN THE LIFE

 The alarm shook Linda out of a dream. Shafts of light pierced the window blinds in her room. She shut off the alarm, rose, and raised the blinds. A world of color splashed in. As she stifled a morning sneeze, Linda recalled that yesterday, in psychology class, her teacher had challenged the students to touch their noses with their eyes closed. Linda had succeeded, but Todd had jokingly poked himself in the eye. She remembered the incident and laughed. Her laughter stopped when she remembered that she was going to have a math test today. Then she relaxed. "No sweat; I'm really good at math," she thought. And after school, she had plans to meet some friends. "I wonder if Marc will be there," she pondered. (Linda thought Marc was very attractive.) She reflected sadly that Nick would not be there. Nick had a drug problem, and his parents had convinced him to go to a treatment center for help. Linda sighed to herself, then turned away from the window and went to the kitchen for breakfast. She was hungry.

Sleeping and waking, our perceptions of the worlds within and around us, memory, emotion, attractions between people—these are some of the topics of interest to psychologists. The kinds of questions that psychologists might ask about Linda's thoughts and behavior this morning include the following:

- How did the alarm wake Linda? What happened inside her brain that woke her?
- Linda raised the blinds and her morning became alive with color. How are we able to sense the world outside? Why do most of us see colors while some of us cannot see them?
- Linda touched her nose when her eyes were closed. What body senses enable us to know where our body parts are and what we are doing when our eyes are closed?
- Linda is good at math. Why do some students do well in some high school classes but struggle in others? How are factors such as motivation and intelligence involved?
- Linda was looking forward to meeting her friends. Why do most of us seek friendship? How is our behavior influenced by other people?
- Linda thought Marc was attractive. What is attraction? What is love? Why do we find some people attractive and others less so?
- Nick was involved with drugs. How do drugs affect people psychologically? In what way are drugs harmful?
- Linda was hungry for breakfast. What makes us hungry? Why are some people overweight and others dangerously thin?

Psychologists are so intrigued by these types of questions that they make the attempt to answer them their life's work.

Key Terms

- psychology
- behavior
- cognitive activity
- theory
- basic research
- introspection
- structuralism
- functionalism
- behaviorism
- Gestalt psychology
- psychoanalysis
- biological perspective
- cognitive perspective
- humanistic perspective
- psychoanalytic perspective
- learning perspective
- social-learning theory
- sociocultural perspective

Read the following statements about psychology. Do you think they are true or false? You will learn whether each statement is true or false as you read the chapter.

- Psychologists have very little interest in studying people's emotions.
- A book on psychology, with content similar to that of this textbook, was written by Aristotle more than 2,000 years ago.
- In the Middle Ages, some innocent people were drowned as a way of proving that they were not possessed by the devil.
- Some psychologists view our strategies for solving problems as mental programs operated by our very personal computers—our brains.
- Sigmund Freud's theories continue to influence psychology today.

Why Study *1* Psychology?

What do you hope to learn from the study of psychology? Perhaps you hope to gain a better understanding of why people act as they do, or more specifically, why *you* act as you do. Or perhaps you want to learn more about your thoughts and feelings; in doing so, you might discover more effective ways to handle, or help others handle, the stresses of daily life. Whether your reason is general or specific, the study of psychology will give you new ways to look at and interpret your world and the people who inhabit it.

Behavior and Mental Processes

Psychology is the scientific study of behavior and mental processes. **Behavior** is any action that other people can observe or measure. For example, Linda awakened, rose from her bed, raised the blinds, and laughed. All of these activities are behaviors. All are observable by other people.

Behavior also includes activities such as walking and talking, pressing a switch, turning left or right, sleeping, eating, and drinking. Behavior even includes automatic body functions such as heart rate, blood pressure, digestion, and brain activity. Behavior can be measured by simple observation or by laboratory instruments. Brain activity, for example, can be measured by scientific instruments such as the electroencephalograph (EEG).

Linda also engaged in private mental processes, or **cognitive activities**. These activities include dreams, perceptions, thoughts, and memories. For example, Linda was dreaming when her alarm rang. Brain waves that indicate dreaming can be measured, but dreaming itself is a private mental process—dreams are known only to the dreamer. Linda also perceived a world of color. Activity of the cells in a person's eyes can be measured as they respond to color, but only Linda could see her own mental image of the world. Linda laughed as she remembered the nose-touching psychology lesson. Memories, too, are private mental processes.

Psychologists are also interested in studying people's emotions, or feelings. Emotions can affect both behavior and mental processes. For example, Linda experienced a moment of anxiety when she remembered her math test, and she felt happiness at the thought of seeing Marc. Perhaps Linda's heart raced a bit when she thought about the test or about Marc. Her heart activity was an example of behavior, but her thoughts about the math test and about Marc were private mental processes. We would be unable to observe or measure Linda's thoughts directly. But if she told us about them, we would be observing a behavior—Linda *telling* us about her thoughts.

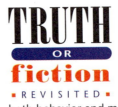
It is not true that psychologists have very little interest in studying people's emotions. Psychologists know that emotions are important because they can influence both behavior and mental processes.

The Goals of Psychology

In general, scientists seek to observe, describe, explain, predict, and control the events they study. Psychologists have the same goals. They observe and describe behavior and mental processes to better understand them. A better understanding of behavior enables psychologists to explain, predict, and control behavior.

An example of how psychologists apply the goals of psychology can be seen in the case of Buffalo Bills placekicker Scott Norwood. Norwood had toiled for many years perfecting his techniques and preparing for the day when he would play in a Super Bowl. For several hours a day, he practiced and improved his form on the field. He kicked field goals from various distances and in all extremes of weather. Then, in 1991, he got his chance—the Bills and the New York Giants met in the Super Bowl. But when Norwood had the opportunity to win the game with a short field goal, he missed, handing the victory to the Giants in the final seconds of the game. Norwood had "choked"—he had lost his composure and was unable to perform under pressure.

Losing one's "cool" and failing to perform effectively in a crucial situation—such as during an important game or while taking a major test—can be very hard on a person. It can hurt an individual's self-esteem and self-confidence.

Sports psychologists help athletes such as Scott Norwood handle performance problems by applying the goals of psychology. First, they observe and describe the behavior. By measuring athletes' heart rates and other body processes, psychologists know that problems may occur when athletes are highly excited. Interviews with athletes reveal that they often feel anxious during big games. They are distracted by the cheers and jeers of the crowd and lose their concentration. They cannot focus on the jobs they are supposed to be doing.

Psychologists then explain the behavior in terms of the feelings of anxiety and the distractions that hinder the athletes' performance. The relationship between anxiety and performance is somewhat complex. A little anxiety is often a good thing. It motivates us to practice for a game or to study for a test. It makes us alert and ready. On the other hand, too much anxiety is harmful. It makes us shaky and distracts us from the task at hand.

Psychologists next predict that athletes will do best when anxiety is moderate and will falter when anxiety becomes too intense. Finally, they help athletes change, and thus control, their behavior and mental processes by teaching them ways of keeping their anxiety at a tolerable level. Psychologists also teach athletes how to filter out the sounds of the fans so they can focus on their task—helping the team win the game.

One method that sports psychologists recommend to help athletes perform more effectively under pressure is called positive visualization. In

Some athletes use positive visualization to help them perform successfully in high-pressure situations such as close games.

this method, athletes imagine themselves going through the motions in a critical game situation. A basketball player might, for example, imagine taking a free throw in overtime during a close game. She concentrates on blocking the noise of the crowd from her mind and focuses on the rim. She sees herself raising the ball with one hand as she guides it with the other. She then imagines releasing the ball and watching it glide through the net.

The goal of "controlling" behavior and mental processes is often misunderstood. Some people mistakenly think that psychologists seek ways to make people behave as the psychologists want them to—like puppets on strings. This is not so. Psychologists know that people should be free to make their own decisions. Although psychologists know much about the factors that influence human behavior, they use this knowledge to help people accomplish their own goals.

Psychology as a Science

Psychology is a social science, but it has foundations in the natural sciences. The social sciences, which also include history, anthropology, economics, political science, and sociology, deal with the structure of human society and the nature of the individuals who make up society. These individuals and their behavior and mental processes are the focus of psychology.

The natural sciences, which include biology, chemistry, and physics, are concerned with the nature of the physical world. Some topics that psychologists study, such as the brain, are closely related to the natural sciences, especially biology. Also, like natural scientists, psychologists seek to answer questions by following the steps involved in scientific research. These steps include conducting experiments, collecting and analyzing data, and drawing conclusions. (See Chapter 2.)

Research As a science, psychology tests ideas through various research methods. Two widely used methods are surveys and experimentation. A survey is a method of collecting data that usually involves asking questions of people in a particular group.

Although most psychologists are interested mainly in human behavior, some focus on animal behavior, such as that of sea snails, pigeons, rats, and gorillas. Some psychologists believe that research findings with certain animals can be applied to human beings. Others argue that humans are so distinct that we can only learn about them by studying people. The truth probably lies somewhere in between. For example, by studying the nerve cells of squid (yes, squid), psychologists have been able to learn about the workings of human nerve cells. Only by studying people, however, can we learn about uniquely human qualities such as morality, values, and love.

Psychologists rely on research to learn whether certain methods will work before they use them with clients. Sometimes the research is conducted only with people, as in the case of research on how to help athletes perform under intense pressure. In such cases, psychologists make every effort to protect the research participants. You will read more about research methods in Chapter 2.

Psychological Theories Psychologists organize their ideas about behavior and mental processes into theories. A **theory** is a statement that attempts to explain why things are the way they are and happen the way they do. Psychological theories discuss principles that govern behavior and mental processes. Psychological theories may include statements about behavior (such as sleeping or aggression), mental processes (such as memories and mental images), and biological processes (such as the effect of chemicals in the brain).

A useful psychological theory allows psychologists to predict behavior and mental processes. For instance, if a theory about fatigue is useful, psychologists can apply it to predict when people will or will not sleep. If a theory does not accurately predict behavior or mental processes, psychologists consider revising or replacing the theory.

In psychology, as in other sciences, many theories have been found inadequate for accurately explaining or predicting the things with which they are concerned. As a result, these theories have been discarded or revised. For example, many psychologists once believed that stomach contractions were the cause of hunger. But then it was observed that many people feel hungry or eat even when they do not have stomach contractions. As a result, psychologists now believe that stomach contractions are only one of many factors in hunger and eating.

Psychologists—as well as others—often conduct surveys to learn about people's behavior and mental processes.

THINKING ABOUT PSYCHOLOGY

1. What is psychology? What are the five goals of psychology?

2. In what way is psychology a social science? How is psychology related to the natural sciences?

3. **Critical Thinking** What do you think is the main value of psychology? Explain your answer.

CASE STUDIES
AND OTHER TRUE STORIES
Parapsychology: Psychology or Not?

Parapsychology is the field of study concerned with the supernatural or other phenomena that science cannot explain. The prefix *para* means "at the side of," so parapsychology is at the side of psychology. Whether parapsychology has a place within psychology is a highly controversial issue.

Imagine how wealthy you could become if you were able to look into the future. You could check next month's stock market reports and know what shares to buy or sell. And imagine what power you would have if you were capable of making objects move simply by seeing them move in your mind.

These are examples of extrasensory perception (ESP). Extrasensory perception refers to the perception of objects or events through means other than sensory organs, such as the eyes. In theory, there are four forms of ESP:

- precognition—the ability to know about events before they occur
- psychokinesis—the ability to make objects move by thinking of them as moving
- telepathy—the direct transmission of thoughts or ideas from person to person without anything being spoken or written down
- clairvoyance—the ability to perceive objects that are out of the range of human senses

Most psychologists are skeptical about the existence of ESP. To them, ESP is in the realm of magic, not science. Some psychologists, however, believe that ESP may be a valid, scientific area of study (Bem & Honorton, 1994). The issue for them is whether the existence of ESP can be proved in the laboratory.

The best-known ESP researcher was Joseph Banks Rhine, who began studying ESP in the 1920s. In an experiment in clairvoyance, Rhine used a pack of 25 cards that consisted of 5 sets of 5 cards, each of which had a different symbol on it. If you were to guess which card would show up next, you would be correct 20 percent of the time (1 time in 5) by chance alone. But Rhine found that some people guessed correctly more often than that. He thus concluded that these people might be clairvoyant.

Other studies on ESP have focused on telepathy. In a method called the Ganzfeld procedure, one person acts as a "sender" and another person is the "receiver." The sender looks at randomly selected images, such as photographs, and tries to "transmit" an image to the receiver, who is in another room. The receiver is then shown four images and is asked to select the one that was transmitted by the sender. A person guessing which picture was transmitted would be correct one time in four by chance. Yet many studies using this procedure find that receivers identify the correct image somewhat more often (Bem & Honorton, 1994; Honorton et al., 1990).

Overall, however, there remain many reasons to be skeptical of ESP. For one thing, people who support ESP are probably less likely to report results that *fail* to show evidence of ESP. Furthermore, many things that look like ESP are really just coincidence. If you flip a coin indefinitely, eventually you will flip heads 10 times in a row. If you report eventual success and do not report weeks of failure, you might give the impression that you have a special coin-flipping ability.

Most important, experiments in ESP often do not yield the same results twice (Hyman, 1994). Often, people who appear to have ESP with one researcher fail to demonstrate it with another. In fact, from all studies of ESP, not one person has emerged who can reliably show ESP from one occasion to another, and with more than one researcher. As a result, most psychologists do not believe in extrasensory perception. ESP remains only an unproven theory.

Think About It

Describe an instance in which you or someone you know seemed to have ESP. How could you prove whether it really was ESP or not?

2

What Psychologists Do

All psychologists share a keen interest in behavior and believe in the value of scientific research. They also share the belief that theories about behavior and mental processes should be supported by scientific evidence. They accept that something is true only if the evidence shows it is so.

Some psychologists are interested mainly in research. They investigate the factors that give rise to behavior and mental processes. They form theories about why people and animals do the things they do. Then they test their theories by predicting when behaviors will occur.

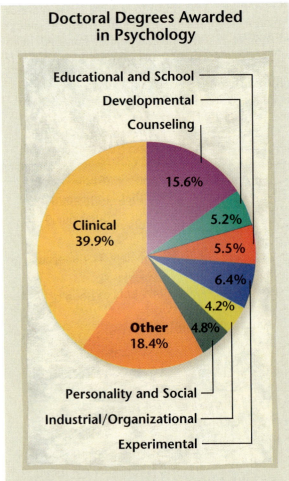

Doctoral Degrees Awarded in Psychology

- Educational and School
- Developmental
- Counseling — 15.6%
- 5.2%
- 5.5%
- 6.4%
- 4.2%
- Clinical 39.9%
- Other 18.4%
- 4.8%
- Personality and Social
- Industrial/Organizational
- Experimental

FIGURE 1.1 *The lion's share of doctoral degrees in psychology tend to be in clinical psychology.*

Source: *Summary Report Doctorate Recipients from United States Universities* (Table W04846), Office of Demographic, Employment, and Educational Research, 1994, Washington, DC: American Psychological Association.

Other psychologists consult. That is, they apply psychological knowledge in the form of therapy to help people change their behavior so that they can better meet their own goals. Still other psychologists teach, sharing their knowledge of psychology in classrooms and workshops.

Clinical Psychologists

Clinical psychologists make up the largest group of psychologists. (See Figure 1.1.) Clinical psychologists are the people most of us think of when we hear the term *psychologist.*

Clinical psychologists help people with psychological problems, such as anxiety or depression, or severe psychological disorders, such as schizophrenia. Clinical psychologists help their clients overcome problems and adjust to the demands of their lives. They also help people who have problems with relationships, drug abuse, or weight control. Most likely, a clinical psychologist was helping Linda's friend Nick overcome his drug problem.

A DAY IN THE LIFE

Clinical psychologists are trained to evaluate psychological problems through the use of interviews and psychological tests. Then these psychologists help clients understand their problems and resolve them by changing ineffective or harmful behavior. (See Chapter 19.)

Clinical psychologists work in hospitals, in prisons, and in college and university clinics. Many clinical psychologists are in private practice. Some clinical psychologists divide their time among clinical practice, teaching, and research.

Clinical psychologists should not be confused with psychiatrists. A psychiatrist is a medical doctor who specializes in the treatment of psychological problems and who can prescribe medication for clients. Psychologists also specialize in the treatment of psychological problems, but because they are not medical doctors, they may not prescribe medication for their clients.

Counseling Psychologists

Like clinical psychologists, counseling psychologists use interviews and tests to identify their clients' problems. Counseling psychologists typically treat people who have adjustment problems rather than serious psychological disorders. For example, a counseling psychologist's clients may have difficulty making decisions about their careers, or they may find it hard to make friends. They may be experiencing conflicts with family members, teachers, employers, or colleagues. Counseling psychologists help their clients clarify their goals, overcome their adjustment problems, and meet challenges. Counseling psychologists often are employed in businesses and in college and university counseling and testing centers.

School Psychologists

Your school district may employ one or more school psychologists. School psychologists identify and help students who have problems that interfere with learning. Typical problems that school psychologists deal with include peer group and family problems, psychological problems, and learning disorders, which are problems in learning to read, write, or do math.

School psychologists identify students with problems by talking with teachers, parents, and the students themselves. School psychologists may also administer tests, such as intelligence tests and achievement tests. These tests, which are usually given to large groups of students, help identify students with special abilities as well as students who need assistance. For example, the psychologist at Linda's school noticed her exceptional results on the math section of an achievement test and recommended placing Linda in an advanced math class.

School psychologists also observe students in the classroom to see how they interact with their teachers and peers. After gathering the information they need, school psychologists advise teachers, school officials, and parents about how to help certain students reach their potential or overcome their learning difficulties.

In addition, school psychologists make recommendations regarding the placement of students in special classes and programs. In some school districts, student placement is the major responsibility of the school psychologist.

Educational Psychologists

Like school psychologists, educational psychologists are concerned with helping students learn. But they generally focus on course planning and instructional methods for an entire school system rather than on designing a program of study for an individual student.

School psychologists may administer various types of tests to find out about students' abilities. Educational psychologists may help construct such tests.

Educational psychologists are concerned with theoretical issues that relate to learning, measurement of abilities, and child and adolescent development. Their research interests include the ways in which learning is affected by

- psychological factors, such as motivation, emotions, creativity, and intelligence;
- cultural factors, such as beliefs;
- economic factors, such as the level of income earned by a person's family; and
- instructional methods used in the classroom.

Some educational psychologists help prepare standardized tests, such as the Standard Assessment Test (SAT). They study various tests to determine the type of test that can most effectively predict success in college. They may also examine individual test items to determine whether these items make a useful contribution to the test as a whole.

Developmental Psychologists

Developmental psychologists study the changes that occur throughout the life span. These changes can be of the following types:

- physical (examples include changes in height and weight, adolescent growth, sexual maturity, physical aspects of aging)
- emotional (for instance, development of self-concept and self-esteem)

- cognitive (such as changes from childhood to adulthood in mental images of the world outside, or how children learn right and wrong)
- social (such as formation of bonds between parents and children, relationships with peers, or intimate relationships between adults)

Developmental psychologists also attempt to sort out the relative influences of heredity and the environment on development. (See Chapters 3 and 10.)

Some developmental psychologists are especially interested in the challenges of adolescence. For example, how do adolescents handle the competing, and often contradictory, messages of peers (who pressure them to act in one way) and parents (who want them to act in another way)? How can psychologists help parents and school officials encourage adolescents to avoid activities that may be harmful to their physical and psychological well-being? What are the causes of depression and suicide among teens? How can people help prevent these painful situations from occurring?

Personality Psychologists

Personality psychologists identify characteristics, or traits. Shyness and friendliness are examples of traits. Personality psychologists look for the many different traits people have and study the development of these traits. Personality psychologists share with clinical psychologists an interest in the origins of psychological problems and disorders. These psychologists are also concerned with issues such as anxiety, aggression, and gender roles. Gender roles are the behavior patterns expected of women and men in a given culture.

Social Psychologists

Social psychologists are concerned with people's behavior in social situations. They would be interested, for example, in studying the reasons for Linda's attraction to Marc. Whereas personality psychologists tend to look within people for explanations of behavior, social psychologists tend to focus on external influences. Social psychologists study the following issues:

- the ways in which women and men typically behave in a given setting
- the physical and psychological factors that attract people to one another
- the reasons people tend to conform to group standards and expectations
- how people's behavior changes when they are members of a group
- the reasons for and the effects of prejudice and discrimination within various groups and from one group to another
- the situations in which people act aggressively and those in which they help others

Experimental Psychologists

Psychologists in all specialties may conduct experimental research. However, experimental psychologists conduct research into basic processes such as the functions of the nervous system. Other basic processes include sensation and perception, learning and memory, and thinking and motivation.

Experimental psychologists would be interested in exploring the pathways by which Linda's alarm clock woke her. They would want to know what triggered her memory of the psychology teacher's nose-touching demonstration. In addition, experimental psychologists would be interested in the biological and psychological factors that contributed to Linda's feeling of hunger.

Some experimental psychologists focus on the relationships between biological changes (such as the release of hormones into the bloodstream) and psychological events (such as feelings of anxiety or depression). These experimental psychologists are called biological psychologists.

Experimental psychologists are more likely than other psychologists to engage in basic research. **Basic research** is research that has no immediate application and is done for its own sake. The findings of experimental psychologists are often put into practice by other psychological specialists. Basic research into motivation, for example, has helped clinical and counseling psychologists develop ways of helping people control their eating habits. Basic research into learning and memory has helped educational psychologists enhance learning conditions in schools.

Other Specialists

You have already read about sports psychologists and how they can help athletes. There are several other specialties in psychology.

Industrial and Organizational Psychologists

Industrial psychologists focus on people and work. Organizational psychologists study the behavior of people in organizations, such as business firms. Industrial psychology and organizational psychology are closely related. Psychologists in these fields often are trained in both areas.

Industrial and organizational psychologists are employed by business firms to improve working conditions and increase worker output. They may assist in hiring, training, and promoting employees. They may also devise psychological tests for job applicants and conduct research into the factors that contribute to job satisfaction. In addition, some industrial and organizational psychologists have counseling skills and help employees who have problems on the job.

Environmental Psychologists
Does crowding in cities make people irritable? Does smog have an effect on people's ability to learn? Environmental psychologists ask these types of questions. They focus on the ways in which people influence, and are influenced by, their physical environment. Environmental psychologists are concerned with the ways in which buildings and cities serve, or fail to serve, human needs. They investigate the psychological effects of extremes of temperature, noise, and air pollution.

Consumer Psychologists
Consumer psychologists study the behavior of shoppers to explain and predict their behavior. They also assist others to apply their findings. For example, they work with advertisers to create effective newspaper ads and television commercials. They advise store managers about window displays and shelf arrangement to attract customers. Have you ever noticed that in many supermarkets, milk is shelved far away from the store entrance? That is because milk is an item that many people buy frequently. Its placement at the rear of the store ensures that shoppers will pass—and hopefully buy—other items on the way to the milk shelf.

Forensic Psychologists
When an attorney wants an expert witness to testify whether a person accused of a crime is or is not competent to stand trial, the attorney might call on a forensic psychologist. Forensic psychologists work within the criminal justice system. In addition to testifying about the psychological competence of defendants to stand trial, they may explain how certain kinds of

A worker clears rubble from the site of a collapsed building. What types of psychologists might be interested in studying the effects of such work?

psychological problems give rise to criminal behavior. Psychologists are also employed by police departments to

- assist in the selection of police officers;
- help police officers cope with job stress; and
- train police officers in the handling of dangerous situations such as suicide threats, hostage crises, and family violence.

Health Psychologists
Health psychologists examine the ways in which behavior and mental processes are related to physical health. They study the effects of stress on health problems such as headaches and heart disease. Health psychologists try to explain why some people follow their doctor's advice and other people do not. Health psychologists also help people adopt healthful behaviors such as exercising and quitting smoking.

THINKING ABOUT PSYCHOLOGY

1. In what way do psychiatrists and psychologists differ?
2. List three subspecialties of psychology and describe the work of each.
3. **Critical Thinking** If you decided to become a psychologist, what subspecialty of psychology would you prefer and why?

A History of Psychology

3

People have always been interested in the behaviors of other people, and thus psychology is as old as human history. Interest in the actions, motives, and thoughts of human beings can be traced as far back as the philosophers and scientists of ancient times.

Roots from Ancient Greece

More than 2,000 years ago, Plato (428–348 or 347 B.C.), a student of Socrates in ancient Greece, recorded his teacher's advice—"Know thyself"—a phrase that has remained a motto of psychological thought ever since. Socrates suggested that we can learn much about ourselves by carefully examining our thoughts and feelings. Psychologists call this method of learning **introspection**, which means "looking within."

One of Plato's students, the Greek philosopher Aristotle (384–322 B.C.), continued in this line of inquiry about human behavior. He raised many issues that are still discussed today (as, for example, in this textbook). One of Aristotle's works is called *Peri Psyches*, which means "about the mind." Aristotle's approach was scientific. He argued that human behavior, like the movements of the stars and the seas, is subject to certain rules and laws. He believed one such universal law was that people are motivated to seek pleasure and to avoid pain—a view still found in some modern psychological theories. *Peri Psyches* begins with a history of psychological thought. Then it explores topics such as personality, sensation and perception, thought, intelligence, needs and motives, feelings and emotions, and memory.

Socrates encouraged people to examine their thoughts and feelings—to "know themselves."

It is true that a book on psychology, with content similar to that of this textbook, was written by Aristotle more than 2,000 years ago. The name of that book is *Peri Psyches,* which means "about the mind."

The ancient Greeks also theorized about various psychological problems, such as confusion and bizarre behavior. Throughout human history, many people have attributed such disorders to supernatural forces. The ancient Greeks generally believed that the gods punished people for wrongdoing by causing them confusion and madness. The Greek physician Hippocrates (c. 460–c. 377 B.C.) was an exception. He suggested that such problems are caused by abnormalities in the brain. But this idea that biological factors can affect our thoughts, feelings, and behavior was to lie dormant for more than 2,000 years.

The Middle Ages

During the Middle Ages, most Europeans believed that problems such as agitation and confusion were signs of possession by demons. A popular belief of the time was that possession by the devil was punishment for sins or the result of deals made with the devil.

Certain "tests" were used to determine whether a person was possessed. One of the most famous tests, the water-float test, was based on the principle that pure metals sink to the bottom during smelting whereas impure metals float to the surface. Individuals who were suspected of being possessed were thrown into deep water. Suspects who managed to keep their heads above water were assumed to be impure and in league with the devil. They were then executed for associating with the devil. Those who sank to the bottom, on the other hand, were judged to be pure. Unfortunately, they enjoyed no better fate—they drowned.

TRUTH OR fiction ■ REVISITED ■

It is true that in the Middle Ages some innocent people were drowned as a way of proving that they were not possessed by the devil. The method was based on a water-float test used to judge the purity of metals.

The Birth of Modern Science

The 1500s, 1600s, and 1700s witnessed a movement away from belief in demons and possession. Great scientific and intellectual advances were made during this period. In the 1500s, for instance, Polish astronomer Nicolaus Copernicus challenged the view that the sun revolved around the earth, suggesting instead that the earth revolved around the sun. In the 1600s, British scientist Sir Isaac Newton formulated the laws of gravity and motion; philosopher John Locke theorized that knowledge is not inborn but is learned from experience. In the late 1700s, Antoine Lavoisier founded the science of chemistry and explained how animals and plants use oxygen in respiration.

The scientific approach also led to the birth of modern psychology in the 1800s. Psychologists argued that ideas about human behavior and mental processes should be supported by evidence. In the late 1800s, psychological laboratories were established in Europe and the United States. In these laboratories, psychologists studied behavior and mental processes using methods similar to those Lavoisier had used to study chemistry. Most historians of psychology point to the year 1879 as the beginning of psychology as a laboratory science. In that year, Wilhelm Wundt established his laboratory in Leipzig, Germany.

Wilhelm Wundt and Structuralism

Wilhelm Wundt (1832–1920) and his students founded a field of psychology that came to be known as **structuralism**. Structuralists were concerned with discovering the basic elements of conscious experience. Wundt broke down conscious experience into two separate categories: objective sensations and subjective feelings. Objective sensations, such as sight and taste, were assumed to accurately reflect the outside world. Subjective feelings were thought to include emotional responses and mental images.

Wilhelm Wundt

Structuralists believed that the human mind functioned by combining these basic elements of experience. For example, a person can experience an apple objectively by observing its shape, color, texture, and taste. The person can also experience the apple subjectively by remembering how good it feels to bite into it. Using the method of introspection, Wundt and his students carefully examined and reported their experiences.

William James and Functionalism

A decade after Wundt, introspection convinced Harvard University professor William James (1842–1910) that experience cannot be broken down the way structuralists believed. James maintained that experience is a fluid and continuous "stream of consciousness." He focused on the relationships between experience and behavior and described his views in *The Principles of Psychology*. The book, which was published in 1890, is considered by many people to be the first modern psychology textbook.

William James

James was one of the founders of the school of **functionalism**. Functionalists were concerned with how mental processes help organisms adapt to their environment. They stressed the application of their findings to everyday situations.

Calvin and Hobbes
by Bill Watterson

Functionalism differed from structuralism in several ways. Whereas structuralism relied only on introspection, the methods of functionalism included behavioral observation in the laboratory as well as introspection. The structuralists tended to ask, "What are the elements (structures) of psychological processes?" The functionalists, on the other hand, tended to ask, "What are the purposes (functions) of behavior and mental processes? What do certain behaviors and mental processes accomplish for the person (or animal)?"

Functionalists proposed that adaptive behavior patterns are learned and maintained because they are successful. For example, some students continue to study because they have learned that studying leads to good grades. Less adaptive behavior patterns drop out, or are discontinued. For example, if you ask someone for a date repeatedly and are refused each time, eventually you will probably stop asking the person out.

Adaptive (successful) actions are repeated and eventually become habits. The formation of habits is seen in such acts as turning doorknobs or riding a bicycle. At first, these acts require our full attention. But through repetition—and success—they become automatic. The multiple tasks involved in learning to type on a keyboard or to write in longhand also become routine through successful repetition. We then perform them without much attention. Habit allows us to take the mechanics of typing or writing for granted and to concentrate instead on *what* we are writing.

John B. Watson and Behaviorism

Picture a hungry rat in a maze. It moves along until it reaches a place where it must turn left or right. If the rat is consistently rewarded with food for turning right at that place, it will learn to turn right when it arrives there—at least, when it is hungry. But what does the rat *think* when it is learning to turn right at that place in the maze?

Does it seem absurd to try to place yourself in the mind of a rat? It did to John Broadus Watson (1878–1958), when he was asked by examiners to consider this question as a requirement for his doctoral degree in psychology.

John B. Watson

He was asked this question because functionalism was the dominant school of psychology at the time. Functionalists were concerned with the stream of consciousness as well as with behavior. Although Watson agreed with the functionalist focus on the importance of learning, he believed that it is unscientific to study consciousness—especially the consciousness of animals. He saw consciousness as a private event that is known only to the individual. He asserted that if psychology was to be a natural science, like physics or chemistry, it must be limited to observable, measurable events—that is, to behavior. As the founder of the school of **behaviorism**, Watson defined psychology as the scientific study of observable behavior.

B. F. Skinner and Reinforcement

Harvard University psychologist B. F. Skinner (1904–1990) added to the behaviorist tradition by introducing the concept of reinforcement. Skinner

EXPLORING
DIVERSITY

Bringing Diversity into Psychology

In the past, psychology—like many other fields—was the domain primarily of White males. Not only were the psychologists themselves mostly White men, but most of their research used White male participants and tended to explore issues that were relevant primarily to White men. In recent decades, however, that has changed. Today many psychologists are women and members of traditionally under-represented ethnic groups. In fact, White males now obtain fewer than two in five doctoral degrees in psychology.

Not only are psychologists as a group more diverse now than they used to be—so is their research. A great deal of psychological research today deals with questions of gender, culture, prejudice, stereotypes, and so on. The work of African American psychologist Kenneth Clark exemplifies such research.

Kenneth Bancroft Clark was born in the Panama Canal Zone in 1914, the son of West Indian parents. Miriam Clark, his mother, brought her children to the United States for their education. They settled in the Harlem section of New York City.

Although most African American children at the time were advised to attend vocational high schools, where they could learn specific job skills, Kenneth Clark attended an academic high school. He went on to Howard University in Washington, D.C., where he majored in psychology and married Mamie Phipps. The Clarks then attended Columbia University, where they both earned Ph.D. degrees in psychology.

In 1946, the Clarks founded the Northside Center for Child Development. Kenneth and Mamie Clark's clinical work led to several studies showing the negative effect of segregation on the

Kenneth B. Clark

self-esteem of African American children. In one well-known study (Clark, 1947), African American children were asked to choose between white and brown dolls after being given instructions such as "Give me the pretty doll" or "Give me the doll that looks bad." The Clarks reported that most children preferred the white dolls over the brown ones and concluded that the children were demonstrating their feelings that society as a whole preferred White people.

In 1951, Kenneth Clark began working with the National Association for the Advancement of Colored People (NAACP) to end school segregation. In 1954, when the Supreme Court overturned the "separate but equal" doctrine, it cited Clark's work on the effects of discrimination on the personality development of African American and White children. In his book *Prejudice and Your Child*, published in 1955, Clark described the effects of segregation on White children as well as on African American children.

Clark's later work concerned the quality of education and the problems of juvenile delinquency and crime. He was among the first experts to recommend preschool classes, after-school programs, and community participation.

Think About It

Kenneth Clark is only one of the many people who have contributed to psychology's growing diversity. Select one of the following psychologists and prepare an oral report on his or her life and work: J. Henry Alston, Mary Whiton Calkins, Lillian Comas-Diaz, Beverly Greene, Gilbert Haven Jones, Christine Ladd Franklin, Jorge Sanchez, Stanley Sue, Margaret Floy Washburn.

B. F. Skinner

showed that when an animal is reinforced, or rewarded, for performing an action, it is more likely to perform that action again in the future. He demonstrated that laboratory animals, such as rats and pigeons, are capable of learning complex behavior patterns if they are reinforced in the right ways. Behaviorists have taught animals to peck buttons, turn in circles, climb ladders, push toys across the floor, and even shoot baskets by rewarding the animals for performing the desired behavior.

According to Skinner, people learn in the same way animals do. Like animals, people learn to behave in certain ways because they have been reinforced for doing so.

The Gestalt School

Look at the two drawings in Figure 1.2 and answer the questions posed in the caption. These drawings demonstrate the idea that the context in which something occurs affects the way we perceive it. For example, in Drawing A, the circles in the centers of the two sets are the same size. However, we may think they are different sizes because of the contexts in which they appear. That is, one circle is surrounded by larger circles and the other is surrounded by smaller circles.

In Drawing B, the second symbols in the two rows are identical. The symbol in the top row may look like the letter B because it is with the letters A, C, and D. However, when the identical symbol is with the numbers 12, 14, and 15, it may look more like the number 13. Even though the two symbols are identical, the context in which each one appears influences what we perceive it to be.

German psychologists Max Wertheimer, Kurt Koffka, and Wolfgang Köhler were fascinated by the ways in which context influences people's interpretation of information. In the 1920s, they founded the school of **Gestalt psychology**. The psychology of *Gestalt*, which means "shape" or "form" in German, is based on the idea that perceptions are more than the sums of their parts. Rather, they are wholes that give shape, or meaning, to the parts. As such, Gestalt psychology rejects the structuralist idea that experience can be broken down into individual parts or elements.

Gestalt psychologists also reject the behaviorist notion that psychologists should concentrate only on observable behavior. In addition, Gestalt psychologists believe that learning is active and purposeful. They disagree with the behaviorist view that learning is mechanical.

These circus lions probably learned how to do their tricks by being reinforced, or rewarded, for each behavior that contributed to the overall effect the trainers were trying to achieve.

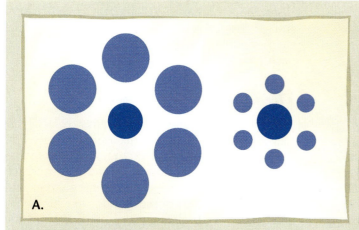

A.

B.

FIGURE 1.2 *Look at Drawing A. Are the circles in the centers of the two sets of circles the same size? In Drawing B, what is the second symbol in each line? We perceive images in terms of the contexts in which they occur, so two images that are identical may appear to be different if their surroundings are different.*

Köhler and the other founders of Gestalt psychology demonstrated that much learning, especially problem solving, is accomplished by insight, not by mechanical repetition. Insight is the reorganization of perceptions that enables an individual to solve a problem. In other words, insight is the sudden appearance of the Gestalt, or form, that enables the individual to see the solution.

Sigmund Freud and the School of Psychoanalysis

Sigmund Freud

Sigmund Freud (1856–1939), a Viennese physician, was perhaps the most famous of the early psychologists. The school of thought he founded—called **psychoanalysis**—emphasizes the importance of unconscious motives and internal conflicts in determining human behavior.

Freud's theory, more than the others, has become a part of popular culture. You may be familiar with several Freudian concepts. For example, have you ever tried to "interpret" a slip of the tongue, or have you ever tried to figure out the "meaning" of a dream you had? The ideas that people are driven by hidden impulses and that verbal slips and dreams represent unconscious wishes largely reflect Freud's influence on popular culture.

Structuralists, functionalists, behaviorists, and Gestalt psychologists all conducted their research in the laboratory. Freud, however, gained his understanding of human behavior through consultations with patients. Freud was astounded at how little insight these patients had into their own ideas and feelings. He came to believe that unconscious processes, especially sexual and aggressive urges, are more important than conscious experience in governing people's behavior and feelings.

Freud thought that most of what fills an individual's mind is unconscious and consists of conflicting impulses, urges, and wishes. According to Freud's theories, people's behavior is aimed at satisfying these impulses, even though some of them seem socially inappropriate or even unacceptable. But at the same time, people want to see themselves as good and decent human beings. Thus, they often fool themselves about the real motives for their behavior. Freud attempted to help people gain insight into their unconscious conflicts and find socially acceptable ways of expressing their wishes and meeting their needs.

THINKING ABOUT PSYCHOLOGY

1. Describe the main differences between structuralism and functionalism.

2. Why do behaviorists object to schools of psychology that study consciousness?

3. **Critical Thinking** Identify one example of the influence of Sigmund Freud's psychoanalytic theory on popular culture.

4
Contemporary Perspectives

Today we no longer find psychologists who describe themselves as structuralists or functionalists. And although the school of Gestalt psychology inspired current research in perception and problem solving, few would consider themselves Gestalt psychologists. The numbers of traditional behaviorists and psychoanalysts also have been declining. Many current psychologists in the behaviorist tradition have modified the theories of Watson and Skinner. Similarly, many contemporary psychoanalysts do not use the methods Freud did.

Nevertheless, the historical traditions of psychology find expression in contemporary perspectives on psychology. The most important of these are the biological, cognitive, humanistic, psychoanalytic, learning, and sociocultural perspectives. Each perspective emphasizes different topics of investigation and has different approaches.

The Biological Perspective

The **biological perspective** emphasizes the influence of biology on our behavior. Psychologists assume that our mental processes—our thoughts, fantasies, and dreams—are made possible by the nervous system. They point especially to its key component, the brain. Biologically oriented psychologists look for the connections between events in the brain, such as the activity of brain cells, and behavior and mental processes. They use several techniques, such as CAT scans and PET scans, to show which parts of the brain are involved in various mental processes. (See Chapter 3.) Biological psychology has shown that certain parts of the brain are highly active when we listen to music, other parts are active when we solve math problems, and still other parts are involved with certain psychological disorders. Biological psychologists have also learned that certain chemicals in the brain are connected with the storage of information—that is, the formation of memories.

Moreover, biological psychologists are interested in the influences of hormones and genes. Hormones are chemicals that glands release into the bloodstream to set in motion various body functions, such as growth and digestion. Genes are the basic units of heredity. Biological psychologists study the influences of genes on personality traits such as intellectual or artistic talent, psychological health, and various behavior patterns.

The Cognitive Perspective

The **cognitive perspective** emphasizes the role played by thoughts in determining behavior. Cognitive psychologists study mental processes to understand human nature. They investigate the ways in which people perceive information and make mental images of the world, solve problems, and dream and daydream. Cognitive psychologists, in short, study what we refer to as the mind.

The cognitive tradition has roots in Socrates' maxim "Know thyself" and in his method of introspection for learning about the self. Cognitive psychology also has roots in structuralism, functionalism, and Gestalt psychology. Each of these schools of thought has addressed issues that are of interest to cognitive psychologists.

Today many psychological theories have roots in the cognitive perspective. One of these is the developmental theory of Swiss psychologist Jean Piaget. Piaget showed how a child's mental picture of the world grows more sophisticated as the child matures. (See Chapter 10.)

Another aspect of the cognitive perspective involves information processing. Many cognitive psychologists have been influenced by computer science. Computers process information to solve problems. Information is first fed into the computer. Then it is placed in the working memory while it is being worked on, or manipulated. Finally, the information is stored more or less permanently on the computer's hard drive or on a floppy disk.

Many psychologists speak of people as having working memories and storage facilities (or long-term memories). If information has been placed in computer storage or in a person's long-term memory, it must be retrieved before it can be worked on again. To retrieve information from computer storage, people must know the name for the data file and the rules for retrieving data files. Similarly, say cognitive psychologists, people need certain cues to retrieve information from their long-term memories. Otherwise, the information is lost to them.

Cognitive psychologists sometimes refer to our strategies for solving problems as our "mental programs" or "software." In this computer metaphor, our brains are the "hardware" that runs our mental programs. In other words, our brains are our own *very* personal computers.

Cognitive psychologists believe that people's behavior is influenced by their values, their interpretations, and their choices. For example, an individual who interprets a casual remark as an insult may react with hostility. But the same remark directed at another person might be perceived very differently by that person and thus may meet with a different reaction.

The Humanistic Perspective

The **humanistic perspective** stresses the human capacity for self-fulfillment and the importance of consciousness, self-awareness, and the capacity to make choices. Consciousness is seen as the force that shapes people's personalities.

Humanistic psychology considers people's personal experiences to be the most important aspect of psychology. Humanistic psychologists believe that self-awareness, experience, and choice permit us to "invent ourselves." In other words, they enable us to fashion our growth and our ways of relating to the world as we go through life. Unlike the behaviorists, who assume that behavior is caused largely by the stimuli that act on us, humanistic psychologists believe that we are free to choose our own behavior.

The humanistic perspective views people as basically good and helpful to others. Humanistic psychologists help people get in touch with their feelings, manage their negative impulses, and realize their potential.

Critics of the humanistic perspective, especially behaviorists, insist that psychology should be scientific and address only observable events. They argue that people's inner experiences are unsuited to scientific observation and measurement. Humanistic psychologists, however, insist that inner experience is vital to the understanding of human nature.

Some cognitive psychologists are interested in the ways in which children view the world.

The Psychoanalytic Perspective

The **psychoanalytic perspective** stresses the influence of unconscious forces on human behavior. In the 1940s and 1950s, psychoanalytic theory dominated the practice of psychotherapy and greatly influenced psychology and the arts. Although psychoanalytic thought no longer dominates psychology, its influence continues to be felt. Psychologists who follow Sigmund Freud's approach today focus less on the roles of unconscious sexual and aggressive impulses and more on conscious choice and self-direction.

Freud believed that aggressive impulses are common reactions to the frustrations of daily life and that we seek to vent these impulses on other people. Because we fear rejection or retaliation, we put most aggressive impulses out of our minds. But by holding aggression in, we set the stage for future explosions. Pent-up aggressive impulses demand

Contemporary Psychological Perspectives

Perspective	Subject Matter	Key Assumption
Biological	Nervous system, glands and hormones, genetic factors	Biological processes influence behavior and mental processes.
Cognitive	Mental images, information processing, thinking, language	Perceptions and thoughts influence behavior.
Humanistic	Subjective experience	People make free and conscious choices based on their unique experiences.
Psychoanalytic	Unconscious processes, early childhood experiences	Unconscious motives influence behavior.
Learning	Environmental influences, habitual behavior, observational learning	Personal experience and reinforcement guide individual development.
Sociocultural	Ethnicity, gender, culture, socioeconomic status	Sociocultural, biological, and psychological factors create individual differences.

FIGURE 1.3 *Contemporary psychologists differ in their approaches to psychological thought. These six broad perspectives are the most common ways to view behavior today.*

outlets. Partial outlets can be provided by physical activity—for example, sports—but we may also direct hostile impulses toward strangers. (That guy who intentionally bumped into you in the hallway, according to Freud, might be venting unconscious anger toward his parents.)

The Learning Perspective

The **learning perspective** emphasizes the effects of experience on behavior. In the views of many psychologists, learning is the essential factor in observing, describing, explaining, predicting, and controlling behavior. The term *learning,* however, has different meanings to different psychologists. For example, traditional behaviorists and social-learning theorists have different attitudes toward the role of consciousness in learning.

John B. Watson and other behaviorists found no role for consciousness. They believed that people do things because of their learning histories and the influence of their situations, not because of conscious choice. Behaviorists are not concerned with what an organism *knows.* They are concerned with what the organism *does.* Behaviorists emphasize the importance of environmental influences and focus on the learning of habits through repetition and reinforcement.

In contrast, **social-learning theory** suggests that people can change their environments or create new ones. Furthermore, social-learning theory holds that people can learn intentionally by observing others. Social-learning theorists believe that conscious observational learning provides people with a storehouse of responses to life's situations. People's expectations and values, however, influence whether they *choose* to do what they have learned how to do. Since the 1960s, social-learning theorists have gained influence in the areas of development, personality, and methods of therapy.

Psychologists who take the learning perspective believe that behavior is learned either from direct experience or by observing other people. For example, people will behave a certain way when they expect to be rewarded for that behavior. Social-learning theorists have a cognitive leaning, however. Like cognitive theorists, social-learning theorists believe that people act in a particular way only when they recognize that the circumstances call for that behavior. For example, we act with hostility when we have been provoked, or we act with friendliness when we have been treated well.

The Sociocultural Perspective

The **sociocultural perspective** addresses such issues as ethnicity, gender, culture, and socioeconomic status. It is based on the idea that these factors have a significant impact on human behavior and mental processes.

Studies of the experiences of various ethnic groups in the United States highlight the influences of social forces on the individual. The following items are among the issues related to ethnicity that sociocultural psychologists study:

- inclusion of people from various ethnic groups in psychological research studies

- bilingualism

- ethnic differences in views of the world or in various types of achievement

- ethnic differences in susceptibility to physical and psychological problems

- multicultural issues in the practice of psychotherapy and treatment

- prejudice

The study of such topics enables people to appreciate the cultural heritages of various ethnic groups and understand the challenges they face.

Sociocultural theorists also examine gender—the state of being male or being female. Gender is not simply a matter of anatomy. It involves a complex web of cultural expectations and social roles that affect people's self-concepts and behavior. One reason for the importance of gender studies is that such studies address issues concerning similarities and differences between males and females.

Historically, much of the scientific research into gender roles and gender differences assumed that male behavior represented the norm for all people (Ader & Johnson, 1994; Matlin, 1993; Walsh, 1993). Women traditionally have been channeled

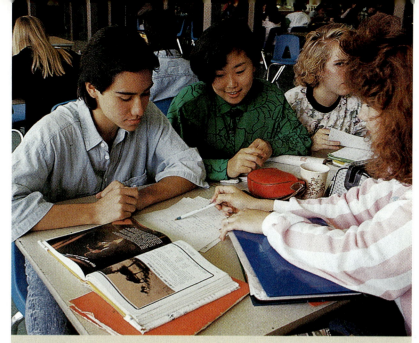

One topic explored by followers of the sociocultural perspective is how people of different ethnicities and genders interact with each other.

into domestic careers, regardless of their wishes. Not until relatively modern times has higher education been seen as a suitable pursuit for women. Women have attended college in the United States only since 1833, when Oberlin College in Ohio first admitted women. Today more than half of postsecondary students in the United States are women.

Contemporary women have also succeeded in academic and professional fields—such as medicine, law, and engineering—that traditionally were reserved for men. In the United States, women now account for 40 percent of medical and law students and for 1 in 6 engineering graduates (Matlin, 1993). By contrast, in the 1970s, women accounted for only 1 engineering graduate in 25 (Morrison & Von Glinow, 1990).

THINKING ABOUT PSYCHOLOGY

1. How do cognitive psychologists compare people's mental processes to the working of computers?

2. How would a psychoanalyst explain aggression?

3. Explain how the humanist and social-learning perspectives support the view that people are free to make choices.

4. **Critical Thinking**   How does knowledge of cultural differences enrich the study of psychology?

Chapter 1 REVIEW

SUMMARY

Psychology is the study of behavior and the factors that affect behavior.

I. Why Study Psychology?

A. Psychology is the scientific study of behavior and mental processes.

B. Psychology aims to observe, describe, explain, predict, and control behavior.

C. Psychology is a social science that has its foundations in the natural sciences.

D. Two widely used methods of psychological research are surveys and experimentation.

E. Psychologists propose theories to explain behavior and mental processes. They then seek evidence to support their theories.

II. What Psychologists Do

A. Clinical psychologists evaluate and help people overcome various mental and emotional problems.

B. Counseling psychologists generally help people with adjustment problems.

C. School psychologists help students who have problems that interfere with learning.

D. Educational psychologists are concerned with theoretical issues that relate to learning, measurement of abilities, and child and adolescent development.

E. Developmental psychologists study the physical, emotional, cognitive, and social changes that occur during the life span.

F. Personality psychologists study the effects of personality traits on behavior.

G. Social psychologists look at the influence of social factors on people's behavior.

H. Experimental psychologists conduct research into basic human processes to understand their effects on behavior.

I. Other areas of specialization include industrial, organizational, environmental, consumer, forensic, and health psychology.

III. A History of Psychology

A. Socrates suggested that human beings learn about themselves by examining their thoughts and feelings.

B. The 1500s, 1600s, and 1700s witnessed the birth of modern science.

C. In the late 1800s Wilhelm Wundt founded structuralism, which sought to discover the basic elements of conscious experience.

D. William James founded functionalism, which focused on how mental processes help adaptation to the environment.

E. John B. Watson founded behaviorism, which maintained that organisms behave in certain ways because they are reinforced for doing so.

F. Gestalt psychologists believed that experience cannot be broken down into parts.

G. Sigmund Freud, the founder of psychoanalysis, believed that human behavior is determined by unconscious motives.

IV. Contemporary Perspectives

A. The biological perspective emphasizes the importance of biological factors in determining behavior.

B. The cognitive perspective studies mental processes to explain human nature.

C. The humanistic perspective stresses human consciousness, experience, and self-awareness in helping people make life choices.

D. The psychoanalytic perspective has roots in Freud's theories, but psychoanalysts today are less concerned with unconscious motives and are more concerned with conscious choice and self-direction.

E. The learning perspective maintains that people learn through experience or by observing others.

F. The sociocultural perspective examines the effects of ethnicity, gender, culture, and socioeconomic status on human behavior and mental processes.

TERM & CONCEPT REVIEW

1. What is the difference between behavior and cognitive activities? Give one example of each.
2. What are the five goals of psychology?
3. What is a psychological theory? When is a psychological theory useful?
4. Compare and contrast the work done by clinical psychologists and counseling psychologists.
5. What method did Socrates suggest for gaining self-knowledge? How does this method work?
6. What view held by the ancient Greek physician Hippocrates was ahead of its time?
7. How is behaviorism similar to functionalism? How is it different?
8. How is the image of a lightbulb going on in a person's head related to Gestalt psychology?
9. How does the research method used by psychoanalysis differ from the methods used by other schools of psychology?
10. How do humanistic psychologists view the study of consciousness?

CRITICAL THINKING

1. List four qualities you think a psychologist should possess. Give reasons for each selection.
2. Sports psychology and substance abuse counseling are examples of relatively new areas of psychological specialization. What do you think might be important areas for psychology in the years ahead? Explain your choices.
3. Compare the Gestalt psychologists' viewpoint on learning with the viewpoint of the behaviorists. What do you think is the major difference between the two viewpoints?
4. Describe a commonly held belief about gender differences that sociocultural psychologists might want to research. How might they go about proving or disproving this belief?

APPLYING SKILLS IN PSYCHOLOGY

1. **Writing About Psychology** A tip line is a telephone service people can call to hear a recording of helpful information. Write a three-minute script for a consumer tip line on the services different types of psychologists provide. Types of psychologists you might want to provide information about include clinical psychologists, counseling psychologists, school psychologists, developmental psychologists, industrial psychologists, organizational psychologists, environmental psychologists, consumer psychologists, forensic psychologists, health psychologists, and sports psychologists. In writing your script, consider the kinds of problems and concerns people might want to discuss with each type of psychologist. Tape-record your script and present it in class.

2. **Reading About Psychology** Find three newspaper and/or magazine articles that discuss the work done by different psychologists. For example, you might read about a psychologist testifying in a criminal court case or about a psychologist called in to help students cope with the death of a classmate. You might find a column on parenting skills written by a psychologist. Summarize the articles for an oral presentation in class. Identify which type of psychologist is described in each article.

3. **COOPERATIVE LEARNING Using Your Observation Skills** As a class, agree to watch the same program on television. The next day, organize small groups of students to discuss the characters on the program. What behaviors did you observe? How did you find out about the characters' thoughts (cognitive activities) and feelings (emotions)? Did everyone in the group interpret the characters in the same way? Why or why not? Choose one person in your group to record the group's ideas on the role of observation in understanding differences among people. Share your group's ideas in class.

Chapter 2

PSYCHOLOGICAL METHODS

Objectives

1 List and explain the steps scientists follow in conducting scientific research.

2 Explain the survey method and the importance of proper sampling techniques.

3 Compare and contrast various methods of observation, and discuss the use of correlation in analyzing results.

4 Describe the purpose and elements of an experiment.

5 Evaluate the ethical issues involved in psychological research.

A DAY IN THE LIFE

Dan and Marc were at Todd's, and Dan noticed a new fish tank in Todd's room. "Hey, Todd, when did you get this?"

"Last week," explained Todd. "I finally made enough money at the restaurant to be able to buy a fish tank and some fish. I've wanted fish since I was little."

"Cool! What do you have to do to take care of them?" Marc asked.

"You know, feed them, monitor the water temperature, generally watch over the fish and make sure they're doing okay. Like last week, I noticed that they seemed to be acting a little sluggish. They were eating less than usual, so I figured it was because they didn't like the food I was feeding them. I switched to a different kind of fish food."

"Did it help?"

"It seemed to, although it took a couple of days."

"What kind of fish are in here?" Dan asked.

"Some tetras and a Siamese fighting fish. I wanted to get more than one of the fighting fish, but the salesperson at the pet store said that probably wasn't a good idea."

"Why? What would they do to each other?" Dan wanted to know.

"I'm not sure. Attack each other, I think," Todd speculated.

"Too bad the fish can't tell us!" Dan joked.

Marc was quiet as he watched the fish swim around. "Do you have a mirror?" he asked suddenly.

Todd got a small hand mirror, wondering what Marc was up to. Then Marc held up the mirror so the fighting fish could see its reflection. The fish fanned out its fins menacingly, puffed up its cheeks, and started to dart toward its reflection. Marc moved the mirror away.

"I bet that was its attack reaction! It didn't realize that the other fish was only a reflection of itself," Todd exclaimed excitedly. "It thought it was a rival fish, and it prepared itself to fight!"

"I guess fighting fish really do fight each other," concluded Dan.

"Or maybe Todd just has a weird fish," teased Marc.

* * *

Todd, Marc, and Dan were having fun. They did not realize that they were actually conducting scientific research. By creating the right conditions, Todd and his friends were able to observe the fish and how it reacted to changes in the environment. Similarly, psychologists sometimes bring animals or people into laboratory environments where they can observe them under carefully controlled conditions. At other times, psychologists study the behavior of organisms in the field—that is, where the organisms live naturally. In addition, psychologists sometimes get information by conducting experiments, much as the boys did with the fighting fish. There are many different approaches to research. This chapter explores several of them.

Key Terms

- hypothesis
- replicate
- survey
- target population
- sample
- random sample
- stratified sample
- volunteer bias
- case study
- longitudinal method
- cross-sectional method
- naturalistic observation
- laboratory observation
- correlation
- positive correlation
- negative correlation
- experiment
- variable
- independent variable
- dependent variable
- experimental group
- control group
- controlled experiment
- placebo
- single-blind study
- double-blind study
- ethics
- informed consent

Conducting Research

Psychology, like chemistry and biology, is an experimental science. In an experimental science, assumptions (such as about the behavior of chemical compounds, cells, or people) must be supported by evidence. It is not enough to argue that something is true just because someone says it is. Psychologists and other scientists make it their business to be skeptical. It is part of their job to doubt claims that are not supported by actual scientific evidence.

Psychologists use a variety of research methods to study behavior and mental processes. These methods differ from each other in a number of ways. But regardless of what method psychologists are using, they tend to follow the same general procedure in conducting their research. This procedure consists of five steps: forming a research question, forming a hypothesis, testing the hypothesis, analyzing the results, and drawing conclusions.

Forming a Research Question

Psychologists begin a study by forming a research question. Many research questions arise from daily experience. For example, Todd, Marc, and Dan

came up with a research question while they were watching Todd's fish: What do fighting fish placed together do to each other?

Other research questions arise out of psychological theory. According to social-learning theorists, for example, people learn by observing others. Thus, these theorists might ask, what effects (if any) does watching television violence have on viewers?

Research questions also arise from folklore and common knowledge. For example, questions might arise from such well-known—and often-repeated—statements as "Two heads are better than one," "Opposites attract," and "Beauty is in the eye of the beholder." Psychologists ask, is it true that pairs or groups of people solve problems more effectively than people working alone? Are people with opposite personality traits really attracted to each other? Is beauty a matter of individual preference, or are there common standards for beauty?

Forming a Hypothesis

After psychologists ask a research question, they form a hypothesis about the answer to the question. A **hypothesis** is an educated guess. The accuracy of a hypothesis can be tested.

Todd's hypothesis about what two fighting fish would do to each other was that they would attack. Although Todd did not know for sure, he had reasons for thinking this. He may have based the hypothesis on the fact that the fish were called "fighting" fish. He also probably based his hypothesis on the advice of the salesperson at the pet shop not to put more than one fighting fish in the same tank. Perhaps the salesperson had even told him that two fighting fish placed together would attack each other. But because Todd had not actually seen this for himself, he could not know for sure. Thus, his suspicion was only a hypothesis, not a certainty.

Testing the Hypothesis

Because psychology is a science, psychological knowledge rests on carefully examined human experience. No matter how good a hypothesis sounds and no matter how many people believe it, a hypothesis cannot be considered to be correct until it has been scientifically tested and proved to be right. Psychologists do not rely on people's opinions. Instead, they examine the evidence and draw their own conclusions.

Psychologists answer research questions or test hypotheses through a variety of methods. To test the hypothesis that two fighting fish would attack each other, the best method would probably be to put two real fish in the same tank. But Todd did not have another fighting fish, so this was not possible. Marc suggested using a mirror to create the illusion of another fighting fish. He hoped that Todd's fish would react to its reflection in the same way it would react to a real fish, so that he, Todd, and Dan would be able to find out whether it is true that fighting fish do attack each other. Thus, holding up a mirror in front of the fish was the method Marc chose to test the boys' hypothesis.

Analyzing the Results

After psychologists have tested their hypotheses, they analyze their results. In other words, they ask what their findings mean. After Todd, Marc, and Dan saw the fighting fish fan out its fins and puff up its cheeks in reaction to seeing the image of another fish, they had to figure out how to interpret that reaction. Todd interpreted the fish's actions as going into attack position.

In most psychological studies, psychologists collect a great deal more information, or data, than Marc, Dan, and Todd did with the fish. For example, they would test their hypothesis on more than one fish. They might spend weeks, months, or even years gathering data. The more information collected, the more complex a task it is to analyze it. Often, psychologists look for patterns and relationships in the data. They must decide which data support their hypothesis and which data do not.

Drawing Conclusions

Once psychologists have analyzed their research observations, they draw conclusions about their

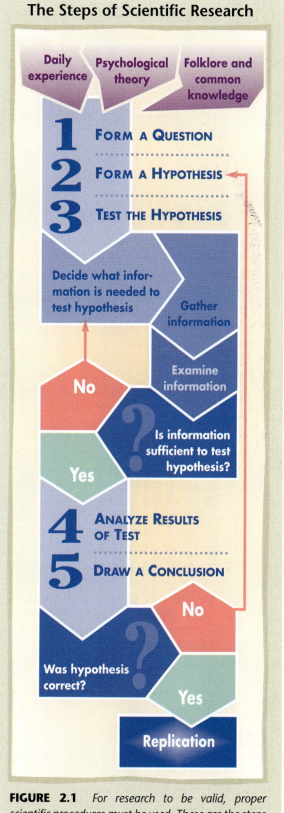

FIGURE 2.1 *For research to be valid, proper scientific procedures must be used. These are the steps that researchers generally follow.*

Despite the claims of fortune-tellers, little scientific evidence supports the existence of precognition or other forms of ESP. Studies that seem to support ESP usually cannot be replicated.

questions and their hypotheses. When their observations do not support their hypotheses, they often must change the theories or beliefs from which the hypotheses were derived. Therefore, psychologists need to keep open minds. They must be willing to adjust or modify their hypotheses if their findings make it necessary to do so.

In the fish example, once the boys had seen how the fighting fish reacted to the image of another fish and had interpreted that reaction as an attack reaction, they concluded that, yes, fighting fish do fight each other. They were satisfied that Todd's hypothesis was correct. If the fighting fish had not had an attack reaction, Todd, Marc, and Dan would not have been able to conclude that the hypothesis was correct. They would not necessarily have been able to prove that the hypothesis was *incorrect*, however. Maybe the fighting fish realized that it was only looking at a reflection and not at a real fish, but they could not have known for sure. Thus, they would have had to do more research, this time perhaps with two or more actual fish.

Replication

Even when a study carefully follows proper procedures, its findings might just represent a random occurrence. As Marc put it, maybe Todd just had a weird fish; maybe other fighting fish would react differently. For the findings of a study to be confirmed, the study must be **replicated**. That is, the study must be repeated—and it must produce the same results as before.

When scientists replicate a study but obtain different results than were obtained the first time, the findings of the first study are questioned. This is one reason that most psychologists do not believe that extrasensory perception (ESP) is a valid scientific phenomenon, even though some isolated studies have supported the existence of ESP. These studies have not yielded the same results when replicated. (See Chapter 1.)

TRUTH OR **fiction** ∎ REVISITED ∎ *It is true that you have to do a study more than once to be sure its results are valid.* The repeating of an experiment is called replication. If a study does not produce the same results more than once, the results may not have been accurate.

Sometimes scientists repeat a study under slightly different circumstances than those in the original study. In the fish example, to confirm the hypothesis that fighting fish attack each other, it would probably be best to replicate the experiment by using two or more real fish rather than one fish and its reflection.

Sometimes researchers repeat a study using a different set of participants. Todd, Marc, and Dan could have tried the same experiment with a few other fighting fish. If these fish acted differently than Todd's did, that would indicate that Todd's fish was somehow unusual. The boys might even try the experiment with different *types* of fighting fish, to see if the fish all have the same reaction. They might also try the experiment with both male and female fighting fish. In many animal species, males have different behavior patterns than females. Thus, it is important to study both males and females if the goal is to make generalizations about all members of the species.

In a study in which people are the participants, researchers might want to replicate the study using participants who differ not only in gender but also in such characteristics as age level, ethnicity, social and economic background, level of education, geographic setting, and so on. For example, if a study was done for the first time only with teenagers, the researchers might include participants from other age groups the next time. That way, the researchers could be sure that the findings held across a variety of age groups.

New Questions

Whether the findings of a research study support or contradict the hypothesis of that study, they are likely to lead to new research questions. Once Todd, Marc, and Dan had performed their fish experiment, they might have asked any number of other questions. For example, *why* do fighting fish attack each other? Does it have to do with mating, with turf, or with something else entirely? Is it a reaction they have instinctively from birth, or do they learn it as they mature? Are there any circumstances under which fighting fish do *not* attack each other? Do any other animals have similar attack reactions? Do people ever act like that?

Even if Todd's fish had totally ignored its reflection, that too would have raised new questions. Would it also ignore a real fish? And if so, why is it called a fighting fish? Under what circumstances does it fight?

Once new questions have been asked, the process begins all over again. The researchers must propose a new hypothesis about the answer to the new question. And once again, the hypothesis must be tested.

The rest of this chapter explores the different types of research methods that psychologists use to test hypotheses. These methods include the survey method, various observational methods, and the experimental method. Each of these methods has advantages and disadvantages, and some methods are better suited to certain kinds of research studies than are other methods. It might be convenient if there were one perfect method that could be used in all circumstances. But human beings are complex, and the human experience has many dimensions. Thus, several different research methods are needed to study it.

THINKING ABOUT PSYCHOLOGY

1. List and describe the five steps that scientists follow in conducting research.
2. Why is replication of a research study important?
3. **Critical Thinking** Locate a newspaper or magazine article that discusses the findings of a recent research study. Summarize the study, then list two new questions that might be asked based on the findings of the study.

2
Surveys, Samples, and Populations

When Todd, Marc, and Dan wanted to know what fighting fish would do to each other, it would have been convenient (as Dan pointed out) if they could have just asked the fish. But, of course, fish cannot talk. People, on the other hand, *can* talk. Thus, when psychologists want to find out about people's attitudes and behaviors, one possible way to gather information is to ask people directly.

The Survey Method

Gathering information by asking people directly is usually accomplished by means of a survey. In a **survey**, people are asked to respond to a series of questions about a particular subject.

Psychologists D. L. DuBois and B. J. Hirsch (1990), for example, used the survey method to examine mixed-race friendships among high school students. (See Figure 2.2.) The survey asked high school students to identify the races of their friends. More than 80 percent of White and African American students reported having a friend of the other race in school. However, fewer students

Friendship Patterns Among High School Students

Students	White	African American
Have a friend of another race in school	87%	82%
Have a friend of another race outside of school	23%	42%

FIGURE 2.2 *Research indicates that although many students have friends of a different race, fewer students see those friends outside of school.*

Source: "School and neighborhood friendship patterns of Blacks and Whites in adolescence" by D. L. DuBois and B. J. Hirsch, 1990, *Child Development*, 61, pp. 524-536.

Calvin and Hobbes   by Bill Watterson

I'M FILLING OUT A READER SURVEY FOR *CHEWING* MAGAZINE.

SEE, THEY ASKED HOW MUCH MONEY I SPEND ON GUM EACH WEEK, SO I WROTE, "$500." FOR MY AGE, I PUT "43," AND WHEN THEY ASKED WHAT MY FAVORITE FLAVOR IS, I WROTE "GARLIC/CURRY."

THIS MAGAZINE SHOULD HAVE SOME AMUSING ADS SOON.

I LOVE MESSING WITH DATA.

reported seeing these friends outside of school. DuBois and Hirsch concluded that the reason may be that even though many of the respondents attended integrated schools, the neighborhoods they lived in may have been segregated.

Psychologists conduct surveys by asking people to fill out written questionnaires or by interviewing people orally. By distributing questionnaires or by conducting interviews over the telephone or in person, researchers can rapidly survey thousands of people. Computers often aid in the analysis of the information collected.

The findings of interviews and questionnaires are not necessarily completely accurate. People may not be honest, for whatever reasons, about their attitudes or behavior. Some people may fear that their responses will not be kept confidential. Thus, they answer only what they are willing to reveal to the world at large. Other respondents may try to please the interviewers. They say what they think the interviewers want to hear.

This became clear from the results of a 1960s survey about tooth-brushing habits. If people had brushed their teeth as often as they claimed, and used the amount of toothpaste they said they used, three times as much toothpaste would have been sold in the United States as was actually sold at that time (Barringer, 1993). Why would people misrepresent their tooth-brushing behaviors? Perhaps because they did not want the interviewers to know that they did not brush their teeth as often as their dentists advised.

Populations and Samples

When researchers conduct any type of study, they must consider what group or groups of people they wish to examine and how respondents will be selected. This is particularly true with surveys.

Imagine that your town or city is about to hold a referendum on whether to institute a 10:00 P.M. curfew for people under the age of 18. How might you most accurately predict the outcome of the referendum? You might conduct a poll by asking people how they are planning to vote. But whom would you select to be in the poll?

Researchers who conduct studies in densely populated areas have a large pool of possible participants from which to draw.

Suppose you only polled the students in your psychology class. Do you think you would be able to make an accurate prediction? Probably not. Many of the people in your psychology class are probably under the age of 18 and thus might be particularly likely to oppose the curfew because they think it would restrict their freedom. In addition, most cannot vote. But, of course, the voters in the actual referendum would all be at least 18. And since the curfew would not restrict them, they might be more inclined to vote for it. Thus, a poll of your psychology class would probably not be very useful for predicting the outcome of this particular referendum.

To accurately predict an outcome, it is necessary to study a group that represents the target population. A **target population** is the whole group you want to study or describe. In the curfew example, the target population consists of all possible voters on the referendum. It does not consist of nonvoters, such as children. The question is not whom the referendum will affect if passed, but whether the referendum will be passed or not. Thus, only voters are relevant to the question.

However, it would be costly and difficult—if not impossible—to interview or question every member of the target population (in this case, all voters in the area). Instead, researchers study a **sample**, which is only part of the target population.

Selecting Samples

Psychologists and other scientists select samples scientifically to ensure that the samples represent the populations they are supposed to represent. In other words, a sample should be as similar as possible to the target population. Otherwise, researchers will be unable to use the sample to make accurate predictions about the population from which the sample is drawn.

A high school class does not represent all people in the town or city where the school is located, particularly in terms of opinions on an issue that pertains to age (such as a curfew for people under 18). Thus, the answers of people in a high school class would be biased. In this case, they would probably be biased against the curfew. On the other hand, researchers probably could predict the outcome of the referendum by interviewing a large number of people who represent all voters in the town or city.

One way that scientists try to obtain a sample that represents the target population is by using a random sample. In a **random sample**, individuals are selected by chance from the target population. Each member of the population has an equal chance of being chosen. If the random sample is big enough, chances are that it will accurately represent the whole population.

Researchers can also use a stratified sample. In a **stratified sample**, subgroups in the population are represented proportionally in the sample. For instance, about 12 percent of the American population is African American. A stratified sample of the American population would thus be about 12 percent African American. (See Figure 2.3.)

A large random sample is likely to be accurately stratified even if researchers take no special steps to ensure that it is. A random sample of 1,000 to 1,500 people will usually represent the general American population reasonably well. A sample of 5 million motorcycle owners, however, would not. A large sample size by itself does not necessarily guarantee that a sample represents a target population, particularly if the sample is not a random sample. Motorcycle owners probably do not represent all people in the United States.

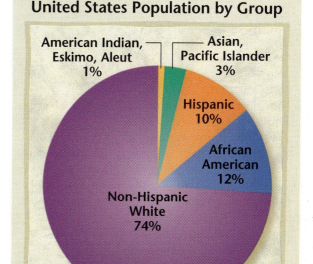

United States Population by Group

American Indian, Eskimo, Aleut 1%

Asian, Pacific Islander 3%

Hispanic 10%

African American 12%

Non-Hispanic White 74%

FIGURE 2.3 *In a stratified sample of the U.S. population, various groups should be represented in the same proportions as they are represented in the whole population. In a stratified sample consisting of 100 people, how many African Americans would you expect, based on this pie chart, to find in the sample?*

Source: Statistical Abstract of the United States 1995. Figures have been rounded.

EXPLORING

DIVERSITY

Representing Human Diversity in Research

Throughout the history of psychology, men have been included as research participants more often than women. Why is this? One probable reason has been prejudice—the notion that men are more important than women or that men represent people as a whole more than women do.

Another reason has been availability. Many research study participants have traditionally been drawn from the armed services and universities. The majority of people in the armed services are male. And only in recent years

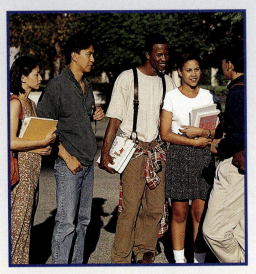

Many research studies draw their participants from college campuses, which have grown increasingly diverse in recent years.

have the numbers of women in colleges and universities grown equal to (and in some cases exceeded) those of men.

Health, in particular, is an area in which there has been much more research with men than with women. Areas in which more research with women is needed include the promotion of women's health (including disease prevention), women and depression, and women and addiction (including alcohol and other substances).

Violence against women is another area that requires more research. Large numbers of women are assaulted—slapped, beaten, choked, or attacked with a weapon—by their spouses or boyfriends. More research is needed to determine how this violence affects women's lives. Another area of research concern is women and work. Women are more likely than men to put in a "double shift" every day. That is, many women put in a full day on the job. Then they put in a whole other shift of grocery shopping, cooking, cleaning, and

otherwise caring for their families. Further research is needed on the effects of this overload on women.

Psychology once mistakenly generalized findings of research done only with men to women. Most psychologists now recognize the flaws of this generalization (Ader & Johnson, 1994). Problems with overgeneralization remain, however. Some psychologists overgeneralize findings of research done only with middle-aged, middle-income White women to all women (Yoder & Kahn, 1993). Because of age-related, socioeconomic, and cultural differences, the behavior and mental processes of women may vary from group to group. When these distinctions are not made, issues of importance to some groups of women—and possibly to all women—tend to be ignored.

The American Psychological Association (1994b) recommends that the write-up of a study's results include a clear description of the research sample in terms of ethnicity, gender, and any other potentially relevant characteristics. For example, if a sample uses only male participants, the report should include this information. When such descriptions are included, the reader is less likely to assume that what is true for one group is also true for another.

THINK ABOUT IT

What might be some ways to increase the number of participants from traditionally underrepresented groups in psychological studies?

It is not true that asking the students in your psychology class for their opinions on a topic is a good way to figure out how people in the larger community feel about that topic. To find out how community members feel about a topic, you would need to select a sample that represents the community. Your psychology class probably does not.

Men and women might tend to prefer different types of cars, so a study of people's car preferences would need to have both male and female participants.

Generalizing Results

Sometimes, for one reason or another, researchers do not use a sample that represents an entire population. In some cases, the researchers want to know about only one group within the population and thus have no reason to study other groups. In other cases, it may be impractical or impossible to obtain a random or stratified sample.

In such cases, researchers are cautious about generalizing their findings to groups other than those from which their samples were drawn. For example, because their sample used only one fish, Todd, Marc, and Dan could not conclude that *all* fish would fight each other or even necessarily that all Siamese fighting fish would. Todd's one fish could not be assumed to represent all fish. Thus, the boys could not know for sure whether they would get the same results if they used other types of fish.

The same is true with people. Researchers cannot learn about the preferences of all people by studying only one group of people, such as men. In a study about car preferences, for example, psychologists would avoid generalizing from a sample that was made up only of men because men's preferences for cars might not be the same as women's. In other words, if researchers found that men prefer certain types of cars, the researchers could not conclude that women will prefer those same types of cars if the study did not include women.

The gender of the people in the sample is not the only characteristic that researchers must take into account. For instance, researchers cannot learn about the attitudes of Americans in general if they limit their observations to people who live in one part of the country (for example, the Midwest) or to people from one socioeconomic background (for example, wealthy people).

Volunteer Bias

Researchers often have little control over who responds to surveys or participates in research studies. Although the researchers may choose whom to give a questionnaire to, for example, they usually cannot force people to *complete* the questionnaire. Thus, another factor that psychologists must take into account regarding the participants of a study has to do with **volunteer bias**. That is, people who volunteer to participate in research studies often differ from people who do not.

For one thing, volunteers are usually more willing than other people to disclose personal information. Volunteers may also be more interested in research than people who do not volunteer. Furthermore, they may have more spare time to participate in research studies than other people. Depending on what the study is about, any or all of these factors—as well as others—could skew the results. That is, these factors could slant the results in a particular direction.

Have you ever filled out and returned a questionnaire printed in a magazine? Popular magazines such as *Glamour, Seventeen,* and *Psychology Today* often survey readers' attitudes about various topics

The Survey Method

Research Method	Description	Advantages	Disadvantages
Survey Method	People respond to a series of questions about a particular subject.	Enables the researcher to gather information about large numbers of people.	People may not be entirely honest in answering questions. Survey samples are not always representative of the population as a whole.

FIGURE 2.4   *One way to learn about people's behaviors and attitudes is simply to ask them. Psychologists often do just that by conducting surveys. Surveys, however, have some disadvantages.*

and behaviors in certain circumstances. Such a questionnaire might, for instance, ask readers about how they like to spend their leisure time. Do they prefer to go to the movies, visit with friends, read magazines, or listen to music?

Thousands of readers complete these types of questionnaires and send them in. However, do they represent the general population of the United States? Probably not. In a magazine survey, a disproportionate number of responses to the question posed above would probably be "read magazines." After all, the questionnaire itself comes from a magazine. People who do not like to read magazines probably would not fill out the questionnaire in the first place. They would not have seen it.

Such magazine surveys are affected by volunteer bias. For example, readers who have enough time to fill out the questionnaire may tend to have different leisure preferences than people who are too busy to fill out the questionnaire. This might affect the findings.

THINKING ABOUT PSYCHOLOGY

1. What are two different ways by which surveys are conducted?

2. Explain the importance of random and stratified sampling.

3. **Critical Thinking**   Give an example of a survey that might produce different results depending on whether participants volunteered or were selected randomly. How might the results differ, and what would account for the difference?

3 Methods of Observation

Almost everyone, at one time or another, observes other people. We observe people as they talk, eat, work, play, and interact with others and with us. Based on our observations of other people (and also of ourselves), we tend to make generalizations about human behavior and human nature.

Our observations and generalizations usually serve us fairly well in our daily lives. But no matter how many experiences we have had, most of our personal observations are fleeting and haphazard. We sift through experience for things that interest us, but we often ignore the obvious because it does not fit our ideas about how things ought to be. Thus, we cannot draw scientific conclusions based only on our own unstructured observations.

Even the most respected psychologists may use their personal observations as a starting point for their research and as the basis for their hypotheses. Once they have begun their investigations, however, they use more careful methods of observation. The survey method, discussed above, is one such method of observation. Other methods of observation include the testing, case-study, longitudinal, cross-sectional, naturalistic-observation, and laboratory-observation methods.

The Testing Method

Psychologists sometimes use psychological tests to learn about human behavior. There are several types of psychological tests. Intelligence tests measure general learning ability. Aptitude tests measure specific abilities and special talents, such as musical ability and mechanical skills. Still other tests measure vocational interests.

Personality tests are another type of psychological test psychologists use. Personality tests measure people's character traits and temperament. For example, personality tests might be used to assess whether people are socially outgoing or aggressive. Personality tests might also be used to diagnose psychological problems such as anxiety and depression. (See Chapter 15.)

The Case-Study Method

Another research method psychologists use is the case-study method. A **case study** is an in-depth investigation of an individual or a small group. To learn about the people who are being studied, researchers may observe or speak with them, interview others who know them, find out more about their backgrounds and personal histories, and so on. Psychologists use what they learn in a case study to generalize broader principles that apply to the larger population.

Sigmund Freud developed psychoanalytic theory largely on the basis of case studies. Freud carefully studied the people who sought his help. He interviewed some of them for many years, developing as complete a record of their childhoods as he could. He also looked for the factors that seemed to contribute to their current problems.

Some case studies focus on rare circumstances or events. One such case study involved a girl named Genie. When she was only 20 months old, her father locked her in a small room. She was kept there until she was rescued at the age of 13 (Rymer, 1993). Her social contacts were limited to her mother, who fed her, and her father, who often beat her. No one spoke to her. And in all those years, she herself did not say a word.

After her rescue, Genie's language development followed the normal sequence of language development. (See Chapter 8.) Genie never learned to use language as well as most people, however. This case study suggests that there is a special period in early childhood when it is easiest for people to learn language.

Although case studies can sometimes offer great insights, psychologists are cautious about generalizing from case studies. This is particularly true of case studies that cannot be replicated, such as

Some aptitude tests measure the test taker's physical or perceptual abilities.

Genie's. Because of the rarity and cruelty of Genie's experience, scientists would never repeat this study. Thus they cannot know for sure, on the basis of Genie's experience alone, whether the theory about a special language-learning period in childhood is correct. Perhaps other, unknown factors were responsible for Genie's apparent inability to achieve full language competence.

Furthermore, case studies lend themselves to some of the same pitfalls that surveys do, particularly when the case studies are based on interviews of people about their past experiences. Most people's recollections are filled with gaps and inaccuracies. Some of these inaccuracies occur because people tend not to remember the details of events. Some people even intentionally distort their pasts to impress the researcher. And sometimes without meaning to, researchers subtly encourage people to answer in certain ways to fulfill the researchers' expectations. For example, some psychoanalysts have been criticized for encouraging people to interpret their behavior according to Freud's psychoanalytic theory (Bandura, 1986).

Longitudinal and Cross-Sectional Methods

Just as Freud studied some of his patients over a matter of years, so too do some psychological studies observe participants over a long period of time. Some research topics, such as those concerned with development throughout the life span, deal with how people or other organisms change over time.

To study such topics, psychologists often use the **longitudinal method**. In this method, researchers select a group of participants and then observe those participants over a period of time, often years or even decades. By using this method, psychologists can observe the ways in which individuals change over time.

Usually the observations are conducted at intervals, perhaps once a year. For example, if psychologists wanted to find out more about how people learn language, they might select a group of six-month-olds who do not yet know how to use language. Then once a month, say, the researchers might observe the children to find out how their language skills are changing over time. By the time the children are three or four years old and they are no longer learning language at such a rapid pace, the psychologists might observe them only once or twice a year.

TRUTH OR fiction REVISITED

It is true that some psychological studies take years or even decades to complete. These studies may be longitudinal studies, which examine the ways in which individuals change by observing them over a long period of time.

Needless to say, longitudinal studies are extremely time-consuming. Imagine how much patience you would need to know that even if you started a study right now, you would not get conclusive results for another 5, 10, or 15 years. Moreover, longitudinal studies tend to be expensive, and they are risky. There is often no guarantee that participants will remain available over the long time period that they are to be studied.

To avoid some of the problems with longitudinal studies, psychologists may use the cross-sectional method to find out about changes over time. In the **cross-sectional method**, instead of following a set of individuals over a number of years, researchers select a sample that includes people of different ages. The researchers then compare the behavior of the participants in the different age groups. For example, in the language-learning example, psychologists might select 12-month-olds, 14-month-olds, 16-month-olds, and so on. They would then observe the language skills of members of each age group and compare the groups with one another in order to make generalizations about how children learn language over time.

Information gained in cross-sectional studies is less reliable than information from longitudinal studies. When psychologists study one individual over a period of time, as in a longitudinal study, they know that any changes they observe in that individual are due to her or his experiences or development. But when they compare groups of people of different ages at the same time, as in a cross-sectional study, psychologists cannot be certain what factors are responsible for differences among the participants. Perhaps the differences are due to developmental changes, but perhaps the participants were simply different to begin with.

The Naturalistic-Observation Method

One way that psychologists sometimes find out about children's language skills is to observe children as they use language naturally, such as while they interact with other children and adults in play groups. This is called **naturalistic observation**, or field study. People often use naturalistic observation in their daily lives without even knowing it. That is, they observe other people or animals in the "field"—in their natural habitats. In the case of people, field settings include homes, schools, office buildings, restaurants—anyplace where people spend time.

A DAY IN THE LIFE

If Todd had wanted to use naturalistic observation to observe fish, he would have had to go to a river, a lake, or an ocean—someplace where fish exist naturally. But without realizing it, Todd used naturalistic observation all the time to watch *people*. In his job at the restaurant, Todd could not avoid noticing the different ways in which customers ate their food. Some people gobbled down their meals quickly, almost without pausing. Others ate delicately, carefully chewing each bite. He wondered what accounted for these differences in people's eating habits.

Psychologists, too, wonder about such questions. They have, like Todd, used naturalistic observation to study how people eat. They have watched people in restaurants to learn, for example, whether slender people and heavy people eat their food differently. Such field research has shown that heavy people tend to eat somewhat more rapidly than slender people. Heavy people also chew less often and leave less food on their plates.

This type of study has led to suggestions about how heavy people might diet more effectively. For example, they might eat more slowly and take less food to begin with so that when they clean their plates, they have eaten less. (See Chapter 13.)

This researcher uses naturalistic observation to study a meerkat, a small mammal native to Africa.

In naturalistic observation, psychologists do not interfere with the organisms they are observing. In the restaurant example, psychologists would not ask the diners questions or encourage them to eat a particular food. They would simply observe the people eating.

The Laboratory-Observation Method

Some matters simply cannot be studied in a naturalistic setting. For example, Todd could not realistically have observed his tropical fish in their natural habitat.

Sometimes it is more useful for a psychologist to observe behavior in a laboratory rather than in the field. This is called the **laboratory-observation** method. Laboratories are not necessarily sterile rooms tended by people in white coats; a laboratory is any place that provides the opportunity for observation or experimentation. As such, many laboratories are quite informal.

In fact, even Todd's fish tank was a type of laboratory, a small artificial lake. To make the environment suitable for the fish, Todd had to do many things, such as monitor the temperature and acid content of the water. Once he had set up his laboratory, he was able to observe the behavior of the fish. He watched the fish dart under the protecting leaves. He saw how they created and defended their

turf. He observed their mating behavior and watched them breed. Sometimes their behavior amazed him—such as when they immediately swam to the surface of the water when he turned on the light. In just a few days after Todd had brought the fish home, they had learned that they would be fed when the light went on.

Like Todd, psychologists often study animals by using the laboratory-observation method. B. F. Skinner created special enclosed environments, which became known as Skinner boxes, to study the behavior of rats. In one of these miniature laboratories, a food pellet drops into the box when the rat in the box presses a lever. Rats learn quickly to press the levers, especially when they are hungry. Other psychologists have built mazes for rats to see how effectively they learn routes through the mazes. (See Chapter 6.) Both the Skinner box and the maze are examples of laboratories.

Psychologists sometimes use a laboratory to control the environment of a study. For example, if they wanted to see whether the amount of light in a room affects how much people eat, they would need to be able to control the lighting in the room where people were eating. Similarly, Todd's fish tank was a place where he could observe the behavior of the fish while he controlled what happened in the environment. He could, for instance, observe how the fish responded if he changed the temperature of the water or the type of food he fed them.

Six Methods of Observation

Research Method	Description	Advantages	Disadvantages
Testing Method	Several types of tests measure various elements of human behavior such as abilities, interests, and personality.	Enables researchers to gain insight to certain aspects of an individual's abilities or behavior.	Does not always provide a complete or accurate representation of an individual's true abilities or personality.
Case-Study Method	Researchers conduct in-depth investigations of individuals or small groups.	Provides insight to specific cases.	May focus on isolated circumstances or events that cannot be replicated. People interviewed in case studies may distort their past experiences. Researchers may unintentionally encourage people to answer questions a certain way.
Longitudinal Method	A group of participants are observed at intervals over an extended period of time.	Enables researchers to see how individuals change over time.	Time-consuming and expensive. Participants may not be available for the duration of the study.
Cross-Sectional Method	Researchers compare the differences and similarities among people in different age groups at a given time.	Less time-consuming than the longitudinal method for studying changes over time.	Differences between the members of the sample cannot necessarily be attributed to age or development.
Naturalistic-Observation Method	Researchers observe the behavior of people or animals in their natural habitats.	Enables researchers to witness the behavior of people or animals in settings that are not artificial.	Researchers have no control over the setting or the events that occur.
Laboratory-Observation Method	Participants are observed in a laboratory setting.	Enables researchers to control certain aspects of the study.	Laboratories cannot duplicate real-life environments.

FIGURE 2.5 *Researchers employ several types of observation methods to test their hypotheses.*

Analyzing Observations

Once psychologists have made their observations, they must analyze and interpret them. One method they use is correlation. **Correlation** is a measure of how closely one thing is related to another. The stronger the correlation between two things, the more closely those two things are related. For example, there is a strong correlation between height and ability to reach items that are located on the top shelf of a cabinet. The taller the person, the greater that person's ability to reach the top shelf.

In psychology, researchers often look for correlations between various characteristics or traits. For instance, are people with a stronger need than others for achievement more likely to advance in their jobs? What is the relationship between stress and health? Between grades earned by students and extracurricular involvement?

Positive and Negative Correlation   To determine whether there is a correlation between achievement and occupational success, a researcher might compare need for achievement as measured by a personality test with the salaries of the test takers. There is, in fact, a correlation between the need for achievement and salaries, and it is a **positive correlation**. (See Figure 2.6.) That is, as one goes up, so does the other. Generally speaking, people who feel a greater need to achieve earn more money (Ginsburg & Bronstein, 1993; Gottfried et al., 1994).

There are, of course, some exceptions. Some people are highly motivated to achieve, but they do not have high-paying jobs. Others are average in their need for achievement but earn very high incomes. Therefore, factors other than a need for achievement also contribute to high salaries. One such factor is the type of job one has; people in some kinds of jobs earn more than people in other kinds of jobs. In addition, for people to succeed, they also have to know how to interact with others, how to manage people, and how to manage multiple tasks at one time (Collier, 1994; Sternberg et al., 1995). Thus, there is a positive correlation between success and a variety of factors.

In contrast, there is a **negative correlation** between stress and health. As one goes up, the other goes down. (See Figure 2.6.) As the amount of stress on people increases, their immune systems become less capable of fighting off illness—thus, the greater the stress, the poorer the health. This is why students under stress are more likely than other students to get colds (Cohen et al., 1993).

Positive and Negative Correlations

Positive Correlation

Generally speaking, people who have a higher need for achievement achieve higher salaries.

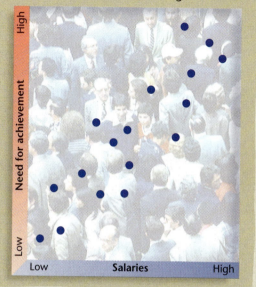

Negative Correlation

Generally speaking, the immune systems of people who are under high amounts of stress tend to function more poorly than the immune systems of people who are under less stress.

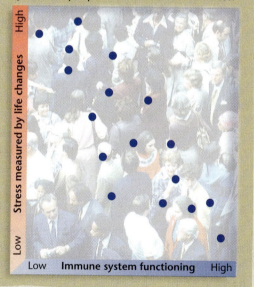

FIGURE 2.6   *Each dot represents an observation of one person. When two factors show a positive correlation, one rises as the other rises. When two factors show a negative correlation, one of the factors rises as the other one falls.*

Correlation Versus Cause and Effect

FIGURE 2.7 *Although a correlation may exist between high grades and extracurricular involvement, this does not mean that one causes the other.*

Limits of Correlation Correlation describes relationships. It does not, however, reveal cause and effect. Just because two things are related does not necessarily mean that one causes the other.

For example, suppose you were conducting a study in your school and discovered a positive correlation between students' grades and their level of involvement in extracurricular activities. In other words, suppose you found that students who earn high grades in their classes also participate heavily in extracurricular activities. Does this mean that earning high grades *causes* students to become involved in extracurricular activities, or that involvement in extracurricular activities *causes* students to earn high grades? Not necessarily. It might be that there are other factors—such as a general desire to succeed—that encourage or cause *both* high grades and extracurricular involvement. (See Figure 2.7.) Thus, we cannot conclude on the basis of the correlation alone that one causes the other.

When Todd noticed a correlation between the amount of food his fish were eating and the way they were behaving—they were eating less and were acting sluggish—Todd assumed that the fish were sluggish because they were not eating enough. In other words, he assumed that one factor (decreased amount of food eaten) was causing the other (sluggish behavior). On the basis of this assumption, Todd changed the type of food he was feeding the fish.

But Todd's assumption may have been mistaken. Perhaps, for example, the fish were sick and their illness was causing both the odd behavior and the lack of appetite. There could have been a hidden factor at work that was acting on both of the other factors to create a correlation between them. As you will see, experiments allow us to draw conclusions about cause and effect.

THINKING ABOUT PSYCHOLOGY

1. What is a case study? Name one drawback of the case-study method.

2. What is the difference between the naturalistic-observation method and the laboratory-observation method?

3. **Critical Thinking** Suppose you wanted to find out if there was a correlation between age and volume level for listening to music for people between the ages of 15 and 55. Which observational methods might you use to study this?

4
The Experimental Method

The method researchers use to answer questions about cause and effect is the experiment. In an **experiment**, participants receive what is called a treatment, such as a change in room temperature or a new drug. Researchers then carefully observe the participants to determine how the treatment influences their behavior (if at all).

When Todd switched fish foods to see if the new food would make the fish eat more and stop acting sluggish, he was conducting an experiment. Changing the food was the treatment. Similarly, when Marc used a mirror to see how the fighting fish would react, that was an experiment too. Holding up the mirror was the treatment.

As with other research methods, the experimental method has some limitations. For example, the conditions created in an experiment may not accurately reflect conditions in real life. Almost by their very nature, experiments must simplify things somewhat in order to yield useful information about cause and effect. Nevertheless, experiments do yield useful information much of the time, and for that reason, psychologists frequently turn to the experimental method in their research.

Independent and Dependent Variables

Experiments contain **variables**, which are factors that can vary, or change. In an experiment, the **independent variable** is the factor that researchers manipulate so that they can determine its effect. Suppose researchers are testing the hypothesis that warm temperatures cause aggression in humans. In that experiment, temperature is the independent variable because that is what researchers are manipulating to observe its effect.

In the same experiment, level of aggression is the dependent variable. As you might guess from its name, a **dependent variable** depends on something—the independent variable. The researchers want to find out whether level of aggression depends on temperature.

In Todd's experiment with the fish food, the type of food he was using was the independent variable. The extent to which the fish acted sluggish and the amount they ate were dependent variables.

Experimental and Control Groups

Ideal experiments use experimental and control groups. Members of an **experimental group** receive the treatment. Members of a **control group** do not. Every effort is made to ensure that all other conditions are held constant for both the experimental group and the control group. This method makes it possible for researchers to conclude that the experimental results are caused by the treatment, not by something else.

Researchers randomly assign participants to one group or the other. For example, in an experiment about students' grades and extracurricular involvement, some students would be randomly assigned to participate in extracurricular activities. These students would make up the experimental group. Others would be randomly assigned to *not* participate in extracurricular activities. These students would be the control group. Once researchers ensured that all other factors—such as educational background—were the same for the two groups,

they could then compare the groups to see whether involvement in extracurricular activities makes a difference in the grades participants earn.

When an experiment uses control groups as well as experimental groups, it is called a **controlled experiment**. When Todd switched foods to see if a different food would change the behavior of the fish, he was *not* conducting a controlled experiment. Because the fish acted less sluggish after he switched their food, he assumed that the new food was responsible. But what if another factor caused the change in their behavior? Perhaps they had been sick and had recovered naturally. Or perhaps the temperature of the water had changed without Todd's realizing it.

To know for sure whether the food was responsible for the changed behavior of the fish, Todd would have to do a controlled experiment. First, he would have to randomly organize the fish into two groups. He would give the experimental group the new food. The control group would receive the usual food. If he separated the groups with a piece of glass in the tank, he could keep all other factors —such as water temperature and acidity—the same for both groups of fish. (See Figure 2.8 on page 42.) If after a period of time the fish that received the new food were no longer acting strange, but the fish that received the old food still were, he could conclude that the new fish food had made the difference. But if all of the fish continued to act strange, or if they all started to act normal again, something other than the new food must be the cause.

Another example of a study in which it is useful to have a control group concerns a key question for psychologists: Does psychotherapy work? In other words, do people who undergo therapy feel better, or feel better faster, than people who do not?

Millions of people seek help from psychologists. Many of them believe their therapists have helped them. For example, a former patient might say, "I was in terrible shape before therapy, but I feel much better now." Yet we do not know what would have happened if this person had not sought help. Many people, of course, feel better about their problems as time goes on, with or without therapy. In other words, an individual's involvement in therapy is not part of a controlled experiment. There is no control group—an identical person who has *not* gone to a therapist. Of course, we could never find such a person because no two people are exactly the same.

However, researchers can make up for this by conducting an experiment on the effects of therapy

FIGURE 2.8 *In an experiment to test the hypothesis that a different food changes the behavior of fish, the fish might be divided at random into two groups. The groups are separated by a piece of glass. Except for the type of food received, all other factors, such as water temperature, are kept the same for both groups.*

using a large number of people. In such an experiment, some people would be randomly assigned to an experimental group and would receive therapy. Others, with the same problems as those in the first group, would be assigned to a control group and would not receive therapy. Even though the people in the experimental group would not be identical to the people in the control group, individual differences would probably average out as long as the groups were large enough. Thus, researchers could determine whether people who receive therapy fare better than those who do not. It would be a controlled experiment.

The Placebo Effect

The question of whether psychotherapy works is further complicated by the fact that people who seek psychotherapy usually expect it to work. Imagine that a person who has a problem is about to see a therapist about it. Chances are, the person is expecting that the visit will be helpful. Otherwise, why would he or she be going?

In research studies and in our daily lives, our expectations affect what happens to us. Feeling better simply because we expect to feel better—and for no other reason—is an example of the placebo (pluh-SEE-boh) effect. A **placebo** is a substance or treatment that has no effect apart from a person's belief in it. For example, one type of placebo is a tablet that appears to contain a real drug but actually has no medicinal value. Someone who has a headache and takes the tablet to feel better might start to feel better even though the tablet does not contain any medicine—as long as the person *thinks* it contains medicine.

People undergoing therapy might find it helpful not only because of the therapy itself but also because of the expectation that it will help.

Single-Blind Studies

One way that researchers can avoid the influence of expectations is by keeping participants unaware of, or blind to, the treatment they are receiving. In a **single-blind study**, participants do not know whether they are receiving the treatment or not. In other words, they do not know whether they are in the experimental group or the control group. For example, if a researcher wanted to test the effects of a particular drug, the experimental group would receive the drug, and the control group would receive a placebo. Neither group would know for sure which one they were given.

Figure 2.9 shows experimental conditions in which some people are given a real drug and others are given a placebo. In this example, half of those given the real drug are deceived. They are told they are taking the placebo. Half of those given the placebo also are deceived. They are told they are taking the drug. The rest of the participants are told the truth about what they are taking.

What does it mean if the people taking the new drug improve faster, regardless of what they have been told, but people who take the placebo do not? It means the drug is effective. What does it mean if all the people who are told they are taking the drug get better faster, regardless of whether they are taking the drug or the placebo? It means that they improve because of their expectations—because of a belief that they are taking a helpful drug—and not because of the effects of the drug itself. Thus, the drug in and of itself has few if any benefits.

Double-Blind Studies

Participants may not be the only people involved in an experiment who have expectations. Researchers themselves may also have expectations, such as about the effectiveness of a particular treatment. It is therefore useful if the people observing the participants are also unaware of who has had the treatment and who has had the placebo. A study in which both participants and experimenters are unaware of who has obtained the treatment is called a **double-blind study**.

Double-blind studies are required by the Food and Drug Administration before new drugs can be put on the market (Carroll et al., 1994). People in these studies are assigned at random to take the real drug or the placebo. Neither the participants nor the people who measure the results know who is taking what. Thus, the people who measure the

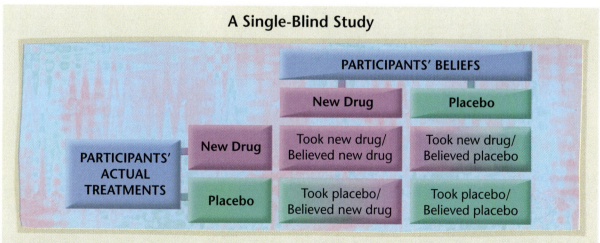

A Single-Blind Study

PARTICIPANTS' BELIEFS

PARTICIPANTS' ACTUAL TREATMENTS		New Drug	Placebo
	New Drug	Took new drug/ Believed new drug	Took new drug/ Believed placebo
	Placebo	Took placebo/ Believed new drug	Took placebo/ Believed placebo

FIGURE 2.9 *In a single-blind study testing the effectiveness of a drug, participants are divided into four groups. People in one group receive the drug and are told that they are receiving the drug. Members of the second group receive the drug and are told that they are receiving a placebo. Participants in the third group receive a placebo but are told that they are receiving the drug. People in the fourth group receive a placebo and are told that they are receiving a placebo.*

The Experimental Method

Research Method	Description	Advantages	Disadvantages
Experimental Method	Researchers administer a treatment, then carefully observe the participants to determine how the treatment influences their behavior, if at all.	Researchers are able to manipulate variables to determine cause and effect. Laboratory setting enables researcher to monitor and record all stages of the experiment.	Conditions created in the laboratory may not accurately reflect the conditions of real life. Experiments may be subject to volunteer bias, researcher bias, and the placebo effect.

FIGURE 2.10   *The experimental method allows researchers to determine cause and effect.*

effects can remain unbiased. After the final measurements are made, an impartial panel (made up of people who *do* know who had the real drug and who did not) determines, on the basis of the measurements of the unbiased observers, whether the effects of the drug differed from those of the placebo.

THINKING ABOUT PSYCHOLOGY

1. Define *independent variable* and *dependent variable*. Give an example of each.
2. What is a controlled experiment? What is the difference between an experimental group and a control group?
3. **Critical Thinking**   Design an experiment that uses a double-blind procedure.

5
Ethical Issues

Ethics are standards for proper and responsible behavior. Psychologists follow ethical standards to promote the dignity of the individual, foster human welfare, and maintain scientific integrity. Ethical standards prevent scientists from undertaking research or treatments that will be harmful to human participants. Specific ethical guidelines have been established by the American Psychological Association (APA). The APA is a scientific and professional organization of psychologists.

Research with People

Ethical standards limit the type of research that psychologists may conduct. Imagine trying to study whether early separation of children from their mothers impairs the children's social development. Scientifically, such a study might provide important information. But it would be unethical to purposefully separate infants from their mothers to study the effects of such a separation. Thus, psychologists would not seriously consider running an experiment that involved intentional separation.

One alternative research approach to such a study might be to observe the development of children who have already been separated from their mothers from an early age. However, it would be difficult to draw conclusions from such research. The same factors that led to the separation—such as the death of the parents—may have influenced a child's development as much as (or more than) the separation itself. Even if there was a positive correlation between separation from the mother and impaired social development, we could not prove cause and effect—that one caused the other.

What are the ethical standards researchers adhere to? The APA has provided some guidelines about what is needed to make a study ethical (APA, 1994a). These guidelines include two important principles: confidentiality and informed consent.

Confidentiality   Psychologists treat the records of research participants and clients as confidential. In other words, the records are private. This is

CASE STUDIES
AND OTHER TRUE STORIES

The Hawthorne Plant Study: A Flawed Experiment

In 1927, researchers began a study in the Hawthorne plant of the Western Electric Company in Cicero, Illinois. They had been called in by the factory's managers to find out what conditions in the factory might be changed to boost productivity. The researchers designed a study in which productivity was the dependent variable and length of rest periods, workday, and workweek were the independent variables.

The researchers selected five women as participants in the study. The women were to work as a team in a room where they could be observed. The researchers introduced rest pauses of varying lengths throughout the workday. They observed the women to see how their productivity was affected. The researchers then began to shorten the workday and, later, the workweek. Again, they observed the changes in productivity.

At first, the researchers observed that as they increased rest periods and shortened the workday and workweek, the women's overall output increased. It appeared that, with more rest, workers returned to their jobs refreshed and therefore were able to produce more. To check their findings, the researchers slowly returned to the original schedule—with shorter rest periods, a longer workday, and a longer workweek.

To the surprise of the researchers, the women's output remained higher than it had been at the beginning of the study. How could that be? The research team concluded that the increase in output was caused not by the independent variables (length of rest pauses, workday, and workweek) but by another variable—the women's awareness that they were being observed. They felt special because of the unusual attention they were receiving; thus, they worked harder.

This phenomenon came to be known as the "Hawthorne effect." It was a valuable finding, and led to the theory that one effective way to increase worker productivity was simply to pay more attention to the workers. However, its value notwithstanding, the finding was accidental and a result of a flawed study design.

To test the variables they wanted to test, the researchers could have conducted a blind study. In such a study, at least some of the participants would not have known they were being observed. Alternatively, the researchers could have established a control group—a group of participants who knew they were being observed but did not receive any of the treatments that the members of the experimental group received.

The design of the Hawthorne study had some other flaws as well. For one thing, the experimental group was exceedingly small. A sample size of five is really not large enough to be able to generalize conclusions about the larger population. Furthermore, the sample did not remain constant over the course of the whole experiment. Two of the women in the group were replaced in the middle of the study because they talked too much, their productivity was low, and they were considered a negative influence on the others. Their removal may well have biased the results in favor of increased productivity.

Moreover, the researchers may have misinterpreted the results of the study. The conclusion that productivity remained high even after the women returned to the original schedule was not completely correct. Total output stayed about the same, but it was achieved in more hours. In other words, hourly productivity actually *dropped*. In addition, the researchers never considered that the longer one does a job, the more skilled one becomes. That in itself may increase productivity.

Because of these flaws, the existence of the Hawthorne effect has been called into question (Jones, 1992). The Hawthorne effect remains only a hypothesis.

THINK ABOUT IT

How might you redesign the Hawthorne study to eliminate its flaws?

Participants in psychological studies sign consent forms to indicate that they understand the research.

or not to participate. The provision of information and the opportunity to choose give people some degree of control and make participation less stressful (Dill et al., 1982).

Deception On the other hand, some psychological experiments cannot be run without deceiving people. For instance, new drug experiments and other blind studies cannot be conducted without keeping participants unaware of the treatment they are receiving or of the nature of the study. In order for the study to be valid, some participants must be deceived. In drug experiments, for example, participants might be told they are taking a real drug when they are actually taking a placebo, or vice versa.

Psychologists have debated the ethics of deceiving participants in research (Fisher & Fyrberg, 1994). According to the APA's statement of ethical principles, psychologists may use deception only under specified conditions:

- when they believe that the benefits of the research outweigh its potential harm
- when they believe that the individuals might have been willing to participate if they had understood the benefits of the research
- when participants receive an explanation of the study after it has occurred

Explaining what happened in the study once it is over helps avoid misunderstandings about the research. Explanations also reduce participants' anxieties and let the participants maintain their dignity (Blanck et al., 1992).

because psychologists respect people's right to privacy and also because people are more likely to disclose true information and feelings when they know that what they say will remain confidential (Blanck et al., 1992).

In certain very rare circumstances, such as when a client reveals plans to harm someone, a psychologist may disregard confidentiality in order to protect the well-being of the client or of other people. Such situations, however, are definitely the exception rather than the rule. Even when they do arise, psychologists must think long and hard about whether breaking confidentiality is the appropriate thing to do.

Informed Consent The APA has distinct restrictions against research studies that could pose a serious threat to the physical or psychological health of participants or that might have long-term, irreversible effects on them. However, the APA acknowledges that some worthwhile studies may cause participants to experience some discomfort or other short-term potentially negative effects. To help avoid situations in which people volunteer to participate in research without knowing that such effects are possible, the APA generally requires that the participants provide informed consent. **Informed consent** means that people agree, or consent, to participate in a research study only after they have been given a general overview of the research and have been given the choice of whether

TRUTH
OR
fiction
■ REVISITED ■

It is true that psychologists sometimes have to deceive participants in a study. Deception may be needed to prevent participants from purposefully or accidentally distorting the outcome of the research. But there are strict rules about deception in research.

Research with Animals

Needless to say, the experiments Todd, Marc, and Dan conducted were done with animals—Todd's fish. Most studies that use animals (such as those in which researchers have rats run through mazes to find out how they learn) do not harm the animals at all. Even the boys' fish experiments did not harm the fish. Marc's idea of using a mirror to find out about the fighting fish was a much more ethical method than using another real fighting fish. Marc was able to move the mirror, but if he had used another real fish, the two fish might have fought to the death.

Sometimes, however, psychologists and other scientists conduct research that may be harmful to animals. Such research studies often use animals because they cannot be carried out with people for ethical reasons. Experiments on the effects of early separation of children from their mothers are an example. These experiments could not be done with people, but they have been done with monkeys and other animals (e.g. Harlow, 1959). Such research has helped psychologists investigate the formation of bonds of attachment between parents and children. (See Chapter 10.)

There are other examples of psychological studies that rely on animals in order to avoid harming humans. Psychologists and biologists who study the brain sometimes destroy parts of the brains of laboratory animals to learn how those parts influence the animals' behavior. For example, damage to one part of a rat's brain will cause the rat to overeat (Keesey, 1986). Damage elsewhere will cause the rat to stop eating (Margules & Olds, 1962). (See Chapter 13.) Psychologists believe that, in characteristics such as appetite, people are similar enough to animals that the results may be applied to people. Researchers hope that these experiments with animals will lead to solutions to human problems, such as eating disorders.

Psychologists use animals only when there is no alternative and when they believe that the potential benefits outweigh the harm. Some researchers argue that many advances in medicine and psychology could not have taken place without harming animals (Fowler, 1992; Pardes et al., 1991). Yet many people believe that it is no more ethical to harm animals than it is to harm humans. Although the APA has rules of ethics for how animals used in research should be treated, controversy continues to surround the use of animals in scientific research.

In many studies that use animals, researchers are careful to treat the animals kindly.

Ethics in Using Data

Another area in which psychologists follow strict rules about ethics is in how they produce and present their data. When researchers conduct a study, they need to be as objective as possible in planning their study, in collecting their data, and in analyzing their data. Without this objectivity, the researchers may bias their study, perhaps unintentionally, in favor of their hypothesis.

Even more importantly, when information collected by researchers contradicts their hypothesis, they must be willing to discard their hypothesis in light of the evidence. It might be tempting to toss out all the evidence that contradicts the hypothesis and present to others only the evidence that supports the hypothesis. But this would be misleading and thus unethical. It might also become an obstacle to others' attempts to study psychology.

THINKING ABOUT PSYCHOLOGY

1. Explain the purpose of ethical standards in the profession of psychology.
2. Why are confidentiality and informed consent important to psychological research?
3. **Critical Thinking** Do you believe that it is ethical or unethical to deceive people about the purposes of research studies? Explain your answer.

Chapter 2 REVIEW

SUMMARY

Psychologists use a variety of methods to study behavior and mental processes.

I. Conducting Research

A. Psychologists generally follow five basic steps in conducting research.
 1. First, psychologists form a research question from daily experience, psychological theory, other research studies, or common knowledge.
 2. Next, psychologists form a hypothesis, or an educated guess, about the answer to the question.
 3. Then psychologists test their hypothesis using one of several methods.
 4. After psychologists have tested their hypothesis, they analyze the results.
 5. Finally, psychologists draw conclusions based on their observations or findings.

B. Additional steps involve confirming the findings through replication and forming new questions for study.

II. Surveys, Samples, and Populations

A. Surveys use interviews and questionnaires to gather information from large groups of people.
B. The group to be studied or described is called the target population.
C. Sample populations are scientifically selected to accurately represent the group under study.
D. Researchers use caution when generalizing results to the population at large.
E. Volunteer bias may skew a study's results.

III. Methods of Observation

A. The testing method uses psychological tests to learn about human behavior.
B. The case-study method investigates an individual or a small group in depth.

C. A longitudinal study is used to see how an individual or a group changes over time; a cross-sectional study includes participants of different ages.
D. Psychologists using the naturalistic-observation method study people and animals in their natural environments.
E. In the laboratory-observation method, psychologists study people and animals in a controlled environment.
F. Observations are analyzed through correlations, which indicate the extent to which one thing is related to another.

IV. The Experimental Method

A. Experiments contain variables, or factors that can change.
B. Researchers establish experimental groups and control groups to ensure that the results of an experiment are caused by the treatment and not by something else.
C. The expectations of participants and researchers can interfere with the effects of an experimental treatment.

V. Ethical Issues

A. Psychologists follow standards for proper and responsible behavior that have been established by the American Psychological Association (APA).
 1. Confidentiality protects the participants' right to privacy and encourages them to give truthful answers.
 2. Informed consent is generally required for research with people.
 3. Sometimes participants must be kept in the dark about the true nature of the research. The APA has strict guidelines for these situations.

B. The use of animals in scientific research continues to be a subject for debate.
C. Psychologists must take certain considerations into account when they interpret their research findings.

TERM & CONCEPT REVIEW

1. What steps do psychologists follow in conducting research?
2. How do random samples and stratified samples differ? Why is it important for researchers to select study participants scientifically?
3. How might volunteer bias affect the results of a survey?
4. Identify an advantage and a disadvantage of the survey method.
5. List three types of tests used by psychologists.
6. Explain the difference between positive correlation and negative correlation.
7. When is the experimental method preferable to observational methods?
8. Define the terms *single-blind study* and *double-blind study.*
9. What purposes do ethical standards serve in psychological research?
10. Under what circumstances might a psychologist break the promise of confidentiality?

CRITICAL THINKING

1. Read each of the following hypotheses. Then describe how you could test each one.
   a. College students exercise less than high school students.
   b. A hungry rat will find the food at the end of a maze more quickly than a rat who has recently been fed.
   c. Understanding foreign cultures and traditions reduces prejudice.
2. Surveys are often used to predict future events, such as election outcomes. How might these surveys affect the outcome of the events?
3. If correlations do not explain cause and effect, why are they useful?
4. What are some potential sources for error in conducting research?

APPLYING SKILLS IN PSYCHOLOGY

1. **COOPERATIVE LEARNING Research in Psychology** Working in small groups, design and conduct a survey that will gather information about the students in your school. For example, you might find out about their views on a particular issue, their buying habits, or their ideas for ways to increase student participation in school activities. Decide on a format for your survey—printed questionnaire or face-to-face interviews—and give everyone in the group a role in preparing and distributing the questionnaires or in planning and conducting the interviews. Analyze the results as a group and write a summary of the project for the school newspaper.

2. **Using Your Observation Skills** Use the naturalistic-observation method to study the behavior of your classmates. Think of a hypothesis you could test, such as "Students tend to socialize with the same group of people." Then choose a field setting, such as the hallways, the cafeteria, or a sports event, in which to conduct your observations. Keep a written record of your observations and, after a week, analyze your observations and draw a conclusion based on them.

3. **Reading About Psychology** Check newspapers and magazines for articles about negative and positive correlations, such as between the amount of time spent watching television and violent behavior or between a sports team's seasonal success (or failure) and attendance at the games. Summarize your findings and share them in class.

4. **Writing About Psychology** Write an essay in which you defend or argue against the use of animal subjects in psychological research. Do some background reading so that you can support your position with facts. Read your essay to the class as part of a class discussion about the ethics of research with animals.

REVIEW

IDENTIFYING PEOPLE AND IDEAS

Explain the significance of each of the following people or terms to the study of psychology.

1. behavior
2. cognitive activity
3. theory
4. basic research
5. functionalism
6. John B. Watson
7. Gestalt psychology
8. Sigmund Freud
9. biological perspective
10. sociocultural perspective
11. hypothesis
12. replicate
13. target population
14. sample
15. case study
16. naturalistic observation
17. correlation
18. variable
19. control group
20. placebo
21. ethics
22. informed consent

HANDS-ON PSYCHOLOGY

Individual Project

Formulate a hypothesis about a type of behavior that interests you. For example, you might want to study the television viewing habits of adults or the ways in which your classmates spend their free time. After you have formulated your hypothesis, conduct a written or oral survey to collect data about the behavior you have chosen to study. Carefully consider what types of questions you will need to ask in order to test your hypothesis. Then, choose a target population for your survey. Finally, select a random sample of participants from that target population.

After you have completed your survey, write a report in which you explain your study. You should begin by stating your hypothesis. Then describe your sampling techniques, including your target population and the size of your random sample. Finally, explain the results of your survey. Attach a copy of your questionnaire (or the questions you asked if it was an oral survey). When writing your report, consider the following questions:

1. Did the results of the survey coincide with your expectations of how people would respond? Why or why not?

2. What did you learn about people's behavior? (You may discuss the behavior tested in your survey, or you may want to discuss people's willingness or unwillingness to participate in your survey.)

3. Do you think your respondents were affected by volunteer bias? If so, explain how the bias was demonstrated. How could you improve your survey method?

BUILDING YOUR PORTFOLIO

Individually or in a group, complete the following project to demonstrate your understanding of the psychology concepts involved.

Using Research Techniques

As you learned in this unit, psychologists use various research methods to test their theories. Select a specific area of psychology that interests you, such as developmental psychology. For that specific area, formulate a research question from your daily experience. Then form a hypothesis, test the hypothesis, analyze the results, and draw a conclusion based on your results. Prepare an oral report supported by written and visual materials analyzing your research question, method, and results. Consider the following questions:

1. How does your research question relate to the specialized area of psychology you selected? What other areas of psychology could possibly benefit from your findings? Give examples to support your answer.

2. State your hypothesis. How did you test your hypothesis? Explain, in detail, the method you chose and the steps you followed to test your hypothesis. What do you believe your findings or observations indicate? Did you collect enough data to analyze your results accurately and completely? What conclusions can you draw from your findings? If your findings or observations did not support your hypothesis, how should you change your theory or hypothesis?

Organize your materials and present your report to the rest of the class.

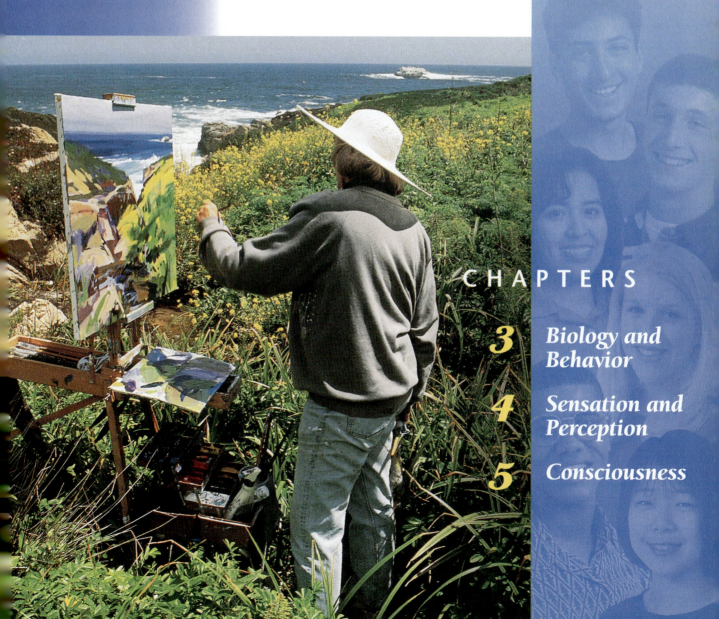

UNIT 2

BODY AND MIND

2

3 Chapter

BIOLOGY AND BEHAVIOR

Objectives

1 Explain how messages are transmitted by neurons, and describe the functions of the spinal cord and the peripheral nervous system.

2 Identify the major structures of the brain, and explain the functions of each structure.

3 Identify the hormones secreted by the major glands of the endocrine system and the role each one plays.

4 Explain the role of chromosomes and genes in heredity, and evaluate the methods used by psychologists to study the role of heredity in determining traits.

A DAY IN THE LIFE

 Marc was rushing through the halls to reach class on time. As he ran, thoughts of Linda floated through his mind. He was in some classes with her, and he was beginning to think that she was very attractive. Distracted by these images of Linda, Marc rounded a corner and bumped into Todd, who stepped down hard on Marc's big toe. Marc grabbed his sneakered foot in his hands, then started to rub his toe, which throbbed with pain. In addition, he felt his heart begin to race. Todd cringed and said, "Oh, sorry. I didn't even see you." Still holding his foot, Marc grunted, "Hey, don't worry. It's no big deal."

• • •

No big deal? At first glance, this incident between Marc and Todd seems very simple, but much more actually occurred than meets the eye. The way in which Marc's body responded to having his foot stepped on is of great interest to psychologists. This may seem surprising—after all, what does biology have to do with psychology? In fact, biological functioning has much to do with psychology.

The ways in which our bodies and minds work in relation to each other are quite remarkable. Biological psychologists (sometimes called biopsychologists) study the ways in which our behavior and psychological processes are linked to biological structures and processes. For example, sensation, perception, memory, and thinking are all psychological processes that have at least a partly biological basis. (You will read about these topics in greater depth in later chapters.)

A major area of study for biological psychologists concerns the workings of the nervous system. The nervous system, which includes the brain, is involved in psychological processes such as thought and emotion, movement and sensation, and much more. Based on our knowledge of the nervous system, we can explain how messages were sent from Marc's toe to his brain and back to his foot, causing him to grab his foot and begin to massage his injured toe.

In addition to the nervous system, biological psychologists study the endocrine system. This system is responsible for the secretion of hormones. Hormones serve a wide variety of functions, such as influencing emotions. Marc's emotional response to having his foot stepped on was due in part to the endocrine system.

Biological psychologists are also interested in heredity and how it affects us both physically and psychologically. Heredity influences not only how we look but also how we act. Biological psychologists study the interactions between our heredity and the environments in which we live.

Key Terms

- central nervous system
- peripheral nervous system
- neuron
- cell body
- dendrite
- axon
- myelin
- axon terminal
- synapse
- neurotransmitter
- spinal cord
- somatic nervous system
- autonomic nervous system
- medulla
- pons
- cerebellum
- reticular activating system
- thalamus
- hypothalamus
- limbic system
- cerebrum
- cerebral cortex
- corpus callosum
- association area
- endocrine system
- hormone
- heredity
- gene
- chromosome

TRUTH OR fiction?

Read the following statements about psychology. Do you think they are true or false? You will learn whether each statement is true or false as you read the chapter.

- Individual cells in the human body can be several feet long.
- Anxiety can give you indigestion.
- A person with brain damage may be able to report that he or she has seen a face but may not be able to identify that it was the face of a close friend.
- Some people are "left-brained" and others are "right-brained."
- The father's genetic contribution—not the mother's—determines the sex of the offspring.

The Nervous System

The human nervous system is involved in thinking, dreaming, feeling, moving, and much more. It is working when we are active or still, awake or asleep. The nervous system regulates our internal functions. It is also involved in how we react to the external world. Even learning and memory are made possible by the nervous system. When we learn a new behavior or acquire new information, the nervous system registers that experience and changes to accommodate its storage.

The nervous system has two main parts: the central nervous system and the peripheral nervous system. The **central nervous system** consists of the brain and the spinal cord. The **peripheral nervous system** is made up of nerve cells that send messages between the central nervous system and all the parts of the body. In order to understand how the central and the peripheral nervous systems work, we must first understand how nerve cells communicate with one another and how their messages travel through the body.

Neurons

Nerve cells, called **neurons**, run through our entire bodies and communicate with each other. Neurons send and receive messages from other structures in the body, such as muscles and glands. These messages can affect events ranging from the sensation of a pinprick to the first steps of a child, from the writing of a poem to the memory of a past event. Each of us has more than 100 billion neurons, most of which are found in the brain.

Components of a Neuron   Neurons are somewhat like trees in structure. Parts of neurons resemble the branches, trunk, and roots of a tree. And, as

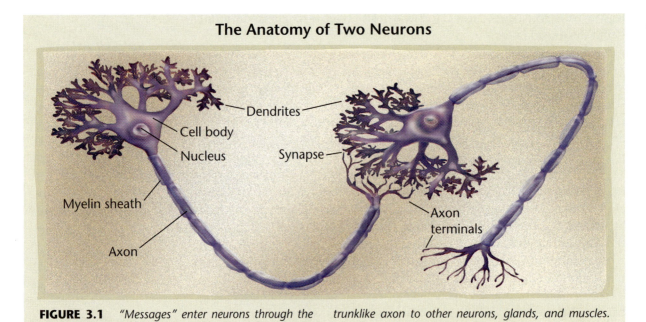

The Anatomy of Two Neurons

Dendrites

Cell body

Nucleus

Synapse

Myelin sheath

Axon

Axon terminals

FIGURE 3.1   *"Messages" enter neurons through the dendrites. These messages are transmitted along the trunklike axon to other neurons, glands, and muscles. The myelin sheath protects the axon.*

in forests, many nerve cells lie alongside one another like a thicket of trees. Unlike trees, however, neurons can also lie end to end. Their "roots" are intertwined with the "branches" of neurons that lie below. (See Figure 3.1.)

Every neuron consists of a cell body, dendrites, and an axon. The **cell body** produces energy that fuels the activity of the cell. Branching out from the cell body are thin fibers called **dendrites**. The dendrites receive information from other neurons and pass the message through the cell body.

While the dendrites carry information *to* the cell body, the **axon** carries messages *away*. A neuron has many dendrites but usually only one axon. Axons vary greatly in length. Some are just a tiny fraction of an inch, while others stretch to several feet. Because of the length of their axons, some neurons in your legs are several feet long.

. . . .

TRUTH
OR
fiction
. REVISITED .

It is true that individual cells in the body can be several feet long. These cells are nerve cells, or neurons, that are long because they have long axons. Some of these neurons are in the leg and are several feet long, stretching from the lower spine to the toes.

. . . .

Many axons are covered with **myelin**, a white fatty substance that insulates and protects the axon. This myelin sheath, or casing, also helps to speed up the transmission of the message. At the end of the axon, smaller fibers branch out. These fibers are called **axon terminals**.

The Communication Process   Messages are sent from the axon terminals of one neuron to the dendrites of other neurons. In order for a message to be sent from one neuron to another neuron, it must cross the **synapse**. The synapse is a junction between the axon terminals of one neuron and the dendrites of another neuron. Messages travel in only one direction. Thus, messages are received by the dendrites and travel through the cell body and the axon to the axon terminals. From there, they cross synapses to the dendrites of other neurons. (See Figure 3.2.) New synapses can develop between neurons that were not previously connected, as when we learn something new.

The information that is sent and the place to which it goes depend on a number of factors. These

The Synapse

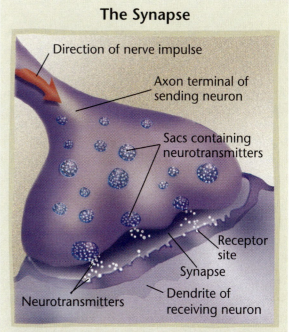

Direction of nerve impulse

Axon terminal of sending neuron

Sacs containing neurotransmitters

Receptor site

Synapse

Dendrite of receiving neuron

Neurotransmitters

FIGURE 3.2   *There is no physical connection between neurons. A neuron relays its message across a junction called a synapse by releasing chemicals called neurotransmitters. They are received by the next neuron.*

factors include the locations of the neuron in the body and the events that produced the message. For

A DAY IN THE LIFE

example, the pain in Marc's toe was transmitted to his brain through sensory neurons. Sensory neurons are nerve cells that carry information received by the senses *to* the central nervous system. Motor neurons, on the other hand, are nerve cells that carry information *from* the central nervous system to the muscles and the glands and influence their functioning. Motor neurons took the message to Marc's foot so that he pulled up on it and began to rub it. Other motor neurons stimulated Marc's glands, making his heart beat faster. Still other neurons in his brain enabled him to think over the matter and to decide that Todd should be forgiven.

Occasionally, something happens to disrupt the message-sending process. For example, a hard blow to the head from a car accident or a sports injury can cause a concussion—an injury in which the soft tissue of the brain hits against the skull. Sometimes, the person is affected for only a few seconds. Other times, the person may experience effects for a much longer time. In 1993, Dallas Cowboys quarterback Troy Aikman received a concussion during a game in the National Football League playoffs. He

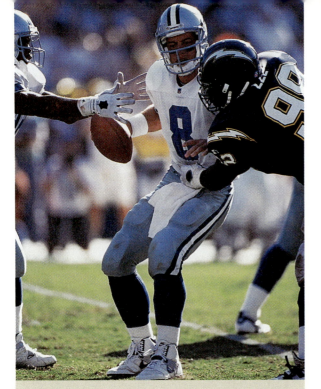

Troy Aikman's concussion in the 1993 football play-offs interfered with his memory of the event.

remembers being at the game, but he cannot remember what happened during the game. Such experiences show that memory is in large part a biological process. (See Chapter 7.)

Neurotransmitters: Chemical Messengers

Neurons send messages across synapses through the release of **neurotransmitters**. Neurotransmitters are chemicals that are stored in sacs in the axon terminals. A neuron fires, or sends its message, by releasing neurotransmitters—much like droplets of water shooting out of a spray bottle. This can occur hundreds of times every second.

There are several types of neurotransmitters. Each has its own specific structure and fits into a receptor site on the next neuron, similar to the way in which a key fits into a lock. The message is converted into an electrical impulse that travels the length of the neuron. The message is then transmitted to the next neuron by neurotransmitters. The process continues until the message arrives at its destination, which in many cases is the brain. This whole process takes only a fraction of a second.

Neurotransmitters are involved in everything people do. Whenever a person waves a hand, yawns, or thinks about a friend, neurotransmitters

are involved in the underlying biological process. In addition, some diseases and psychological disorders may be caused by the presence of too much or too little of various neurotransmitters.

Researchers have identified dozens of neurotransmitters and their functions. For example, acetylcholine is a common neurotransmitter that is involved in the control of muscles. It is used by the motor neurons of the spinal cord and stimulates skeletal muscles. The release of acetylcholine was what led to Marc's response of grabbing his foot.

Dopamine is another neurotransmitter. It is involved primarily in motor behavior. A deficiency in dopamine levels plays a role in Parkinson's disease, which is characterized by tremors and uncoordinated, rigid movements. An excess of dopamine may contribute to the psychological disorder schizophrenia. (See Chapter 18.)

Other neurotransmitters include noradrenaline, which is primarily involved in preparing the body for action, and serotonin, which is involved in emotional arousal and sleep.

Though we are often unaware of the processes in our bodies, we can be sure that our bodies are hard at work whether we are running or sitting still. At

Long-distance runners experience a "runner's high," which may be connected with the release of endorphins. Endorphins are neurotransmitters similar in function to the drug morphine. They have a tranquilizing and painkilling effect on the body.

any given moment, billions of neurons are shooting neurotransmitters across synapses and sending complicated messages to various parts of the body. These messages are carried via the spinal cord and the peripheral nervous system.

The Central Nervous System

Figure 3.3 shows the central nervous system, which consists of the neurons of the spinal cord and the brain. (The brain is discussed in Section 2.) The **spinal cord** extends from the brain down the back. It is a column of nerves about as thick as a thumb, and it is protected by the bones of the spine. It transmits messages between the brain and the muscles and the glands throughout the body.

The spinal cord is also involved in spinal reflexes. A spinal reflex is a simple, automatic response to something. For example, if a person touches a hot stove, a message goes immediately from his or her hand to the spinal cord. A message to remove the hand is then sent back to motor neurons in the hand. The removal of the hand is a spinal reflex. (The person may also register pain in his or her brain. But the pain is not what causes the reflex. In fact, the pain may not even be felt until after the hand has been removed.)

Many of our simple actions are reflexive. Have you ever wondered why you blink when you get a speck of dust in your eye? Or why some people sneeze when they sniff pepper? Physicians sometimes test people's reflexes to learn whether their nervous systems are functioning properly. When a doctor taps just below the knee to see if you kick, the purpose is to check your knee-jerk reflex to make sure your neurons are responding the way they are supposed to.

The Peripheral Nervous System

The peripheral nervous system lies outside the central nervous system and is responsible for transmitting messages between the central nervous system and all parts of the body. The two main divisions of the peripheral nervous system are the somatic nervous system and the autonomic nervous system. (See Figure 3.4 on page 58.)

The Somatic Nervous System   The **somatic nervous system** transmits sensory messages to the central nervous system. It is activated by touch, pain, changes in temperature, and changes in body position. The somatic nervous system enables us to

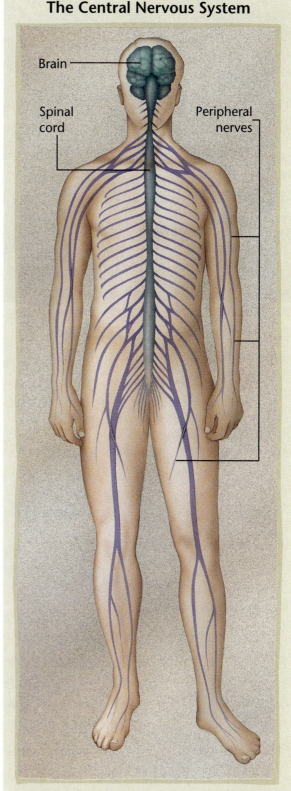

The Central Nervous System

Brain

Spinal cord

Peripheral nerves

FIGURE 3.3   *Your spinal cord is protected by a column of bones called vertebrae. Similarly, your brain is protected by the skull.*

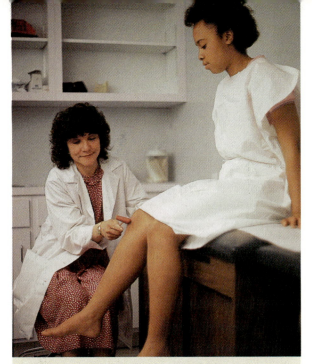

When the doctor hits your knee joint, sensory neurons carry the message from the muscles to the spinal cord and the brain. Motor neurons carry a message from the brain back to the muscles, making your leg move.

experience the sensations of hot and cold and to feel pain and pressure. For example, we can feel the softness of a cat's fur, warmth if the cat is sitting on our lap, and pain if the cat scratches us. The somatic system also alerts us that parts of the body have moved or changed position. It sends messages to the muscles and the glands and helps us maintain posture and balance.

The Autonomic Nervous System   The word *autonomic* means "occurring involuntarily," or automatically. The **autonomic nervous system** regulates the body's vital functions, such as heartbeat, breathing, digestion, and blood pressure. We generally do not have to think about these activities—they occur automatically and are essential for keeping us alive.

Psychologists are interested in the autonomic nervous system because of its involvement in the experience of emotion. The response of the autonomic nervous system is particularly important when a person experiences something stressful in the environment.

The autonomic nervous system has two divisions: the sympathetic and the parasympathetic nervous systems. (See Figure 3.4.) These systems generally have opposing functions. The sympathetic system is activated when a person is going into action, perhaps because of some stressful event. It prepares the body either to confront the situation or to run away. This is sometimes called the "fight-or-flight" response. For example, when a person is suddenly attacked by a large angry dog, the sympathetic nervous system is aroused.

The sympathetic nervous system prepares the body by suppressing digestion, increasing the heart

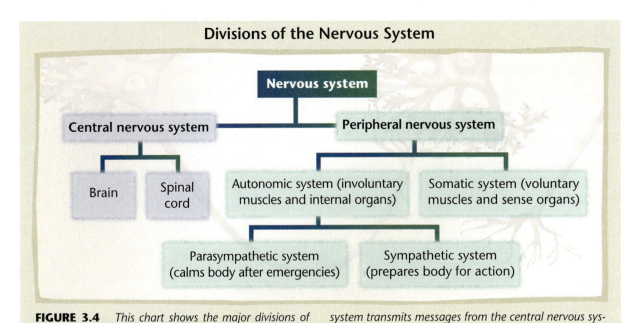

Divisions of the Nervous System

Nervous system

Central nervous system

Peripheral nervous system

Brain

Spinal cord

Autonomic system (involuntary muscles and internal organs)

Somatic system (voluntary muscles and sense organs)

Parasympathetic system (calms body after emergencies)

Sympathetic system (prepares body for action)

FIGURE 3.4   *This chart shows the major divisions of the nervous system. The central nervous system consists of the brain and the spinal cord. The peripheral nervous system transmits messages from the central nervous system to all parts of the body.*

and respiration rates, and elevating the blood pressure. Do you ever feel queasy when you are in a stressful situation—such as when your teacher springs a surprise quiz on you? This is because your sympathetic nervous system has kicked into action and has suppressed your digestive processes. And when Todd stepped on Marc's toe, Marc felt his heart start to race—another result of the activation of the sympathetic nervous system.

It is true that anxiety can give you indigestion. Anxiety may cause indigestion by inducing activity of the sympathetic nervous system, which suppresses digestion.

In contrast to the sympathetic system, the parasympathetic nervous system restores the body's reserves of energy after an action has occurred. Heart rate and blood pressure are normalized, breathing is slowed, and digestion returns to normal. If you are having trouble remembering which system is which, perhaps it will help to keep in mind that "sympathetic" and "stress" both start with the letter *s,* while "parasympathetic" and "peace" both begin with *p.* The sympathetic system reacts to stress; the parasympathetic system restores peace.

THINKING ABOUT PSYCHOLOGY

1. How do messages travel from one neuron to another?
2. Identify the systems that make up the peripheral nervous system.
3. **Critical Thinking**   In what way do the parasympathetic and the sympathetic nervous systems work together?

2
The Brain: Our Control Center

Every person is unique in part because of the capacities for learning and thought made possible by the human brain. In ancient times, hundreds of years before scientists had learned much about how the brain functions, people did not attribute human psychological processes such as thinking to the working of the brain. People thought that what was inside a person's body was not very different from what was inside an animal's body. Therefore, they reasoned, the abilities that make people different from animals—such as creative thought, art, and analytical abilities—could not be explained in biological terms. Instead, it was widely believed that the body was inhabited by souls or demons.

The ancient Egyptians believed that a little person dwelled within the skull and regulated behavior. The Greek philosopher Aristotle thought that the soul had set up living quarters in the heart. B. F. Skinner (1987) noted that the English language still reflects the belief in the heart as the seat of will, thought, hunger, and joy. We use expressions such as "deep in one's heart," "to know something by heart," "to look into someone's heart," and "to have a change of heart."

Today, however, we recognize that the mind, or consciousness, dwells within the brain (Goldman-Rakic, 1995; Sperry, 1993). We know that when thoughts of Linda ran through Marc's mind, something was happening in his brain. We now have greater understanding of the brain and the links between biological processes and psychological phenomena.

Parts of the Brain

The human brain is composed of many parts that work together to organize our movements, create our thoughts, form our emotions, and produce our behaviors. The brain is divided into three sections: the hindbrain, the midbrain, and the forebrain. (See Figure 3.5 on page 60.) The hindbrain is the lower portion of the brain and is involved in many vital functions such as heart rate, respiration, and balance. The midbrain includes areas that are involved in vision and hearing. The forebrain, the front area of the brain, is involved in complex functions such as thought and emotion.

The Hindbrain   The medulla, the pons, and the cerebellum are important structures of the hindbrain. The **medulla** is involved in vital functions such as heart rate, blood pressure, and breathing. The **pons** is located in front of the medulla and is involved in regulating body movement, attention, sleep, and alertness.

Parts of the Human Brain

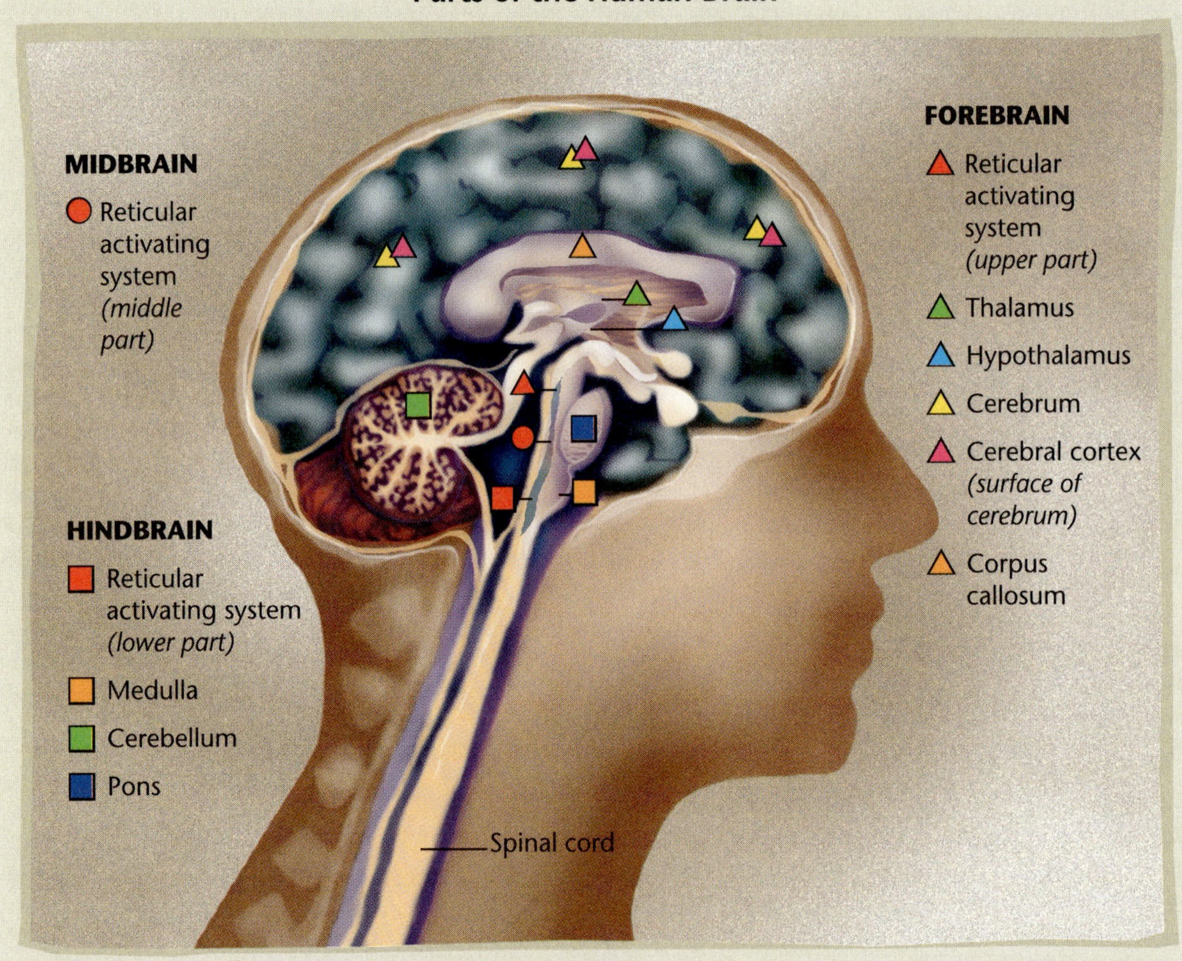

MIDBRAIN

🔴 Reticular activating system *(middle part)*

HINDBRAIN

🟧 Reticular activating system *(lower part)*

🟧 Medulla

🟩 Cerebellum

🟦 Pons

FOREBRAIN

🔺 Reticular activating system *(upper part)*

🔺 Thalamus

🔺 Hypothalamus

🔺 Cerebrum

🔺 Cerebral cortex *(surface of cerebrum)*

🔺 Corpus callosum

Spinal cord

FIGURE 3.5 *The average human adult brain weighs about 3 pounds and has more than 10 billion cells, many of which are neurons. Although the brain makes up about 2 to 3 percent of a person's body weight, it requires about 20 percent of the blood's oxygen supply.*

Cerebellum is the Latin word for "little brain." The **cerebellum** looks like the larger part of the brain (the cerebrum), under which it rests, but it is much smaller. It is involved in balance and coordination. A person whose cerebellum is injured may have trouble with coordination. The person may walk unevenly and even occasionally fall down.

The Midbrain The midbrain is located between the hindbrain and the forebrain. Areas within the midbrain are involved in vision and hearing. Eye movement, for example, is controlled by an area in the midbrain. In addition, the midbrain contains part of the **reticular activating system**. The reticular activating system begins in the hindbrain and rises through the midbrain into the lower part of the forebrain. This system is important for attention, sleep, and arousal. Stimulation of the reticular activating system makes us alert. It affects arousal by increasing heart rate and blood pressure, and it increases brain activity. Some drugs, such as alcohol, reduce the activity of the reticular activating system, thus affecting alertness and reaction time.

Sudden, loud noises stimulate the reticular activating system and can awaken a sleeping person. However, the reticular activating system can screen out some noises. A person who lives in the city may not be awakened by the sounds of traffic roaring by. This same person may, however, awaken to sounds that are more out of the ordinary, such as a bird singing, even if these sounds are fairly soft.

The Forebrain Four major areas of the forebrain are the thalamus, the hypothalamus, the limbic system, and the cerebrum. Certain parts of the forebrain are very well developed in human beings. The forebrain is the part of the brain that makes it possible for humans to engage in complex thinking processes.

Thalamus is a Latin word meaning "inner chamber." The **thalamus** is a critical structure of the brain because it serves as a relay station for sensory stimulation. Most of the messages coming from the sense organs go through the thalamus on the way to the higher levels of the brain (those areas responsible for mental processes such as thinking and reasoning). The thalamus transmits sensory information, such as the pain from Marc's big toe, to the areas of the brain that interpret and respond to the information. The thalamus also relays sensory input from the eyes and the ears to the appropriate parts of the brain for interpretation of the input.

Hypo- is a Greek prefix meaning "under." Thus, the **hypothalamus** lies below the thalamus. The hypothalamus is very tiny, but it is extremely important because it is involved in many aspects of behavior and physiological functions. It is vital to the regulation of body temperature, the storage of nutrients, and various aspects of motivation and emotion. It is also involved in hunger, thirst, sexual behavior, caring for offspring, and aggression. Disturbances within the hypothalamus can lead to unusual drinking and eating behaviors.

Among lower animals, stimulation of parts of the hypothalamus triggers behaviors such as fighting, mating, or nest building. Although the hypothalamus is also important to people, our behavior is less mechanical and tends to be influenced by cognitive functions such as thought, choice, and value systems.

The **limbic system** forms a fringe along the inner edge of the cerebrum. It is involved in learning and memory, emotion, hunger, sex, and aggression. If a particular part of the limbic system is damaged, people can recall old memories but do not create new memories. For example, a person with damage to that area may have vivid childhood memories of playing with his or her sister but may not be able to remember that this same sister visited earlier that day. Researchers have also found that destruction of another specific area of the limbic system can lead animals to show passive behavior. Destruction of a different area of the limbic system causes some animals to behave aggressively, even when there seems little reason to do so.

The **cerebrum** (Latin for "brain") is the crowning glory of the brain. Only in human beings does the cerebrum make up such a large part of the brain. The cerebrum accounts for about 70 percent of the weight of the brain. The surface of the cerebrum is wrinkled with ridges and valleys. This surface is the **cerebral cortex**. (*Cortex* is the Latin word for "bark of a tree.") The cerebral cortex is the outer layer of the brain, just as bark is the outer layer of a tree.

The cerebral cortex is the part of the brain that we tend to think of when we talk about the brain. It is the part that makes us uniquely human, the part that thinks. In addition to thinking, the cerebral cortex is also concerned with memory, language, emotions, complex motor functions, perception, and much more.

The Cerebral Cortex: What Makes Us Unique

The cerebral cortex is composed of two sides—a left side and a right side. Each side is called a hemisphere. (The Greek *hemi-* means "half." Thus, each half of the brain is half a sphere, just as each half of planet Earth is a hemisphere.) To visualize the cerebral cortex, think of a walnut. The shell of the walnut is like the skull. Just as the walnut has two sides that are connected, so does the brain. In the brain, the structure that connects the two hemispheres is called the **corpus callosum**.

Interestingly, information received by one side of the body is transmitted to the *opposite* hemisphere of the brain. For example, if you touch something with your left hand, that information is sent to the right side of your brain. Conversely, if you touch something with your right hand, the left hemisphere of your brain receives the information. The corpus callosum aids in getting information from one side of the brain to the other.

Each hemisphere of the cerebral cortex is divided into four parts, or lobes. The frontal lobe lies behind the forehead, and the parietal lobe lies to the top and rear of the head. The temporal lobe lies to the side, just below the ears. The occipital lobe is at the back of the head. (See Figure 3.6 on page 62.)

Some sensations, such as visual sensations, are received primarily in one lobe. However, each lobe does not necessarily act independently from the others. Some functions require the interplay of several lobes. The involvement of the cerebral cortex in the senses and motor behavior is a good illustration of this interaction.

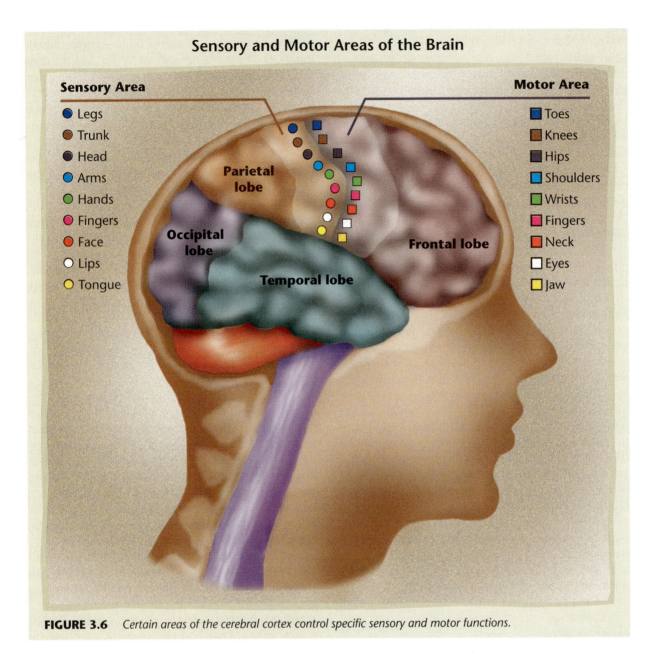

Sensory and Motor Areas of the Brain

Sensory Area

- Legs
- Trunk
- Head
- Arms
- Hands
- Fingers
- Face
- Lips
- Tongue

Motor Area

- Toes
- Knees
- Hips
- Shoulders
- Wrists
- Fingers
- Neck
- Eyes
- Jaw

Parietal lobe

Occipital lobe

Temporal lobe

Frontal lobe

FIGURE 3.6   *Certain areas of the cerebral cortex control specific sensory and motor functions.*

Senses and Motor Behavior   The occipital lobe contains the primary visual area of the cerebral cortex. When light strikes the eyes, neurons in the occipital lobe fire, enabling us to see. We also "see" flashes of light if neurons in the occipital lobe are stimulated by electricity.

Damage to different parts of the occipital lobe can create unusual conditions. People with damage to one area may be able to recognize an object, but they may be unable to differentiate it from another object that is similar. For example, if shown a key, they may know that what they see is a key, but they may not be able to tell it apart from another key that looks different. People with damage to another area may be able to report that they have seen a face, but they may not be able to identify that it is the face of a close friend.

It is true that a person with brain damage may be able to report that he or she has seen a face but may not be able to identify that it was the face of a close friend. Damage to a particular area in the occipital lobe of the cerebral cortex can create this condition.

The hearing, or auditory, area of the cortex lies in the temporal lobe. Sounds are relayed from the ears to the thalamus to the auditory area. When this occurs, we hear sounds. If a specific area of the temporal cortex is damaged, a person may not be able to recognize very common sounds, such as a doorbell ringing.

Messages received from the skin senses (see Chapter 4) are projected to the sensory cortex in the parietal lobe. These sensations include warmth and cold, touch, and pain. Different neurons fire, depending on whether you have scratched your nose, touched a hot stove, or been stung by a bee. When Todd stepped on Marc's toe, the pain message was relayed from the toe to the parietal lobe of Marc's brain.

The motor cortex in the frontal lobe, however, was involved when Marc grabbed his foot and started rubbing it. Neurons in the motor cortex fire when we move certain parts of our body. When we clap our hands or wiggle our toes, different parts of the frontal lobe are stimulated.

Association Areas   Much of the cerebral cortex is composed of areas that are directly responsible for sensory and motor functions. Other areas, called **association areas**, serve mainly to shape information into something meaningful on which we can act. For example, some association areas piece together sensory information. Certain neurons in the occipital lobe fire when we view vertical lines. Others fire when we see horizontal lines. Activity in the association areas then integrates the information so that we see a meaningful form such as a tree, the ground, a swing set, or a letter of the alphabet. Other association areas make possible such complex psychological functions as thought and language.

Language Abilities   Although the left and the right hemispheres of the brain have many of the same functions, they differ in a number of ways. For example, for nearly all right-handed people, language functions are based in the left hemisphere. Language functions are also based in the left hemisphere of about two out of three left-handed people. Thus, only in a very small percentage of people are language functions based in the right hemisphere.

Within the hemisphere containing the language functions, two key language areas are Broca's area and Wernicke's area. Damage to either area is likely to cause an *aphasia*, a difficulty with specific aspects of understanding or producing language.

Wernicke's area, which is located in the temporal lobe, pieces together sounds and sights. People with damage to this area may find it difficult to understand speech. They may be able to speak, but their speech often is meaningless. For example, when asked to describe a picture of two boys stealing cookies behind a woman's back, one person responded: "Mother is away her working her work to get her better, but when she's looking the two boys looking the other part. She's working another time" (Geschwind, 1979).

Broca's area is located in the frontal lobe near the section of the motor cortex that controls the areas of the face used for speaking. When Broca's area is damaged, people speak slowly and laboriously, using simple sentences. Comprehension is quite good, but they may speak only key words. For example, a person with Broca's aphasia who wants to say "the three bananas are lying on the table" may produce only "bananas lie table."

Left Versus Right Hemispheres   The same hemisphere that contains most language functions also is usually more involved in logic, problem solving, and mathematical computation than is the other hemisphere (Borod, 1992; Hellige, 1990). The nonlanguage hemisphere is relatively more concerned with the imagination, art, feelings, and spatial relations.

In our society, people often speak of certain abilities as belonging to the right brain or to the left brain. Thus, people who are very logical are said to be "left-brained," while people who are particularly creative are called "right-brained." This idea, however, has become greatly exaggerated. Although some differences do exist, the hemispheres do not act independently of each other (Hellige, 1990). Even though each hemisphere is capable of functioning by itself, the brain functions better when the two hemispheres work together. One hemisphere does play a special role in language, while the other hemisphere plays a special role in feelings. However, both hemispheres are involved in logic, creativity, and intuition.

It is not true that some people are "left-brained" and others are "right-brained." Both hemispheres of the brain are involved in most human activities and abilities.

A common belief is that people who are very logical (such as judges) are "left-brained" whereas people who are more creative (such as artists) are "right-brained." This belief, however, has little scientific validity.

Much of what psychologists have learned about left- and right-hemisphere functioning comes from people who have had split-brain operations. In a split-brain operation, the corpus callosum, which connects the two hemispheres, is cut. This procedure, although performed only rarely, is sometimes used to help people with serious neural disorders such as severe cases of epilepsy. People with epilepsy experience seizures, which are bursts of abnormal neuron firings that generally occur in one hemisphere and then spread to the other. Cutting the corpus callosum can reduce the severity of the seizures by preventing them from spreading. After the surgery, patients usually function quite effectively despite their hemispheres' inability to communicate with each other.

However, the surgery does have some subtle effects on functioning. For example, people may be able to describe verbally the objects they hold in their right hand but not what they hold in their left hand (Gazzaniga, 1992). This is because if an object is held in the right hand, the information is sent to the left hemisphere, which (in most people) contains language abilities. However, if the same object is held in the left hand, this information is projected to the right hemisphere, which has very little language ability. It is important to remember that for people with intact corpus callosums, the hemispheres usually work together. Thus, most people can describe objects held in either hand.

Methods of Studying the Brain

Much of our earlier understanding of the brain came from studies of people with head injuries. Today, researchers increase their knowledge of the brain and its functions by using a variety of techniques to study damaged and intact brains.

Accidents   One way that researchers have been able to see how the brain is related to psychological functions is through the study of accidents and brain damage. Brain damage from head injuries can result in loss of vision and hearing, confusion, or loss of memory. In some cases, the loss of large portions of the brain may result in relatively little loss of function. Yet the loss of vital, smaller parts can result in language problems, memory loss, or death. In other words, which particular area is damaged may have a greater effect than the amount of the damage.

Electrical Stimulation of the Brain   Electrical stimulation of the brain has shown that specific areas are associated with specific types of sensations (such as seeing light or feeling a tap on the arm) or motor activities (such as walking).

Classic research by José Delgado (1969) used electrical stimulation of the brain to show how an animal could be made to change behavioral patterns. The researchers implanted an electrode into a

CASE STUDIES
AND OTHER TRUE STORIES
Is Phineas Gage Still the Same Man?

The ability of the brain to withstand some accidents is nothing less than remarkable. In some instances, people have not only survived severe injuries to the brain, but they have continued to live fairly normal lives. Sometimes, though, the victim is not quite the same as before the accident. Consider the case of Phineas Gage.

Young Mr. Gage was a promising railroad worker. His character was outstanding and he was well liked. But all that changed one day in 1848. While he was tamping down the blasting powder for a dynamite charge, Gage accidentally set the powder off, and an inch-thick metal rod shot upward through his brain and out the top of his head.

The rod landed many yards away. Gage fell back in a heap. Yet he was not dead. His coworkers watched in shock as he stood up a few moments later and spoke. They drove him by oxcart to a local doctor, John Harlow. As the doctor marveled at the hole through Gage's head, Gage asked when the doctor thought he'd be able to return to work.

Everyone, including the doctor, was surprised that Phineas Gage even survived the accident. Two months later, the physical effects of Gage's wounds had healed. He walked about, spoke normally enough, and was aware of his surroundings. However, Gage had changed. He no longer was a dependable worker. He had also become foul-mouthed and ill-mannered. It had become clear that the accident had had some serious psychological consequences.

Gage died 13 years later during an epileptic seizure. Dr. Harlow persuaded Gage's family to donate his skull to the Warren Medical Museum at

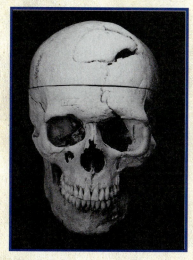

Gage's skull

Harvard University. Generations of biologists and psychologists have studied the skull and wondered how Gage's changes in personality might have been caused by damage to his brain.

According to biologists Hanna and Antonio Damasio (1992), the way in which the rod had entered the brain had spared the parts of the frontal lobes that were involved in language and motor behavior. Thus, Gage was able to speak normally and move about easily. However, the rod had severely damaged a part of the underside of the frontal lobes, causing the disturbance in personality. The Damasios note that people who suffer damage to the same part of the brain today experience similar changes in personality. These individuals are often unable to censor their thoughts before speaking. As a result, they may blurt out thoughts that they would have kept to themselves before their brains were injured.

Other researchers also have found changes in patients' personalities after brain injuries. In general, damage to right frontal areas can produce impulsive and rule-breaking behaviors, such as interrupting conversations (Kolb & Taylor, 1981). People with frontal-lobe injuries are also less likely to make spontaneous facial expressions. The combination of excessive talking and lack of facial expressions may make these individuals seem like different people than they were before.

Think About It

If a person suffers a major head injury in an accident and then acts differently afterward, can we assume that brain damage was responsible for the personality change? Why or why not?

bull's brain. When the brain was stimulated, the bull dramatically stopped his charge and circled to the right.

In another classic study, James Olds and Peter Milner (Olds, 1969) used rats who had electrodes implanted in their brains to learn about the functions of the hypothalamus. When the rats pressed a lever, the electrodes stimulated the portion of the hypothalamus where they were implanted. As it turned out, the rats found this stimulation pleasurable—so pleasurable that the rats would press the lever up to 100 times a minute just to receive the stimulation. In some cases, hungry rats chose electrical stimulation over food. The part of the hypothalamus where the electrodes were implanted thus became known as a "pleasure center."

Electrical stimulation of the brain is not always reliable as a research tool. Stimulation in the same place can produce different effects at different times. On one occasion, a rat may eat when a portion of the brain is stimulated, but on another occasion it may drink. The areas that produce pleasant and unpleasant sensations in people may also vary from person to person and from day to day.

The Electroencephalogram The electroencephalogram (EEG) is a device that records the electrical activity of the brain. Electrodes attached to the scalp with tape or paste detect small amounts of electrical activity called brain waves. Researchers have learned that certain brain wave patterns are associated with feelings of relaxation and with sleep. (See Chapter 5.) Researchers and physicians can use electroencephalogram readings to help diagnose some kinds of psychological disorders and to help locate tumors.

Scans In recent years, scientists have designed new techniques for examining the brain. These techniques use computers to generate images of the brain from various sources of information (Goleman, 1995; Posner & Raichle, 1994). Images of the brain can provide information about brain damage and other abnormalities. Imaging techniques can also be used for early diagnoses of cancers and other problems. In addition, physicians can use imaging to aid them during difficult and intricate surgeries.

In computerized axial tomography (CAT) scans, a moving ring passes X-ray beams around and through the head. The density of the brain tissue determines how much radiation is absorbed. Computers measure the amounts of radiation and piece together a three-dimensional view of the brain that can be displayed on a video monitor.

In magnetic resonance imaging (MRI), a person lies in a very powerful magnetic field. Radio waves then cause parts of the brain to give off extra energy. This energy is measured from multiple angles and is translated by computer into a visual image of the brain's anatomy. MRI is more powerful than a CAT scan and can show details more clearly. For example, MRI is more effective at revealing small injuries and abnormalities in hard-to-see areas.

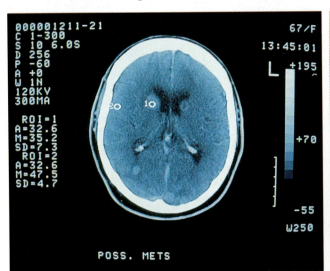
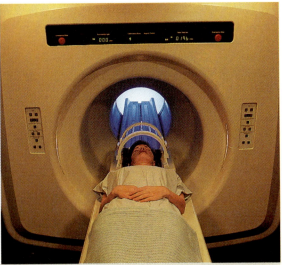

The photograph at left shows an image obtained by a CAT scan. By producing a three-dimensional view of the brain, a CAT scan can reveal hidden brain damage. The photograph on the right shows a person entering MRI apparatus. For people who fear enclosed spaces, the time spent lying in the MRI field can be uncomfortable.

Positron emission tomography (PET) scans differ from CAT scans and MRI because they show the activity of the brain rather than a snapshot of the brain at a given time. Scientists can see the brain actually at work. The person is injected with radioactive sugar. As the sugar reaches the brain, more of it is used where brain activity is greater. A computer image is generated based on the activity. The PET scan has been used by researchers to see which parts of the brain are most active when we are listening to music, working out a math problem, using language, or playing chess (Goldman-Rakic, 1995; Raichle, 1994). The PET scan reveals which parts of the brain are activated while the event is actually taking place. So, if you raise your hand, the computer will show activity in one area. If you suddenly start to sing a song, another area will light up.

Using these research techniques, psychologists have learned that the mind is a product of the brain. Today, it is generally agreed that for every mental event, such as a thought or a feeling, there are accompanying, underlying biological events. Imaging techniques have allowed us to explore more deeply how the nervous system, particularly the brain, functions while we are thinking, feeling, and moving. The study of brain abnormalities has also revealed that the brain has great flexibility. In other words, when parts of the brain have undergone damage, other areas of the brain can sometimes take over the functions of the damaged areas.

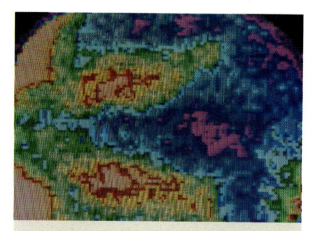

A PET scan shows brain activity as it occurs.

THINKING ABOUT PSYCHOLOGY

1. Why is the cerebral cortex important?
2. Describe two differences between the left hemisphere and the right hemisphere of the cerebral cortex.
3. List three different imaging techniques used to study the brain.
4. **Critical Thinking** Why do you think it benefits people to have brains that are flexible? What would happen if brains were not flexible?

3
The Endocrine System

The **endocrine system** consists of glands that secrete substances, called **hormones**, into the bloodstream. The word *hormone* is derived from the Greek *horman*, meaning "to stimulate" or "to excite." Hormones stimulate growth and many kinds of reactions, such as changes in activity levels and moods. Because hormones affect behavior and emotional reactions, psychologists who study the biology of behavior are also interested in the endocrine system.

Like neurotransmitters, hormones have specific receptor sites. Although the various hormones circulate throughout the body, they act only on hormone receptors in certain places. Hormones are produced by several different glands. These glands include the pituitary gland, the thyroid gland, the adrenal glands, and the testes and the ovaries. (See Figure 3.7 on page 68.)

The Pituitary Gland

The pituitary gland lies just below the hypothalamus. It is about the size of a pea, but it is so important that it has been referred to as the "master gland." The pituitary gland, which is stimulated by the hypothalamus, is responsible for the secretion of many different hormones that affect various aspects of behavior.

Growth hormone, for example, regulates the growth of muscles, bones, and glands. Children whose growth patterns seem abnormally slow often catch up to others the same age when doctors give them growth hormone.

Some hormones affect females in relation to pregnancy and mothering. Prolactin stimulates production of milk in nursing women. Oxytocin is responsible for stimulating labor in pregnant women. Sometimes when a pregnant woman is overdue, an obstetrician may induce labor by injecting the woman with oxytocin.

The Endocrine System

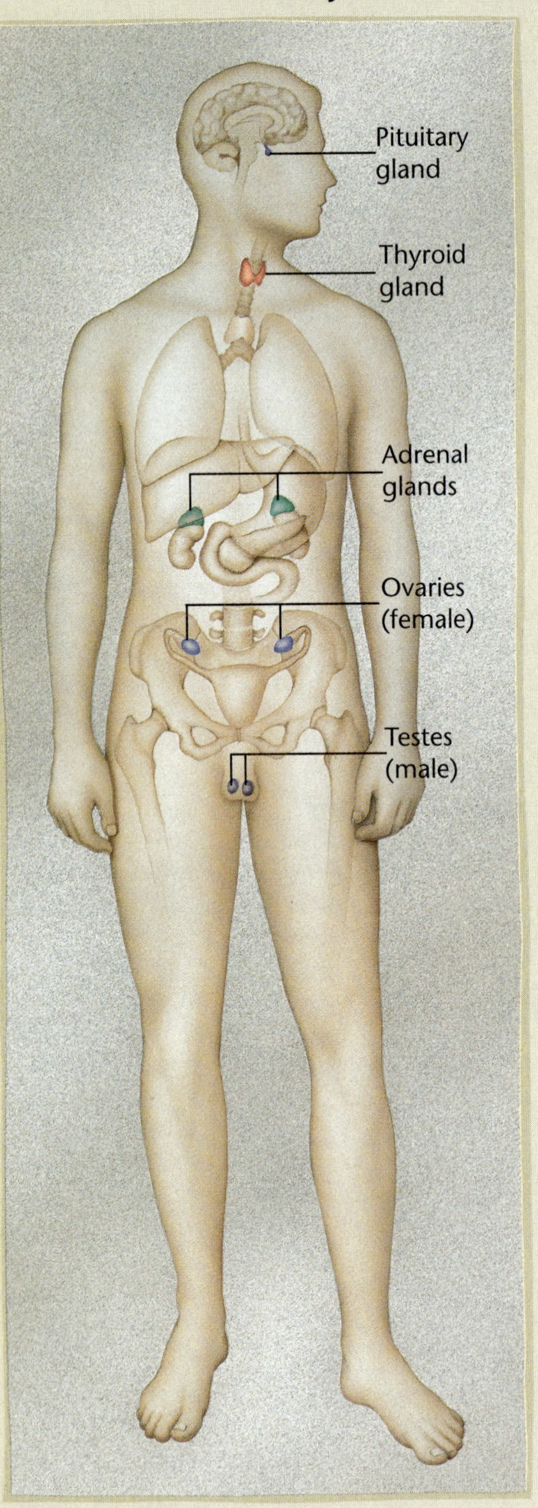

Pituitary gland

Thyroid gland

Adrenal glands

Ovaries (female)

Testes (male)

FIGURE 3.7 *The glands of the endocrine system secrete hormones that stimulate various body functions. Why do you think psychologists are interested in the endocrine system?*

Oxytocin and prolactin have been shown in some lower mammals to be connected to maternal behaviors such as caring for young (Kimble, 1992). The role of these hormones, if any, in human maternal behaviors remains unclear, however.

The Thyroid Gland

The thyroid gland produces thyroxin. Thyroxin affects the body's metabolism—its rate of converting food to energy. The production of too little thyroxin can lead to a condition called hypothyroidism. People with hypothyroidism often are overweight. For children, too little thyroxin can cause a condition called cretinism, which is characterized by stunted growth and mental retardation.

People who produce too much thyroxin may develop hyperthyroidism. Hyperthyroidism is characterized by excitability, inability to sleep, and weight loss.

The Adrenal Glands

The adrenal glands are located above the kidneys. The Latin prefix *ad-* means "toward" or "at," and *renal* derives from the Latin *renes,* meaning "kidneys."

The outer layer, or cortex, of the adrenal glands secretes cortical steroids. Cortical steroids increase resistance to stress and promote muscle development. They also cause the liver to release stored sugar, making energy available for emergencies.

The adrenal glands also produce adrenaline and noradrenaline. When a person faces a stressful situation, the sympathetic nervous system causes the adrenal glands to release a mixture of adrenaline and noradrenaline. These hormones help arouse the body, enabling the person to cope with the stressful situation. When Todd stepped on Marc's toe, for example, Marc's adrenal glands produced the adrenaline-noradrenaline mixture to help Marc deal with the situation.

Adrenaline also plays a role in the emotions people experience. It can intensify emotions such as fear and anxiety. Another function of noradrenaline is to raise blood pressure. In the nervous system, it also acts as a neurotransmitter.

The Testes and the Ovaries

Other glands are the testes (in males) and the ovaries (in females). These glands produce the hormones testosterone, estrogen, and progesterone.

Adrenaline and noradrenaline help people deal with emergencies, such as when parents must rush a child to the hospital.

Testosterone Testosterone is a male sex hormone, although females have small amounts of this hormone as well. Testosterone is produced by the testes in males. Small amounts of it are also secreted by the ovaries in females. Testosterone plays an important role in development, particularly during the prenatal period and during adolescence.

In the prenatal period, testosterone influences development of the sex organs. About six weeks after fertilization, if testosterone is secreted, it stimulates development of male sex organs. If testosterone is not secreted, however, then female sex organs develop.

In adolescence, testosterone aids the growth of muscle and bone as well as the development of primary and secondary sex characteristics. Primary sex characteristics are directly involved in reproduction. Secondary sex characteristics, such as beard growth, distinguish males and females but are not directly involved in reproduction.

Testosterone is a kind of steroid. A small number of athletes use steroids to enhance their athletic ability. Steroids affect muscle mass, heighten resistance to stress, and increase the body's energy supply. Because our society is highly competitive, some people are tempted to use steroids, but their use has serious medical and ethical implications. Steroid use carries significant health risks. Links have been reported between steroid use and sleep disturbances, liver damage, heart disease, and other medical problems. Ethically, most people believe that the use of steroids is unnatural and unfair to athletes who do not use them.

Estrogen and Progesterone Estrogen and progesterone are female sex hormones, although low levels are found in males as well. The ovaries in females produce estrogen and progesterone. Estrogen is also produced in smaller amounts by the testes in males.

Estrogen fosters the development of primary and secondary sex characteristics, such as breast enlargement. Progesterone, meanwhile, has multiple functions. It stimulates growth of the female reproductive organs. It also helps prepare the body for pregnancy. Together, estrogen and progesterone regulate the menstrual cycle and vary greatly during that cycle. Changes in levels of estrogen have been linked to premenstrual syndrome (PMS) in some women. PMS is a collection of symptoms (such as irritability, depression, and fatigue) that some women experience before menstruating.

THINKING ABOUT PSYCHOLOGY

1. List and describe the role of the hormones produced by the pituitary gland, the thyroid gland, the adrenal glands, and the testes and the ovaries.
2. **Critical Thinking** What might psychologists learn about behavior by studying the sex hormones?

4
Heredity:
Our Genetic Background

Heredity is the transmission of characteristics from parents to offspring. Psychologists are interested in studying heredity, along with the brain and hormones, as a means to understanding how and why people behave as they do. Heredity plays a key role in the development of traits both in people and in animals. The traits we inherit shape our behavior and also place limits on it.

Heredity is vital in the transmission of physical traits such as height, hair texture, and eye color. Heredity is also related, to some extent, to some psychological traits (Lykken et al., 1992; Plomin &

DNA: The Genetic Code

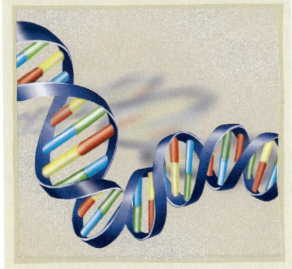

FIGURE 3.8 *The threadlike molecules of DNA that make up chromosomes contain the codes for the development of particular traits.*

Rende, 1991). Researchers have found that some psychological traits such as shyness, leadership, aggressiveness, and even an interest in arts and crafts are influenced by heredity. It is very important, though, to keep in mind that the environment also plays an important role in shaping these traits.

Heredity has been shown to be one factor involved in many psychological disorders, including anxiety and depression, schizophrenia, bipolar disorder, and alcoholism (Carey & DiLalla, 1994; Clark et al., 1994; Sher & Trull, 1994). (See Chapter 18.)

Despite some level of retardation, children with Down syndrome enjoy many of the same activities that other children do.

Genes and Chromosomes

Genes are the basic building blocks of heredity. Traits are determined by pairs of genes, with one gene in each pair inherited from each parent. Some traits, such as blood type, are controlled by a single pair of genes. Complex psychological traits, such as intelligence, involve combinations of genes, as well as environmental factors.

Genes are found in threadlike structures called **chromosomes**, which are composed of deoxyribonucleic acid (DNA). DNA takes the form of a double helix. (See Figure 3.8.) Most normal human cells contain 46 chromosomes that are organized into 23 pairs. In each of the 23 pairs, one chromosome comes from the father and the other chromosome comes from the mother. Each chromosome contains instructions for the development of particular traits in the individual.

Researchers have learned that 22 of the 23 pairs of chromosomes are similar in males and females. The 23rd pair, the sex chromosomes, determines whether we are female or male. In males, the 23rd pair consists of an X chromosome (so called because of its X shape) and a Y chromosome (because of its Y shape). Females have two X chromosomes, so they always pass an X chromosome on to their offspring. The chromosome that comes from the father, therefore, determines the sex of the offspring. If the father contributes an X chromosome, then the offspring is female. If the father contributes a Y chromosome, then the offspring is male.

TRUTH
OR
fiction
■ R E V I S I T E D ■

It is true that the father's genetic contribution—not the mother's—determines the sex of the offspring. The mother always contributes an X chromosome. Thus, it is the X or the Y chromosome from the father that determines the sex of the child.

When a child is born without 46 chromosomes in each cell, physical and behavioral disorders may result. One of the most common disabilities of this type occurs when there is an extra, or third, chromosome on the 21st pair. When this happens, a baby will be born with Down syndrome. People with Down syndrome usually have some level of mental retardation and may have heart and respiratory problems.

DILBERT reprinted by permission of United Feature Syndicate, Inc.

The Nature-Nurture Debate

Throughout history, philosophers and scientists have debated the role of biology in determining who we are, as people. This discussion is often called the "nature-nurture debate." *Nature* refers to what people inherit—the biological groundwork that prepares a person to develop in certain ways. *Nurture* refers to environmental factors—what a person is exposed to in life. Nurture includes a variety of factors such as family, education, culture, living conditions, everyday individual experiences, and a variety of other factors that are all part of people's environment.

People who support the "nature" side of the debate argue that people's traits and personality are primarily determined by their biological makeup. The argument is that our inherited characteristics determine the kind of people we are. Supporters of the "nurture" side, on the other hand, argue that the environment we live in and our everyday experiences—not our biological inheritance—determine how we behave and think.

Both of these views are extreme, and today, most psychologists agree that the influences of both nature and nurture determine our psychological traits. Biology influences us to act in certain ways, but our environment can modify these plans. It is the interaction of heredity and environment that determines who we are. A person who has the genetic potential to write a brilliant novel will never write that novel if he or she is never taught to read or write. An athlete who has the genetic potential to win a gold medal in figure skating will never win the medal if he or she has never been to a skating rink (or a solidly frozen pond).

Although most psychologists agree that genes and the environment interact, the extent of the role that heredity plays is still a controversial topic. Some psychologists believe that many of our traits, including intelligence, are determined largely by genetics. Others have criticized this view and are concerned about its implications. The heredity view can be interpreted to suggest that we cannot control our destiny because it is determined by our biology. Taken to the extreme, the heredity view might suggest, for example, that we should not try to change something about ourselves with which we are not satisfied. However, most psychologists are careful to note that heredity is not destiny. They emphasize that the environment does play a role in determining how a person develops, even though heredity is involved as well.

Kinship Studies

The most common way to sort out the roles that heredity and environment play in determining a trait is to do kinship studies. Kinship refers to the degree to which people are related, based on the genes they have in common. Identical twins share 100 percent of their genes. A parent and his or her child share 50 percent of their genes, as do full brothers and sisters, on average. Aunts and uncles related by blood share an average of 25 percent of their genes with nieces and nephews, and first cousins share an average of 12.5 percent.

Psychologists use this information to determine how much a trait is influenced by genetics and how much by environment. They study certain traits or behavioral patterns in individuals and then compare them to those of relatives. If genes are involved in a certain trait, then people who are more closely related, and who share more genes, should be more likely to exhibit the same trait than people who have less overlap in genes or who are not related. Two common types of kinship studies are twin studies and adoptee studies.

Identical twins share the same genetic makeup.

Twin Studies   The study of identical and fraternal twins is a useful way to learn about the relative influences of nature and nurture. Because identical twins share the same genetic makeup, differences between identical twins must be the result of the environment. For example, if one of the identical twins loves jazz, but the other twin prefers rock, that difference must be due to the twins' different experiences in the environment—not their heredity.

In contrast, fraternal twins, like other brothers and sisters, share an average of 50 percent of their genes. Thus, differences between fraternal twins might stem from heredity or the environment. The premise behind twin studies is that if identical twins are more similar on a certain trait than are fraternal twins, then that trait is influenced by genetics.

Researchers have found that identical twins resemble one another more strongly than fraternal twins in certain traits, including shyness and activity levels, irritability, and sociability (Emde, 1993; DeFries et al., 1987; Goldsmith, 1993). Thus, these traits appear to be influenced by heredity.

Identical twins are also more likely than fraternal twins to share psychological disorders such as autism, substance dependence, and schizophrenia. In one study on autism, a disorder characterized by limited social and communication abilities, both twins were likely to be autistic in 96 percent of the identical twin pairs. In contrast, both twins were likely to be autistic in only 24 percent of the fraternal twin pairs (Ritvo et al., 1985). This evidence strongly suggests a role for heredity in autism.

Adoptee Studies   One problem with twin studies is that identical twins tend to be treated similarly and are exposed to similar environments (Coon et al., 1990; Segal, 1993). Because they share the same environment as well as the same heredity, it is sometimes difficult to determine whether their similarities are due to nature or nurture.

One way to try to eliminate the effects of common backgrounds is to study children who have been adopted. Children who have been separated from their parents at an early age and then raised elsewhere provide special opportunities for sorting out the effects of nature and nurture. Psychologists look for the relative similarities between children and their adoptive and biological families. If the children act more like their biological families—with whom they share genes—than their adoptive families—with whom they share the environment—then their behavior may be largely influenced by heredity.

Twins Reared Apart   One of the most useful types of kinship studies examines twins who have been reared apart. Twins reared apart are less likely than twins reared together to share common experiences. Thus, similarities are probably due to genetic factors. In a major study that began in 1979, Thomas Bouchard and his colleagues (1990) examined twins who were reared apart. They found that many psychological and personality traits—including intelligence, traditionalism (following rules), risk avoidance, aggression, and leadership—are influenced by heredity.

Twins reared apart even share many of the same mannerisms, such as how they sit or stand. In one study, one pair of twins each wore seven rings, two bracelets on one wrist, and a bracelet and watch on the other wrist (Holden, 1980). Most researchers, however, acknowledge that the environment also has an important effect on the development of traits and mannerisms.

THINKING ABOUT PSYCHOLOGY

1. Define *gene* and *chromosome*.
2. Describe two methods used to study the role of heredity in determining traits.
3. **Critical Thinking**   Some traits such as extreme shyness have been shown to be partially determined by heredity. What aspects of the environment might also affect whether a person is shy?

PSYCHOLOGY

DOES HEREDITY DETERMINE OUR PERSONALITIES?

In 1979, Thomas Bouchard and several colleagues began conducting the Minnesota Study of Twins Reared Apart (Bouchard et al., 1990). The purpose of the study was to discover the extent to which heredity and environment were each involved in determining various psychological and personality traits. More than 100 pairs of identical and fraternal twins who were separated in infancy and reared apart participated in the study. The researchers examined similarities and differences in numerous traits such as intelligence, leadership abilities, and reaction to stress. They also studied social attitudes such as religious beliefs and the tendency to follow tradition.

In the report, Bouchard emphasized the importance of studying twins reared apart:

Monozygotic [identical] and dizygotic [fraternal] twins who were separated early in life and reared apart are a fascinating experiment of nature. They also provide the simplest and most powerful method for disentangling the influence of environmental and genetic factors on human characteristics.

Bouchard and his colleagues drew several conclusions from their research:

The study of these reared-apart twins led to two general and seemingly remarkable conclusions concerning the sources of the psychological differences—behavioral variation—between people: (i) genetic factors exert a pronounced and pervasive influence on behavioral variability, and (ii) the effect of being reared in the same home is negligible for many psychological traits. . . . For almost every behavioral trait so far investigated, from reaction time to religiosity, an important fraction of the variation among people turns out to be associated with genetic variation.

In other words, the results of the study suggested that heredity plays a greater role than environment in determining personality traits and behavior. Bouchard and his colleagues also noted, however, that the strong influence of heredity on psychological traits does not necessarily mean that environmental factors in general—and parenting in particular—play no role whatsoever. Commenting on the role parents play in determining personality traits in their children, the researchers stated:

Psychologists have been surprised by the evidence that being reared by the same parents in the same physical environment does not, on average, make siblings more alike as adults than they would have been if reared separately in adoptive homes. It is obvious that parents can produce shared effects if they grossly deprive or mistreat all their children. It seems reasonable that charismatic, dedicated parents, determined to make all their children share certain personal qualities, interests, or values, may sometimes succeed. Our findings, and those of others, do not imply that parenting is without lasting effects. The remarkable similarity in [identical twins reared apart] in social attitudes (for example, traditionalism and religiosity) does not show that parents cannot influence those traits, but simply that this does not tend to happen in most families.

The study, which lasted more than a decade, indicated that identical twins reared apart are as similar as identical twins reared together, and that identical twins are more similar than fraternal twins. Based on these results, Bouchard and many other psychologists believe that personality, intelligence, and social attitudes are largely determined by heredity, rather than environment.

Think About It

One of the findings of the Bouchard study was that children raised in the same family do not necessarily have similar social attitudes or personalities. Why might differences occur?

Chapter 3 REVIEW

SUMMARY

Biological psychologists, or biopsychologists, study the ways in which the nervous system, the brain, the endocrine system, and heredity affect human behavior, thought, and emotions.

I. The Nervous System

A. The nervous system is the body's internal communication system. It consists of two main parts: the central nervous system and the peripheral nervous system.

B. Neurons are made up of a cell body (which produces energy for cell activity), dendrites (which receive information), and axons (which carry messages away).

C. Neurotransmitters are chemicals that aid neurons in sending messages across synapses (the junction between the axon terminals of one neuron and the dendrites of another neuron).

D. The spinal cord is a thick column of nerves that transmits messages between the brain and the muscles and the glands throughout the body.

E. The peripheral nervous system transmits messages between the central nervous system and all parts of the body. Its two main divisions are the somatic nervous system and the autonomic nervous system.

II. The Brain

A. The human brain consists of three sections. The hindbrain regulates vital functions such as heart rate and respiration. The midbrain is involved in vision and hearing. The forebrain, which contains the cerebrum, is responsible for complex functions such as thought and emotions.

B. The cerebral cortex is the outer layer of the cerebrum. The cerebrum consists of two sides, or hemispheres. Although each hemisphere contains different functions, the two sides are interdependent.

C. Researchers learn about the brain by studying people with head injuries, by applying electrical stimulation to the brain, by measuring brain waves, and by using computers to create images of the brain.

III. The Endocrine System

A. The endocrine system consists of glands that secrete chemicals called hormones into the bloodstream. Hormones stimulate many kinds of reactions.

B. The pituitary gland secretes several different hormones. The thyroid gland produces the hormone thyroxin, which affects metabolism. The adrenal glands release hormones that help a person deal with stress.

C. The testes in males and the ovaries in females produce the hormones testosterone, estrogen, and progesterone.

IV. Heredity

A. Heredity is the transmission of characteristics from parents to offspring. Psychological traits and disorders, as well as physical traits, may be influenced by heredity.

B. Traits are determined by pairs of genes within the chromosomes of each human cell. Complex psychological traits may be controlled by combinations of genes.

C. The "nature-nurture debate" is a long-standing controversy in human psychology. Supporters of the "nature" approach believe that psychological traits are largely the result of heredity. Supporters of the "nurture" approach, on the other hand, believe that environment determines how a person develops. Most psychologists today agree that nature and nurture interact to produce a person's traits and personality.

D. Researchers use kinship studies to try to determine the influences of heredity and environment on psychological traits.

TERM & CONCEPT
REVIEW

1. Why is the nervous system referred to as a communication system?
2. Give an example of a spinal reflex, and explain how the nervous system functions in this reflexive action.
3. Where is the pons located, and what functions is it involved in?
4. What is the reticular activating system, and what does it do?
5. Which brain structures might be called "little brain" and "big brain"? Why? Besides their size, how are these structures different?
6. List the four lobes of the cerebral cortex and one function of each.
7. What happens if a person's corpus callosum is cut or removed?
8. How are the nervous system and the endocrine system related? Give an example.
9. Why are psychologists interested in heredity?
10. What is meant by the "nature-nurture debate"?

CRITICAL
THINKING

1. Messages travel in only one direction from neuron to neuron. What happens if the message-sending process is disrupted?
2. Why do you think the sympathetic and parasympathetic nervous systems have opposing functions?
3. Imagine that you have to give an oral report in class. Describe how you might feel and act before and after the report. How does your knowledge of the nervous system help you understand your reactions?
4. What is the danger of adhering to an extreme heredity view of psychological traits?
5. Which type of kinship study probably yields the most reliable results? Why? What might be some drawbacks of this type of study?

APPLYING SKILLS
IN PSYCHOLOGY

1. **COOPERATIVE LEARNING**   **Reading About Psychology**   With two or three of your classmates, look for magazine and newspaper articles that deal with biology and behavior. For example, you might find an article describing research that indicates schizophrenia is caused by a chemical imbalance in a person's body, or you might see an article describing a surgical procedure that relieves the tremors of Parkinson's disease. Present a summary of the article to the class. Then place the article in a class file on biology and behavior.

2. **Using Your Observation Skills**   During the next week, watch for spinal reflexive behavior, either in yourself or in others. Describe your observations in a journal or a notebook. Share them with other students in your class, and discuss whether the behaviors qualify as spinal reflexes. In what way is having reflexes beneficial?

3. **Research in Psychology**   Look in several psychology and anatomy books for illustrations of neurons. Then, using clay or papier-mâché, create a model of a neuron for a classroom display. Include a written explanation of how neurons transmit messages.

4. **Putting Psychology to Use**   Make a list of 10 traits that "run in your family." Include physical and personality traits, abilities, interests, and habits of various family members including stepparents, stepsiblings, and half siblings. For example, your list may have items such as *brown eyes, many freckles, highly athletic, generous, good in math, like to work with hands, shy, talkative, very neat, tendency to procrastinate.* For each item on your list, write "H" if you think that trait is primarily the result of heredity or "E" if you think that trait is primarily the result of environmental influences. Alongside each item, write a brief explanation of your decision. Share your list with family members to see if they agree or disagree.

Chapter 4

SENSATION AND PERCEPTION

Objectives

1 Distinguish between sensation and perception, and explain how they contribute to an understanding of our environment.

2 Explain how the eye works to enable vision.

3 Describe the process of hearing.

4 Identify the chemical, skin, and body senses, and explain how these senses work.

5 Summarize the laws of sensory perception.

A DAY IN THE LIFE

Linda and Marc were on their first date. They were getting settled in their seats at the movie theater. The movie was about to start, and voices buzzed all around them. Still, Marc did not really hear any of them. He was paying attention to what Linda was saying, and it seemed as if no one else was there at all. The other moviegoers were just gray, colorless shapes in the dim light. Marc hardly even noticed that the popcorn was a little too salty and that the gummy spot under his feet made the soles of his shoes stick to the floor. Instead, he was thinking about how much he liked the smell of Linda's cologne and the touch of her hand, although even these sensations faded into the recesses of Marc's mind as he listened to her speak.

Suddenly a darkened shape said "Excuse me" and squeezed in front of them to find a seat. A moment later, Marc's toe throbbed with pain, and for the second time in less than a week, Todd was saying, "Oh gee, I'm sorry!" Once again, Todd had accidentally stepped on Marc's foot.

Although Marc was annoyed, he grunted, "It's okay. It's dark in here. I guess you couldn't see." Yet that did not really help his toe, which was still throbbing. However, when Linda asked, "Are you all right, Marc?" her concerned voice practically made the pain in his toe disappear. All of a sudden, he was almost glad the whole accident had happened.

* * *

Like Marc in the movie theater, we all experience the world with our senses. A common belief is that people have five senses: vision, hearing, smell, taste, and touch. But you will learn that people actually have more than five senses. Touch, for example, includes several skin senses—pressure, warmth, cold, and pain. Still other senses tell us the position our body is in without our having to look.

Once we take in information through our senses, we do something with that information to interpret it. What we do depends on many factors—the circumstances, our mood, even our cultural background. Marc, for example, tuned out the buzzing in the theater because the only thing he was interested in hearing was Linda's voice. Then, when Todd stepped on his toe, he was both surprised and annoyed. These intense feelings heightened his perception of pain. But just a few seconds later, Linda's concern seemed to drive away the pain.

Psychologists call these two different processes sensation (the feeling) and perception (the interpretation of the feeling). As you read this chapter, you will learn more about these two concepts.

- sensation
- perception
- absolute threshold
- difference threshold
- signal-detection theory
- sensory adaptation
- pupil
- lens
- retina
- photoreceptor
- blind spot
- visual acuity
- complementary
- afterimage
- cochlea
- auditory nerve
- conductive deafness
- sensorineural deafness
- olfactory nerve
- gate theory
- kinesthesis
- vestibular sense
- closure
- proximity
- similarity
- continuity
- common fate
- stroboscopic motion
- monocular cue
- binocular cue
- retinal disparity

1

Sensation and Perception: The Basics

A DAY IN THE LIFE

When Todd stepped on Marc's toe, the sensation of pain was registered by sensory neurons in his skin. **Sensation** is the stimulation of sensory receptors and the transmission of sensory information to the central nervous system (the spinal cord and brain). Sensory receptors are located in sensory organs such as the eyes and ears and elsewhere in the body. The stimulation of the senses is automatic. It results from sources of energy like light and sound or from the presence of chemicals, as in smell and taste.

Marc perceived the pain in his brain. **Perception** is the psychological process through which we interpret sensory stimulation. Imagine that you are standing at one end zone of a football field while a play is going on. Some of the players are close and rushing toward you; other players are at the other end of the field. Those players who are far away look very small compared to those players who are barreling down on you. Still, you know that the quarterback, who has just thrown a pass from the other end of the field, is not actually tiny. How do you know? The answer is that you know through experience. Perception reflects learning, expectations, and attitudes.

Stimulation of the senses and the ways in which people interpret that stimulation is affected by several concepts. These concepts include absolute threshold, difference threshold, signal-detection theory, and sensory adaptation.

Absolute Threshold

Have you ever had your hearing tested? If so, try to remember the experience. There you were, sitting in a booth or quiet room with earphones on your head. At first, you heard nothing, and perhaps you began to wonder what was going on. Then suddenly, a beep. You had just discovered your absolute threshold for hearing that kind of sound. **Absolute threshold** is the weakest amount of a stimulus that can be sensed. Even before you heard that first beep, the person testing you was trying different beeps, but you simply could not hear them. The first one you heard was the weakest one you were capable of hearing.

Did you know that dogs can hear certain whistles that people cannot? This is because a dog's absolute threshold for certain sounds is different from that of a human being.

Absolute thresholds for humans have been determined for the senses of vision, hearing, smell, taste, and touch. (See Figure 4.1.) However, the absolute threshold for a particular stimulus can differ from person to person. Some people are more sensitive to certain sensory stimuli than others. These differences stem from psychological and biological factors.

If absolute thresholds differed much from what they are, we might sense the world very differently. For example, if our ears were more sensitive, we might hear collisions among molecules of air. If our sense of smell was as sensitive as a dog's, we might be able to track down someone just by sniffing a piece of his or her clothing.

Difference Threshold

For us to function well in the world, we need absolute thresholds low enough to see, hear, smell, taste, and feel what is going on around us—but not so low that our senses are overloaded with information we cannot use. We also need to be able to detect small differences between stimuli—what makes one stimulus different from another stimulus. The minimum amount of difference that can be detected between two stimuli is known as the **difference threshold**.

Absolute Thresholds for Humans

SENSE	STIMULUS	RECEPTORS	THRESHOLD
Vision	Electromagnetic energy	Rods and cones in the retina	A candle flame viewed from a distance of about 30 miles on a dark night
Hearing	Sound waves	Hair cells of the inner ear	The ticking of a watch from about 20 feet away in a quiet room
Smell	Chemical substances in the air	Receptor cells in the nose	About one drop of perfume diffused throughout a small house
Taste	Chemical substances in saliva	Taste buds on the tongue	About 1 teaspoon of sugar dissolved in 2 gallons of water
Touch	Pressure on the skin	Nerve endings in the skin	The wing of a fly falling on a cheek from a distance of about 0.4 inch

FIGURE 4.1 *This table shows humans' absolute threshold for various stimuli and five senses.*

Source: Adapted from "Contemporary Psychophysics," by E. Galanter, 1962, in R. Brown and others (Eds.), *New Directions in Psychology*, New York: Holt, Rinehart and Winston.

For example, imagine that someone shows you two dark blue paint chips. You may think they are the same color, even if they are slightly different. But now imagine that one of the paint chips is removed and replaced with another chip that is just a bit lighter or darker. Do the two paint chips still seem the same color? No. The smallest amount of difference you can see in order to distinguish between the two shades of blue is your difference threshold. Just as with absolute threshold, people's individual difference thresholds vary slightly.

Signal-Detection Theory

As you might imagine, it is easier to hear a friend talking in a quiet room than in a room where other people are laughing loudly. And when your nose is stuffy from a cold, your dinner may seem to have little flavor. In the first case, the setting has made a difference in your sensation and perception. In the second case, your physical condition has made the difference. **Signal-detection theory** is a method of distinguishing sensory stimuli that takes into account not only their strengths but also such elements as the setting, your physical state, your mood, and your attitudes.

Signal-detection theory also considers psychological factors such as motivations, expectations, and learning. For example, even if the place where you are now reading is buzzing with distracting signals such as a breeze against your face, the shadow of passing clouds, or the voices of passersby, you will be able to ignore those influences as long as you are motivated to keep reading. Similarly, people who smell perfumes for a living have learned through years of experience how to detect subtle differences others would not be able to smell.

We focus on whatever we consider important. Marc's toe hurt a great deal when Todd stepped on it, but when Linda asked him if he was in pain, her voice was all that interested him. As another example, suppose that you attend a recital at school. A student you do not know plays the piano. Your mind may wander as you listen. But do you think the student's parents let their minds wander? You can be pretty sure that they do not—the performance is much more important to them than it is to other members of the audience.

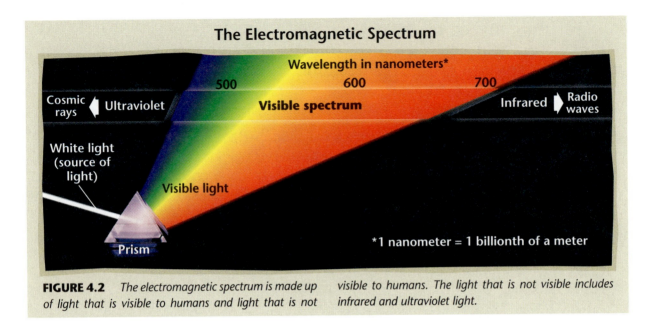

The Electromagnetic Spectrum

Wavelength in nanometers*

500　　　600　　　700

Cosmic rays　Ultraviolet　Visible spectrum　Infrared　Radio waves

White light (source of light)

Visible light

Prism

*1 nanometer = 1 billionth of a meter

FIGURE 4.2　*The electromagnetic spectrum is made up of light that is visible to humans and light that is not* visible to humans. The light that is not visible includes infrared and ultraviolet light.

Sensory Adaptation

A DAY IN THE LIFE

When Marc and Linda first walked into the darkened movie theater, they could see little except the colorless shapes of the other moviegoers. As time passed, they became able to see the faces of people around them and the features of the theater. And if Todd had waited a few minutes before trying to find a seat, his eyes would have adapted to the darkness and he might not have stepped on Marc's toe.

Our sensory systems adapt to a changing environment. **Sensory adaptation** is the process by which we become more sensitive to weak stimuli and less sensitive to unchanging stimuli. As time went on, Marc, Linda, and Todd could see the people around them better—the people were weak stimuli. On the other hand, as we adapt to lying on the beach, we become less aware of the unchanging stimulus of the lapping of the waves. Similarly, if we live in the city, we adapt to the sounds of traffic (unchanging stimuli) except for the occasional car backfire or fire engine siren.

THINKING ABOUT PSYCHOLOGY

1. Define *absolute threshold*.
2. Give two examples of sensory adaptation.
3. **Critical Thinking**　Describe a recent situation where you were so involved in something that you did not notice your surroundings. How does that experience relate to signal-detection theory?

2 Vision

Those of us fortunate enough to have good vision usually consider information from vision to be more essential than that from our other senses. No other sense allows us to gather so much information from nearby and distant sources. To understand vision, it is important to know how light works and how our eyes function.

Light

Light is electromagnetic energy. It is described in wavelengths. Not all light is visible to humans. In fact, the light that humans can see makes up only a small part of the spectrum of electromagnetic energy. The wavelengths of cosmic rays are only a fraction of an inch long. The wavelengths of some radio waves extend for miles. The wavelengths of visible light are in between. (See Figure 4.2.)

You have probably seen sunlight broken down into colors as it filters through water vapor—this is what makes a rainbow. Sunlight can also be broken down into colors by means of a glass structure called a prism. The main colors of the spectrum, from longest to shortest wavelengths, are red, orange, yellow, green, blue, indigo, and violet. For generations, people have remembered the order by using the made-up name *Roy G. Biv,* which comes from using the first letter of each of the colors.

It is true that when you look at a rainbow, the wavelength of light determines the colors you see. The wavelength for red is longer than that for orange, and so on through the spectrum of visible light to violet, which has the shortest wavelength.

The Eye

When you take a picture with a camera, light enters through an opening and is focused onto a sensitive surface—the film. Chemicals on the film are changed by the light and create a lasting impression of the image that entered the camera.

Your eye is very similar. (See Figure 4.3.) As in a camera, light enters the eye and then is projected onto a surface. The amount of light that enters is determined by the size of the opening in the colored part of the eye. This opening is called the **pupil**. When you look into someone's eyes, the black circles you see in the middle are the pupils. They may look solid to you, but actually they are holes.

The size of the pupil adjusts automatically to the amount of light entering the eye. Try the following experiment. With a friend, go into bright light, stay there for a few minutes, then go into a much darker area. Notice how the size of your friend's pupils changes. In the bright light, the pupils become very small. This is because the light is bright enough that the eyes need only a bit of it. In the dark, however, the pupils become very large because they need to let in as much light as possible. Pupil size is also sensitive to our emotions. We can be literally

The Human Eye

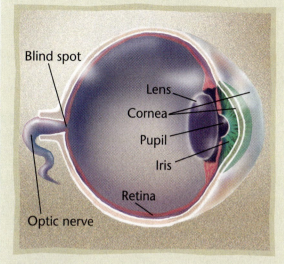

FIGURE 4.3 *In the human eye, light travels through the pupil to the lens and is then reflected onto the retina. The optic nerve sends the visual information to the brain.*

"wide-eyed with fear," meaning that the pupils open widely when we are afraid.

Once light has entered the eye, it encounters the lens. The **lens** adjusts to the distance of objects by changing its thickness. Hold a finger at arm's length and then bring it slowly toward your nose. You will feel tension in the eye as the thickness of the lens adjusts to keep the finger in focus. When people squint to look at something, they are adjusting the thickness of the lens.

These changes project a clear image of the object onto the retina. The **retina** is the sensitive surface in the eye that acts like the film in a camera. However, the retina consists of neurons—not film. Neurons

©1995 United Feature Syndicate, Inc. (NYC)

Sonic Navigation Systems

Technology is constantly at work to assist people with disabilities. It has, for example, assisted Dr. Reginald Golledge, who has been blind since the mid-1980s. These days, Dr. Golledge carries a very special backpack when he walks over the campus of the University of California at Santa Barbara. Inside that backpack is a computer, one part of which is called a "personal navigation system."

Programmed into the computer is a map of the campus, with all the different buildings and other objects a person walking there would encounter. As Dr. Golledge walks across the campus, these structures seem to call out to him through the headphones connected to the computer. "Psychology building here, psychology building here," or "Bench here, bench here," they might say. The computerized messages guide him as he moves along: the psychology building is to his right; the bench is on the left. Though he still takes his cane, he needs to use it less, and he is able to venture into unfamiliar territory with more confidence than he had before.

Widespread use of a system like this is probably years away, but Dr. Golledge, who is a geographer, and psychologist Dr. Roberta Klatzky are working to make it a reality for people who are blind. They are focusing on ways to make the backpack lighter—it currently weighs about 28 pounds—and the system easier to use. For example, they are trying to determine the types of messages that work best: "The psychology building is 40 feet ahead, 30 feet ahead, 20 feet ahead," or compass readings such as "The psychology building is at 30 degrees."

Dr. Golledge makes use of the sonic navigation system.

How does the system work? A device in the backpack sends signals to Global Positioning System satellites in orbit around the earth. These satellites sense the precise location on the earth of the person wearing the backpack. They then transmit this information to the computer in the backpack. The computer already has a map of the area programmed into it and can use the information about the person's location on the earth to calculate where the person is on the map. It can also calculate the person's location in relation to various objects in the area, which are part of the computerized map.

The nearer the person comes to an object, the louder the messages become. If a structure is to the person's right, the sounds will be louder in the right ear. If the structure is to the left of the person, the sounds will be louder in the left ear. As a result, the person can quickly sense a structure's direction and distance and use that information for guidance. Those who have tried the system say they quickly adapt to locating an object through the sounds.

Although researchers are excited about this new system, they realize that it will never completely replace the cane or the Seeing Eye dog. The sonic navigation system cannot, for example, announce the location of items—such as other people—that have not been programmed into the computer.

Think About It

What effects, beyond navigation itself, might this system have on the lives of people who are blind?

that are sensitive to light are called **photoreceptors**. Once the light hits the photoreceptors, a nerve carries the visual input to the brain. In the brain, the information is relayed to the visual area of the occipital lobe. (See Chapter 3.)

The Blind Spot   Look again at Figure 4.3 and find the point where the optic nerve leaves the eye. When light hits that point, the eye registers nothing because that area lacks photoreceptors. Thus it is called the **blind spot**. We all have one. If we did not, we would never be able to "see" anything—no visual input would reach the brain through the optic nerve for interpretation.

Rods and Cones   Remember how Marc saw only the gray outlines of the other people in the dimly lit movie theater? This was because of the way the photoreceptors in the retina work. There are two kinds of photoreceptors: rods and cones. Rods are sensitive only to the brightness of light. They allow us to see in black and white. Cones provide color vision.

If you are a camera buff, you know that when lighting is low, you get a clearer image with black-and-white film than with color film. In the same way, rods are more sensitive to light than are cones. Therefore, as the lighting grows dim, as in a movie theater when the lights go down, objects lose their color before their outlines fade from view.

Dark and Light Adaptation   When you first enter a movie theater, it may be too dark for you to find a seat. As time passes, however, you come to see the seats and the other people more clearly. This adjustment to lower lighting is called dark adaptation. Your ability to see in low light continues to improve for up to 45 minutes.

But what happens when you first move from the dark into the light? Imagine turning on the lamp next to your bed in the middle of the night. At first, you blink, and it almost hurts, but within only a minute or two, you have adapted. Adaptation to bright light happens much more quickly than adaptation to the dark.

Visual Acuity   The sharpness of vision is called **visual acuity**. Visual acuity is determined by the ability to see visual details (in normal light). When people have their eyes examined, they have to read the letters on a chart like the one shown above. This is the Snellen Chart. It is used to measure visual

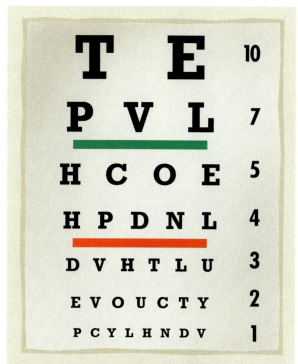

If you have ever had your eyes examined, you probably looked at the Snellen Chart, which is used to measure visual acuity.

acuity. If you were to stand 20 feet from the Snellen Chart and could only read the T or the E, we would say that your vision is 20/100. This means that what a person with normal vision could see from a distance of 100 feet away, you could see from no more than 20 feet away. In such a case, you would be nearsighted—you would have to be particularly close to an object to make out its details. A person who is farsighted, on the other hand, needs to be farther away from an object than a person with normal vision to see it clearly.

You may have noticed that older people often hold newspapers or books at more of a distance from their eyes than younger people. As people reach middle age, their lenses become relatively brittle. Therefore, it is more difficult for them to focus, especially on nearby objects. As a result, many older people are farsighted.

Color Vision

Look around. The world is a place of brilliant colors—the blue of the sky, the reds and yellows of autumn leaves, the vivid greens of spring. The wavelength of light determines the color. People with normal color vision see any color in the spectrum

The Color Circle

FIGURE 4.4 *The colors across from each other on the color circle are called complementary colors. What is the complement of green?*

enable us to perceive color. Some cones are sensitive to blue, some to green, and some to red. When more than one kind of cone is stimulated at the same time, we perceive other colors of the spectrum, such as yellow and violet.

This is similar to the way color television sets convey colors to the viewer. Although you may not be aware of it, the images you see on a television screen actually consist of thousands of very small dots. Each of these dots is either blue, green, or red—the same colors that are perceived by the different types of cones in the eye. There are no yellow, purple, or even black or white dots in the television images. These and other colors are created only through various combinations of blue, green, and red dots.

Afterimages   Look at the strangely colored flag in Figure 4.5 for at least half a minute. Then look at a sheet of white paper. What do you see? If your color vision is working properly and if you looked at the flag long enough, you should see a flag composed of the familiar red, white, and blue. The flag you perceive on the white sheet of paper is an afterimage of the first flag. The **afterimage** of a color is its complementary color. You perceive an afterimage when you have viewed a color for a while and then the color is removed. The same holds true for black and white. Staring at one will create an afterimage of the other.

of visible light. But what about animals? You may be surprised to find out that dogs and cats see far fewer colors than you do but that insects, birds, fish, and reptiles experience a wide variety of colors.

The Color Circle   Look at Figure 4.4. What you see is called the color circle. It is the colors of the spectrum bent into a circle. The colors across from each other are called **complementary**. Red-green and blue-yellow are the major complementary pairs. If we mix complementary colors together, they form gray. You may have learned in art class that mixing blue and yellow creates green, not gray. But this is true only with *pigments,* or substances such as crayons or paints. Here we are talking about *light,* not about pigments.

- - - - - - - - - - - - -

TRUTH
OR
fiction
■ R E V I S I T E D ■

It is not true that you get green light by mixing blue light and yellow light. You do get a green pigment when you mix pigments of blue and yellow, but pigments are substances, not light. Mixing blue light and yellow light forms gray.

- - - - - - - - - - - - -

Cones and Color Vision   Cones, one of the two types of photoreceptors in the retina of the eye,

Color Blindness

If you can see the colors of the visible spectrum, you have normal color vision. People who do not have normal color vision are said to be "color blind."

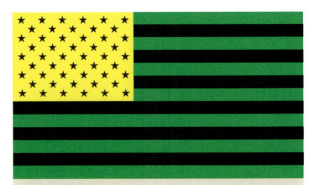

FIGURE 4.5 *Stare at the center of this flag for 30 seconds, then look at a white piece of paper. You should see a more familiar image—the red, white, and blue American flag. The afterimage of a color is that color's complement.*

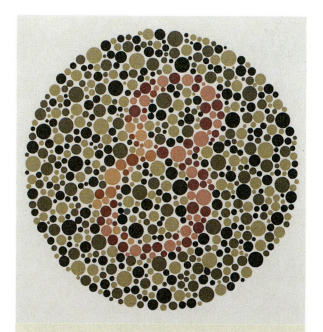

FIGURE 4.6 *This image resembles a test for color blindness. In the actual test, which would be conducted by a trained professional, a person with normal color vision would see an 8, a person with red-green color blindness would see a 3, and a person with total color blindness would see no number.*

These people are partially or totally unable to distinguish color due to an absence of, or malfunction in, the cones. People who are totally color blind are sensitive only to light and dark and see the world as most people do on a black-and-white television set. Total color blindness is rare.

Partial color blindness, on the other hand, is fairly common. People who are partially color blind see some colors but not others. Particularly common is red-green color blindness, in which a person has difficulty seeing shades of red and green. Figure 4.6 shows one of the types of tests that are used to check for color blindness.

THINKING ABOUT PSYCHOLOGY

1. What is visible light?

2. What is the retina, and what is its function?

3. Explain how we are able to see color.

4. **Critical Thinking** Imagine that you became completely color blind. How might your life be different from the way it is now? How would you have to adjust? What occupations or hobbies might become difficult for you?

3 Hearing

Do you know how you are able to hear your phone ringing? a baby crying? leaves rustling? Sound travels through the air in waves. It is caused by changes in air pressure that result from vibration. Anything that makes a sound—the whisper of your voice, the hum of a tuning fork, the strumming of a guitar—causes vibrations. Each of these vibrations is called a cycle or a sound wave. Every sound has its own pitch and loudness.

Pitch

Sound waves can be very fast, occurring many times per second. The pitch of a sound—how high or low the sound is—depends on its frequency, or the number of cycles per second. The more cycles per second, the higher the pitch of a sound.

Try this experiment. Cut a rubber band into two segments—one long, one short—then stretch each one out and twang it. The shorter one has a higher sound, right? In the same way, women's voices usually have a higher pitch than those of men because women's vocal cords tend to be shorter and therefore vibrate at a greater frequency. Similarly, the strings of a violin are shorter and vibrate at a higher frequency than the strings of a cello. Therefore, the violin's sound is higher in pitch than the sound made by the cello.

The human ear can hear sound waves that vary from 20 to 20,000 cycles per second. Many animals, including dogs and dolphins, hear sounds well beyond 20,000 cycles per second. Although we cannot hear them, dolphins emit sounds that help them locate objects. The sound pulses echo back from fish and other objects.

Loudness

What is the softest sound you can hear? What is the loudest? The loudness of a sound is determined by the height, or amplitude, of sound waves. The higher the amplitude of the wave, the louder the sound. The loudness of a sound is measured in decibels, a unit that is abbreviated *dB*. Zero dB is considered the threshold of hearing. Zero dB is about as loud as the ticking of a watch 20 feet away in a very quiet room. (See Figure 4.7 on page 86.)

The Ear

Just as the eye is the human instrument for seeing, the ear is the instrument for sensing all the sounds around us. In fact, the ear is shaped to capture sound waves, to vibrate with them, and to transmit sound to the brain. What we normally think of as the ear is actually the outer ear. We also have a middle ear and an inner ear. (See Figure 4.8.)

The eardrum is the gateway from the outer ear to the middle ear. It is a thin membrane that vibrates when sound waves strike it. As it vibrates, it transmits the sound to three small bones in the middle ear: the hammer, the anvil, and the stirrup. (The stirrup is the smallest bone in the human body.) These bones then also begin to vibrate and transmit sound to the inner ear.

The inner ear consists of the cochlea (COH-klee-uh). The word *cochlea* comes from the Greek word for "snail." Look at Figure 4.8 again, and you will see why—it is shaped just like the shell of a snail. The **cochlea** is a bony tube that contains fluids as well as neurons that move in response to the vibrations of the fluids. The movement generates neural impulses that are transmitted to the brain via the **auditory nerve**. Within the brain, auditory input is projected onto the hearing areas of the cerebral cortex. (See Chapter 3.)

Locating Sounds

Did you ever sit in front of a stereo, and for some reason, all the sound seemed to come from one side instead of from straight ahead? What you probably did was adjust the balance knob until the sound seemed equally loud in each ear.

Balancing a stereo set is similar to locating sounds. If a sound seems louder from the right, you think it is coming from the right because you are used to a sound from the right side reaching the right ear first.

But what if a sound comes from directly in front of you, from behind, or from above? All such sounds are equally loud and distant from each ear. So what do you do? Simple—you usually turn your head just a little to determine in which ear the sound increases. If you turn to your right and the

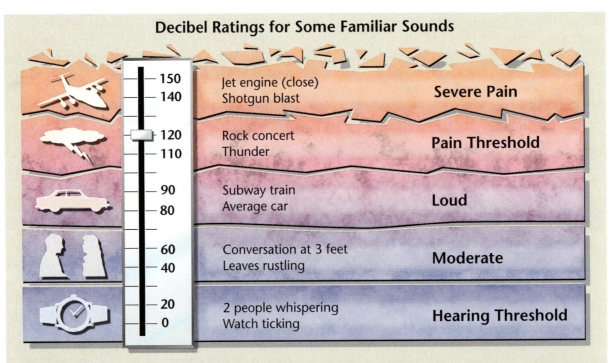

Decibel Ratings for Some Familiar Sounds

dB	Sound	Category
150 / 140	Jet engine (close) / Shotgun blast	Severe Pain
120 / 110	Rock concert / Thunder	Pain Threshold
90 / 80	Subway train / Average car	Loud
60 / 40	Conversation at 3 feet / Leaves rustling	Moderate
20 / 0	2 people whispering / Watch ticking	Hearing Threshold

FIGURE 4.7 *Zero dB is the threshold for hearing. Prolonged exposure to sounds greater than 85 dB will cause some hearing loss. Sounds of 130 dB can cause immediate hearing loss.*

The Human Ear

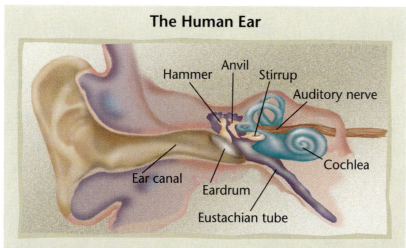

FIGURE 4.8 *Sound enters the outer ear and is funneled to the eardrum. Inside the middle ear, the hammer, anvil, and stirrup vibrate, transmitting the sound to the inner ear.*

ears? This may have meant that neurons had been lost in your ears. The same thing can happen to workers who operate certain drilling equipment or drive loud vehicles. The next time you are exposed to loud sounds, remember to cover your ears.

Devices called experimental cochlear implants, or "artificial ears," contain microphones that sense sounds and electronic equipment that stimulates the auditory nerve directly. However, if the auditory nerve itself is damaged, a cochlear implant cannot help.

loudness increases in your left ear, the sound must be in front of you. Of course, you also use information from vision and other cues in locating the source of sounds. If you hear the roar of jet engines, most of the time you can be fairly certain that the airplane is overhead.

Deafness

Not everyone perceives sound. About 2 million Americans are deaf. Deafness may be inherited or caused by disease, injury, or old age.

Conductive Deafness   If we see an older person with a hearing aid, we can assume that he or she is probably suffering from conductive deafness. **Conductive deafness** occurs because of damage to the middle ear. Since this part of the ear amplifies sounds, damage to it causes people not to hear sounds that are not loud enough. Fortunately, people with conductive deafness often are helped by hearing aids. These aids provide the amplification that the middle ear does not.

Sensorineural Deafness   Many people do not perceive sounds of certain frequencies. This is a sign of sensorineural deafness. **Sensorineural deafness** usually is caused by damage to the inner ear. Most often, the neurons in the cochlea are lost. Sometimes sensorineural deafness is due to damage to the auditory nerve, either through disease or through prolonged exposure to very loud sounds.

Have you ever attended a high-volume rock concert and left with a ringing sensation in your

Deafness in the World Today   In recent years, people who are deaf have been able to come more into the mainstream of sensory experience as a result of their own efforts, the efforts of others, and new technology. For example, Heather Whitestone, who lost most of her hearing in infancy, became the

Heather Whitestone, the Miss America of 1995, lost most of her hearing as an infant.

These students at a school for the deaf make the sign for friends as part of a school performance. More and more people are becoming familiar with the signs of American Sign Language.

Miss America of 1995. Whitestone is a dancer of classical ballet. She uses the vibrations of the music to dance in rhythm.

Interpreters are often on hand to translate speeches into languages (such as American Sign Language) used by members of the audience who are hearing impaired. More and more schools are offering courses in American Sign Language. Many television shows are now "closed captioned," which means that special decoders make the captions visible on the screen. And, as you have just read, scientists are always trying to find new ways to counteract damage inside the ear.

THINKING ABOUT PSYCHOLOGY

1. What determines the loudness of a sound? How is loudness measured?
2. Define *eardrum* and explain its function.
3. Describe the two kinds of deafness.
4. **Critical Thinking**   Describe a situation in which you or someone you know seemed confused about the direction from which a sound was coming. How was the confusion resolved?

4
Other Senses

Vision and hearing are just two of many human senses. Others are smell, taste, and the skin and body senses. Smell and taste are called the chemical senses. With vision and hearing, physical energy in the form of light and sound waves stimulates our sensory receptors. With smell and taste, however, we sense molecules of substances. The skin detects touch through pressure, temperature, and pain. Body senses alert us to our posture and movement.

Smell

People do not have as strong a sense of smell as many animals. Dogs use seven times as much of the cerebral cortex for smell as people do. Some dogs even earn a living by sniffing out drugs in suitcases or using scent to track lost children or objects.

But smell is important to people too. Without smell, you would not be able to taste as much as you do. For example, if your sense of smell were not working, an onion and an apple would taste very much alike to you.

Odors of substances are detected by receptor neurons high in each nostril. Receptor neurons react when molecules of the substance in the form of a gas come into contact with them. The receptors send information about the odors to the brain via the **olfactory nerve**.

Our sense of smell adapts quickly. In the movie theater, Marc soon lost awareness of Linda's cologne. We adapt rapidly even to annoying odors. This may be fortunate if we are in a locker room. It may not be fortunate if harmful fumes, such as from cars, are present—we may lose awareness of the smoke or fumes even though danger remains. One odor can also be masked by another, which is how air fresheners work.

Taste

Why would your dog gobble up a piece of a candy bar, but your cat turn up its nose at it? Dogs can taste sweetness, but cats cannot.

The four basic taste qualities are sweetness, sourness, saltiness, and bitterness. Do you think that you taste more than these four qualities? What

It is not true that people often lose their sense of taste as they grow older. **What they usually lose is their sense of smell,** which is why their food seems to lack flavor.

you are experiencing is the *flavor* of food, which involves odor, texture, and temperature as well as taste. If you have a cold, for example, food tastes flat because you cannot smell it. The reason older people sometimes complain that their food has little "taste" is usually that they have experienced a loss of the sense of smell, not taste. Thus they perceive less of the flavor of their food.

Taste is sensed through receptor neurons located on taste buds on the tongue. Taste buds specialize. Those that are responsive to sweetness are located at the tip of the tongue. Receptors for bitterness are at the back of the tongue. Sourness is sensed along the sides of the tongue, and saltiness overlaps the areas sensitive to sweetness and sourness. (See Figure 4.9.) This might explain why you lick an ice cream cone but not, say, a pickle. Ice cream is sweet, so using the tip of your tongue to lick it makes sense. But a pickle is salty and sour, so you would not taste much if you simply licked it—you need to touch the pickle with other parts of your tongue in order to taste it. Try sucking a lemon, and see whether you feel the sour taste at the sides of your tongue.

The Skin Senses

What we normally call "touch" is better called the "skin senses" because touch is a combination of pressure, temperature, and pain. Our skin senses are vitally important to us. Studies have shown that premature infants grow more quickly and stay healthier if they are touched (Field et al., 1986). And older people seem to do better if they have a dog or cat to stroke and cuddle (Pearlman, 1994).

Pressure   Your body is covered with hairs, some of them very tiny. Sensory receptors located around the roots of hair cells fire where the skin is touched. Other structures beneath the skin are also sensitive to pressure. Different parts of the body are more sensitive to pressure than others. The fingertips, lips, nose, and cheeks are more sensitive than the shoulders, thighs, and calves.

The Taste Buds

Bitter

Sour

Sweet

Salty

FIGURE 4.9   *Different areas on the tongue are especially sensitive to each of the four taste sensations: sweetness, sourness, saltiness, and bitterness.*

CASE STUDIES

AND OTHER TRUE STORIES

Compensating for Lost Senses: Helen Keller's Story

Most, if not all, of our knowledge of the world comes to us through our senses. What happens, then, if we lose one or more of those senses? Perception may not be lost if other senses can be used to compensate for the missing sense or senses. The life of Helen Keller serves as an excellent example.

Helen Keller was born in Tuscumbia, Alabama, in 1880. She was walking and had just started to learn a few words when suddenly, in February 1882, she became very ill. Despite the doctor's prediction that she would die, the child survived, but she had become both deaf and blind.

It is hard to imagine what it must be like to wake up one day and find nothing but silence and darkness where once you heard sounds and saw objects and people. Not surprisingly, the young Keller became difficult to manage. Fearful, she clung to her mother's apron, and at times she had violent temper tantrums.

When Keller was almost seven, her life changed dramatically. Anne Sullivan arrived in Tuscumbia to teach the child. Sullivan had once been nearly blind herself, and she had attended the Perkins Institute for the Deaf and Blind in Boston. Although two operations had restored her eyesight, she understood what it was like to be blind, and she was eager to teach her new pupil.

The situation did not look promising at first. Keller was rude to her new teacher, and she would not sit still to have Sullivan use the manual alphabet. In the manual alphabet, which is still used with people who are deaf and blind, the "speaker" makes the signs right into the hand of the "listener," using the sense of touch to communicate. At first, Sullivan tried the word *doll* when she gave the child a doll as a gift. Keller simply took the present and ran off. Eventually, however, she began to imitate Sullivan. Within days, she signed several words, although she still had some difficulty connecting the words spelled in her hand with the actual objects.

One day, while Sullivan put her pupil's hand under running water, she spelled the word *w-a-t-e-r* into Keller's palm over and over. Suddenly Keller realized that w-a-t-e-r was the "cool something" that was running over her hand, and a breakthrough had occurred. Within one hour, she learned 30 new words.

From that beginning came a long life of both learning and teaching. The easiest words to learn were those that described objects or things Keller could taste or smell. It was harder for the young girl to understand that her feelings—such as anger and love—also had names.

For the first few years, Anne Sullivan was Keller's only teacher, but Keller was eager to learn. At the age of 10, Keller decided that she needed to learn to speak. To do so, she took lessons from a teacher of people who were deaf. Eventually, Keller learned to speak by "hearing" the vibrations made when she placed her fingers on Sullivan's larynx. Keller also learned to "listen" to others speak by putting her middle finger on the speaker's nose, her forefinger on the speaker's lips, and her thumb on the speaker's larynx.

Helen Keller wanted to attend Radcliffe College, but to do so she had to complete regular high school. Sullivan accompanied her to class and signed the lectures into Keller's hand. Keller passed her exams and was admitted to Radcliffe. Later, Keller and Sullivan traveled and lectured around the world. They never rested in their efforts to improve the lives of people with deafness and blindness. Most people who are deaf and blind today agree that Helen Keller, who died in 1968, is a powerful symbol.

Think About It

In what ways do you think Keller's life and experiences were different from the lives and experiences of most people who are deaf and blind today? How have people's attitudes and expectations changed over the past 100 years?

A DAY IN THE LIFE

The sense of pressure undergoes rapid adaptation. In the movie theater, Marc and Linda held hands, but after a little while they became so used to the feelings of their fingers in each other's hands that they hardly noticed. They had adapted.

Temperature Sensations of temperature are relative. When your body temperature is at a normal 98.6°F, you might perceive another person's skin as being warm. When you are feverish, though, the other person's skin might seem cool.

The receptors for temperature are neurons just beneath the skin. When skin temperature increases because you touch something warm, receptors for warmth fire. Decreases in skin temperature, such as those that occur when you put a cool, moist cloth on your forehead, cause receptors for cold to fire.

We adapt to differences in temperature. Have you ever walked out of an air-conditioned building into the hot sun? At first, the heat really hit you, but soon the sensation faded as you adapted to the warmth. In the same way, when you first jump into a swimming pool, the water may seem cold. Yet, after a few moments, the water feels warmer as your body adjusts to it.

Pain When Marc's toe was stepped on, he knew it. Pain told him that something was wrong. Pain is also adaptive— it motivates us to do something to stop it. That is why Marc pulled back his leg.

Headaches, backaches, toothaches—these are only a few of the types of pain most of us experience from time to time. Other, more serious health problems—such as arthritis, cancer, or wounds—also cause pain. Not all areas of the body are equally sensitive to pain. The more pain receptors located in a particular area of our skin, the more sensitive that area is. (See Figure 4.10.)

Once a person gets hurt, everything happens very quickly. Pain originates at the point of contact, as with Marc's toe. The pain message is sent from the point of contact to the spinal cord to the

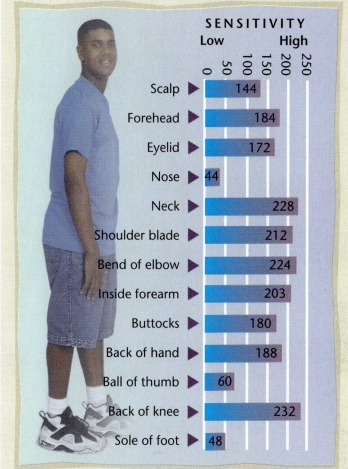

Distribution of Pain Receptors

SENSITIVITY
Low — High

Body part	Value
Scalp	144
Forehead	184
Eyelid	172
Nose	44
Neck	228
Shoulder blade	212
Bend of elbow	224
Inside forearm	203
Buttocks	180
Back of hand	188
Ball of thumb	60
Back of knee	232
Sole of foot	48

FIGURE 4.10 *Some parts of the body are more sensitive to pressure and pain than others. Which part of the body has the fewest pain receptors?*

Source: Strughold, H. (1924). On the density and thresholds in the areas of pain on the epidermis in the various regions of the body. *Z. Biol*, 80, 367–380. (In German.)

thalamus in the brain. Then it is projected to the cerebral cortex, where the person registers the location and severity of the pain. Chemicals called prostaglandins help the body transmit pain messages to the brain. Aspirin and ibuprofen are common pain-fighting drugs that work by curbing production of prostaglandins.

Simple remedies like rubbing and scratching an injured area sometimes help relieve pain. Marc rubbed his toe. Why? One possible answer lies in the gate theory of pain. **Gate theory** suggests that only a certain amount of information can be processed by the nervous system at a time. Rubbing or scratching the area transmits sensations to the brain that compete with the pain messages for

Gymnasts rely heavily on their vestibular sense, particularly on the balance beam.

space. Thus, many neurons cannot get their pain messages to the brain. It is as if too many calls are flooding a switchboard. The flooding prevents many or all of the calls from getting through.

TRUTH OR fiction

■ R E V I S I T E D ■

It is true that pinching your arm can help relieve the pain in your toe. According to the gate theory of pain, the pinching may flood the nervous system with messages so that the news of the pain in your toe does not get through to the brain.

Another fascinating aspect of pain sensation is called phantom-limb pain. About two out of three combat veterans with amputated limbs report pain in the missing, or "phantom," limbs. Although the limbs are gone, the pain is real enough. Phantom-limb pain appears to reflect the activity of the neurons in the brain that store memories connected with the missing limb. Scientists, however, do not yet completely understand this phenomenon.

Body Senses

Body senses are the senses that people are least aware of. But do not let that fool you. Without them, you would have to pay attention just to stay upright, to lift your leg to go down some stairs, or even to put food in your mouth.

The Vestibular Sense   Stand up. Now close your eyes. Do you have to look in a mirror to be certain that you are still upright? No, of course not. Your **vestibular sense** tells you whether you are physically upright without your having to use your eyes. Sensory organs located in the ears monitor your body's motion and position in relation to gravity. Your vestibular sense enables you to keep your balance. It tells you whether you are upside down or not and lets you know when you are falling. It also informs you of whether your body is changing speeds, such as in an accelerating automobile.

TRUTH OR fiction

■ R E V I S I T E D ■

It is true that you have a sense that keeps you upright. It is the vestibular sense. Sensory organs in the ears monitor the body's position in relation to gravity.

Kinesthesis   Ask some friends to close their eyes. Then ask them to touch their noses with their index fingers. How close to their noses did they come? Many of them were probably right on the mark, while others came close.

How did they locate their noses? Their eyes were closed, so they could not see their hands moving. They were able to touch their noses through kinesthesis. **Kinesthesis** is the sense that informs people about the position and motion of parts of their bodies. The word *kinesthesis* comes from the Greek words for motion (*kinesis*) and perception (*aisthesis*). In kinesthesis, sensory information is fed to the brain from sensory organs in the joints, tendons, and muscles.

THINKING ABOUT PSYCHOLOGY

1. How does the sense of smell work?
2. What is the vestibular sense?
3. **Critical Thinking**   How might our daily lives be different if we did not have kinesthesis? Give an example.

5
Perception

Every minute of every day, countless impressions are made on our various senses. Imagine the confusion if we did not find ways to organize all that information. Perception is the way in which we organize or make sense of our sensory impressions.

Rules of Perceptual Organization

Gestalt psychologists applied the principle that "the whole is more than the sum of its parts" to the study of perception. Using this principle, they noted many different ways in which people make sense of sensory information. These ways are called the rules of perceptual organization and include closure, figure-ground perception, proximity, similarity, continuity, and common fate.

Closure   Study Figure 4.11. Do you see random blotches of ink or a dog sniffing the ground? If you perceive the dog, it is not just because of the visual sensations provided by the drawing. Those are actually quite confusing. The pattern is not very clear. Despite the lack of clarity, however, you can still see a dog. Why? The answer is that you are familiar with dogs and that you try to fit the pieces of information into a familiar pattern.

What you are doing with this picture is filling in the blanks. Gestalt psychologists refer to this as the

FIGURE 4.12   *Do you see a vase or the profiles of two faces looking at each other? This figure illustrates the Gestalt principle of figure-ground perception.*

FIGURE 4.11   *Do you see meaningless ink blotches or a dog sniffing? Although the pattern is unclear, you will probably see a dog because dogs are familiar to you and you fill in the blanks.*

principle of closure. **Closure** is the tendency to perceive a complete or whole figure even when there are gaps in what your senses tell you.

Figure-Ground Perception   Now take a look at Figure 4.12. What do you see? In the center of the drawing, you probably see a vase. If you look again, though, you may see more than a vase. Can you see the two profiles that form the sides of the vase?

This drawing is one of psychologists' favorite illustrations of figure-ground relationships. Figure-ground perception is the perception of figures against a background. When you saw a vase, it was a light-colored figure against a dark background. The profiles, on the other hand, were dark figures against a light background.

We experience figure-ground perception every day. If we look out a window, we may see people, buildings, cars, and streets or perhaps grass, trees, birds, and clouds. We see these objects as figures against a background, such as white clouds against a blue sky or a car in front of a brick building. What we perceive as the figure and what we perceive as the background influence our perception.

Other Rules of Organization   Without reading further, describe Part A of Figure 4.13 on page 94. Did you say that Part A consisted of six lines, or did you say that it was three pairs of lines? If you said three pairs of lines, you were influenced by the **proximity**, or nearness, of some of the lines to each other. There is no other reason to perceive them in pairs since all of the lines are the same in every other respect.

Now describe Part B of the figure. Did you perceive it as a six-by-six grid or as three columns of *x*'s and three columns of *o*'s? If you said three columns, then you were grouping according to the law of **similarity**, which says that people think of similar objects as belonging together.

What about Part C? Is this a series of half-circles, every other one turned down? Or did you see a wavy line and a straight line? If you saw the wavy line and the straight line, you were probably organizing your perceptions according to the rule of **continuity**. People usually prefer to see smooth, continuous patterns (like lines and waves), not disrupted ones (like the alternating half-circles).

Finally, there is the law of **common fate**. Have you ever noticed how when you see things moving together, you perceive them as *belonging together*? For example, a group of people running in the same direction would appear to have the same purpose. You assume that they are part of the same group and that they are all running to the same place—that they have a common fate.

Perception of Movement

The next time you are in a car or a bus that is stopped at a traffic light, pay attention to what happens when the vehicle in the next lane begins to move forward. Do you think at first that your vehicle, not the other one, is moving? Is it unclear whether your car or bus is moving backward or the other one is moving forward?

To be able to sense movement, humans need to see an object change its position relative to other objects. We all know that the earth is moving, but do we really feel it? To early scientists, whose only instrument for visual observation was the naked eye, it seemed logical that the sun circled the earth. After all, that is what they seemed to be seeing. To observe that it is the earth that moves around the sun, we would have to be somewhere in outer space. We cannot observe it while standing on the earth itself.

So how do you decide which vehicle is beginning to move at the traffic light? One way is to look for objects that you know are stable, like structures on the side of the road—buildings, signs, or trees. If you are steady in relation to them, then your vehicle is not moving. You might also try to sense motion in your body. You could close your eyes and decide whether you feel a lurching or rolling motion or vibration from the wheels. Try it sometime. Can you hear the sound of the tires? Do you feel the bumps in the road? Clues like these help you know that you are moving.

Stroboscopic Motion

We have been talking about perception of real movement—movement that actually occurs.

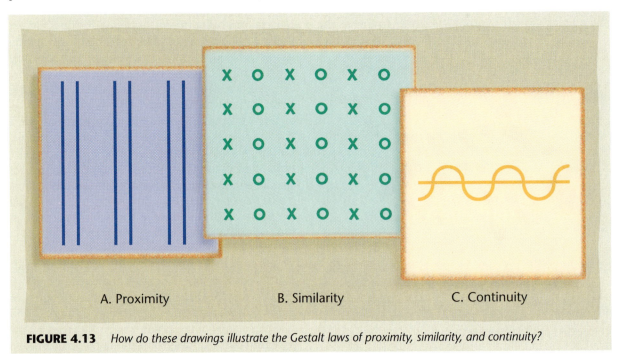

A. Proximity B. Similarity C. Continuity

FIGURE 4.13 *How do these drawings illustrate the Gestalt laws of proximity, similarity, and continuity?*

Psychologists have also studied *illusions* of movement. One such illusion of movement is called stroboscopic motion. In **stroboscopic motion**, the illusion of movement is produced by showing the rapid progression of images or objects that are not moving at all. Have you ever seen one of those little books designed to be flipped through quickly so that the figures on the pages appear to move? These books work because of stroboscopic motion.

Movies work in a similar way. Despite the name *movie*, movies do not consist of images that move. Instead, the audience is shown 16 to 22 pictures, or frames, per second.

In a motion picture, frames of stationary images pass at the rate of about 16 to 22 per second, giving the illusion of motion.

Each frame is just slightly different from the previous one. Showing the frames in rapid succession creates the illusion of movement. Why? Because of the law of continuity, humans prefer to see things as one continuous image. Perception smoothes over the interruptions and fills in the gaps.

Depth Perception

A DAY IN THE LIFE

Imagine trying to go through life without being able to judge depth or distance. Like Todd in the theater, you might bump into other people or step on their toes. You would have trouble going up or down stairs without stumbling. Depth, in this case, has little to do with the way people sometimes use the word *deep*. It is not, for instance, the depth of a lake or a hole. Depth here means "distance away." For example, without really thinking about it, you decide how far away a glass of juice is from you. Can you just reach out and pick it up, or do you have to get out of your chair? You perceive the depth of objects through both monocular and binocular cues.

Monocular Cues for Depth   **Monocular cues** need only one eye to be perceived. Artists use monocular cues to create an illusion of depth. These cues create the illusion of three dimensions, or depth, on two-dimensional, or flat, surfaces. Monocular cues cause certain objects to appear more distant from the viewer than others. These cues include perspective, clearness, overlapping, shadow, and texture gradient.

If you take two objects that are exactly the same size and place one of them far away from you and the other nearby, the object that is farther away will stimulate a smaller area of your retina than the one that is near. Even though the objects are the same size, the amount of sensory input from the more distant object is smaller because it is farther away. The distances between far-off objects also appear to be smaller than the same distances between nearby objects. For this reason, the phenomenon known as perspective occurs. Perspective is the tendency to see parallel lines as coming closer together, or converging, as they move away from us. However, experience teaches us that objects that look small when they are far away will seem larger when they are close, even though their size does not actually change. In this way, our perception of a familiar object's size also becomes a cue to its distance from us.

The clearness of an object also helps in telling us how far away it might be. Nearby objects appear to be clearer, and we see more details. Faraway objects seem less clear and less detailed. Thus, the clearer a familiar object seems to be, the closer it is to us.

Overlapping is another monocular cue that tells us which objects are far away and which ones are near. Overlapping is the placing of one object in front of another. Nearby objects can block our view of more distant objects. Experience teaches us to perceive partly covered objects as being farther

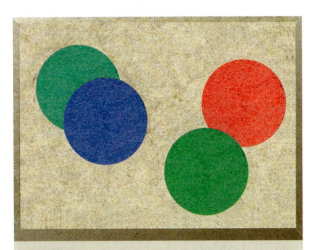

FIGURE 4.14 *Which circles—the complete circles or those that are partially covered—seem closer to you? Why?*

away than the objects that block them from view. (See Figure 4.14.)

Shadows and highlights also give us information about objects' three-dimensional shapes and where they are placed in relation to the source of light. Look at Figure 4.15. What do you see on the left compared to the right? Your answer probably is that you see a two-dimensional circle on the left and a three-dimensional sphere on the right. What is the difference between the two? The right part of the figure shows a circle with a highlight on its surface and a shadow underneath. Because of these cues, you perceive the highlighted central area to be closest to you.

Still another monocular cue is texture gradient. Texture, of course, is the surface quality and appearance of an object. A gradient is a progressive change. Texture that is farther away from us appears to be denser than texture that is closer, and we see less detail. Therefore, closer objects are perceived as having a more varied texture than objects that are farther away.

The most complex of monocular cues of depth is called motion parallax. It is more complex because, as you probably have guessed by the name, it involves not a stationary picture but the image of something as the viewer moves. Motion parallax is the tendency of objects to seem to move forward or backward depending on how far away they are from the viewer.

If you have the opportunity to take a drive in the countryside, pay attention to what happens to various objects as you move past them. You will notice that distant objects, such as mountains, the moon,

and stars, appear to move forward with you. Objects at an intermediate distance seem to stand still. Nearby objects, such as roadside markers, rocks, and trees, go by quite rapidly. If you did not know better, you might think that they were moving backward. Through experience, we realize that objects that appear to move with us are at a greater distance than those that pass quickly.

Binocular Cues for Depth   Whereas monocular cues can be perceived with just one eye, both eyes are required to perceive **binocular cues** for depth. Two binocular cues for depth are retinal disparity and convergence.

Hold a finger at arm's length. Now slowly bring it closer until it almost touches your nose. If you keep your eyes relaxed as you do this, you will seem to see two fingers. An image of the finger will be projected onto the retina of each eye. Each image will be slightly different because the finger will be seen at different angles. This difference is referred to as **retinal disparity**. The closer your finger comes, the farther apart the "two fingers" appear to be. Thus, the amount of retinal disparity we detect gives us a cue about the depth of an object. However, retinal disparity serves as a cue to depth only for objects that are within a few feet of us, not for objects that are farther away.

The other binocular cue we use is called convergence. Convergence is associated with feelings of tension in the eye muscle. When we try to maintain a single image of the approaching finger, our eyes must turn inward, or converge on it, giving us a cross-eyed look. The closer we feel our eyes moving

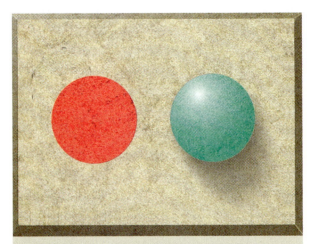

FIGURE 4.15 *The addition of a highlight and a shadow gives us the sense that the circle on the right is three-dimensional, or has depth.*

If you look at a Magic Eye poster in the right way, a three-dimensional image may appear. The image that comes from this poster is of two dolphins, one jumping through a hoop and one in the water.

toward each other, the nearer the object they are looking at is. Like retinal disparity, convergence has stronger effects when objects are close.

Have you seen one of those posters that on the surface seems to consist of images of a crazy, swirled pattern, but when you stare at the images just the right way, three-dimensional figures pop out at you? Such pictures, which are created by a computer and are known as *Magic Eye,* make use of retinal disparity and convergence. Each eye, in fact, sees a slightly different image from the other, and if you can relax your eyes enough, those two images fuse into a three-dimensional picture.

Perceptual Constancies

Imagine that you are just leaving school and that you see your friends waiting for you under a tree some distance away. As you run over to them, they get closer and look larger because, as you have just learned, the image of your friends takes up more and more space on your retina. Why don't you think your friends are literally growing in inches? This would certainly appear to be the case judging from the sensory input. Or consider the problems of

a pet owner who might recognize his or her dog from the side but not from above because the dog's shape would differ from above. The reason you know your friends are not actually getting taller by the second, and the pet owner recognizes the dog from every angle, is experience. Each person's experience creates perceptual constancies—constancies of size, color, brightness, and shape.

Size Constancy   The image of a dog seen from a distance of 20 feet occupies about the same amount of space on the retina as an inch-long insect crawling in the palm of the hand. Yet we do not perceive the dog to be as small as the insect. Similarly, we may say that people on the ground look like ants when we are at the top of a tall building, but we know they remain people even if the details of their form are lost in the distance.

Through experience, people acquire a sense of size constancy. Size constancy is the tendency to perceive an object as being of one size no matter how far away the object is, even though the size of its image on the retina varies with its distance. Through experience, humans learn about perspective—that the same object seen at a great distance

FIGURE 4.16 *Although the two gray squares are identical, the one on the left is perceived as brighter because it appears against a dark background.*

the distance. The pygmy guide mistook the buffalo for insects and would not believe Turnbull when he told him otherwise. The reason? Experience. The pygmy had seen buffalo before. However, having lived in a dense forest, he was not used to seeing them at great distances. He had therefore not developed size constancy in the way a plains dweller would have.

Color Constancy Imagine that Marc was wearing a tan sweatshirt and Linda had on a red blouse. Even in the darkened movie theater, Marc and Linda still knew that their shirts were tan and red. Because of their previous experience, they perceived their shirts as remaining tan and red even though they appeared gray in the darkness of the theater. Color constancy is the tendency to perceive objects as keeping their color even though different light might change the appearance of their color.

Brightness Constancy Brightness constancy is the tendency to perceive an object as being equally bright even when the intensity of the light around it changes. Look at Figure 4.16. Does the gray square in the black frame look brighter than the one in the white frame? If it does, it is because we judge the

from the viewer will appear much smaller than when it is nearby.

How do we know that size constancy is something we learn? Some evidence comes from a study of the pygmies in Africa, who live in a dense forest. When anthropologist Colin Turnbull (1961) took one of the pygmy guides out of the forest and onto a wide plain, they happened to see some buffalo in

FIGURE 4.17 *When a door is closed, it looks like a rectangle. When it is open, it is trapezoidal. But because of shape constancy, we still perceive the door as being rectangular whether it is open or not.*

brightness of an object by the brightness of other objects around it. For example, a black object really looks almost gray in very bright sunlight, but we still perceive it as being black because everything else around it is also much brighter.

Shape Constancy Take a glass and look at it from directly above. You see a circle, right? Now move back slightly; it becomes an ellipse. When you look at the glass straight on, the image of the top of it is a line. So why do you still describe the rim of the glass as being a circle? Because of shape constancy—the knowledge that an item has only one shape no matter what angle you view that item from. Figure 4.17 shows another example. A door is a rectangle only when you view it straight on. When you move to the side or open it, the left or right edge comes closer and appears to be larger, changing the retinal image of the door to a trapezoid. Yet because of shape constancy, you continue to think of doors as being rectangular.

Visual Illusions

Do your eyes sometimes "play tricks on you"? Actually, your eyes are not to blame, but your brain's use of perceptual constancies is at fault. Your brain tricks your eye through visual illusions.

Part A of Figure 4.18 shows the Müller-Lyer illusion. Look at the two lines at the top of the illustration. Do you think they are the same length? To most people, the line on the right, with its reversed arrowheads, looks longer. Why? Again, because of experience. In this culture, we are used to living in rooms in buildings. The line on the right may remind us of how a far corner of a room looks, while the line on the left reminds us of the outside near corner of a building. The rule of size constancy is that if two objects seem to be the same size and one is farther away, the farther object must be larger than it actually seems. How did psychologists come to the conclusion that we are reminded of buildings and rooms in this illusion? Because they found that the illusion does not work

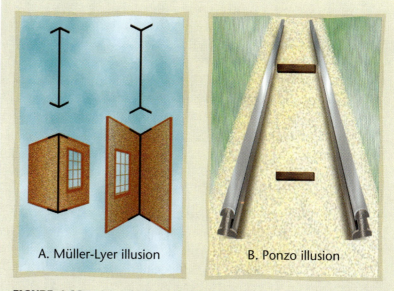

A. Müller-Lyer illusion   B. Ponzo illusion

FIGURE 4.18 *(A) Which line at the top is longer? If you measure them, you will find that they are exactly the same. Notice how the line on the left resembles the near corner of a building and the line on the right looks like the far corner of a room. (B) The two horizontal lines are equally long, but the top line seems longer. Why?*

in cultures that do not live in the same types of structures that we do (Segall, Campbell, & Herskovits, 1966).

Now turn to Part B of Figure 4.18, which shows the Ponzo illusion. Which of the two horizontal lines do you think is longer? Do you perceive the top line as being longer? The rule of size constancy may also afford insight into this illusion. Perhaps the converging lines strike you as receding into the distance. If so, you assume from experience that the horizontal line at the top is farther down the track—farther away from you. The rule of size constancy is at work again.

SUMMARY

People come to understand and organize their environment through sensation and perception.

I. Sensation and Perception

A. Absolute threshold is the weakest amount of a stimulus that can be sensed.
B. Difference threshold is the minimum amount of difference that can be detected between two stimuli.
C. Signal-detection theory suggests that perception of sensory stimuli is influenced by factors such as setting and expectations.
D. Because of sensory adaptation, we become more sensitive to weak stimuli and less sensitive to unchanging stimuli.

II. Vision

A. Light is electromagnetic energy.
B. In the eye, light is projected onto the retina, which consists of photoreceptors.
  1. The blind spot, which lacks photoreceptors, is the point at which the optic nerve leaves the eye.
  2. Rods and cones are photoreceptors.
  3. Visual acuity is the sharpness of vision.
C. People with normal color vision see any color in the spectrum of visible light.
  1. The color circle is the spectrum of light bent into a circle.
  2. The afterimage of a color is its complementary color.
D. People can be partly or totally color blind.

III. Hearing

A. A sound's pitch depends on its frequency.
B. The loudness of a sound is determined by the height of sound waves.
C. Sound travels through the outer, the middle, and the inner ear before its message reaches the brain.
D. We locate some sounds by determining which ear the sound strikes most loudly.
E. Two kinds of deafness are conductive deafness and sensorineural deafness.
  1. People with conductive deafness cannot hear soft sounds.
  2. People with sensorineural deafness cannot hear sounds of certain frequencies.

IV. Other Senses

A. Odors are detected by neurons in each nostril that send information to the brain.
B. Receptor neurons for taste are located on the taste buds of the tongue.
C. The skin senses include pressure, temperature, and pain.
D. The vestibular sense enables us to keep our balance. Kinesthesis cues us about the position and motion of parts of our body.

V. Perception

A. Closure is the tendency to perceive a complete or whole figure.
B. Figure-ground perception is the tendency to see objects against a background.
C. Other perceptual rules include proximity, similarity, continuity, and common fate.
D. We sense movement by seeing an object change its position relative to other objects.
E. Stroboscopic motion is an illusion made by a rapid progression of still images.
F. Monocular and binocular cues allow people to perceive depth.
  1. Monocular cues include perspective, clearness, overlapping, shadows and highlights, texture gradient, and motion parallax.
  2. Binocular cues include retinal disparity and convergence.
G. Size, color, brightness, and shape constancies are created through experience.
H. Principles of perception sometimes trick us, as in visual illusions.

TERM & CONCEPT REVIEW

1. What is the difference between sensation and perception?
2. Describe signal-detection theory.
3. Explain how the pupils adjust to the amount of light available.
4. What are the two types of photoreceptors? What function does each type serve?
5. Define *pitch* and *loudness*.
6. How are smell and taste related?
7. How do the skin senses of pressure and temperature function?
8. Explain how pain reaches the brain.
9. What is stroboscopic motion?
10. What is the difference between monocular cues and binocular cues? Give examples of each.

CRITICAL THINKING

1. What do you think life would be like if human beings lacked sensory adaptation?
2. What would happen if our eyes were unable to control the amount of light that entered them?
3. The process of hearing is considered a chain reaction. Why?
4. How might people's perceptions and senses affect their choice of a career?
5. Describe a situation in which you used one or more monocular cues to determine how far away an object was.

APPLYING SKILLS IN PSYCHOLOGY

1. **Writing About Psychology** Recall an experience in which one of your senses produced such an impact that you still remember it. Write two or three paragraphs to recreate the experience in vivid detail.

2. **Research in Psychology** Conduct an experiment to show the relationship of the senses of taste and smell. Ask several friends and family members to participate. Select four foods that are similar in texture, such as an apple, an onion, a pear, and a potato. Peel and cut the food into bite-size pieces. Blindfold one of the participants and ask the person to hold his or her nose. Place a piece of each food in front of the participant. Guide the person's hand to each bit of food and ask him or her to taste it and guess what it is. Repeat the procedure until all the participants have tasted all of the foods. Did they consistently guess or miss the same foods? Report your findings to the class.

3. **Research in Psychology** With a partner, go to a local day-care center or elementary school. Ask the teachers or assistants for permission to collect samples of artwork from several young children of different ages between 3 and 10 years old. Note the age of each child on his or her drawing. Then analyze the drawings in terms of perspective, color, shape, proportional size, and shadows. What do these drawings tell you about how children of various ages perceive their environment? Can you detect any trends in how perception changes as children get older? Make a chart showing the results of this cross-sectional study.

4. **COOPERATIVE LEARNING Using Your Observation Skills** With three classmates, take a 10-minute walk outside. Stay together, but do not talk to one another or take any notes. After the walk, divide a sheet of paper into four columns. Write the following headings at the top of each column: *See, Hear, Smell, Feel*. Try to recall what you saw, heard, smelled, or felt during your walk and write these items in the appropriate columns. Compare your list with those of the others in your group. How do people exposed to the same stimuli perceive them differently?

CONSCIOUSNESS

Objectives

1 Analyze the nature of consciousness.

2 Describe the stages of sleep and list possible sleep problems.

3 Explain how meditation, biofeedback, and hypnosis relate to consciousness.

4 Describe the various kinds of drugs and their effects on consciousness.

A DAY IN THE LIFE

November 9

"I had an extremely strange dream last night," Linda said as she, Marc, and Todd were standing around at school waiting for the bell to ring.

"What was it about? Was I in it?" Marc wanted to know.

"Sorry, Marc, you weren't," Linda replied. "Actually, you know who was in it? Nick. And it was weird because it was Nick the way he used to be before he had the drug problem, before he started spacing out all the time. Back when you could talk to him and know that he was actually listening."

The group was silent for a few seconds while they recalled the way Nick used to be. They were all glad his parents had convinced him to go to a treatment center for help.

"But Nick wasn't the only person in my dream," Linda continued. "The thing is, I can't remember who else was there. It was someone I know, but I can't think of who!" She was obviously annoyed.

"Hey, in a movie I saw last weekend, this guy used hypnosis to help a woman remember her dreams," said Todd.

"Did it work?" asked Linda.

"Well, in the movie it did," said Todd. "But I read in a magazine article that you can only be hypnotized if you want to be."

"How did he hypnotize her in the movie?" Linda wanted to know. "What kind of things did he do?"

"Well, first he got out a chain with something hanging from it. He began to swing it slowly back and forth in front of the woman's eyes, and he told her to concentrate on it. Then he told her that she was getting sleepy, very sleepy, and that her eyelids were getting heavy. Once he'd put her in a trance, he asked her some questions about her dreams, and she was able to answer them. It was amazing."

"Huh," pondered Linda. "Sounds a little creepy to me." Just then the bell rang, and everyone went off to class. Linda never did figure out who else had been in her dream.

• • •

Linda's dream, Nick's behavior while on drugs, and Todd's description of hypnotism all have to do with **consciousness**, or awareness of things inside and outside ourselves. Many psychologists believe that we cannot capture the richness of the human experience without talking about consciousness.

You may be fairly certain that you are conscious right now. For example, you are conscious, or aware, that you are reading this page. But what about tonight, when you are asleep? Sleeping and dreaming are related to consciousness. There are also several altered states of consciousness, such as those that occur when a person is in a hypnotic trance or is under the influence of certain drugs. These topics and others that have to do with consciousness will be discussed in this chapter.

Read the following statements about psychology. Do you think they are true or false? You will learn whether each statement is true or false as you read the chapter.

- If it were not for cues such as the sunrise and sunset, people would act as if a day were 25 hours long.
- The only time people dream is just before they wake up.
- It is possible to hypnotize any person at any time.
- People who are drunk always know that they are drunk.
- Smoking leads to more deaths in the United States than automobile accidents do.

1

The Study of Consciousness

Psychologists have not always thought that consciousness should be part of the study of psychology. In 1904, William James wrote an article called "Does Consciousness Exist?" In this article, James questioned the value of studying consciousness because he could not think of a scientific way to observe or measure another person's consciousness. His point was that even though we can see other people talking or moving around, we cannot actually measure their consciousness.

John Watson, the founder of behaviorism, agreed with James. In 1913 Watson wrote an article called "Psychology as the Behaviorist Views It." In this article, he stated, "The time seems to have come when psychology must discard all references to consciousness" (p. 163). Watson, like James, questioned whether consciousness could be studied scientifically. He chose instead to focus only on observable behaviors.

Consciousness as a Construct

Not all psychologists dismissed the possibility of studying consciousness. Today many psychologists believe that consciousness can be studied because it can be linked with measurable behaviors such as talking and with brain waves.

Consciousness is a psychological construct. A **construct** is a concept used to talk about something we cannot see, touch, or measure directly. Along with consciousness, intelligence and emotion are also psychological constructs. None of them can be seen, touched, or measured directly. They are known by their effects on behavior. That is, when people behave in certain ways, we may conclude that the behaviors result from, say, intelligence even though there is no way to be certain. Although consciousness cannot be seen or touched, it is real enough to most people.

Meanings of Consciousness

Generally speaking, consciousness means awareness. But there is more than one type of awareness. Thus, the term *consciousness* is used in a variety of ways. Sometimes consciousness refers to sensory awareness. At other times, consciousness may mean direct inner awareness. A third use of the term consciousness refers to the sense of self that each person experiences.

Consciousness as Sensory Awareness When you see a raindrop glistening on a leaf, when you hear your teacher's voice, or when you smell pizza in the cafeteria, you are *conscious* of all of these sensations around you: sights, sounds, smells, and so on. Your senses make it possible for you to be aware of your environment. Therefore, one meaning of consciousness is sensory awareness of the environment. In other words, you are conscious, or aware, of things outside yourself.

Yet you are not *always* aware of your environment. If you do not pay attention to it, you can be unaware of sensory stimulation. Although the world is full of sensory stimuli, you are focusing on this page and probably not much else right now. To pay attention in class, you must screen out the rustling of paper and the scraping of chairs. To get your homework done, you must pay more attention to your assignments than to your hunger pangs or the songs coming from a radio playing in the background.

We tend to be more conscious of some things than others. We tend to be particularly conscious of sudden changes, as when a cool breeze enters a sweltering room. We also tend to be especially conscious of unusual stimuli—for example, a dog entering the classroom. Intense stimuli—such as bright colors, loud noises, or sharp pains—also tend to get our attention.

Consciousness as Direct Inner Awareness

Imagine jumping into a lake or a swimming pool on a hot day. Can you feel the cool, refreshing water all around you? Although this image may be vivid, you did not really experience it. No sensory organs were involved. You are conscious of the image through what psychologists call direct inner awareness.

Anytime you are aware of feeling angry, anytime you remember a best friend you had when you were younger, anytime you think about abstract concepts such as fairness or love, you do so through direct inner awareness. In other words, you do not hear, see, smell, or touch thoughts, images, emotions, or memories. Yet you are still conscious of them. This meaning of consciousness, then, is being aware of things inside yourself.

Consciousness as Sense of Self

Have you ever noticed how young children sometimes refer to themselves by their names? For example, they do not say, "I want milk" but "Taylor wants milk." It is only as they grow older that they begin to understand that they are unique individuals, separate from other people and from their surroundings. From then on, they have a sense of self, no matter how much they or the world around them might change. In some uses of the word, *consciousness* is this sense of self in which we are aware of ourselves and our existence.

Levels of Consciousness

So far, we have discussed only one level of consciousness—the level at which people are aware of something and are aware of their awareness. But many psychologists speak of other levels of consciousness as well. These include the preconscious level, the unconscious level, and the nonconscious level. At these levels of consciousness, awareness is more limited.

The Preconscious Level

What if someone asked you what you wore to school yesterday? Or what you did after school? Your class schedule? Your next vacation? Although you were not consciously thinking about any of this information before you were asked about it, you will probably be able to come up with the answers. **Preconscious** ideas are not in your awareness right now, but you could recall them if you had to. You can make these preconscious bits of information conscious simply by directing your inner awareness, or attention, to them.

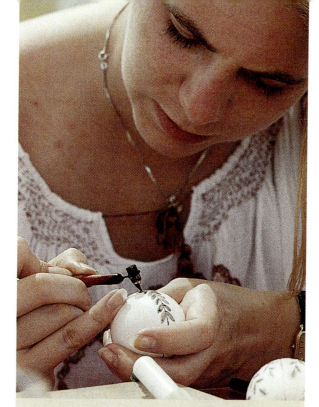

When people are engaged in activities that require close attention to detail, they screen out many sensations to stay focused on the task at hand.

The Unconscious Level

Sigmund Freud theorized that people have an unconscious mind. Information stored in the **unconscious** (sometimes called the subconscious) is unavailable to awareness under most circumstances. In other words, this information is hidden. For example, imagine that you are planning to go to a party. Without realizing why, you find yourself continually distracted from getting ready. First, perhaps, you cannot find a pair of shoes. Then maybe you become involved in a lengthy phone call. Can you guess what information was stored in your unconscious? It may be that, for some reason, you did not want to go to the party. But this desire to avoid the party was unconscious—you were not aware of it.

Freud believed that certain memories are painful and that some of our impulses, such as aggressiveness, are considered unacceptable. He stated that we use various mental strategies, called defense mechanisms, to push painful or unacceptable ideas out of our consciousness. In this way, we protect ourselves from feelings of anxiety, guilt, and shame. (See Chapter 14.)

The Nonconscious Level

Many of our basic biological functions exist on a **nonconscious** level.

Freud's Levels of Consciousness

CONSCIOUS LEVEL
Perceptions
Thoughts

PRECONSCIOUS LEVEL
Memories
Stored knowledge

UNCONSCIOUS LEVEL
Selfish needs
Violent motives
Immoral urges
Fears
Irrational wishes
Shameful experiences
Unacceptable desires

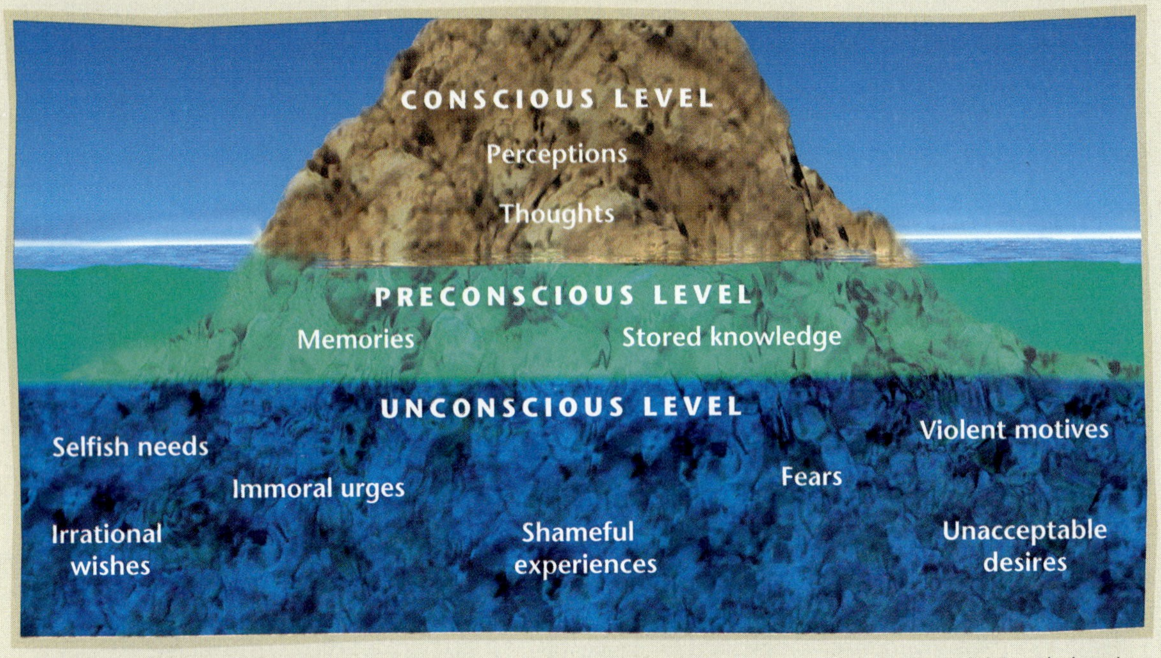

FIGURE 5.1   *According to Sigmund Freud, many memories, impulses, and feelings exist below the level of conscious awareness. On what level did Freud place irrational wishes?*

For example, even if you tried, you could not sense your fingernails growing or the pupils in your eyes adjusting to light. You know that you are breathing in and out, but you cannot actually feel the exchange of carbon dioxide and oxygen. You blink when you step from the dark into the light, but you cannot feel your pupils growing smaller. It may be just as well that these events are nonconscious. After all, how much can a person hope to keep in mind at once?

Altered States of Consciousness

The word *consciousness* sometimes refers to the waking state—the state in which a person is awake. Yet there are also several **altered states of consciousness**, in which a person's sense of self or sense of the world changes. When you doze off, you are no longer conscious of what is going on around you. Sleep is one altered state of consciousness. When Nick was under the influence of drugs, he also experienced altered states of consciousness. Other altered states of consciousness occur through meditation, biofeedback, and hypnosis. The rest of this chapter explores these altered states of consciousness.

A DAY IN THE LIFE

THINKING ABOUT PSYCHOLOGY

1. Explain what is meant by a psychological construct.

2. List and describe three levels of consciousness at which awareness is limited.

3. **Critical Thinking**   Do you think that a person can study or understand the consciousness of another person? Why or why not?

2
Sleep and Dreams

Are you aware that you spend about one third of your life asleep? Why do we sleep? Why do we dream? Why do some of us have trouble getting to sleep or experience nightmares?

Much of how people, animals, and even plants function is governed by **circadian rhythms**, or biological clocks. The word *circadian* comes from the Latin words *circa*, meaning "about," and *dies*, meaning "a day." The circadian rhythms in humans include a sequence of bodily changes, such as those

The Stages of Sleep

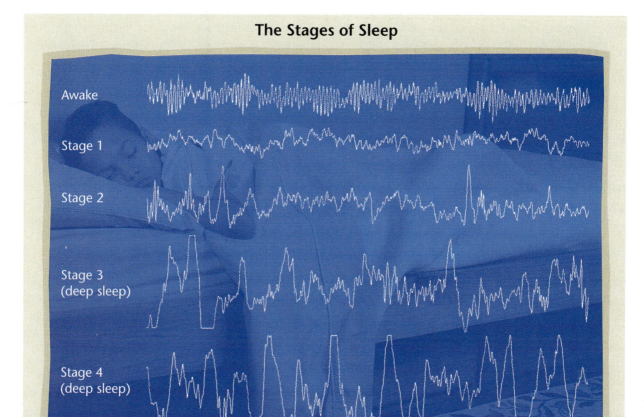

Awake

Stage 1

Stage 2

Stage 3 (deep sleep)

Stage 4 (deep sleep)

REM sleep

└─┘ = 1 second

FIGURE 5.2 *These are the typical EEG patterns for the stages of sleep. During rapid-eye-movement, or REM, sleep, EEG patterns resemble those of stage 1 sleep. Most people dream or have nightmares during REM sleep.*

in body temperature, blood pressure, and sleepiness and wakefulness, that occurs every 24 hours. The human circadian rhythms usually operate on a 24-hour day. For example, body temperature falls to its lowest point between 3:00 A.M. and 5:00 A.M. each day.

The most-studied circadian rhythm is that of the sleep-wake cycle. Because people normally associate periods of wakefulness and sleep with the rotation of the earth, a full sleep-wake cycle is 24 hours. However, when people are removed from cues that signal day or night (such as clocks, television programs, sunrise, and sunset), their cycle tends to expand to about 25 hours (Kimble, 1992). The reason this happens is unclear. This and many other issues concerning sleep have been, and continue to be, the subject of much research.

It is true that if it were not for cues such as the sunrise and sunset, people would act as if a day were 25 hours long. Because of the earth's rotation, a day is 24 hours. For reasons not fully understood, however, people may be more suited to a 25-hour day.

The Stages of Sleep

Sleep researchers have discovered that we sleep in stages. (See Figure 5.2.) Sleep stages are defined in terms of brain wave patterns, which can be measured by an electroencephalograph (EEG). Brain waves, like other waves, are cyclical, and they vary on the basis of whether we are awake, relaxed, or sleeping. Four different brain-wave patterns are beta waves, alpha waves, theta waves, and delta waves.

When we are awake and alert, the brain emits beta waves, which are short and quick. As we begin to relax and become drowsy, the brain waves slowly move from beta waves to alpha waves, which are a little slower than beta waves. During this relaxed state, we may experience visual images such as flashes of color or sensations such as feeling as if we are falling. This state is followed by five distinct stages of sleep.

Stage 1 is the stage of lightest sleep. As we enter stage 1 sleep, our brain waves slow down from the alpha rhythm to the slower pattern of theta waves. This transition may be accompanied by brief dreamlike images that resemble vivid photographs. Because stage 1 sleep is light, if we are awakened during this stage, we will probably recall these images and feel as if we have not slept at all.

If we are not awakened, we remain in stage 1 sleep no more than 30 to 40 minutes. Then we move into sleep stages 2, 3, and 4. During stages 3 and 4, sleep is deep, and the brain produces delta waves—the slowest of the four patterns. Stage 4 is the stage of deepest sleep, meaning that it is the one during which someone would have the greatest difficulty waking us up.

After perhaps half an hour of stage 4 sleep, we begin a relatively quick journey back to stage 3 to stage 2 to stage 1. About 90 minutes will have passed since we fell asleep. Now something strange happens. Suddenly, we breathe more irregularly,

blood pressure rises, and the heart beats faster. Brain waves become similar to those of stage 1 sleep. Yet this is another stage of sleep—the stage called **rapid-eye-movement sleep**, or REM sleep, because beneath our closed lids, our eyes are moving rapidly. The preceding four stages are known as non-rapid-eye-movement, or NREM, sleep because our eyes do not move as much during them.

During a typical eight-hour night of sleep, most people go through these stages about five times, each of which constitutes one sleep cycle. (See Figure 5.3.) As the night goes on, periods of REM sleep become longer. The final period of REM sleep, toward morning, may last half an hour or longer.

Why Do We Sleep?

People need sleep to help revive the tired body and to build up resistance to infection. Sleep also seems to serve important psychological functions. It may, for example, help us recover from stress. We seem to need more sleep when we have problems in school, with our families and friends, or at work.

What would happen if people forced themselves to go without sleep? In 1964, Randy Gardner, age 17, tried to find out as part of a science project. Under the supervision of a physician, Randy stayed awake almost 11 days. He became irritable, could not focus his eyes, and had speech difficulties and memory lapses. (Because of these types of effects and others that are potentially dangerous, sleep deprivation experiments like Gardner's should be conducted only by trained professionals in laboratory settings.) William Dement, an early sleep

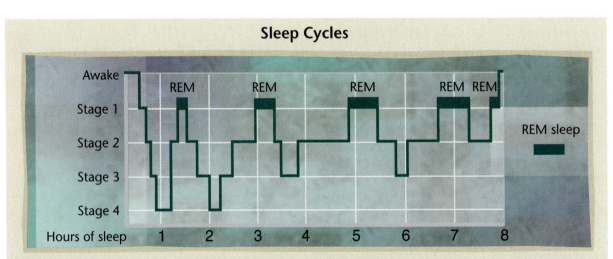

FIGURE 5.3 *This is a typical sleep pattern. Most people go through the cycle five times in eight hours.* *As the night progresses, stages 3 and 4 become shorter and REM sleep becomes longer.*

The mystery of dreams has occupied artists, philosophers, and scientists for centuries. "Desert Dream," a painting by contemporary American artist Michael Parkes, shows a variety of dreamlike images.

researcher, tracked Gardner's recovery. He found that Gardner slept an extra 6.5 hours for the first three days following the experiment. On the fourth night he slept 2.5 extra hours (Gulevich, Dement, & Johnson, 1966).

In some studies, animals or people have been deprived only of REM sleep. People and animals deprived of REM sleep tend to show what psychologists call REM-rebound. They catch up on their REM sleep by having much more of it when they sleep later on. REM sleep seems to serve particular psychological functions. Animals and people who are deprived of REM sleep learn more slowly than usual. They also forget more rapidly what they have learned (Adler, 1993b; Winson, 1992). Other research findings suggest that REM sleep may help brain development in infants and "exercise" brain cells in adults (McCarley, 1992).

Dreams

 It is during REM sleep that we have the most vivid dreams. Linda's dream, for example, probably occurred while she was in REM sleep. Dreams are a mystery about which philosophers, poets, scientists, and many others have theorized for centuries.

Did you know that dreams can be in black-and-white or in full color? Some dreams seem very realistic. You may have had a dream of going to class and suddenly realizing that there was going to be a test in the class. You had not studied. You started to panic. Then you woke up. The dream felt very real, and you were relieved to find that it was only a dream after all. Other dreams are disorganized and seem less real.

We dream every time we are in REM sleep. During REM sleep, dreams are most likely to have clear imagery and plots that make sense, even if some of the events are not realistic. During NREM sleep, plots are vaguer and images more fleeting.

TRUTH OR fiction
■ R E V I S I T E D ■

It is not true that the only time people dream is just before they wake up. The most vivid dreams occur during REM sleep, the final part of the sleep cycle. Most people go through the sleep cycle about five times a night.

Interestingly, if the events in a person's dream seemed to last 10 minutes, she or he was probably dreaming for 10 minutes. That is, people seem to dream in "real time." Although some dreams involve fantastic adventures, most of the dreams people have—particularly REM-sleep dreams experienced early in the night—are simple extensions of the activities of the day. The characters in dreams are more likely to be friends and neighbors than spies, monsters, or princes. Linda suspected that the other person in her dream was someone she knew, and she was probably right.

Like Linda, we sometimes have difficulty recalling all, or even a few, of the details of our dreams. This may be because we are often unable to hold on to information from one state of consciousness (in this case, sleeping/dreaming) when we move into another (in this case, wakefulness).

The Freudian View   Have you ever heard the song "A Dream Is a Wish Your Heart Makes" from the Disney film *Cinderella*? Is it true that your dreams reveal what you really want? Sigmund Freud thought so—he theorized that dreams reflect a person's unconscious wishes and urges—"wishes your heart makes."

However, some unconscious wishes may be unacceptable, perhaps even painful. Those, Freud thought, would be the ones that would most likely appear in dreams, although not always in direct or obvious forms. Freud believed that people dream in

symbols. He thought that these "symbolic" dreams give people a way to deal with painful material that they cannot deal with consciously.

The Biopsychological Approach   Some psychologists believe that dreams begin with biological, not psychological, activity. According to this view, during sleep, neurons fire in a part of the brain that controls movement and vision. These neuron bursts are random, and the brain tries to make sense of them. It does so by weaving a story—the dream. When neurons fire in the part of the brain that controls running, for example, we may dream we are running toward or away from something.

The biopsychological approach suggests an explanation for why people tend to dream about events that took place earlier in the day. The most current activity of the brain concerns the events or problems of the day. Thus, the brain uses everyday matters to give structure to the random bursts of neurons during REM sleep.

Today most psychologists caution that there are no hard-and-fast rules for interpreting dreams. And we can never be sure whether a certain interpretation is correct.

Sleep Problems

Even when we need sleep, we may have trouble getting to sleep or sleeping soundly. When these troubles last for long periods of time or become serious, they are considered to be sleep problems.

Insomnia   **Insomnia** is the inability to sleep. The word comes from the Latin *in-,* meaning "not," and *somnus,* meaning "sleep." The most common type of insomnia is difficulty falling asleep. People with insomnia are more likely than others to worry and to have "racing minds" at bedtime. For many people, insomnia comes and goes, increasing during periods of anxiety or tension and decreasing or disappearing during less stressful periods.

People can actually make insomnia worse by *trying* to get to sleep. The effort backfires because it increases tension. We cannot force ourselves to fall asleep. We can only set the stage by lying down and relaxing when we are tired. Yet millions of people go to bed each night dreading the possibility that they will not be able to fall asleep.

Some people use sleeping pills to cope with insomnia, but many psychologists believe that the safest, simplest, most effective ways of overcoming insomnia do not involve medication. Psychologists recommend that people with insomnia try the following techniques:

- Tense the muscles, one at a time, then let the tension go. This helps relax the body.
- Avoid worrying in bed. If worrying persists, however, get up for a while.
- Establish a regular routine, particularly for getting up and going to sleep each day.
- Use pleasant images or daydreams to relax. These may occur naturally, or people may have to focus on creating them.

Many psychologists also note that occasional insomnia is fairly common and is not necessarily a problem. It becomes a problem only if it continues for long periods of time.

Nightmares and Night Terrors

You have probably experienced one or more nightmares in your lifetime. Common nightmares involve snakes or murderers. Some nightmares are specific to a particular activity or profession. For example, the "actor's nightmare" involves being on stage in front of an audience. The dreamer (an actor, naturally) has no idea what play is being presented, much less what any of the lines are.

In the Middle Ages, nightmares were thought to be the work of demons who were sent to make people pay for their sins. Today we know that nightmares, like most other dreams, are generally products of REM sleep. In one study, college students kept dream diaries and reported having an average of two nightmares a month (Wood & Bootzin, 1990). Upsetting events can produce nightmares, as reported in a study of people who experienced the San Francisco earthquake of 1989 (Wood et al., 1992). People who are anxious or depressed are also more likely to have nightmares.

Night terrors (also called sleep terrors) are similar to, but more severe than, nightmares. Dreamers with night terrors feel their hearts racing, and they gasp for air. They may suddenly sit up, talk incoherently, or thrash about. They do not fully wake up. In the morning, they may recall a feeling or an image from the night terror. Unlike the case with nightmares, however, memories of night terror episodes usually are vague.

Night terrors also differ from nightmares in when they occur. Night terrors tend to occur during deep sleep (stages 3 and 4), whereas nightmares occur during REM sleep. Night terrors happen during the first couple of sleep cycles, nightmares more toward morning. Night terrors are most common

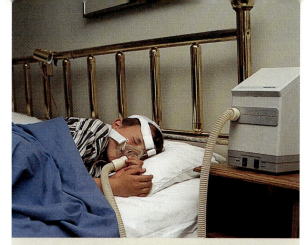

This person with sleep apnea is hooked up to equipment that applies continuous pressure through the nose to keep airways open during sleep.

among young children and may reflect immaturity of the nervous system.

Sleepwalking

Many children walk in their sleep. Sleepwalkers may roam about almost nightly during stages of deep sleep. They may respond to questions while they are up and about, but when they wake up they typically do not remember what they did or said. Contrary to myth, there is no evidence that sleepwalkers become violent or upset if they are awakened. However, because sleepwalkers are not fully conscious and thus may be prone to accidentally hurting themselves, they should be supervised if possible.

Most children outgrow sleepwalking as they mature. As is true of night terrors, sleepwalking may reflect immaturity of the nervous system.

Sleep Apnea

We all have occasional apneas, or interruptions in breathing. **Sleep apnea** is a breathing interruption that occurs during sleep. People with sleep apnea do not automatically start breathing again until they suddenly sit up and gasp for air. Once they begin breathing again, they fall back asleep. They usually do not wake up completely, so they may not even be aware of what has happened during the night. However, they often feel tired during the day.

Sleep apneas occur when a person's air passages are blocked. Thus, they are sometimes accompanied by snoring. A nasal mask that provides a steady air flow can help prevent breathing interruptions.

Some experts believe that sleep apnea may be linked to sudden infant death syndrome (SIDS). In SIDS, an infant dies during his or her sleep for no obvious reason.

Narcolepsy Narcolepsy is a rare sleep problem in which people suddenly fall asleep no matter what time it is or where they are. One minute they are awake. The next their muscles completely relax, and they are in REM sleep. Drug therapy and frequent naps have been used to treat narcolepsy.

Although people usually awaken from an episode of narcolepsy feeling refreshed, such episodes may be dangerous. For example, they can occur while people are driving or operating machinery. No one knows for sure what causes narcolepsy, but it is believed to be a genetic disorder of REM-sleep functioning.

THINKING ABOUT PSYCHOLOGY

1. Describe the five stages of sleep.
2. Describe three kinds of sleep problems.
3. **Critical Thinking** Compare and contrast nightmares and night terrors. Why might it be difficult to differentiate between the two in a young child?

3
Meditation, Biofeedback, and Hypnosis

People who are asleep and dreaming are in an altered state of consciousness. Other altered states of consciousness occur when we are awake. These states of consciousness can be achieved through meditation, biofeedback, and hypnosis.

Meditation: Narrowing Consciousness

Meditation is a method some people use to try to narrow their consciousness so that the stresses of the outside world fade away. Numerous techniques have been used to accomplish this. The ancient Egyptians gazed upon an oil-burning lamp. (This is the origin of the fable of Aladdin's magic lamp.) The yogis of India stare at an intricate pattern on a vase or carpet. Other meditators repeat pleasing sounds called mantras, such as *om* or *sheereem,* and mentally focus on these sounds.

All of these methods of meditation share a common thread—they focus on a peaceful, repetitive stimulus. This focus helps people narrow their consciousness and become relaxed. By narrowing their consciousness, people can suspend planning, worrying, and other concerns. Meditation is an important part of some religions, such as Buddhism. Some meditators claim that meditation helps them achieve "oneness with the universe," pleasure, or some great insight. These claims have never been scientifically proven, but evidence does suggest that meditation can help people relax. A study led by Herbert Benson, for example, found that meditation can help people lower blood pressure, heart rate, and respiration rate (Benson et al., 1973).

Biofeedback: Feeding Back Information

Biofeedback is a system that provides, or "feeds back," information about something happening in the body. Through biofeedback training, people have learned to control certain bodily functions, such as heart rate. Some people have used biofeedback to learn to create the brain waves produced when relaxing—alpha waves—as a way of coping with tension (Budzynski & Stoyra, 1984). Figure 5.4 shows a biofeedback system designed to record the tension in the forehead muscle of a person who suffers from headaches. As the forehead muscle relaxes, the line on the screen levels off. The patient's task is to keep the line as level as possible—in other words, to keep the forehead muscle relaxed. Using biofeedback, people have learned not only to treat tension headaches, but also to lower their heart rates or blood pressure. However,

A monk meditates in Thailand. Meditation is important in both Buddhism and Hinduism.

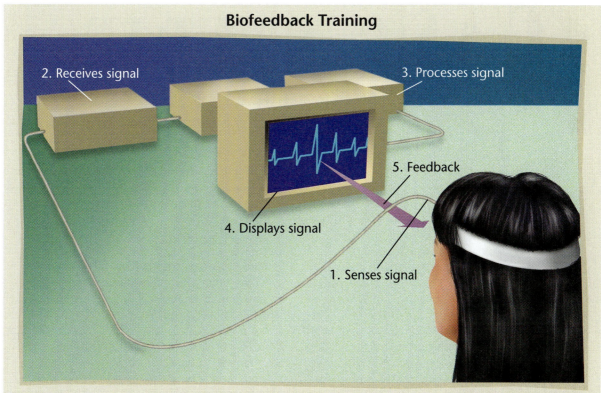

Biofeedback Training

2. Receives signal

3. Processes signal

5. Feedback

4. Displays signal

1. Senses signal

FIGURE 5.4 *By using a biofeedback system to monitor the level of tension in the forehead muscle, a person can learn to control the level of tension and thereby cut down on tension headaches.*

as with all treatments, biofeedback should be attempted only under the direct supervision of a medical professional.

Hypnosis: Myths and Realities

Perhaps you have seen movies like the one Todd described to Linda, in which one character hypnotized another. Or perhaps you have seen audience members hypnotized in a magic show. If so, chances are you found that these people seemed unable to open their eyes, could not remember their own names, acted out scenes from childhood, or behaved in other unusual manners. But hypnosis is not always what it seems to be in movies and magic shows.

What Is Hypnosis? The word *hypnosis* is derived from the Greek *hypnos,* meaning "sleep." Some psychologists believe that **hypnosis** is an altered state of consciousness during which people respond to suggestions and behave as though they are in a trance. Other psychologists, however, wonder whether hypnosis truly is an altered state of consciousness. Studies have shown that some of the same effects achieved by hypnosis can also occur without hypnosis. Furthermore, brain wave patterns (as measured by an EEG) of people in hypnotic states look the same as brain wave patterns produced in the waking state.

Hypnosis began with the ideas of Austrian physician Franz Mesmer in the late 1700s. The word *mesmerize* comes from his name. Mesmer thought that the universe was connected by forms of magnetism. To cure his patients, he would pass magnets over their bodies. Some of them would fall into a trance, then awaken feeling better. Eventually, scientists decided that Mesmer's so-called cures had little scientific basis.

Hypnotism, however, may have more validity than Mesmer's magnet treatment. Today, hypnotism may be used in a variety of ways. For example, some doctors use hypnosis as an anesthetic in certain types of surgery. Some psychologists use it to help clients reduce anxiety, manage pain, or overcome fears. Nevertheless, there is still a great deal about hypnosis that is not understood. Thus, hypnosis should be left in the hands of professionals. Do not attempt hypnotism on your own.

CASE STUDIES
AND OTHER TRUE STORIES

Taking Psychology to Heart Through Biofeedback

Suppose that someone told you to lift your arm. Could you do it? Of course—all you would have to do is decide to do it. Lifting your arm is an example of *voluntary* behavior. Walking and talking are other examples. You can walk and talk simply by deciding that you are going to.

But suppose someone told you to lower your blood pressure or your heart rate. Could you do *that*? Perhaps, but not directly. To lower your blood pressure, you might eat less salt, lose weight, or lie down and relax. To lower your heart rate, you might sit down and take it easy for a while. But you cannot lower your blood pressure or heart rate directly. Blood pressure and heart rate are *involuntary* forms of behavior.

Or are they?

A few decades ago, psychologists thought they knew the difference between voluntary and involuntary behavior of the body. They thought voluntary behaviors (such as lifting an arm or a leg) were conscious. People could make them happen simply by directing their attention to having them happen. Psychologists thought other behaviors, such as heartbeat and blood pressure, were involuntary. They were automatic. They could not be consciously controlled, at least not on an immediate basis.

Then, in 1969, psychologist Neal E. Miller made an exciting discovery. He was able to train laboratory rats to increase or decrease their heart rates voluntarily. But why would rats do such a thing in the first place? Miller already knew that there is a pleasure center in the hypothalamus of a rat's brain. Whenever a rat was given a small burst of electricity in this center, the rat felt pleasure, and it wanted more.

Because the rats would do whatever they could to continue feeling this pleasure, they quickly learned that whenever they pressed a lever in their cage, they received this bit of pleasure-producing electric shock. Miller's rats pressed this lever to the point of exhaustion.

Miller designed a study to find out what the rats would do for pleasure. He implanted electrodes in the rats' pleasure centers. Then some of the rats were given shocks whenever their heart rates happened to increase. Other rats received shocks when their heart rates happened to decrease. In other words, some rats were rewarded when their heart rates were faster, whereas others were rewarded when their heart rates were slower. After a training session that took only 90 minutes, the rats learned to change their heart rates—either up or down, depending on when they had been rewarded—by as much as 20 percent. In other words, they seemed to be *voluntarily* changing their heart rates.

Miller's research was an example of biofeedback training (BFT). If it could be done with rats, could people, too, control bodily behavior thought to be involuntary? Instead of implanting electrodes in people's brains, researchers used monitors to let people know when, for example, their heart rates were slower. A biofeedback system does not actually control any of the bodily behaviors. Instead, like a mirror, the biofeedback monitor reflects a person's own efforts and enables him or her to see how various voluntary behaviors affect the involuntary ones. For example, a person might be able to observe that breathing slower reduced his or her heart rate. Indeed, some people have learned to control their heart rates using biofeedback.

Studies have shown that biofeedback has numerous other applications. Even people who are paralyzed below the neck can reduce their blood pressure with the help of biofeedback. And biofeedback is moderately effective in reducing the intense pain of migraine headaches and other painful conditions.

Think About It

What does biofeedback have to do with the topic of consciousness?

How Is Hypnosis Achieved?

Professional hypnotists may put people in a state of consciousness called a hypnotic trance by asking them to focus on something specific—a spot on the wall, an object held by the hypnotist, or merely the hypnotist's voice. Hypnotists usually suggest that people's arms and legs are becoming warm, heavy, and relaxed. They may also tell people that they are becoming sleepy or are falling asleep. Hypnosis is not sleep, however. People who are sleeping have very different brain waves from people in trances. But hearing the word *sleep* often does help a person enter a hypnotic trance.

People who are easily hypnotized are said to have hypnotic suggestibility. They can focus on the instructions of the hypnotist without getting distracted. Suggestible people also usually *like* the idea of being hypnotized and are not resistant to it. Todd was correct when he told Linda that people can only be hypnotized if they want to be.

It is not true that it is possible to hypnotize any person at any time. People must have a positive attitude toward hypnosis and a willingness to cooperate with the hypnotist for hypnosis to be successful.

How Can We Explain Hypnosis?

Psychologists offer various explanations for the behavior of people under hypnosis. According to Freud, hypnotized people permit themselves to return to childish ways of behaving. For instance, they allow themselves to put fantasy and impulse before fact and logic. Therefore, they believe what the hypnotist tells them. They also enjoy becoming passive and waiting for the hypnotist to tell them what to do.

According to another view, called role theory, people who are hypnotized are playing a part as if they are in a play. However, unlike actors in a play, hypnotized people may believe that what they are doing is real. Research suggests that many people in hypnotic trances may *not* be faking it (Kinnunen et al., 1994). Rather, they become engrossed in playing the part of a hypnotized person. They use their imaginations to try to experience what the hypnotist tells them to experience. If they are told that they are blind, for example, and then are handed a

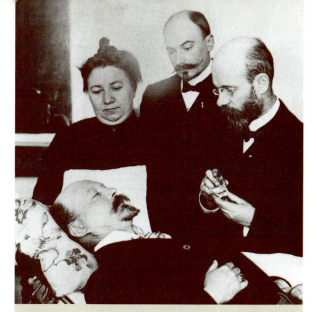

This photograph shows French doctors putting a patient into a trance in the 1890s. Hypnosis gained widespread popularity in the late 1800s.

book, they may think of a white curtain coming down over the page. Then they believe they cannot see or read anything. People with vivid imaginations are especially suggestible.

Is Hypnosis Effective?

Psychologists continue to debate whether hypnosis has a scientific basis. They also continue to research what hypnosis can and cannot do. Some of the research on hypnosis has addressed the effects of hypnosis on memory, on feelings of pain, and on the quitting of habits such as smoking or overeating.

Hypnosis and Memory

Police have occasionally used hypnosis to jog the memories of witnesses to a crime. At times this approach has worked with dramatic success. Nevertheless, studies have shown that unhypnotized people are just as likely as hypnotized people to remember details of a crime. More importantly, hypnotized people are just as likely to make *mistakes* about those details as are others. Many psychologists thus argue that material recalled under hypnosis should not be used as testimony in trials.

One interesting finding about hypnosis and memory has to do with memory of events that occur during the hypnotic trance itself. If so directed by the hypnotist, many people will act as if they do not recall what happened while they were hypnotized. They may not even remember that they were hypnotized at all.

Reprinted with special permission of King Features Syndicate

Hypnosis and Pain Prevention Under certain circumstances and with careful application, hypnosis has been used to help people prevent feelings of pain. For example, dentists have used hypnosis successfully to help people avoid feeling pain during certain procedures. Some people are so suggestible that they can even undergo surgery without anesthesia if they are hypnotized and told they feel no pain. On the other hand, some studies have shown that a similar effect can sometimes be achieved through relaxation techniques.

Hypnosis and Quitting Habits To help someone quit a habit such as overeating or smoking, a therapist may use **posthypnotic suggestion**. In this technique, the therapist gives instructions during hypnosis that are supposed to be carried out after the hypnosis session has ended. Often, psychologists link the habit with something repulsive, something that would make the person feel ill or disgusted. Then, whenever she or he lights a cigarette, for example, that sickening image appears. Sometimes hypnotists give more positive posthypnotic suggestions—for example, telling a person that he or she now has the willpower to resist sweets. Hypnosis has had some success in helping people quit habits, but it is not reliable.

4
Drugs and Consciousness

Linda recalled that Nick had started "spacing out" when he had a drug problem. Drugs have a wide range of effects. Some of them slow down the nervous system. Others spur it into rapid action. Some drugs, such as alcohol and nicotine (the drug found in tobacco), are believed to be connected with serious diseases, including cancer and heart disease. Many drugs are addictive. **Addiction** to a drug means that after a person takes that drug for a while, his or her body craves it just to feel normal. Alcohol, nicotine, and many other drugs are considered addictive.

Drugs also have a number of effects on consciousness. They may distort people's perceptions, change their moods, or cause them to see or hear things that are not real. Categories of drugs that affect consciousness include depressants, stimulants, and hallucinogens.

Depressants

Depressants are drugs that slow the activity of the nervous system. They generally give people a sense of relaxation but can have many negative effects. Depressant drugs include alcohol and narcotics.

Alcohol   Few drugs are as widely used in the United States as alcohol. Alcohol is a depressant. Small amounts of alcohol may have little effect, or they may be relaxing. High doses of alcohol can put a person to sleep. Too much alcohol can be lethal, either in the long term or the short term—people have died from drinking too much at one time.

Alcohol also intoxicates. **Intoxication** is another word for drunkenness. The root of the word *intoxication* is *toxic,* which means "poisonous." Alcohol does have some poisonous effects on the body, on the brain, and on consciousness. Intoxication slurs people's speech, blurs their vision, makes them clumsy, and makes it difficult for them to concentrate. They may bump into things or be unable to write. It also affects their judgment. In fact, they may not even realize that they are intoxicated. Therefore, they may try to do things that require a clear mind and good coordination, such as drive a car, when they are incapable of doing these things correctly. Alcohol is involved in more than half of all fatal automobile accidents in the United States.

These Civil War casualties may have been treated with morphine, a painkiller introduced during the war.

. . . .

TRUTH
OR
fiction
■ R E V I S I T E D ■

It is not true that people who are drunk always know that they are drunk. Because intoxication impairs judgment, people who are drunk may believe that they can drive just as well as they can when they are sober.

. . . .

Some drinkers do things they would not do if they were sober. Why? When intoxicated, people may be less able to focus on the consequences of their behavior. Alcohol can also bring feelings of elation that wash away inhibitions. Furthermore, it provides an excuse for behaviors that sober people know are unwise. Drinkers may place the blame for their behavior on the alcohol. But, of course, drinkers *choose* to drink. Thus, people remain responsible for actions taken while intoxicated.

Regardless of why people start drinking, regular consumption of alcohol can lead to addiction. Once people become addicted to alcohol, they may continue drinking to avoid withdrawal symptoms such as tension and trembling.

Narcotics   The word *narcotic* comes from the Greek *narke,* meaning "numbness" or "stupor." **Narcotics** are addictive depressants that have been used to relieve pain and induce sleep.

Many narcotics—such as morphine, heroin, and codeine—are derived from the opium poppy plant. Morphine is a narcotic that was introduced during the Civil War to deaden the pain from battle wounds. Therefore, addiction to morphine became known as the "soldier's disease."

Heroin, also introduced in the 1800s, was hailed as the "hero" that would cure addiction to morphine. It was named heroin because it made people feel "heroic." This drug, which is now illegal, is a powerful narcotic that can give the user feelings of pleasure. However, coming off heroin can plunge the user into a deep depression. Furthermore, high doses impair judgment and memory and cause drowsiness and stupor. High doses of heroin can also depress the respiratory system so much that they lead to loss of consciousness, coma, and, in some cases, even death.

The use of heroin can also lead to death indirectly because it is often taken intravenously—that is, injected with a needle into a vein. Sometimes such needles are shared among users. If one user is infected with the virus that causes AIDS, needle sharing can infect other users as well.

People who are addicted to narcotics experience withdrawal symptoms when they try to stop using them. These withdrawal symptoms may include tremors, cramps, chills, rapid heartbeat, insomnia, vomiting, and diarrhea.

Stimulants

Stimulants, in contrast to depressants, increase the activity of the nervous system. They speed up the heart and breathing rate. Stimulants include nicotine, amphetamines, and cocaine.

Nicotine   Nicotine, the drug found in tobacco leaves, is one of the most common stimulants. The leaves are usually smoked in the form of cigarettes, cigars, and pipe tobacco. They can also be chewed, as in chewing tobacco.

Nicotine spurs the release of the hormone adrenaline, which causes the heart rate to increase. As a stimulant, nicotine may make people feel more alert and attentive, but research has shown that it does not improve the ability to perform complex tasks, such as solving difficult math problems.

Nicotine reduces the appetite and raises the rate at which the body changes food to energy. For these reasons, some smokers do not try to quit for fear that they will gain weight. But weight gain can be controlled by diet.

Through regular use, people can become addicted to nicotine. In fact, evidence suggests that cigarette smoking is as addictive as the use of heroin. People who stop smoking can experience symptoms such as nervousness, drowsiness, loss of energy, headaches, lightheadedness, insomnia, dizziness, cramps, heart palpitations, tremors, and sweating. Nonetheless, many people have successfully quit smoking.

Smoking has also been associated with serious health risks. All cigarette advertisements and packs sold in the United States carry a message such as: "Warning: The Surgeon General Has Determined

That Cigarette Smoking Is Dangerous to Your Health." Each year, more than 400,000 Americans die from smoking-related diseases. This is more than the number who die from motor-vehicle accidents, abuse of alcohol and all other drugs, suicide, homicide, and AIDS combined.

TRUTH
OR
fiction
■ R E V I S I T E D ■

It is true that smoking leads to more deaths in the United States than automobile accidents do. In fact, almost one out of every five deaths in the United States is caused by smoking. Lung cancer and heart disease are the most common smoking-related diseases.

Heavy smokers are about 10 times as likely as nonsmokers to die of lung cancer. Moreover, the substances in cigarette smoke have been shown to cause several other kinds of cancer in laboratory animals. Cigarette smoking is also linked to death from heart disease, chronic lung and respiratory diseases, and other illnesses. Pregnant women who smoke risk miscarriage, premature birth, and babies with birth defects. Perhaps due to the risks involved in smoking, the percentage of American adults who smoke has declined from more than 40 percent in the 1960s to about 25 percent in the 1990s.

Research indicates that secondhand smoke, the cigarette smoke exhaled by smokers, can even increase the health risk of nonsmokers who inhale it. Secondhand smoke is connected with lung cancer, breathing problems, and other illnesses. It accounts for more than 50,000 deaths per year. Because of the effects of secondhand smoke, smoking has been banned from many public places such as government buildings, airports, and restaurants.

Amphetamines   **Amphetamines** are another kind of stimulant. They are especially known for helping people stay awake and for reducing appetite. Amphetamines are made from the chemical alpha-methyl-beta-phenyl-ethyl-amine, which is a colorless liquid made up of carbon, hydrogen, and nitrogen.

Amphetamines were first used by soldiers during World War II to help them remain awake and alert during the night. Sometimes called "speed" or "uppers," amphetamines can produce feelings of pleasure, especially in high doses.

EXPLORING
DIVERSITY

Multicultural Perspectives on Consciousness

Visions, dreams, meditation, and hallucinations are important parts of many cultures, reflecting the human desire to reach beyond what the senses can directly perceive. The methods for reaching these altered states of consciousness, however, are as diverse as the people who inhabit this planet.

The Aborigines of Australia believe that there are two worlds: the ordinary, physical world and another world called Dreamtime. Ritual songs, dances, stories, and dreams create the Dreamtime world. Frans Hoogland, a Dutchman who lived for 15 years among the Aborigines, described the process: "We start with nothing—a total emptiness—a void. Then we have some singing and dancing. . . . [T]he singing creates the sound and the vibration forms a shape; and the dancing helps solidify it. . . . The process, the Dreaming itself, becomes a reality." (Maybury-Lewis, 1992, pp. 197–202) For the Aborigines, dream and actuality are just different states of the same consciousness.

The Maulavis, a Muslim sect in Turkey, also use dancing to create an altered state of consciousness. The Maulavis are known as whirling dervishes because they whirl around until they are in a trance. This trance, they believe, brings them closer to Allah, God.

Some religions use meditation to achieve an altered state of consciousness. According to the yoga school, a part of Hinduism, every human being consists of two parts. The first is a person's body, mind, and conscious self. The second part is the soul—pure, empty consciousness. The yoga school uses certain exercises, including bodily postures, control of breathing, and meditations, to help teach people understanding of their soul.

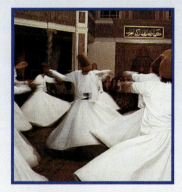

Accompanied by music, Maulavis, or whirling dervishes, spin around until they are in a trance.

The followers of Buddhism meditate to achieve a state of enlightenment called *nirvana.* Buddhists believe that nirvana can be achieved through control of the mind, or mental discipline. Certain yoga techniques help followers achieve this control.

People in some cultures use drugs to produce a religious trance. The Incas in the Andean highlands of South America use a drug called yage while a shaman, or holy man, watches them. Once past an initial drug-induced nausea, they begin to hallucinate. The hallucinations range from pleasurable to terrifying. The Incas will endure even the terrifying visions because they believe that terror is something that needs to be overcome in order to gain knowledge, look into the future, and communicate with the spirit world.

The Huichol Indians in central Mexico make a sacred pilgrimage to a place hundreds of miles from their homes. Once they arrive, they fast, pray, dance, and chant. The next day, they hunt for peyote, a strong stimulant that comes from a cactus plant. They then sit with their shaman-priest, talk, eat peyote, and begin to hallucinate. They believe that the hallucinations help them achieve a state of fusion with their ancestors and the universe. The shaman must always be present to help them return from the experience. Many fear that if they stay too long "in paradise," their souls will be lost forever.

Think About It

In some cultures, people view altered states of consciousness as something to be avoided whenever possible, not something to be sought out. Why do you think some people feel this way?

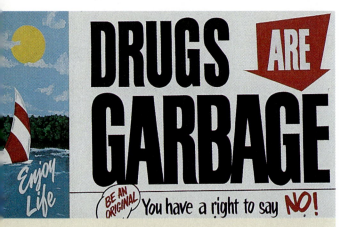

DRUGS ARE GARBAGE

Enjoy Life

BE AN ORIGINAL You have a right to say NO!

Various advertising campaigns have helped make people more aware of the dangers of drugs. Posters such as this one encourage people to refuse drugs and enjoy life without them.

Amphetamines can be taken in the form of pills. They can also be injected directly into the veins in the form of liquid methedrine, the strongest form of the drug. People who take large doses of amphetamines may stay awake and "high" for days. Such highs must come to an end, however. People who have been on prolonged highs usually "crash." That is, they fall into a deep sleep or depression. Some people even commit suicide when crashing. Nick's spaced-out, inattentive behavior may have been the result of his coming down from an amphetamine high.

A DAY IN THE LIFE

High doses of amphetamines can cause restlessness, insomnia, loss of appetite, and irritability. They also affect consciousness. For example, people who have taken amphetamines sometimes experience frightening hallucinations. A **hallucination** is a perception of an object or a sound that seems real but is not. One hallucination that people under the influence of amphetamines commonly experience is that bugs are crawling all over them.

Use of amphetamines can also cause the user to have delusions. A **delusion** is a false idea that seems real. If you thought you could fly (without the aid of an airplane), that would be a delusion. Overdoses of amphetamines are sometimes connected with delusions of being in danger or of being chased by someone or something.

Cocaine Cocaine is a stimulant derived from the leaves of the coca plant, which grows in the tropics of South America. Cocaine produces feelings of pleasure, reduces hunger, deadens pain, and boosts self-confidence. Because cocaine raises blood pressure and decreases the supply of oxygen to the heart while speeding up the heart rate, it can sometimes lead to death.

Cocaine has been used as a painkiller since the early 1800s. It came to the attention of Sigmund Freud in 1884. Freud, then a young neurologist, first used the drug to overcome depression. He even published an article on cocaine called "Song of Praise." But Freud's excitement about cocaine's healing powers was soon cooled by his awareness that the drug was dangerous and addictive.

Overdoses of cocaine can cause symptoms including restlessness, insomnia, trembling, headaches, nausea, convulsions, hallucinations, and delusions. A particularly harmful form of cocaine is known as "crack." Crack is very powerful. However, crack is impure, and therefore it is even more dangerous than other forms of cocaine. Because of the strain crack and other forms of cocaine can put on the heart, overdoses of these drugs are sometimes fatal.

Hallucinogens

A **hallucinogen** is a drug that produces hallucinations. In addition, hallucinogens may cause relaxation or feelings of pleasure. However, hallucinogens can also cause feelings of panic. Marijuana and LSD are examples of hallucinogens.

Marijuana Marijuana is a hallucinogenic drug produced from the leaves of the *cannabis sativa* plant, which grows wild in many parts of the world. Marijuana may produce feelings of relaxation and mild hallucinations. Hashish, or "hash," comes from the sticky part of the plant. Hashish has stronger effects than marijuana.

Marijuana impairs perception and coordination, making it difficult to operate machines, including cars. It also impairs memory and learning. In addition, marijuana can cause anxiety and confusion. It increases the heart rate up to 140 to 150 beats per minute and in some people raises blood pressure. These effects thus pose a particular threat to people with high blood pressure or heart problems.

One hundred years ago, marijuana was used by some people almost the way aspirin is used today— to treat headaches and other minor aches and pains. It could be bought without a prescription in any drugstore. Because it carries a number of health risks, marijuana use and possession are now illegal in most states.

Marijuana has distinct effects on consciousness. People who are very intoxicated with marijuana may think time is passing more slowly than usual. A song might seem to last an hour rather than a few minutes. Some people experience increased consciousness of bodily sensations such as heartbeat. Experiencing visual hallucinations is also fairly common while under the influence of marijuana.

Strong intoxication gives some marijuana smokers frightening experiences. Sometimes marijuana smokers become confused and lose their sense of self—their consciousness of who and where they are. Some fear they will lose themselves forever. Consciousness of a rapid heart rate leads others to fear that their hearts will "run away."

LSD   Lysergic acid diethylamide (LSD) is a hallucinogen. LSD is sometimes simply called "acid." It is much stronger than marijuana and can produce intense hallucinations. Some of these hallucinations can be quite bizarre. Users of LSD claim that it expands consciousness and "opens new worlds." Sometimes people are convinced that they have achieved great insights while using LSD. But when its effects wear off, they often are unable to recall or use these "discoveries."

LSD's effects are not predictable. Some LSD experiences are so frightening that the users, in a state of panic and confusion, injure themselves seriously or even commit suicide. In addition, some users of LSD experience lasting side effects. These side effects include memory loss, violent outbursts, nightmares, and feelings of panic.

Another long-term effect of LSD use is the experience of flashbacks. Flashbacks are hallucinations that happen weeks, months, or even years after the LSD was used. Some psychologists believe that flashbacks stem from LSD-induced chemical changes in the brain.

Treatments for Drug Abuse

Treatment for drug abuse varies, depending on the drug abused. Forms of treatment include detoxification, maintenance programs, and therapy. Some people also join support groups.

Detoxification   One form of treatment for drug abuse is detoxification. **Detoxification**, the removal of the harmful substance from the body, is a way of weaning addicts from the drug while restoring their health. This treatment is most commonly used with people addicted to alcohol and narcotics.

Many hospitals have chemical dependency units to help treat drug abusers.

Maintenance Programs   Maintenance programs are sometimes used for people addicted to narcotics. Participants in these programs are given controlled and less dangerous amounts of the drug or some less addictive substitute. This treatment is very controversial because the users never actually become completely free of drugs.

Counseling   Counseling can be conducted either individually or in a group. Both individual and group methods are used for treating stimulant and depressant abuse.

Support Groups   Support groups usually consist of several people who share common experiences, concerns, or problems. These individuals meet in a group setting to provide one another with emotional and moral support. Alcoholics Anonymous is an example of a support group that encourages members to live without drugs—in this case, alcohol—for the rest of their lives.

THINKING ABOUT PSYCHOLOGY

1. Describe the effects of depressants, stimulants, and hallucinogens. Give examples of each type of drug.
2. **Critical Thinking**   Do you think people use drugs to heighten consciousness or to escape from it? Explain your answer.

Chapter 5 REVIEW

SUMMARY

The concept of consciousness has several meanings. Consciousness also takes several forms.

I. The Study of Consciousness

A. The term *consciousness* has several different meanings.
   1. Sensory awareness is an awareness of the environment.
   2. Direct inner awareness allows people to remember and to think about feelings or abstract ideas.
   3. Consciousness is also a sense of self as a unique individual.
B. There are levels of consciousness in which awareness is limited.
   1. At the preconscious level, information that a person might not be thinking of can be recalled if necessary.
   2. At the unconscious level, information is not usually available to consciousness.
   3. Bodily functions that people cannot bring into awareness are at the nonconscious level.

II. Sleep and Dreams

A. Sleep occurs in five stages.
B. Sleep helps revive tired bodies. People deprived of sleep become irritable and have speech problems and memory lapses.
C. Most dreams occur during REM sleep.
   1. Freud theorized that dreams reveal unconscious wishes and urges.
   2. According to the biopsychological approach, dreams occur because neurons fire in different parts of the brain.
D. Sleep problems include insomnia, nightmares, night terrors, sleepwalking, sleep apnea, and narcolepsy.
   1. Insomnia is the inability to sleep.
   2. Nightmares occur during REM sleep. Night terrors usually happen in stage 3 or stage 4 sleep.
   3. Sleepwalkers roam about during stages of deep sleep.
   4. People suffering from sleep apnea briefly stop breathing.
   5. People with narcolepsy fall suddenly and unexpectedly asleep.

III. Meditation, Biofeedback, and Hypnosis

A. Meditation is a method of narrowing consciousness. It can lead to relaxation.
B. People have used biofeedback to lower their blood pressure or to decrease their heart rates.
C. Psychologists are divided over the question of whether hypnosis is an altered state of consciousness.
   1. Psychologists offer various explanations for the behavior of hypnotized people.
   2. The effects of hypnosis are not fully understood.

IV. Drugs and Consciousness

A. Depressants slow down activity of the nervous system.
   1. Alcohol is an addictive depressant.
   2. Narcotics are addictive depressants. They include morphine and heroin.
B. Stimulants increase the activity of the nervous system.
   1. Nicotine is addictive and unhealthy.
   2. Amphetamines may cause hallucinations and delusions.
   3. Cocaine is addictive. Crack is a particularly powerful form of cocaine.
C. Hallucinogens produce hallucinations.
   1. Marijuana can produce relaxation but carries a number of health risks.
   2. LSD is unpredictable. People may experience flashbacks years after using it.
D. Treatments for drug abuse include maintenance programs, detoxification, and counseling. In addition, some drug users join support groups.

TERM & CONCEPT REVIEW

1. What does it mean to say that consciousness is a construct?
2. What are circadian rhythms, and how do they influence human behavior?
3. What are the five stages of sleep? What brain-wave patterns occur in each stage?
4. Describe two different theories of dreaming.
5. List and describe six sleep problems.
6. Why do people meditate?
7. In what way is biofeedback training useful?
8. Define *hypnosis* and discuss what it can and cannot do.
9. Identify one of the three major groups of drugs. Then describe the drugs in the group, including their effects and problems.
10. Describe one treatment for drug abuse.

CRITICAL THINKING

1. In your own words, write a one-sentence definition of consciousness.
2. Compare and contrast REM and NREM sleep.
3. Why do you think many people use medication to try to overcome insomnia? Why might medication not be an effective cure?
4. Identify the pros and cons of using biofeedback instead of medication to reduce high blood pressure.
5. Why do you think some people drink or use other drugs even though they know that the drugs can be harmful?

APPLYING SKILLS IN PSYCHOLOGY

1. **Using Your Observation Skills** Many famous authors, such as James Joyce and William Faulkner, have used a writing technique known as *stream of consciousness*. In this technique, the author writes down his or her ideas, thoughts, memories and sensations as they enter the mind. Attempt to write your own stream of consciousness essay. For 15 minutes, concentrate on nothing other than the thoughts and images that enter your mind. As ideas come to you, write them down. Your essay should be an unstructured series of sentences and phrases that record your thoughts. After 15 minutes of uninterrupted writing, stop and examine your essay. Write a paragraph answering the following questions: How would you characterize your stream of consciousness essay? Were you able to concentrate only on your thoughts and ideas without becoming distracted? What does your essay reveal about consciousness?

2. **Research in Psychology** For two weeks, keep a record of the number of hours you sleep each night. If possible, record the number of hours other members of your family sleep, and note the age of each person. At the end of the two-week period, calculate the average number of hours of sleep obtained per night by each person in your study, including yourself. Compare your data with the data collected by your classmates. Do any patterns emerge? If so, how do you account for these patterns?

3. **COOPERATIVE LEARNING** **Writing About Psychology** Imagine that a female friend tells you the following dream: She is lying on a beach with her boyfriend. They are sunbathing. She is warm and content, and her eyes are closed. Suddenly other people on the beach begin screaming, so she opens her eyes and sees a huge tidal wave that completely blocks out the horizon. Before she can stand up and run, she feels herself being swept away. Working in groups, use the Freudian and biopsychological theories about dream interpretation to analyze the dream. Then write a summary of the analysis, comparing and contrasting the interpretations suggested by each dream interpretation approach. Finally, share your group's analysis with the class.

UNIT 2
R E V I E W

IDENTIFYING PEOPLE AND IDEAS

Explain the significance of each of the following people or terms to the study of psychology.

1. neuron
2. central nervous system
3. peripheral nervous system
4. cerebral cortex
5. Phineas Gage
6. endocrine system
7. heredity
8. absolute threshold
9. photoreceptor
10. sensorineural deafness
11. gate theory
12. kinesthesis
13. closure
14. stroboscopic motion
15. retinal disparity
16. altered state of consciousness
17. rapid-eye-movement sleep
18. insomnia
19. meditation
20. biofeedback
21. Franz Mesmer
22. hallucinogen

HANDS-ON PSYCHOLOGY

Individual Project

Design, but do not actually do, an experiment or survey to study the effects that altered states of consciousness have on sensation and perception. You may wish to focus on one or more altered states of consciousness, such as sleep and dreams. You may also wish to focus on one or more types of sensation (including vision, hearing, smell, taste, and the skin senses) and perception. Begin by asking a question. For example, you might ask, "How do people perceive pain when they are dreaming?" After you have asked your question, form a hypothesis about the answer to the question. Write three or four sentences explaining your hypothesis. Then design an experiment or survey that would test the hypothesis. Write a detailed description of the experiment or survey. At the end of your description, include a paragraph analyzing what results would indicate that your hypothesis was correct.

BUILDING YOUR PORTFOLIO

Individually or in a group, complete the following project to show your understanding of the psychology concepts involved.

The Body Politic

You may have heard the term *the body politic,* which refers to a group of people organized into a collective unit such as a nation. Now that you have read about the makeup of the human body and mind, evaluate the extent to which they are similar to an entire nation—the United States. Prepare an oral report, supported by written and visual materials, analyzing similarities and differences between the two entities. In putting together your report, you will need to consider the following questions.

1. What is the "biology" of the United States? Does the United States have "neurons," and if so, what are they? Does the nation have a nervous system? A brain? What about an endocrine system? What aspects of the United States might be considered a result of heredity, and what aspects might be due to "nature"? Create two graphic organizers that, side by side, compare the makeup of the human body with that of the United States. One will illustrate the biological components of the human body and brain; the other will show the social, political, and/or economic components of the United States.

2. How does the United States sense and perceive information? Does it have equivalents to the senses of vision, hearing, smell, and taste? Does it have skin senses and body senses? Once the nation takes in information, how does it process it? What principles of perceptual organization does it use? To what extent is it subject to illusions? Present your comparisons between humans and the nation regarding sensation and perception in a chart.

3. To what extent does the United States have consciousness similar to that of individual people? What are the different ways in which the nation is conscious? Does the nation ever experience "altered states of consciousness," and if so, what are they? How are they caused? Write an essay comparing and contrasting individuals' consciousness with "national" consciousness.

Organize your materials and present your report to the rest of your class.

UNIT 3

LEARNING AND COGNITION

CHAPTERS

6 Learning

7 Memory

8 Thinking and Language

9 Intelligence

Chapter 6

LEARNING

Objectives

1 Explain the principles of classical conditioning, and describe some of its applications.

2 Explain the principles of operant conditioning, and describe some of its applications.

3 Discuss cognitive factors in learning, including latent learning and observational learning.

4 Identify and implement the steps of the PQ4R method of learning.

A DAY IN THE LIFE

Linda, Marc, Dan, and Janet were in the library studying after school. "I don't feel like studying," Marc complained. "Let's shoot some hoops instead."

"Come on," Linda protested. "It's interesting stuff—it's all about how people learn. And don't you want to get a good grade on Thursday's psychology test?"

"Yeah, I suppose," Marc said, playing with his pencil. "But why do we even care about grades anyway? I mean, they're just letters. They don't really *mean* anything."

"Try saying that to the college admissions officers or at a job interview," chimed in Janet. "Even though a grade doesn't mean anything by itself, it means a lot in terms of what it can get you."

"And don't forget the district's new rule—you *have* to get at least a C in order to be on a sports team. Marc, the soccer team can't afford to lose you this year—you *have* to do well in the class," Dan pleaded.

"But what happens if I study a lot and *still* don't do well on the test? That's what happened to me last week on that test in Ms. Kramer's class. I studied for *hours* the night before, and I *still* only got a C on the test. So what's the point in studying if it's not going to help anyway?" asked Marc gloomily.

"There's more to good studying than just memorizing," Linda pointed out. "Hey, why don't we all study together? We can review the chapter and quiz one another. And when we're finished, we can do something fun. Any suggestions?"

Dan made a face. "Anything that doesn't involve eating ice cream. I ate a whole half-gallon of ice cream Monday night, and now the thought of it makes me sick."

"I wasn't thinking about food anyway. How about Marc's idea of playing basketball? Or maybe we could go to a movie," suggested Linda. "But we can't go until we really know the chapter."

"If I knew I'd get to do something fun every time I studied, maybe I'd study more often," Dan reflected thoughtfully.

Marc, Linda, and the others were studying material about learning. When you hear the word *learning*, you probably think of school—of listening to teachers and studying and taking tests. But people are learning all the time.

Learning is achieved through experience. Anything we are born knowing how to do is not a result of learning. For example, babies do not learn to cry. But people do need experience to learn how to walk, how to speak the languages of their parents and communities, and how to read. The experiences through which we learn all of these things, however, can vary. Sometimes we learn to do things by trying them ourselves; at other times, we learn by watching others or by reading books. This chapter explores several types of learning and the processes involved in each type.

Key Terms

- stimulus
- response
- conditioning
- classical conditioning
- unconditioned stimulus
- unconditioned response
- conditioned response
- conditioned stimulus
- taste aversion
- extinction
- spontaneous recovery
- generalization
- discrimination
- flooding
- systematic desensitization
- counterconditioning
- operant conditioning
- reinforcement
- primary reinforcer
- secondary reinforcer
- positive reinforcer
- negative reinforcer
- schedule of reinforcement
- continuous reinforcement
- partial reinforcement
- shaping
- latent learning
- observational learning

TRUTH? OR fiction

Read the following statements about psychology. Do you think they are true or false? You will learn whether each statement is true or false as you read the chapter.

- Becoming sick from eating a certain food can be a genuine learning experience.
- If you are afraid of snakes, it may help to surround yourself with them.
- Pigeons were used to guide missiles during World War II.
- Negative reinforcement is the same thing as punishment.
- People who watch a lot of violence on television are more likely to be violent themselves than people who watch less violence on television.

1
Classical Conditioning

A DAY IN THE LIFE Presumably, Linda and her friends were hoping to get a good grade on the psychology test they were studying for. But Marc wanted to know why grades mattered, and it was a good question. After all, people are not born with instinctive attitudes regarding letters used for grades, such as A and F. So why do most students like A's and try to avoid F's?

As Janet and Dan pointed out by mentioning the relationship between grades and college, jobs, and participation in team sports, grades have meaning because they are associated with other things. Most of us are familiar with this concept of association. Have you ever been listening to the radio and heard a song that was popular a few years ago—maybe a song that you really liked back then? Did you feel a rush of the sensations that you used to feel back when the song was popular?

If so, this reaction was probably a result of associations between the song and the events of the time in your life when the song was popular. In other words, the song served as a stimulus. A **stimulus** is something that produces a reaction, or a **response**, from a person or an animal. In this case, the response consisted of the feelings brought about by hearing the song.

Here is a simple experiment that also demonstrates associations. Think of a food you really like—say, lasagna or enchiladas. Is your mouth watering? If it is, you are experiencing the results of **conditioning**, or learning. Conditioning works through the pairing of different stimuli. In particular, your reaction demonstrates a type of conditioning known as classical conditioning. **Classical conditioning** is a simple form of learning in which one stimulus (in this case, the thought of the food) comes to call forth the response (your mouth watering) usually called forth by another stimulus (the actual food). This occurs when the two stimuli have been associated with each other.

Ivan Pavlov Rings a Bell

Some of the earliest findings about classical conditioning resulted from research somewhat similar to your own experiences in thinking of food. However, that early research was with dogs, not people. Russian physiologist Ivan Pavlov (1849–1936) discovered that dogs, too, learn to associate one thing with another when food is involved.

Does the sight of this pasta make your mouth water? If so, the reaction is a result of classical conditioning.

FIGURE 6.1 *Pavlov strapped dogs into harnesses and collected their saliva in a tube. After several pairings of a bell and meat powder, the dogs learned to salivate at the sound of the bell by itself.*

Pavlov did not set out to learn about learning. Rather, he was interested in the relationship between the nervous system and digestion. In particular, Pavlov was studying salivation, or mouth-watering, in dogs. He knew that dogs would salivate if meat was placed on their tongues because saliva aids in the eating and digestion of the meat. In other words, meat on the tongue is a stimulus for the production of saliva.

But Pavlov discovered that the dogs did not always wait until they had received meat to start salivating. For example, they salivated in response to the clinking of food trays. The dogs would also salivate when Pavlov's assistants entered the laboratory. Why? Because the dogs had learned from experience that these events—the clinking of the trays, the arrival of the assistants—meant that food was coming.

At first, Pavlov viewed the dogs' unwanted salivation as a nuisance because it was getting in the way of what he was trying to study. But soon he decided that the "problem" was worth looking into. If the dogs could learn to salivate in response to the clinking of food trays because this clinking was associated with the bringing of meat, could they learn to salivate in response to any stimulus that signaled meat? Pavlov predicted that they could. He set out to show that he could train his dogs to salivate in response to any stimulus he chose.

The stimulus Pavlov chose was the ringing of a bell. He strapped the dogs into harnesses and rang a bell. (See Figure 6.1.) Then about half a second after the bell rang, meat powder was placed on the dogs' tongues. As expected, the dogs salivated in response to the meat powder. Pavlov repeated this process several times.

After several pairings of the meat and the bell, however, Pavlov changed the procedure: he sounded the bell but did not follow the bell with the meat. Yet the dogs salivated anyway—they had learned to salivate in response to the bell alone.

US, UR, CR, and CS: Letters of Learning

The dogs' salivation in response to the bell demonstrates classical conditioning. Terms that are important in understanding classical conditioning include unconditioned stimulus, unconditioned response, conditioned response, and conditioned stimulus.

The meat in Pavlov's research was an example of an unconditioned stimulus. An **unconditioned stimulus** (US) is a stimulus that causes a response that is automatic, not learned. That automatic response, in turn, is called an **unconditioned response** (UR). Salivation in response to the meat was an unconditioned response. In other words, the dogs did not *learn* to salivate in response to the meat—they did so naturally, by reflex, because of their biology.

The dogs' salivation in response to the bell was a conditioned response. A **conditioned response** (CR) is a learned response to a stimulus that was previously neutral, or meaningless. In Pavlov's research, the bell was a neutral stimulus. That is, before Pavlov associated it with the meat, it might have made the dogs' ears perk up, but it would not have made the dogs salivate because it had nothing to do with food. Through repeated association with meat, however, the bell became a learned stimulus, or a **conditioned stimulus** (CS), for the response of salivation.

A conditioned response is often the same as or very similar to an unconditioned response. With Pavlov's dogs, for example, salivation in response to the meat was the UR. But salivation in response to the bell was the CR. In other words, salivation was both the UR and the CR. (See Figure 6.2.)

Adapting to the Environment

Classical conditioning helps organisms adapt to the surrounding environment. For example, just as Pavlov's dogs learned that the bell signaled meat, a person's pet dog may learn that the sound of a can opener (CS) means that dog food (US) will soon appear in the dog's bowl. Thus, the dog comes running to the bowl (CR).

Sometimes classical conditioning helps animals and people avoid or deal with danger. For example, a bear cub may learn to associate a particular scent (CS) with the appearance of a dangerous animal (US). The cub can then hide or run away (CR) when it catches the scent. Or a new car owner may hear his or her car alarm go off (CS). Thinking that someone is breaking into the car (US), the car owner calls the police (CR).

Taste Aversions   One form of classical conditioning that can be particularly useful to people is called a taste aversion. A **taste aversion** is a learned avoidance of a particular food. Have you ever eaten a food that made you ill, perhaps because it was spoiled? Did you then stay away from that food for a long time? If so, you had probably developed a taste aversion to it.

Often when foods make us ill, it is because they are unhealthy, even poisonous. A taste aversion helps us avoid these foods by keeping us away from

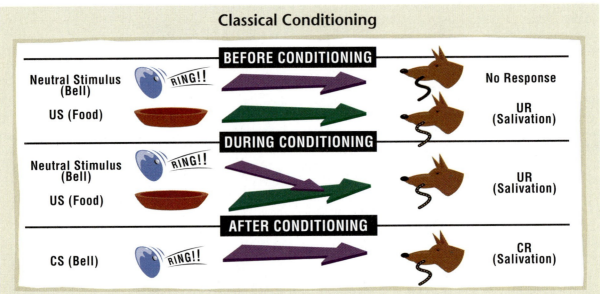

FIGURE 6.2   *Before conditioning, food (US) elicits salivation (UR). The bell (a neutral stimulus at first) elicits no response. Then, during conditioning, the bell precedes the food. After several repetitions, the bell (now a CS) elicits salivation (CR). What do US, UR, CS, and CR stand for?*

A DAY IN THE LIFE

them. Psychologists would call Dan's response to eating a half-gallon of ice cream all at one time a taste aversion. Dan had felt nauseated after eating so much ice cream. Ice cream was the unconditioned stimulus (US) that had caused the unconditioned response (UR) of nausea. As a result of his one experience, even the thought of ice cream served as a conditioned stimulus (CS) that made him feel nauseated (CR). The taste aversion was strong. Even though Dan knew that he could probably eat smaller amounts of ice cream safely, the thought of ice cream made him feel ill.

It is useful for people and animals to develop taste aversions readily. With other examples of classical conditioning, an association must be made several times before the conditioned response occurs. Pavlov had to pair the bell with meat several times before the dogs would begin to salivate at the sound of the bell. In taste aversions, however, just one pairing of food and illness may be all that is necessary to create the aversion.

TRUTH OR fiction

▪ REVISITED ▪

It is true that becoming sick from eating a certain food can be a genuine learning experience. Avoidance of a food that once caused illness is called a taste aversion. Taste aversions are a result of classical conditioning.

Extinction   Classical conditioning helps people and animals adapt to their environments. But times can change, and what once was dangerous may no longer be so. What threatens a bear cub may lose its menace once the bear matures. Or the signal for

danger may lose its meaning. A car alarm may be set off so often by accident (such as by a harmless gust of wind) that the car owner no longer rushes to call the police.

When a conditioned stimulus (such as the scent of an animal or a car alarm) is no longer followed by an unconditioned stimulus (a dangerous animal, the car being broken into), it will eventually lose its ability to bring about a conditioned response. In classical conditioning, this is called **extinction**. Extinction occurs when the conditioned stimulus

Researchers used classical conditioning to teach coyotes not to eat sheep by feeding them poisoned lamb meat. Because the poisoned meat made the coyotes sick, they developed a taste aversion to the lamb. Thus, they no longer attacked the livestock, solving an economic problem for ranchers.

Key Concepts in Classical Conditioning

	Procedure	Result
Classical Conditioning	A neutral stimulus is paired with an unconditioned stimulus (US). It brings forth an unconditioned response (UR).	The neutral stimulus becomes a conditioned stimulus (CS). It brings forth the conditioned response (CR).
Example	A child waits for his parents to come home. He hears the car drive up (neutral stimulus) and then his parents come inside (US). He gets excited (UR) to see his parents.	After many occasions of the parents coming inside after the car drives up, the child hears the car (CS) and automatically gets excited (CR).
Related Concepts	Taste aversion, extinction, spontaneous recovery, generalization, discrimination	

FIGURE 6.3 *If the strength, timing, and frequency of an expected stimulus are varied, the response changes. What do you think happens if a conditioned stimulus is repeatedly presented without an unconditioned stimulus?*

(CS) is disconnected from the unconditioned stimulus (US). As a result, the conditioned stimulus (CS) no longer causes the conditioned response (CR) to occur.

Pavlov found that with repeated ringing of the bell (CS) not followed by meat (US), the dogs eventually stopped salivating (CR) when they heard the bell (CS). The dogs had learned that the bell no longer meant that food was on the way. The conditioned response of salivating at the sound of the bell had been extinguished.

Spontaneous Recovery An extinguished response is not necessarily gone forever. In what psychologists have termed **spontaneous recovery**, organisms sometimes display responses that were extinguished earlier. This revival of the response follows a period in which the conditioned stimulus was not presented. For example, after the response of salivating at the sound of the bell had been extinguished in Pavlov's dogs, a day or two passed during which the dogs did not hear the bell at all. After this rest period, the bell was rung again. Even though the salivation response had earlier been extinguished, it was now back. It was, however, a little weaker than it had been when it was in full force—the dogs produced less saliva.

Think again of the song that brought back old feelings. If the song were again to become popular and you started hearing it every day, you probably would no longer experience the same rush of feelings after hearing it over and over. After all, your life has changed now, and when the song is continually played without actually transporting you into the past, it loses the ability to spark those old feelings—the response has undergone extinction. But if a month passes without your hearing the song at all, the next time you hear it, those old feelings may well return. In other words, they will have been spontaneously recovered.

Generalization and Discrimination Dan's half-gallon of ice cream was probably all one flavor, perhaps chocolate. But Dan did not say, "I can eat any flavor of ice cream except chocolate." Rather, he wanted to avoid ice cream of all flavors. This is called generalization. **Generalization** is the act of responding in the same ways to stimuli that seem to be similar, even if the stimuli are not identical.

In a demonstration of generalization, Pavlov first conditioned a dog to salivate when it was shown a circle. On several occasions, the dog was shown a circle (the CS), then given meat (the US). After several pairings, the dog salivated when presented with only the circle. Pavlov demonstrated that the dog would also salivate in response to the sight of many other geometric figures, including ellipses, pentagons, and squares. The more closely the figure resembled a circle, the greater the strength of the response (the more drops of saliva that flowed).

The dog's weaker response to figures that looked less like a circle was an example of discrimination. **Discrimination** is the act of responding differently to stimuli that are not similar to each other. Dan did not want to eat ice cream, but he probably would not have objected to eating other types of food—say, chocolate pudding. This is because ice cream and pudding are sufficiently different that Dan was able to discriminate them from each other.

Both generalization and discrimination help people and animals adapt to their environments. For example, a bear cub who has a bad experience with a wolf may generalize from that experience that all big furry animals that growl (other than adult bears) should be avoided. On the other hand, the bear cub probably discriminates between the wolf and a mouse. The mouse might be furry, but it is not big and does not growl. Thus, the mouse is not a danger. A child who has been frightened by a dog may generalize and stay away from all dogs. But because of discrimination, the child continues to play with his or her stuffed animals, even the ones that look like dogs.

Applications of Classical Conditioning

Classical conditioning is the means by which stimuli come to serve as signals for other stimuli. It is a major avenue of learning in our daily lives. It also can be used to solve specific problems that people have. For example, classical conditioning can help people overcome their fears of various objects and situations. It can even help children stop wetting their beds.

Flooding and Systematic Desensitization
Many fears—such as fear of heights, of snakes, and of speaking in front of the class—are out of proportion to the harm that could happen. Some people fear looking out of windows in tall buildings, even though they cannot fall. Many people fear snakes, even snakes that are small and nonpoisonous.

People on a roller coaster discriminate between the real danger of an automobile careening out of control and the ride in an amusement park.

Two methods for reducing such fears are based on the principle of extinction. In the method called **flooding**, a person is exposed to the harmless stimulus until fear responses to that stimulus are extinguished. A person with a fear of heights might look out from a sixth-story window until she or he is no longer upset by it. A person with a fear of snakes might be put in a room with lots of harmless snakes crawling around in the room.

It is true that if you are afraid of snakes, it may help to surround yourself with them. This is a method of therapy called flooding. In flooding, an application of classical conditioning, a person is exposed to a fear-provoking but harmless stimulus until the fear is extinguished.

Although flooding is usually effective, it tends to be quite unpleasant. When people fear something, forced exposure to it is the last thing they want. For this reason, psychologists usually prefer to use

CASE STUDIES
AND OTHER TRUE STORIES

The Story of Little Albert

In 1920, psychologists John B. Watson and Rosalie Rayner published an article describing an experiment they had done with an infant named Albert. The experiment had such an impact on the field of psychology that the boy became known as "Little Albert" and the story of the experiment became a classic. Even today, psychologists and psychology students are still familiar with it.

What was the experiment? It was a very small but very significant demonstration that emotional reactions such as fears can be acquired through principles of classical conditioning.

Albert was the 11-month-old son of one of Watson's and Rayner's acquaintances. Watson and Rayner observed that Albert did not become easily frightened. They also observed that he had a white laboratory rat for a playmate. To demonstrate that fears can be learned through associations, Watson and Rayner decided to see if they could condition Albert to fear the white rat rather than be amused by it. All they had to do, they reasoned, was pair the rat with something that Albert would find frightening.

What does an 11-month-old instinctively find frightening? Loud, harsh noises—such as the clanging of steel bars. Every time Albert played with the rat, Watson clanged steel bars behind the infant. Sure enough, after seven pairings, Albert showed fear of the rat even when there was no more clanging. The rat had at first brought pleasure to Little Albert. Now, through no fault of its own, it had become a source of fear and trembling. Through association, the animal had taken on the meaning of the jangling, jarring steel bars to Little Albert.

In the terms used in classical conditioning, the clanging of the steel bars was the unconditioned

Why do children fear some objects but not others?

stimulus (US) that led to the unconditioned response (UR) of fear. The rat was the conditioned stimulus (CS) that, through association with the clanging of the bars, also led Albert to feel fear—now the conditioned response (CR).

Little Albert's newfound fear, however, did not stop with the innocent rat. It spread, or generalized, to objects similar in appearance to the rat, such as a rabbit and a fur coat. Because of his experiences with the rat and the steel bars, Albert learned to fear other objects that were white and furry.

Unfortunately, Watson and Rayner never had the chance to help Little Albert overcome his conditioned fear of rats. Therefore, his fear may never have become extinguished. Somewhere out there may be an older man who cringes at the sight not only of rats but also of little girls wearing fluffy sweaters, of small dogs, or maybe even of Santa Claus's beard. Moreover, because the conditioning was carried out at such a tender age, Little Albert—now Big Albert?—may have no idea why he fears these things. He would not remember the original experience.

Was it ethical for Watson and Rayner to experiment on such a small child—especially when the experiment involved repeatedly frightening him and teaching him to fear something that had previously given him pleasure? Today most psychologists would say no, it was not ethical. For this reason, this experiment would never be duplicated today. Psychologists would have to find some other way of demonstrating their theories.

Think About It

How might a psychologist demonstrate the same phenomenon shown by Watson and Rayner using a more ethical method?

systematic desensitization to help people overcome their fears. In this method, people are taught relaxation techniques. Then they are exposed gradually to whatever stimulus they fear while they remain relaxed. For example, people who fear snakes are shown pictures of snakes while they are relaxed. Once they can view pictures of snakes without losing the feeling of relaxation, they are shown some real snakes from a distance. Then, after some more time, the snakes are brought closer, and eventually the people no longer fear snakes. Systematic desensitization takes longer to work than flooding, but it is not as unpleasant.

Counterconditioning Can cookies help children overcome their fears? Perhaps. Early in this century, University of California professors Mary Cover Jones (1924) and Harold Jones reasoned that if fears could be conditioned by painful experiences, perhaps fears could be counterconditioned by pleasant experiences. In **counterconditioning**, a pleasant stimulus is paired repeatedly with a fearful one, counteracting the fear.

The Joneses tried out their idea with a two-year-old boy named Peter, who feared rabbits. The Joneses gradually brought a rabbit closer to Peter while they fed Peter candy and cookies. Peter seemed nervous about the rabbit, but he continued to eat his treat. Gradually, the animal was brought even closer. Eventually, Peter ate treats and petted the rabbit at the same time. Apparently, his pleasure at eating the sweets canceled out his fear of the rabbit. Dentists might caution against overusing this "cookie treatment," however. While it might help children overcome their fears, it might also give them cavities.

The Bell-and-Pad Method for Bed-Wetting
By the time children are five or six years old, most of them wake up when their bladders are full. They stop themselves from urinating, which is an automatic response to bladder tension, and go to the bathroom. But some children do not respond to sensations of a full bladder when they are asleep. They remain asleep and often wet their beds.

To help children stop wetting their beds, psychologists came up with the bell-and-pad method. This method teaches children to wake up in response to bladder tension. A child with a bed-wetting tendency sleeps on a special pad placed on his or her bed. When the child starts to urinate, the water content of the urine triggers a bell, and the ringing wakes the child up.

Unlike the case in Pavlov's experiments with the dogs, in which the bell was a conditioned stimulus, the bell in the bell-and-pad method is an unconditioned stimulus (US). That is, it wakes up the child because of the child's biological makeup; people instinctively wake up when they hear loud noises. Waking up to the bell is the unconditioned response (UR).

Because of repeated pairings, a stimulus that precedes the bell becomes associated with the bell. It also gains the capacity to wake up the child. What is this stimulus? It is the sensation of a full bladder. In this way, bladder tension is the conditioned stimulus (CS) that comes to wake up the child even though the child is asleep during the classical conditioning procedure. Waking up in response to bladder tension is the conditioned response (CR).

After a couple of weeks of using the bell-and-pad method, most children no longer wet their beds. Similar methods have been used to aid in the toilet training of children.

THINKING ABOUT PSYCHOLOGY

1. Describe Pavlov's classic experiment with dogs using the following terms: *unconditioned stimulus, unconditioned response, conditioned response, conditioned stimulus.*

2. Explain what is meant by extinction, spontaneous recovery, generalization, and discrimination in classical conditioning.

3. **Critical Thinking** People acquire certain behavior patterns through classical conditioning. Explain how this might happen. Give an example to support your explanation.

2
Operant Conditioning

In classical conditioning, we learn to associate one stimulus with another. Pavlov's dogs learned to associate a bell with meat. Because of classical conditioning, the response made to one stimulus (for example, meat) is then made in response to the other (for example, the bell).

Classical conditioning, however, is only one type of learning. Another type of learning is operant conditioning. In **operant conditioning**, people and animals learn to do certain things—and not to do others—because of the results of what they do. In other words, they learn from the consequences of their actions. Linda and Janet, for example, had learned that studying would result in good grades. Because they desired good grades, they studied. In operant conditioning, organisms learn to engage in behavior that results in desirable consequences, such as food, an A on a test, or social approval. They also learn to avoid behaviors that result in negative consequences, such as pain or failure.

A DAY IN THE LIFE

In classical conditioning, the conditioned responses are often involuntary biological behaviors, such as salivation or eye blinks. In operant conditioning, however, voluntary responses—behaviors that people and animals have more control over, such as studying—are conditioned.

B. F. Skinner's Idea for the Birds

The ideas behind a secret war weapon that was never built will help us learn more about operant conditioning. The weapon was devised by psychologist B. F. Skinner, and it was called Project Pigeon. During World War II, Skinner proposed training pigeons to guide missiles to targets. The pigeons would be given food pellets for pecking at targets on a screen. Once they had learned to peck at the targets, the pigeons would be placed in missiles. Pecking at similar targets on a screen in the missile would adjust the missile's flight path to hit a real target. However, the pigeon equipment was bulky, and plans for building the missile were abandoned.

TRUTH *OR* **fiction** ▪ R E V I S I T E D ▪ It is not true that pigeons were used to guide missiles during World War II. B. F. Skinner, however, proposed that with the proper conditioning, pigeons would be able to guide missiles by pecking at targets on a screen.

Although Project Pigeon was scrapped, the principles of learning Skinner applied to the project are a fine example of operant conditioning. In operant conditioning, an organism learns to do something because of its effects or consequences. Skinner reasoned that if pigeons were rewarded (with food) for pecking at targets, then the pigeons would continue to peck at the targets.

Reinforcement

To study operant behavior, Skinner devised an animal cage that has been dubbed the "Skinner box." A Skinner box is ideal for laboratory experimentation. Treatments can be carefully introduced and removed, and the results can be carefully observed.

In a classic experiment, a rat in a Skinner box was deprived of food. The box was designed so that when a lever inside was pressed, some food pellets would drop into the box. At first, the rat sniffed its way around the box and engaged in random behavior. The rat's first pressing of the lever was accidental. But lo and behold, food appeared.

Soon the rat began to press the lever more frequently. It had learned that pressing the lever would make the food pellets appear. The pellets are thus said to have reinforced the lever-pressing behavior. **Reinforcement** is the process by which a stimulus (in this case, the food) increases the chances that the preceding behavior (in this case, the lever pressing) will occur again. After several reinforced responses, the rat pressed the lever quickly and frequently, until it was no longer hungry.

In operant conditioning, it matters little why the person or animal makes the first response that is reinforced. It can be by chance, as with the rat in the Skinner box, or the person or animal can be physically guided into the response. In training a dog to sit on command, the dog's owner may say, "Sit!" and then push the dog's rear end down. Once sitting, the dog's response might be reinforced with a pat on the dog's head or a food treat.

People, of course, can simply be told what they need to do when they are learning how to do things such as boot up a computer or start a car. In order for the behavior to be reinforced, however, people need to know whether they have made the correct response. If the computer does not turn on or the car lurches and stalls, the learner will probably think he or she has made a mistake and will not repeat the response. But if everything works as it is supposed to, the response will appear to be correct, and the learner will repeat it next time. Knowledge of results is often all the reinforcement that people need to learn new skills.

Types of Reinforcers

The stimulus that encourages a behavior to occur again is called a reinforcer. There are several different types of reinforcers. Reinforcers can be primary or secondary. They can also be positive or negative.

Key Concepts in Operant Conditioning

	Procedure	Result
Operant Conditioning	A behavior is followed by a consequence of reinforcement.	The behavior increases in frequency.
Example	When a child cleans his room, his parents read him a story.	The child cleans his room more often, so as to hear more stories.
Related Concepts	Primary and secondary reinforcers, positive and negative reinforcers, schedules of reinforcement, extinction	

FIGURE 6.4 *In classical conditioning, a neutral stimulus becomes a conditioned stimulus that brings forth the desired behavior. In operant conditioning, on the other hand, reinforcements are used to bring forth the desired behavior from the organism.*

Primary and Secondary Reinforcers

Reinforcers that function due to the biological makeup of the organism are called **primary reinforcers**. Food, water, and adequate warmth are all primary reinforcers. People and animals do not need to be taught to value food, water, and warmth.

The value of **secondary reinforcers**, however, must be learned. Secondary reinforcers initially acquire their value through being paired with established reinforcers. Money, attention, and social approval are all usually secondary reinforcers. Money, for example, is a secondary reinforcer because we have learned that it may be exchanged for primary reinforcers such as food and shelter.

Sometimes secondary reinforcers acquire their value only through a long chain of associations. Janet pointed out that good grades (secondary reinforcers) were important because they could help with college admission or jobs. College admission and jobs (also secondary reinforcers) might lead to money or social approval (other secondary reinforcers). As a result of such a chain of associations, secondary reinforcers—such as good grades—sometimes come to be desired in and of themselves.

Positive and Negative Reinforcers

Reinforcers can also be positive or negative. **Positive reinforcers** increase the frequency of the behavior they follow when they are applied. Food, fun activities, and social approval are usually examples of positive reinforcers. In positive reinforcement, a behavior is reinforced because a person (or an animal) receives something he or she wants following the behavior.

Different reinforcers work with different people. For people who enjoy sports, for example, receiving the opportunity to participate in a sport is a positive reinforcer. For people who do not enjoy sports, however, receiving the opportunity to participate in a sport would not be an effective reinforcer. Similarly, what serves as a reinforcer at one time for a person may not be effective at another time for that same person. When a person is hungry, for example, food will work well as a positive reinforcer. But once the person has eaten and is full, food will no longer have an effect.

Unlike with positive reinforcement, with negative reinforcement, a behavior is reinforced because something unwanted *stops* happening or is removed following the behavior. **Negative reinforcers** increase the frequency of the behavior they follow when they are removed. Negative reinforcers are unpleasant in some way. Discomfort, fear, and social disapproval are negative reinforcers.

Daily life is filled with examples of negative reinforcement. When we become too warm in the sun, we move into the shade. When we are tired at the end of the day, we go to sleep. When a food particle is stuck between our teeth, we floss to remove it. And when we have an itch, we often scratch it (even when advised not to do so). All of these situations involve some uncomfortable stimulus—a negative reinforcer—that we act on to make the discomfort disappear. When a specific behavior reduces or

Reinforcement and Punishment

	Behavior		Result		Change
Positive Reinforcement	Studying	➡	Enjoyment of the material (Positive reinforcer)	➡	Student studies more. (Increase)
Negative Reinforcement	Studying	➡	Fear of doing poorly on test (Negative reinforcer)	➡	Student studies more. (Increase)
Punishment	Littering	➡	Person has to pay fine. (Punishment)	➡	Person stops littering. (Decrease)

FIGURE 6.5 *Both positive and negative reinforcers increase the frequency of a behavior. Punishment, however, is intended to decrease or eliminate a particular behavior. Which type of reinforcer increases the behavior when it is removed?*

removes the discomfort, that behavior is reinforced, or strengthened. We learn, for example, that flossing is an effective way of removing a piece of food stuck between our teeth.

Linda wanted to study for her psychology test in part because she thought the material was interesting. In this case, her interest in the material was a positive reinforcer for her. She was studying because it brought her pleasure. But Linda was also probably studying because she did not want to do poorly on the test. In this case, fear of doing poorly was a negative reinforcer. She wanted to study because studying would remove her fear of getting a bad grade.

Rewards and Punishments

Many people believe that being positively reinforced is the same as being rewarded and that being negatively reinforced is the same as being punished. Yet there are some differences, particularly between negative reinforcement and punishment.

Rewards When Linda suggested that she and her friends do something enjoyable after they finished studying, she was proposing that they give themselves a reward. Rewards, like reinforcers, increase the frequency of a behavior, and some psychologists do use the term *reward* interchangeably with the term *positive reinforcement*. But Skinner preferred the concept of reinforcement to that of reward because the concept of reinforcement can be explained without trying to "get inside the head" of an organism to guess what it will find rewarding. A list of reinforcers is arrived at by observing what kinds of stimuli increase the frequency of a behavior.

Punishments While rewards and positive reinforcers are similar, punishments are quite different from negative reinforcers. Both negative reinforcers and punishments are usually unpleasant. But negative reinforcers increase the frequency of a behavior by being removed. Punishments, on the other hand, are unwanted events that decrease the frequency of the behavior they follow when they are applied. (See Figure 6.5.)

It is not true that negative reinforcement is the same thing as punishment. Both punishments and negative reinforcers are unpleasant, but negative reinforcers encourage a behavior by being removed. Punishments, on the other hand, discourage a behavior by being applied.

In school districts such as Marc's that tie participation in athletic programs to academic grades, both punishment and negative reinforcement are involved. To the athlete on the team who does not achieve the required grades, being removed from the team is a punishment. But once the student is off the team, the disappointment of being banned from participation is a negative reinforcer. The student may work harder to raise his or her class grades in order to gain permission to rejoin the team, thus ending the disappointment.

Strong punishment can rapidly end undesirable behavior. Yet many psychologists believe that in most cases punishment is not the ideal way to deal with a problem. They point to several reasons for minimizing the use of punishment:

- Punishment does not in itself teach alternate acceptable behavior. A child may learn what not to do in a particular situation but does not learn what to do instead.
- Punishment tends to work only when it is guaranteed. If a behavior is punished some of the time but goes unnoticed the rest of the time, the behavior probably will continue.
- Severely punished people or animals may try to leave the situation rather than change their behavior. Psychologists warn that children who are severely punished by their parents, for example, may run away from home.
- Punishment can create anger and hostility. A child who is punished may take out such anger on other children.
- Punishment may have broader effects than desired. This can occur when people do not know why they are being punished and what is wanted of them.
- Punishment may be imitated as a way of solving problems. As discussed in the next section, people learn by observing others. Psychologists warn that when children are hit by angry parents, the children may learn not only that they have done something wrong, but also that people hit other people when they are upset. Thus, children who are hit may be more likely to hit others themselves.
- Punishment is sometimes accompanied by unseen benefits that make the behavior more, not less, likely to be repeated. For instance, some children may learn that the most effective way of getting attention from their parents is to misbehave.

Most psychologists believe that it is preferable to reward children for desirable behavior than to punish them for unwanted behavior. For example, parents and other authority figures should pay attention to children, and praise them, when the children are behaving well. If good behavior is taken for granted, and only misbehavior receives attention, misbehavior may be getting reinforced.

Psychologists also point out that children need to be aware of, and capable of performing, the desired behavior. Consider a situation in which parents punish a child for not listening to directions only to find out much later that the child has a hearing problem and could not *hear* the directions.

Schedules of Reinforcement

A major factor in determining how effective a reinforcement will be in bringing about a behavior has to do with the **schedule of reinforcement**— when and how often the reinforcement occurs.

Continuous and Partial Reinforcement Up to now, we primarily have been discussing **continuous reinforcement**, or the reinforcement of a behavior every time the behavior occurs. For

An effective way of encouraging someone to "keep up the good work" is to reward them, as with a prize.

example, the rats in the Skinner box received food every time they pressed the lever. If you walk to a friend's house and your friend is there every time, you will probably continue to go to that same location each time you want to visit your friend because you have always been reinforced for going there. New behaviors are usually learned most rapidly through continuous reinforcement.

It is not, however, always practical or even possible to reinforce a person or an animal for a behavior every single time the behavior occurs. Moreover, a person or animal who is continuously reinforced for a behavior tends to maintain that behavior only as long as the reinforcement is still there. If for some reason the reinforcement stops occurring, the behavior disappears very quickly. For example, if you walk to your friend's house only to find that your friend no longer lives there, you almost certainly will not return to that house again in search of your friend.

The alternative to continuous reinforcement is partial reinforcement. In **partial reinforcement**, a behavior is not reinforced every time it occurs. People who regularly go to the movies may not enjoy every movie they see, for example, but they continue to go to the movies because they enjoy at least *some* of the movies. Behaviors learned through partial reinforcement tend to last longer after they are no longer being reinforced at all than do behaviors learned through continuous reinforcement.

There are two basic categories of partial reinforcement schedules. The first category concerns the amount of time (or interval) that must occur between the reinforcements of a behavior. The second category concerns the number of correct responses that must be made before reinforcement occurs (the ratio of responses to reinforcers).

Interval Schedules   If the amount of time—the interval—that must elapse between reinforcements of a behavior is greater than zero seconds, the behavior is on an interval schedule of reinforcement. There are two different types of interval schedules: fixed-interval schedules and variable-interval schedules.

In a fixed-interval schedule, a fixed amount of time—say, five minutes—must elapse between reinforcements. Suppose a behavior is reinforced at 10:00 A.M. If the behavior is performed at 10:02, it will not be reinforced at that time. However, at 10:05, reinforcement again becomes available and will occur as soon as the behavior is performed. Then the next reinforcement is not available until five minutes later, and so on. Regardless of whether or how often the desired behavior is performed during the interval, it will not be reinforced again until it occurs at least five minutes after the last time it was reinforced.

The response rate falls off after each reinforcement on a fixed-interval schedule. It then picks up

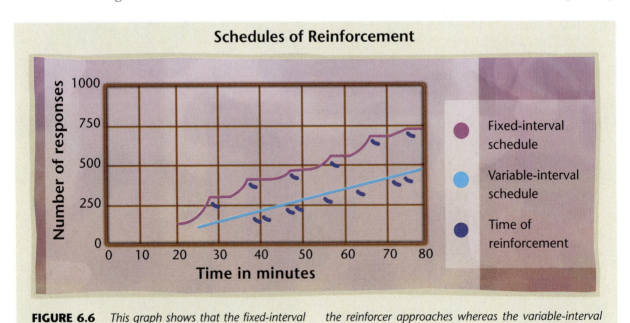

Schedules of Reinforcement

- ● Fixed-interval schedule
- ● Variable-interval schedule
- ● Time of reinforcement

FIGURE 6.6   *This graph shows that the fixed-interval schedule produces increased responses as the time for the reinforcer approaches whereas the variable-interval schedule leads to a relatively steady rate of response.*

Source: Skinner, B. F. (1961). Teaching machines. *Scientific American*, 205, 90–102.

As harvest time draws nearer, the corn farmer begins to check the crop increasingly often. Typically, by late summer, the corn crop will have been completely harvested and the farmer will not have to check it again until after the next year's replanting. What type of reinforcement schedule do the corn farmer's actions indicate?

as the time when reinforcement will be dispensed draws near. For example, in a one-minute fixed-interval schedule, a rat may be reinforced with food the first time it presses the lever after a minute has elapsed since the previous reinforcement. After each reinforcement, the rat's rate of lever pressing slows down, but as a minute approaches, lever pressing increases in frequency. It is as if the rat has learned that it must wait a while before reinforcement is available. Similarly, if you know that your teacher gives a quiz every Friday, you might study only on Thursday nights. After a given week's quiz, you might not study again until the following Thursday. You are on a one-week fixed-interval schedule.

Farmers and gardeners are quite familiar with one-year fixed-interval schedules. If a particular type of fruit ripens only in the spring, for example, the farmer probably will not check to see if the fruit is ripe in the autumn or winter. However, as spring begins, the farmer will probably check more and more frequently to see if the fruit is ripe. Once all the fruit has ripened and been picked, the farmer will stop checking for it until the next spring.

In a variable-interval schedule, varying amounts of time go by between reinforcements. For example, a reinforcement may occur at 10:00, then not again until 10:07 (7-minute interval), then not again until 10:08 (1-minute interval), then not again until 10:20 (12-minute interval). In variable-interval schedules, the timing of the next reinforcement is unpredictable. Therefore, the response rate is steadier than with fixed-interval schedules. (See Figure 6.6.) If your teacher gives unpredictable pop quizzes, you are likely to do at least some studying fairly regularly because you do not know when the next quiz will be. And if it turns out to be tomorrow, you want to be prepared.

Ratio Schedules If a desired response is reinforced every time the response occurs, there is a one-to-one (1:1) ratio of response to reinforcement (one response:one reinforcement). If, however, the response must occur more than once in order to be reinforced, there is a higher response-to-reinforcement ratio. For example, if a response must occur five times before being reinforced, the ratio is 5:1. As with interval schedules, there are fixed-ratio schedules and variable-ratio schedules.

In a fixed-ratio schedule, reinforcement is provided after a fixed number of correct responses have been made. The rat in the box would have to press the lever, say, five times, and always exactly five times, in order to receive the food. Some stores use fixed-ratio schedules to encourage people to buy more. A video rental store, for instance, may promise customers a free video rental with every five rentals paid for.

With a fixed-ratio schedule, the person or animal tends to try to get its fixed number of responses "out of the way" as quickly as it can to get to the reward. With the free video rental offer, for example, a customer may rent the five required videos as soon as possible so as to get to the free one sooner. If the ratio is very high, however, it is often less effective, particularly with people.

In a variable-ratio schedule, reinforcement is provided after a variable number of correct responses have been made. Sometimes the rat might have to press the lever five times to receive the food; at other times, eight times; and at still other times, 14 times. The rat cannot predict how many times the lever must be pressed because the number changes each time.

With a variable-ratio schedule, reinforcement can come at any time. This unpredictability maintains a high response rate. Slot machines tend to work on variable-ratio schedules. Even though the players do not know when (or even if) they will win, they continue to drop coins into the machines. And when the players do win, they often continue to play because the next winnings might be just a few lever-pulls away.

Extinction in Operant Conditioning

In operant conditioning, as in classical conditioning, extinction sometimes occurs. In both types of conditioning, extinction occurs because the events that had previously followed a stimulus no longer occur.

In operant conditioning, the extinction of a learned response results from repeated performance of the response without reinforcement. In Skinner's experiment with the rats, lever pressing was followed by—and reinforced by—food. But if a rat presses a lever repeatedly and no food follows, it will eventually stop pressing the lever. The lever-pressing behavior will have been extinguished.

Marc's reluctance to study for the psychology test may have been an example of extinction. The previous week, he had studied very hard for a test in another class but had done poorly on the test anyway. In other words, his studying behavior had not been reinforced by doing well on the test. As a result, he began to question whether studying was helpful at all. If Linda and the others had not been there to persuade him that it was necessary to study, he might very well not have studied for the psychology test. Marc's studying behavior would have been

A DAY IN THE LIFE

extinguished because of the previous week's lack of reinforcement. After a rest period, though, it might have been spontaneously recovered, as in classical conditioning.

Applications of Operant Conditioning

As we have seen, even people who have never had a course in psychology use operant conditioning every day to influence other people. For example, parents frequently use rewards, such as a trip to the park, to encourage children to perform certain tasks, such as cleaning their rooms.

Techniques of operant conditioning also have widespread application in the field of education. Some specific applications of operant conditioning in education include shaping, programmed learning, and classroom discipline.

Shaping   If you have ever tried to teach someone how to do a complex or difficult task, you probably know that the best way to teach the task is to break it up into parts and teach each part separately. When all the parts have been mastered, they can be put together to form the whole. Psychologists call this shaping. **Shaping** is a way of teaching complex behaviors in which one first reinforces small steps in the right direction.

Learning to ride a bicycle, for example, involves the learning of a complex sequence of behaviors and can be accomplished through shaping. First, people must learn to move the bike forward by using the pedals. Then they must learn to balance the bicycle and then to steer it. You may remember when you learned to ride a two-wheeler, or you may have seen a parent help a young child by holding the seat as the child learned to pedal. At first, each of these steps seems difficult, and people must pay close attention to each one. After many repetitions, though, and much praise and reassurance from the instructor, each step—and eventually bicycle riding itself—becomes habitual. Close attention no longer needs to be paid.

Psychologists have used shaping to teach animals some complex behavior patterns. For example, they have trained rats to pedal toy cars by first reinforcing the rats' behavior of turning toward the cars. Next they wait until the rats approach the cars before providing further reinforcement. Then they wait until the rats touch the cars, and so on. In this way, rats have been trained to run up ramps, cross bridges, climb ladders, and the like.

PSYCHOLOGY

B. F. SKINNER:
Theories of Control

B.F. Skinner was not only a psychologist, but also a philosopher. Many of his philosophies were rooted in his belief that all human behaviors are learned through reinforcement.

Skinner explained his ideas in numerous writings. The following excerpt is from his novel *Walden Two* (1948), a fictional account of a group of people who use behavioral engineering—the carefully planned use of reinforcements—to create a perfect community. A member of the community, Frazier, explains:

". . . It's what the science of behavior calls 'reinforcement theory.'. . . If it's in our power to create any of the situations which a person likes or to remove any situation he doesn't like, we can control his behavior. When he behaves as we want him to behave, we simply create a situation he likes, or remove one he doesn't like. As a result, the probability that he will behave that way again goes up, which is what we want." (p. 244)

The character explained how the leaders of the community applied the technique of reinforcement to maintain the natural curiosity of the children in the society and to shape their behavior:

"We made a survey of the motives of the unhampered child. . . . Our engineering job was to preserve them by fortifying the child against discouragement. We introduce discouragement . . . beginning at about six months. Some of the toys in our air-conditioned cubicles are designed to build perseverance. A bit of a tune from a music box, or a pattern of flashing lights, is arranged to follow an appropriate response—say, pulling on a ring. Later the ring must be pulled twice, later three or five or ten times. It's possible to build up . . . perseverative behavior without encountering frustration or rage." (pp. 114)

In essence, the children learned to continue a behavior (in this case, pulling on the ring), even though they were not rewarded for the behavior every time they performed it.

Skinner believed that reinforcement could be used for the good of society, as he tried to show in *Walden Two*. He also believed, however, that reinforcement could be used, and had been used, in ways that were harmful. He discussed this in his 1971 book *Beyond Freedom and Dignity:*

Reinforcement can also be misused. . . . Certain schedules [of reinforcement] generate a great deal of behavior in return for very little reinforcement, and the possibility has naturally not been overlooked by would-be controllers. . . . In the incentive system known as piece-work pay, the worker is paid a given amount for each unit of work performed. . . . This . . . schedule of reinforcement can be . . . used to generate a great deal of behavior for very little return. It induces the worker to work fast and the ratio can then be 'stretched'—that is, more work can be demanded for each unit of pay without running the risk that the worker will stop working. His ultimate condition [is] hard work at very little pay. (p. 32)

Skinner argued that through reinforcement, human behavior was constantly being controlled by outside forces. In Skinner's view, such control was unavoidable, but some types of control were better than others. In fact, some types of control could even be beneficial. He noted, "The problem is to free men, not from control, but from certain kinds of control" (pp. 39–40). Although Skinner's theories about control have been widely criticized, most people agree that they are worth studying.

Think About It

Which schedule of reinforcement is portrayed by the example of the children playing with the ring? Which schedule of reinforcement is portrayed by the example of the piece-work pay?

Building on a squirrel's natural tendency to use its paws, this animal was taught to ride a remote-controlled hang glider. What steps do you think were reinforced to produce this final behavior?

Programmed Learning B. F. Skinner developed an educational method called programmed learning that is based on shaping. Programmed learning assumes that any task, no matter how complex, can be broken down into small steps. Each step can be shaped individually and combined to form the more complicated whole.

In programmed learning, a device called a teaching machine presents the student with the subject matter in a series of steps, each of which is called a frame. Each frame requires the student to make some kind of response, such as answering a question. The student is immediately informed whether the response was correct. If it was correct, the student goes on to the next frame. If the response was incorrect, the student goes back over that step until he or she learns it correctly.

Teaching machines can be mechanical hand-held devices. They can also be books or papers, such as worksheets. These days, however, teaching machines are most likely to be computers that are programmed so that the material can branch off in several different directions, depending on where the student needs the most instruction and practice. The use of computers in learning is called computer-assisted instruction.

Programmed learning does not punish students for making errors. Instead, it reinforces correct responses. Eventually, all students who finish the program earn "100 percent," but they do so at their own pace. The machines are infinitely patient with the learner. They are also highly efficient. Most people, however, believe that teaching machines

should not be used to replace human teachers—only to assist them.

Classroom Discipline Sometimes when we think we are reinforcing one behavior, we are actually unknowingly reinforcing the opposite behavior. For instance, teachers who pay attention to students who misbehave may unintentionally give these students greater status in the eyes of some of their classmates (Wentzel, 1994). Some teacher training programs show teachers how to use principles of learning to change students' negative patterns of behavior. In these programs, teachers are taught to pay attention to students when they are behaving appropriately and to ignore their misbehavior as long as the misbehavior is not harmful to themselves or to others. If misbehavior is ignored, or unreinforced, it should become extinct, according to the theory.

Teacher attention and approval may have more influence with elementary school students than with high school students, however. Among some adolescents, peer approval can be more powerful than teacher approval. Peer approval may reinforce misbehavior even when teachers ignore it. Moreover, ignoring misbehavior may only encourage other students to become disruptive as well.

Instead of ignoring misbehaving adolescents, therefore, teachers may decide to separate them from the rest of the class or group. Teachers and parents frequently use a technique called time-out to discourage misbehavior. Time-out involves placing students in dull, confining environments for a short period of time, such as 10 minutes, when they misbehave. Students who are isolated cannot obtain the attention of peers or teachers, and no reinforcing activities are available.

THINKING ABOUT PSYCHOLOGY

1. Explain the differences between classical conditioning and operant conditioning.

2. Name four types of reinforcers.

3. How are fixed schedules of reinforcement different from variable schedules of reinforcement?

4. **Critical Thinking** How do parents and teachers use rewards and punishments to influence children's behavior? Give an example of a reward or punishment that works with some people but not with others.

Cognitive Factors in Learning

If B. F. Skinner had heard Dan speculate that he might study more often if he got to do something enjoyable every time he studied, Skinner probably would have paid little attention. For Skinner, what was important was what organisms actually do, not what they say or think they might do. Skinner was interested only in organisms' behaviors.

Cognitive psychologists, however, are willing to speak about what people and animals know because of learning—not just about what they do. Cognitive psychologists see learning as purposeful, not mechanical. They believe that a person can learn something simply by thinking about it or by watching others. They see people and even some animals as searching for information, weighing evidence, and making decisions. Two kinds of learning that involve cognitive factors are latent learning and observational learning.

Latent Learning

How do you know where objects are in your home, in your school, or in your neighborhood? You probably have a mental picture, or "cognitive map," of the area. Because you are very familiar with your school, for example, you know the locations of your locker, the main office, the cafeteria, the gymnasium, and your psychology classroom. Chances are, no one has reinforced your creation of a mental picture of the school's layout; you have simply created it on your own.

In the past, many psychologists argued that organisms only learn behaviors that are reinforced. Today, however, most psychologists believe that much learning can occur without reinforcement. Support for this view came from the work of E. C. Tolman. Tolman showed that rats will learn about their environments even in the absence of reinforcement. Tolman trained some rats to run through mazes to reach food. Other rats were simply permitted to explore the mazes. They received no food or other rewards. After the unrewarded rats had run around in the mazes for 10 days, food was placed in a box at the far ends of the mazes. The previously unrewarded explorers reached the food as quickly as the rewarded rats after only one or two reinforced efforts (Tolman & Honzik, 1930).

Tolman concluded that the rats had learned about the layouts of the mazes even when they were unrewarded for their learning. Tolman distinguished between what organisms learn and what they do. Rats would learn about the mazes even when they roamed about without a goal. However, they had no reason to run efficient routes to the far ends of the mazes until they were rewarded for doing so. Therefore, even though they had knowledge of the rapid routes all along, this knowledge had been hidden, or latent, until the rats had reason to use it—when there was food at the ends. Learning that remains hidden until it is needed is called **latent learning**.

On your way to school each morning, you may pass a particular street corner at which you have never had any reason to stop. But if a friend wants to meet you at that corner on Saturday, you will still know how to get there, even though you may never have stopped there before. This is an example of latent learning.

A mouse in a maze might know where the maze's end is even if there is no food there.

Observational Learning

How many things have you learned from observing other people, from reading books, and from watching films and television? No doubt you have picked up a few ideas about how to act or what to say in certain situations or how to do certain things. Certainly, cooking programs on television or how-to home-improvement books are based on the premise that people learn by watching or being told how others do things.

Albert Bandura   In his research on social learning, Albert Bandura (1925–) has shown that we acquire knowledge and skills by observing and imitating others (Bandura et al., 1963). Such learning is called **observational learning**. Aggression, for instance, may be learned by watching others who display aggression. In fact, children are more likely to imitate what their parents *do* than to heed what they *say*. If adults say they disapprove of aggression but smash furniture or hit each other when they are frustrated, children are likely to learn that aggression is the way to handle frustration.

Observational learning accounts for much human learning, far beyond aggression. Children learn to speak, eat, and play at least partly by observing their parents and others do these things.

Many people believe that because cartoons are aimed at young children, cartoon violence should be kept to a minimum or eliminated altogether.

You learn to pronounce words in your foreign language class by hearing your teacher pronounce them. We may not always be able to do something perfectly the first time we try it, but if we have watched others do it first, we probably have a head start over people who are coming into it without any previous exposure.

Learning from the Media   Observational learning is often proposed as a cause of violence in society. Studies show that children who watch two to four hours of television a day will have seen 8,000 murders and another 100,000 acts of violence by the time they have finished elementary school (Eron, 1993). If children learn by watching others, are they learning how to be violent themselves from watching all this violence on television?

Although exposure to violence in the media is usually not the sole cause of violent behavior, most psychologists agree that media violence does contribute to aggression (Huesmann, 1993). In study after study, people who are exposed to violence in the media behave more aggressively than people who are not (DeAngelis, 1993; Liebert et al., 1989). Observational learning is partly responsible: television violence supplies models of aggressive "skills." Classic experiments have shown that children tend to imitate the aggressive behavior they see on television (Bandura et al., 1963).

TRUTH OR fiction
■ R E V I S I T E D ■

It is true that people who watch a lot of violence on television are more likely to be violent themselves than people who watch less violence on television. People often imitate the behaviors of others they see, including television characters. This is called observational learning.

Media violence also provides viewers with aggressive scripts—that is, ideas on how to behave in situations that seem to parallel those they have observed (Huesmann & Miller, 1994). Furthermore, people tend to become used to repetitious stimuli. Repeated exposure to television violence may decrease viewers' emotional response to real violence (Huesmann, 1993). If children think of violence as normal because they are constantly being exposed to it, they are less likely to condemn violence and restrain their own aggressive urges (Eron, 1993; Huesmann, 1993).

Just as observational learning may contribute to violent behavior, it may also be used to prevent it. Television networks, for example, have recently made some attempts to limit the amount of violence in programs intended for children. But it is probably not practical to hope to shield children from all violence—after all, even religious texts, the evening news, and classic works such as Shakespeare's *Macbeth* contain violence. Instead, young people can be informed that the violence they see in the media does not represent the behavior of most people. Most people resolve their conflicts without resorting to violence. Children also can be told that the violence they see on TV shows is not real; it involves camera tricks, special effects, and stunts.

A person who has observed a behavior in others does not necessarily begin to display that behavior himself or herself. There is a difference between what people learn and what they do. Of all the children who are exposed to media violence, only a few of them become violent. Furthermore, it may be that people who *choose* to watch violent television programs are more likely to be violent in the first place. It is difficult to prove a cause-and-effect relationship based only on correlation. (See Chapter 2.) If young people consider violence wrong for them, they will probably not be violent, even if they know how to be violent. The same applies to other behaviors as well.

THINKING ABOUT PSYCHOLOGY

1. How might studying a cookbook for fun be a form of latent learning?

2. Provide an example of observational learning that takes place in school.

3. **Critical Thinking** How much violence have you witnessed over the past year on television or in the movies? Has observation of violence in the media affected your behavior? If so, how?

4
The PQ4R Method: Learning to Learn

If you put a sponge in a bathtub, it will soak up the water. Many students assume that simply by being in a course (such as history, biology, or even psy-

chology) they will somehow soak up the subject matter of that course. Not so. Students are not sponges. Courses are not bathtubs.

Students learn more when they take an active approach to learning. One such active approach is called the PQ4R method. Based on the work of educational psychologist Francis P. Robinson, the PQ4R method has six steps: *Previewing, Questioning, Reading, Reflecting, Reciting,* and *Reviewing.* Following these six steps will help you get the most out of your textbooks.

Preview

Previewing the subject matter in a textbook means getting a general picture of what is covered before you begin reading a chapter. If you are in the library or the bookstore looking at books to decide which ones you would like to read for pleasure, you may flip rapidly through the pages to get some idea of what the books are about. Thumbing through the pages is one way of previewing the material. In fact, many textbooks are designed with devices that encourage students to preview chapters before reading them.

This book, for instance, has chapter objectives, Truth-or-Fiction sections, lists of key terms, major and minor section heads in each chapter, section review questions, and chapter reviews. If drama and suspense are your goals, read each chapter page by page. But if learning the material is your aim, it may be more effective to first read the objectives, skim the pages, and read the questions in the section and chapter reviews.

Familiarity with the overall picture will give you a cognitive map of a chapter. Your map will have many blank areas, but it will have an overall structure. You can fill in the details of the map as you read through the chapter page by page.

Question

Learning is made easier when we have goals in mind, when there is something in particular we want to learn. When we want to learn something, we become active learners.

One way to create goals is to phrase questions about the subject matter in each chapter. You may ask: how is it possible to come up with the questions without reading the chapter first? Look at each heading. Write down all the headings in a notebook. If a book you are reading does not have helpful headings, you might try looking at the first sentence of each paragraph instead. Phrase questions as you proceed. With practice, you will develop questioning skills, and your questions will help you grasp the subject matter.

The following questions are based on the major and minor headings at the beginning of this chapter: What is classical conditioning? Who is Ivan Pavlov? (See Figure 6.7.) You may have come up with different questions after reading the headings. Your questions might have been as useful as these, or more useful; there is always more than one "right" question. As you study, you will learn what works for you.

Read

Once you have formulated your questions, read the chapter with the purpose of answering them. A sense of purpose will help you focus on the key points of the material. As you answer each question,

you can jot down a few key words in your notebook that will remind you of the answer when you recite and review later on.

You may find it helpful to keep two columns in your notebook: one column for the questions themselves and the other column for the key words that relate to the answer to each question.

Reflect

Reflecting on subject matter is an important way to understand and remember it. As you are reading, think of examples or create mental images of the subject matter.

One way to reflect is to relate new information to old information. You may remember some facts about B. F. Skinner from Chapter 1, for example. What you learned about him there can serve as a springboard for you to learn about him and about his work in greater detail in this chapter. Take advantage of what you already know.

Another way to reflect is to relate new information to events in your personal life. For instance, you can reflect on classical conditioning by thinking of times when you have experienced it. Then you will find it easier to remember that classical conditioning involves learning through the association of stimuli with each other.

Even if you cannot think of any way to relate the material to your own life, you probably know other people who provide examples of the kinds of behavior discussed throughout this book. To help yourself understand and remember the subject matter of psychology, think of ways in which the behavior of people described in the text and by your teacher is similar to—or different from—the behavior of people you know.

Recite

Do you remember when you learned the alphabet? If you were like many children, you probably learned it by saying it—or singing it to the tune of the "Alphabet Song"—over and over again. This is an example of how reciting something can help a person learn. The same thing can work with your textbook. (You will have to make up your own song, however.)

Once you have read a section and have answered your questions, reciting the answers will help you understand and remember them. You can recite aloud or repeat words silently to yourself. You can also do your reciting alone or with others. Many

Using PQ4R

I. What is classical conditioning?
   A. Who is Ivan Pavlov?
   B. What do US, UR, CR, and CS mean?
   C. How is adaptation to the environment related to conditioning?
      1. What is a taste aversion?
      2. What is extinction?
      3. What is spontaneous recovery?
      4. How do generalization and discrimination relate to classical conditioning?
   D. What are some applications of classical conditioning?
      1. What are flooding and systematic desensitization?
      2. What is counterconditioning?
      3. How does the bell-and-pad method for bed-wetting work?

FIGURE 6.7 *An actual PQ4R notebook might include a column for answers in addition to the questions.*

students learn by quizzing each other with their questions, taking turns reciting the answers. This may have been what Linda had in mind when she suggested that she and her friends study together for the psychology test.

Review

When Marc said that he had been studying for the test in Ms. Kramer's class the night before the test, he may have given the explanation for why he did not do as well on the test as he would have liked. For one thing, learning takes time. That means that we usually have to repeat or reread things before we know them cold.

Second, "distributed" learning is more effective than "massed" learning. That is a scientific way of saying what most students already know but that Marc apparently did not: it is more effective to study regularly (to distribute the learning over several days or weeks) than to try to cram just before a test (to mass all the learning at once). Actually, distributed learning usually takes no more work than cramming. But it means that we have to plan ahead and try to stick to some sort of schedule.

Review the material for each subject you are studying according to a reasonably regular schedule, such as once a week. Reviewing leads to relearning, and relearning on a regular schedule is easier than learning something the first time. By reviewing material regularly, we understand and remember it better.

It may seem like a large time commitment to study regularly when there is no apparent immediate need to do so, but it will reduce the amount of time you have to study right before a test. It may also help reduce the amount of anxiety you feel about the test the day before (negative reinforcement) because you know that you have already mastered at least some of the material. And it also helps keep you prepared for pop quizzes.

Once you have set aside enough time to review the material, you will need to figure out what review techniques will help you most. One way to review the material is to go back to the questions and key words in your notebook. Cover up the answer column and read the questions in the left column as though they were a quiz. Recite your answers and check them against the key words in the right column. When you forget an answer or get an answer wrong, go back and reread the subject matter in the textbook. (In this technique, your notebook

The PQ4R method helps students take an active approach to learning.

becomes a type of teaching machine used in programmed learning.)

Another way of reviewing the subject matter, as already mentioned, is for you and other classmates to quiz each other. By taking a more active approach to learning, you may find that you are earning higher grades and gaining more pleasure from the learning process.

THINKING ABOUT PSYCHOLOGY

1. What are the steps in the PQ4R method?

2. What purposes does it serve for a person to reflect on information she or he has read about? What purposes does reciting the information out loud serve?

3. **Critical Thinking** Prepare a learning and studying schedule for yourself for one of your classes. Use PQ4R as a basis for the schedule.

6 REVIEW

SUMMARY

Organisms learn through several different processes.

I. Classical Conditioning

A. In classical conditioning, a previously neutral stimulus acquires the ability to produce a response originally produced by another stimulus.

B. Russian physiologist Ivan Pavlov pioneered research in classical conditioning in a famous experiment with dogs.

C. *Unconditioned stimulus (US), unconditioned response (UR), conditioned stimulus (CS),* and *conditioned response (CR)* are important terms in classical conditioning.

D. Classical conditioning helps organisms adapt to the surrounding environment. It is especially useful in helping people or animals avoid or deal with danger.

　1. Conditioned responses may be extinguished when the unconditioned stimulus is no longer paired with the conditioned stimulus. However, an extinguished conditioned response may recover spontaneously at a later time.

　2. Generalization occurs when people (and animals) respond in the same way to similar stimuli. Discrimination is the act of responding differently to stimuli that are not similar.

E. Flooding, systematic desensitization, and counterconditioning are techniques of classical conditioning that can help people overcome their fears.

II. Operant Conditioning

A. Operant conditioning is a type of learning based on the consequences of actions.

B. Psychologist B. F. Skinner developed many of the principles of operant conditioning.

C. In operant conditioning, people and animals learn as a result of the reinforcement they receive following a behavior.

D. Reinforcers encourage behavior to occur again. They can be primary or secondary, positive or negative.

E. Positive reinforcement and rewards are similar. Negative reinforcers and punishment are both unpleasant, but negative reinforcers encourage a behavior by being removed while punishments discourage a behavior by being applied.

F. When and how often a reinforcement occurs is a major factor in determining its effectiveness.

　1. The schedule of reinforcement may be continuous or partial.

　2. Types of partial reinforcement schedules are fixed-interval, variable-interval, fixed-ratio, and variable-ratio schedules.

G. In operant conditioning, extinction results from repeated performance of a response without reinforcement.

H. Techniques of operant conditioning—including shaping, programmed learning, and classroom discipline—are widely used in the field of education.

III. Cognitive Factors in Learning

A. Cognitive psychologists believe that people learn something by thinking about it or by watching others.

B. In latent learning, a kind of learning that involves cognitive factors, learning remains hidden until it is needed.

C. Research by psychologist Albert Bandura has shown that people acquire knowledge and skills by observing and imitating others. This type of learning is called observational learning.

IV. The PQ4R Method: Learning to Learn

A. The PQ4R method of learning can help students get the most from textbooks.

B. The six steps of PQ4R are preview, question, read, reflect, recite, and review.

TERM & CONCEPT
REVIEW

1. How do people and animals learn responses through classical conditioning?
2. In what way is a taste aversion different from other examples of classical conditioning?
3. Under what conditions might a conditioned response become extinct? Give an example.
4. Use the following terms to describe how researchers might teach laboratory rats to press a lever in a Skinner box to obtain food pellets: *positive reinforcement, primary reinforcer,* and *continuous reinforcement.*
5. How does a fixed-interval schedule of reinforcement differ from a fixed-ratio schedule?
6. What is programmed learning? On what principle of operant conditioning is it based?
7. What are two types of learning that involve cognitive factors? Explain each type.
8. How did E. C. Tolman demonstrate latent learning in rats?
9. In what way is previewing a chapter in a textbook an effective study skill?
10. List the six steps of the PQ4R method and explain the purpose of each step.

CRITICAL
THINKING

1. How might a therapist help cigarette smokers quit smoking by using each of these types of learning: classical conditioning, operant conditioning, and cognitive learning?
2. How might the principles of classical conditioning lead to the formation of superstitions? How might the principles of operant conditioning help keep superstitions alive?
3. Explain how flooding, desensitization, and counterconditioning can help a person overcome a problem. Give one example for each.
4. Many psychologists believe that punishment is not the ideal way to change behavior. Do you

agree or disagree with this position? Give examples to support your opinion.

APPLYING SKILLS
IN PSYCHOLOGY

1. **Using Your Observation Skills** Make three columns on a sheet of paper. Label them Classical, Operant, and Cognitive. During the next week, look for examples of each type of learning at home, in school, or in the community. Write each example in the appropriate column. At the end of the week, share your observations with the class.
2. **Research in Psychology** Find information about other applications of operant conditioning such as biofeedback, behavior modification, and weight control. Write a brief report explaining how operant conditioning is used in one of the applications.
3. **Using Your Observation Skills** Many movies and television shows portray scenarios in which heroes use violence to destroy "the bad guys." Usually, at the end of the movies or shows, the heroes are rewarded in some way for their efforts, regardless of the means they used. You have read about how witnessing violence in the media may encourage viewers to become violent themselves because of observational learning, but how might operant conditioning in such movie plots also play a role?
4. **Writing About Psychology** Write a brief two-act play about observational learning. In the first act, show a young child observing the behavior of one or more teens. In the second act, show the same child demonstrating the observed behavior in a different setting. Ask several classmates to help you perform the play for the class.
5. **COOPERATIVE LEARNING** **Reading About Psychology** Form a study group with two or three other students in your psychology class. Using material from Chapter 6, practice the recite step of the PQ4R method.

7

MEMORY

Objectives

1 Compare and contrast the three kinds of memory, and give an example of each kind.

2 Explain the three processes of memory.

3 Identify the three stages of memory, and explain how they are related to each other.

4 Describe the various kinds of forgetting, and suggest ways to improve your memory.

"Flashbulb memory" is a type of episodic memory in which an event can be recalled in great detail. When people see a photograph of the Challenger explosion, for example, they may remember what they were doing on January 28, 1986.

instrument, and driving a car are other examples of procedural memory. Once such a skill has been learned, it usually stays with you for many years. Even if you do not use the skill for a long time, you are unlikely to forget it. Once skills have been learned, they tend to stay remembered for many years—perhaps even a lifetime.

TRUTH
OR
fiction
▪ R E V I S I T E D ▪

It is true that once people learn to ride a bicycle, they probably never will forget how. Once people learn a skill, there is little chance they will ever forget it. Skill memories tend to last, even when they are not used regularly.

THINKING ABOUT PSYCHOLOGY

1. Describe the three kinds of memory.
2. Explain what flashbulb memory is.
3. **Critical Thinking** Write down the three kinds of memory you have learned about so far. Next to each, give an example of how you have used that type of memory recently.

usually do not remember *when* we acquired the information in our generic memory. We probably cannot remember when we first learned about George Washington, for instance.

A DAY IN THE LIFE

The memory Marc had at Hannah's party was a generic memory. He remembered that Marina Crossley wrote the song, not Ashley Austin, as Linda had thought. Most likely, Marc did not remember when he learned that Marina Crossley wrote the song. Still, he remembered correctly that she did.

Here are two more examples of generic memory. You remember the alphabet, but you probably do not remember where, when, or how you learned it. So, too, you may remember that humans need oxygen to breathe, even though you may not recall learning this piece of information. Most of what you have learned in your classes at school has become part of your generic memory.

Procedural Memory

The third kind of memory is **procedural memory**. It consists of the skills, or procedures, you have learned. These skills might include throwing a ball, riding a bicycle, skipping rope, or swimming. Skills such as typing, using a computer, playing a musical

2
Three Processes of Memory

Computers and people both process information. Computers use electronic circuits to process the information they receive, while people use their brains. But the processes used by computers and people are the same. Computers and people both encode, store, and retrieve information.

Encoding

Imagine writing an essay or a story on a computer. You use the keyboard to type information in the form of letters and words. The information is usually stored on a hard drive or a floppy disk. But if you were to put the hard drive or floppy disk under a microscope, would you be able to see the letters or words you typed? No. This is because the computer

Computers use electronic circuits to process information; humans use their brains. Both use similar processes of encoding, storing, and retrieving information.

changes, or encodes, the information into a form that it can store. **Encoding** is the translation of information into a form in which it can be stored. When people place information in their memory, they, like computers, encode it. For both the computer and the human brain, encoding is the first stage of processing information.

Initially, we receive information through our senses in a physical form—such as light waves or sound waves. When we encode it, we convert the physical stimulation we have received into psychological formats that can be mentally represented. To do so, we use different types of codes.

On a sheet of paper, write this list of letters:

OTTFFSSENT

Look at the letters for 30 seconds and memorize as much of the list as you can in that time. Then continue reading this section to find out which type of code—visual, acoustic, or semantic—you used to remember the letters.

Visual Codes   When you tried to memorize the letters, did you attempt to see them in your mind as a picture? If you did, you used a visual code. That is, you tried to keep a mental picture of the letters in your mind.

Acoustic Codes   Another way that you may have tried to remember the letters might have been to read the list to yourself and repeat it several times. That is, you may have said the letters (either out loud or silently) one after another: O, T, T, and so forth. This way of trying to remember the letters uses an acoustic (or auditory) code. An acoustic code records the letters in your memory as a sequence of sounds.

Semantic Codes   Still another way that you may have tried to remember the list might have been to attempt to make sense of the letters, that is, to figure out what they might mean. For example, you may have noticed that the last four letters spelled the word *sent*. You may then have tried to see if the letters made up a phrase or sentence with the word *sent* in it. The word *semantic* means "relating to meaning," so this type of code is called a semantic code. A semantic code represents information in terms of its meaning. If you tried to figure out a possible meaning for the letters, you were searching for a semantic code.

Another way that you could try to remember the letters by using a semantic code would be to find words that begin with each of the letters in the list and then make up a sentence using those words. Such an approach might result in a sentence that begins "Only Tiny Tots Feel Friendly. . . ." By using all 10 letters in a sentence, you would then have to remember only the sentence, not the list of letters.

Yet another way you might use semantic coding to remember the letters would be to use the phrase "other flowers sent" and then make a few changes in the spelling—that is, "OTTher FFlowerS SENT." You would then have to remember the phrase with its "OTTities" (oddities) of spelling!

What you may *not* have realized when you first examined the list is that the letters **OTTFFSSENT** stand for the first letter of the series of numbers from one (O) through ten (T)—that is, One, Two, Three, Four, Five, Six, Seven, Eight, Nine, Ten. Obviously, if you had known that in the first place, remembering the letters would have been much easier. All you would have had to remember was that the letters were the first letters of the numbers 1 through 10. Remembering this rule would certainly be easier than remembering an apparently meaningless list of 10 letters. By using semantic (meaningful) codes, you can memorize lists of letters and other items more easily and will probably remember them for a longer amount of time than you would otherwise.

Storage

After information is encoded, it must be stored. **Storage**, the second process of memory, is the maintenance of encoded information over a period of time. As with encoding, human storage of information is not completely different from a computer's storage of information. With a computer, however, the user must instruct the machine to save information in its memory. Otherwise, it will lose the newly encoded information when the user shuts off the computer. People who want to store new information in their memory use a variety of strategies. These strategies are related closely to the strategies people use for encoding.

Maintenance Rehearsal

As Dan found out at the party when he tried to remember the phone number of the girl he had met, once we encode information we need to do something more to keep from forgetting it. If you were in a similar situation in which you wanted to remember a name or phone number, how would you do it? One way would be to keep repeating the name or number to yourself to keep it in your memory. If you were concerned that you might forget it before you could write it down, you might need to repeat it several times. Repeating information over and over again to keep from forgetting it is called **maintenance rehearsal**.

The more time spent in rehearsing, or repeating information, the longer the information will be remembered. Actors and actresses know this well. That is why they rehearse their lines again and again until they know them as well as they possibly can. Because maintenance rehearsal does not try to make information meaningful by connecting it to past learning, however, it is a relatively poor way to put information in permanent storage.

Elaborative Rehearsal

A more effective and lasting way to remember new information is to make it meaningful by relating it to information already well known (Woloshyn et al., 1994). This method, called **elaborative rehearsal**, is widely used in education because it has proved to be a much more effective method than maintenance rehearsal. For example, language arts and foreign language teachers recommend elaborative rehearsal when they encourage their students to use new vocabulary words in sentences instead of just repeating individual words by themselves.

Organizational Systems

Memories that you store become organized and arranged in your mind for future use. If you are a fairly organized person, you probably have a place for everything. When you bring items home, you probably do not just throw them on the floor or stick them haphazardly in a closet. You probably sort them and put them in their place. That way you have a better chance of finding them when you need them. You have probably learned from experience that not knowing where items are means that you end up spending a lot of time looking for them when you need them.

In some ways, your memory resembles a vast storehouse of files and file cabinets in which you store what you learn and need to remember. The more you learn, the more files you need and the more elaborate your filing system becomes. When you started attending school, the first facts you learned about American history, for example, may have been about Pocahontas, the Pilgrims, or George Washington. Your first "American history" file probably had only a couple of pieces of information in it.

However, as you progressed and learned more about American history, you had to expand your filing system. As you learned about the presidents, for example, you found new ways to file the information in your memory. You may have filed the presidents in chronological order, that is, in the order in which they held office. In that file you put Washington first, followed by others such as Jefferson, Lincoln, and Theodore Roosevelt. You may also have filed more recent presidents according to the events in American history with which they are associated, such as Franklin Roosevelt with the New Deal and World War II, Richard Nixon with Watergate, and George Bush with the Persian Gulf War.

As your memory develops, it organizes the information you learn into files and then files within files. Your memory organizes the new information it receives into certain groups, or classes, according to common features. For example,

The "American history" file in your brain might remind you that Mount Rushmore has the largest figures of any statue in the world and that the faces are those of Washington, Jefferson, Theodore Roosevelt, and Lincoln.

mammals share certain features. They are warm-blooded, and they nurse their young. If you knew that whales are warm-blooded and nurse their young, you probably filed them in your memory as mammals. If you did not know that about them, you might have filed them as fish because they swim and live in the water.

Classes can contain smaller classes and also can be part of a larger class. For example, the class mammals includes monkeys, rats, and other warm-blooded, nursing creatures. At the same time, mammals are part of a larger class—animals. Much of our generic memory that is stored as we get older and acquire more knowledge is organized into groups or classes.

Filing Errors   Our ability to remember information—even when we are healthy and functioning well—is subject to error. Some memory errors occur because we "file" information incorrectly. Psychologists have discovered that when we classify pieces of information accurately, that is, when we place items in the correct file, we have a much better chance of recalling accurate information about them (Hasselhorn, 1992; Schneider & Bjorklund, 1992). Nevertheless, filing systems are not perfect. Have you ever misplaced a paper? For example, have you ever brought home a science paper and mistakenly filed it in your history folder? Our mental filing systems sometimes make similar errors.

A DAY IN THE LIFE

Linda's memory had made a filing mistake. This became evident at the party when she said that Ashley Austin wrote the song that reminded her of being back in the seventh grade. Todd knew the song had not been written by Ashley Austin, but he was unable to remember who did write it. Marc was the one who finally came up with the right answer—Marina Crossley. Linda had apparently put the "wrong label"—Ashley Austin rather than Marina Crossley—on her file of information about the song.

Retrieval

The third memory process is retrieval. **Retrieval** consists of locating stored information and returning it to conscious thought. Retrieving information stored in our memory is like retrieving information stored in a computer. To retrieve information stored in a computer, we have to know the name of the file and the rules for retrieving information. Retrieval of information stored in our memory requires a similar knowledge of proper procedures.

Some information in our memory is so familiar that it is readily available and almost impossible to forget. Examples of this type of information include our own names and those of our friends and family members. But when it comes to trying to remember lines from a play or a mathematical formula, retrieval may be more difficult.

Remember the list of letters discussed earlier in the section? What were they? Write them down now. How did you retrieve them from your memory? The method of retrieval you used might have had to do with the way you encoded them to begin with. If you had encoded the series of letters—OTTFFSSENT—as a three-word phrase ("other flowers sent"), you would try to retrieve the letters by recalling the three words and the rule you needed to use to convert them into the 10 letters. But you might make a mistake. For example, you might recall "other flowers senD" rather than "other flowers senT." Or you might correctly recall "other flowers sent" but then not remember that you have to double the T and the F.

However, by remembering the semantic code that the letters stand for the numbers 1 through 10, your memory could accurately recall, or retrieve, the letters. Using this semantic code may be more complex than seeing the list in your mind's eye (using a visual code), and it might take you a little longer to reconstruct the list of letters. However, by using the 1–10 device, you have a much better chance of remembering the letters—and of remembering them for a longer time.

Before reading on, take this very brief spelling quiz: Which of the following words is spelled correctly—*retrieval* or *retreival*? Because you know how the word is pronounced, regardless of how it is spelled, saying the word to yourself (using an acoustic code) will not help you remember the correct spelling, which is retri*e*val. How might you go about remembering the correct spelling? Repeating it over and over (maintenance rehearsal) is certainly one way, and that method might work. However, a much better way would be to remember a spelling rule, such as "*i* before *e* except after *c,*" as a semantic code. That rule enables you to reconstruct the correct spelling without having to memorize the order of the letters.

Context-Dependent Memory   Have you ever been to a place that brought back old memories? Perhaps you went back to your elementary school or to the neighborhood where you once lived. The memories that came back to you in that place are called **context-dependent memories**. The context of a memory is the situation in which a person first had the experience being remembered. Such memories are dependent on the place where they were encoded and stored. If you had not returned to the place where your memories were encoded, you probably would not have retrieved them.

A fascinating experiment in context-dependent memory involved some students who belonged to a swimming club. They were asked to memorize lists of words while they were in the water of a pool (Godden & Baddeley, 1975). Other students in the club tried to memorize the lists while they were out of the water. Later, the students who had studied the lists in the water did a better job of remembering them when they were in the water again. Students who had worked on the lists out of the water, on the other hand, remembered more words when they were dry. These findings suggest that the ability to retrieve memories is greater when people are in the place or situation in which they stored the memories to begin with.

Another study of context-dependent memory indicated that students do better on tests when they study for a test in the room where the test will be given (Smith et al., 1978). If possible, try to do some studying for your tests in the classrooms where you will take the tests. Of course, you should study in a variety of other settings as well to

Context-dependent memories are dependent on the place where they were encoded and stored. This teenager may be remembering childhood friends and the games they played here years ago.

improve your recollection of the material after the tests are over.

In addition, when police and lawyers ask witnesses to describe a crime, they ask the witnesses to describe the scene as clearly as possible. By doing this, witnesses are better able to recall details that they might otherwise have forgotten. Police sometimes take witnesses to the scene of the crime in the hope that such visits will improve their memories of what they witnessed.

A DAY IN THE LIFE

At Hannah's party, Linda heard the song that brought back memories of being in the seventh grade. Seventh grade was when she heard the song (probably many times), encoded it, and stored it in her memory. Hearing the song again brought back context-dependent memories connected to that earlier period in her life. As she put it, "Hearing it almost makes me feel 13 again." That is one reason why some people like to hear familiar music. It brings back old and happy memories.

State-Dependent Memory   Not only do people tend to retrieve memories better when they are in the same place they were in when they first stored the memories, but people also retrieve memories better when they are in the same emotional state they were in when they first stored the memories. Memories that are retrieved because the mood in which they were originally encoded is recreated are called **state-dependent memories**. For example, feelings of happiness tend to bring back memories from other times when we were happy, feelings of sadness can trigger memories from other times when we were sad.

To demonstrate this phenomenon, Gordon Bower (1981) conducted experiments in which study participants were instructed, while in a hypnotic trance, to experience happy or sad moods. Then, while still in the trance, the participants tried to memorize a list of words. People who had studied the list while in a happy mood were better able to recall it when they were put into a happy state again. People who had studied the list while in a sad mood showed better recall when placed back in a sad mood. Bower's explanation of these results is that moods influence memories.

Not only is memory better when people are in the same moods as when the memories were acquired, it is also better when people are in the same states of consciousness. Drugs, for example, alter a person's state of consciousness and thus result in state-dependent memories. (See Chapter 5.) Things that happen to somebody under the influence of a drug may be remembered most accurately when the person is back under the influence of that drug (Atkinson et al., 1996).

On the Tip of the Tongue

At Hannah's party, when Linda said she used to think Ashley Austin wrote the song just for her, Todd knew it was not an Ashley Austin song. However, when he then went on to say who did write it, he could not think of the artist's name. "It's on the tip of my tongue," he said.

As in Todd's experience, memories can sometimes be difficult to retrieve. Either they are not very well organized, or they are incomplete. Trying to retrieve such memories can be highly frustrating. Sometimes we come so close to retrieving information that it seems as though the information is on the "tip of the tongue." Psychologists call this the **tip-of-the-tongue phenomenon**. It is sometimes also referred to as the "feeling-of-knowing experience." You feel you know something. In fact, you are sure you know it. However, you just cannot seem to verbalize it. It is on the tip of your tongue, but that is as far as it goes.

Because the files in our memory have labels, so to speak, that include both the sounds and the meanings of words, we often try to retrieve memories that are on the tip of our tongue by using either acoustic or semantic cues. Sometimes we try to summon up words that are similar in sound or meaning to a word that is on the tip of the tongue. We might make a remark like Todd's: "I can't think of her name. It starts with an M. Mary? Maria? Something like that."

3 Three Stages of Memory

We do not store in our memory everything we experience. The world provides us with a rich display of colors, sounds, tastes, and other sources of stimulation, but we can only take in and remember so much. How much of what our senses experience will we encode and remember? That depends on what happens to the information as it flows through each of the three stages of our memory. The three stages of memory are sensory memory, short-term memory (STM), and long-term memory (LTM).

Sensory Memory

Sensory memory is the first stage of memory. It consists of the immediate, initial recording of information that enters through our senses. If we were to see a row of letters or numbers flash briefly on a screen, the memory trace—or impression made on our senses by the row—would last for only a fraction of a second. A memory trace of a visual stimulus held in our sensory memory decays within a second. So if we want to remember it, we have to do something with the information very quickly.

Psychologists believe that all of our senses have sensory registers. The mental pictures we form of visual stimuli are called *icons*. Icons are held in a sensory register called **iconic memory**. Iconic memories are like snapshots. They are accurate, photographic memories. However, these iconic memories are extremely brief—just a fraction of a second. The ability to remember visual stimuli over long periods of time (what most of us think of as photographic memory) is called **eidetic imagery**.

About 5 percent of children have eidetic imagery. They can look at a photograph and remember it in remarkable detail several minutes later. It is as if they were still looking at it (Haber, 1980). This keen ability usually declines with age, however. By adolescence it is nearly gone.

Mental traces of sounds, called *echoes*, are held in a sensory register called **echoic memory**. While icons (memory traces of visual stimuli) are held only for a fraction of a second, echoes can last for several seconds. For this reason, acoustic codes are easier to remember than visual codes. That is, it is easier to remember a spoken list of letters than to try to remember a mental picture of the letters. Saying things to yourself or out loud makes them easier to remember.

Short-Term Memory

If you pay attention to iconic and echoic memories held ever so briefly in a sensory register, you can transfer that information into your **short-term memory**. The information will remain there after the sensory memory trace has faded away. Short-term memory is also called working memory.

A DAY IN THE LIFE

At Hannah's party, Dan tried to use his short-term memory to help himself remember the phone number of the girl he had met. After she gave him her number, he converted that echoic memory, which lingered in his sensory register for a few seconds, into his short-term memory. He hoped to keep it there until he could find a piece of paper and write it down.

We use our short-term memory a great deal of the time. Whenever you are thinking about something, it is in your short-term memory. When you are trying to solve a math problem, the elements of the problem are in your short-term, or working, memory. When you meet someone new, you put the person's name in your short-term memory, perhaps by using the name or by repeating it to yourself several times. Similarly, when a teacher assigns homework or changes the date on which a paper is due, you place that information in your short-term memory until you can write it down or store it in long-term memory.

When you are told a new phone number, you can keep it in short-term memory by repeating it over and over. Repeating the number will give you time to look for a pencil and paper. The more times you rehearse a piece of information, the more likely you are to remember it. If you rehearse information often enough, as actors do when they learn lines, you will probably remember it for a long time.

When you look up a number in the phone book and then walk across the room to reach the phone, you try to keep the number in your short-term memory long enough to dial it. You may repeat or rehearse the number on your way across the room

After people look up a phone number, they keep it in short-term memory until it has been dialed.

to improve your chances of keeping it in your short-term memory. If the number you dial is busy, you can dial it again a few minutes later if you have been able to keep it in your short-term memory. Otherwise, you will have to look it up again.

Information in short-term memory begins to fade rapidly after several seconds. If you want to remember it longer, you need to keep rehearsing the information or take other steps to prevent it from fading. People can sometimes keep visual images in short-term memory. But it is usually better to encode information as sounds so that you can rehearse or repeat the sounds.

 At the party, Dan probably would have remembered the phone number of the girl he had just met if he had been able to repeat it until he could write it down. Instead, unable to contain his excitement about meeting her, he stopped to share the good news with his friends. That was Dan's mistake. Talking to Linda and Todd prevented him from rehearsing the number enough to keep it in his short-term memory.

The Primacy and Recency Effects

When we try to remember a series of letters or numbers, our memories of the first and last items tend to be sharper than our memories of the middle items of the list. The tendency to recall the initial items in a series of items is called the **primacy effect**. (The root *prim-* means "first.") Perhaps we remember the first few items of a series better because, due to their placement early in the list, we have more time to rehearse them than we do for later items. Also, we may remember first items better because our minds are fresher when we first see or hear them.

The tendency to recall the last items in a series is called the **recency effect**. Since the last items in a series are likely to have been perceived and rehearsed most recently, they tend to be fresher in our memory and therefore probably more easily remembered than items in the middle of a series.

Chunking

When we try to keep something in our short-term memory by rehearsing it, it is usually better to organize the information into manageable units that are easy to remember. **Chunking** is the organization of items into familiar or manageable units. Return for a moment to **OTTFFSSENT**. If you tried to remember it letter by letter, there were 10 distinct pieces, or chunks, of information to retain in your short-term memory. When you tried to repeat the list as consisting of 10 meaningless

chunks, you probably had a difficult time. It is not easy to repeat 10 meaningless letters, let alone remember them.

If you tried to encode **OTTFFSSENT** as "other flowers sent" you reduced the number of chunks you needed to remember from 10 to 3. (Of course, you also needed to remember the variations in spelling.) Psychologist George Miller (1956) found that the average person can hold a list of seven items in short-term memory. This, conveniently, is the number of digits in local telephone numbers. Nearly everyone can remember a ZIP code, which is five numbers long. Some people can remember a list of nine items, but very few people can remember more than nine.

Businesses try to obtain telephone numbers with as many zeroes or repeated digits as possible because they are easier to remember. For example, 222-2000 is easier for customers to remember than 792-6873. Numbers with zeroes and repeated digits contain fewer chunks of information. Alternatively, a business may try to get a telephone number that can be spelled out as a word or phrase (because each digit on the telephone is associated with a set of letters). Thus, people need only remember the word or phrase, not the seven numbers. For instance, a clinic that helped people quit smoking was able to get a telephone number that spelled out the phrase NO SMOKE. This phrase worked well as a semantic code.

How do people remember long-distance telephone numbers? With area codes included, phone numbers are 10 digits long. Actually, most people do not try to remember the numbers as a series of 10 separate items. They try to remember the area code as a single, separate chunk of information. They become familiar with the area codes of surrounding areas and places where their long-distance friends and relatives live. When they know where someone lives, they sometimes already know and remember the area code.

If you had known that **OTTFFSSENT** stood for the first letters of the numbers 1 through 10, you could have reduced the number of chunks of information you needed to hold in short-term memory from 10 down to 1. That one chunk would have been a single rule: make a list of letters in which each letter is the first letter of the numbers 1 through 10. Of course, your ability to remember the 10 letters rested on the fact that you already knew the numbers 1 through 10 (and how to spell them). But most likely, you learned this information by heart when you were much younger.

Three Stages of Memory

Rehearsal

Sensory input

Sensory registers

Attention

Rehearsal

Storage

Retrieval

Sensory Memory

Short-Term Memory

Long-Term Memory

FIGURE 7.2 *Psychologists have identified three stages of memory. Outside stimuli first enter sensory memory. Here most stimuli are forgotten. A few pieces of information, however, enter short-term memory, where they* *remain if they are rehearsed. Information that is not rehearsed is forgotten. Information needed for future use is stored in long-term memory, where it can be retrieved when necessary.*

Interference Short-term memory is like a shelf that holds only so much. Once a shelf is full, you cannot put something on it without shoving something else off. Only a limited amount of information at a time can be retained in short-term memory. **Interference** occurs when new information appears in short-term memory and takes the place of what is already there.

A classic experiment by Lloyd and Margaret Peterson (1959) showed how new information can cause problems with what is stored in short-term memory. The Petersons asked college students to remember three-letter combinations, such as ZBT. Because most students can remember seven chunks of information, this task was fairly easy. Nearly 100 percent of the students could recall the three-letter sequences when asked to repeat them immediately. But then the Petersons asked the students to count backward from a number such as 142 by threes (142, 139, 136, 133, and so forth). After a certain amount of time passed, the students were then asked to stop counting backward and to report the letters they had been asked to remember. After only three seconds of this interference, the percentage of students who could recall their letters dropped by about half. After 18 seconds had elapsed, practically nobody could recall the letters. The numbers that entered the students' short-term memory while they were counting backward had displaced the letters in nearly all cases.

Interference was what happened to Dan at Hannah's party. His conversation with Linda and Todd, especially when Todd asked him the time, interfered with his short-term memory of the phone number. When Dan looked at his watch and told Todd it was 9:37, it was as if the new numbers bumped the old numbers off the shelf of his short-term memory.

Short-term memory is very useful, but it is only a temporary solution to the problem of remembering information. It allows us just enough time to find a way to store the information more permanently. Short-term memory is the bridge between sensory memory and long-term memory.

Long-Term Memory

Long-term memory is the third, and final, stage of memory of information. (Figure 7.2 shows all three stages of memory.) If you want to remember something more than just briefly, you have to take certain steps to store it in your long-term memory. Mechanical repetition (maintenance rehearsal) is one way of transferring information from short-term memory to long-term memory. Relating new information to information that you already know (elaborative rehearsal) is another.

New information is constantly being transferred into your long-term memory. Your long-term memory already contains more information than an encyclopedia or a computer's hard drive. It holds names, dates, places, the memory of how you teased the student in front of you in second grade, and the expression on your mother's face when you gave her the picture you drew of her in fourth grade. Your long-term memory contains more words, pictures, sounds, smells, tastes, and touches than you could count.

When Linda heard the song at the party, it brought back images and feelings stored in her long-term memory. The song reminded her of being back in the seventh grade. Had she been asked to reminisce about what she remembered, she probably could have talked for a long time about many of the feelings and experiences she had when she was 13, with all their rich sights, sounds, smells, and even tastes.

Capacity of Memory
Our long-term memory holds the equivalent of vast numbers of videos and films of our lifetime of experience. All of them are in color (as long as we can perceive color). They also come with stereo sound (as long as we can hear), with smells, tastes, and touches thrown in. This is a light and sound show that will never fit on any stage. But all of it is contained comfortably within our long-term memory. And there is room for more, much more. How much more? Psychologists have yet to discover a limit to how much can be stored in long-term memory.

It is true that there is no known limit to how much information a person can remember. There seems to be no restriction on the capacity of long-term memory.

Although there is apparently no limit to how much we can remember, we do not store all of our experiences permanently. Not everything that reaches our short-term memory is transferred to our long-term memory. Our memory is limited by the amount of attention we pay to things. We are more likely to remember the things that capture our attention. If we are distracted or uninvolved with what is occurring around us, we are not going to remember as much as we will if we are interested and paying attention. The memories we have stored in our long-term memory are the incidents and experiences that have had the greatest impact on us.

Memory as Reconstructive
Some psychologists once thought that nearly all the perceptions and ideas people had were stored permanently in their memory. Supporters of this view often pointed to the work of Wilder Penfield (1969), a brain surgeon. Many of Penfield's patients reported that they had experienced images that felt like memories when parts of their brain were stimulated electrically during surgery. From this information, some observers inferred that experiences become a physical part of the brain and that proper stimulation can cause people to remember them.

Today psychologists recognize that electrical stimulation of the brain does not bring about the accurate replay of memories. Memory expert Elizabeth Loftus, for example, notes that the memories stimulated by Penfield's instruments had little in the way of detail and were often factually incorrect (Loftus, 1983; Loftus & Loftus, 1980).

We now know that memories are not recorded and played back like videos or movies. Rather, they are reconstructed from the bits and pieces of our experience. When we reconstruct our memories, we tend to shape them according to the personal and individual ways in which we view the world. Thus, we tend to remember things in accordance with our beliefs and needs. That is, we put our own personal stamp on our memories. This is one of the reasons brothers and sisters can have differing memories of the same family events. Each sibling has interpreted the information differently.

Schemas
The mental representations that we form of the world by organizing bits of information into knowledge are called **schemas**. To understand better what is meant by a schema, take out the sheet of paper on which you wrote the names of the objects you saw in Figure 7.1. Without looking back at Figure 7.1, draw the items on your sheet of paper. Try to make your drawings as similar to the originals as you can. (But again, no peeking!)

Now turn to Figure 7.3 on page 166. Are your drawings more similar to those in Group 1 or those in Group 2? Because of the labels you had already written on the sheet of paper, your drawings probably look more like the ones in Group 1. The labels

Eyewitness Testimony

Eyewitnesses are often asked to describe what happened when they observed a crime. Sometimes they are asked to identify the person who committed the crime. As you can imagine, lawyers, judges, and police are very concerned about the accuracy of eyewitness testimony.

Eyewitnesses do not have mental video cameras. Instead, they reconstruct their memories from the bits and pieces of what they saw. The words and even the tone of voice used by the questioner can influence what witnesses remember. For example, if a questioner asks a witness to describe what he or she saw when a defendant "forced his way into" the store, the question has a slant, or schema, that invites the witness to assume that the store was entered by force. If a questioner asks a witness what he or she saw when a defendant "entered" the store, the question has a different slant. When a judge thinks the questioner is slanting a question too much, the judge will rule that the questioner is leading the witness and will ask that the questioner rephrase the question.

Sometimes police try to hypnotize witnesses to help them remember the details of a crime. Unfortunately, hypnosis can often distort memories. Eyewitnesses tend to accept suggestions made by the hypnotist. Also, hypnotized people sometimes report made-up stories as convincingly as if they were real memories (Loftus, 1994).

Witnesses tend to pay more attention to people's clothing than to their facial features and body shapes. In one experiment, psychologists showed people a videotape of a simulated crime and then asked the viewers to identify the criminal. Most witnesses incorrectly identified a certain man as the criminal because he wore the same T-shirt and eyeglasses as the real criminal. The actual

Even when witnesses believe they are telling the truth, their memories may be inaccurate

criminal wore something else when it was time to be identified and was picked out less often (Sanders, 1984). Eyewitnesses are even more likely to identify the wrong people when they are of a different racial or ethnic background than the witnesses' own (Egeth, 1993).

Eyewitnesses tend to be believed more often when they insist that they are sure of their testimony (Wells, 1993). However, it has yet to be proved whether insistence really equals truth.

Eyewitness testimony is more useful when certain things are kept in mind. First of all, eyewitness testimony is more accurate when different witnesses confirm each other's testimony (Leippe, 1985; Lindsay et al., 1986). It is also more reliable when witnesses are asked simply to describe in their own words what happened rather than being given suggestions by the questioner as to what happened (Sanders & Chiu, 1988).

Law enforcement and legal professionals can be more certain that witnesses are making correct identifications by first giving them a "blank" lineup, that is, one that does not contain the suspect. If the witnesses make no identifications in the blank lineup, they are more likely to identify the suspect in later lineups (Wells, 1993).

Even with these safeguards, however, eyewitness testimony can never be 100 percent accurate. But it is accurate enough that most people consider the risks acceptable. Eyewitness testimony is an important part of the criminal justice system. If witnesses could not testify in criminal trials, many criminals would go free.

Think About It

How do you think eyewitness testimony could be made more reliable?

served as schemas for the drawing—they helped you mentally represent the objects. When you drew the items, you did not draw them exactly from memory. Rather, you drew them to fit the schemas. Therefore, you did not recall them exactly. You reconstructed them from your ideas about what eyeglasses and hourglasses look like. People who have been told that the initial drawings are of a dumbbell and a table, on the other hand, reconstruct drawings more similar to those in Group 2 (Carmichael, Hogan, & Walter, 1932).

Elizabeth Loftus and J. C. Palmer (1974) conducted a classic experiment on the role of schemas in memory. They showed people a film of a car crash. Then they asked them to complete questionnaires about the film. One question asked for an estimate of how fast the cars were going when they collided. However, the phrasing of the question differed for different participants. Some participants were asked how fast the cars were going when they "hit" each other. Other participants were asked how fast the cars were going when they "smashed" into each other.

The participants who had been asked how fast the cars were going when they "hit" each other estimated an average speed of 34 miles per hour. Those who had seen the word "smashed," on the other hand, estimated an average speed of 41 miles per hour. In other words, which schema people used—"hit" or "smashed"—influenced how they mentally reconstructed the crash.

The participants were questioned again a week later. They were asked if they had seen any broken glass. There was no broken glass in the film; thus, a yes answer was incorrect. Of participants who had been told that the cars had hit each other, 14 percent incorrectly said yes, there was broken glass. However, 32 percent of those who had been told that the cars had smashed into each other—more than twice the percentage of the other group—incorrectly reported seeing broken glass. Schemas influence both the ways we perceive things and the ways our memories store what we perceive.

THINKING ABOUT PSYCHOLOGY

1. What are the three stages of memory?

2. How does information move through each of the three stages of memory?

3. **Critical Thinking**   Give an example of a situation in which a schema might distort a person's memory.

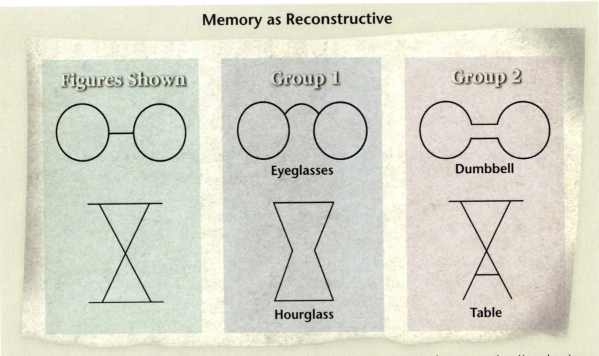

Memory as Reconstructive

FIGURE 7.3 *Are your drawings more like those in Group 1 or those in Group 2? Although you may not have recalled the drawings exactly, you reconstructed them* *from a schema, or mental representation. Your drawings were probably more like those in Group 1 because of the labels you copied from Figure 7.1.*

4
Forgetting and Memory Improvement

Forgetting is the flip side of memory. Forgetting may seem simple enough. If you do not think about something, you forget it, right? Not really. It is not that simple.

Forgetting can occur at any one of the three stages of memory—sensory, short-term, or long-term memory. Information encoded in sensory memory decays almost immediately unless you pay attention to it and transfer it into short-term memory. A memory trace in a visual sensory register decays in less than a second, and a sound recorded in echoic memory lasts no more than a few seconds.

Information in short-term memory does not last much longer. It will disappear after 10 or 12 seconds unless you find a way to transfer it into your long-term memory. As Dan found out at the party, information stored in short-term memory is lost when it is displaced, or crowded out, by new information.

Information in long-term memory also can be lost. Since long-term memory holds such vast amounts of material and because the material is represented in an abstract form, forgetting and other memory errors (such as recalling information incorrectly) occur. Sometimes new information becomes mixed with material you already know. Old learning can interfere with new learning. For example, if you study a new foreign language, your knowledge of a language you already know or are studying at the same time can interfere with your new learning. This is more likely to happen if the languages are somewhat similar.

Consider the example of French, Spanish, and Italian. All three are closely related to each other because they are all based on Latin, the language of the ancient Romans. French, Spanish, Italian, and Latin have similar roots and spellings. Anyone who has ever tried to learn two or more of these languages, especially at the same time, knows how easy it is to confuse them.

Basic Memory Tasks

Do you know what DAL, RIK, and KAX are? They are nonsense syllables, or meaningless sets of two

In long-term memory, old learning can interfere with new learning. If you try to learn more than one foreign language at a time, especially similar ones such as the Romance languages, you might become confused.

consonants with a vowel in the middle. Nonsense syllables provide psychologists with a way to measure three basic memory tasks: recognition, recall, and relearning.

The first researcher to use nonsense syllables to study memory and forgetting was German psychologist Hermann Ebbinghaus (1850–1909). Today his experiments are regarded as the first scientific study of forgetting, and psychologists continue to use nonsense syllables in their studies. Because nonsense syllables are meaningless, remembering them depends on acoustic coding (saying them out loud or in one's mind) and mechanical repetition (maintenance rehearsal). These tasks play a part in recognition, recall, and relearning.

Recognition One of the three basic memory tasks is **recognition**, which involves identifying objects or events that have been encountered before. It is the easiest of the memory tasks. That is why multiple-choice tests are often considered easier than other tests. In a multiple-choice test, you need only recognize the right answer. You do not have to come up with the answer on your own.

In some experiments on recognition, psychologists ask people to read a list of nonsense syllables. The participants then read a second list of nonsense syllables and are asked whether they recognize any syllables in the second list as having appeared in the first list. In this instance, forgetting is defined as failure to recognize a nonsense syllable that had been read before.

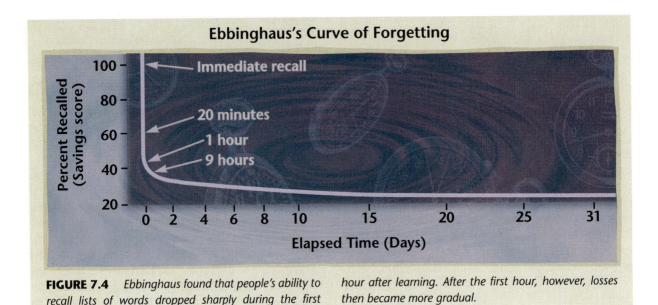

Ebbinghaus's Curve of Forgetting

Percent Recalled (Savings score)

100 — Immediate recall
80 —
60 — 20 minutes
  1 hour
40 — 9 hours
20 —

0 2 4 6 8 10   15   20   25   31

Elapsed Time (Days)

FIGURE 7.4 *Ebbinghaus found that people's ability to recall lists of words dropped sharply during the first hour after learning. After the first hour, however, losses then became more gradual.*

A classic study by Harry Bahrick and his colleagues (1975) examined recognition using a different technique. Bahrick took pictures from the yearbooks of high school graduates and mixed them in with four times as many photos of strangers. Recent graduates correctly picked out their former classmates 90 percent of the time. Graduates who had been out of school for 40 years recognized their former schoolmates less often, but not by too much—they recognized them 75 percent of the time. Keep in mind that only one photo in five was actually of a former schoolmate. Thus, if the graduates had been guessing, they would have picked out former schoolmates only 20 percent of the time. The participants recognized the photos of their former classmates far more easily than they recalled their classmates' names. The study showed that the ability of people to recognize familiar faces remains strong and lasting.

Recall The second memory task is recall. To **recall** something means to bring it back to mind. In recall, you do not simply recognize whether you have come across something before. Rather, you try to reconstruct it in your mind.

Hermann Ebbinghaus sometimes studied his own recall ability. For example, he would read a list of nonsense syllables aloud to himself while a metronome (an instrument that marks exact time) was ticking. He would then see how many nonsense syllables he could recall from memory. After reading through his list one time, Ebbinghaus could typically recall seven nonsense syllables. As you know,

this is the number of items most people can keep in short-term memory.

If a person memorizes a list of nonsense syllables or words and is asked to repeat the list immediately, there is generally no memory loss. But the ability to recall the list drops dramatically within an hour after learning it. In fact, about half of the nonsense syllables or words on the list are forgotten within the first hour. After that first hour, memory loss becomes more gradual. For instance, the amount of material a person remembers is cut in half again in about a month. The person continues to forget as time goes on, but the rate of forgetting slows down considerably. (See Figure 7.4.)

Psychologists also use paired associates to measure recall. Paired associates are lists of nonsense syllables, as shown in Figure 7.5. In this method, people read a list pair by pair. Later they are given the first member in each pair and are asked to recall the other one. That is, the people try to retrieve one syllable with the other serving as the cue.

Learning the vocabulary of a foreign language is something like learning paired associates. For example, a student studying Spanish might try to remember a Spanish word by pairing it with an English word that has a similar meaning. The student could most easily remember that the Spanish word *mano* means "hand" by creating a meaningful link between the words. She or he could do that by remembering that to do something *manually* is to do it by *hand*. Otherwise, the only way to remember the foreign word is by mechanical repetition (maintenance rehearsal).

Relearning The third basic memory task is **relearning**. Sometimes we do not remember things we once knew. For example, people who have been out of school for 25 years might not remember the algebraic formulas they learned when they were in high school. However, they could probably relearn them very quickly if someone showed them how to use them again. We can usually relearn fairly rapidly things we once knew but have forgotten.

Ebbinghaus (1885) used nonsense syllables to study relearning and other memory tasks. First, he would record how many repetitions a particular person needed to memorize a list of nonsense syllables. Then, after a few months had passed, Ebbinghaus would check on the person again. Typically, the person could not recall or even recognize the list of nonsense syllables that she or he had memorized. However, Ebbinghaus found that the person was able to relearn the list more quickly than she or he had learned it the first time.

Different Kinds of Forgetting

Much of the time, forgetting is due to interference or decay. As you have already learned, interference occurs when new information shoves aside or disrupts what has been placed in memory. **Decay**—the fading away of a memory—is similar to a burning candle. The candle burns down until it goes out. Both decay and interference are part of normal forgetting. They occur when memory traces fade from sensory or short-term memory. Memory loss also occurs in long-term memory when something that has been stored there cannot be retrieved. However, there are more extreme kinds of forgetting. These include repression and amnesia.

Repression

According to Sigmund Freud, the founder of psychoanalytic theory, we sometimes forget things on purpose without even knowing we are doing it. Some memories may be so painful and unpleasant that they make us feel anxiety, guilt, or shame. To protect ourselves from such disturbing memories, said Freud, we forget them by pushing them out of our consciousness. Freud called this kind of forgetting *repression*. For example, a person might forget to go to a dentist appointment because he or she expects the experience to be unpleasant. However, the extent to which repression occurs—and even *whether* repression occurs—is controversial in contemporary psychology.

FIGURE 7.5 *Psychologists often use paired associates, such as those shown here, to measure recall. The task is to recall the second syllable in the pair when given the first syllable as a cue.*

Amnesia

Psychoanalysts believe that repression is responsible for a rare but severe kind of forgetting called dissociative amnesia. Amnesia is severe memory loss caused by brain injury, shock, fatigue, illness, or repression. Dissociative amnesia is thought to be caused by psychological trauma (an extremely upsetting experience or series of experiences). Other kinds of amnesia include infantile amnesia, anterograde amnesia, and retrograde amnesia.

Infantile Amnesia Some people think that they can remember special events that took place in their infancy, but they cannot. After many years of hearing his patients talk about their childhoods, Freud found that they could not remember things that had happened to them before the age of three. This forgetting of early events is called **infantile amnesia**.

People who think that they can remember their birth have probably constructed the memory from other memories. For example, they may remember being told about their birth by a parent or another family member. Or they may remember the birth of a younger sibling and then use that information to create a memory of their own birth.

The reason people have infantile amnesia is not that the events happened a long time ago. People in their 70s and 80s have many precise memories of their life between the ages of 6 and 10, even though the events they remember occurred 60 or 70 years earlier. College freshmen, meanwhile, have difficulty remembering events that occurred before the age of 6, even though these events occurred only 13 or 14 years earlier (Wetzler & Sweeney, 1986). Thus, failure to recall events from infancy or early childhood is not simply a matter of gradually forgetting information over many years.

Freud explained infantile amnesia in terms of repression. He believed that young children often have aggressive and sexual feelings toward their parents but that they forget these feelings as they get older. However, repression may not be the reason, or at least the only reason, people forget events from their earliest years. The fact that people tend to forget boring and bland events from their early childhoods casts doubt on Freud's theory.

Many psychologists believe that infantile amnesia is primarily the result of biological and cognitive factors. For one thing, the part of the brain most involved in memory (the hippocampus) remains underdeveloped until people are about two years old, so infants may be biologically incapable of forming memories. For another, infants tend to live in the present. They are not all that interested in remembering events or weaving them into the stories that become memories (Hudson, 1993; Neisser, 1993). Nor can infants use language to encode events. All these factors help explain infantile amnesia.

· · · · · · · · · · · · · · · · · ·

 It is not true that you can remember important events from the first two years of life. Apparent infant memories are reconstructed and probably inaccurate. Many factors contribute to and help explain this memory loss during the first two years of life.

· · · · · · · · · · · · · · · · · ·

Note that infantile amnesia refers to memory of specific events (episodic memory). We certainly learn and remember many other things during infancy and early childhood using generic and procedural memory. For example, we learn who our parents are and learn to have strong feelings for them. We learn and remember the language spoken at home. We learn how to encourage other people to care for us. We learn how to get from one part of the home to another. We remember such information and skills quite well.

Anterograde Amnesia   Trauma to the brain caused by a blow to the head, electric shock, or brain surgery can cause memory loss of events that took place both before and after the trauma. Memory loss from trauma that prevents a person from forming new memories is called **anterograde amnesia**. Certain kinds of brain damage, such as damage to the hippocampus, have been linked to anterograde amnesia (Corkin et al., 1985; Squire et al., 1984).

Retrograde Amnesia   In **retrograde amnesia**, people forget the period leading up to a traumatic event. For example, many people who are injured in auto accidents do not remember that they were in the car before the accident. Similarly, athletes who are knocked unconscious during a game often have no memory of what happened before the play in which they were injured. Some cannot even remember starting the game.

In the most severe cases of retrograde amnesia, the person cannot remember a period of several *years* prior to the traumatic incident. One man with retrograde amnesia received a head injury in a motorcycle accident (Baddeley, 1982). When he woke up after the accident, he had no memory of anything that had happened since he was 11 years old. As a matter of fact, he thought that he was still 11. Over a period of months, he regained much of his memory, but he never did remember what happened just before the accident.

Improving Memory

Memory can be improved, and there are specific ways to go about it. As a result of studies of memory and forgetting, psychologists have been able to identify different strategies people can use to improve their memory. Some of the methods they recommend are discussed in the rest of this section. You may find them helpful.

Drill and Practice   One basic way to remember information is by going over it again and again, that is, by repetition, or drill and practice. Repetition is one fairly effective way to transfer information from sensory memory to short-term memory and from short-term memory to long-term memory.

CASE STUDIES
AND OTHER TRUE STORIES

The Case of H.M.

Studies of people who have undergone brain surgery to reduce epileptic seizures have helped provide a clearer picture of the relationship between amnesia and damage to certain parts of the brain. In the operations, which are now performed only rarely, the patients had one or both of their temporal lobes surgically removed to stop the epileptic seizures. One of the most famous of these cases was that of a man known by his initials: H.M.

H.M. suffered from severe epileptic seizures beginning at the age of 16. His seizures became worse as he reached adulthood. By the time he was 27, he could no longer function at work or live a normal life. At that point, he agreed to undergo surgery to reduce the rate and severity of the seizures. Surgery was performed to remove part of his hippocampus.

Following the operation, H.M.'s personality and mental functioning seemed to be normal. However, as time went on, it became increasingly difficult for him to process new information. His memory of events during the year leading up to the operation was weak, and his ability to learn and store new information was almost nonexistent. For example, two years after the surgery, H.M. thought he was still 27 years old. His memory was so poor that he forgot something as soon as he was distracted from rehearsing it.

When he moved with his family to a new home, he could not remember his new address or how to reach his new home. When his uncle died, he expressed appropriate grief at the loss. However, he then began asking about his uncle and wanting to know why he did not visit. Each time he was told that his uncle was dead, H.M. grieved as if he were hearing the information for the first time.

The formal testing that was done on H.M. showed that he could remember verbal information for as long as 15 minutes if he was allowed to rehearse it. However, it soon became clear that H.M.'s operation had caused him to lose the ability to transfer information from his short-term memory to his long-term memory. As soon as his short-term memory capacity reached its limit, or he was distracted from the rehearsing he had to do to keep new information in his short-term memory, he would forget the information. His capacity to remember nonverbal material was even more impaired. With or without distractions, he forgot even simple figures, such as circles, squares, and triangles.

Despite this severe memory loss, H.M. retained a limited capacity to learn, although the learning process was very slow and difficult. For example, H.M. had to exert great effort to learn to navigate a very short visual maze. What took most people only a couple of trials to master took H.M. 155 trials. Surprisingly, a week after he did so, H.M. remembered what he had painstakingly learned. Two years later he still retained some of what he had learned. At that time, it took him only 39 trials to relearn his way through the maze (116 fewer trials than he had needed to learn it originally).

H.M. showed learning ability in other situations as well. When he was asked to trace the drawing of a star by looking at its reflection in a mirror, he completed the task successfully. Not only did he draw the star as well as other people do, but his ability to retain what he had learned was also normal. For example, on the second and third days, he performed as well on the first trial of the day as he had on the last trial of the day before. That was evidence that there was no memory loss from day to day. Apparently, the operation he had did not significantly impair his ability to retain motor skills even though his ability to transfer information from short-term memory into long-term memory was impaired.

Think About It

What other tests can you think of for assessing the extent of H.M.'s memory loss?

JUMP START reprinted by permission of United Feature Syndicate, Inc.

Mechanical repetition may sound boring. Nevertheless, it was by repetition that we all learned the alphabet and how to count. We can memorize the spellings and meanings of new vocabulary words by repeating them over and over again. Math students can memorize formulas by writing and rewriting them. They can then use their time on tests to figure out how to use the formulas rather than spending time trying to remember what they are.

You can remember facts in social studies and other courses by pairing different pieces of information with each other and then drilling yourself on the connections between the items. This is what flash cards do. Use flash cards and write each word or phrase from the pair on a different side of a card. For example, write, "The U.S. president during the Persian Gulf War" on one side of the card and "George Bush" on the other. If you make a set of flash cards and then go over them again and again, drilling yourself on the information, eventually you will know it by heart.

You can use this method to learn new vocabulary words as well. Put the words on one side of the cards and the definitions on the other, and then test yourself both ways. You can read the definitions first and see if you know the words that go with them. Then you can read the words and see if you can remember their definitions. You might then want to go on to practice using the words in sentences. If you rehearse what you have learned by going through this procedure with the cards at regular intervals, including just before a test, you should do well on the test.

Douglas Herrmann (1991) has some advice about how to remember the names of people you meet. He recommends using the names right away. This will help you remember them later. If you are introduced to a new person, for example, say his or

her name aloud when you are introduced. Instead of saying, "Glad to meet you," say, "Glad to meet you, Sam." You can also use his or her name in a question, such as, "Where do you live, Sam?" As you continue to talk, use the person's name some more. You might find it even more helpful, says Herrmann, to write the name down, if you can, at the end of the conversation. If you need to remember the names of several different people you meet, you may want to write down a brief description of each person next to the listing of the person's name.

At Hannah's party, Dan concentrated so hard on remembering the telephone number of the girl he had met that he ended up forgetting her name as well as her number. He forgot her number because he did not write it down fast enough while it was still in his short-term memory. He then forgot her name, too, because he was so confident he would remember it that he did not bother to rehearse it sufficiently to keep it in his short-term memory.

Relate to Things You Already Know Relating new information to what you already know (elaborative rehearsal) is not as mechanical and repetitious as drill and practice (maintenance rehearsal). Relating new information to what you already know requires you to think more deeply about the new information (Willoughby et al., 1994). As a result, you may remember the new information better.

There are many situations in which elaborative rehearsal can be helpful. For example, if you were trying to remember the spelling of the word *retrieve*, you would probably do it by recalling the rule "*i* before *e* except after *c*." But then how would you remember the spelling of the word *weird*, which does not follow the rule? One way would be to use elaborative rehearsal on the word by recalling that it does not follow the "i before e" rule because it's a "weird" word.

Learning to expand our knowledge by relating new information to things we already know begins early. For instance, children learn that a lion is like a house cat, only bigger (and more dangerous).

Form Unusual Associations
It is sometimes easier to remember a piece of information if you can make an unusual or even humorous association between that piece of information and something else. That will make it stand out from ordinary things and thus help you recall it. For example, suppose that you wanted to memorize the symbol for the chemical element tin. You could remember that *Sn* is the symbol for tin by thinking of a *snake* in a *tin* can. The more unusual the association, the more effective it will probably be.

Sometimes people can enhance memory by forming a group of unusual associations. Suppose that you need to buy groceries but do not have time to write out a shopping list. How will you remember what items to buy? First, think of a group of related images, such as the parts of your body. Then picture each dish you plan to cook as hanging from a different body part. For example, you might envision lasagna hanging off your left shoulder. When you are at the supermarket, mentally go through the body parts you have designated and see what is connected to each one. When you get to the left shoulder and envision the lasagna, tick off the items you want to buy in order to make the lasagna: lasagna noodles, tomato paste, mozzarella cheese, and so forth.

Construct Links
Constructing links between items is another way elaborative rehearsal can help improve memory. You may find it easier to remember vocabulary words from a foreign language if you construct a meaningful link between each foreign word and its English equivalent (Atkinson, 1975). One way to create such a link is to find part of the foreign word and construct a sentence or phrase that includes that part of the word in English. For example, suppose that you are trying to remember that a *peso* (PAY-soh) is a unit of Mexican money. You might note that *peso* contains the letters *pe,* and then construct the following sentence: "*Pe*ople pay with money." Then, when you come across the word *peso,* you recognize the *pe* and retrieve the sentence that serves as the link. From that sentence, you can then reconstruct the meaning of the word *peso* as "a unit of money."

Use Mnemonic Devices
All these methods for improving memory are called *mnemonics* (nih-MAH-nicks). Mnemonic devices are systems for remembering information. Such devices usually combine chunks of information into a format, such as an acronym, phrase, or jingle. For example, as you learned in Chapter 4, many psychology students have used the acronym *Roy G. Biv* to remember the colors of the spectrum (*red, orange, yellow, green, blue, indigo,* and *violet*).

In biology, you can remember that dromedary camels have one hump, whereas Bactrian camels have two humps. How? Just turn the uppercase letters D and B on their sides and count the "humps" in each one. In geography, the acronym HOMES stands for the Great Lakes: *H*uron, *O*ntario, *M*ichigan, *E*rie, and *S*uperior.

Douglas Herrmann (1991) recommends using a mnemonic device to remember the name of someone new. He suggests that you make up a little rhyme that uses the name. For example, suppose the name of the girl Dan met at the party was Kate. When he stopped talking to her, he might have made up this rhyme: "I've met my next date; her name is Kate." However, he wanted to remember her telephone number as well as her name. Since poetry and telephone numbers do not mix very well, a poem would not have been much help in this case.

A DAY IN THE LIFE

TRUTH OR fiction
■ REVISITED ■

It is true that there are certain tricks you can use to improve your memory. Such tricks are called mnemonic devices. These devices provide people with systems for remembering information.

THINKING ABOUT PSYCHOLOGY

1. Explain how psychologists use nonsense syllables to study both memorization and forgetting.

2. Define *repression.*

3. What are the differences between infantile, anterograde, and retrograde amnesia?

4. **Critical Thinking** How can you test whether you really remember something that happened in early childhood?

SUMMARY
. . . .

There are three kinds, three processes, and three stages of memory.

I. Three Kinds of Memory

A. Episodic memory consists of events that people have experienced or witnessed. "Flashbulb memory" is a special kind of episodic memory.

B. Generic memory is memory of general knowledge.

C. Procedural memory consists of the skills, or procedures, that people have learned.

II. Three Processes of Memory

A. In encoding, the brain translates incoming information into visual, acoustic, or semantic codes.

B. Storage refers to the maintenance of information in memory over a longer period of time. Memory stores new information it receives in groups, or classes, according to common features.

C. Retrieval is the returning of stored information to consciousness.

III. Three Stages of Memory

A. Sensory memory consists of the immediate, initial recording of information that has entered through a person's senses. The person must pay attention to the information in some way or it rapidly disappears.

B. Short-term memory, or working memory, is the bridge between sensory memory and long-term memory. Holding information in short-term memory allows a person enough time to find a way to store it more permanently.

    1. Rehearsing, or repeating, information enables a person to keep it from fading from short-term memory. Organizing the information into chunks also makes it easier to remember.

    2. Short-term memory can retain only a limited amount of information at one time. A person forgets things in short-term memory when new information interferes with it or takes the place of what is already there.

C. Long-term memory contains the information a person wants to remember more than just briefly.

    1. Long-term memory contains a vast amount of information, and there seems to be no limit to the amount of information that can be stored.

    2. Memories are reconstructed from the bits and pieces of a person's experience. People use their own schemas, or ways of thinking about the world, to reconstruct their memories.

IV. Forgetting and Memory Improvement

A. Three basic memory tasks are recognition, recall, and relearning.

B. Normal forgetting occurs as a result of interference (new information shoves aside what has already been placed in memory) and decay (the fading away of a memory).

C. Repression and amnesia are more extreme kinds of forgetting.

    1. Repression, or pushing disturbing memories from the conscious mind, may be a way to protect against feelings of anxiety, guilt, or shame.

    2. Because of infantile amnesia, people cannot remember events from their infancy and early childhood.

    3. Anterograde amnesia prevents a person from forming new memories following a trauma. In retrograde amnesia, people forget the period leading up to the traumatic injury.

D. Psychologists recommend various techniques, such as the use of mnemonic devices, to help improve memory.

TERM & CONCEPT
REVIEW

1. What is memory?
2. How is a flashbulb memory like a photograph? Give two reasons why flashbulb memories are so distinct.
3. Describe the three ways in which a person encodes information.
4. What are maintenance rehearsal and elaborative rehearsal?
5. What might a person do to retrieve a context-dependent memory? What might a person do to retrieve a state-dependent memory?
6. What are icons? Where are they held?
7. What are the primacy and recency effects?
8. Define *recognition, recall,* and *relearning.*
9. What is amnesia? What are its causes?
10. What are mnemonics? Give an example.

CRITICAL
THINKING

1. Name the type of memory involved in each of the following situations: (a) You can recite the capitals of every U.S. state. (b) You and your friends laugh every time you think about the fun you had last summer. (c) You know how to program a VCR to tape your favorite TV show.
2. Why might you and another family member have different memories of the same vacation?
3. Which type of forgetting is usually to blame when people cannot find their car keys?
4. If you were asked to identify all the students in a photo of your third-grade class, which memory task would be involved? Why might the task be easier if you were supplied with a list of their names?
5. Give several reasons why you may be unable to recall your fifth birthday.
6. Make up three mnemonic devices that you could use to remember information discussed in this chapter.

APPLYING SKILLS
IN PSYCHOLOGY

1. **Research in Psychology** Ask your parents or older adults to describe where they were and what they were doing when they heard the news that President John F. Kennedy had been shot (November 22, 1963). Ask them to describe details surrounding the event, such as what they were doing or who else was with them. What kind of memory is involved here? Why are people able to recall so vividly something that happened more than 30 years ago?

2. **Using Your Observation Skills** Interview a person who must memorize a great deal of information in order to perform a task or job well. For example, you might interview a classmate who acts in school plays or a person who works for the U.S. Postal Service. Ask the person what techniques he or she uses to memorize material. Compare these techniques with information you read in this chapter. Write up your findings in a "helpful tips" column for the school newspaper.

3. **COOPERATIVE LEARNING** **Research in Psychology** Working in small groups, conduct an experiment on the primacy and recency effects. Make up a list of 15 items, such as the names of 15 animals. Have everyone in the group show a copy of the list to friends and family members, and then see how many items the friends and family members can remember and write down. Pool your findings and, as a group, calculate what percentage of participants were able to recall the first item, the second item, and so on. Make a line graph of the results. Does the graph demonstrate the primacy and recency effects?

4. **Putting Psychology to Use** Identify a fact or concept that you need to know for one of your classes. Then write an acronym, a phrase, or a jingle that will help you remember it. Make a poster showing your mnemonic device and display it in the classroom.

8

THINKING AND LANGUAGE

Objectives

1 Explain the role that symbols, concepts, and prototypes play as units of thought.

2 Describe several methods people use to solve problems, and identify obstacles to problem solving.

3 Differentiate between deductive reasoning and inductive reasoning.

4 Analyze the strategies used in decision making.

5 Identify the basic elements of language, and summarize the stages of language development.

A DAY IN THE LIFE

"I can*not* figure out this trig problem!" Dan sighed. He, Marc, Linda, and Hannah were studying. "This is so frustrating!"

"I know what you mean," replied Hannah. "I'm stumped on this crossword puzzle assignment for World History. Here's one of the clues: 'The _____ Republic.' Five letters, C _ _ C H. What could that be?"

After a brief pause, Linda blurted out, "The *Czech* Republic!"

"Oh, of course. The CZ was throwing me off," stated Hannah.

Dan smiled and said, "Very good, Linda. Now does someone want to help with my trig problem?"

"I have problems of my own to solve," said Marc. "Like whether to take Japanese or creative writing next semester. Hannah, how hard will Japanese be?"

"How should I know?" she asked.

"Because you speak Korean, right? Korea and Japan are pretty near each other, so I figured the languages would be similar."

"As far as I know, Korean and Japanese are completely different."

"Oh. That's no help, then. Well, either way, I have to figure out how to tell Mr. Hochberg I'm not taking computer science, which is what *he* suggested I take." Mr. Hochberg was the school's guidance counselor.

"Mr. Hochberg will understand. When I talked to him last year about what courses to take, he was very open to my ideas," said Linda.

"Oh!" Dan exclaimed. "I just figured out the trig problem. Weird. I had stopped thinking about it."

"I think we should all stop thinking about studying for a moment," Linda stated. "Tonight is my night to cook dinner for my family. What am I going to make?"

"How about making macaroni and cheese?" Dan suggested.

"Had it last night," said Linda.

"Tacos?" put in Hannah.

"My sister doesn't eat red meat," Linda replied.

"Chicken stew?" Marc proposed.

"I don't have all the ingredients."

"So go to the store and get them!" the other three said together.

"I guess I could do that," Linda reflected. "That sounds like a pretty good idea, come to think of it."

• • •

This chapter is about thinking. When you are awake, you are probably thinking nearly all the time. But the type of thinking you are doing may vary from moment to moment. You may be solving a problem, such as Dan's math problem, Hannah's crossword puzzle, or Linda's dinner dilemma. Or you may be reasoning—using information to draw a conclusion. Or perhaps you are making a decision, such as Marc's decision about which course to take. Problem solving, reasoning, and decision making are three types of thinking explored in this chapter. And because thinking often relies on language, this chapter also deals with language.

Key Terms

- thinking
- symbol
- concept
- prototype
- algorithm
- heuristic
- difference reduction
- means-end analysis
- analogy
- insight
- incubation effect
- mental set
- functional fixedness
- convergent thinking
- divergent thinking
- reasoning
- deductive reasoning
- premise
- inductive reasoning
- confirmation bias
- representativeness
- availability
- anchoring
- framing effect
- language
- phoneme
- morpheme
- syntax
- semantics
- overextension
- overregularization
- language acquisition device

Read the following statements about psychology. Do you think they are true or false? You will learn whether each statement is true or false as you read the chapter.

- The most reliable way of solving a problem correctly is not always the best way of solving it.
- If you do not see the answer to a problem right away, you will probably not be able to solve it.
- Scientists can never prove for certain that their theories are true.
- Most people easily change their opinions when presented with convincing arguments.
- Once a child learns the correct form of a word, he or she will never use the incorrect form.

1
What Is Thinking?

Thinking is the mental activity that is involved in the understanding, processing, and communicating of information. But how is all this accomplished? Thinking is made possible through the use of symbols, concepts, and prototypes. These are all units of thought.

Symbols

When we think, we use symbols to represent the things about which we are thinking. A **symbol** is an object or an act that stands for something else. As you are probably aware, symbols are a part of our daily lives. Your school mascot and the American flag are both examples of symbols. Different types of symbols are found in mathematics. Plus and minus

signs, for example, are both symbols: the plus sign signifies "add," and the minus sign signifies "subtract." Dan probably was all too familiar with various mathematics symbols from his trigonometry class.

Letters and words are also symbols. After all, a word actually stands for something else—it is not the thing itself. For example, the word *plate* is not itself a plate—it only refers to an object that is called a plate in English.

Even your mental images are a type of symbol. If you picture a dog in your mind, that image stands

Shown here is the Greek letter psi—the symbol of the American Psychological Association.

for a dog, but of course it is not itself a dog. If it were not for symbols, we would be unable to think about things that were not present.

Concepts

What do dogs, horses, and elephants have in common? You may say that they are all animals, or perhaps you may say that they are all mammals. When we think, we tend to mentally group together objects, events, or ideas that have similar characteristics, as dogs, horses, and elephants do. Such a grouping is called a **concept**. "Animal" and "mammal" are both examples of concepts.

Much thinking involves categorizing new items and manipulating the relationships among them. Think of a new kind of animal, for instance—just make one up. What makes it an animal? You have used the concept "animal" to create a new item that fits into the "animal" category. Now imagine your new animal in a tree eating a piece of fruit. You are thinking about relationships among concepts (your animal, the tree, and the fruit).

People organize concepts in hierarchies, series of levels that go from broad to narrow. As we saw above, dogs, horses, and elephants can be grouped both as animals and as mammals. The "animal" concept is higher up in the hierarchy than is the "mammal" concept because it is broader, or contains more elements. Sparrows, goldfish, and spiders are all animals, but they are not mammals.

People learn concepts through experience. Simple concepts such as "ball" and "vegetable" are taught by means of examples. We point to a baseball or a basketball and say, "Ball" or "This is a ball" to a child. We point to broccoli or carrots and say, "Eat your vegetables." Communication of the meaning of abstract concepts such as fairness, beauty, and goodness may require detailed explanations, a variety of personal experiences, and many examples. Even then, people may still disagree about what is fair, beautiful, or good.

Prototypes

Often when we think about a concept, we have an image in our minds of a particular example of that concept, even though a concept is a category and contains many different examples. For instance, picture a shoe in your mind. What does the shoe you pictured look like? Does it have shoelaces, straps, or neither? Does it have a heel, or is it flat-soled?

The shoe you imagined was a **prototype**—an example of a concept that best exemplifies that concept. A prototype does not have to be an actual, experienced example, such as a particular shoe you have seen. Instead, a prototype can be more like an average of all experienced examples. You may never have seen a shoe that looks exactly like your shoe prototype, but your prototype probably contains elements of many different shoes you have seen.

Which do you think is a better example of a shoe: a loafer or a slipper? You probably said a loafer. Why? Because a loafer is probably closer to your "shoe" prototype than is a slipper. Most people think of shoes as items that are worn outside or in public, and slippers usually are worn only around the house. But a slipper is a type of shoe.

THINKING ABOUT PSYCHOLOGY

1. Define *thinking*.
2. List and describe three units of thought.
3. **Critical Thinking** Is a concept a type of a symbol? Why or why not?

Even though there are many, many different types of shoes, you probably picture only one type when you hear the word shoe. What you picture is your prototype of a shoe.

2
Problem Solving

People solve many different kinds of problems. Some, such as Dan's trigonometry problem, are in

math and science. In such cases, people often use formulas and scientific facts to solve the problems. For example, they may need to know the formula for the area of a circle or how many protons oxygen contains.

Other problems concern fitting things into a busy schedule or paying for what we need. Such problems are best solved by budgeting. Still other problems are social problems, such as how Marc should approach Mr. Hochberg about his choice of an elective for next semester. How should Marc tell Mr. Hochberg that he really wants to take Japanese or creative writing rather than computer science?

These problems may seem very different. But they all present a set of facts. They all have a goal.

And they all require people to manipulate the facts until they arrive at the goal.

Figure 8.1 on the next page shows some more problems. Try to solve them now. If you have difficulty with any of them, don't worry—you will learn the answers as you read.

Algorithms and Heuristics

In many cases, people do not go straight from a problem to its solution in one giant leap. Rather, they move toward the solution in a series of steps. Ideally, each step taken moves the problem solver closer to the solution. But how do people know what steps to take? If they do not know the solution to begin with, how can they even know where to start?

Through experience, people know that different types of problems must be approached in different ways. By simply identifying the type of problem it is, people have an idea of which method to use— which steps to take—in solving the problem.

Algorithms Some types of problems are best approached with the use of an algorithm. An **algorithm** is a specific procedure that, when used

Six Problems to Solve

A Naomi, Marquita, and Kim are planning to go to a party, and they want to prepare for the party together. The party is across the street from Naomi's home, so the three meet there an hour before the party. When, at the end of the hour, they are ready to go to the party, they discover that it has started to rain heavily. None of them wants to get wet because they are all wearing nice clothing. Unfortunately, they only have one umbrella for the three of them, and the umbrella is big enough to protect only two people from the rain. How can all three of them get to the party without becoming drenched?

B Imagine that you are a doctor. One of your patients has a stomach tumor that must be destroyed if the patient is to live. Certain rays will destroy the tumor if they are intense enough. To reach the tumor, however, the rays need to pass through the healthy tissue that surrounds it, and at the intensity needed to destroy the tumor, the rays will also destroy the healthy tissue. How can you use the rays to destroy the tumor without damaging the healthy tissue? (Adapted from Duncker, 1945)

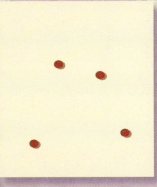

C Copy this dot formation on a sheet of tracing paper. Then connect all four dots with two straight lines without lifting your pencil from the paper.

D Imagine that you are in a room with a candle, a box of matches, and some thumbtacks. Your task is to use these objects to attach the candle to the wall. How do you do it? (Adapted from Duncker, 1945)

E Imagine that you are in a room in which two strings are hanging from the ceiling. Your task is to tie the two strings together, but they are so far apart that you cannot reach both of them at the same time. The only other object in the room is a pair of safety scissors. How can you tie the strings together? (Adapted from Maier, 1931)

F An airplane crashes on the border of Mexico and the United States. Where do you bury the survivors?

FIGURE 8.1 *Try solving these problems. You will learn the answers as you read the section.*

properly and in the right circumstances, will always lead to the solution of a problem.

Formulas are examples of algorithms. If you know the radius (r) of a circle and you want to find the area of that circle, you can apply the formula πr^2 to get the correct answer. As long as you know the formula and how to use it correctly, you need know nothing else to solve the problem.

Many algorithms are more complex and time-consuming than simple formulas, however. One such complex algorithm is called a systematic search. In a systematic search, each possible solution to a problem is tried and tested according to a certain set of rules.

People who do crossword puzzles regularly know of several heuristics that often help lead to solutions quickly. For example, if a word ends in G, the previous two letters are likely to be I and N.

For example, suppose that you, like Hannah, are working on a crossword puzzle. You are trying to fill in a word for which you have all but one letter—say, C L _ F F. Using a systematic search, you would try putting every letter of the alphabet, starting with A, in that blank middle space until you found the letter that formed a word that fit the clue. In other words, first you would try C L A F F, then you would try C L B F F, then C L C F F, and so on, until you came to the right letter, which would probably be an I (C L I F F). It might take some time, but as long as you had all the other letters in the word correct and as long as you were able to recognize the word once you found it, this method would be guaranteed to work.

Heuristics   While algorithms are guaranteed to work, they are not always practical. Suppose, for example, that you were missing not one, but two letters of your crossword puzzle word—C _ _ F F. In order to have success with the systematic search, not only would you have to try every letter of the alphabet in each of the two spaces, but you would have to fill in one of them with a placeholder while you tried letter after letter in the other space.

In other words, first you would have to fill the first blank space with an A, then you would have to run through all 26 letters in the second blank space. And when that did not work, you would have to try

a B in the first space, and then run through all the letters *again* in the second space. By the time you arrived at C L I F F, you would have already run through 294 other possible solutions.

Needless to say, although this algorithm would eventually lead to success, it would not be a very efficient way to do a crossword puzzle, nor would it be very interesting or rewarding. This is why, for many types of problems, people use heuristics rather than algorithms. **Heuristics** are rules of thumb that often, but not always, help us find the solution to a problem. They are shortcuts.

In the first crossword puzzle problem, where only one letter is missing, you probably would use the following heuristic: in a five-letter word in which four of the letters are consonants, the fifth letter is probably a vowel. Thus, instead of trying *eight* possible combinations before you arrived at the letter I, you would try only *two*: A and E (the only vowels that precede I). In the second crossword puzzle problem, in which two letters are missing, a heuristic might involve deciding that certain letters of the alphabet (B, C, D, F, and so on) would be unlikely to follow the first letter C, and thus you would not even try them as possibilities. Rather, you might focus on the letters that you know are likely to follow C.

Heuristics are faster than algorithms, but they are not as reliable. For example, we might forget that if C is the first letter of a word, the letter L (a consonant rather than a vowel) might be the second. And in some circumstances, we might miss some more unusual words. This is probably what happened to Hannah with **C _ _ C H**. She did not try a **Z** in the first blank space because the letter **Z** usually does not directly follow the letter **C**. As Hannah put it, "The **CZ** was throwing me off." Thus, she was unable to come up with the word **C Z E C H**.

■ ■ ■ ■ ■ ■ ■ ■ ■ ■ ■ ■ ■ ■ ■ ■ ■ ■

TRUTH
OR
fiction
■ R E V I S I T E D ■

It is true that the most reliable way of solving a problem correctly is not always the best way of solving it. Algorithms are guaranteed to lead to the solution eventually, but they can be time-consuming. Heuristics are less reliable, but when they do work, they are more efficient than algorithms.

■ ■ ■ ■ ■ ■ ■ ■ ■ ■ ■ ■ ■ ■ ■ ■ ■ ■

Problem-Solving Methods

Algorithms and heuristics are general approaches to problem solving. There are also specific methods of problem solving. Systematic searching, which we have already discussed, is one of these methods. Others include trial and error, difference reduction, means-end analysis, working backward, and use of analogy.

Trial and Error   Sometimes we have little choice but to resort to trial and error in solving a problem. We know what our goal is, but we have absolutely no idea how to reach it, and all we can do is try different things and see what happens with each one until we arrive at our goal more or less by chance. Trial and error is somewhat similar to systematic searching, except that it is more haphazard and less reliable. In trial and error, we often do not keep track of which possibilities we have already tried.

If you have ever tried to work on a complicated maze puzzle, you probably found that the only thing you could do was just to pick one possible route and see where it took you. When you hit a dead end, you came back and tried something else. In other words, you used trial and error—trying one thing until it is proved to be an error.

Difference Reduction   In a method called **difference reduction**, we identify our goal, where

we are in relation to it, and the direction we must go to move closer to it. In other words, we want to *reduce the difference* between our present situation (problem unsolved) and our desired situation (problem solved).

Suppose you are standing blindfolded on the side of a hill. Your goal is to get to the top of the hill, but because you cannot see, you do not know which way to go. So what do you do? You take a step. If you feel yourself moving downward, then you know that you are going the wrong way and that you must change direction. But if you feel a pull in your legs that means you are moving upward, you know you are getting closer to the top of the hill. You have identified which direction to go in to move closer to your goal.

The difference-reduction method is a heuristic, however, and thus is not always reliable. Sometimes we may think we have reached our goal when we have not. Suppose that the hillside levels off for a bit and then continues upward to the top, for instance. You may think you have reached the top when you arrive at this level patch, and you may stop there. You do not know that there is more hill ahead.

Furthermore, sometimes we have to take what seems to be a step away from our goal in order to

This woman will probably use trial and error to figure out which key is the correct one.

achieve that goal. For example, to straighten up your desk, you might have to take everything out of the drawers first, to organize the contents—even though this would seem to be a step in the wrong direction (since at first things will become messier rather than neater). Similarly, what seems to be moving us closer to a goal may actually be moving us farther away.

Problem A in Figure 8.1 highlights some of the pitfalls of the difference-reduction method. In order for Naomi, Marquita, and Kim to get to the party dry, two of them (say, Marquita and Kim) must cross the street to the party first, leaving the third one (Naomi) back at Naomi's home. But then either Marquita or Kim must *leave* the party and go back with the umbrella for Naomi. In other words, they must temporarily increase, rather than decrease, the difference between the goal (all three of them at the party) and their present situation (two of them at the party but one of them not). One of the two currently at the party must temporarily leave the party.

When people set out to cook or bake something, they use means-end analysis to break the task down into individual steps.

Means-End Analysis Another heuristic problem-solving technique is called means-end analysis.

A DAY IN THE LIFE

In **means-end analysis**, we know that certain things we can do (means) will have certain results (ends). If the stew Linda is making for dinner seems bland, adding pepper will probably help. Adding water probably will not.

As with the difference-reduction method, means-end analysis aims to reduce the difference between where we are and where we want to be. But means-end analysis goes beyond difference reduction in its awareness that a particular action will have a particular effect. Whereas the difference-reduction user asks, "What direction must I move in to get from here to there?", the means-end-analysis user asks, "What can I do to get there?"

Means-end-analysis users often break a problem down into parts and then try to solve each part individually, recognizing that solving each of the parts will contribute to solving the entire problem. We do this all the time without realizing it.

Once Linda had decided to make chicken stew for dinner, for example, she first had to identify the ingredients she needed. Then she had to figure out how to obtain these ingredients—a trip to the grocery store seemed necessary. Next, she had to figure out which store to go to, how to get there, how to find what she needed once she arrived at the store, and how to pay for what she bought. Finally, she had to figure out how to put the ingredients together in the way that would yield the taste and flavor she was trying to achieve—in other words, she had to do the actual cooking. Each of these steps was one means toward the end of serving chicken stew for dinner.

Working Backward Related to means-end analysis is the technique known as working backward. As in means-end analysis, working backward involves breaking a problem down into parts and then dealing with each part individually. In working backward, however, the problem solver starts by examining the final goal, then works back from the final goal to the present position to determine the best course of action.

This method is particularly useful when we know what we want to accomplish but are not sure how best to begin. Working backward helps ensure that we start off on the right path and avoid having to retrace our steps if we discover that the path we have chosen does not lead where we want to be.

THINKING AND LANGUAGE **183**

Suppose that you need to cross a stream that has no bridge and is too wide to leap across. There is, however, a series of stepping stones that you can use to cross the stream. If you start by selecting one stone near your side of the bank, then select another stone to step to from there, and so on, you may find yourself ending up at a stone that is too far away from the opposite bank (your destination) for it to be useful.

A better approach might be to work backward from the opposite bank. Start off by identifying the stone that is nearest the opposite bank. Then find the stone that is nearest to that one, and so on, working back to your own side of the stream. This way you can avoid getting stuck in the middle of the stream with no place to go except back.

Analogies   People also solve some problems by analogy. An **analogy** is a similarity between two or more items, events, or situations. Linda, for example, saw an analogy between her situation last year, when she went to talk to Mr. Hochberg about what courses to take, and Marc's situation this year.

When people have successfully solved one problem, they may try to use the same approach in solving another problem if it is similar enough to the first one. For example, if you observe that studying early and getting a good night's rest helps you do well on a test for one class, you may try that technique again the next time you have a test, even if the next test is in a different class. Many analogies, however, are much less obvious, and the trick is to find one that works.

Problem B in Figure 8.1 (the ray-tumor problem) is not an easy one, and people typically have difficulty solving it. However, when they are provided with a story to use as an analogy, they often can solve the problem (Gick & Holyoak, 1980). Such a story might be as follows:

A dangerous group of terrorists barricaded themselves in a building in the middle of a town. Government officials considered it necessary to capture the terrorists, even though the operation would require a large force of agents to storm the building. Furthermore, the terrorists had planted mines on all of the streets that led to the building. If the entire force passed over any one of the streets, the mines would explode, killing not only the agents but also the people who lived in the surrounding area. Thus the officials decided to divide the force into smaller units and send each unit on

a different street leading to the building. Timing was arranged so that all of the units arrived at the building at the same time, and the terrorists were captured.

(If you still cannot figure out the solution to the problem in Figure 8.1B, refer to Figure 8.2.)

A famous example of problem solving by analogy involves the ancient Greek scientist Archimedes (ar-kuh-mee-DEEZ). As legend has it, Archimedes had been trying to find a way of measuring the volume of the king's crown, but the crown's irregular shape made it difficult, and Archimedes could not figure out what to do.

One day, as Archimedes climbed into his bath, some water overflowed from the filled tub onto the floor. Suddenly, Archimedes saw an analogy between what had just happened and the crown problem he was working on, and the solution to the problem came to him. He could measure the volume of the crown by placing it in water and then collecting and measuring the amount of water that overflowed. Archimedes had realized that the volume of water displaced by an object equals the

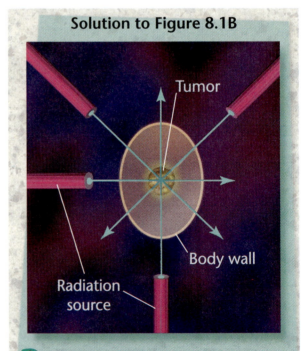

Solution to Figure 8.1B

Tumor

Body wall

Radiation source

B **FIGURE 8.2** *Weak rays sent from several points meet at the tumor site. Radiation will be intense at this site, thereby destroying the tumor. But because the rays are weak individually, healthy tissue surrounding the tumor will not be damaged.*

At first, the chimpanzee cannot reach the bananas hanging from the ceiling. After some time has passed, however, the chimpanzee experiences a "flash of insight." The chimp suddenly stacks the boxes, climbs up on them, and reaches the fruit. What does it mean to say that a problem has been solved by insight?

volume of the object—whether the object is a human body or a king's crown. He was said to be so happy that he shouted, "Eureka," which means, "I have found it."

Insight and Incubation

Not only was Archimedes' experience an example of problem solving by analogy, it was also an example of **insight**, or sudden understanding. Usually we solve a problem by breaking it down into steps. Sometimes, however, we seem to arrive at the solution to a problem all of a sudden, as Archimedes did. Often we have little conscious awareness of how we found the solution—it just seems to come to us on its own.

Have you ever pondered a problem for a while, then had the solution come to you suddenly? Did it seem to come in a flash? This is what seemed to

happen to Dan, with his trig problem—suddenly he just knew how to solve it. When this happens, we have experienced insight. Often we express our delight and surprise by exclaiming "Aha!" or something similar. As a result, experiences of insight are also known as "Aha!" experiences.

Psychologist Wolfgang Köhler pioneered studies into this type of experience. During World War I, Köhler was marooned on one of the Canary Islands, off the northwest coast of Africa. While stranded,

Köhler worked with a colony of chimpanzees that the Prussian Academy of Science kept there. His research with these animals demonstrated to him that much learning is achieved by insight.

In one of Köhler's experiments, a chimpanzee was placed in a room in which some bananas were hanging from the ceiling. The chimp clearly wanted the bananas and tried to reach them by jumping. But the bananas were too high up to be reached this way. The chimp walked around, looked at the bananas, walked around some more, noticed some boxes that were also in the room, and sat down for a while. The chimp seemed to be doing nothing related to the problem of reaching the bananas. Then, all of a sudden, the chimp got up, stacked the boxes, and climbed up on them to reach the bananas. Apparently, the chimp had suddenly seen the situation in a new way. That is, the chimp had had a flash of insight.

Köhler's findings suggested that animals and people set up problems in their minds and play with them until they are solved. Once the parts of the problem fit together in the right way, the solution seems to come in a flash.

Sometimes, as with Dan and his trig problem and also as with Köhler's chimps and the bananas, we need to get away from a problem for a while before a solution comes to us. When we arrive at the solution to a problem when we have not even been consciously working on the problem, we have experienced the **incubation effect**. An incubator warms

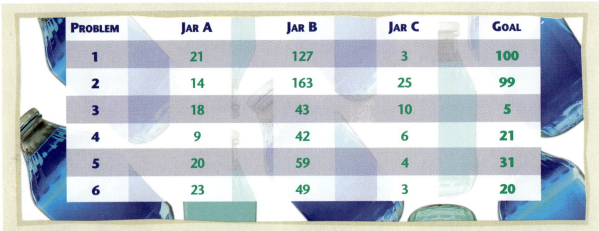

PROBLEM	JAR A	JAR B	JAR C	GOAL
1	21	127	3	100
2	14	163	25	99
3	18	43	10	5
4	9	42	6	21
5	20	59	4	31
6	23	49	3	20

FIGURE 8.3 *For each of the six problems, how can you use some combination of the amounts of water (shown here in ounces) in Jars A, B, and C—and a tap—to obtain the precise number of ounces of water indicated as the goal in the column at the far right? The jars have no markings on them.*

Source: Adapted from *Rigidity of Behavior* (p. 109) by Abraham S. Luchins and Edith H. Luchins, 1959, Eugene: University of Oregon Press.

eggs so that they will hatch. Incubation in problem solving means standing back from a problem for a period of time while some unconscious process within us continues to work on it. Later, the answer may occur to us in a flash—it will have "hatched" on its own.

Because of the incubation effect, psychologists sometimes recommend that people take a break from work on a difficult problem. After taking such a break, they may come back to the problem refreshed, and a new point of view or approach may have incubated (Azar, 1995).

TRUTH OR fiction ·REVISITED·

It is not true that if you do not see the answer to a problem right away, you will probably not be able to solve it. In fact, it is common for people to have greater success in solving a problem if they go away from it for a little while. This is called the incubation effect.

Obstacles to Problem Solving

Sometimes we have trouble finding the solution to a problem simply because the problem is difficult or perhaps because we have little experience in solving that type of problem. At other times, particular obstacles get in our way of solving a problem. Two of these obstacles are known as mental set and functional fixedness.

Mental Set   As we know from our discussion on problem solving by analogy, people often try to solve new problems in ways that worked for similar problems. The tendency to respond to a new problem with an approach that was successfully used with similar problems is called **mental set**. While mental set can sometimes help us solve a problem, it can also sometimes get in the way.

Take a moment to work out each of the six problems in Figure 8.3. You have three jars—A, B, and C. They each hold the amount of water you see in the figure. For example, for Problem 1, Jar A holds 21 ounces of water, Jar B holds 127 ounces of water, and Jar C holds 3 ounces. Your goal for Problem 1 is to get 100 ounces. You can fill or empty any of the three jars as many times as you wish.

How did you solve the six problems? You probably discovered that one formula—B – A – 2C—works for all six problems. However, if you are like most people, you did not realize that the final problem, Problem 6, can be solved much more simply, using the formula A – C. Because of your work on problems 1 through 5, you had a mental set on the B – A – 2C formula. In this case, your mental set allowed you to solve the problem, but it prevented you from using the most efficient method. In other cases, mental set may block a person from solving a problem altogether.

For example, were you able to solve Problem C in Figure 8.1? If not, mental set may have been responsible. From past experience, you probably perceived the four dots as the corners of a quadrilateral, and thus it may not have occurred to you that the lines could go beyond the dots. (See Figure 8.4.)

Functional Fixedness Another obstacle to problem solving is called functional fixedness. **Functional fixedness** is the tendency to think of an object as being useful only for the function that the object is usually used for.

Problems D and E in Figure 8.1 are challenging because of functional fixedness. In Problem D, the solution is to tack the box of matches to the wall and then use it to support the candle. (See Figure 8.5.) But people have trouble arriving at this solution because they think of the box as a container and not as something they can actually use. In other words, they are fixed on the function of the box as a container because that is usually what it is.

Similarly, in Problem E in Figure 8.1, the solution is to tie the safety scissors to one of the strings and then to set the string swinging so that it will reach you as you hold the other string. (See Figure 8.6). But again, most people are fixed on the function of the scissors as something to cut with, not as a weight to make the string swing.

Problem Solving and Creativity

Functional fixedness can often be overcome by creativity—the ability to come up with new or unusual ways of solving a problem. Thinking of the box of matches as a support platform rather than as a container, for example, is creative; this is not how matchboxes are usually used.

Creativity requires divergent thinking rather than convergent thinking (Guilford, 1967). With **convergent thinking**, thought is limited to available facts. One tries to narrow one's thinking to find the single best solution. With **divergent thinking**, however, one associates more freely to the various elements of a problem. One follows "leads" that run in various directions; perhaps one of them will lead to the solution unexpectedly. Linda may have used divergent thinking when she helped Hannah figure out the correct answer in the crossword puzzle. And Marc almost certainly will find divergent thinking useful if he decides to take creative writing next semester.

Successful problem solving may require both divergent and convergent thinking. At first, divergent thinking produces many possible solutions. Convergent thinking is then used to select the most probable solutions and to reject the others.

Solutions to Figures 8.1C, D, and E

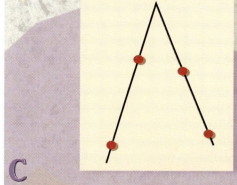

FIGURE 8.4 *The lines connecting the four dots must extend beyond the dots.*

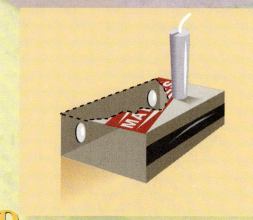

FIGURE 8.5 *To solve this problem, you have to overcome functional fixedness and think of the box as a platform, not a container.*

FIGURE 8.6 *To solve this problem, tie the safety scissors to one of the strings and set the string swinging. Then catch the swinging string.*

The ABCDEs of Problem Solving

What is the best way to solve a problem? Some psychologists advise following these steps:

A: *A*ssess the problem.

B: *B*rainstorm approaches to the problem.

C: *C*hoose the approach that seems most likely to work.

D: *D*o it—try the most likely approach.

E: *E*valuate the results.

Assessing the Problem Assessing a problem means examining its parts and making sure that you understand it. Often the first assessment we make about a problem is the *type* of problem it is.

Did you figure out the answer to the question in Figure 8.1F? The answer, of course, is that you don't bury the survivors anywhere at all—the survivors are still alive. But many listeners get this problem wrong, suggesting answers such as, "In their hometowns." (Try it on your friends!)

The reason that most people get this problem wrong when they first hear it is that they have assessed it incorrectly. They assess it to be a *political* problem; they hear the word *border* and assume that the problem has to do with territorial concerns. People who give the correct answer, however, have assessed it to be a trick question. They look for the trick (the word *survivor*) and find it.

Brainstorming Approaches Brainstorming is the free, spontaneous production of possible approaches or solutions to a problem. Often brainstorming is done in a group; people are free to call

out ideas as they think of them. When Dan, Hannah, and Marc were trying to help Linda figure out what to make for dinner, they brainstormed. That is, they called out ideas as the ideas occurred to them.

Brainstorming can also be done individually. It helps to have a sheet of paper handy so that you can jot down your ideas as they occur to you.

With brainstorming, anything goes. The more ideas, the better. The purpose of brainstorming is to encourage creativity; brainstorming stimulates a large number of ideas, even wild ideas. The more ideas that are suggested, the more likely one of them is to help solve the problem. With Linda, it took a few tries, but eventually she found a dinner idea that seemed possible.

Choosing an Approach Once a number of possible approaches have been proposed through brainstorming, the problem solver must choose which approach to take and which course of action to follow. The choice is made on the basis of which approach seems most likely to work.

Doing the Problem Once the approach has been chosen, the next step is to actually do the problem—to try out the approach.

Evaluating the Results The final step in problem solving is evaluating the results. Has the goal been achieved? Does the end point make sense? Has the problem been solved? If not, we must figure out what went wrong. Did we assess the problem incorrectly? Did we choose the wrong approach or carry it out incorrectly? We may need to go back and repeat any or all of the earlier steps of the problem-solving process.

A group of people may find a "brainstorming session" to be a productive way of accomplishing a task.

THINKING ABOUT PSYCHOLOGY

1. What is the primary advantage of using heuristics rather than algorithms in solving problems? What is the primary disadvantage?

2. In what way do convergent thinking and divergent thinking differ?

3. **Critical Thinking** Select one of the specific problem-solving methods discussed in the section. Describe a problem you have solved or seen others solve using that method.

3
Reasoning

A DAY IN THE LIFE

When Marc was trying to figure out how hard it would be to learn Japanese, he assumed that Japanese and Korean were similar. Thus, he also assumed that Hannah, who spoke Korean, would be able to tell him how hard Japanese would be. Whether Marc knew it or not, he had used reasoning in his thought process. **Reasoning** is the use of information to reach conclusions. There are two main types of reasoning: deductive reasoning and inductive reasoning.

Deductive Reasoning

In **deductive reasoning**, the conclusion is true if the premises are true. A **premise** is an idea or statement that provides the basic information that allows us to draw conclusions. Here is an example of deductive reasoning:

1. South Korea is in Asia.
2. The city of Seoul is in South Korea.
3. Therefore, Seoul is in Asia.

The first two statements of this example are the premises, while the third statement is the conclusion. The conclusion is said to be *deduced* from the premises; if South Korea is in Asia and Seoul is in South Korea, then Seoul must be in Asia. (See Figure 8.7A.)

In deductive reasoning, the conclusion is always true when the premises are true. However, if the premises are incorrect, then the conclusion may be incorrect as well. Marc's reasoning about Japanese and Korean went as follows:

1. Countries that are near each other have similar languages.
2. Japan and Korea are near each other.
3. Therefore, Japan and Korea have similar languages.

Logically, Marc's reasoning was sound. He made a statement about a category (countries that are near each other), then he assigned something (Japan and Korea) to the category. He was right to assume that whatever was true for the category as a whole would be true for members of the category. (See Figure 8.7B.) But his first premise—that countries that are near each other have similar languages—was faulty. Countries that are near each other do not necessarily have similar languages. Thus, Marc's conclusion was incorrect. Japan and Korea are near each other, but their languages are not very similar.

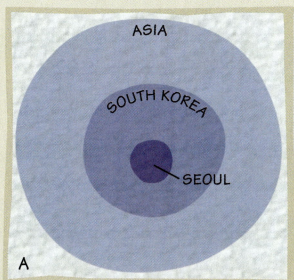
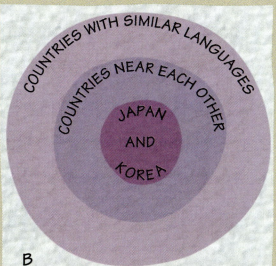

ASIA
SOUTH KOREA
SEOUL
A

COUNTRIES WITH SIMILAR LANGUAGES
COUNTRIES NEAR EACH OTHER
JAPAN AND KOREA
B

FIGURE 8.7 *Venn diagrams such as these use circles to show simple relationships among sets. Overlapping regions show the intersection of sets. (A) This diagram illustrates the Seoul–South Korea–Asia deductive reasoning. If South Korea is in Asia, and Seoul is in South Korea, then Seoul is in Asia. (B) In deductive reasoning, if the premises are incorrect, the conclusion may be incorrect as well. Marc's first premise, that countries near each other have similar languages, was faulty, so his conclusion that Japanese and Korean are similar was incorrect.*

Inductive Reasoning

In deductive reasoning, we usually start out with a general statement or principle and reason down to specifics that fit that statement or principle. In **inductive reasoning**, on the other hand, we reason from individual cases or particular facts to reach a general conclusion.

In inductive reasoning, the conclusion is sometimes wrong, even when the premises are correct. Marc's assumption that countries that are near each other have similar languages was probably based on inductive reasoning. His thinking may have been:

1. Spain and Portugal are near each other, and they have similar languages.
2. Sweden, Denmark, and Norway are near each other, and they all have similar languages.
3. Therefore, countries that are near each other have similar languages.

But just because *some* countries that are near each other have similar languages, this does not mean that *all* countries that are near each other do. (See Figure 8.8.) In effect, Marc's statement that countries that are near each other have similar languages was really only a hypothesis, or an educated guess, rather than a conclusion. And Hannah proved the hypothesis wrong—Japan and Korea are near each other yet do not have similar languages.

Assume for a moment that Marc's hypothesis was correct—that countries that are near each other have similar languages. How could Marc have proved that hypothesis? Only with great difficulty—by comparing the languages of every single country in the world and showing that *all* countries that are near each other have similar languages. However, it was quite easy to prove that Marc's hypothesis was *wrong*—by providing only one example of countries that are near each other and have different languages.

It is often impossible to prove an assumption reached by inductive reasoning to be true. We can only prove it false. But people often fail to realize this. As a result, they seek to prove, or confirm, their hypotheses rather than disprove them. This tendency is called **confirmation bias**.

Even though inductive reasoning does not allow us to be certain that our assumptions are correct, we use inductive reasoning all the time. And until we prove a hypothesis false, we assume it to be true. For example, if we have read two books by a particular author and enjoyed both books, we conclude that a third book by the same author also will be enjoyable. And until we find a book by that author that we do not enjoy, we will probably go on reading that author's books. Inductive conclusions do not follow logically from premises, as deductive

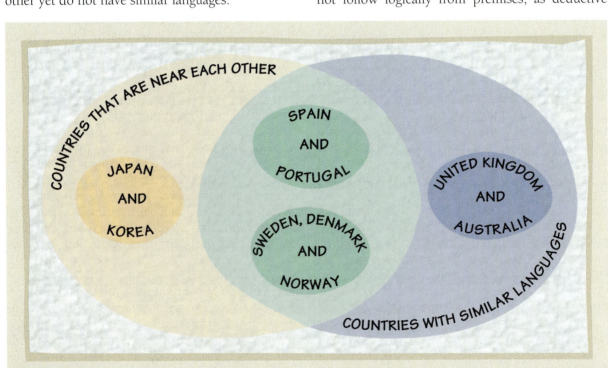

FIGURE 8.8 *In inductive reasoning, the conclusion can be wrong even when the premises are correct.* *Some, but not all, countries that are near each other have similar languages.*

conclusions do. Yet they are accurate often enough that we can rely on them in our daily lives.

Most sciences, including psychology, rely on inductive reasoning. Scientists gather specific pieces of information, and then they come up with general theories that explain the information. However, no matter how much information scientists have to support a particular theory, they can never know for sure if the theory is true for all times and all situations. There might still be some information not yet collected that would prove the theory false.

It is true that scientists can never prove for certain that their theories are true. They can only gather evidence that supports their theories. On the other hand, it *is* possible to prove a theory false.

THINKING ABOUT PSYCHOLOGY

1. What is reasoning?

2. Define *premise*. What role do premises play in deductive reasoning?

3. **Critical Thinking** Give an example of a conclusion that you have reached using inductive reasoning. What evidence would prove your conclusion to be incorrect?

4

Decision Making and Judgment

Life is filled with decisions. Most of these decisions are fairly minor in the general scheme of things. Should we take an umbrella with us when we go out or leave it at home? Should we walk or take the bus? Which route should we take to school or work?

Other decisions, of course, are relatively major. Should we go to college or get a job right after high school? What career do we want to pursue? Which political candidates should we vote for? People use a variety of methods to make decisions. Some methods are more effective than others.

Weighing the Pluses and Minuses

Making decisions means choosing among goals or courses of action to reach goals. When we are making careful decisions, we weigh the pluses and minuses of each possible course of action. We think about the importance of our goals and our abilities to overcome the obstacles in our paths. To make good decisions, we often need to gather more information about our goals. We also need to learn more about our abilities to attain our goals.

The use of a balance sheet—a listing of various reasons for or against making a particular choice—can help us make sure that we have considered the information available to us. A balance sheet might be a list of the pluses and the minuses of taking an action. For example, if you are trying to decide whether to participate in a certain extracurricular activity, you might make a list of the advantages (such as gaining experience and having fun) and the disadvantages (such as losing time that might be needed for studying) of doing so.

A balance sheet can also be useful when a person is trying to decide between two or more alternatives. Listing all the alternatives and the reasons for each one may help the person visualize which of the alternatives is the better course of action. The balance sheet may also help indicate areas where more information is needed.

When Marc was trying to decide whether to take creative writing or Japanese, it might have helped him to put together a balance sheet listing the potential benefits of each class. After he had completed the list, he could have based his decision on which option appeared to have greater rewards. Or he might have discovered that there was still some information he needed to collect before he could make an informed decision. (See Figure 8.9 on page 192.)

Shortcuts in Decision Making and Judgment

Weighing the pluses and minuses may be the best thing to do whenever we want to be sure to make the right decision. But weighing the pluses and minuses can be time-consuming and is not always practical. Furthermore, in order to weigh the pluses and minuses, we need to know what they are, and often we have to make decisions based on somewhat limited information. In such cases, we use heuristics. That is, we take shortcuts.

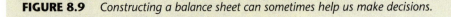

Reasons for Taking Japanese	Reasons for Taking Creative Writing
Learn about different cultures.	Gain greater skills in writing.
Prepare for travel to foreign countries.	Writing skills may be more practical than Japanese.
Impressive for college and job applications.	Also impressive for college and job applications.
Fear of not being able to come up with creative ideas to write about in creative writing.	Foreign languages have always been difficult for me, and Japanese might be even more difficult.

Information Still Needed to Finalize Decision

• Does my schedule allow for the time when each class is offered?

• If I take Japanese now, can I continue to study it later?

• Exactly what types of writing will I be able to learn in creative writing?

FIGURE 8.9 *Constructing a balance sheet can sometimes help us make decisions.*

The Representativeness Heuristic Imagine that you are taking a true-false quiz. The quiz has six items. Which of the following answer sequences (**T** stands for true and **F** stands for false) do you think is most likely to appear on the quiz?

T T T T T T

F F F T T T

T F F T F T

You probably said the third one. Why? For one thing, you know that six "trues" in a row are unlikely (assuming your teacher is not trying to play games with you). Second, you probably assume that your teacher wrote a quiz that had a random mix of true and false answers. The sequence **T F F T F T** looks random. The **T T T T T T** and **F F F T T T** sequences do not. Most people would thus select the **T F F T F T** sequence because it looks *representative*. It seems to represent a random sequence.

Based on the **representativeness** heuristic, people make decisions about a sample according to the population that the sample appears to represent. In all the true-false quizzes and tests you have ever taken—in other words, in the entire population of true-false tests you have seen—more answer sequences have looked like the third one (on your sample quiz) than like either of the other two. Thus the third answer sequence best *represents* the type of sequence you have come to expect, based on all of your previous experiences with true-false tests.

The representativeness heuristic can be misleading, however. Assuming that your teacher really has written a quiz with a random mix of true and false answers—with a 50-50 chance of either a true or a false answer on any given quiz item—each of the three sequences listed above is *equally likely*. For each item, the chance that the answer will be true is

Even if you flip "heads" 20 times in a row, the chance that you will flip it the next time is still 50 percent.

one in two, just as the chance that the answer will be false is also one in two. The likelihood of attaining *any* specific sequence—whether **T T T T T** or **T F F T F T**, say—is the same (1 in 64, in fact).

It is true that the likelihood of attaining a random-looking answer sequence is greater than that of attaining a nonrandom-looking sequence. But that is because there are a greater number of random-looking sequences than of nonrandom-looking sequences—out of 64 possible sequences, most of them look random. For example, **T F F T F T**, **F T F T T F**, and **T T F T F F** all look random. But the likelihood of attaining any *one* sequence—whether it looks random or not—is the same as that of attaining any other sequence.

So what does this have to do with decision making? Well, imagine taking that quiz again. Suppose that you know the answers to the first five items and that they are all true. But the sixth item has you stumped, and you have to guess at the answer. Do you guess true, which would mean six "trues" in a row? Or do you guess false because you figure that it is unlikely that six "trues" in a row would occur? The temptation may be strong to go with the "false." But if the answers were assigned randomly, it really doesn't matter. Regardless of the answers to the previous five items, the answer to the final item has a 50-50 chance of being true and a 50-50 chance of being false. You might as well flip a coin.

The Availability Heuristic

People also make decisions on the basis of information that is available to them in their immediate consciousness. This is called the **availability** heuristic.

For example, what percentage of the students at your school would you estimate are involved in extracurricular activities? Unless you go to a very small school, your answer to this question will probably reflect your personal knowledge of students who do, and do not, participate in extracurricular activities. Knowledge of these individuals is available to you. Rather than going out of your way to find out whether all the students you do *not* know participate in activities, you base your answer on what you already know.

Thus, if most of the students you know participate in extracurricular activities, you may think that most of the students in the school as a whole do too. But this is not necessarily true—the sample of students you know may not be representative of all students in the school.

Events that are more recent or better publicized than others also tend to be more available. For

The publicity plane crashes receive may lead people to overestimate how often such crashes occur compared to the number of flights made safely.

example, whenever a plane crashes, the event is very well publicized. Car accidents, however, cause far more deaths than airplane crashes in the United States. But because of the publicity given to the airplane crashes, people are more likely to fear flying than they are to fear driving. They overestimate the risk of flying and underestimate the risk of driving.

The media also tend to focus on acts of violence, such as murder. As a result, people tend to overestimate the amount of violence in the United States (Silver et al., 1994).

The Anchoring Heuristic

Another shortcut that people sometimes take in making decisions is called the **anchoring** heuristic. When using the anchoring heuristic, people make decisions based on certain ideas or standards they hold, ideas or standards that serve as an anchor for them. For example, people often decide to go along with the things they learn early in life. Early learning serves as an anchor in thinking.

If you have grown up in a family in which everyone else votes in elections, you probably expect to vote, too. That expectation is an anchor in your life. Beliefs about politics, religion, and way of life are common anchors. When something happens that makes people question the beliefs they have grown up with, they may change their beliefs a bit. But most people change only reluctantly.

When people form judgments or make estimates, they begin with an initial view, called a presumption. The initial view serves as the anchor. As they receive additional information, they make adjustments. But such adjustments are often difficult for people to make, and sometimes people are unwilling to make them.

The Framing Effect

Suppose that once Linda arrived at the store, she "chickened out" of making chicken stew from scratch and decided instead to buy canned stew. She noticed that there were two brands to choose from. One brand called the stew "zesty" and "hearty." The other brand simply contained the name of the stew. As far as Linda could tell, the two brands were identical in every other respect. Which one do you think Linda decided to buy? Probably the zesty, hearty one.

If so, this decision was based on the framing effect. The **framing effect** refers to the way in which wording affects decision making. Advertisers try to use the framing effect to get people to decide to buy a particular product. They are very careful in choosing what words to put on a product. Foods with fewer calories, for example, are advertised as being "light," not "thin." A "thin" food does not sound as appetizing as a "light" food.

Advertisers are not the only people who use the framing effect to their advantage. Political groups also are very aware of the framing effect. Most political groups, for example, pick names that sound positive—they know that people are more likely to support a cause that they feel good about rather than a cause that merely opposes something. This is why groups are usually "pro" something rather than "anti" something.

Experienced parents, too, know all about the framing effect, particularly when dealing with very young children. They know that they have to choose their words very carefully in order to encourage the children to give the desired responses. Thus, when parents want the child to take a bath, they might say, "Mr. Duck is waiting for you in the tub!" and not "You'll be cleaner after your bath."

Overconfidence

People tend to have a great deal of confidence in their decisions, whether the decisions are right or wrong (Gigerenzer et al., 1991; Lundeberg et al., 1994). For instance, many students refuse to change their opinions about how well they did on a test they have just taken even when other students point out that their answers were wrong. And have you ever known anyone who kept unrealistic confidence in a baseball team, even though the team was far behind in the standings?

There are a number of reasons why people tend to be overconfident, even when they are wrong:

- People are often unaware of how flimsy their evidence is.
- People tend to pay attention to examples that confirm their opinions and to ignore examples that do not.
- People tend to bring about things they believe in. If students believe that they are capable of

The way information is presented, or framed—such as on product labels—can affect our decisions.

getting an A on next week's test, for example, they are more likely to study for the test and prepare for it in ways that might just help get them that A.

- Even when people are told that they tend to be overconfident in their decisions, they usually do not make use of this information (Gigerenzer et al., 1991).

TRUTH OR fiction REVISITED

It is not true that most people easily change their opinions when presented with convincing arguments. To the contrary, people tend to stick to their opinions even when they are presented with evidence that suggests that they might be wrong.

THINKING ABOUT PSYCHOLOGY

1. What is the main drawback of basing decisions on the availability heuristic?
2. Give two reasons why people tend to be overconfident about their decisions.
3. **Critical Thinking**   How has the anchoring heuristic affected one or more decisions that you have made?

5
Language

Language is the communication of ideas through symbols that are arranged according to rules of grammar. Language makes it possible for people to share knowledge. People can use language to describe what they ate for breakfast or what they thought of the movie they just saw. They can use language to set down the learning of past generations and store it for people who will live hundreds or even thousands of years in the future. Language also permits people to use the eyes and ears of other people to learn more than they ever could from their own individual experiences.

The Basic Elements of Language

Languages contain three basic elements: phonemes (sounds), morphemes (basic units of meaning), and syntax (grammar). Combinations of these units create the words, phrases, and sentences that people use to communicate ideas.

Phonemes   The basic sounds of a language are called **phonemes**. (Languages that do not consist of sounds, such as American Sign Language, do not have phonemes.) There are 26 letters in the English alphabet, but there are many more than 26 phonemes. Phonemes include consonants, such as the *d* and *g* in *dog*. They also include vowels, such as the *o* in *dog* and the *o* in *no*. Even though *no* and *dog* each contain an *o*, the *o* sound is different in each word, and thus the two *o* sounds are two different phonemes. Other phonemes in the English language cannot be represented by a single letter—for example, the sound *sh*.

English contains some phonemes and phoneme distinctions that are not found in other languages. French has no equivalent for the English *th*, for example, which is why native French speakers often use a *z* sound to approximate the *th* in an English word: "Zee book is on zee table." Chinese does not distinguish between a *p* sound and a *b* sound; Japanese does not distinguish between *r* and *l*.

Morphemes   The units of meaning in a language are called **morphemes**. Morphemes are made up of phonemes. Some morphemes, such as *car* and *bike,* are words in and of themselves. Other morphemes are prefixes (for example *pre,* which means "before"), while still others are suffixes (for example, *-ness* and *-ence*). Many words use combinations of morphemes. English uses morphemes such as *z* and *s* to make objects plural. Adding the *z* morpheme to *car* makes the word plural; adding the *s* morpheme to *bike* makes it plural.

In English, the past tense of regular verbs is formed by adding the *ed* morpheme to the end of the present-tense verb. The past tenses of *walk* and *talk,* for example, are *walked* and *talked.* Verbs such as *to be, to run,* and *to think* do not follow this rule, however. Thus they are considered irregular verbs.

Syntax   The way in which words are arranged to make phrases and sentences is **syntax**. The rules for word order are the grammar of a language. English syntax usually follows the pattern of subject, verb, and object of the verb. For example:

Linda (subject)→cooked (verb)→dinner (object).

Many other languages have a different word order. Whereas in English the verb usually goes in the middle of the sentence, between the subject and the object, in German the verb often is placed at the end of a sentence. In the vast majority of languages, however, the subject precedes the object. And in no languages does the object appear first in a sentence (Slobin, 1983).

Semantics

Compare these two sentences:

It will be a long time before dinner is served.

The members of Linda's family long for a tasty dinner.

In the first sentence, *long* is an adjective. The sentence means that there is still much time before dinner. In the second sentence, on the other hand, *long* is a part of a verb—"to long for." The word *long* has more than one meaning.

The study of meaning is called **semantics**. Semantics involves the relationship between language and the things depicted in the language. Words that sound alike, such as *right* and *write,* can have different meanings, depending on how they

are used. So can words that are spelled alike, as we saw with *long.*

How a sentence is structured also affects meaning. Compare these two sentences:

Linda's chicken is ready to eat.

Linda's family is ready to eat.

The first sentence probably means that Linda has prepared the chicken and that it is ready to be eaten. The second sentence looks similar, but it most likely means that Linda's family is hungry—that the members of her family want to eat as soon as possible.

Sentences have a surface structure and a deep structure. The surface structure is what you see, the actual words of a sentence. Both "ready to eat" sentences have the same surface structure. The deep structure of a sentence is its deeper meaning, the message the speaker is trying to communicate. The "ready to eat" sentences differ in meaning.

Some sentences, such as "Make me a sandwich," have an unclear surface structure—you cannot be certain of the deep structure based on the surface structure. If you ask someone with a sense of humor to make you a sandwich, don't be surprised if the reply is, "Poof! You're a sandwich!"

The Stages of Language Development

Children develop language in a sequence of steps. The sequence is the same for nearly all children. It begins with crying, cooing, and babbling, then moves into the learning of words, and finally, the learning of grammar.

Crying, Cooing, and Babbling   Crying, cooing, and babbling are not considered true language because they do not use symbols with specific meanings. Nevertheless, crying is a highly effective form of verbal expression for newborn infants—it usually gets the attention of caregivers.

During their second month, babies begin to coo. Coos are vowel-like and resemble "oohs" and "ahs." Cooing seems to express feelings of pleasure. Tired, hungry babies do not coo. Different cries and coos can communicate discomfort, hunger, or enjoyment of being rocked, held, or fed.

At about six months of age, infants begin to babble. Unlike crying and cooing, babbling has the sounds of speech. Babies often babble consonant and vowel combinations, as in *ba, ga,* even the

This infant may coo to indicate satisfaction at being fed. Cooing is a form of verbal expression that precedes the development of actual language.

EXPLORING
DIVERSITY

Language and Culture

Nearly all humans are born with the capacity to learn language. But the languages used in different cultures vary widely.

List 10 basic colors. Would it surprise you to know that the Dani, a people who live in New Guinea, do not have words for all the colors you named? In fact, they have only two words for colors: *mili,* used to describe dark, cold shades, and *mola* for bright, warm shades.

You might think that any word in one language can be translated into another language, but this is not true. Many languages contain words that have no direct equivalent in other languages. The Arabic language contains more than 250 words for camel. The Hanunoo people of the Philippines have some 90 words for rice. And the Inuit, who live near the Arctic, have many terms describing different types and conditions of snow.

According to the Whorfian hypothesis (named after its originator, Benjamin Whorf), differences such as these indicate that language determines how people perceive the world. In other words, someone who has many words for snow actually perceives snow differently than someone who only has one word for snow.

Most research evidence, however, does not support the Whorfian hypothesis. The Inuit may have many different words for snow, but that does not mean that they perceive snow differently from other people. Rather, because snow is a basic part of their daily existence, the Inuit may have more of a need and more of a use for several snow terms than do people who have less exposure to snow.

Vocabulary is only one of the ways in which languages differ. Languages also differ from each other in the phonemes, or sounds, they use. The Spanish rolled *r,* for example, does not appear in English and is difficult for some native English speakers to pronounce. Similarly, German contains some vowel sounds (such as *ä, ö,* and *ü*) that are not generally used in English. Zun/wasi, a language of southern Africa, contains four different clicking sounds. And in some languages, even the pitch or tone of the speaker's voice can change the meaning of a word.

Think About It

Think of an item that Americans use many different words to identify. What does the large number of words indicate about the importance of the item in American culture?

Calvin and Hobbes   by Bill Watterson

highly valued *mama* and *dada*. At first, however, combinations with actual meaning, such as *mama* and *dada*, are purely coincidental.

Crying, cooing, and babbling are basic human abilities. Children from cultures whose languages sound different all babble similar sounds, including sounds they have not heard. In fact, children babble phonemes found in languages spoken around the world. By 9 or 10 months of age, however, children pick out and repeat the phonemes used by the people around them. Other phonemes start to drop away.

Babies understand much of what other people are saying before they can talk. They demonstrate understanding with their actions and gestures.

Words, Words, Words

After babbling comes the learning of words—the start of true language. Most children acquire new words slowly at first. After they speak their first word, it may take another three or four months before they have a 10-word vocabulary. By about 18 months of age, children are saying about two dozen words. Most early words are nouns—names for things. Research indicates that reading to children increases their vocabulary.

Studies have shown that reading to children can increase their vocabulary.

It is thus a good idea for parents to pull out the storybooks and read to their children (Arnold et al., 1994; Robbins & Ehri, 1994).

Children sometimes overreach—they try to talk about more things than they have words for. Often they extend the meanings of words to refer to things for which they do not have words. This behavior is called **overextension**. For example, if a child sees a cow but does not know the word *cow,* she or he might call the cow a doggie.

Development of Grammar

The first things children say are usually brief, but they have the meanings of sentences. That is, these utterances have a grammar. Even one word can express a complete thought, such as "Sit!" Children just starting to use language use only the words essential to communicating their meaning.

Sometimes a word will have more than one meaning, depending on the circumstances. For example, *doggie* can mean "There is a dog," "That stuffed animal looks like my dog," or "I want you to give me the dog!" Most children readily teach their parents what they mean with their utterances. They are delighted when parents do as requested and howl when they do not.

As they approach their second birthday, most children begin to use two-word sentences. "That doggie" might seem like just a phrase but is really a sentence in which *is* and *a* are implied: "That (is) (a) doggie." Two-word utterances such as this appear at about the same time in all languages (Slobin, 1983).

Even brief two-word utterances show understanding of grammar. A child who wants his or her mother to sit in a chair says, "Sit chair," not "chair sit." Similarly, the child says, "my doggy," not "doggy my," to show possession. "Mommy go" means Mommy is leaving. "Go Mommy" expresses the desire to have Mommy leave.

Between the ages of two and three, children's sentences expand to include missing words. They add articles (*a, an, the*), conjunctions (*and, but, or*), possessive and demonstrative adjectives (*your, her, that*), pronouns (*she, him, it*), and prepositions (*in, on, over, around, under, through*).

One interesting aspect of how children learn grammar has to do with irregular words. As you know, English has many irregular verbs and nouns. For example, the past tense of *am* is *was,* the past tense of *sit* is *sat,* and the plural of *child* is *children.* Children first learn irregular words by imitating their parents. Two-year-olds often use them correctly. But then a seemingly odd thing happens.

Even though the children have used these words correctly, they soon begin to use them incorrectly (Kuczaj, 1982). What has happened?

What has happened is that they have learned the rules for forming the past tense and plurals (in English, adding *d* or *ed* morphemes to make a word past tense and adding *s* or *z* morphemes to form plurals). Once they have learned these rules, they begin to make errors. For example, three- to five-year-olds may be more likely to say, "I runned away" than "I ran away." They are likely to talk about the "gooses" and "sheeps" they "seed" on the farm.

They make these errors because they have applied the normal rules to all words, even the words for which the rules do not work. This is called **overregularization**. Although it may seem like a bad thing when children begin to incorrectly use words that they previously used correctly, over-regularization represents an advance in the development of grammar. And in another year or two, children will learn the correct forms of the irregular words as well as the regular ones, and overregularization will stop.

TRUTH or fiction
■ REVISITED ■

It is not true that once a child learns the correct form of a word, he or she will never use the incorrect form. Because of overregularization of the rules of grammar, children often begin to use words incorrectly that they once used correctly. However, the errors are only temporary.

How Do We Learn Language?

Billions of children have acquired the languages of their parents and have then proceeded to hand them down to their own children. In this manner, languages pass, with small changes, from generation to generation. How are languages learned? Both heredity and environment play a role.

Hereditary Influences   Many psychologists believe that people have a natural, or inborn, tendency to acquire language. Chomsky (1980, 1991) and some other researchers refer to this tendency as a **language acquisition device** (LAD). Humans have an LAD. Plants, fish, and birds do not.

The LAD enables the brain to understand and use grammar. It enables people to turn ideas into sentences (Pinker, 1990, 1994). People may not be ready for chemistry and algebra until high school, but the LAD makes people most capable of acquiring language between about 18 to 24 months of age and puberty (Lenneberg, 1967). One- and two-year-olds seem to learn languages with ease. In many cases, they learn more than one language.

Environmental Influences   People may have an inborn ability to learn language, but environmental influences are important as well. Learning theorists claim that language learning is similar to other kinds of learned behavior (Gleason & Ratner, 1993). Children learn language, at least in part, by observing and imitating other people. For example, all children babble. But during the first year, children start to babble the sounds they hear around them more often and drop other sounds.

Bilingualism

Hannah speaks both Korean and English. Most likely, she learned Korean at home and English in school, in other public places, and from English-speaking friends. Although most people in the United States speak

It is becoming increasingly common in the United States to see signs in public places printed in several different languages.

CASE STUDIES
AND OTHER TRUE STORIES

Washoe and Kanzi: Chimps with Language?

Language is one of the things that sets people apart from other creatures. Sure, parrots can say a few words like "Polly wants a cracker." And your dog may respond to commands such as "Sit!" But animals cannot use language.

Or can they?

Over the past few decades, various researchers have made a number of attempts to teach language to chimpanzees (the animal that is biologically most similar to humans) and to other apes. One of the earliest efforts was aimed at getting a chimp to speak human words. But several years of work that yielded few positive results led to the conclusion that chimps cannot produce verbal speech (Hayes, 1951). Just because chimps cannot talk, however, does not necessarily mean that they are incapable of understanding language. Subsequent efforts therefore focused instead on teaching chimps to use symbols, such as those of American Sign Language (ASL).

Washoe, a female chimpanzee raised by Beatrice and Allen Gardner (1980), was one of the first chimps reported to use language. By the age of 5, Washoe could use more than 100 ASL signs. These included signs for actions *(come, give, tickle)*, objects *(apple, flower, toothbrush)*, and even for more abstract concepts such as *more*.

Moreover, Washoe could combine the signs to form simple sentences. The sentences were similar to those of two-year-old children: "More tickle," "More banana," "More milk." As time passed, Washoe signed longer sentences such as "Please sweet drink" and "Give me toothbrush hurry." However, Washoe had trouble with word order. One day she might sign, "Come give me toothbrush." The next she might sign, "Hurry toothbrush give me." Even one-year-old children use correct syntax more consistently.

Can chimps use language?

Psychologist Sue Savage-Rumbaugh and her colleagues (1993) had somewhat better luck in terms of grammar with a chimp named Kanzi. Kanzi learned to understand several hundred words and to correctly respond to commands in which these words were put together in ways that Kanzi had not previously heard. For example, he knew the words *dog, bite,* and *snake.* When Kanzi was given a stuffed dog and a stuffed snake and asked to "make the dog bite the snake," he put the snake to the dog's mouth, even though he had never before heard this sentence. Kanzi's grammatical ability, however, never surpassed that of the average two-and-a-half-year-old child.

So the question remains: Can chimps use language? The answer seems to hinge on the definition of language. It seems clear that chimps and even some other types of apes can learn to use signs and symbols and can follow some commands given to them. So if this is considered language, then yes, chimps can use language.

Most psychologists, however, use a more restrictive definition of language: the combination of symbols into original, grammatical sentences. If we use originality and mastery of grammar as the standards for defining language, there is little question that chimps fall short. For now, at least, the theory that language belongs to humans alone remains standing.

Think About It

Think of a type of animal other than an ape that appears to have the ability to communicate, either with humans or with other animals. What evidence suggests that this animal is capable of communication? What elements of language are *not* present in its apparent communication?

Bilingualism in the United States

LANGUAGE SPOKEN IN THE HOME	TOTAL NUMBER OF SPEAKERS AGE 5 AND ABOVE (IN THOUSANDS)		CHANGE (%)
	1980	**1990**	
Spanish	11,549	17,339	50
French[1]	1,572	1,702	8
German	1,607	1,547	-4
Italian	1,633	1,309	-20
Chinese	632	1,249	98
Tagalog[2]	452	843	87
Polish	826	723	-12
Korean	276	626	127
Vietnamese	203	507	150
Portuguese	361	430	19
Japanese	342	428	25
Greek	410	388	-5
Arabic	227	355	57
Hindi, Urdu	130	331	155
Russian	175	242	39
Yiddish	320	213	-34
Thai	89	206	132
Persian	109	202	85
French Creole[3]	25	188	654
Armenian	102	150	46

FIGURE 8.10 *This chart shows the 20 non-English languages most commonly spoken in the United States. It also shows how the percentages of speakers of these languages increased or decreased from 1980 to 1990.*

Source: U.S. Bureau of the Census, 1993.
[1]Spoken commonly in the home in New Hampshire, Maine, and Louisiana.
[2]Main language of the Philippines.
[3]Mainly spoken by Haitians.

only one language, the number of people who (like Hannah) are bilingual, or speak two languages, is growing. In this respect the United States is becoming more similar to other parts of the world. The majority of people around the world speak two or more languages (Snow, 1993).

English is a second language for millions of people in the United States. For many of them, languages such as Spanish, Chinese, and Russian are spoken in the home. For some, these languages are also spoken in the neighborhood. Figure 8.10 shows the 20 non-English languages most commonly spoken in homes in the United States. Much of the increase in the numbers of speakers of foreign languages from 1980 to 1990 was due to immigration from Latin America and Asia.

Evidence suggests that people may benefit from being bilingual. Learning a second language often increases children's expertise in their first language (Lambert et al., 1991). Furthermore, knowledge of different languages expands children's exposure to different cultures and appears to broaden their outlooks (Diaz, 1985).

In general, the earlier in life a person learns a second language, the more likely the person is to become fluent in and sound like a native speaker of that language (Snow, 1993; Taylor & Taylor, 1990). One study found that children who immigrated to England from non-English-speaking countries before the age of 7 learned to speak English with no trace of a foreign accent. Children who learned English at age 14 or above, on the other hand, had noticeable accents (Tahka et al., 1981). Results such as these lend support to the theory that there is a period in life—(a portion of childhood)—during which language acquisition occurs more easily and effectively than during any other period. If Marc decides to study Japanese, he probably will never be able to speak Japanese without an accent. Even if he studies the language for years, he will still have an accent.

A DAY IN THE LIFE

THINKING ABOUT PSYCHOLOGY

1. Identify and explain the three basic elements of language.

2. Define *overextension* and *overregularization.*

3. **Critical Thinking** How do research findings about bilingualism indicate that language acquisition involves both environmental and hereditary influences?

Chapter 8 REVIEW

SUMMARY

Three types of thinking are problem solving, reasoning, and decision making. Thinking is closely related to language.

I. What Is Thinking?

A. Thinking is the mental activity involved in understanding, processing, and communicating information.

B. Symbols, concepts, and prototypes make thinking possible.

II. Problem Solving

A. Problem solving is the process of finding a solution to a given set of facts. Two general approaches to problem solving are algorithms and heuristics.
  1. Algorithms are specific procedures that when used correctly always lead to the solution of a problem.
  2. Heuristics are general rules that often, but not always, lead to the solution of a problem. They are less reliable but more efficient than algorithms.

B. Specific approaches to problem solving include trial and error, difference reduction, means-end analysis, working backward, and analogies.

C. Some problems are solved by insight, or sudden understanding. Other problems are solved after a person takes a break from actively trying to solve them, a phenomenon known as the incubation effect.

D. Mental set and functional fixedness can be obstacles to problem solving.

E. Creativity is the ability to think of new or unusual ways of solving a problem. Creative problem solving requires divergent, not convergent, thinking.

F. Some psychologists advise using the ABCDEs of problem solving: *Assess* the problem. *Brainstorm* approaches. *Choose* an approach. *Do* it. *Evaluate* results.

III. Reasoning

A. Reasoning is the use of information to reach conclusions. Deductive reasoning starts with general statements, or premises, and reasons down to specifics. The conclusion is true if the premises are true.

B. Inductive reasoning moves from individual cases or particular facts to a general conclusion. The conclusion may be incorrect even if the premises are true.

IV. Decision Making and Judgment

A. Weighing the pros and cons of possible courses of action can be helpful in making careful decisions.

B. Three shortcuts people use in making decisions are the representativeness heuristic, the availability heuristic, and the anchoring heuristic.

C. Because of the framing effect, the way words are used can influence a decision.

D. Overconfidence can be a barrier to effective decision making.

V. Language

A. The basic units of language are phonemes, morphemes, and syntax.

B. Semantics is the study of the meaning that phrases and sentences convey.

C. Nearly all children develop language in the same sequence.

D. Both heredity and environment play a role in how people learn language.
  1. Some psychologists believe that people have a natural, or inborn, capacity for learning language.
  2. Other psychologists believe that children learn language as a result of observing and imitating other people.

E. Research indicates that the earlier in life a person learns to speak a second language, the more likely the person is to become fluent in that language.

TERM & CONCEPT
REVIEW

1. Define each of the following terms: *symbol, concept,* and *prototype.*
2. What is the purpose of an algorithm? Give two examples of algorithms.
3. List five approaches to problem solving and describe each one.
4. Define *mental set* and *functional fixedness.* How might they be obstacles to problem solving?
5. How could you use both convergent and divergent thinking to solve a problem?
6. What is confirmation bias, and which type of reasoning does it affect?
7. Explain how people use each of the following shortcuts to make a decision: the representativeness heuristic, the availability heuristic, and the anchoring heuristic.
8. What are the first three stages in language development?
9. What is a language acquisition device?
10. According to various studies on language acquisition, what is the best time to learn a foreign language?

CRITICAL
THINKING

1. How would you teach a child the meaning of an abstract concept such as honesty?
2. Explain how mental set might occasionally help problem solving rather than hinder it.
3. Imagine that you are driving to a strange town to visit a friend who has just moved there. Using the ABCDEs of problem solving, explain how you would plan your trip.
4. In addition to using words and sentences to communicate, human beings use sounds, symbols, gestures, and other means to communicate. Give five examples of how people communicate without using words.
5. Give reasons to support or reject a proposal to teach foreign languages in elementary schools.

APPLYING SKILLS
IN PSYCHOLOGY

1. **COOPERATIVE LEARNING Research in Psychology** With several of your classmates, play a popular board game. Team up with one other person in the group and play as partners. Decide together how you will make your moves. At the end of the game, have each set of partners give examples of the problem-solving techniques they used to make their moves during the game. Discuss how prior familiarity with the game helped or hindered your strategy.
2. **COOPERATIVE LEARNING Putting Psychology to Use** Working in small groups, think of a problem facing your school or community for which there are two or more possible solutions, or courses of action. On a large sheet of paper, create a "balance sheet" listing each possible course of action and its pros and cons. Use the balance sheet to reach a decision, and then present the results of your group decision-making process to the class.
3. **Using Your Observation Skills** During the next week, collect examples of the framing effect. Take note of instances when you think family members, teachers, and friends are trying to shape your decision making through their choice of words. Cut out newspaper and magazine advertisements and circle words that might be particularly effective in persuading consumers to buy a product. Record instances of sales pitches you hear in stores or on television. Share your examples with the class.
4. **Research in Psychology** Tape-record the conversation of a two- or three-year-old child. Then make two columns on a sheet of paper. In one column, transcribe, or write out, the child's words. In the other column, analyze his or her language development. For example, point out instances of overextension and overregularization. Read sections of the conversation to the class to see if your classmates agree with your analysis and examples.

9

INTELLIGENCE

Objectives

1 Define *intelligence,* and explain the various theories of intelligence.

2 Identify various types of intelligence tests, and describe their uses.

3 Identify the characteristics of mental retardation and giftedness, and explain the relationship between giftedness and creativity.

4 Explain how heredity and the environment influence intelligence.

A DAY IN THE LIFE

January 8

Todd and Dan were at Todd's house after school. Todd had decided to go to college six months ago and had already begun applying. Dan, on the other hand, had not decided what he wanted to do. He noticed some of Todd's college catalogs sitting on the table and began looking through them.

"Todd, what made you decide to go to college?" Dan asked.

"I'm not really sure. I've always done well in school and I love studying science. Why do you ask?"

"I don't know. I've just always wondered if I'm intelligent enough for college," Dan replied. "My older brother seems to get good grades without any effort at all, but I have to work hard for every 'A' or 'B' that I get. And we both have the same parents and have had the same upbringing."

"Yeah, but you and your brother aren't identical. You two only share some of the same genes and you've had different experiences, especially in school," Todd said. "Plus, don't you think there might be different types of intelligence?"

"How so?" Dan asked.

"Well, have you ever heard Hannah play the violin?"

"Of course I have," Dan replied. "She's great at it."

"Right. Hannah has a special ability to read the music and play the right notes. You're the same way with sports and you have great communication and people skills."

"But those are talents, not *intelligence*," Dan replied. "Talent is different from intelligence."

"Maybe," Todd pondered. "But I think any kind of learning ability is a type of intelligence."

"Okay then, what if I don't have enough learning ability to go to college? Don't they have some sort of test to tell you if you have enough intelligence for college?" Dan asked.

"I don't know," Todd replied honestly. "When I was younger I took some sort of intelligence test for placement. But I doubt that there are tests to tell you if you're intelligent enough for college. Why don't you talk to Mr. Hochberg, the guidance counselor?"

"I guess I could do that," Dan said. "Thanks, Todd."

"No problem. Hey, I have to work hard for every A that I get, too."

- achievement
- intelligence
- mental age
- intelligence quotient
- reliability
- test-retest reliability
- validity
- mental retardation
- gifted
- creativity
- heritability

• • •

Intelligence is one characteristic that sets humans apart from other forms of life. Intelligence permits us to adapt to changing conditions and to challenge our physical limitations—to move faster and higher than any other animal. The human ability to think about abstract ideas, such as space and time, also sets us apart from all other species. Intelligence has even expanded our senses, enabling us to invent microscopes and telescopes to see things too small or distant for the naked eye to detect. This chapter examines how intelligence is defined and measured. It also discusses differences in intelligence and considers the factors that influence intelligence.

1
What Is Intelligence?

A DAY IN THE LIFE

Todd and Dan raised many interesting points about the nature of intelligence. People can be very intelligent and not know a lot because they have not studied. People can also know a lot because they have worked hard, even if their intelligence is not particularly high. But, what, exactly, is intelligence?

Some people, like Todd, have very strong science or math skills. Others, such as Hannah, are talented in music or art. Still others, including Dan, have the ability to get along well with other people. Are all of these abilities signs of intelligence? Are *any* of them? How many factors are involved in intelligence? Throughout human history, many philosophers and scientists have speculated about the answers to these questions.

Intelligence Versus Achievement

According to psychologists, one thing intelligence is *not* is achievement. **Achievement** refers to knowledge and skills gained from experience. In other words, achievement focuses on the things that you know and can do. Thus, achievement involves specific content, such as Spanish, calculus, history, psychology, biology, art, or music. The relationship between achievement and experience is obvious. If

you have spent a lot of time reading about the Civil War, for example, then you will probably do well on a test about that period in U.S. history. You will have gained knowledge on the subject of the Civil War. But if you were tested on the Revolutionary War instead, you might not do as well. That would be because you had more content knowledge of the Civil War.

Although intelligence is not the same as achievement, intelligence can provide the *basis* for achievement. Intelligence makes achievement possible by giving people the ability to learn. Todd pointed this out when he suggested that intelligence might be involved in Hannah's abilities to read music and to play the right notes on her violin.

Now we know what intelligence is *not*. But what is it? **Intelligence** can be defined as the abilities to learn from experience, to think rationally, and to deal effectively with the environment. Within that general definition, however, psychologists have a number of differing theories about what, exactly, makes up intelligence.

Spearman's Two-Factor Theory

Nearly 100 years ago, British psychologist Charles Spearman suggested that all the behaviors we consider to be intelligent have a common underlying factor. He labeled this factor *g*, which stands for "general intelligence." The *g* factor represents the abilities to reason and to solve problems. Spearman noted that people who do well in one area usually do well in others. Yet even the most capable people are relatively better at some things than at others—writing and music rather than math, for example. For this reason, he suggested that specific, or *s*, factors account for particular abilities.

Thurstone's Theory of Primary Mental Abilities

American psychologist Louis Thurstone believed that nine separate factors make up intelligence. He called them primary mental abilities. These primary mental abilities are as follows:

- visual and spatial ability (the ability to picture shapes and spatial relationships)
- perceptual speed (the ability to understand perceptual information rapidly and to see the similarities and differences between stimuli)
- numerical ability (the ability to calculate and recall numbers)

Thurstone would probably suggest that architects such as this one have visual and spatial ability.

- verbal meaning (knowledge of the meanings of words)
- memory (the ability to recall information, such as words and sentences)
- word fluency (the ability to think of words quickly for such tasks as rhyming or doing crossword puzzles)
- deductive reasoning (the ability to derive examples from general rules)
- inductive reasoning (the ability to derive general rules from examples)

Thurstone believed that people can be high in one factor and low in another. For example, someone may have high word fluency—meaning that she or he can find words that rhyme with one another—but be poor at solving math problems (Thurstone & Thurstone, 1963).

Gardner's Theory of Multiple Intelligences

Contemporary psychologist Howard Gardner (1983; Gardner & Hatch, 1989) believes that intelligence has a broader base and that there are actually seven different kinds of intelligence within us:

- linguistic intelligence
- logical-mathematical intelligence
- visual-spatial intelligence
- body-kinesthetic intelligence
- musical-rhythmic intelligence
- interpersonal intelligence (sensitivity to other people's feelings)
- intrapersonal intelligence (insight into one's own inner feelings)

Gardner refers to each of these as "an intelligence" because they are very different from one

A DAY IN THE LIFE

another. He also believes that each kind of intelligence is based in different areas of the brain. Gardner's theory might help to explain why Dan responds well to other people but might not get the highest grades in school.

Some of Gardner's "intelligences," such as language ability, math ability, and spatial-relations skills, are similar to those proposed by other theorists, including Thurstone. A major difference between Gardner's and Thurstone's theories, however, is that Thurstone believed that the nine factors he identified, when taken together, make up intelligence. Gardner, on the other hand, proposes that the seven different intelligences are independent of each other.

According to Gardner's theory, a person possesses several intelligence potentials that vary in intensity. These skaters probably have highly developed bodily-kinesthetic intelligence. They also probably have sensitivity to each others' feelings.

According to Gardner, a person can be a great mathematician or composer but be average in self-insight and in interpersonal relationships. Gardner would probably say that Todd, Dan, and Hannah are each intelligent in their own way. Todd has strong scientific ability. Dan, as an athlete, has highly developed bodily-kinesthetic skills. And Hannah undoubtedly has special musical ability.

Furthermore, according to Gardner, the seven intelligences exist side by side within each person but vary in intensity. They can also change over time. They are simply intellectual "potentials" that can be tapped given the right environment (Gardner, 1995).

Critics of Gardner's views think that exceptional abilities in the musical or bodily-kinesthetic areas are not really part of intelligence at all. They argue that those skills are talents and that being talented is not the same thing as being intelligent (Neisser et al., 1996). Dan, too, made this distinction when he asserted that talent and intelligence are two different things.

Sternberg's Triarchic Theory

While Gardner talks about separate and distinct intelligences, psychologist Robert Sternberg (1995) believes that different kinds of intelligence all work together. He has created a three-level, or *triarchic*,

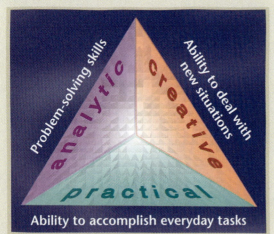

Sternberg's Triarchic Model

Problem-solving skills

analytic

Ability to deal with new situations

creative

practical

Ability to accomplish everyday tasks

FIGURE 9.1 *According to Sternberg, intelligence has three parts: the analytic part that enables us to solve problems, the creative part that allows us to deal with new situations, and the practical part that makes it possible for us to perform everyday tasks. We often use more than one of these parts simultaneously.*

model of intelligence. (See Figure 9.1.) According to Sternberg, intelligence includes analytic, creative, and practical abilities. Analytic intelligence involves the ability to solve problems. Creative intelligence involves the ability to deal with new situations. Practical intelligence involves the ability to accomplish everyday tasks.

Often, we must use more than one of these three types of intelligence at the same time. For example, if you were doing an experiment for an upcoming social studies or science fair, you would use practical intelligence to plan your time and materials to do the project. You would use your analytic intelligence to interpret the results of the experiment and draw conclusions. You would also use creativity to design the display for your project.

TRUTH OR fiction ■ REVISITED ■ *It is true that there may be more than one kind of intelligence.* Both Gardner's and Sternberg's theories discuss the existence of different kinds of intelligences.

Emotional Intelligence

Psychologist Daniel Goleman (1995) is interested in why smart people are not always as successful as might be expected. He proposes yet another kind of intelligence: emotional intelligence. Emotional intelligence, says Goleman, consists of five factors that are involved in success in school or on the job:

- Self-awareness (the ability to recognize our own feelings). If we know when we are happy, sad, or angry, we are better able to cope with our feelings.

- Mood management (the ability to distract oneself from an uncomfortable feeling). Although we may not be able to prevent feelings of anger or sadness, we do have some control over how long the feelings last. Rather than dwell on bad feelings, we can distract ourselves and make changes to reduce the likelihood that we will find ourselves in the same situation again.

- Self-motivation (the ability to move ahead with confidence and enthusiasm). People who are self-motivators sometimes accomplish more than people who obtain higher scores on intelligence tests. (Intelligence tests are discussed later in this chapter.)

PSYCHOLOGY
IN THE WORLD TODAY

Artificial Intelligence

In 1996, world champion chess player Gary Kasparov pitted his skills against an IBM computer. This was not the first time the two had played chess. Last time, Kasparov had won. Would he be able to win again? After several games, the two were tied. Kasparov offered a draw and an end to the competition. His offer was not accepted. Two games later, he had defeated the computer yet again. The human mind had triumphed over the machine. Human intelligence (at least Kasparov's) was superior to artificial intelligence.

Kasparov playing the computer

Artificial intelligence (AI) is a broad field that has been involved in the creation and development of "intelligent machines." These machines include industrial robots and computers such as the one that played chess with Gary Kasparov. Chess-playing computers are considered *expert systems*—computer programs that specialize in some particular field. Expert systems have been created not only to play chess but also to aid in medical diagnosis, the drilling of oil wells, and the mining of minerals. There is even a program for psychologists. The program, called Blue Box, helps pick the best kind of therapy for people who suffer from depression (Gingerich, 1990).

But are these programs anything like human intelligence? Not really. For one thing, expert systems are very limited in their information. Prescriptive computer programs for psychologists are created by human experts who tell programmers all they know about their particular field. Then all the possible psychological symptoms—for depression, for example—and combinations of symptoms are included in the program. Under those limited conditions, the computer does well enough. But it is restricted by what it "knows,"

which is what it has been "told" by the programmer.

The human brain is a complicated machine. We may not be able to calculate numbers as quickly as a computer can, but we can deal with complex ideas and problems with remarkable ability. That is because our brains use what is known as "parallel processing." In other words, our thoughts analyze several different aspects of a problem at once. A computer, on the other hand, uses "serial processing." The computer analyzes only one step at a time. Humans use serial processing, too, but parallel processing is what gives us the decided edge. Even highly sophisticated robots have difficulty moving with speed because it takes them so long to serially analyze all the stimuli necessary for coordinated motion.

Will we ever be able to create a computer or robot that thinks like the human brain? It does not seem likely anytime soon. Despite its electronic brainpower, AI is no match for human intelligence (Pinker, 1994). Powerful computers can handle many problems and vast amounts of information. But they do not have the insights, intuitions, and creativity that humans have (Gelernter, 1994). They follow commands very well, but they have no originality. These limitations become quickly evident when, for instance, computers are asked to write poetry or compose music.

THINK ABOUT IT

If you were creating a new expert system of your own, in what area would it be? To whom would you go for expertise? What sort of problems can you anticipate?

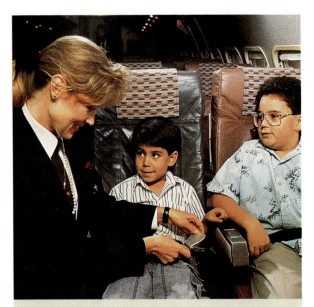

Emotional intelligence includes mood management and people skills, qualities possessed by many airline flight attendants.

- Impulse control (the ability to delay pleasure until the task at hand has been accomplished). A student who resists the temptation to watch television until her or his homework is done may do better in school than a student who puts off homework until later.

- People skills (the ability to empathize, understand, communicate, and cooperate with others). People skills help us get along with others, and getting along with others helps us in school and on the job.

A DAY IN THE LIFE

As Todd pointed out, Dan has exceptional people skills. According to Goleman's theory, Dan would be characterized as emotionally intelligent. Goleman's view has captured the interest of many psychologists and educators. However, research studies still need to be done to confirm Goleman's ideas.

Links Between Different Types of Intelligences

As you have read, a number of psychologists believe that there are several different kinds of intelligences. But what, if any, relationship exists between these different intelligences? Are they totally separate, or are some types of intelligence somehow linked to other types? Research suggests that there may in fact be some links.

Hannah has studied the violin from early childhood. What has happened in Hannah's mind as she learned to play the violin? Has she learned about the music of composers like Mozart and Beethoven? Certainly. Has she gained self-confidence and performance skills when she plays at recitals? Absolutely. But according to recent psychological research, Hannah may also have been enhancing her spatial reasoning ability.

A study done by the research team of Frances Rauscher, Gordon Shaw, and Katherine Ky (1993) has suggested links between musical and spatial reasoning ability. According to the researchers, listening to 10 minutes of a Mozart piano sonata on several occasions enhanced college students' scores on spatial reasoning items of tests they were given.

A follow-up study done by the same group (1994) recruited 19 3- and 4-year-olds. The researchers gave the children eight months of music lessons, including singing and use of a keyboard. Another 15 children served as a control group— they received no music lessons. After the music course was completed, the researchers gave all of the children a task in which they had to put pieces of a puzzle together to form a complete object. The scores of the 19 children who had had the lessons significantly exceeded those of the 15 children who had not received the training in music.

How can we explain these results? How can listening to music or training in music enhance spatial reasoning ability? One view is that the parts of the brain that are involved in music overlap with the parts involved in other cognitive functions, such as spatial reasoning (Blakeslee, 1995c). Musical training thus might help develop the connections between nerve cells in these parts of the brain. The beneficial changes in the nervous system may help children in geometry, art and design, and geography. The changes may even help people fit suitcases into the trunk of a car (Martin, 1994).

THINKING ABOUT PSYCHOLOGY

1. What is the difference between achievement and intelligence?

2. Describe the two factors of intelligence specified in Spearman's theory.

3. **Critical Thinking** Choose an occupation that interests you. List the types of intelligence, as outlined by any of the theories in this section, that a person should have to succeed in that occupation.

2

Measurement of Intelligence

You have probably taken many tests throughout your school career. Some of the tests you have taken or will take are achievement tests—they show what you have learned. Other tests are aptitude tests, which are intended to predict your ability to learn new skills. There are also tests that are designed to measure intelligence. The most widely used intelligence tests are the Stanford-Binet Intelligence Scale and the Wechsler scales. These are probably the types of tests Todd was given when he was younger.

The Stanford-Binet Scales

In the early 1900s, leaders of the French public school system were interested in finding a test that could identify children who were likely to need special educational attention. In response, French psychologist Alfred Binet devised the first modern intelligence test. The original version of the test was first used in 1905.

Binet assumed that intelligence increased with age. Thus, Binet's tests contained questions for children of different age levels. (See Figure 9.2.) Older children were expected to answer more difficult questions. Children earned "months" of credit for correct answers.

Binet's test yielded a score called a mental age. A child's mental age is not the same thing as his or her chronological age. **Mental age** (MA) shows the intellectual level at which a child is functioning. For

Typical Items on the Stanford-Binet Intelligence Scale

Age Level	Item 1	Item 2
2 years	Children know basic vocabulary words. When the examiner says, "Show me the eyes" (or ears), they can point to the proper parts of a doll.	Children can match a model by building a tower made up of four blocks.
4 years	Children show language and classifying ability by filling in a missing word: "Brother is a boy; sister is a _____."	Children show general understanding by answering questions such as: "Why do people have telephones?"
9 years	Children can point out absurdities. For example: "She dug up a coin dated 544 B.C. What is silly about that?"	Children show increased language ability, as shown by answering: "Can you tell me a number that rhymes with *gate?*"
Adult	Adults show knowledge of the meanings of words and conceptual thinking by correctly explaining the differences between word pairs such as "sickness and misery," "house and home," and "integrity and prestige."	Adults show spatial skills by correctly answering questions such as: "If a car turned to the right to head north, in what direction was it heading before it turned?"

FIGURE 9.2 *These items are similar to those that appear on the Stanford-Binet Intelligence Scale. The test includes tasks for age levels from two to adulthood. The test produces an intelligence quotient, or IQ, that reflects the relationship between a person's mental age and his or her chronological age.*

Note: Adapted from Stanford-Binet Intelligence Scale.

example, a child with a MA of 6 is functioning, intellectually, like the typical 6-year-old, even if the child is not 6 years old. The same MA score can mean very different things for children of different ages. A MA of 9 is above average for a 7-year-old. The same MA of 9 is below average for an 11-year-old.

In 1916, Binet's test was brought to the United States and revised by Louis Terman of Stanford University. For this reason, the test became known as the Stanford-Binet Intelligence Scale (SBIS).

The version of the test used today provides an intelligence quotient, not a MA. An **intelligence quotient** (IQ) is a number that reflects the relationship between a child's mental age and his or her actual, or chronological, age (CA).

The IQ is a *quotient* because we use division to obtain the number. The IQ was initially computed using the formula IQ = (mental age divided by chronological age) × 100, or

$$IQ = \frac{\text{Mental Age (MA)}}{\text{Chronological Age (CA)}} \times 100$$

A child with a MA of 9 and a CA of 9 would thus have an IQ of 100. Children who answer test items as well as older children have IQs above 100. For example, an 8-year-old who does as well as the average 10-year-old will attain an IQ of 125. Children who do not do as well as typical children their age attain IQ scores below 100. In other words, people who do better than average for their age attain IQ scores above 100. People who score below average attain scores below 100.

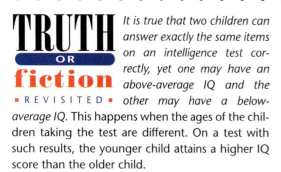

TRUTH OR fiction ■ R E V I S I T E D ■ It is true that two children can answer exactly the same items on an intelligence test correctly, yet one may have an above-average IQ and the other may have a below-average IQ. This happens when the ages of the children taking the test are different. On a test with such results, the younger child attains a higher IQ score than the older child.

The Wechsler Scales

The Stanford-Binet is the "classic" individual intelligence test. Today, however, David Wechsler's scales are more widely used (Watkins et al., 1995). Wechsler developed intelligence tests for children

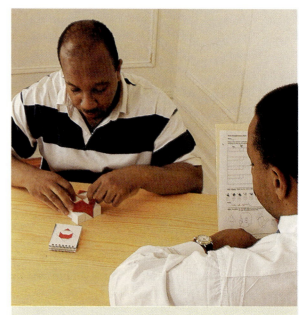

An adult takes one of the performance subtests of the Wechsler scales.

and adults. The most widely used test is the revised Wechsler Adult Intelligence Scale (WAIS-R).

The Wechsler scales consist of several subtests. (See Figure 9.3.) Each subtest measures a different intellectual skill. Some of Wechsler's subtests measure verbal skills. Others assess performance skills. In general, verbal subtests involve words and ideas; performance subtests focus on spatial relations. Both verbal and performance subtests require reasoning ability. The Wechsler scales reveal relative strengths and weaknesses, as well as overall intellectual functioning.

The Wechsler scales differ from the Stanford-Binet test in several important ways. The Wechsler scales do not use the concept of mental age, although they still use the term IQ. The Stanford-Binet test measures verbal ability, whereas the Wechsler scales measure both verbal and nonverbal abilities. Because the Wechsler tests yield three scores (verbal, nonverbal, and combined), they can be used to identify particular learning disabilities. For example, if an individual's verbal score is significantly lower than his or her nonverbal score, this might indicate a reading disability.

Scores on the Wechsler tests are based on a comparison of a person's answers with the answers of others in the same age group. The average score for any age level is 100. About 50 percent of scores fall within a broad range of 90 to 110. About 2 percent of people who take the tests score above 130, and about 2 percent score below 70.

Typical Subtests from the Wechsler Scales

VERBAL SUBTESTS

General Information
1. How many wings does a bird have?
2. How many nickels make a dime?
3. What is steam made of?
4. Who wrote "Tom Sawyer"?
5. What is pepper?

General Comprehension
1. What should you do if you see someone forget his book when he leaves a restaurant?
2. What is the advantage of keeping money in a bank?
3. Why is copper often used in electrical wires?

Vocabulary
This test consists simply of asking, "What is a_____?" or "What does _____ mean?" The words cover a wide range of difficulty.

Similarities
1. In what way are a lion and a tiger alike?
2. In what way are a saw and a hammer alike?
3. In what way are an hour and a week alike?
4. In what way are a circle and a triangle alike?

Arithmetic
1. Sam had three pieces of candy and Joe gave him four more. How many pieces of candy did Sam have altogether?
2. Three women divided eighteen golf balls equally among themselves. How many golf balls did each person receive?
3. If two buttons cost 15¢, what will be the cost of a dozen buttons?

PERFORMANCE SUBTESTS

Digit Symbol
The test taker is asked to learn to associate meaningless figures with numbers.

Block Design
The test taker is asked to copy pictures of geometric designs using multicolored blocks.

Picture Completion
The test taker is asked to identify what is missing from a picture such as this one.

Picture Arrangement
The test taker is asked to arrange pictures such as these in a sequence so that they tell a story.

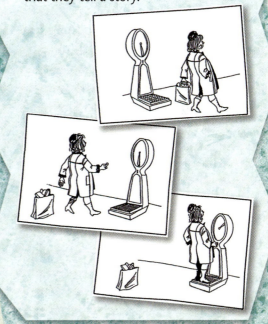

FIGURE 9.3 *These items are similar to those on the revised Wechsler Adult Intelligence Scale (WAIS-R). The WAIS-R contains several subtests; some measure verbal ability and others measure performance. The WAIS-R is now more widely used than the classic Stanford-Binet Intelligence Scale. Because the Wechsler tests place more emphasis on performance than does the Stanford-Binet, they are not as likely to put less verbally oriented people at a disadvantage.*

Reliability and Validity

Before psychologists accept intelligence tests (or other types of psychological tests), the tests must meet two criteria: they must be *reliable* and *valid*.

Test Reliability   Imagine that every time you measured the width of your desk with a tape measure, it showed a different result. If this happened, we would say that the tape measure was an unreliable form of measurement. The **reliability** of a test refers to its consistency. A test or any other method of assessment is reliable if it gives highly similar scores every time it is used. A reliable intelligence test should obtain similar IQ scores on different testing occasions.

There are different ways of showing a test's reliability. One of the most common is called test-retest reliability. **Test-retest reliability** is determined by comparing scores earned by the same person on the same test taken at different times. The Stanford-Binet and Wechsler tests are both highly reliable. For example, if you took the Stanford-Binet in your first year of high school and again in your senior year, your IQ score would probably be nearly the same the second time as it was the first.

Keep in mind that "nearly the same" does not mean "identical." Scores for the same person from different testing occasions may vary somewhat for a variety of reasons. For one reason, a person may be more motivated or attentive one day than another. For a second reason, we may improve our scores from one testing to another because we have become familiar with the test format. For another reason, intelligence is not a fixed item—it varies over time. Some intellectual skills may increase with education; some may decline with age, injury, or various health problems.

Test Validity   A test has **validity** if it measures what it is supposed to measure. To see whether a test is valid, test scores are compared with outside standards or norms. A proper standard for checking the validity of a musical aptitude test might be the ability to learn to play a musical instrument. Tests of musical aptitude therefore should predict ability to learn to play a musical instrument.

What standards might be used to check the validity of intelligence tests? Most people agree that intelligence plays a role in academic success. Intelligence test scores should therefore predict school grades. They do so moderately well (Sattler, 1988). Intelligence is also thought to contribute, in part, to

job success. Scores on intelligence tests have been shown to predict adult occupational status reasonably well (McCall, 1977). Thus, these intelligence tests seem to be reasonably valid. However, because there is considerable disagreement about what intelligence is, some psychologists believe that it is difficult to make definitive statements about the validity of IQ tests.

Problems with Intelligence Tests

Intelligence tests are not perfect. Some test takers do better than others, but not necessarily because they are more intelligent. Other factors—such as education or economic background—can make a difference. For example, on average, lower-income children attain IQ scores that are 10 to 15 points lower than those of middle- and upper-income children (Taylor & Richards, 1991). This may be because they have not had the opportunities to acquire the skills that help raise scores on intelligence tests.

Motivation to do well also contributes to performance on intelligence tests (Collier, 1994). Faced with frequent failure, a person begins to expect to fail and so does not try to succeed. Such a person may think, "Why make the effort when it won't make any difference?" For this reason, some children expect to fail, which affects their motivation to try their best (Tharp, 1991).

 *It is true that when we think we will not succeed at something, we may not try as hard as we can.* We believe that trying will not make a difference anyway.

Some intelligence tests have been criticized for being culturally biased (Helms, 1992). A test that is culturally biased would give an advantage to a particular group. Cultural bias is expressed in several ways. First of all, the words and concepts used on the test might be those used every day by members of one group but not by members of other groups. As a result, some test takers would perform less well on such a test because they might not understand the meanings of some questions or might interpret questions in a way the test makers did not anticipate. Second, questions might be biased toward certain problem-solving methods.

In theory, tests that are free from cultural bias ought to be possible. The challenge is for test makers to develop questions that test the appropriate skills while taking cultural differences into account.

THINKING ABOUT PSYCHOLOGY

1. What is an IQ?
2. What types of skills do the Wechsler subtests measure?
3. Explain what is meant by test reliability and test validity.
4. **Critical Thinking**   Compare and contrast the Stanford-Binet Intelligence Scale and the Wechsler scales.

3
Differences in Intelligence

Despite the limits of intelligence tests, they do have some uses, as Todd recalled. One of the primary functions of intelligence tests is to help identify people whose intelligence is out of the ordinary—at either end of the scale. As noted earlier, the average IQ score is 100. About half of the people in the United States attain scores in the broad average range from 90 to 110. Nearly 95 percent attain scores between 70 and 130. (See Figure 9.4.)

But what of the other 5 percent? People who attain IQ scores of 70 or below are defined by psychologists as mentally retarded. People who attain scores of 130 or above are defined by psychologists as gifted.

Mental Retardation

While having an IQ score at or below 70 is the technical definition of **mental retardation**, there are other indicators of mental retardation as well. According to the American Association on Mental Retardation, mental retardation also is associated with problems in communication, taking care of oneself, social skills, use of leisure time, travel in the community, self-direction, personal hygiene, and vocational training (Michaelson, 1993). There are several levels of mental retardation.

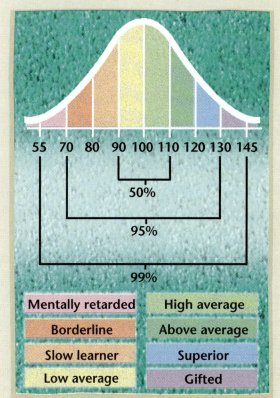

FIGURE 9.4   *Psychologists refer to this bell-shaped curve as a normal curve. Normal curves display the distribution of many traits, including intelligence as measured by IQ tests. The average IQ score is 100. About 50 percent of scores fall within the broad average range from 90 to 110.*

Mild Retardation   About 80 percent of people with retardation are classified as mildly retarded, with an IQ ranging from 50 to 70. Such people often are not obviously retarded, but as children they have more difficulty than most other children in learning to walk, in feeding themselves, and in learning to talk. Most children with mild retardation are able to learn to read and do arithmetic. As adults, they often are able to take care of themselves and hold jobs. They may, however, need occasional guidance and support when under unusual social or economic stress.

Moderate Retardation   People with an IQ of between 35 and 49 have moderate retardation. They can learn to speak, to feed and dress themselves, to take care of their own hygiene, and to work under supportive conditions, as in sheltered workshops. They usually do not learn to read or solve math problems. Children with Down syndrome are most likely to be classified in the moderately retarded range. (See Chapter 3.) Although adults with moderate retardation are usually not capable of self-maintenance, they can participate in simple recreation and travel alone in familiar places.

Severe Retardation   People with severe mental retardation—IQs of 20 to 34—usually require constant supervision. They may have some understanding of speech and be able to respond. Although they can perform daily routines and repetitive activities, they need continuing direction in a protective environment. Some children in this category can respond to training in some basic self-help tasks, such as self-feeding.

Profound Retardation   People with profound retardation—IQs below 20—barely communicate. They may show basic emotional responses, but they cannot feed or dress themselves and are dependent on other people for their care throughout their lives.

Causes of Retardation   Retardation can be caused by any of several factors. Accidents that result in brain damage and difficulties during childbirth can cause retardation. Pregnant women who abuse alcohol or drugs, are malnourished, or who have other health problems may give birth to children who are mentally retarded. Retardation also can be caused by genetic disorders or abnormalities, such as Down syndrome.

Although they sometimes need guidance, most people who are retarded can perform a variety of tasks.

Giftedness

Technically speaking, people who are gifted have IQ scores of 130 or above. However, giftedness (like retardation) may be more than just a matter of IQ. In general, to be **gifted** is to possess outstanding talent or to show the potential for performing at remarkably high levels of accomplishment when compared with other people of the same age, experience, or environment.

Some researchers believe that motivation and creativity contribute to giftedness (Renzulli, 1986). Others emphasize the importance of insight (Davidson, 1986). And many educators consider children with outstanding abilities to be gifted. The abilities can be in specific areas such as music, language arts, mathematics, or science. Children may be gifted in terms of leadership abilities or creativity, or they may exhibit excellence in the visual or performing arts. On the basis of research and experience, educators generally recognize the importance of identifying gifted children early and providing them with rich, varied learning opportunities to help them develop their potential.

Creativity

Giftedness is often linked with creativity. **Creativity** is the ability to invent new solutions to problems or to create original or ingenious materials. Although creativity may be a part of giftedness, a person can

Most doctors today recommend that pregnant women exercise to remain healthy, thereby minimizing chances of giving birth to a child with retardation.

CASE STUDIES
AND OTHER TRUE STORIES

The Exceptional Creator

Harvard psychologist Howard Gardner believes that there are several kinds of intelligences. He decided to study some of the most creative people of the 20th century. In 1993, Gardner published his findings in a book titled *Creating Minds*. In it, Gardner described the characteristics and circumstances that shaped the lives and work of seven major figures: Sigmund Freud, Albert Einstein, Pablo Picasso, Igor Stravinsky, T. S. Eliot, Martha Graham, and Mohandas Gandhi. Each of these people was outstanding in his or her field, and each one also happens to represent one of the seven intelligences in Gardner's theory.

Sigmund Freud, as you know, was a famous psychologist whose intelligence provided insight into his own deepest feelings. Albert Einstein, the physicist who established the theory of relativity, had a special ability in math. Pablo Picasso—a sculptor and potter as well as a painter—had outstanding spatial-relations intelligence. Igor Stravinsky, a composer, had extraordinary musical ability. T. S. Eliot, a poet, had linguistic intelligence. Martha Graham, a dancer, had special bodily-kinesthetic intelligence. Mohandas Gandhi possessed exceptional sensitivity to the feelings and needs of others, which led him to become an influential leader in India in the 1940s.

Using the information he learned about these creative people, Gardner then developed EC. *EC* stands for "Exceptional Creator," an imaginary person who combines the common characteristics of creators. The characteristics are as follows:

- EC comes from outside a major city but not so far removed that she is uninformed.
- EC's family is neither wealthy nor poor but is reasonably comfortable.

Dancer Martha Graham had bodily-kinesthetic intelligence.

- EC's upbringing was fairly strict, and her closest friend is outside her immediate family.
- EC's family is not especially educated, but they value learning and achievement.
- EC discovered her talent at an early age.
- As an adult, EC feels the need to test herself against others in her field, and she moves to the city.
- Once she makes a major breakthrough in her field, EC becomes isolated from her peers.
- EC works nearly all the time and constantly makes tremendous demands on herself.
- EC is self-confident, stubborn, and able to deal with adversity.
- EC has a second major breakthrough in her field about 10 years after the first.
- EC lives a long life, gains many followers, and continues to make contributions in her field until her death.

Most of the famous creators had to struggle to win acceptance for their ideas. When acceptance came too easily, some even made a special effort to be unconventional because they felt it made them more creative.

Gardner admits that his seven people do not represent all cultures or all time periods in history. Also, one cannot expect each and every one of the characteristics to be true for all creative individuals. Even for his seven case studies, there were always differences between them and the imaginary EC. However, Gardner believes that quite a few of the details still hold true.

THINK ABOUT IT

Choose two famous people you admire and write down their names. Below each name list the intelligences that Gardner would apply to that person.

A child who is exceptionally talented at something is often called a prodigy. Wolfgang Amadeus Mozart, who at the age of five began composing music, was known as a prodigy.

be highly creative without being gifted. In fact, a person can even be substantially below average in intelligence and yet have very high creativity.

English psychiatrist Lorna Selfe (1978) identified one such person, a girl named Nadia. Nadia had diminished mental skills and could not speak. However, she had a remarkable talent for drawing, and her creative ability was indisputable. Nadia was a savant—a person who has mental retardation or autism yet who exhibits extraordinary skill, even brilliance, in a particular field.

Research suggests that highly intelligent people are more likely than the average person to be particularly creative. Yet just as a high level of creativity does not guarantee high intelligence, high intelligence does not guarantee high creativity (Sternberg, 1990). For example, a Canadian study of gifted children (ages 9 to 11) found that they generally were more creative than children who were average in intelligence. However, this was only true for the group as a whole. Some of the gifted individuals were no more creative than the children who were average in intelligence (Kershner & Ledger, 1985).

It is not true that intellectually gifted people are by definition highly creative. Gifted people are more likely to be creative than are people of average intelligence. However, not all highly intelligent people are highly creative.

If intelligence does not guarantee creativity, what other factors are involved in creativity? Creative people are flexible, original, and mentally agile—capable of quickly coming up with the right idea or the right word (Azar, 1995). Creative students tend to express their feelings rather than hold them in. They are usually playful and independent. Some creative people are nonconformists. That is, they do not necessarily do what other people do. They go their own ways.

THINKING ABOUT PSYCHOLOGY

1. Define *mental retardation*.
2. Why is it important for educators to identify gifted children early?
3. **Critical Thinking** If highly creative students are not always easily identified as highly intelligent students, how can teachers make sure that they identify students with high creativity and help them reach their potential?

What Influences Intelligence?

A DAY IN THE LIFE

How could Dan's older brother get good grades without any apparent effort while Dan has to study hard for his grades? Why do some people seem to be more intelligent than others? To what extent is it possible to improve a person's intelligence? In order to address these questions, it is necessary to determine where intelligence comes from. Are people born with it, or do they acquire it during their lifetime?

Many psychologists believe that both heredity and environment influence intelligence. Snyderman and Rothman (1987, 1990) surveyed a sample of 1,020 psychologists and educational specialists and found the following:

- Forty-five percent believe that differences in IQ scores among people reflect both genetic and environmental factors.
- Fifteen percent believe that these differences reflect environmental factors alone.
- One percent believe that intelligence is determined entirely by genetic factors.
- Twenty-four percent believe that there is not enough research information to support any particular opinion.

In the case of Dan and his brother, it would be difficult to research the reasons for their differences. As Dan himself pointed out, they both have the same parents and they grew up with similar upbringings. Thus, their differences could not easily be attributed either to heredity or environment alone. Psychologists have, however, been able to conduct some studies on the roles of nature and nurture in the development of intelligence.

Genetic Influences on Intelligence

Are all people born with the same amount of intelligence? How do genetic factors influence the level of intelligence we have? Researchers who study the genetic factors in intelligence have used kinship studies and adoptee studies to explore questions such as these.

Kinship Studies If genetic factors are involved in intelligence, then closely related people should be more alike in terms of IQ scores than distantly related or unrelated people. For this reason, psychologists have studied IQ scores of related people. Identical twins have often been used in these studies. Since they have exactly the same genetic makeup, their test scores should be identical if intelligence is inherited. Any difference in scores means that other factors are also involved.

Bouchard and his colleagues (1990) compiled the results of more than 100 studies on the relationship between heredity and IQ. They found that the IQ scores of identical twins are more similar than those of any other group of people. This finding holds even when the twins are reared apart and therefore in different environments. Similarities in IQ scores between pairs of fraternal twins, other brothers or sisters, and parents and children are moderate. Similarities in IQ between children and

foster parents and between cousins are weak. What does all this mean? It means that genes do seem to play some role in intelligence. But how great a role does inheritance play?

Heritability is the extent to which variations in a trait from person to person can be explained by genetic factors. Most studies suggest that the heritability of intelligence is between 40 percent and 60 percent (Adler, 1993a; Bouchard et al., 1990; Plomin & Rende, 1991). That is, about half of the differences in IQ scores among people can be accounted for by heredity.

Adoptee Studies Some studies have compared the IQ scores of adopted children to those of their biological parents and their adoptive parents (Coon et al., 1990). If children are separated from their biological parents at early ages but their IQ scores remain very similar to those of their biological parents, it is probably because of genetic influences. On the other hand, if the IQ scores of the adopted children are more like those of their adoptive parents, it is probably because of environmental influences. Most studies of adopted children have found that their IQ scores are more like those of the biological parents than those of the adoptive parents (Baker et al., 1983; Horn, 1983; Scarr & Weinberg,

Kinship studies have shown moderate similarities in IQ scores between parents and children.

1983). Thus, there seems to be further evidence for a role for heredity in intelligence.

Psychologists Diana Baumrind (1993) and Jacquelyne Jackson (1993), however, argue that belief in the importance of heredity can undermine parental and educational efforts to help children learn. Parents and educators are most effective when they believe their efforts will improve children's knowledge and skills. Because parents and educators cannot change children's genetic codes, it is useful for them to assume that effective parenting and teaching can make a difference.

Environmental Influences on Intelligence

Bouchard and his colleagues (1990) found that for each type of kinship, from identical twins to parents and children, IQ scores are more alike for pairs of people who were reared together than for pairs who were reared apart. This result holds for identical twins, other brothers and sisters, and even people who are unrelated. These findings suggest that environmental factors also affect intelligence. A variety of studies have examined the influence of home environment, parenting style, schooling, and other environmental factors on intelligence.

Home and Parenting   Studies have shown that home environment and styles of parenting influence the development of intelligence (Coon et al.,

Children in Head Start centers, such as this one in New Mexico, receive educational opportunities that otherwise might not be available to them.

1990; Olson et al., 1992; Steinberg et al., 1992). The following factors apparently contribute to high levels of intellectual functioning in children:

- The parents are emotionally and verbally responsive to their children's needs.
- The parents provide enjoyable and educational toys.
- The parents are involved in their children's activities.
- The parents provide varied daily experiences during the preschool years.
- The home environment is well organized and safe (Bradley et al., 1989).
- The parents encourage the children to be independent—that is, to make their own decisions and solve their own problems whenever possible (McGowan & Johnson, 1984).

Preschool Programs   Many preschool programs are designed to provide young children with enriched early experiences. These experiences are intended to develop intelligence and prepare children for school. Many such programs exist, but one program is particularly well known. That program is Head Start. Begun in the mid-1960s, Head Start was designed to give economically disadvantaged children a better start in school.

Communities throughout the United States operate Head Start centers under the guidance and funding of the U.S. Department of Education. Parental involvement is an important feature of the Head Start program. This program includes health, education, and social services for participating children and their families. In local Head Start centers, children become familiar with books. They also play word and number games; they work with puzzles, drawing materials, toy animals, and dolls; and they interact with teachers in a school-like setting.

Preschool programs such as Head Start have been shown to increase the IQ scores, achievement test scores, and academic skills of participants (Barnett & Escobar, 1990; Hauser-Cram et al., 1991; Zigler, 1995). Preschool programs also appear to have long-term effects. Graduates of these programs are less likely to repeat a grade or be placed in classes for slow learners. They are more likely to finish high school, attend college, and earn high incomes. Participation in such programs even decreases the likelihood of juvenile delinquency and reliance on welfare programs (Schweinhart & Weikart, 1993; Zigler et al., 1992).

Remaining active may help older adults continue to function intellectually at a high level.

Adults and Intelligence

Psychologists are also concerned about factors that affect intelligence among adults, especially older adults. Older people show some drop-off in intelligence as measured by scores on intelligence tests. The decline is most notable in timed test questions—questions that must be answered within a certain amount of time (Schaie, 1994; Schaie & Willis, 1991). On the other hand, vocabulary skills can continue to expand for a lifetime.

Biological changes contribute to some of the decline. However, older people who retain their health have very high levels of intellectual functioning (Schaie, 1994). One study, conducted in Seattle, has been following intellectual changes in adults for nearly 40 years. The Seattle Study has found that intellectual functioning in older people is linked to several environmental factors (Schaie, 1993, 1994):

- level of income
- level of education
- a history of stimulating jobs
- intact family life
- attendance at cultural events, travel, and reading
- marriage to a spouse with a high level of intellectual functioning
- a flexible personality

In general, the more of these factors present in people's lives and the higher and stronger the factors are, the higher the level of intellectual functioning.

All things considered, intellectual functioning in people of all ages appears to reflect many genetic, physical, personal, and social factors. Todd clearly understood this when he reminded Dan that although Dan and his brother share the same parents and similar upbringings, they still have some different genes and have had different experiences, such as in school.

A DAY IN THE LIFE

No matter what genes a person may have inherited, that person's intelligence is not fixed or unchangeable. People such as Hannah, Dan, and Todd can, depending on their education and other factors, improve their intellectual functioning. Genetic factors give each person a range of possibilities. The environment influences the expression of these possibilities. Intelligence remains a complex concept that challenges psychologists, educators, and many others.

THINKING ABOUT PSYCHOLOGY

1. What evidence suggests that genetic factors play a role in intelligence?

2. What are three environmental factors that affect intelligence?

3. **Critical Thinking** Imagine you are a teacher of preschool children. Suggest three activities that you think would provide the children with an important skill or enrich their lives.

SUMMARY

Although psychologists have proposed several theories to explain intelligence, it remains a complex concept that is difficult to define and measure.

I. What Is Intelligence?

A. Intelligence is the capacity to learn from experience, to think rationally, and to deal effectively with the environment. It is not achievement, which is the knowledge and skills gained from experience.

B. Psychologists have proposed several approaches to defining intelligence.
   1. Charles Spearman suggested that intelligence consists of a *g* factor (general intelligence) and an *s* factor (specific intelligence).
   2. Louis Thurstone believed that nine "primary mental abilities" together make up intelligence.
   3. According to Howard Gardner, people have seven kinds of intelligence, examples of which include mental abilities and body-kinesthetic intelligence.
   4. According to Robert Sternberg's triarchic theory, intelligence consists of analytical, creative, and practical abilities, all of which work together.
   5. Daniel Goleman suggests that another kind of intelligence, called emotional intelligence, is as important as mental abilities.

C. Some types of intelligence may be linked to each other.

II. Measurement of Intelligence

A. Intelligence tests are intended to measure intelligence and to predict academic and job success.
   1. The Stanford-Binet Intelligence Scale was devised by Alfred Binet in the early 1900s and revised by Louis Terman of Stanford University in 1916.
   2. The revised Wechsler Adult Intelligence Scale is currently the most widely used intelligence test.

B. Intelligence tests must meet the criteria of reliability and validity.
   1. Reliability means the test gives highly similar scores for the same person every time it is used.
   2. Validity means the test measures what it is supposed to measure.

C. Factors such as economic background and motivation can influence test performance.

D. The methods used in some intelligence tests can give an unfair advantage to certain cultural groups.

III. Differences in Intelligence

A. People who attain IQ scores 70 or below are defined as mentally retarded.
   1. Mental retardation ranges from mild to profound.
   2. Causes of mental retardation include alcohol or drug abuse during pregnancy, health or malnutrition problems during pregnancy, accidents that result in brain damage, and genetic disorders.

B. People with IQ scores of 130 or above are defined as gifted. Many researchers and educators believe that giftedness is more than having a high IQ, however.

C. Giftedness is not the same as creativity, although creativity may be a part of giftedness in some people.

IV. What Influences Intelligence?

A. Kinship studies and adoptee studies show that heredity plays a strong role in determining intelligence.

B. Other studies show that environmental factors such as parenting style and schooling also affect intelligence.

C. Factors such as intact family life, continuing education, and a history of stimulating work can help most older people maintain a high level of intellectual functioning.

TERM & CONCEPT REVIEW

1. What is the relationship between achievement and intelligence?
2. Define the term *primary mental abilities.*
3. Contrast Louis Thurstone's theory of intelligence with that of Howard Gardner.
4. Define *chronological age, mental age,* and *intelligence quotient,* and explain how a person's IQ is calculated on the Stanford-Binet test.
5. Why are the Wechsler scales more widely used than the Stanford-Binet test?
6. What is meant by test-retest reliability?
7. Give one characteristic of each of the following individuals: a person with moderate mental retardation, a person with profound mental retardation, a gifted person, a creative person.
8. Define *heritability.*
9. What have kinship and adoptee studies revealed about the genetic role in intelligence?
10. List three things parents can do to help develop their children's intellectual functioning.

CRITICAL THINKING

1. Which theory of intelligence do you think is the most accurate? Use specific examples to explain your answer.
2. Besides vocabulary and problem-solving methods, what else might cause intelligence tests to be culturally biased?
3. How important do you think motivation is to success? Do you think gifted people can succeed with little motivation? Do you think people of below-average intelligence can succeed if they have a great deal of motivation? Explain your answers.
4. Explain how you might be able to boost your score on an IQ test.

5. What can parents and educators do to encourage highly creative children? How might school programs for these children differ from programs for gifted children?
6. If you were an employer, would you use scores on an IQ test to screen prospective employees? Why or why not?
7. Describe three activities that you could do to help someone who is age 70 or older maintain a high level of intellectual functioning.

APPLYING SKILLS IN PSYCHOLOGY

1. **COOPERATIVE LEARNING** **Research in Psychology** Organize a small group of classmates. Then assign one or more of Gardner's seven "intelligences" to each group member. After providing time for research, have each member tell about a well-known person who appears to exhibit the assigned intelligence. As a group, discuss the strengths and weaknesses of Gardner's theory.
2. **COOPERATIVE LEARNING** **Writing About Psychology** Along with a partner, devise a list of criteria you would use to select the most intelligent students for a student body hall of fame. Share your list with the rest of the class and come up with one class list.
3. **Reading About Psychology** Fetal alcohol syndrome (FAS) is a leading preventable cause of mental retardation. Find out the facts about FAS. Then make a poster warning about the dangers of drinking alcohol during pregnancy. Display your poster in the classroom.
4. **Using Your Observation Skills** Identify a local program that seeks to promote children's intellectual development. For example, there might be a program that shows parents how to interact with their babies. Observe the program in action, and write a brief summary explaining your observations.

UNIT 3
REVIEW

IDENTIFYING PEOPLE AND IDEAS

Explain the significance of each of the following people or terms to the study of psychology.

1. stimulus
2. classical conditioning
3. spontaneous recovery
4. B. F. Skinner
5. positive reinforcer
6. Albert Bandura
7. episodic memory
8. maintenance rehearsal
9. retrieval
10. chunking
11. schema
12. Hermann Ebbinghaus
13. concept
14. difference reduction
15. functional fixedness
16. inductive reasoning
17. syntax
18. language acquisition device
19. achievement
20. intelligence quotient
21. reliability
22. heritability

HANDS-ON PSYCHOLOGY
Cooperative Project

In Chapter 7, you learned that people's ability to retrieve a memory may be greater when they are in the place where the original experience was encoded and stored (context-dependent memory). Organize a group of classmates to help you test this theory. Design an experiment to determine whether people's ability to recall nonsense words they have memorized increases when they are in the same context in which they originally learned the words. Use the experiment with the swimmers on page 159 as a model.

As a group, decide on the setting or context for your test. For example, your group might decide to play music in the background while participants are learning the nonsense words. One student in the group should record the findings. Organize the remaining students into two groups. One group should memorize the list of words in the context you have chosen, while the other group should memorize the list in a different context. For example, if you have chosen the playing of music as your context, the second group should memorize the words in a setting of silence. Then test the memory of the members of both groups by asking them to recall under both conditions the words they have memorized.

As a group, examine the results of your experiment. Do the findings of your experiment support the current theory on context-dependent memory? How can you use context-dependent memory to your advantage in real life situations? Have one student in the group write a description of your group's experiment and conclusions.

BUILDING YOUR PORTFOLIO

Individually or in a group, complete the following project to show your understanding of the psychology concepts involved.

Improving Cognitive Skills

As you learned in this unit, the ways in which people learn, remember, and process information are of great interest to psychologists. By understanding how people's mental processes work, psychologists can help people use their minds as effectively as possible. Formulate a plan that would help parents and educators teach elementary school children in the most effective manner. You may wish to focus on a specific subject area, such as math, writing, or foreign languages, or you could make your report more general. In making your report, consider the following questions:

1. How can the principles of classical conditioning, operant conditioning, and observational learning be applied to specific learning situations? Why would the PQ4R method be more effective in some areas than in others?

2. How can children be taught to improve their memory? How can they minimize the various types of forgetting?

3. How do most children learn to solve problems, reason, make decisions, and use language? Are those methods effective? Why or why not? How could they be improved?

4. What can parents and educators do to help the development of each child's intelligence?

Organize your materials and present your report to the rest of the class.

UNIT 4

DEVELOPMENT

INFANCY AND CHILDHOOD

Objectives

1 Explain the major theories of development.

2 Describe the physical development that occurs during infancy.

3 Describe the social development of infants and children.

4 Identify the stages in Piaget's theory of cognitive development and in Kohlberg's theory of moral development.

A DAY IN THE LIFE

Hannah and her friends were having a discussion with Hannah's three-year-old brother, Eddie. "Why does it get dark outside?" Hannah asked him.

"'Cause I go to sleep," Eddie answered emphatically.

"Why does the sun rise?" Todd asked Eddie.

"'Cause I get up!" Eddie said.

"And why does the sun move in the sky?" Linda asked, taking a turn.

Eddie thought for a moment, "To follow me!" he answered as he scampered off to play with Dan.

"He's really something else," Marc grinned. "It's like he thinks the world revolves just around him."

"You should see some of the other things he does," Hannah said. "The other day, I showed him two rows of pennies. There were five pennies in each row. But in the first row, the pennies were half an inch apart. In the second row, they were two inches apart. I asked Eddie which row had more pennies."

"Bet I know his answer," said Marc. "The longer row, right?"

"Right. But then I asked him to count both rows, which he did, and he counted five pennies in each row. Then I asked him again which row had more pennies. He pointed to the second row again!"

"Makes you wonder how his mind works, doesn't it?" asked Marc.

"He's grown so fast," Hannah replied after a bit. "Not so long ago, he couldn't even sit by himself, then he suddenly started crawling, then standing, then he was walking. Now just look at him go."

"I remember last year when all he wanted to do was stay next to his mother or you," Todd said. "Now all he wants to do is go and explore."

"Yeah," remembered Hannah, laughing. "He used to tug on my leg until I'd pick him up. Now he's so big, I can hardly lift him."

"Bet your parents are spoiling him rotten," said Marc.

"Actually, they're pretty strict. They say it's better for kids."

"Really?" asked Marc. "I don't believe that. I bet it's better just to love them a lot."

Hannah thought for a moment. "Parents can be strict and still love their kids."

"Well," Marc replied, "Eddie is turning out great. Guess your parents are doing something right."

• • •

Hannah and her friends had discovered that Eddie's view of the world was very different from theirs. Psychologists know that preschool children such as Eddie do not think like adults—or like teenagers. Their thinking is truly in a class of its own. Psychologists know this because they have studied people of all ages—throughout the life span. This chapter is about two stages in the life span: infancy, the stage of life that lasts from birth until the second birthday, and childhood, the stage that follows infancy and spans the period from the second birthday to the beginning of adolescence.

1 The Study of Development

Developmental psychology is the field in which psychologists study how people grow and change throughout the life span—from conception, through infancy, childhood, adolescence, and adulthood, and until death. Psychologists are interested in studying the two stages discussed in this chapter—infancy and childhood—for many reasons. One is that early childhood experiences affect people as adolescents and adults. Another is that by studying early stages of development, psychologists can learn about developmental problems, what causes them, and how to treat them. For example, why do some children have low self-esteem? Psychologists can also learn about what types of experiences in infancy and childhood foster healthy and well-adjusted children and adults.

Studying development is also interesting in and of itself. Eddie's thinking would fascinate psychologists just as it intrigued Hannah and her friends. Developmental psychologists study not only people of different ages but also different types of development. These include physical development, social development, and cognitive development.

A DAY IN THE LIFE

Because developmental psychologists study people across the life span, they are interested in seeing how people change over time. Psychologists use two methods to study change: the longitudinal method and the cross-sectional method. Using the longitudinal method, developmental researchers select a group of participants, then observe that same group for a period of time, often years or even decades. Since the longitudinal method is very time-consuming (and also expensive), psychologists often use the cross-sectional method instead. Using this method, researchers select a sample that includes people of different ages. They then compare the participants in the different age groups. (See Chapter 2.)

Developmental psychologists are concerned with two general issues. The first involves the ways in which heredity and environmental influences contribute to human development. The second issue concerns whether development occurs gradually or in stages.

The Roles of Nature and Nurture

Psychologists have long debated the extent to which human behavior is determined by heredity (nature) or environment (nurture). This debate has been particularly relevant to the study of development. Some aspects of behavior originate in the genes people inherit from their parents. In other words, certain kinds of behavior are biologically "programmed" to develop as long as children receive

This infant will not learn to walk until she is biologically ready to walk. The point at which such readiness will occur is influenced by heredity.

WHEN I WAS FOUR MONTHS OLD, I USED TO LIE ON MY STOMACH AND KICK MY FEET..

WHEN I WAS SIX MONTHS OLD, I GOT UP ON MY HANDS AND KNEES, AND I ROCKED BACK AND FORTH...

PRETTY SOON I LEARNED TO CRAWL.. I USED TO CRAWL ALL OVER THE HOUSE..

I THOUGHT CRAWLING WAS GREAT.. IT GAVE ME A NEW FREEDOM.. I CRAWLED EVERYWHERE...

BUT LET ME TELL YOU SOMETHING...

WALKING IS A WHOLE LOT BETTER..

SOURCE: PEANUTS reprinted by permission of United Feature Syndicate, Inc.

adequate nutrition and social experience. Researchers use kinship studies, including studies of twins, to learn about the influence of heredity on human development. (See Chapter 3.)

In the field of human development, heredity manifests itself primarily in the process called maturation. **Maturation** is the automatic and sequential process of development that results from genetic signals. For instance, because of maturation, infants generally sit up before they crawl, crawl before they stand, and stand before they walk. This sequence happens automatically and on its own genetically determined timetable. No matter how much one might try to teach these skills to infants, they will not do these things until they are "ready."

This concept of "readiness" relates to an important term in the study of development: *critical period*. A **critical period** is a stage or point in development during which a person or animal is best suited to learn a particular skill or behavior pattern. For example, much research suggests that there may be a critical period for language development in humans. Young children seem to learn language more easily than older children and adults.

Psychologist Arnold Gesell (1880–1961) believed that maturation played the most important role in development. He focused on many areas of development, including physical and social development. Behavioral psychologists, such as John Watson, took a different view from Gesell's. This school of thought originated with the 17th-century English philosopher John Locke, who believed that the mind of the infant is like a *tabula rasa* (Latin for "blank slate"). That is, when an infant is born, her or his mind is like a blank slate on which the infant's experiences will be written. In this view, "nurture"—or the environment—will have the greatest effect on the newborn's development.

Watson and other behaviorists believed in environmental explanations for behavior. They thought that the influence of nurture was much stronger than that of nature. The influences of nurture, or the environment, are found in factors such as nutrition, family background, culture, and learning experiences in the home, community, and school.

Today nearly all psychologists would agree that both nature and nurture play key roles in children's development. For example, while few psychologists today believe that maturation plays the major role in *all* areas of development, they certainly think it is central in some, such as physical development and motor development.

Stages Versus Continuity

Another topic of debate among psychologists is whether human development occurs primarily in stages or as a continuous process. In other words, is development like climbing a set of stairs to reach the top (each stair being a distinct level), or is it like walking up an inclined plane or hill (a gradual increase up to the top, without distinct levels)?

INFANCY AND CHILDHOOD **229**

A stage, like one step in a staircase, is a period or a level in the development process that is distinct from other levels. Certain aspects of physical development appear to take place in stages. For example, Eddie and most other young children go through sitting, crawling, standing, and walking stages—in that order. When people move from one stage to another, their bodies and behavior can change dramatically.

Maturational theorists, such as Gesell, generally believe that most development occurs in stages. Rapid changes usher in dramatically new kinds of behavior, causing entry into the next stage. For instance, when an infant's legs become strong enough to support him or her, the infant stands and soon begins to walk. A new stage of life has begun—from infant to toddler.

One of the most famous stage theorists was Jean Piaget. His field was cognitive development, and he would have said that Eddie's self-centered way of thinking reflected his cognitive stage of development. Piaget would have further noted that Eddie's thinking would change dramatically when he entered the next stage of cognitive development.

Not all psychologists, however, agree that development occurs in stages. For example, J. H. Flavell and his colleagues (1993) argue that cognitive development is a gradual process. According to Flavell, cognitive development is an example of continuous development, which, like walking up a slope, happens slowly and gradually. For instance, the effects of learning cause gradual changes, such as the addition of new words to a child's vocabulary.

Continuous development can occur almost unnoticed. A child's steady growth in weight and height from the ages of about 2 to 11 years is an example of continuous development that happens so gradually we usually are not aware of the changes as they are occuring.

However, it is not always clear whether development occurs in stages or in a continuous progression. Psychologists still debate the issue, and many questions about it remain to be answered.

THINKING ABOUT PSYCHOLOGY

1. Define *maturation*.
2. Explain what is meant by a stage of development and give an example.
3. **Critical Thinking** What is one kind of development that appears to be gradual?

2 Physical Development

A newborn enters the world possessing certain physical characteristics and equipped with certain abilities. For example, an infant is born measuring a certain length and weighing a certain amount. Both height and weight will increase with time and nourishment. The infant is also born with certain reflexes. A **reflex** is an involuntary reaction or response, such as swallowing. Some of these reflexes the infant keeps; others disappear when they are no longer needed. Changes in reflexes and gains in height and weight are examples of physical development. Motor development and perceptual development are other examples.

Height and Weight

Babies grow at an amazing rate, but the most dramatic gains in height and weight occur even before an infant's birth. During the first eight weeks of the mother's pregnancy, the tiny embryo in her uterus develops fingers, toes, eyes, ears, a nose, a mouth, a heart, and a circulatory system. At eight weeks, the 1 1/2-inch-long embryo becomes a fetus. During the fetal stage (which lasts until birth), the organs of the various body systems, such as the respiratory

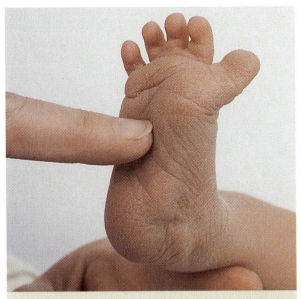

Most babies are born with the Babinski reflex, which means that they fan out their toes when the soles of their feet are touched.

system, develop to the point at which they can sustain the life of the baby after it is born.

During the nine months of pregnancy, the embryo develops from a nearly microscopic cell to a baby about 20 inches in length. A newborn weighs a billion or more times what it weighed at conception.

During **infancy**, the period from birth to age two years, dramatic gains continue in height and weight. Infants usually double their birth weight in about five months and triple it by one year. They grow about 10 inches in height in the first year. During the second year, infants generally gain another four to six inches in height and another four to seven pounds in weight.

TRUTH
OR
fiction
▪ R E V I S I T E D ▪

It is true that most babies triple their birth weights by the time they reach their first birthdays. Babies make dramatic gains in weight and height during their first two years.

After infancy comes **childhood**, the period from two years to adolescence. Following the second birthday, children gain two to three inches and four to six pounds each year until they reach the start of adolescence.

Motor Development

It might seem that, at first, babies are just bundles of reflexes and random movements. Soon, however, as their muscles and nervous systems mature, newborns' random movements are replaced by purposeful activity. The development of purposeful movement is called motor development. Milestones in infants' and children's motor development are shown in Figure 10.1.

Motor development proceeds in stages. Almost all babies roll over before they sit up unsupported, and they crawl before they walk. When Hannah talked about Eddie growing so fast, she was describing the different stages of his motor development: from sitting to crawling to standing to walking.

The point at which these various behaviors occur, however, is different from infant to infant and even from culture to culture. For example, in Uganda, infants usually walk before they are 10

FIGURE 10.1 *Motor development proceeds in an orderly sequence. At birth, an infant's behavior is reflexive. During the first six months, the brain and body mature to enable crawling and, later on, walking. The ages shown here are approximate.*

Cultural factors can influence when certain stages of motor development occur. Infants in some African countries, who spend much of their time being carried upright on their parents' backs, walk (on average) earlier than American infants.

can also breathe consciously if we wish—slowly or quickly, deeply or shallowly. The breathing reflex works for a lifetime. Sneezing, coughing, yawning, blinking, and many other reflexes also continue for a lifetime.

Rooting is another reflex that babies are born with. Because of the rooting reflex, babies turn toward stimuli that touch their cheeks or the corners of their mouths. Once infants locate the source of a stimulus, they automatically begin sucking and swallowing. The sucking and swallowing reflexes are essential to an infant's survival; without them, newborns would not eat. Babies reflexively suck objects that touch their lips and reflexively swallow food in their mouths.

Babies also reflexively withdraw from painful stimuli. They pull up their legs and arch their backs in response to sudden sounds or bumps. This is known as the Moro, or "startle," reflex. Babies also fan their toes when the soles of their feet are touched, a behavior that is called the Babinski reflex. They also eliminate wastes by reflex.

As children develop, many reflexes, such as rooting and sucking, disappear. Other reflexes, such as swallowing, remain. And some reflexes, such as elimination of wastes, come under voluntary control. These changes are all part of the maturation process.

Perceptual Development

Imagine what the world must seem like to a newborn. Prior to birth, the baby has spent several months in a warm, wet, dark place. Now suddenly, it finds itself in a bright, noisy world full of sensory stimuli. Perceptual development is the process by which infants learn to make sense of the sights, sounds, tastes, and other sensations to which they are exposed.

Infants tend to prefer new and interesting stimuli. They seem to be "preprogrammed" to survey their environment and learn about it. For example, a study by Robert Fantz (1961) found that two-month-old infants preferred pictures of the human face to any other pictures, such as newsprint, a bull's-eye, or colored disks without patterns.

Researchers have, however, discovered that infants' perceptual preferences are influenced by their age. For example, 5- to 10-week-old babies look longest at patterns that are fairly complex. It does not matter whether the pattern looks like a human face. What most interests them is the variety and complexity of the pattern. At this age, eyesight

months old, whereas in the United States, babies often do not start walking until around one year of age (Frankenburg et al., 1992). Why might this be? Perhaps because, while American babies spend much of their time lying in cribs, Ugandan babies spend much of their time being carried on their parents' backs. This contact with the parent, the sense of movement, and the upright position the babies maintain as they are being carried may help them learn to walk earlier (Bril, 1986).

Reflexes

Soon after a baby is born, the doctor or nurse places a finger against the palm of the baby's hand. Babies are not told how to respond and do not "know" what to do, of course. Even so, they usually grasp the finger firmly. Grasping is a reflex. Reflexes are inborn, not learned, and they occur automatically, without thinking.

Some reflexes are essential to our survival. Breathing is such a reflex. Although it is a reflex, we is not fully developed, so infants prefer to look at the most complex things they are capable of seeing reasonably well. By 15 to 20 weeks, patterns begin to matter. Babies then begin to stare longer at face-like patterns (Haaf et al., 1983).

These studies illustrate how nature and nurture work together. At first, infants seem to have an inborn preference for moderately complex visual stimuli. That is a result of nature. Their preference for human faces appears after they have had some experience with people. That results from the inter-action of nature with nurture.

Other studies have focused on depth perception in infants. In some of these studies, researchers use what has become known as the "visual cliff." The visual cliff is a special structure, a portion of which has a surface that looks like a checkerboard. Another portion is a sheet of glass with a checker-board pattern a few feet below it. It creates the illu-sion of a drop-off of a few feet—like a cliff.

One classic study with the visual cliff found that very young infants seem to be unafraid (as indicated by heart rate) when they are placed face down on the edge of the apparent drop-off. By nine months, however, infants respond with fear of the drop-off (Campos et al., 1970). Another classic study found that by the time infants learn to crawl, most of them will refuse to move onto the glass portion even when their mothers call them from the other side (Walk & Gibson, 1961). Apparently, crawling and exploring the world have taught the older infants that drop-offs are dangerous and that falling is frightening and painful. Experience has taught them depth perception. (See Chapter 4.)

Vision, of course, is only one type of perception. In general, infants' hearing is much better devel-oped at birth than is their eyesight. When it comes to hearing, most newborns stop whatever they are doing and turn toward unusual sounds. They respond more to high-pitched sounds than to low pitched ones, although they seem to be soothed by the sounds of someone singing softly or speaking in a low-pitched tone (Papousek et al., 1991). No wonder parents often sing lullabies to help their infants go to sleep.

Newborns immediately distinguish strong odors. They spit, stick out their tongues, and wrin-kle their noses at pungent odors (as the rest of us do). But they smile and show licking motions in response to the smells of chocolate, strawberry, and vanilla. They also like sweet-tasting liquid but refuse to suck salty or bitter liquids. A "sweet tooth," it seems, may be part of human nature.

This visual cliff has a glass-covered drop-off. It is used in experiments to test the depth perception of infants. Most infants who can crawl refuse to cross the part that appears to be a cliff even if their mothers call them.

THINKING ABOUT PSYCHOLOGY

1. In what ways do a baby's height and weight change during infancy?
2. Define *reflex* and give two examples.
3. Describe the purpose of research studies that use the visual cliff.
4. **Critical Thinking** Explain why reflexes are necessary for an infant's survival.

3
Social Development

Social development involves the ways in which infants and children learn to relate to other people. For example, infants usually can be comforted by being held, and they soon respond to their mothers' voices. At first, they might cling to their mothers, but after a few months they venture out to explore the world and make contact with strangers. Infants tend to play with toys by themselves, even when other children are around. As they grow older, how-ever, they begin to play with others. All of these changes are part of social development.

Many important factors affect social development. Such factors include attachment, parenting styles, child care, child abuse and neglect (for some children), and self-esteem.

Attachment

Feelings of **attachment** are the emotional ties that form between people. Feelings of attachment keep people together. Since infants are basically helpless and are totally dependent on others to fulfill their needs, feelings of attachment are essential to their survival.

Infants and children try to stay in contact with the people to whom they are attached. That may be why Eddie used to tug on Hannah's pant leg.

Development of Attachment   Psychologist Mary Ainsworth studied attachment in infants around the world (Ainsworth & Bowlby, 1991). What she observed in every place she studied was that, at first, infants prefer being held or even just being with someone—anyone—over being alone. By about four months of age, however, infants develop specific attachments to their mothers. This

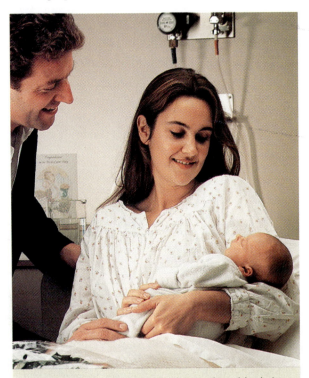

Newborn infants can usually be comforted by being held. In the months to come, this infant will learn to respond to her mother's voice.

attachment grows stronger by six to seven months. Once they reach this point, infants and children try to maintain contact with their mothers and cry or complain when they are separated.

By the age of about eight months, some infants develop a fear of strangers. This is known as **stranger anxiety**. Infants who experience stranger anxiety cry and reach for their parents if they are near strangers. Their anxiety is somewhat less if the person to whom they are attached is holding them (Thompson & Limber, 1990). The closer they are to the strangers, however, the more upset they become (Boccia & Campos, 1989). They are most distressed when the strangers actually touch them.

At about the same age, infants may also develop separation anxiety. **Separation anxiety** causes infants to cry or behave in other ways that indicate distress if their mothers leave them. Why do infants become so attached to their primary caregivers? Research suggests that at least two factors are involved: contact comfort and imprinting.

Contact Comfort   For a long time, psychologists thought that infants became attached to those who fed them. But then psychologist Harry F. Harlow observed that infant monkeys without mothers or companions became attached to pieces of cloth in their cages—even though, of course, the pieces of cloth did not provide food. The monkeys held on to their pieces of cloth and were upset when the cloth was taken away. Harlow conducted several experiments to find out why, and what types of objects the monkeys would and would not become attached to (Harlow, 1959).

In one study, Harlow placed infant monkeys in cages, each of which had two "mother" objects. One object was made from wire and held a baby bottle. The other, which had no bottle, was made of soft terry cloth. The monkeys spent most of their time clinging to their cloth "mother," even though it did not feed them. Harlow thus concluded that the monkeys had a basic need for **contact comfort**, which is the instinctual need to touch and be

In Harlow's study of the importance of contact comfort, monkeys spent most of their time with their cloth "mother" even though it did not feed them.

moving object they see. The moving object is said to become imprinted on the infant animal. **Imprinting** is the process by which some animals form immediate attachments during a critical period.

Researchers have shown that animals can become imprinted on some rather unusual objects. Using imprinting, researcher Konrad Lorenz (1937) acquired a family of goslings for himself. How did he do it? He was present when the goslings hatched, and he then allowed them to follow him. The critical period for imprinting in geese and some other animals begins when they can first move about on their own. Lorenz's "family" followed him wherever he went. They ran to him when they were frightened. They honked loudly when he left them alone—just as human infants cry when they are left by the people to whom they are attached.

touched by something soft, such as skin or fur. This need seems to be even stronger than the need for food. In other words, the monkeys and perhaps human babies may cling to their mothers because of the need for contact comfort rather than just because they are hungry. Based on such findings, researchers have concluded that attachment grows more from body contact than from feeding.

Bonds of attachment between mothers and infants also appear to provide a secure base from which the infants can explore their environments. Harlow and Zimmerman (1959) placed toys, such as stuffed bears and wooden insects, in cages with infant monkeys. Some of the cages had wire "mothers," and the others had terry cloth "mothers." The monkeys who were alone or with wire mothers cringed in fear as long as the bears or insects were in the cage. Infant monkeys in cages with terry cloth mothers, on the other hand, cringed for a while but eventually began to explore the bears or insects. The terry cloth mothers apparently gave the infant monkeys a sense of security that enabled them to explore the world around them.

Imprinting   For many animals, attachment is an instinct. Instinctive behavior develops during a critical period shortly after birth. Ducks, geese, and some other animals become attached to the first

Imprinting involves animals forming attachments during a critical period. Konrad Lorenz was present when these goslings hatched. Because he was the first moving object they perceived and could follow, they became attached to him.

Although the development of attachment may also be instinctive in people (Ainsworth & Bowlby, 1991), human attachments develop somewhat differently than attachments among ducks and geese. For example, children do not imprint on the first person they see or are held by. For humans, it takes several months before infants become attached to their mothers. There is also no known critical period for attachment in humans. Children can become strongly attached to their adoptive parents even when they are adopted after infancy.

Secure Versus Insecure Attachment   When mothers or other primary caregivers are affectionate and reliable, infants usually become securely attached (Cox et al., 1992). Infants with secure attachment are very bonded to their caregivers. They cry or protest if the parent or caregiver leaves them. When the caregiver returns, the infants welcome that person back and are happy again.

When caregivers are unresponsive or unreliable, the infants are usually insecurely attached. They often do not seem to mind when the caregivers leave them. When the caregivers return, the infants make little or no effort to seek contact with them. Some insecure infants may cry when picked up, as if they are angry with the caregiver (Ainsworth, 1973, 1979; Ainsworth et al., 1978).

Secure infants may mature into secure children. Secure children are happier, friendlier, and more cooperative with parents and teachers than insecure children are. They get along better with other children than insecure children do (Belsky et al., 1991; Thompson, 1991a). Secure children are also less likely to misbehave and more likely to do well in school than insecure children (Lyons-Ruth et al., 1993; Youngblade & Belsky, 1992).

Styles of Parenting

Styles of parenting differ along two separate dimensions. One dimension is warmth-coldness; the other is strictness-permissiveness (Baumrind, 1991a, 1991b; MacDonald, 1992). Warm parents can be either strict or permissive, as can cold parents.

Warm or Cold?   Warm parents show a great deal of affection to their children. For example, they hug and kiss them and often smile at them. They show their children that they are happy to have them and enjoy their company. Cold parents may not be as affectionate toward their children or appear to enjoy them as much.

Research suggests that children fare better when their parents are warm to them (Dix, 1991). The children of warm parents are more likely to be well adjusted. They are also more likely to develop a conscience—a sense of moral goodness or a sense of responsibility when they do wrong (MacDonald, 1992; Miller et al., 1993). Children of cold parents, on the other hand, are usually more interested in escaping punishment than in doing the right thing for its own sake.

Strict or Permissive?   If you have younger brothers and sisters, you probably know that children do many things that anger or annoy other people. For example, they may make noise when other people are trying to sleep or concentrate on a difficult task. Sometimes they make messes. Children may also engage in behaviors that are unhealthy to themselves. They may have poor eating habits or watch too much television. They may neglect their schoolwork or play with dangerous objects.

Some parents are extremely strict when it comes to such behaviors. They impose many rules and supervise their children closely. Permissive parents, on the other hand, impose fewer rules and watch their children less closely. Permissive parents tend to be less concerned about neatness and cleanliness than are strict parents.

Parents may be strict or permissive for different reasons. Some extremely strict parents cannot tolerate disorder. Others fear that their children will run wild and get into trouble if they are not taught self-discipline. Some parents are permissive because they believe that children need freedom to express themselves if they are to become independent. Other parents are permissive because they do not care or have time to monitor their children's activities. Without clear and consistent guidance, these children may become confused about which behaviors are acceptable and which are not.

Strictness can have positive and negative results, depending on how it is used. Strictness is not necessarily the same as meanness—as Hannah pointed out, parents can be strict but still love their children. Research suggests that consistent and firm enforcement of rules can foster achievement and self-control, especially when combined with warmth and support (Putallaz & Hefflin, 1990). But physical punishment or constant interference may lead to disobedience and poor grades in school (Olson et al., 1992; Westerman, 1990).

Authoritative (meaning with authority) parents combine warmth with positive kinds of strictness. The children of authoritative parents are often more independent and achievement oriented than other children. They also feel better about themselves (Baumrind, 1991b; Dumas & LaFreniere, 1993). Parental demands for responsible behavior combined with affection and support usually pay off. Apparently, Hannah's parents knew this, and were raising Eddie with both strictness and warmth.

Be careful not to confuse the term *authoritative* with the word *authoritarian,* which means "favoring unquestioning obedience." **Authoritarian** parents believe in obedience for its own sake. They have strict guidelines that they expect their children to follow without question. Often they are rejecting and cold. Children of authoritarian parents may become either resistant to other people or dependent on them (Baumrind, 1989). They generally do not do as well in school as children of authoritative parents. They also tend to be less friendly and less spontaneous (DeKovic & Janssens, 1992; Maccoby & Martin, 1983).

Child Care

In the United States today, many parents—both fathers and mothers—work outside the home. As a result, many children are cared for by others while parents are at work. Often they are cared for in special child care facilities outside the home. Psychologists have studied the effects of such care on bonds of attachment between parents and children. They have also looked into the effects of child care by people other than parents on children's social development.

Studies of the effects of child care have found that children who become accustomed to being cared for by people other than their parents are less upset than other children when their mothers leave them temporarily. They are also less likely to run to

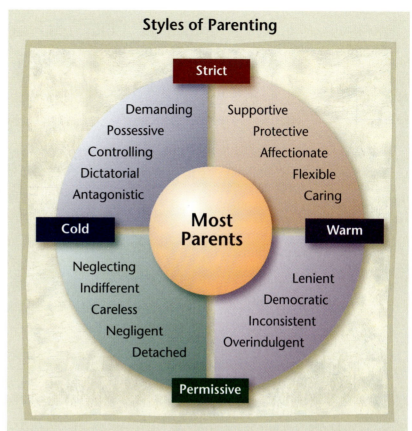

Styles of Parenting

Strict

Demanding
Possessive
Controlling
Dictatorial
Antagonistic

Supportive
Protective
Affectionate
Flexible
Caring

Cold

Most Parents

Warm

Neglecting
Indifferent
Careless
Negligent
Detached

Lenient
Democratic
Inconsistent
Overindulgent

Permissive

FIGURE 10.2 *Styles of parenting can be classified along the dimensions of warm-cold and strict-permissive. Both dimensions are continuums, and most parents do not lie at the extremes but cluster in the middle.*

their mothers excitedly when their mothers return. Does this mean that the children who are in child care are less attached to their mothers? Many psychologists believe that becoming accustomed to one's mother's goings and comings is a sign of positive adjustment, not of a lack of attachment or of a social problem (Field, 1991; Lamb et al., 1992; Thompson, 1991b). Most children in full-time non-parent child care appear to be securely attached to their mothers (Clarke-Stewart, 1989).

Nonparent care seems to have mixed effects on other aspects of children's social development, however. For example, some studies show that children in child care facilities are more sociable with other children, more likely to share their toys, and more independent and self-confident than children who spend the day at home (Clarke-Stewart, 1991; Field, 1991). In these studies, child care seemed to make children more interested in other children and to help them develop social skills.

On the other hand, another study found that children in child care facilities were somewhat less

The Importance of Being a Father

With many mothers returning to work after the birth of their babies, fathers are becoming more actively involved in the rearing of children than ever before in American culture. In fact, six-month-old infants are generally just as attached to their fathers as they are to their mothers (Lamb, 1977).

Although fathers are as good as mothers at such things as bottle-feeding, once the baby comes home, the mother is usually still the one who does most of the caregiving. Caregiving includes feeding, diapering, and bathing infants. So if men generally do not spend the time they have with their children in caregiving, what is it they do? Most fathers play—and they are very good at it.

The way fathers play turns out to be very different from the way mothers play with their children. Whereas mothers usually use toys or word games, fathers tend to play in a rough-and-tumble way. They bounce and lift their children. They move their arms and legs (Parke, 1981). Psychologists have discovered that as infants grow, they come to prefer those sorts of games. By the time most children are 30 months old, they often are more cooperative, excited, and interested in play with their fathers than with their mothers (Clarke-Stewart, 1978).

But do fathers make a difference in the development of their children? They most certainly do. A father's involvement has an effect in at least two major areas: social development and cognitive development. Socially, children whose fathers play with them tend to be more popular and have better relationships with their peers (MacDonald & Parke, 1984). During physical play with their fathers, children learn to figure out other people's emotions and expressions and to regulate

Fathers tend to play with children in a rough-and-tumble way.

their own emotions. Therefore, fathers help teach them how to get along with their friends and other people. Children whose fathers are involved with them also generally grow up to be more empathic (Koestner, 1990). Empathy is the ability to understand another person's point of view and imagine what that person might be feeling.

When it comes to cognitive development, a father's influence is most noticeable in boys. If a boy has a close relationship with his father, he often does better at solving problems and taking cognitive tests (Radin, 1981).

Because of the influence fathers have on their children's development, psychologists have argued that a parental leave of absence from work for fathers is very important. Other changes in the workplace, such as shorter workweeks and flexible hours, may make it easier for fathers to spend time with their children (Parke, 1981b). And in 1993, Congress passed the Family and Medical Leave Act. This legislation enables new parents to take 12 weeks of unpaid leave. Still, most fathers do not take advantage of this. Some of them simply cannot afford to go without pay for that long. Others may worry that their employers will think they are not committed enough to their jobs if they take time off.

This may change over time. In Sweden, where both parents are guaranteed parental leave, over 40 percent of fathers take time off from their jobs to be with their newborn children. In the 1970s this figure was only 2 percent.

THINK ABOUT IT

How might it benefit fathers to take an active role in rearing their children?

cooperative and more aggressive than children cared for at home (Vandell & Corasaniti, 1990). Children in child care facilities may receive less attention or fewer resources than they would like. As a result, they may become more aggressive as they compete with the other children for attention and resources. Some psychologists, however, interpret the greater aggressiveness of children in child care facilities as a sign of independence rather than maladjustment.

Of course, the quality of child care by people other than parents varies widely. In general, children seem to do better in environments that are stimulating. Also, the more adults per child there are and the more sensitive the caregivers are, the higher the quality of the child care (National Institute of Child Health and Human Development Early Child Research Network, 1996).

Child Abuse and Neglect

Most parents are kind and loving to their children. Yet child abuse—either physical or psychological—is unfortunately widespread. In a national poll of 1,000 parents, 5 percent of the parents surveyed admitted to physically abusing their children (Lewin, 1995). Physical abuse is the beating, hitting, or kicking of another person that results in bodily injury.

Even more common than child abuse is child neglect—the failure to give children adequate food, shelter, clothing, emotional support, or schooling. Physical abuse is horrifying because the results—bruises, burns, and broken bones—are visible. Yet more injuries, illnesses, and deaths result from neglect than from abuse (Finkelhor & Dzuiba-Leatherman, 1994; Wolock & Horowitz, 1984).

Why do some parents abuse or neglect their children? Psychologists have found the following factors to be associated with child abuse and neglect:

- stress, particularly the stresses of unemployment and poverty (Lewin, 1995; Trickett et al., 1991)
- a history of child abuse in at least one parent's family of origin
- acceptance of violence as a way of coping with stress
- lack of attachment to the children
- substance abuse
- rigid attitudes about child rearing (Belsky, 1993; Kaplan, 1991)

Studies have shown that children who are abused may run a higher risk of developing psychological problems than other children (Malinosky-Rummell & Hansen, 1993). For example, abused children tend to be insecure. They are less likely than other children to venture out to explore the world (Aber & Allen, 1987) and they tend to have less self-confidence (Cicchetti & Olson, 1990). Abused children are also more likely to develop feelings of anxiety and depression (Malinosky-Rummell & Hansen, 1993; Stone, 1993). Physically abused children are also more likely to become aggressive themselves (Dodge et al., 1990; Rothbart & Ahadi, 1994).

Child abuse tends to run in families (Simons et al., 1991). There are many possible reasons for this pattern. For one thing, children may imitate their parents' behavior. If children see their parents coping with feelings of anger through violence, they are likely to do the same. They are less likely to seek other ways of coping, such as humor, verbal expression of negative feelings, deep breathing, or silently "counting to 10" before reacting, thus giving the feelings of anger time to subside.

Children also often adopt their parents' strict ideas about discipline. Abused children may come to see severe punishment as normal. They may come to believe the old saying "Spare the rod; spoil the child," which means that a child who is not punished (or hit, as with a rod) will grow up spoiled. As a result, when they have children of their own, they may continue the pattern of abuse and neglect.

This does not mean, however, that all people who were abused as children will become abusers themselves. Most children who are abused do not later abuse their own children (Kaufman & Zigler, 1989). One study found that mothers who had been abused as children but were able to break the cycle of abuse with their own children were likely to have received emotional support from a nonabusive adult during childhood. They were also likely to have participated in therapy and to have a nonabusive mate (Egeland et al., 1988).

It is not true that most abused children become child abusers themselves when they grow up. Although some children of abuse do become abusers, most do not.

Self-Esteem

The development of self-esteem begins in early childhood. **Self-esteem** is the value or worth that people attach to themselves. Self-esteem is important because it helps to protect people against the stresses and struggles of life. Although everyone experiences failure now and then, high self-esteem gives people the confidence to know that they can overcome their difficulties.

Influences on Self-Esteem

What factors influence self-esteem? Secure attachment plays a major role. Young children who are securely attached to their parents are more likely to have high self-esteem (Cassidy, 1988).

The ways in which parents react to their children can also make a difference. Research suggests that authoritative parenting contributes to high self-esteem in children (Baumrind, 1991). Children with high self-esteem tend to be close to their parents because their parents are loving and involved in their lives. Their parents also teach and expect appropriate behavior and thus encourage them to become competent individuals.

Psychologist Carl Rogers noted that parents can give their children two types of support—unconditional positive regard or conditional positive regard. **Unconditional positive regard** means that parents love and accept their children for who they are—no matter how they behave. Children who receive unconditional positive regard usually develop high self-esteem. They know that even if they do something wrong or inappropriate, they are still worthwhile as people.

On the other hand, children who receive conditional positive regard may have lower self-esteem. **Conditional positive regard** means that parents show their love only when the children behave in certain acceptable ways. Children who receive conditional positive regard may feel worthwhile only when they are doing what their parents (or other authority figures) want them to do.

Once these children grow up, they often continue to seek the approval of other people. Excessive need for approval from other people is linked to low self-esteem (Ellis & Dryden, 1987). It is unrealistic for people to expect everyone to like and respect them. If they understand that it is natural for others to not always appreciate them, they may have higher self-esteem in the long run.

A sense of competence also increases self-esteem. By the age of about four, children begin to

When children are encouraged and given the means to develop skills, such as tending a garden, their self-esteem may rise.

judge themselves according to their cognitive, physical, and social competence (Harter, 1990). Children who know that they are good at something usually have higher self-esteem than others. Children may feel good about themselves if they are good at puzzles or counting (cognitive skills), if they are good at tying their shoelaces or swinging (physical skills), or if they have friends (social skills).

Both heredity and environment play roles in individual differences in skills. Some people are more physically coordinated than others and therefore naturally good at sports. Other people may take lessons and train to improve their athletic abilities. Part of becoming competent is setting realistic goals. Warmth and encouragement from parents and teachers can help children reach high levels of competence and self-esteem.

Gender and Self-Esteem

By the ages of five to seven, children begin to value themselves on the basis of their physical appearance and performance in school. Once in grade school, girls tend to display greater competence in the areas of reading and general academic skills. Boys tend to display competence in math and physical skills (Eccles et al., 1993; Marsh et al., 1991). (See Chapter 9.)

Does this mean that girls are genetically better in reading and boys better in math and sports? No. It may be that the reason girls and boys show greater competence, and thus higher self-esteem, in these areas is that people around them have suggested that this is what girls and boys are *supposed* to be good at. For example, girls predict that they will do better on tasks that are considered "feminine," and boys predict better performance for themselves when tasks are labeled "masculine" (Lips, 1993). When people feel they will do well at a particular task, they often do. People generally live up to the expectations they have for themselves—and that others have for them. Such expectations often become self-fulfilling prophecies.

Age and Self-Esteem   Children gain in competence as they grow older. Through experience they learn more skills and become better at them. Even so, their self-esteem tends to decline during the elementary school years. Self-esteem seems to reach a low point at about age 12 or 13 and increases again during adolescence (Harter, 1990; Pomerantz et al., 1993). How can we explain this pattern?

It appears that young children, such as Hannah's brother Eddie, assume that others see them as they see themselves. Thus, if they like themselves, they assume that other people like them too. As children develop, however, they begin to realize that some people might not see them the way they see themselves. They also begin to compare themselves to their peers. If they see themselves as less competent in some areas, their self-esteem may decrease.

It is true that children's self-esteem tends to decrease as they go through elementary school. As children develop and mature, they begin to compare themselves to others of the same age. Sometimes they feel they do not measure up to their peers.

THINKING ABOUT PSYCHOLOGY

1. Define the terms *attachment, contact comfort,* and *imprinting.*

2. What is the difference between authoritative and authoritarian parenting?

3. **Critical Thinking**   Identify three things you think parents and teachers can do to help children keep self-esteem high throughout the school years.

4 Cognitive Development

In addition to social development, psychologists are also interested in studying cognitive development, or the development of people's thought processes. Two psychologists who are famous for their work on children's cognitive development are Jean Piaget and Lawrence Kohlberg.

Piaget's Theory of Cognitive Development

Jean Piaget

When Jean Piaget (1896–1980) was in his early 20s, he was employed at the Binet Institute in Paris. At the institute he worked on the Binet intelligence test, trying out potential test questions on children.

Before long, Piaget realized that the children he questioned gave certain types of wrong answers and that these wrong answers fit patterns from child to child. Piaget was so interested in these patterns that the study of children's thinking became his life's work.

Assimilation and Accommodation   Piaget believed that human beings organize new information in two ways: through assimilation and through accommodation. **Assimilation** is the process by which new information is placed into categories that already exist. For example, a child might know the word *doggie* because the family has a pet collie. If that child sees a Great Dane on the street and says "Doggie," she or he has assimilated the new information about the Great Dane into the category "dog"—even though the Great Dane looks and may act different from the collie familiar to the child.

If the same child sees a cat and says "Doggie" again, some adults most likely will correct the child. Through such corrections, the child will learn that the category "dog" does not apply to cats and that a new category is needed. This adjustment is an example of **accommodation**—a change brought about because of new information.

Object permanence means understanding that objects exist even when they are out of sight. This toddler realizes that his brother still exists even when he is hidden behind the cushions.

Piaget theorized that children's thinking develops in a sequence of stages. Some children are more advanced than others at a given age. However, the developmental sequence is the same for everyone. Piaget identified four stages in the sequence: sensorimotor, preoperational, concrete operational, and formal operational.

The Sensorimotor Stage The behavior of newborns is mainly reflexive. They are capable only of responding to their environment and cannot initiate behavior. Instead of "acting," infants "react." By about one month of age, however, infants begin to act with purpose. As they coordinate vision with touch, for example, they will look at objects they are holding.

The first stage of cognitive development is characterized mainly by learning to coordinate sensation and perception with motor activity. Infants begin to understand that there is a relationship between their physical movements and the results they sense and perceive. That is why Piaget called this stage the **sensorimotor stage**.

Infants who are three and four months old are fascinated by their own hands and legs. They are easily amused by watching themselves open and close their fists. If they hear an interesting sound, such as a rattle, they might do something to sustain the sound. By four to eight months, infants are exploring cause-and-effect relationships. They might, for example, hit mobiles that hang over their cribs so that the mobiles will move.

Perhaps you have heard the expression "Out of sight; out of mind." Before infants are six months old, objects out of their sight are truly out of their minds. The infants do not realize that objects out of sight still exist. They might stare at a stuffed animal, but if you were to put the stuffed animal behind a piece of paper, they would not look behind the paper or reach to find it. By eight months to a year, however, infants understand that things that have been taken away still exist. For example, a 10-month-old child probably would search for a stuffed animal that was hidden behind a screen. Piaget called this **object permanence**—the understanding that objects exist even when they cannot be seen or touched.

According to Piaget's theory, object permanence occurs because infants are able to hold an idea in mind. For instance, they learn that "stuffed animal" is a soft, fuzzy object. They can mentally picture a stuffed animal even when it is no longer in view. Therefore, they know to look for it when it is hidden behind a screen.

The Preoperational Stage The sensorimotor stage ends at about the age of two years, when children begin to use words and symbols (language) to represent objects. At this point, children enter the **preoperational stage**.

A DAY IN THE LIFE

As we saw with Eddie, preoperational thinking is very different from more mature forms of thinking. Children's views of the world are different from those of adolescents and adults. For example, preoperational thinking is one-dimensional. In other words, preoperational children can see only one aspect of a situation at a time.

This one-dimensional thinking is most evident in the fact that in the preoperational stage children do not understand the law of **conservation**. The law says that key properties of substances, such as their weight, volume, and number, stay the same even if their shape or arrangement are changed. That is, the basic properties are *conserved*. Children in the preoperational stage cannot comprehend all the aspects at once, so they focus only on the most obvious one—the way a substance looks.

When preoperational children are shown two identical tall, thin glasses of water, each filled to the same level, they know that both glasses hold the

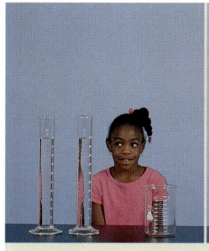

In the first photograph, the child looks at two tall glasses filled to the same level and understands that both glasses contain the same amount of liquid. In the second photograph, the child watches as the liquid from one of the tall glasses is emptied into a shorter glass. In the third photograph, the child indicates a belief that the tall glass that is still full contains more liquid than the short one simply because the taller glass *looks* bigger.

same amount of water. However, if water from one of the tall glasses is poured into a short, squat glass, the children say that the other tall glass contains more liquid than the short one. They say this even if they have *watched* the water being poured. Because they can focus only on what they are seeing at a given moment—and on one dimension at a time—they incorrectly think that the tall glass now contains more water than the short glass. Their thinking is that it looks as if there is less water in the short glass (because the water level is lower) and therefore it must be so. Children in the preoperational stage do not realize that increases in one dimension (such as width) can make up for decreases in another (such as height).

A DAY IN THE LIFE Eddie—who at three years of age is in the preoperational stage—did not understand the law of conservation, as demonstrated by Hannah's experiment with the five pennies. Eddie insisted that the row of five pennies that was stretched out had more pennies in it than the row in which the pennies were close together. He said so even when Hannah had him count the pennies in both rows, which he did correctly.

Another characteristic of children in the preoperational stage is **egocentrism**—the inability to see another person's point of view. Remember how Eddie thought it became dark because he went to sleep and that the sun rose because he woke up? Preoperational children assume that other people see the world just as they do. They cannot imagine that things might happen to others that do not happen to them. They think that the world exists to meet their needs. Egocentrism is a consequence of the preoperational child's one-dimensional thinking. Egocentrism is not the same as selfishness. When a preschooler sits down in front of the television set blocking everyone's else's view, he or she is not being rude. The child simply thinks you can see exactly what he or she can see.

Preoperational children are also artificialistic and animistic. They think that natural events such as rain and thunder are made by people (artificialism). They also think objects such as the sun and the moon are alive and conscious (animism).

The Concrete-Operational Stage Most children enter the **concrete-operational stage** at about the age of seven. In this stage, children begin to show signs of adult thinking. Yet they are logical only when they think about specific objects, not about abstract ideas. Their thinking is still grounded mostly in concrete experiences. This is one reason why many teachers assign them hands-on projects. Seeing, touching, and manipulating objects often help concrete-operational children understand abstract concepts.

Children at the concrete-operational stage can focus on two dimensions of a problem at the same time. For this reason, they understand the laws of conservation. They understand that a short, wide glass might contain the same amount of water as a tall, thin glass. They can focus on both the height

Examples of Preoperational Thought

Kind of Thinking	Sample Questions	Typical Answers
Egocentric (thinking that the world exists to meet one's own needs)	Why does it get dark out?	So I can go to sleep.
	Why does the sun shine?	To keep me warm.
	Why is there snow?	For me to play in.
	Why is grass green?	Because that's my favorite color.
	What are TV sets for?	To watch my favorite shows and cartoons.
Animistic (thinking that inanimate objects are alive and conscious)	Why do trees have leaves?	To keep them warm.
	Why do stars twinkle?	Because they're happy and cheerful.
	Why does the sun move in the sky?	To follow children and hear what they say.
	Where do boats go at night?	They sleep like we do.
Artificialistic (thinking that natural things and events are made by people)	Why is the sky blue?	Somebody painted it.
	What is the wind?	A man blowing.
	What causes thunder?	A man grumbling.
	What makes it rain?	Somebody emptying a watering can.

FIGURE 10.3 *The second stage of Piaget's theory of cognitive development is the preoperational stage. At about two years of age, the child begins to use words and symbols to represent things. Thinking tends to be one-dimensional, however. The child believes that the world exists to meet his or her needs.*

and the width of the glasses at the same time. They can therefore recognize that a gain in width compensates for a loss in height. Similarly, in a few years, Eddie will conserve number. He will understand that the two rows have the same number of pennies in them, even though one row is longer because the pennies are spaced farther apart.

Concrete-operational children are less egocentric than children in earlier stages. They can see the world from another person's point of view. They understand that people may see things differently because they have different experiences or are in different situations.

The Formal-Operational Stage The final cognitive stage in Piaget's theory begins at about puberty and represents cognitive maturity. It is the **formal-operational stage**.

People in the formal-operational stage think abstractly. They realize that ideas can be compared and classified mentally just as objects can. For example, they understand what is meant by the unknown quantity x in algebra. They can work on geometry problems about lines, triangles, and squares without concerning themselves with how the problems relate to the real world. They can also deduce rules of behavior from moral principles. They focus on many aspects of a situation simultaneously when reasoning and solving problems.

During the formal-operational stage, people are capable of dealing with hypothetical situations. They realize that they may be able to control the outcome of a situation in several different ways. Therefore, if one approach to solving a problem does not work, they will try another. They think ahead, imagining the results of different courses of action before they decide on a particular one.

Criticism of Piaget's Theories Over the years, a number of psychologists have questioned the accuracy of Piaget's views. Some believe his methods caused him to underestimate the abilities of children. Recent research using different methodology indicates that preschoolers are less egocentric

CASE STUDIES

AND OTHER TRUE STORIES

The Story of the Cups

Adults do not usually blame people for breaking things by accident. But Jean Piaget discovered that preoperational children differ greatly from adults in their reactions to accidents. He studied their reasoning by telling them stories and then asking them questions about the stories. Here are two stories Piaget used (adapted from Piaget, 1932, pp.125–130):

John's Story   A little boy, who was called John, was in his room. He was called to dinner. He went downstairs to the dining room. However, behind the dining-room door, which was closed, was a chair, and on the chair was a tray holding 15 cups. John did not know what was behind the door when he pushed open the door. The door knocked against the tray. Bang went the 15 cups and they all broke.

Henry's Story   Once there was a little boy named Henry. One day when his mother was out, Henry tried to reach some jam in the cupboard. He climbed onto a chair and stretched out his arm. But the jam jar was too high up and he could not reach it. But while Henry was trying to reach the jar, he knocked over a cup. The cup fell to the floor and broke.

After Piaget told the stories, he asked the children some questions. The dialogue typically went as follows when the listener was six years old:

Piaget: *Have you understood these stories? Let me hear you tell them.*

Child: *A little child was called in to dinner. There were 15 plates on a tray. He didn't know. He opens the door and he breaks the 15 plates.*

Piaget: *. . . And now the second story?*

Child: *There was a child. {He} wanted to go and get some jam. He gets onto a chair. His arm catches onto a cup, and it gets broken.*

Piaget: *Are those children both naughty, or is one not so naughty as the other?*

Child: *Both just as naughty.*

Piaget: *Would you punish them the same?*

Child: *No. The one who broke 15 plates.*

Piaget: *And why would you punish the other one . . . less?*

Child: *The first one broke lots of things, the other fewer.*

Piaget: *How would you punish them?*

Child: *The one who broke the 15 cups, two slaps. The other one, one slap.*

Piaget said that this kind of reasoning was based on objective responsibility. This means that younger children focus only on the amount of damage done. The greater the damage, the greater the punishment. Intentions do not matter.

With older children, however, the dialogue went differently:

Piaget: *Which is the naughtiest?*

Child: *The second, the one who wanted to take the jampot, because he wanted to take something without asking.*

Piaget: *Did he [actually get the jam]?*

Child: *No.*

Piaget: *Was he the naughtiest all the same?*

Child: *Yes.*

Piaget: *And the first [child]?*

Child: *It wasn't his fault. He didn't do it on purpose.*

This kind of response, typical of older children, Piaget called reasoning by subjective responsibility. It means that older children take the intentions of wrongdoers into consideration.

THINK ABOUT IT

Use Piaget's theory of cognitive development to explain the differences in reasoning between younger children and older children.

than Piaget's research suggested. Some psychologists also assert that several cognitive skills appear to develop more continuously than Piaget thought. Nonetheless, his theories are still respected.

Kohlberg's Theory of Moral Development

Psychologist Lawrence Kohlberg (1927–1987) devised a cognitive theory about the development of children's moral reasoning. Kohlberg used the following story in his research:

A woman was near death from a special kind of cancer. There was one drug that the doctors thought might save her. It was a form of radium that a pharmacist in the same town had recently discovered. The drug was expensive to make, but the pharmacist was charging 10 times what the drug cost him to make. He paid $200 for the radium and charged $2,000 for a small dose of the drug. The sick woman's husband, Heinz, went to everyone he knew to borrow the money, but he could raise only about $1,000—half the amount he needed. He told the pharmacist that his wife was dying and asked him to sell it cheaper or let him pay later. But the pharmacist rejected the man's plea saying that he had discovered the drug and intended to make money from it. Heinz became desperate and broke into the man's store to steal the drug for his wife. (Adapted from Kohlberg, 1969, p. 379).

Should Heinz have stolen the drug? Was he right or wrong? Kohlberg believed that there was no simple answer. Heinz was involved in what Kohlberg called a moral dilemma. In this case, laws against stealing contradicted Heinz's strong human desire to save his wife.

Kohlberg was not particularly interested in whether children thought Heinz was right or wrong to steal the drug. More important to Kohlberg were the reasons *why* children thought Heinz should or should not steal the drug. People arrive at answers for different reasons. Kohlberg classified these reasons according to levels of moral development.

Kohlberg, like Piaget, was a stage theorist. He believed that the stages of moral development always follow a specific sequence. People do not skip any stages or go backward. Children advance at different rates, however, and not everyone reaches the highest stage. Kohlberg theorized that there are three levels of moral development and two stages within each level.

The Preconventional Level   According to Kohlberg, through the age of nine, most children are at the preconventional level of moral development. Children who use **preconventional moral reasoning** base their judgments on the consequences of behavior.

In stage 1, children believe that what is "good" is what helps one avoid punishment. Therefore, children at stage 1 would argue that Heinz was wrong because he will be caught for stealing and sent to jail.

At stage 2, "good" is what satisfies a person's needs. Stage 2 reasoning holds that Heinz was right to steal the drug because his wife needed it.

The Conventional Level   People who are at the level of **conventional moral reasoning** make judgments in terms of whether an act conforms to conventional standards of right and wrong. These standards are created by the family, religion, and society at large.

At stage 3, "good" is what meets one's needs and the expectations of other people. Moral behavior is what most people would do in a given situation. According to stage 3 reasoning, Heinz should steal the drug because a good and loving husband would do whatever he could to save the life of his wife. But stage 3 reasoning might also maintain that Heinz should not steal the drug because good people do not steal. Both conclusions show conventional thinking. Kohlberg found stage 3 moral judgments most often among 13-year-olds.

Stage 4 moral judgments are based on maintaining the social order. People in this stage have high regard for authority. Stage 4 reasoning might insist that breaking the law for any reason sets a bad example and undermines the social order. Stage 4 judgments occurred most often among 16-year-olds (Kohlberg, 1963).

The Postconventional Level   Reasoning based on a person's own moral standards of goodness is called **postconventional moral reasoning**. Here, moral judgments reflect one's personal values, not conventional standards.

Stage 5 reasoning recognizes that laws represent agreed-upon procedures, that laws have value, and that they should not be violated without good reason. But laws cannot bind the individual in exceptional circumstances. Stage 5 reasoning might suggest that it is right for Heinz to steal the drug, even though it is against the law, because the needs of his wife have created an exceptional situation.

Kohlberg's Stages of Moral Development

Stage	Moral Reasoning Goal	What Is Right?
preconventional level		
1	Avoiding punishment	Doing what is necessary to avoid punishment
2	Satisfying needs	Doing what is necessary to satisfy one's needs
conventional level		
3	Winning approval	Seeking and maintaining the approval of others using conventional standards of right and wrong
4	Law and order	Moral judgments based on maintaining social order High regard for authority
postconventional level		
5	Social order	Obedience to accepted laws Judgments based on personal values
6	Universal ethics	Morality of individual conscience, not necessarily in agreement with others

FIGURE 10.4 *According to Lawrence Kohlberg, people's moral development follows a specific sequence. Not every person reaches the highest stage.*

ment than do girls. Does this mean that boys are morally superior to girls? No. It may mean instead that Kohlberg's stages and scoring system were biased to favor males.

Psychologist Carol Gilligan argues that the differences between boys and girls are created because of what adults teach children about how they should behave as boys or girls (1982; Gilligan et al., 1989). For example, girls are often taught to consider the needs of others over simple right or wrong. Therefore, a girl might worry that both stealing the drug and letting Heinz's wife die are wrong. Such reasoning—involving empathy for others—would be classified as stage 3.

Boys, however, are often taught to argue logically rather than with empathy. Therefore, a boy might set up an equation to prove that life has greater value than property. This would be considered reasoning at stage 5 or even stage 6.

Gilligan suggests, however, that girls' reasoning is at as high a level as that of boys. Girls have, in fact, thought about the same kinds of issues boys considered. In the end, they have chosen to be empathetic, not because their thinking is simpler, but because it is very complex—and because of what they have been taught is appropriate for girls. Shortly before his death in 1987, Kohlberg had begun to correct the gender bias in his theory.

Stage 6 reasoning regards acts that support the values of human life, justice, and dignity as moral and good. People at stage 6 rely on their own consciences. They do not necessarily obey laws or agree with other people's opinions. Using stage 6 reasoning, a person might argue that the pharmacist was acting out of greed and that survival is more important than profit. Therefore, Heinz had a moral right to steal the drug to save his wife's life even though he broke the law to do so. Postconventional moral reasoning rarely occurs before adolescence and is found most often in adults.

Bias in Kohlberg's Theory Some studies have found that according to Kohlberg's stages, boys appear to reason at higher levels of moral develop-

THINKING ABOUT PSYCHOLOGY

1. Identify and briefly describe Piaget's four stages of cognitive development.

2. List the three levels of moral development, as theorized by Kohlberg.

3. **Critical Thinking**   In what way are Piaget's preoperational stage and Kohlberg's stage 2 similar?

Chapter 10 REVIEW

SUMMARY

Studying the physical, social, and cognitive development of infants and children gives psychologists insight into human behavior.

I. The Study of Development

A. Developmental psychologists study how people grow and change throughout the life span.

B. One debate among developmental psychologists concerns which has a greater effect on development: nature or nurture.
   1. The role of nature, or heredity, is seen primarily in maturation.
   2. The role of nurture, or environment, is seen in nutrition, family and cultural backgrounds, and education.

C. Developmental psychologists also disagree about whether human development occurs in stages or in a continuous progression.

II. Physical Development

A. From birth to age two, children make dramatic gains in height and weight.

B. Motor development in infants and children proceeds in universal stages.

C. Infants are born with certain reflexes that are essential for their survival.

D. Infants and children have an inborn capacity to perceive and learn from sensory stimuli in their environment.

III. Social Development

A. During their first months of life, infants develop attachments to their mothers or other primary caregivers.
   1. By eight months, infants may show a fear of strangers and anxiety when separated from their mothers.
   2. Two types of attachment are contact comfort and imprinting.
   3. Attachment may be secure or insecure. Infants develop secure attachment to affectionate and reliable caregivers.
   4. Secure infants develop into happier, friendlier, and more cooperative children than do insecure infants.

B. Studies show that nonparent child care has mixed effects on children. Quality of nonparent child care plays a large role in whether nonparent child care affects children positively or negatively.

C. The kind of parenting a child receives, the development of a sense of competence, and gender and age can influence a child's level of self-esteem.

IV. Cognitive Development

A. Psychologist Jean Piaget theorized that children's thinking develops in four stages.
   1. During the sensorimotor stage (infancy to two years), children learn to coordinate what they perceive with motor activity.
   2. During the preoperational stage (two to seven), children first use words and symbols to represent objects.
   3. During the concrete-operational stage (seven to puberty), children can think logically about specific objects.
   4. The formal-operational stage (begins in puberty and continues throughout adulthood) deals with abstract thinking.

B. Psychologist Lawrence Kohlberg believed that children's moral development follows a specific sequence.
   1. At the preconventional level, children base their moral judgments on the consequences of behavior.
   2. At the conventional level, children base moral judgments on standards created by family, religion, or society at large.
   3. At the postconventional level, people rely on their own consciences and values to make moral decisions.

C. Both Piaget's and Kohlberg's theories have been subject to some criticism.

TERM & CONCEPT REVIEW

1. What is the main focus of developmental psychology?
2. How do maturational theorists believe development occurs?
3. List three "nurture" influences on development.
4. Define *stranger anxiety* and *separation anxiety*. Why would you expect an older infant to exhibit these fears?
5. How does an authoritarian parenting style differ from an authoritative parenting style?
6. What is unconditional positive regard? What is conditional positive regard?
7. According to Piaget's theory of cognitive development, how do assimilation and accommodation help people organize information?
8. Define *object permanence*. When do infants acquire it? According to Piaget, what enables object permanence to occur?
9. What is meant by the law of conservation in developmental psychology?
10. Define *egocentrism* as it occurs in preoperational children. Give an example.

CRITICAL THINKING

1. Explain how a child's learning to read might be the result of both maturation and nurture.
2. Secure attachment occurs when mothers or other primary caregivers are warm and affectionate. How do infants unknowingly encourage warmth and affection from their caregivers?
3. Describe how each of the following types of parents might react to their child drawing a picture on the wall with crayons: a warm-permissive parent, a warm-strict parent, a cold-permissive parent, a cold-strict parent.
4. Jean Piaget believed that cognitive development occurs in distinct stages. How might you show that cognitive development occurs gradually?

5. Psychologists often study a specific area of child development, such as physical development, social development, or cognitive development. In reality, these areas overlap and influence one another. Give an example of how a child's physical development might influence his or her social development.

APPLYING SKILLS IN PSYCHOLOGY

1. **Research in Psychology**   Conduct an experiment in which you test the law of conservation on a child in the preoperational stage of cognitive development. You can repeat one of the experiments mentioned in the chapter or create your own. Write a description of your experiment. Include the age of the child, the materials and procedures used, an analysis of the results, and your conclusions.
2. **COOPERATIVE LEARNING** **Research in Psychology**   Working in small groups, construct an imaginary situation in which a moral judgment must be made. Have one person in the group write out the scenario the group created and make a copy for each group member. Then have each group member read the situation to a young child, an adolescent, and an adult, and record their responses. As a group, share the responses and compare them with Kohlberg's levels and stages of moral development.
3. **Reading About Psychology**   Look in your local newspaper for reports about programs and events that attempt to raise the self-esteem of children. Share your articles with the class.
4. **Using Your Observation Skills**   Arrange to visit a child care facility in your community. Before your visit, divide a sheet of paper into three columns and label them Physical, Social, and Cognitive. During your observation, record in the proper column examples of activities or events that promote each type of development. Discuss your observations in class.

11

Chapter

ADOLESCENCE

Objectives

1 Identify the physical changes that occur in males and females during adolescence, and examine the psychological effects of these changes.

2 Describe the role that parents and peers generally play in the lives of adolescents.

3 Define identity formation, and describe the four categories of adolescent identity status.

4 Describe some of the important challenges that adolescents face in today's society.

A DAY IN THE LIFE

Linda and Hannah feel very much a part of their circle of friends, which they often refer to as "the group." They are friendly with classmates outside the group, but when it comes to discussing the people and ideas they care about most, they talk to each other more than to anybody else except their parents. When they were concerned about Nick and his problems with drugs and alcohol, they could always talk to each other about it.

As it turned out, Nick wasn't the only one of their classmates they were concerned about. Linda and Hannah were eating lunch one day when Linda asked Hannah quietly, "Can I tell you something?"

"Sure," said Hannah. "Don't tell me Marc actually did something wrong. I thought he was supposed to be 'perfect.'"

Linda laughed. "Hardly. No, Marc is wonderful." Her expression turned serious. "It's about Annie."

"Oh, Annie," said Hannah. "I bet I know what you're going to say."

They both liked Annie although she wasn't really a part of their group. She was a bright, quiet girl, well liked by her teachers—and everyone else for that matter.

"I'm worried about her," said Linda. "She keeps losing weight."

"I know," said Hannah.

"You've noticed too?" Linda asked with concern.

"How can you not notice it?" replied Hannah.

"She says she's on a diet. But she looks like a skeleton."

"I know," Hannah responded. "She's been skipping gym a lot too. I asked her when she was going to stop dieting. She said her weight was nearly where she wanted it to be and that she had never felt better."

"I don't know," said Linda. "Something's not right. Maybe I should talk to my parents about it. They might know how to help her."

"You're right," said Hannah. "We really should do something."

* * *

This chapter is about adolescence—the time between childhood and adulthood. For many teenagers, adolescence can be a rich and fulfilling time of life. Close friendships may develop. New opportunities to learn and grow present themselves. Most teenagers look to the future and see it as a time of hope and promise. However, adolescence can also be a confusing and difficult period. Rapid physical growth and sexual development bring dramatic changes. Teenagers must define who they are and what they stand for as they begin to establish identities as young adults. Even though they may be old enough to reproduce and be as big, or bigger, than their parents, adolescents sometimes feel they are treated like "big children." At other times, they must make adult decisions when they do not feel ready to make them. This chapter explores the physical changes that occur during adolescence, adolescent social development and identity formation, and the special challenges of adolescence.

Key Terms

- adolescent growth spurt
- puberty
- primary sex characteristic
- secondary sex characteristic
- menarche
- clique
- crowd
- identity crisis
- identity status
- identity moratorium
- identity foreclosure
- identity diffusion
- identity achievement
- anorexia nervosa
- bulimia
- juvenile delinquency
- status offense

TRUTH OR fiction?

Read the following statements about psychology. Do you think they are true or false? You will learn whether each statement is true or false as you read the chapter.

- Boys begin their adolescent growth spurt before girls do.
- Boys who mature early have certain advantages over their peers.
- Adolescents are in a constant state of rebellion against their parents.
- Girls are more likely than boys to have close friendships.
- Many adolescents follow the example of their peers in matters of clothing, hairstyles, speech patterns, and musical tastes.
- Excessive dieting may be a sign that a person has an eating disorder.

1
Physical Development

In earlier times in Western societies (and in some developing countries today), the period of transition from childhood to adulthood was very brief. Most people took over adult responsibilities—going to work, caring for children, and so on—shortly after they reached sexual maturity. The transition to adulthood was often marked by an elaborate ceremony that symbolized the passage from childhood to adulthood.

In the 20th century, however, all that has changed. In Western societies, required education has been extended, and the status and duties of adulthood have been delayed. As a result, adolescence has come to cover most of the teen years. Today, the period known as adolescence is sometimes subdivided into smaller categories. These categories include early adolescence (ages 11 through 14), middle adolescence (15 through 18), and late adolescence (18 through 21).

The biological changes that occur during adolescence are greater than those of any other time of life, with the exception of infancy. In some ways, however, the changes in adolescence are more dramatic than those that occur in infancy—unlike infants, adolescents are aware of the changes that

are taking place and of what the changes mean. But no teenager can ever be quite sure how all these physical changes will turn out. There are many variables to consider. Different adolescents begin their growth spurts at different ages, and they grow at different rates. Even the different parts of an adolescent's body grow at different rates. Most adolescents can only wonder about the final shape and size of their body.

The Adolescent Growth Spurt

During adolescence the stable growth patterns in height and weight that mark early and middle childhood come to an end. Stability is replaced by an abrupt burst of growth. This **adolescent growth spurt** usually lasts two to three years. During this time of rapid growth, most adolescents grow 8 to 12 inches in height.

Girls begin the adolescent growth spurt earlier than boys. The growth spurt usually begins in girls at about the age of 10 or 11 and in boys about 2 years later. As a result, girls tend to be taller and heavier than boys during early adolescence. Then, during middle adolescence, most boys catch up and grow taller than their female classmates. However, the exact time when this growth will occur for any individual—boy or girl—is difficult to predict (Etaugh & Rathus, 1995).

TRUTH OR fiction ▪ REVISITED ▪

It is not true that boys begin their adolescent growth spurt before girls do. Most boys begin their spurt at about 12 or 13 years of age, two years later than most girls.

A DAY IN THE LIFE

By the time Linda entered her senior year of high school, she had been at her full height for about four years. At the same time, Marc had been at his full height for only about two years. In eighth grade, when Marc first noticed Linda, she was taller than he was. But then he caught up and passed Linda in height. His voice deepened, and by the time they were juniors, they seemed to be more or less equal in their level of physical maturity.

This period of sudden adolescent growth can be awkward for both boys and girls because different parts of their bodies grow and mature at different rates. For example, hands and feet may grow before arms and legs do. This growth spurt may cause adolescents to feel as if their hands or feet are too big or to worry that they "just don't look right."

Although some teenagers may feel that they look awkward, they tend to be well coordinated during adolescence. As adolescents become older and complete the growth spurt, the various parts of their bodies usually reach their correct proportions. Once this has happened, the seeming awkwardness of the early teens becomes a thing of the past. Some psychologists believe that only a small percentage of adolescents—no more than about 15 percent—have difficulty adjusting to the adolescent growth spurt (Petersen, 1987).

Sexual Development

Adolescence begins with the onset of puberty. **Puberty** refers to the specific developmental changes that lead to the ability to reproduce. This biological stage of development ends when physical growth does.

During puberty the reproductive organs of both males and females develop and dramatically change the body of an adolescent. Characteristics that are directly involved in reproduction are called **primary sex characteristics**. Other characteristics that distinguish males and females but are not directly involved in reproduction—called **secondary sex characteristics**—also develop during puberty. These characteristics include the growth of hair on certain parts of the body, the deepening of the voice in males, and the rounding of the hips and breasts in females.

These changes are linked to changes in hormone levels. All hormones are present in children of both sexes from birth. During puberty, however, boys begin to produce higher levels of some hormones, while girls begin to produce higher levels of other hormones.

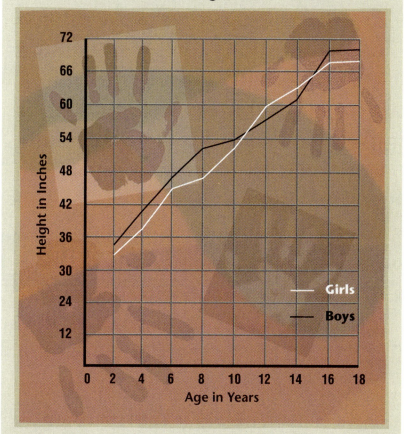

Average Growth Rates for Boys and Girls from Childhood Through Adolescence

FIGURE 11.1 *Throughout childhood, girls and boys are similar in height, with boys being slightly taller. At puberty, girls surge ahead for a short time. At about age 14, boys surge back ahead of the girls.*

Source: Tanner, J.M. (1978). *Fetus into man: Physical growth from conception to maturity.* Cambridge, MA: Harvard University Press. (p. 118)

Changes in Males   In boys, hormones from the pituitary gland cause the testes to increase output of the hormone testosterone. This causes boys' sexual organs to grow, their voices to deepen, and hair to grow on their faces and later on their chests. During the period of rapid growth, boys develop broader shoulders and thicker bodies. They also develop more muscle tissue and larger hearts and lungs.

Changes in Females   In girls, hormones from the pituitary gland stimulate the ovaries to secrete more estrogen. Estrogen spurs the growth of breast tissue and supportive tissue in the hips and buttocks. As a result, the pelvic region widens and the hips become rounder. Girls also produce small amounts of androgens, which are similar to testosterone, in the adrenal glands. Androgens stimulate

ADOLESCENCE   **253**

Adolescents develop physically at different rates. Both early- and late-maturing adolescents may experience difficulties associated with their rates of development, but these problems usually fade over time.

the growth of pubic and underarm hair. Estrogen and androgens work together to spur the growth of the female sex organs.

The production of estrogen, which becomes cyclical in puberty, regulates the menstrual cycle. The first menstruation, or **menarche**, is a major life event for most girls, and most societies consider it the beginning of womanhood. It usually occurs between the ages of 11 and 14.

Differences in Maturation Rates

Some adolescents reach physical maturity at a relatively early age, while others reach it later. Research suggests that boys who mature early have certain advantages over boys who mature later (Alsaker, 1992). They tend to be more popular and to be leaders within their circle of friends. Their greater size and strength may give them a competitive edge in sports. They also tend to be more self-assured and relaxed. Because they have matured early, they no longer need to worry about maturing later than their peers. This may boost their self-esteem.

However, boys who mature early physically are not necessarily more mature than their peers in some other ways, such as in how they approach and

handle problems. Also, coaches, friends, and others may pressure them to perform beyond their abilities. They may not be prepared to live up to the expectations of others (Kutner, 1993). Early-maturing boys may even be more likely than other boys to engage in types of problem behaviors (Andersson & Magnusson, 1990).

Furthermore, although early-maturing boys may have some advantages over their peers who develop later, these advantages fade over time. In fact, some longitudinal studies indicate that boys who mature later show better adjustment as adults than boys who mature early (Livson & Peskin, 1972). Of course, not all early-maturing boys have problems, either as adolescents or as adults.

TRUTH OR **fiction** ▪ R E V I S I T E D ▪

It is true that boys who mature early have certain advantages over their peers. For example, they tend to be more popular and self-assured than their peers. However, early maturity may also carry certain disadvantages.

Early maturation is somewhat different for girls. Early-maturing girls may feel awkward because they are taller than their classmates, both male and female. They may be teased about their height. Early-maturing girls may be tempted to associate with older teens, even when they are not emotionally ready for such associations. Moreover, older boys may assume that these girls are more mature than they really are and may expect them or pressure them to do things they do not want to do.

Needless to say, not all girls who mature early encounter problems. In any case, the differences between early- and late-maturing girls usually do not last long. Once their peers catch up to them, the issue of differences in maturity generally disappears (Simmons & Blyth, 1987).

THINKING ABOUT PSYCHOLOGY

1. List three characteristics of the adolescent growth spurt.
2. What physical changes occur in males during puberty? In females?
3. **Critical Thinking** Identify some long-term effects of early maturity for girls and for boys.

EXPLORING
DIVERSITY

Rites of Passage

A rite of passage is a ceremony that marks a person's entrance into a new stage of life. Rites of passage include ceremonies such as baptism, graduation, and marriage. For many Americans, rites of passage such as school graduations and weddings signify the end of one period of life and the beginning of another.

Most rites of passage are characterized by three stages. In the first stage, the participant is separated from his or her previous status. The next stage is a transitional stage in which the participant learns the behavior and ideas appropriate to his or her new status. In some African societies, for example, boys who are on the verge of adulthood are separated from others for days or even months while they learn tribal traditions and skills. After the completion of the second stage the participant is formally admitted into his or her new status. This is often marked by an elaborate ceremony.

People often pass through the stages of a rite of passage as a group. For example, in many graduation ceremonies in the United States, the graduating students sit together in a special area separated from their families and friends. The walk across the stage to receive their diploma symbolizes the transition from student to graduate. In some ceremonies, in which the graduates wear academic caps and gowns, they switch the tassels on the caps from one side to the other to signify their entrance into the society of graduates.

Many cultures have special ceremonies to mark young people's passage from childhood to adulthood. In some societies, teenagers celebrate certain birthdays as rites of passage. For example,

In some Hispanic cultures, a girl's 15th birthday marks her passage into adulthood. The girl, her family, and the community celebrate at an event called the quinceañera.

the 15th birthday is an important occasion for many Hispanic girls. It is celebrated by the girl, her family, and community members in an event called the *quinceañera.* A ceremony, usually in a church, is followed by a party.

Jewish adolescents mark their entrance into the adult religious community in a ceremony called (for boys) a bar mitzvah, which means "son of the commandment," or (for girls) a bat mitzvah, which means "daughter of the commandment." When a Jewish child reaches age 13, he or she is expected to observe the religious customs and obligations of Jewish adulthood. After much preparation, Jewish teens show what they have learned about Judaism.

Several Christian traditions—including Roman Catholicism, Eastern Orthodox Christianity, Lutheranism, and Episcopalianism—also have an initiation ceremony. It is called a confirmation, and it confers full adult membership in the church. At the confirmation service, young people renew, or confirm, promises made for them at baptism.

For many American teenagers, rites of passage are neither formal nor religious. Rather, they are a series of "first" events that signify assuming more responsibility and receiving adult treatment. Obtaining one's driver's license is one example. Getting one's first after-school job is another.

Think About It

Besides the examples mentioned above, what are some other rites of passage for adolescents in the United States?

Social Development

2

About 100 years ago, G. Stanley Hall, the founder of the American Psychological Association, described adolescence as a time of *Sturm und Drang*. These are German words that mean "storm and stress." Hall attributed the conflicts and distress some adolescents experience to biological changes.

Research suggests that the hormonal changes of adolescence do have some effect on the activity levels, mood swings, and aggressive tendencies of many adolescents. However, contemporary studies suggest that cultural and social influences may have more of an effect on adolescent behavior than hormones do (Buchanan et al., 1992).

Adolescence is a psychological concept as well as a biological concept. Psychologically, the adolescent period ends when people become adults and take on adult responsibilities. How long adolescence lasts varies with each individual. For some people, adolescence may be quite extended; for others, it is quite short. For example, when a teenager finds himself or herself caring for family members, financially supporting the family, or assuming other significant responsibilities, adolescence for that individual has probably been quite short, at least in the psychological sense.

Certainly, adolescence can be a challenging time of life. Some teenagers may experience difficulties at home or at school that lead to psychological and social problems. Nonetheless, the vast majority of teenagers face the many challenges of adolescence and cope with them successfully. They form new friendships, increase their knowledge, build their self-esteem, and develop personal and social skills that enable them to become successful and competent adults.

Relationships with Parents

During adolescence, parent-child relationships undergo redefinition. However, the picture of adolescence as a state of constant rebellion against parents and society is exaggerated. The truth is that most of the changes that occur during adolescence are positive rather than negative (Collins, 1990; Steinberg, 1991).

As adolescents strive to become more independent from their parents, however, some conflicts may arise. This striving for greater freedom often results in bickering, especially in early adolescence (Smetana et al., 1991). Conflicts typically center on such issues as homework, chores, money, appearance, curfews, and dating (Galambos & Almeida, 1992; Smetana et al., 1991). Arguments sometimes arise when adolescents maintain that personal choices, such as those that have to do with clothes and friends, should be made by them, not their parents (Smetana et al., 1991).

The adolescent quest for independence may lead to less time spent with family, greater emotional attachment to people who are not family members, and more activities outside the home. In one study, children ranging in age from 9 to 15 carried electronic pagers for a week so that when signaled they could report to researchers what they were doing and with whom (Larson & Richards, 1991). The study showed that the older the children were, the less time they spent with their families. The 15-year-olds spent only half as much time with their families as the 9-year-olds. For the older boys in the study, time spent with the family tended to be replaced by time spent alone. The older girls, on the other hand, tended to divide the time they spent away from their families between friends and solitude.

Greater independence from parents does not necessarily mean that adolescents withdraw emotionally from their parents or fall completely under the influence of their peers. Most adolescents continue to love, respect, and feel loyalty toward their parents (Montemayor & Flannery, 1991).

A DAY IN THE LIFE

Linda and Hannah spent less time with their parents than they did when they were younger. They also talked to each other more than they did to either one of their parents. Still, they continued to love their parents and depend on them for emotional support. Adolescents who feel close to their parents tend to show greater self-reliance and independence than those who are distant from their parents. Adolescents who retain close ties with parents also tend to fare better in school and have fewer adjustment problems (Davey, 1993; Papini & Roggman, 1992; Steinberg, 1991).

Despite a certain amount of parent-adolescent conflict, parents and adolescents usually share similar social, political, religious, and economic views (Paikoff & Collins, 1991). For example, adolescents tend to share the religion of one or both of their parents. Rarely will a teenager break completely with his or her family and adopt a different

religion. Therefore, while there are frequent parent-adolescent differences of opinion about behavior and rules of conduct, conflict between the generations on broader issues is less common.

It is not true that adolescents are in a constant state of rebellion against their parents. While there may be conflict with parents about family rules, most adolescents are in agreement with their parents about broader issues.

Adolescents tend to interact with their mothers more than they do with their fathers. Most adolescents also see their mothers as more supportive than their fathers, as knowing them better, and as more likely to tolerate their opinions (Collins & Russell, 1991; Noller & Callan, 1990). Teenagers are also more likely to seek and follow advice from their mothers than from their fathers (Greene & Grimsley, 1991).

Relationships with Peers

The transition from childhood to adolescence involves an increase in the importance of peers. While most adolescents maintain good relations with parents, peers become more important in terms of influence and emotional support. For example, fourth-graders consider parents to be their most frequent providers of emotional and social support. If something upsetting happens at school, they are more likely to discuss it with their parents than with anybody else. However, by seventh grade, friends of the same gender are generally seen as providing more support than parents (Furman & Buhrmester, 1992).

Adolescent Friendships Friendship is a very important part of adolescence. Most adolescents tend to have one or two "best friends," but they have other good friends as well. Linda and Hannah probably considered themselves to be best friends, but they had other friends too, such as Annie. Adolescents may spend several

Friends begin to take on greater importance during adolescence. Although most teenagers maintain loving relationships with their parents, they spend more time with friends, either in person or on the phone. Friendships provide adolescents with support and understanding and boost their self-esteem.

also have close friendships, they tend to spend time together in larger, less intimate groups. These gender differences in patterns of friendship continue into adulthood (Dindia & Allen, 1992).

Cliques and Crowds Adolescents not only have close friends, but they also tend to belong to one or more larger peer groups. **Cliques** are peer groups of 5 to 10 people who spend a great deal of time with one another, sharing activities and confidences. Larger groups of people who do not spend as much time together but share attitudes and group identity are called **crowds**.

A DAY IN THE LIFE

Marc, Linda, Hannah, Todd, Dan, Janet, and a few others were members of a clique, which they called "the group." Adolescent cliques often include members of both sexes, which may lead to romantic relationships such as the one between Marc and Linda. Most young people also belong to a larger crowd with whom they go to parties, play basketball or baseball, and participate in other activities.

Some adolescents join certain cliques in their search for the stability and sense of belonging that come from being part of such a group. They may imitate their peers' clothing, hairstyles, and speech, and they may adopt some of their values. They and the other members of the group may even become intolerant of "outsiders"—people not in the group.

hours a day with their friends (Hartup, 1993). When teenagers are not actually with their friends, they are often speaking with them on the telephone.

Friendships serve many purposes for adolescents. One teen girl described her best friend this way: "I can tell her things and she helps me talk. And she doesn't laugh at me if I do something weird—she accepts me for who I am" (Berndt & Perry, 1990, p. 269).

Adolescents also value loyalty as a key aspect of friendship. They say that true friends "stick up for you in a fight" and do not "talk about you behind your back" (Berndt & Perry, 1990, p. 269). In other words, having friends means more to adolescents than just having people to spend time with. Close friends provide support and understanding, strengthen one's ability to be a caring person, and contribute to self-esteem.

Adolescents usually choose friends who are similar to themselves in age, background, educational goals, and attitudes toward drinking, drug use, and sexual activity (Hartup, 1993; Youniss & Haynie, 1992). In addition, adolescents' closest friends are usually of their own sex (Hartup, 1993). The friendships of adolescent girls tend to be closer than those of boys (Berndt & Perry, 1990; Manke, 1993). Girls are more likely than boys to share their secrets, personal problems, and innermost feelings. While boys

Peer Influences Parents often worry that their adolescent children's needs for peer approval will influence them to engage in risky or unacceptable behavior. However, the assumption that parents and peers often pull an adolescent in different directions does not seem to be borne out by reality. In fact, parental and peer influences often coincide to some degree (Brown et al., 1993; Youniss & Haynie, 1992). For example, research suggests that peers are more likely to urge adolescents to work for good grades and complete high school than they are to try to involve them in drug abuse, sexual activity, or delinquency (Brown et al., 1993).

Studies show that whereas girls are more likely to develop close, personal relationships with a couple of other girls, boys are more likely to spend time in a larger group. Girls are also more likely to spend their time together talking and sharing thoughts and feelings, while boys are more likely to engage in an activity, such as basketball.

Nevertheless, adolescents are influenced by their parents and peers in different ways. Adolescents are more likely to follow their peers in terms of dress, hairstyles, speech patterns, and taste in music (Camarena, 1991). However, they are more likely to agree with their parents on issues such as moral values and educational and career goals (Savin-Williams & Berndt, 1990).

TRUTH OR fiction
■ REVISITED ■

It is true that many adolescents follow the example of their peers in matters of clothing, hairstyles, speech patterns, and musical tastes. However, they are likely to agree with their parents on important and broader issues, such as morality and educational goals.

In early adolescence, peer pressure is relatively weak, but it increases in middle adolescence, peaking at about the age of 15. Peer pressure seems to decrease after the age of 17 (Brown et al., 1993; Youniss & Haynie, 1992). Adolescents are strongly influenced by their peers for several reasons. They seek the approval of their peers and feel better about themselves when they receive it. Peers provide standards by which adolescents can measure their behavior as they grow more independent of their parents (Foster-Clark & Blyth, 1991). Also, since peers may share some of the same feelings, they can provide support in times of difficulty (Kirchler et al., 1991; Pombeni et al., 1990).

Dating and Romantic Relationships   Many people begin dating during adolescence. Dating usually develops in stages (Padgham & Blyth, 1991). During the first stage, adolescents place themselves in situations where they will probably meet peers of the other sex—for example, at after-school events. In the next stage, adolescents participate in group dating, such as joining a mixed group at the movies. Finally, they may pair off for traditional two-person dating.

People date for several reasons. Obviously, people may date simply because they enjoy spending time with somebody they like. But dating may also help adolescents learn how to relate positively to other people. Furthermore, dating may help prepare adolescents for the more serious courtship activities that come later in life.

Among younger adolescents, dating relationships tend to be casual and short-lived. But in later adolescence, relationships tend to be more stable and committed (Feiring, 1993). As 18-year-olds, Marc and Linda were most likely thinking in terms of trust, commitment to each other, and honesty.

A DAY IN THE LIFE

THINKING ABOUT PSYCHOLOGY

1. In what ways does a teen's relationship with his or her parents change during adolescence? How does it stay the same?

2. Suggest two reasons why adolescents are influenced by their peers.

3. What are the three stages of dating?

4. **Critical Thinking**   Do you think adolescence is a time of "storm and stress"? Why or why not?

3
Identity Formation

Psychoanalyst Erik Erikson maintained that the journey of life consists of eight stages. (See Chapter 14.) At each stage, there is a task that must be mastered in order for healthy development to continue. Erikson said that young children must deal with issues of trust, autonomy (self-government), and initiative (taking the lead). Once children begin school, their main task becomes the development of competence, which is the sense that they can learn and achieve.

According to Erikson, the main task of the adolescent stage is the search for identity—a sense of who one is and what one stands for. Adolescents seek to identify their beliefs, their values, and their life goals. They also need to identify the areas in which they agree and disagree with parents, teachers, and friends.

Identity Development

According to Erikson, the adolescent task of establishing one's identity is accomplished mainly by choosing and developing a commitment to a partic-

Investigating various career options, such as at a career fair, might be one step toward developing an identity, according to Erikson.

ular role or occupation in life. Accomplishing this task may also involve developing one's own political and religious beliefs.

To find an identity that is comfortable, adolescents may experiment with different values, beliefs, roles, and relationships. They may try out different "selves" in different situations. For example, the way they behave with their friends may be quite different from the way they behave with their parents. Adolescents who take on these different roles may sometimes wonder which one of the selves is the "real" one. Adolescent identity is achieved when different selves are brought together into a unified and consistent sense of self (Conger, 1978).

Erikson believed that teens who do not succeed in forging an identity may become confused about who they really are and what they want to do in life. They may have difficulty making commitments and may drift from situation to situation. Since they do not create a solid sense of self, they may remain overly dependent on the opinions of others.

One key aspect of adolescent identity development is what Erikson called an identity crisis. An **identity crisis** is a turning point in a person's development when the person examines his or her values and makes or changes decisions about life roles. Should I go to college? Which one? What type of job should I look for? What career is right for me? Adolescents can feel overwhelmed by the choices that lie before them and the decisions they must make (Crain, 1992).

Chapter 10 discussed Piaget's four stages of cognitive development. The final stage is the formal-operational stage. It generally begins at puberty and continues through adulthood. Formal-operational thinking involves abstract thinking, such as hypothetical situations. It enables people to find reasonable solutions to problems and to predict the possible consequences of the decisions they make. Formal-operational thinking helps adolescents make important life choices. Because their thinking is no longer tied to concrete experience, adolescents can evaluate the options available to them even though they may not have personally experienced them (Kahlbaugh & Haviland, 1991).

Identity Status

According to psychologist James Marcia (1966, 1991), the adolescent identity crisis arises as teenagers face decisions about their future work, moral standards, religious commitment, or political orientation. Marcia studied the different ways that

CASE STUDIES
AND OTHER TRUE STORIES

Working Teens

In the United States today, more teenagers than ever before are working. Three out of every four high school juniors and seniors hold part-time jobs. The majority of parents and psychologists have supported the idea of teenage employment in the belief that having a part-time job prepares teenagers for adult life and teaches them self-reliance, money management, and the value of hard work. Several panels in the 1970s and 1980s suggested that many of the problems of modern adolescents, including crime, substance abuse, and lack of motivation, could be cured if teens were more actively involved in the working world. Just how does holding a job affect an adolescent?

Research indicates that having a part-time job may help teenagers develop a sense of independence. They may no longer have to rely on their parents for spending money, nor are they as accountable to their parents for how they spend the money they make (Greenberger & Steinberg, 1986). Taking a part-time job can thus be beneficial for teens as they strive to become independent from their parents. Erik Erikson believed that independence from one's parents is an important step in identity development.

However, part-time employment of adolescents may have some drawbacks. Psychologists Ellen Greenberger and Laurence Steinberg (1986) argue that in order for a work experience to be beneficial for teenagers, it should teach them skills or knowledge valuable for adult life. In the past, adolescents worked primarily in farming, factories, or skilled trades and crafts. But today the majority of teens work in food-service and sales jobs. These jobs often do not teach teenage workers specific skills for their future professions as many jobs of the past did. Nor do they give workers much responsibility. There is little room for ambition and little reward for putting in extra effort. As a result of these conditions, teenage employees often develop a negative attitude about work and about its ability to lead to self-fulfillment. Instead of gaining respect for work, teenagers with part-time jobs often come to see work as a necessary evil with no worth in and of itself.

Greenberger and Steinberg also believe that for work to be valuable, it should fill a financial need of the teenager's family, the community, or the teen's own future. But the majority of teens today work to supply themselves with "extras" rather than to help support their families or save for a long-term goal, such as a college education. Because most teens tend to spend their paychecks on luxury items such as CDs and designer clothing, they may develop an unrealistic view of money. Instead of learning the hard reality of life—that there is often little money left over after paying for rent, groceries, and utilities—teens may become accustomed to spending most of their income on nonnecessities.

Perhaps the biggest concern for many people is the effect that working has on teens' grades. While some studies have indicated that students who work excessive hours do worse in school than their nonworking counterparts (Lillydahl, 1995; Steinberg, 1993), evidence suggests that students who have jobs but work fewer than 13.5 hours per week actually do *better* in school than those who do not work (Lillydahl, 1995).

To work or not to work? There is no easy answer. Each teenager and his or her parents should examine the issues—necessity, goals, grades, and time—before deciding. However, many teenagers can benefit from the working experience, especially if they keep school a top priority, avoid working too many hours, save part of the money earned toward future education, and continue to participate in other activities.

Think About It

Do you think it is a good idea for teenagers to work? Why or why not? Use your experiences and those of your friends to support your answer.

adolescents handle commitment and cope with the adolescent identity crisis. He concluded that there are four categories of adolescent **identity status**, or reaction patterns and processes. Adolescents do not remain in a single one of these categories throughout their entire adolescence, nor do they proceed through them in a particular order. Rather, they move in and out of the various categories, from one to another. The four categories are identity moratorium, identity foreclosure, identity diffusion, and identity achievement. (See Figure 11.2.)

Identity Moratorium

A moratorium is a "time out" period. Teens experiencing what Marcia termed **identity moratorium** delay making commitments about important questions. They are actively exploring various alternatives in an attempt to forge their identity. They may even experiment with different behaviors and personalities. Adolescents experimenting with different ways of life in their search for an identity may adopt distinctive ways of dressing or behaving. For example, they may cut or style their hair in a particular way. Or they might adopt a special article of clothing as their "trademark."

Adolescents who remain in moratorium longer than other teens may become somewhat anxious as they struggle to find anchors in an unstable world (Patterson et al., 1992). But for most high school students in moratorium who say, "I don't know what I want to do," it is enough to know that they are heading in a general direction even if they do not know where their journey will end. They may end up attending college, joining the armed services, or doing something completely different to reach their final goals. It is not unusual for young people to actively explore their life alternatives for a decade or more.

Identity Foreclosure

To avoid an identity crisis, adolescents in the **identity foreclosure** category make a commitment that forecloses (or shuts out) other possibilities. These adolescents make a definite commitment, but the commitment is based on the suggestions of others rather than on their own choices. They adopt a belief system or a plan of action without closely examining whether it is right for them. They may simply follow the model set by their parents, peers, teachers, or other authority figures in order to avoid uncertainty. For example, an adolescent who is "foreclosed" might decide to become a lawyer because one or both parents are lawyers. Adolescents in identity foreclosure tend to be inflexible and intolerant of people who do not share their views and commitments (Berzonsky et al., 1993; Marcia, 1991).

Although following a path recommended by a respected adult eliminates the need to make some hard choices, some adolescents become foreclosed too early. After they find themselves dissatisfied with the direction of their lives, they may switch to the moratorium category. For instance, the adolescent who has chosen to be a lawyer simply because both parents are lawyers may discover in law school, or even after becoming a lawyer, that being a lawyer is not really what he or she wants to do or is best suited for. The individual may then enter moratorium to reassess life goals and to decide whether to make a career change.

Identity Diffusion

Adolescents in the category of **identity diffusion** seem to be constantly searching for meaning in life and for identity because they have not committed themselves to a set of personal beliefs or an occupational path. They tend to wander about without goals or interests and seem to live from crisis to crisis.

Identity diffusion is characteristic of children in middle school and early high school. However, if it continues into the 11th and 12th grades, identity diffusion can lead to an "I don't care" attitude. Some adolescents in this category become angry and rebellious. They may reject socially accepted beliefs, values, and goals (Archer & Waterman, 1990; Marcia, 1991).

Identity Achievement

Adolescents in the **identity achievement** category have coped with crises and have explored options. They have then committed themselves to occupational directions and have made decisions about important life questions. Although they have experienced an identity crisis, they have emerged from it with a solid set of beliefs or with a life plan. The plan might be to pursue a course of study that leads to a particular career. Identity-achieved teens tend to have feelings of well-being, high self-esteem, and self-acceptance. They are capable of setting goals and working toward attaining them (Berzonsky et al., 1993; Waterman, 1992). A teenager who decides to become a veterinarian or a businessperson, for example, may choose courses in high school or take an after-school job with that goal in mind.

Many young people do not reach identity achievement until well after high school. It is normal to change majors in college and to change

Marcia's Adolescent Identity Status Categories

Identity Status	Characteristics	Example
Identity Moratorium	Searching for identity Exploring various alternatives Delaying making commitments	"I don't know what I want to do when I graduate, so I'm going to apply to college and for jobs. Then I'll decide which would be best for me."
Identity Foreclosure	Conforming Accepting identity and values from childhood Choosing to identify with others rather than self Making commitments and adopting plans without self-examination Becoming inflexible	"Everyone in my family goes into the military after high school, so that's what I'm planning to do."
Identity Diffusion	Making no commitment Doing no soul-searching Wandering without goals Becoming angry and rebellious	"I really have no idea what I'll do after graduation. I'll just have to see what happens."
Identity Achievement	Exploring options Committing self to direction in life and occupation Finding own identity	"I'm going to start college in the fall. My parents wanted me to go into the family business after I graduated, but I decided that what I really want to do is go to school and become a scientist."

FIGURE 11.2 *By studying the ways in which teenagers handle commitment and cope with the adolescent identity crisis, psychologist James Marcia identified four adolescent identity status categories.*

careers. Such changes, which may even be made several times, do not necessarily mean that these people are indecisive or that they have made wrong decisions. The changes may simply mean that these individuals are continuing to actively explore their options. College, vocational training, and jobs are broadening experiences that expose people to new ways of life, career possibilities, and belief systems. It is common to adjust one's personal goals and beliefs as one matures and views the world from a new or broader perspective.

Gender and Ethnicity in Identity Formation

All adolescents struggle at some point with issues concerning who they are and what they stand for. However, the nature of the struggle is somewhat different for males and females and for adolescents from different ethnic backgrounds.

Gender and Identity Formation According to Erik Erikson's theory, identity development during adolescence means embracing a philosophy of life and a commitment to a career. However, his views of the development of identity were intended to apply primarily to boys (Archer, 1992; Patterson et al., 1992).

Erikson believed that it is in the young adult stage of development that people develop the capacity to form intimate relationships. He also believed that the development of interpersonal relationships was more important than occupational issues and values to women's identity. Erikson, like

The cultural heroes for adolescents from ethnic minority groups are often not as well-known in other groups in society. Some, however—such as professional basketball player Hakeem Olajuwon—are quite well-known and respected.

Prejudice and discrimination can also contribute to problems faced by adolescents from ethnic minority groups in forging a sense of identity. For example, the cultural heroes for these adolescents may not be recognized by members of other groups in society.

Adolescents whose father and mother are from different cultural backgrounds must also wrestle with balancing two cultural heritages (Gibbs, 1992; Johnson, 1992; Miller, 1992). Most adolescents are able to balance the two cultural influences. For some children, however, having a father and a mother from different cultural backgrounds may create emotional conflict.

THINKING ABOUT PSYCHOLOGY

1. What is an identity crisis?
2. Briefly describe the four adolescent identity status categories.
3. **Critical Thinking**   Do you agree that the main task of adolescence is the formation of identity? Why or why not?

Sigmund Freud, believed that women's identities were intimately connected with their roles as wives and mothers. Men's identities, on the other hand, were not assumed to depend on their roles as husbands and fathers (Patterson et al., 1992).

Today many women work outside the home. Research shows that female adolescents are now apt to approach identity formation more like male adolescents than they used to (Archer, 1992). The concern of female adolescents about occupational plans is now about equal to that of males. However, there is a difference. Female adolescents also express concern about how they will balance the day-to-day demands of work and family life (Archer, 1992). Their concern is well-founded. Despite their involvement in the workplace, women in the United States still bear most of the responsibility for rearing the children and maintaining the home (Archer, 1991).

Ethnicity and Identity Formation   Identity formation can have additional dimensions for adolescents from ethnic minority groups (Cross, 1991; Spencer & Markstrom-Adams, 1990). Unlike many other adolescents, those from minority groups often have to face two sets of cultural values: those of their ethnic group and those of the larger society (Markstrom-Adams, 1992; Phinney & Rosenthal, 1992). When these values are in conflict, the adolescent has to reconcile the differences and decide where she or he stands.

4
Challenges of Adolescence

A DAY IN THE LIFE

Adolescence is a rewarding time of life for many young people. Close friendships, such as the one between Hannah and Linda, develop. So do romantic relationships, such as that of Linda and Marc. While there are important choices to be made, the future seems exciting. Yet, for some, adolescence is a difficult time.

Some adolescents have problems that seem too large to handle. Nearly all teenagers know classmates who have school or family problems. Adolescents who are not accepted by their peers often experience loneliness and feelings of low self-esteem. Concerns about getting a good job, being able to support family members, and being accepted into college can be highly stressful.

Some young people, such as Annie, may develop an eating disorder. Others, such as Nick, may abuse alcohol or other drugs. Still others may turn to crime and acts of mischief. Tragically, a few take their own lives.

Eating Disorders

The adolescent growth spurt makes it especially important that teenagers receive adequate nutrition. The average girl needs about 2,200 calories a day, and the average boy needs about 3,000 (Ekvall, 1993). Adolescents also need sufficient protein, carbohydrates, fiber, vitamins, and minerals in their diet. Teens who primarily eat foods such as hamburgers, pizza, potato chips, and candy may not be getting the nutrients their growing bodies need.

Adolescents who develop eating disorders get neither the calories nor the nutrients their bodies need. Some, such as Annie, literally starve themselves. Eating disorders affect many teenagers and young adults, especially females. The two main types of eating disorders are anorexia nervosa and bulimia.

Anorexia Nervosa **Anorexia nervosa** is a life-threatening disorder characterized by self-starvation and a distorted body image. Anorexia results in severe weight loss, malnutrition, and other health problems such as low blood pressure, menstrual irregularity, slow heartbeat, and hair loss. Annie is anorexic. She has an intense fear of gaining weight and perceives herself to be heavier than she actually is. Like other anorexic people, she weighs less than 85 percent of what she would weigh if she were eating properly.

Some anorexic women lose 25 percent or more of their weight in a single year. As a result, they stop menstruating and their overall health declines. The weight loss can become so extreme that about 4 percent of anorexic women die from problems related to their disorder, such as extreme physical weakness and imbalances in their body chemistry (Herzog et al., 1988).

Girls who develop anorexia typically notice some weight gain after menarche and decide that the weight must come off. But after it does, they continue to diet and exercise to excess. Although concerned family members and others may tell them that they are losing too much weight, anorexic women deny that they have a problem and in the process develop a distorted view of their body shapes (Williamson et al., 1993). Whereas other people perceive them to be dangerously thin, anorexics tend to see themselves as overweight and awkward.

Girls are more likely than boys to become anorexic. More than 90 percent of adolescents who have anorexia are girls (Attie, Brooks-Gunn, & Petersen, 1990). Some Freudian psychologists suggest that anorexia represents a young woman's unconscious effort to avoid growing up. Because anorexic females lose body fat, their breasts and hips remain flatter than they normally would, like those of children. Freudian psychologists theorize that anorexic girls are trying to stop the growing-up process and thus avoid separating from their families and assuming adult responsibilities.

Other psychologists suggest that anorexia may stem from an attempt to assert control, particularly over parents—adolescents may reason that parents cannot force them to eat. One study found that girls with eating disorders were more likely than other girls to be in conflict with their mothers (Pike & Rodin, 1991). Other evidence further supports the idea that the causes of anorexia go beyond food and weight. Even before they start dieting, people who become anorexic tend to be shy and have low self-esteem (Leon & Dinklage, 1989).

However, many psychologists see anorexia simply as an excessive fear of putting on weight. This fear may result from a need or a desire to live up to the ideal of the slender female represented by models and movie stars (Vitousek & Manke, 1994). Women with large, or even average, figures may feel great pressure to slim down, perhaps because of the images portrayed in magazines and on television (Bordo, 1993; Wolf, 1991). This ideal may become so internalized that a girl who does not have a weight problem will see herself as being overweight.

For many young women who want to be slender, well-known female supermodels represent the ideal they want to reach. But most of these supermodels are much taller and slimmer than the average woman (Brenner, 1992). To look like these models, the average adolescent female would not only have to lose weight, but also grow several inches taller. Attempts to look like supermodels and reach an unnatural body weight are unhealthy and dangerous.

Researchers Agras and Kirkley (1986) have documented that interest in weight loss has significantly increased in recent times. They counted the number of diet articles that appeared in three leading women's magazines that have been published since 1900. These magazines published no articles on dieting until the 1930s. During the 1930s and the 1940s, there was about one diet article for every 10 issues. During the 1950s and the 1960s, the number of diet articles increased to one in every other issue. During the 1980s, the number jumped

Anorexia nervosa and bulimia are much more common in adolescent girls than in boys, but boys can suffer from them as well. Wrestlers are more likely to develop eating disorders than boys in general because their sport demands that they stay in a certain weight class during wrestling season.

to more than one article per issue. That's a great deal of advice on losing weight—and a great deal of social pressure on women to do so.

TRUTH
OR
fiction
■ R E V I S I T E D ■

It is true that excessive dieting may be a sign that a person has an eating disorder. Anorexia nervosa is an eating disorder characterized by self-starvation and a distorted body image. It can be life-threatening.

Bulimia   Another severe and dangerous eating disorder is bulimia. **Bulimia** is characterized by binging, or compulsive overeating followed by purging, or self-induced vomiting or the use of laxatives. Bulimia has some similarities to anorexia. Like anorexics, bulimics are overly concerned about their weight and body shape (Gleaves et al., 1993). Also, like anorexia, bulimia mainly affects females (Katzman, Wolchik, & Braver, 1984).

However, unlike anorexia, which often begins in early adolescence, bulimia generally begins in the middle or late teen years. Some bulimics start out as anorexics but then change the pattern of self-starvation by beginning to binge and purge.

Bulimics generally engage in their binge-purge behavior in secret. Many people with bulimia may deal with the disorder from the moment they wake up each morning to the moment they fall asleep at night. Bulimics' first thought upon waking is likely to be whether they will be able to get through the day without becoming obsessed with thoughts of food or the desire to go on an eating binge. They may eat a fairly normal breakfast and lunch. However, when evening comes they may binge on foods such as cookies, doughnuts, and candy bars. They may also consume several bowls of cereal and milk. Their binge will end only when they cannot eat any more. They will then purge—rid their bodies of the food they have consumed.

Some researchers speculate that bulimia may result from an attempt to cope with feelings of alienation from parents. Purging may serve as a symbolic way of ridding oneself of one's feelings of anger toward the family. The part of the disorder that involves excessive eating may be a way to re-experience the security that went with being fed and nurtured by one's mother when one was a child (Humphrey, 1986).

Treatment   Whatever the causes, eating disorders are severe health problems, and people who have them require professional assistance to overcome them. Often a school psychologist or counselor can suggest possible courses of action.

Sometimes health professionals will give students with eating disorders a choice—either to enter a treatment program (where their caloric intake is closely monitored) or to remain in school as long as they stop losing weight and receive counseling. They may have to see a psychologist on a regular basis and have their weight checked weekly. Treatment for eating disorders is often a long and difficult process. Many issues are involved, including several that have nothing to do with food.

Substance Abuse

Some teenagers use drugs because they think drugs are enjoyable or they want to earn the approval of peers who also use drugs. Others use drugs to try to escape from emotional stress (Hussong & Chassin, 1993). Adolescents who are under stress may be drawn to alcohol, marijuana, and tranquilizers (Novacek et al., 1991). Adolescents with low self-esteem may seek out stimulants, such as amphetamines and cocaine. But alcohol and drug use greatly increases the likelihood of injury and death. In fact, alcohol-related incidents are the leading cause of death among adolescents.

Moreover, these substances provide only temporary relief from stress and other problems. In fact, alcohol and drugs lead to additional problems. Use of these substances can cause or contribute to poor grades, social problems, and motor vehicle accidents (Burkett, 1980; Chase, Jessor, & Donovan, 1980). Drug users often fall into a vicious cycle. Drinking and drugs only make their problems worse. As the users' troubles multiply, they seek more relief in alcohol and drugs.

Regular use of alcohol and some other drugs may cause teenagers, such as Linda's and Janet's friend Nick, to become addicted to them. Addicts experience intense cravings for the substances when their effects have worn off. Soon after a person starts using alcohol or another drug, the substance may take control of that person's life.

Peer counseling is a valuable way of preventing substance abuse in teenagers. Scare tactics by adults can often backfire by making students more curious and disbelieving. Teenagers may be more willing to believe the warnings of other students who have actually used illegal substances.

Gender Differences in Substance Abuse
Male teenagers are more likely than females to use illegal drugs. Males also tend to use them in heavier doses than females.

However, when it comes to smoking, the opposite is true. High school girls are more likely than high school boys to smoke cigarettes (Newcomb & Bentler, 1992). In recent years, the percentage of boys who smoke has declined, while the percentage of girls who smoke has risen. Evidence shows that smokers greatly increase their risk of getting lung cancer, heart disease, and other serious illnesses (Bartecchi et al., 1994). Smoking also decreases bone density in women, thus increasing the risk of fractures of the hip and back later in life (Hopper & Seeman, 1994).

Treatment
Withdrawing from alcohol and other drugs can be a physically and psychologically painful experience for people of any age. After someone such as Nick is admitted to a hospital or a treatment center, the first step in his or her treatment is detoxification—the removal of the toxic, or poisonous, substance from the body. During this process, the person is gradually and carefully taken off the drug. Both medical treatment and emotional support are very important to help the individual through the process.

Another important aspect of the treatment of adolescents with substance abuse problems is psychological. Therapists can help young people understand the meaning of their drug use. For example, they can learn to recognize that they might be using drugs or alcohol to avoid facing the difficult issues in their lives: How are they doing in school? How are their relations with their family? How do they feel about themselves? Therapy can help teenagers recognize that low self-esteem may be at the root of their problems.

Drug Prevention
Most school prevention programs are aimed at stopping the use of "gateway drugs." These drugs include alcohol, cigarettes, and marijuana. They are called gateway drugs because they are typically tried first—before teenagers "open the gate" to more powerful drugs, such as heroin and cocaine.

Research on the effectiveness of prevention programs shows mixed results. Attempts to scare students by warning them about the dangerous consequences of using drugs can backfire, possibly because scare tactics can arouse their curiosity and disbelief (Kazdin, 1993). Peer counseling is often effective because students are generally more willing to believe other students who have actually

In the United States, nearly a million babies are born to teenage mothers every year. Rearing a child is always challenging, even without the additional burdens teen parents usually face, such as a lack of money, education, and emotional maturity.

used the substances they are being warned against (Hawkins et al., 1992; Perry, 1991).

Sexuality

Many adolescents wrestle with issues of how and when to express their sexual feelings. But they receive mixed messages. Their bodies may be giving them a powerful "go-ahead" signal at the same time that their parents and other adults are advising them of the dangers of early sexual relationships and encouraging them to practice abstinence. Yet other messages may come from media images—models in advertisements, television shows that seem to revolve around sex, and popular songs with lyrics that contain powerful sexual messages. Many teenagers may assume that sexual activity is more widespread among their peers than it actually is. The truth is, however, that many adolescents are not sexually active.

People today often start dating and "going steady" at a younger age than people of earlier times. Adolescents who begin dating young are more likely to engage in sexual relations during

high school (Brooks-Gunn & Furstenberg, 1989; Miller et al., 1986). About 10 percent of American girls between the ages of 15 and 19 become pregnant each year. This amounts to nearly a million pregnancies a year.

Teenage pregnancies can be devastating for adolescent mothers, their children, and society at large. Life for many teenage mothers is an uphill struggle. Teenage mothers are more likely to live in poverty and lack hope for their futures than teenagers of the same age who do not have children (Desmond, 1994; Grogger & Bronars, 1993). Half of all adolescent mothers quit school and go on welfare (Kantrowitz, 1990). Few receive financial or emotional help from the fathers of their children. The fathers—sometimes also adolescents—often cannot support themselves, much less a family. Adolescents themselves see teenage parenthood as disastrous (Moore & Stief, 1992).

Several factors contribute to the likelihood of teenage pregnancy (Etaugh & Rathus, 1995). These include the following:

- problematic relationships with parents or rebellion against parents
- emotional problems, such as feelings of emptiness or loneliness
- problems in school or lack of educational or vocational goals
- societal loosening of traditional prohibitions against adolescent sexuality and the portrayal of sexual themes in the media
- pressure from peers who are engaging in sexual activity
- misunderstanding or lack of knowledge about reproduction

Some adolescent girls intentionally become pregnant to try to strengthen relationships with their boyfriends or fill an emotional void with a child. However, the relationships with the fathers usually come to an end. Premature motherhood tends to make emotional problems worse, not better. It also has serious implications for the offspring. Teen mothers are more likely to give birth to premature babies and to babies who are below average in weight (Osofsky, Osofsky, & Diamond, 1988).

Juvenile Delinquency

The term **juvenile delinquency** refers to many illegal activities committed by children or adolescents. The most extreme acts of delinquency include robbery, rape, and homicide, which are considered criminal acts regardless of the age of the offender. Less serious offenses, known as **status offenses**, are illegal only when they are committed by minors. Status offenses include truancy (unexcused absence from school), drinking, smoking, and running away from home.

Some people assume that teenagers from poor neighborhoods are more likely to break the law than other teens. However, this is not true. Research shows that low income is not a factor (Hinshaw, 1992; Zigler et al., 1992). Another common belief is that children whose mothers work outside the home are more likely to engage in delinquent behavior. Once again, research shows that this is not the case (Silverstein, 1991).

Many delinquent acts do not lead to arrest and prosecution, but they have other serious consequences. Status offenses tend to be handled by school officials, social workers, parents, and other such authorities. When adolescents *are* arrested and prosecuted, they are often referred to mental-health agencies and are not formally labeled as delinquents. Nonetheless, between 25 percent and 30 percent of the serious crimes in the United States are committed by teenagers under the age of 18 (Siegel & Senna, 1994).

Factors that contribute to juvenile delinquency are similar to those that contribute to substance abuse. They include the following:

- low self-esteem and feelings of alienation (Krueger et al., 1993)
- lack of affection, lax and ineffective discipline, and use of severe physical punishment in the home (Kopera-Frye et al., 1993)
- behavior problems that began at an early age (Brook et al., 1993)
- poor grades and lack of educational or vocational goals (Zigler et al., 1992)
- pressure from peers who engage in delinquent behavior (Etaugh & Rathus, 1995)
- having a parent or sibling who has been convicted of criminal behavior (Butterfield, 1992)

Avoiding Problems

Most adolescents who have clear educational and vocational goals manage to steer clear of problems. Adolescents who fear the onset of a particular problem are usually better off if they can talk things over with a trusted adult—a parent or another relative, a teacher, or a guidance counselor.

The most successful programs for dealing with juvenile delinquency are those that try to address potential problems early. It is more difficult to stop delinquent behavior after a pattern has been established than before it begins.

Unfortunately, many programs developed to deal with juvenile delinquency are established after the delinquent behavior pattern is already well established. At that late date, it is more difficult to help adolescents turn themselves around. The most successful prevention programs are those that address the potential problems early. These programs provide classes and support groups for parents, make home visits to families, and provide other effective services. And they encourage parents to become involved in the activities of their children both in and out of school.

Research shows that children who participate in prevention programs do better in school and are more likely to graduate from high school, go to college, and work at a steady job. They also seem less inclined to commit crimes (Zigler et al., 1992).

THINKING ABOUT PSYCHOLOGY

1. Describe the similarities and differences between anorexia and bulimia.

2. How do status offenses differ from other acts of delinquency?

3. List three factors that contribute to juvenile delinquency.

4. **Critical Thinking** Why do you think girls are more likely than boys to develop eating disorders?

11 REVIEW

SUMMARY

For the majority of young people, adolescence is a time of many changes and challenges including rapid physical growth, widening social relationships, and identity formation.

I. Physical Development

A. During adolescence, boys and girls generally experience rapid growth in height and weight referred to as the "adolescent growth spurt."

B. Adolescence begins with puberty (the onset of the ability to reproduce).

C. While most adolescents achieve physical and sexual maturity at about the same time, some adolescents mature earlier or later than others.

II. Social Development

A. While parents and adolescents may disagree on rules of conduct and dress, they tend to agree on broader matters, such as religion and politics.

B. During adolescence, peers become more important as a source of influence and support and as people to spend time with.

    1. Adolescents generally choose friends who have backgrounds, values, and interests similar to their own.

    2. In addition to having close friendships, adolescents belong to larger peer groups that provide standards for behavior.

    3. Parents and peers influence adolescents in different ways, but most of the time these influences are not contradictory.

    4. Dating and the formation of romantic relationships often begin during the adolescent years.

III. Identity Formation

A. Psychoanalyst Erik Erikson believed that the main developmental task of adolescence is the search for identity.

    1. According to Erikson, a teen who does not establish a firm identity may become confused about his or her identity, goals, and role in life.

    2. The point at which an adolescent must make decisions about life roles is called an identity crisis.

B. Psychologist James Marcia identified four different identity statuses, or ways adolescents deal with identity crises.

    1. Adolescents in identity moratorium delay making a commitment about the important questions they face.

    2. Adolescents in identity foreclosure make a commitment that shuts out other possibilities.

    3. Adolescents in identity diffusion wander about without goals or interests and seem to live from crisis to crisis.

    4. Adolescents in identity achievement have contemplated and made decisions about important life questions.

C. Questions of identity have additional dimensions for female adolescents and members of minority groups.

IV. Challenges of Adolescence

A. Adolescents who are overly concerned about their weight and body shape may have an eating disorder such as anorexia nervosa or bulimia.

B. Some teens use illegal drugs to help them win peer approval, to escape from emotional stress, or to bolster their self-esteem. By doing so, they often create worse problems for themselves.

C. Failure to control sexual feelings can have negative consequences for adolescents.

D. Problems at home and at school, along with low self-esteem and feelings of alienation, can lead teenagers to engage in delinquent behavior.

E. Adolescents who have clear goals in life usually avoid major problems.

TERM & CONCEPT
REVIEW

1. Why do some adolescents feel awkward during the adolescent growth spurt?
2. What is the difference between a primary sex characteristic and a secondary sex characteristic? Give an example of each.
3. List two ways in which adolescents are likely to follow their peers. List two ways in which they are likely to agree with their parents.
4. What is the difference between a clique and a crowd?
5. Identify three reasons for adolescent dating.
6. What does it mean to find one's identity?
7. What does the word *moratorium* mean? How is this term related to finding an identity?
8. List the characteristics of two eating disorders.
9. Describe the detoxification process in the treatment of substance abuse.
10. What is a status offense? Give an example.

CRITICAL
THINKING

1. Why do you think adolescence has become prolonged in Western society?
2. List several types of peer relationships that develop during adolescence. What are some of the advantages and disadvantages of each of these types of relationships?
3. What factors might help a teenager in his or her search for identity?
4. Gender differences in the physical development of males and females are a biological fact of life. What seem to be some gender differences in other types of development of adolescent males and females?
5. Why might peer counseling be an effective way of helping teenagers deal with the challenges of adolescence? What other methods might also help a teenager resolve some of these challenges or conflicts?

APPLYING SKILLS
IN PSYCHOLOGY

1. **COOPERATIVE LEARNING Research in Psychology** Working in small groups, survey the contents of several recent teen magazines. Identify the types of articles, features, and advertisements that appear most frequently. Discuss the overall message these magazines send to teenagers. Also consider whether the material appearing in the magazines is representative of the issues students at your high school face. Have one person in your group report your findings to the class.
2. **Writing About Psychology** Imagine that you are the writer of a newspaper column in which you answer letters from teens seeking advice. Think of a problem or concern that a teen might have. Compose a letter to "Dear (*your name*)" briefly describing the background of the problem. Then write a response that suggests a way to deal with the situation. Read your letter and response in class.
3. **Using Your Observation Skills** Collect examples of the ways in which adolescents are portrayed in comic strips, on television shows, and in the movies. Along with your classmates, discuss whether or not these portrayals are fair and accurate.
4. **Reading About Psychology** Read a novel that features an adolescent as its main character. (Ask your school librarian or English teacher for suggestions on appropriate books.) As you read, try to connect the character to information you learned in this chapter about adolescent development and the challenges of adolescence. For example, is the character having an identity crisis? Is the character dealing with negative peer pressure? If the novel is historical, describe ways in which adolescence has changed since the novel was written. If the novel is contemporary, consider whether it accurately depicts adolescence. Write a profile of the character exploring these issues.

12 ADULTHOOD

Chapter

Objectives

1 List the characteristics and issues of young adulthood.

2 Describe the changes that occur and issues that are faced in middle adulthood.

3 Analyze the changes that occur and the concerns of people in late adulthood.

4 Explain the attitudes and issues related to death and dying.

A DAY IN THE LIFE

 Marc and Linda had decided to volunteer at the local residential community for senior citizens. They had just finished for the day and were comparing experiences while they waited for the bus.

"So what did you do today?" asked Marc.

"I visited with the patients in the nursing home," said Linda. "At first it was upsetting because it reminded me of visiting my grandmother in the hospice before she died. I didn't think I'd ever get over missing her, but I guess I've adjusted."

"That must have been hard," Marc sympathized.

"I used to love spending time with my grandmother," Linda mused. "She would always think of fun things for us to do. Until she got sick, she was very energetic."

"She sounds like the people I met today," said Marc. "I was helping some of the people who live in their own apartments over by the recreation center. There was a man there in his late 70s who was doing yard work. He told me that he walks about five miles every day—he says that regular exercise keeps him

healthy. I hope I'm as fit as he is when I'm that age."

"My dad will be happy to hear about him," said Linda. "When Dad turned 40, he began worrying about aging. He started doing all these things he'd never done before, like exercising and taking classes. It's funny, but I really think he's actually happier now than he was when he was younger."

"That's fantastic," said Marc. "Turning 40 seems to make people really think about their lives."

"Yeah," answered Linda. "Janet said that when her parents hit their 40s, they finally realized how unhappy they were with each other."

"How's Janet been doing since her parents' divorce, by the way?" asked Marc.

"Well, it was really hard for her at first, but she's basically fine now. In fact, she told me she feels closer than ever to her mom."

Marc and Linda were both silent for a moment.

"Do you realize we'll be in our 20s soon?" asked Linda.

"I know. We'll be on our own then—we'll be independent," said Marc, obviously anticipating the arrival of that day.

Marc and Linda had just been confronted with what it means to be an adult, grow older, and eventually die. Development is a process that continues throughout one's lifetime. Many theorists believe that adult development, like childhood and adolescence, follows certain stages. Others believe that there is no "standard" life cycle with predictable life stages. Nowadays, people are living longer and, in some ways, are freer than ever to make their own life choices. The adult years are generally divided into three broad stages: young adulthood, middle adulthood, and late adulthood.

Key Terms

- patriarchy
- generativity
- midlife transition
- midlife crisis
- empty-nest syndrome
- menopause
- programmed theories
- cellular damage theories
- free radical
- cross-linking
- dementia
- senile dementia
- Alzheimer's disease
- ego integrity
- hospice
- euthanasia
- living will
- bereaved

1 Young Adulthood

Young adulthood, also called early adulthood, covers a span of approximately 20 years—from about age 20 to about age 40. Most people reach their physical peak in their 20s. During their 20s and early 30s, they are faster, stronger, better coordinated, and have more endurance than they have ever had or will ever have again. Many people also are at the height of their cognitive powers during this period (Simonton, 1988).

Young adulthood is characterized by a desire to try new ways of doing things and by changing relationships with parents. In their late teens and early 20s, some people assume that they must live the way their parents do if they want to succeed in life. Some also assume that their parents will always be there to rescue them if their plans fail. As time passes, however, young adults learn to become independent and to take responsibility for themselves and the decisions they make.

Studies indicate that, in the United States, becoming independent from parental authority is a key goal of development for most young adult men (Guisinger & Blatt, 1994). Although Marc is still in high school, his remark anticipating independence indicates that he, too, shares this goal. Women are generally less

concerned with seeing themselves as separate, independent individuals. They tend to be more interested in creating relationships with others (Gilligan et al., 1990, 1991; Jordan et al., 1991). Of course, these are generalizations only; many women in their 20s become independent and develop as individuals (Helson & Moane, 1987). The creation and maintenance of relationships are also important concerns for many men.

Reassessment

Adults in their 20s often believe they have chosen the course in life that is exactly right for them. As they reach their 30s, however, they often reevaluate the decisions they have made in an effort to determine whether their chosen course is really the one that is right for them. Levinson (1978, 1996) has labeled the period of the late 20s and early 30s the "age 30 transition." For many young adults, this is a time to reassess earlier choices. People often ask themselves, "Why am I doing this?" or "Where is my life going?" Sometimes they find that the life paths they chose in their 20s are no longer the paths they truly want to follow.

This period of reassessment may bring about major life changes. Some people change jobs or start new careers. Many single people feel that this is the time to find a mate. People who have been working in the home, perhaps raising children, may feel the urge to find a job outside the home. Couples who are without children may now think about starting a family (Sheehy, 1995).

Women in particular may find themselves reassessing their lives in their 30s. Some women in their 30s begin to think about the biological changes that lie ahead. Many women become concerned about how many childbearing years they have left, especially if they have not already had children. Furthermore, during their early 30s, many women begin to feel that they have been controlled by others and that they have never had the chance to shape their own lives (Helson & Moane, 1987). Today, as in years past, it is still mostly women who take care of family and household chores. As a result, women in the workforce may feel overwhelmed by the double duties of caring for their families and maintaining jobs.

In addition, research suggests that some working women have mixed feelings about success on the job. Even though the great majority of women are in the workplace, some still feel they must sacrifice their family lives to advance their careers. Although working men also have less time to spend with their families, many people still consider it more acceptable for men to work long hours than for women to do the same (Levinson, 1996).

Settling Down

After the upheaval of the early 30s, the middle-to-late 30s are often characterized by settling down or "planting roots" (Levinson, 1978). People in their 30s may increase the financial and emotional investments they make in their lives. Many have been employed long enough to gain promotions and pay raises. They often become more focused on advancing their careers and gaining stability in their personal lives.

Figure 12.1 on page 276 lists some of the developmental tasks of young adulthood. Every individual does not necessarily experience all of these tasks. Nor does every young adult follow them in a particular order. For example, many people today choose to remain single or to postpone (or forgo) having and rearing children.

Marriage and Intimate Relationships

An important part of adolescence and young adulthood is the development of an identity—who you are and what you stand for (your values). Identity brings the personal stability that is needed to form lasting relationships. (See Chapter 11.) According to Erik Erikson (1963), one of the key tasks of young adulthood is the forming of relationships.

Relationships can be difficult to sustain when one or both of the people involved lack personal stability, which may be one reason why teenage marriages suffer a higher divorce rate than adult marriages. However, young adults who have developed a firm sense of identity during adolescence may be ready to join their lives with those of other

It is not unusual for women to feel torn between their obligations to their jobs and to their families. Many women still have the primary responsibility for taking care of the family and home in addition to working full-time.

people through friendships and marriage. Erikson believed that people who do not develop intimate relationships may risk falling into a pattern of isolation and loneliness. An intimate relationship is not necessarily a physical relationship. Rather, it is a trusting, close friendship with another person in which one can be honest without fear of rejection.

In the United States, most people marry. Only about one in four people over the age of 18 has never been married (Norton & Moorman, 1987). However, with more people delaying marriage in favor of pursuing educational and career goals, the median age at first marriage has risen in recent decades. In the past 25 years, it has gone from about 23 to 27 for men and from about 21 to 25 for women (Norton & Moorman, 1987; Tanfer, 1987).

TRUTH OR **fiction** ▪ R E V I S I T E D ▪

It is true that people in the United States have been marrying later than people did a few generations ago. Many people now wait until they have finished college or have their careers under way before they marry.

History of Marriage

In most Western cultures, men have traditionally played the dominant role in marriage as well as in society. This system is known as a **patriarchy**. Over the past several decades, however, this situation has changed, and spouses are now more likely to be considered equal partners in marriage.

Marital roles in modern society are still changing. Some couples continue to adhere to roles in which the husband is the breadwinner and the wife is the homemaker. Other couples have begun to share, and even sometimes reverse, these roles. And many single or divorced individuals are alone responsible for fulfilling these roles.

In the United States today, most people marry primarily for love. The concept of romantic love as a reason for marriage, however, did not become widespread in Western society until the 1800s. In the 1600s and 1700s, most marriages were arranged by the parents of the bride and groom, generally on the basis of how the marriage would benefit the two families. This practice permitted the orderly transition of wealth from one family to another and from one generation to the next. Another purpose of marriage was to provide a stable home life in which to have and rear children.

TRUTH OR fiction
▪ REVISITED ▪

It is true that romantic love is a relatively new reason for marrying. Historically, marriage was seen as an institution for rearing children and for providing for the transmission of wealth from one generation to another. Marriage was not viewed as an expression of love.

Today, however, companionship and intimacy are central goals in most marriages. Marriage generally provides feelings of security and opportunities to share experiences and ideas with someone special. Research has found that most young adults

Developmental Tasks of Young Adulthood

- Exploring adult roles
- Becoming independent
- Developing intimate relationships
- Adjusting to living with another person
- Starting a family and becoming a parent
- Assuming the responsibilities of managing a home
- Beginning a career or a job
- Assuming some responsibilities in the larger community—for example, participating in local government or religious organizations
- Creating a social network of friends and coworkers

FIGURE 12.1 *Erikson believed that each stage of life has its own developmental tasks. This chart lists some of the tasks associated with young adulthood. Not all young adults experience all of these tasks, nor do they experience them in a particular order.*

strongly believe marriage should be a lifetime commitment (Moore & Stief, 1992).

Choosing Spouses

Unlike in times past, in which marriages were arranged by the family, today young people in the United States typically select their own mates. Parents may, however, have at least some degree of influence over the choice.

People are also influenced in their marital decisions by factors such as ethnicity, level of education, social class, and religion. Generally, people marry others who are similar to themselves. For example, Americans tend to marry people who are from the same geographical area and social class—perhaps because they are more likely to meet such people in the first place.

People also tend to be like their mates in race and religion. Less than 3 percent of marriages are between people of different races. The majority of marriages are between people of the same religion. Marital partners also tend to be similar in physical attractiveness, attitudes, personality traits, and intelligence. They are usually even similar in height and weight (Buss, 1994; Lesnik-Oberstein & Cohen, 1984; Schafer & Keith, 1990).

PSYCHOLOGY

LOVE STORIES

Some couples seem perfectly happy. Then suddenly, to the surprise of all their friends, they divorce. Other couples seem to fight all the time and constantly complain about each other. Yet they stay married. Why does this happen? That is the question psychologist Robert Sternberg asked himself. After interviewing many people he formed the theory that "love is a story."

Sternberg maintains in his article "Love Stories" (1996) that through the interaction of our personalties and the environment, we create stories about love, which we then try to fulfill. Various potential spouses fit these stories to a greater or lesser degree. According to Sternberg, marriages tend to last when the partners fulfill the roles they have created for themselves in their love stories.

Sternberg explains how we develop these stories and why they are very different from culture to culture:

> The stories we invent draw on elements from our experience of living in the world—from the fairy stories we heard as young children, from the models of love relationships we observe around us in parents and relatives, from television and movies, from conversations with other people about their relationships, and so on. (p. 62)

According to Sternberg, love is not just a single story. He has come up with 24 stories but cautions that there are probably many more. Two of Sternberg's stories are the "fantasy" story and the "gardening" story. The fantasy story is similar to a fairy tale. A woman who has a fantasy story expects her mate to be a "knight in shining armor" to protect her from danger. A man with a fantasy story expects his mate to be a "princess." The potential for the success of such a union depends on how much the people expect the fantasy to continue. If their expectations are too high, they may become disappointed.

In the "gardening" story, both partners tend and nurture the relationship as they would a beautiful rose. According to Sternberg, this relationship

has potential for success as long as the partners continue to tend the "garden" (marriage).

Although people have created these stories, they are not aware that they have done so. Sternberg suggests what happens when we meet a person who might be a potential partner:

> . . . if our story is a fantasy story then the slot we want to fill is reserved for a knight or princess. . . . Thus . . . we are attracted to a person who (we think) can fill a slot in our story line and we will stay attracted as long as the person continues to fill the slot. (pp. 71–72)

If the potential mate does not meet our story ideals, we probably will not even consider him or her, but if the person comes close, we might fall in love. What matters more than the individual story itself is that both partners believe in the same story. That is what is needed for the success of the union, as stated in the following excerpt:

> Love stories have complementary roles. We look for someone who shares our story or who at least has a compatible story that can more or less fit it. (p. 69)

Sternberg's story theory might explain why some women stay with abusive husbands:

> Abused individuals might stay with partners not only for reasons of finances or fear, but because they truly believe—perhaps from what they have seen as children or in movies—that abuse is part of love. (p. 73)

It is possible that both people in an abusive relationship share a terrible story—that love includes hurt and abuse. And stories, explains Sternberg, are hard to change or break.

Think About It

What might be some other common love stories? Give three examples, then explain what kind of roles people would play in those stories.

Many wedding ceremonies blend modern and traditional customs.

People also tend to choose marriage partners who are near their own age (Michael et al., 1994). This is especially true for couples who marry in early adulthood. People who meet in school and then marry each other tend to be similar in age. Most bridegrooms are about two to five years older than the women they are marrying (Buss, 1994). People who marry later in life or who remarry after being divorced or widowed are less likely to select partners who are as close in age.

Marriages between similar people may have a greater chance at survival because the partners probably share the same values and attitudes (Michael et al., 1994). Dissimilar couples, however, can work to overcome the differences that divide them by developing shared interests and mutual respect for those differences. Evidence that similarity between spouses is beneficial in the long run—the entire course of the marriage—remains somewhat limited (Karney & Bradbury, 1995).

Divorce

A DAY IN THE LIFE

Although most couples marry for love, a great many marriages in the United States—such as the one between Janet's parents—end in divorce or permanent separation. The most common reasons given for divorce are problems in communication and a lack of understanding. The divorce rate in the United States rose steadily through much of the 20th century before leveling off in the 1980s. About one fourth of the children in the United States below the age of 18 live in single-parent households (Facts on File, 1994).

Reasons for Divorce   Why is divorce such a common occurrence when most couples believe in marrying for life? One reason may be that obtaining a divorce has become easier than it used to be. Many states now have "no-fault" divorce laws. That means that a judge can grant a divorce without having one or both partners blaming the other. If both partners agree on issues of child custody, financial support, and the distribution of the couple's assets, the marriage is legally dissolved.

The increased economic independence of women also may have contributed to the rise in the divorce rate. Just 30 years ago, most women were homemakers with little or no work experience outside the home. Because there were relatively few opportunities for women to enter the paid workforce at that time, many women probably doubted whether they would be able to support themselves and their children on their own. Thus, they may have been inclined to remain in troubled marriages because they perceived that they had no realistic alternative. Today, however, more women have jobs outside the home and are therefore more likely to have the economic independence that makes it easier for them to break away.

Increasingly high expectations may also have made divorce more likely. Today many couples expect marriage to be constantly gratifying—and to be easy. Relationships, however, require work and commitment. Some couples no longer feel committed enough to the marriage to try to make it work. Of course, there are numerous other reasons why people get divorced, including spouse abuse, child abuse, infidelity, strains brought about by illness or financial hardship, or an inability to communicate effectively (Cherlin, 1992).

The Costs of Divorce   Divorce has many financial and emotional costs. When a household splits, the financial resources, such as income and property, are usually divided. Often, neither partner can afford to maintain the standard of living he or she had while married. A woman who does not have an established career may find herself struggling to compete with younger, more experienced workers as she enters the workforce.

Women generally are granted custody of the couple's children. Thus, divorced mothers often face the primary responsibility for rearing the children and may need to increase income to make ends meet. These responsibilities can be extremely stressful. Divorced fathers, meanwhile, may find it difficult to pay child support and alimony (financial support paid to a former spouse).

Divorce can lead to feelings of failure, loneliness, fears about the future, and depression. Married people (especially happily married people) are usually better able to cope with the stresses of life, perhaps because they lend each other emotional support. Divorced and separated people have higher rates of physical and psychological disorders than do married people (Nevid et al., 1997).

Yet, for some people, divorce is a time of personal growth and renewal. When partners are convinced they cannot save their marriage, divorce may enable them to establish new and more rewarding lives. Despite the difficulties in adjusting to a divorce, most divorced people eventually recover. The majority remarry. Yet, research suggests that remarriages are even more likely than first marriages to end in divorce (Lown & Dolan, 1988). This may be because divorced people—having set a precedent in their first marriage—are inclined to leave a troubled second marriage fairly quickly. People in first-time marriages, on the other hand, may be more inclined to persist even if the marriage is difficult. In addition, many divorced people who remarry have alimony and child-support obligations that often place a financial strain on their new marriages.

The Children of Divorce Divorce can be difficult for children, even when they are almost adults, as Janet was when her parents divorced. Still, like Janet, most children overcome an initial period of pain about their parents' divorce and eventually stop doubting their ability to adjust to their new situation. Children of divorce usually fare better when both parents maintain an interest in them and set aside marital differences to agree on childrearing practices (Wallerstein & Blakeslee, 1989). Children also benefit when divorced parents encourage each other to remain involved in their children's lives and when they avoid saying negative things about the other parent to the children.

Nevertheless, some research suggests that nearly half of all the children of divorced parents experience problems such as anxiety, poor grades, low self-esteem, and anger (Wallerstein & Blakeslee, 1989). Many children blame themselves for their parents' divorce. Boys tend to have more problems than do girls in adjusting to parents' divorces. They may become disruptive in school and aggressive in their relationships with others. Both boys and girls tend to experience increased anxiety, depression, and dependence (Grych & Fincham, 1993; Holden & Ritchie, 1991).

Some effects of divorce on children are not immediately evident. Some children appear to adjust well to divorce. In early adulthood, however, they may find it difficult to trust the commitment of a potential partner and thus may be reluctant to become deeply involved with other people. This delayed reaction is called a "sleeper effect" (Wallerstein & Blakeslee, 1989).

Some researchers attribute children's problems following divorce not only to the divorce itself but also to the changes that may follow the divorce. Sometimes a stepfamily introduces new relationships and changes the dynamics of the existing ones; such changes can put strain on the children in the family. In addition, parents may have to work more to financially support the family and therefore may have less time to spend with the children.

Should parents in conflict remain married for the sake of the children? There is no easy answer to that question. Divorce may have negative effects on

Some people believe that parents in unhappy marriages should stay together for the sake of the children. While divorce can take its toll on children, so can living in a household with parents who are in constant conflict with each other.

children, but so do marital conflicts (Amato & Keith, 1991; Davies & Cummings, 1994). Marital problems often spill over into parents' relationships with their children (Erel & Burman, 1995). Parents are sometimes so overwhelmed by stress that they grow impatient with the children or make the children part of the conflict by asking them to take sides. Both situations are hurtful to children.

THINKING ABOUT PSYCHOLOGY

1. How do men and women differ in their views about becoming independent from parental authority?

2. According to Erikson, what are the risks for people who do not develop intimate relationships during young adulthood?

3. **Critical Thinking**   Agree or disagree with the following statement: "Parents in conflict should remain together for the sake of the children." Provide evidence to support your answer.

2
Middle Adulthood

Middle adulthood spans the years from 40 to 65. By age 40, most people have begun to lose some of the strength, coordination, and stamina they had in their 20s and 30s. This decline in physical ability is generally so gradual that it is hardly noticeable. It is often only of concern to people who rely on physical fitness for their livelihoods or interests, such as athletes. However, middle adulthood can also be the time when many people first *begin* to work on developing their physical potential, as Linda's father did when he was 40. Even someone who has been inactive for years might decide at 45 to train for a marathon. People who work at their conditioning can maintain excellent health and strength throughout middle adulthood.

Generativity

Figure 12.2 on page 281 summarizes some of the developmental tasks of middle adulthood, according to Erik Erikson. Erikson believed that the greatest challenge for middle-aged adults is **generativity**—the ability to

create, originate, and produce. According to Erikson, generativity adds meaning to the lives of adults, and it helps them to maintain and enhance their self-esteem.

Adults can be creative, or generative, in various areas of their lives, such as their career, their family, and their community. People in middle adulthood are often also in positions in which they can exercise a particularly important influence on the world around them. As experienced workers, they may improve methods and relationships in the workplace. As parents, they guide the next generation. As voters and residents, they can help make their communities safer, friendlier places. Erikson also believed that adults who are not generative become stagnant. Stagnation—lack of advancement or development—can result in feelings of emptiness and meaninglessness.

Transition

Some psychologists have noted that many people experience a midlife transition around the ages of 40 to 45. The **midlife transition** is a period in middle adulthood when people's perspectives change in a major way. Some adults in their 40s are struck with the dramatic realization that they have lived about half their lives. They see themselves as being at a turning point. Previously, they have probably thought of their ages mostly in terms of how many years had elapsed since their birth. Once the midlife transition occurs, however, they begin to think of their ages in terms of how many years they may have left.

People in their 30s may still think of themselves as the older sibling of brothers or sisters in their 20s. Then, in their early 40s, a critical event often occurs. It may be a serious illness, a change at work, the death of a friend or a parent, or even just losing at basketball to one's child. Whatever the event, it triggers a 40-year-old's realization that he or she has made a generational shift. For example, the death of a parent may mean that the 40-year-old is now the head of the family. Similarly, losing at basketball to one's child may trigger the realization that "I'm not a kid anymore."

Women tend to undergo their midlife transitions about five years earlier than men do, at about age 35 instead of 40 (Reinke et al., 1985; Sheehy, 1995). What makes the mid-30s so special for women? For some women, 35 is about the age when they have sent their youngest child off to grade school, an event that can illustrate that their children are quickly growing up. Many women, of course, are not finished (or have not begun) having children by the age of 35, and for women who become pregnant at age 35 or older, doctors advise routine fetal testing for Down syndrome and other chromosomal disorders. (See Chapter 3.) Thirty-five is often also the age at which women are given a baseline mammogram (a specialized X ray for early detection of breast cancer) and are considered at greater risk for various types of cancer. These are all events that can cause women to reflect on their age and mortality.

With the thought that their lives may be close to half over, many people—men and women—come face-to-face with their limitations. They may acknowledge that dreams they had when they were younger may never be realized. For instance, they probably will never be a professional baseball player, a movie star, or president of the United States. People begin to adjust to the idea that they are growing older. For some adults, entering midlife may trigger a sense of urgency—"a last chance" to do certain things.

Midlife Crisis or Age of Mastery?

In some people, the midlife transition triggers a second period of reassessment, often referred to as a **midlife crisis**. The middle-aged professional who sees younger people advancing at a faster rate may become seriously depressed. The parent with two or three teenagers may feel less needed by her or his children. Both may feel trapped and think they have lost their purpose in life.

The concept of the midlife crisis has often been treated as something generally negative. It suggests that people are overwhelmed by the crushing realities and the limits of their lives. Yet journalist Gail Sheehy (1995) is quite positive about the years from 45 to 65. She calls these years the "age of mastery."

Sheehy maintains that during these years, people are frequently at the height of their creative and productive powers. In many cases, they need only

Developmental Tasks of Middle Adulthood

- Helping one's children make the transition from home life to the outside world

- Strengthening one's relationship with one's spouse

- Helping make the world a better place by assuming leadership roles in social and civic activities

- Achieving mastery in one's career

- Adjusting to the physical changes that occur in middle age

- Making decisions about how to spend one's "second adulthood"

- Pursuing one's passions

- Coping with one's aging parents

FIGURE 12.2 *Earlier in the chapter you read a list of what Erikson believed are the developmental tasks of young adulthood. Erikson also believed that middle adulthood has developmental tasks. The focus of these tasks is on improving one's quality of life and strengthening relationships, both personal and in the community.*

find new outlets for their talents and experience. Therefore, Sheehy believes, the key task for middle-aged adults is to decide what they will do with the remainder of their lives. Because people are living longer than people did in previous generations, most American adults have 30 to 40 healthy years left after they reach middle adulthood. Men and women can continue to have fulfilling lives if they find careers, hobbies, or other activities that bring satisfaction, and if they pursue these newfound interests wholeheartedly.

"Middlescence"

But how do people go about recognizing and finding these interests? The term *middlescence* is sometimes used to describe a period of searching that in some ways resembles adolescence. Both middlescence and adolescence are periods of transition. Just as a key task of adolescence is the formation of identity in becoming an adult, middlescence involves a search for a *new* identity, or a *second* adulthood.

By the time they reach their early 40s, women have already dealt with some of the fears and

TONIGHT'S TOPIC:

LIFE STAGES ←

HE SAYS YOUR LIFE GOES IN CYCLES.

OF COURSE! AS SOON AS YOU KNOW WHAT YOU'RE DOING, EVERYTHING CHANGES.

THAVES 3-19

E-mail: FandEBobT@AOL.COM

© 1996 by NEA, Inc.

FRANK & ERNEST reprinted by permission of Newspaper Enterprise Association, Inc.

uncertainties that are only just starting to confront men (Helson & Moane, 1987). As women emerge from middlescence in their 40s and 50s, they frequently experience a renewed sense of self. Many women in this age group feel confident and secure. They extend their interests. For example, they may become more involved in their communities. They are committed to what they are doing and feel productive, effective, and powerful.

The Empty-Nest Syndrome

In the past, psychologists placed great emphasis on the so-called empty-nest syndrome. **Empty-nest syndrome** is the term applied to the feelings of emptiness and loss mothers (and sometimes fathers) supposedly feel after the children have left home to establish their own lives. For mothers who have never worked outside the home, it can be particularly difficult to adjust to the departure of the

While parents do encounter some adjustment problems when their youngest child leaves home, many actually experience a new sense of freedom.

children whose upbringings have been a full-time job. After years of being totally committed to being a wife and mother, some women seem to lose their sense of purpose and become depressed after their children go out on their own.

Contemporary research findings, however, reveal a much more optimistic picture. Once the "nest" is empty, many women report that they are happier with their marriages and other aspects of their lives. Many women mention positive changes such as greater peace of mind, self-confidence, and personal stability (Reinke et al., 1985). Many middle-aged women become more self-assertive and achievement oriented. Furthermore, most women whose children have left home are already employed. With more energy and time to spend outside the home, many women become more influential in politics and careers. Many others return to school. And although there may be some problems of adjustment once children leave, those problems affect both parents, not just mothers.

TRUTH
OR
fiction
▪ R E V I S I T E D ▪

It is not true that most parents feel a great sense of loss and loneliness when the youngest child leaves home. Instead, many parents experience a new sense of opportunity.

There is much variation, of course. Some people in middle age feel hopeless and drained. But often middle age is a time of increased freedom. Many people have been successful enough to be free of financial worries. Many begin to travel extensively. They may have the leisure time to take up new hobbies or explore old interests. Therefore, middle age does not need to be a painful period. Rather, it can be a time to enjoy new freedoms and opportunities for self-development.

Menopause

Menopause, the end of menstruation, usually occurs in a woman's late 40s or early 50s, although it can occur earlier or later. It is caused by a decrease in the secretion of the hormones estrogen and progesterone. After menopause, a woman no longer produces egg cells that can be fertilized. Other body changes also occur. Breast tissue decreases, and the skin becomes less elastic. There may also be a loss in bone density that can lead to brittle bones—a condition called osteoporosis.

In some women, the hormonal changes of menopause may cause discomfort, such as hot flashes (sudden sensations of warmth, often accom-panied by reddening and sweating), fatigue, and mood swings. However, in most cases, these symptoms are relatively mild. Some women cope with the more severe changes of menopause by taking doses of hormones to replace those the body no longer produces (hormone replacement therapy).

The psychological meaning of menopause to a woman is often more important than the physical changes she experiences. Some women feel that they have become less attractive or even that they are losing their identity as women. These women are likely to be more distressed by menopause than those who do not have such feelings (Rathus et al., 1997). Women who feel that their primary purpose in life was birthing and rearing children are also likely to find menopause stressful.

Figure 12.3 highlights some myths and realities about menopause. Notice that all the myths are negative. The reality, however, is often positive. For

Myths and Realities About Menopause

Myth	Reality
Menopause is abnormal.	Menopause is a normal development in women's lives.
Doctors consider menopause to be a disease.	Not so. Menopause is now conceptualized as a "deficiency syndrome" because of the drop-offs in estrogen and progesterone.
After menopause, women need estrogen replacement therapy.	Not necessarily. Some estrogen is still produced by the adrenal glands and other parts of the body. Estrogen replacement therapy is recommended only occasionally.
Menopause is accompanied by depression and anxiety.	Not necessarily. Much of a woman's response to menopause reflects its psychological aspects rather than biological changes.
At menopause, women suffer crippling hot flashes.	Not necessarily. Many women do not experience any hot flashes. Women who do experience them usually find them mild.
Menopause ends a woman's sex drive.	Not at all. In fact, many women feel a renewal of sexual interest.
A woman's general level of activity is lower after menopause.	Not so. Many women report having more energy after menopause.

FIGURE 12.3 *The left-hand side of this table shows several of the myths about menopause. The realities of menopause are shown on the right-hand side. Why do you suppose people have so many misconceptions about menopause? How might these misconceptions influence the way menopausal women are treated?*

example, many women report having more energy —not less—after menopause.

When people are referred to as "menopausal," it is usually the mood swings and increased irritability that are being talked about. Unfortunately, this simplifies what menopause is all about for women, and it also reinforces the stereotype of menopause as a time when women are not in control of their emotions. Such stereotypes and myths often do not have anything to do with the biology or psychology of aging.

Do men undergo menopause? The quick answer is "of course not" since men have never menstruated. Yet, occasionally one hears of a so-called male menopause. Men do experience a hormone decline. At about age 40 or 50, testosterone levels in men begin to decline. They may reach one third or one half of their peak levels by age 80 (Brody, 1995c). However, this is a gradual drop-off. It does not resemble the sharp plunge in estrogen levels that women experience.

The decline in a man's testosterone level may be connected with such other age-related changes as loss of strength, weight gain, reduced energy, and decreased fertility. Some of these changes, however, could just as well be due to a gradual loss of the human growth hormone rather than a diminishing testosterone level.

Life Expectancy of Americans from 1900 to 2000

FIGURE 12.4 *By the year 2000, the life expectancy of the average American will have risen by almost 30 years since 1900. What do you think are some of the reasons Americans are living longer?*

Source: U.S. National Center for Health Statistics, *Vital Statistics of the United States,* annual, and *Monthly Vital Statistics Reports;* U.S. Public Health Service, 1900-1967, *Vital Statistics of the United States, 1967;* and U.S. Bureau of the Census, *Current Population Reports.*

THINKING ABOUT PSYCHOLOGY

1. How does generativity contribute to a healthy middle adulthood?
2. What is the midlife transition and why does it sometimes result in a "crisis"?
3. **Critical Thinking**   Do you think middle age is a time of crisis or a period of new opportunities? Explain your answer.

3
Late Adulthood

Age 65 marks the beginning of late adulthood. As Figure 12.4 shows, people are living longer than ever before. In 1900, only one American in 30 was over 65. By the year 2020, nearly one American in five will be age 65 or older (Heckler, 1985).

Some people view the later years as the beginning of the end of life, but they can be much more. In fact, the later years provide many opportunities for self-fulfillment. Ronald Reagan became the U.S. president when he was 70; comedian George Burns performed his comedy routines into his late 90s.

Physical Changes

Many physical changes take place in late adulthood. Wrinkles and skin folds occur as the skin becomes less elastic. Some of the senses become less sharp. In general, older people do not see and hear as well as younger people. A decline in the sense of smell leads many older people to add more spices to their food for flavor. The reflexes and the reaction time of older people also tend to be a little slower than those of younger people.

A few of the physical changes cause health problems. For example, as bones become more brittle, they fracture more easily, and the risk is greater that they will break if the person falls. As people grow older, their immune systems also become less effective as a barrier against disease.

However, older adults can do many things to maintain their health, strength, and energy levels.

Regular exercise and a healthful diet can contribute to making older adults feel well and also help them fight disease. The man whom Marc met doing yard work is a good example of the benefits of exercise.

Exercise helps people maintain flexibility and fitness at any age—including the years of late adulthood. Because brittle bones and stiff joints are part of the aging process, many older people may prefer walking and swimming to more weight-bearing exercises such as running and bicycling. The latter activities tend to cause more stress on bones and joints (Pena & Bricklin, 1990).

It is not true that it is good for older people not to exercise. Exercise helps people maintain flexibility and fitness at any age. Many older adults enjoy walking and swimming.

Why Do People Age?

Why do some people seem to age faster than others? Many scientists hope that by understanding the process of aging, we may eventually be able to slow it down or even reverse some of its negative effects. Theories of aging fall into two categories: programmed theories and cellular damage theories.

Programmed Theories The developmental theories that maintain that aging is the result of genetics are called **programmed theories**. These theories of aging view people as having biological clocks that move forward at a predetermined pace. Studies show that people whose parents lived long lives are more likely to have long lives themselves. This suggests that genetics plays a significant role in the length of one's life.

Heredity influences our cells, our hormones, and our immune systems. The cells in our bodies divide and repair themselves only a specific number of times. After that, they become inactive and eventually die. Some researchers believe that the limitation on the number of times a cell can divide is less important than the fact that the cells are aging. As they age, cells become less able to repair themselves. This makes people vulnerable to diseases that involve cellular breakdown, such as cancer (Lehrman, 1995).

Exercise is beneficial at every stage of life, especially late adulthood. Regular exercise can help older people stay healthy, flexible, and energetic.

Heredity also affects our hormones. Hormonal changes in later life may leave the body more vulnerable to certain health problems, such as diabetes, osteoporosis, and heart disease. Researchers are investigating the possible role of certain hormones—such as melatonin and the human growth hormone—in the aging process.

In addition, heredity influences the immune system. According to programmed theories, genetics may predetermine the decline in our immune systems. Such a decline makes the body less able to fight off disease.

Cellular Damage Theories In contrast to programmed theories, **cellular damage theories** of aging suggest that cells malfunction as a result of damage, not heredity. The damage may come from internal body changes or from external causes, such as trauma or poisons.

The cells in our bodies are affected by the environment. If they are exposed to poisons or cancer-causing agents for long periods of time, they become less able to repair themselves and more vulnerable to disease. As time passes, cells and vital organs are worn down, like machines whose parts eventually wear out from constant use.

Some scientists blame free radicals for damage to our bodies. **Free radicals** are unstable molecules in our bodies. They are normally produced as a by-product of digestion. They may also be produced by exposure to environmental agents, including

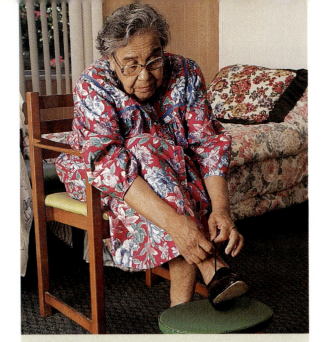

Sometimes older people have difficulty with certain tasks, such as tying shoes, not because of cognitive factors but because of physical ones, such as arthritis.

ultraviolet light, air pollution, pesticides, or even extreme heat. According to this view, aging occurs because free radicals accumulate in the body. These molecules eventually damage cells, causing people to age faster and to become vulnerable to various diseases (Hayflick, 1994; Lehrman, 1995).

Another cause of aging may be **cross-linking**. According to this view, proteins within a cell bind together, toughening body tissues. This toughening eventually leads to the breakdown of various bodily processes and causes aging (Lamb, 1993).

Aging is a complex biological process. It may not be due to a single cause. It may not be explainable by a single theory. Aging may result from a combination of the processes described here, or it may involve factors we are not even aware of yet. For these reasons, researchers continue to study the aging process.

Cognitive Changes

Some older adults occasionally experience memory loss, but most memory loss is not serious. Many older people do have some general decline in intellectual ability, as measured by scores on intelligence tests. The drop-off is sharpest on items that require people to rapidly perform tasks, such as piecing puzzles together. However, changes in cognitive functioning are not generally as significant as many people assume they are (Benson, 1995).

The great majority of older people have no serious decline in intellectual skills. Accumulated knowledge and vocabulary, for example, continue to expand throughout a person's lifetime. Moreover, many older people develop new cognitive skills (Berger, 1994). For example, as they grow older, people often become more tolerant and thoughtful than they were in earlier years. By using the valuable insights from their years of experience, they become wiser. Many older people have more leisure time than they did earlier in life and find a new appreciation for nature and the arts.

All in all, most older people do quite well intellectually. Late adulthood is a time to discover new skills and ways of thinking. Unfortunately, some older people do have cognitive problems, such as senile dementia and Alzheimer's disease.

Senile Dementia   Serious loss of cognitive functioning is called a **dementia**. People with dementia show major losses in memory. They may also have speech problems or be unable to perform simple tasks, such as tying their shoes or buttoning a shirt, even if they are physically able to perform such tasks. They may also have difficulty concentrating or making plans.

Dementia that occurs after the age of 65 is called **senile dementia**. Only a minority of older people have senile dementia, sometimes called senility. Most cases occur in people over the age of 80 (Nevid et al., 1997).

Although dementia is more common among older people than younger people, it is not a normal part of the aging process. Of about 70 known causes of dementia, not one is simply a result of growing older. The onset of dementia has more to do with chance and probability: the longer a person lives, the more time there is for dementia to show up and thus the greater chance that it will. Aging does not cause dementia. Some malfunction does. As the life expectancy of the population has increased, dementia has become more frequent simply because there is now more time in people's life spans for it to occur (Cummings, 1995).

It is not true that everyone who lives long enough will eventually become senile. Senile dementia (sometimes called senility) is not an automatic result of aging.

Alzheimer's Disease   The most common cause of dementia is **Alzheimer's disease**. Alzheimer's disease affects about 10 percent of people in the United States over the age of 65 (Teri & Wagner, 1992). The risk increases sharply with advanced age (Selkoe, 1992). Alzheimer's disease, like other kinds of dementia, is connected with aging, but it is not a normal part of the aging process.

The onset of Alzheimer's disease is usually gradual. It is linked to the deterioration of cells in a part of the brain (the hippocampus) that produces the neurotransmitter acetylcholine (ACh). The hippocampus and ACh are involved in memory. One of the key symptoms of Alzheimer's disease is memory loss and confusion. People with Alzheimer's disease often become lost—even in their own homes. Eventually, they are unable to recognize family members. They become childlike and unable to take care of themselves.

The precise causes of Alzheimer's disease are somewhat unclear. Heredity seems to play a role, as do certain viral infections and aluminum poisoning. Researchers are looking into ways of helping people with Alzheimer's disease. They are experimenting with medications, special diets, and even cell transplants—the transplanting of cells that produce ACh in the brain (Tanzi, 1995).

The second most common kind of dementia is vascular dementia. Vascular dementia can be caused by the bursting of a blood vessel in the brain (also called a stroke) or by a decrease in the blood supply to the brain. Such a decrease happens when fatty deposits collect in the blood vessels that go to the brain. The deposits cause the blood vessels to narrow, impeding the blood flow. Various infections can also cause dementia.

Social Changes

Aging also involves many social changes. People have to make decisions about their retirement, how much time to spend with their children and grandchildren, and where they should live.

Retirement   Many people dream of retirement, the period when they no longer need to wake up early in the morning and go to work. Other people dread the idea of retirement, wondering what they will do with all their free time. In many cases, retirement is voluntary. But people in some jobs, including teachers in most school systems, must retire when they reach a certain age, usually 65 or 70. In other cases, older people find themselves forced out of jobs because of discrimination or for other reasons related to age.

Some people turn their attention to leisure activities when they retire. Others continue in part-time work, either paid or voluntary. Research indicates that there may be some common experiences involving retirement (Atchley, 1991). When people first retire, they often undergo a "honeymoon" phase. They feel very positive about their newfound freedom, and they do many of the things they had dreamed about doing once they had the time. During this honeymoon period, people are often quite busy.

After a while, however, many people become disillusioned with retirement. Their schedules slow down, and they discover that the things they had fantasized about are less stimulating than they had thought they would be. Retirement can also place stress on a marriage because spouses may suddenly be spending a great deal more time together than they ever have before. As people encounter such experiences, they tend to develop a more realistic view of retirement. They may join volunteer groups and participate more in community activities. Sometimes they begin entirely new careers—painting or writing, for example. In general, people establish a new routine and stability sets in.

Grandparenthood   Grandparents often have more relaxed relationships with their grandchildren than they had with their children. Their perspectives may have become broader as they have grown older. Many have become more tolerant and understanding over the years. And because they do not usually have to shoulder the major responsibility for the grandchildren, grandparents usually can enjoy them. Of course, due to a variety of circumstances, increasing numbers of grandparents are in fact taking on the major responsibility for raising their grandchildren.

 Grandparents are frequently valued by their children for the roles they play with the grandchildren. For example, retired grandparents who live nearby can help baby-sit. Grandparents also often serve as special sources of wisdom and love for grandchildren, as Linda remembered about her own grandmother.

For many older adults, balancing a need for independence with a need to stay involved with their children and grandchildren is an important job. Older people sometimes hand over control of their finances to their children. How often they see

To grandchildren, grandparents often serve as a source of love and understanding—and enjoyment.

the children and grandchildren and whether they have the right to make "suggestions" become key issues. Although many older people worry that their families might no longer want them around, they are not usually rejected by their children. Most older people see or talk to their children regularly (Berger, 1994).

Living Arrangements   Some Americans hold certain stereotypes about older people's living arrangements. One stereotype portrays older people living with their children. Another has them in nursing homes and other institutions (Stock, 1995). Still another stereotype is that older people buy condominiums or move to retirement communities in areas with warmer climates.

In contrast to the stereotypes, most older people are independent. Many of them are financially secure and own their own homes. It is true that nearly 30 percent of older people will spend some time in a nursing home (Kemper & Murtaugh, 1991). However, the populations of nursing homes usually consist of people who are 80 or older.

Most older people also remain in their home-towns rather than moving to other areas of the United States. They prefer to live in familiar sur-roundings where they have social and cultural ties (U.S. Bureau of the Census, 1995).

Successful Aging

Some people age more successfully than others. Psychologists have found that "successful agers" have several characteristics that can inspire all peo-ple to lead more enjoyable and productive lives.

Ego Integrity   Erik Erikson (1963) believed that people in late adulthood, like those in other stages of life, face certain developmental tasks. (See Figure 12.5 on page 290.) He believed that one challenge facing people in late adulthood is the maintenance of **ego integrity**—the belief that life is meaningful and worthwhile even when physical abilities are not what they used to be. A person with ego integrity is able to accept his or her approaching death as part of life.

People spend most of their lives developing rela-tionships and gathering possessions. Erikson believed that ego integrity enables people to let go of relationships and objects as the end of life approaches. Older people who do not maintain ego integrity risk falling into despair because they feel as if they are losing everything that matters to them. Ego integrity is connected with the wisdom to accept that one's life span is limited and to realize that nothing will last forever. Successful agers have this wisdom.

Aging and Adjustment   Most people in their 70s report being largely satisfied with their lives (Margoshes, 1995). Despite the physical changes that occur with aging, more than 75 percent rate their health as good or excellent.

Older people tend to be more satisfied with their lives when they are in good health and when they are financially secure. In fact, there is a correlation between socioeconomic status and health (Leary, 1995). Economically disadvantaged people at any age are more likely to report ill health than people of higher socioeconomic status. People who are financially secure are usually able to afford better health care and preventive services. They tend to worry less, and their stress is reduced. It may also be true that throughout life, people who are healthy are able to work harder and earn higher incomes. Most older people have some degree of financial security, but about 13 percent of people age 65 or older do live below the poverty line.

Among older people, as among younger people, a strong connection exists between social support and personal well-being. Social support is provided by various relationships. Spouses, children, and

CASE STUDIES
AND OTHER TRUE STORIES

Making the Most of Old Age

Old age does not mean the end of achievement. In fact, many people reach the height of their productivity and accomplishments in late adulthood. Three people who have proved just how valuable the contributions of older people can be are Pablo Picasso, Mother Teresa, and Thurgood Marshall.

Pablo Picasso (1881–1973)

Many people consider Pablo Picasso to be the most influential artist of the 1900s. This Spanish-born artist experimented with various styles of painting, sculpture, and ceramics. His innovative art styles were sometimes viewed with surprise, even horror, as so often happens when something different is introduced. Throughout Picasso's life and career, he never stopped trying new things. The last major exhibition of his work during his own lifetime was mounted in 1970, when he was 90. As with earlier shows, the public was once again surprised by the newness of his artistic vision. Many of the works in the 1970 exhibit were early expressions of a style that came to dominate the art of the early 1980s. Picasso never stopped working. He died in his sleep. Next to his bed was a bundle of crayons—placed there in case he woke with an inspiration. As he once said: "The painter never finishes . . . you can never write 'The End'" (Marks, 1984, p. 675).

Mother Teresa (1910–)

Mother Teresa became a nun when she was only 18 years old. Known as Sister Teresa early on, she found herself in India teaching the daughters of middle-class Indians. Then one day she received what she refers to as "a call from God." She believed that God wanted her to serve only the poorest people, the dying, and the homeless for the rest of her life. She left the convent with only the clothes she was wearing. In 1948, Sister Teresa opened her first school. Two years later, she founded the Order of the Missionaries of Charity, a congregation of women dedicated to helping the poor. She established schools and opened health centers for the care of the blind, the elderly, the sick, and the dying. In 1989, when she was 79, Mother Teresa suffered a heart attack and, soon after, resigned as head of the order. But by the end of 1990, she had returned to her post in India. Although Mother Teresa is a small, frail-looking woman, old age has not weakened her. At the time she returned to the order, the Missionaries of Charity had more than 3,000 nuns.

Thurgood Marshall (1908–1993)

Thurgood Marshall was another extremely influential figure whose contributions continued throughout his life. He first made his mark as a young lawyer when he became the head attorney for the National Association for the Advancement of Colored People (NAACP). Although it was often dangerous to do so, Marshall traveled across the country to ensure that courts protected the constitutional rights of African Americans. He became famous for his leading work on the 1954 case of *Brown* v. *Board of Education of Topeka,* which resulted in the famous Supreme Court declaration that segregation in the nation's public schools is unconstitutional.

In 1967, Marshall himself was appointed to the Supreme Court, the first African American to receive such an appointment. He worked unselfishly to end political, economic, and social injustices in this country. Despite several serious illnesses, he continued to serve, noting that he had "a lifetime appointment." However, during his 80s, Marshall's health declined, and he was compelled to retire from the bench in 1991. He will always be remembered for his strong convictions, especially regarding civil rights.

Think About It

What factors enable a person to maintain a vigorous level of activity well into old age?

Developmental Tasks of Late Adulthood

- Adjusting to physical changes and keeping (or becoming) physically active

- Maintaining concern about other people so that one does not become preoccupied with one's own physical changes

- Shifting interests from work to retirement or leisure activity

- Adjusting to changes in financial status

- Establishing fulfilling living arrangements

- Learning to live with one's husband or wife in retirement (in that both spouses may now be home much of the day)

- Adjusting to the illness or the death of one's husband or wife

FIGURE 12.5 *Erikson also believed that late adulthood has its own particular developmental tasks. Acceptance and adjustment are primary tasks at this time in life.*

Paul and Margret Baltes (1995) note that successful agers no longer try to compete with younger people in certain activities, such as athletics or business. Rather, they focus on matters that allow them to maintain a sense of personal control. Moreover, they find ways to make up for their losses. If their memories are not quite what they used to be, they may make notes or use other types of reminders. If their senses are no longer as sharp as they once were, they use devices such as hearing aids or eyeglasses. Some older people even develop creative solutions to their problems. The great pianist Arthur Rubinstein performed well into his 80s, even after he had lost much of his speed. To make up for this lack, he would slow down as he approached a passage in the music that required him to play faster. In this way, he gave the impression of speed during the more rapid passages (Margoshes, 1995).

friends may all provide social support, helping out in both practical and emotional ways when necessary. This may help explain the research finding that older couples generally are happier than older single or widowed people (Berger, 1994). Once couples are retired, they tend to spend more time together. Their relationships thus take on greater importance in their lives. When one spouse dies, however, children often are able to give needed support to the surviving spouse.

Reshaping One's Life   Another component of successful aging is reshaping one's life to focus on what is important. Laura Carstensen's (1995) research on people aged 70 and above revealed that successful agers formulate specific goals that bring them satisfaction. For example, rather than becoming involved with many different causes or hobbies, they may focus on one particular interest. Successful agers may have less time left than people in earlier stages of adulthood, but they tend to spend it more wisely (Garfinkel, 1995).

A Positive Outlook   Still another component of successful aging is a positive outlook. For example, some older people blame their occasional aches and pains on specific causes, such as a cold. Others simply blame old age itself. Not surprisingly, those who attribute their problems to specific causes are more optimistic that they will get better. Thus, they have a more positive outlook or attitude.

Researcher William Rakowski (1995) followed 1,400 people aged 70 and above who had common health problems, such as aches and pains. He found that those who blamed the problems on aging were more likely to die sooner than those who blamed the problems on specific factors.

Self-Challenge   Yet another component of successful aging is challenging oneself. Many people look forward to late adulthood as a time when they can rest from life's challenges. However, sitting back and allowing the world to pass by is a prescription for becoming passive and for not living life to its fullest extent.

This view was confirmed in a study conducted by Curt Sandman and Francis Crinella (1995). They randomly assigned 175 participants, whose average age was 72, either to a foster-grandparent program or to a control group. They then followed the participants for 10 years. As compared to people in the control group, the foster grandparents faced greater physical challenges, such as walking a few miles each day. They also had new social experiences by getting to know the children and their families. The results of the study showed that people in the foster-grandparent program improved their overall cognitive functioning, including their memories. They even slept more soundly.

Withdrawing from life and avoiding challenges is clearly not the route to well-being and good health for older people. Focusing on what is important, maintaining a positive attitude, and accepting new challenges are as important for older people as for younger people.

THINKING ABOUT PSYCHOLOGY

1. What is the difference between programmed theories of aging and cellular damage theories of aging?
2. Why is ego integrity an important part of healthy aging?
3. **Critical Thinking** Many older people experience minor and temporary memory losses. What are some memory aids older people can use to keep track of their medication and remember important telephone numbers or directions to the doctor's office?

Death and Dying

We all must face death at some point in our lives. Yet most of us seem to want to turn away from such a thought. According to psychiatrist Elisabeth Kübler-Ross (1969), the subject of death is often avoided. We seem to do all kinds of things to avoid confronting the reality of death. For example, prior to burial, cosmetics are used to make the deceased person look as if he or she is asleep.

Because death often brings sadness, some people send their children away to friends or relatives so that they need not face the sadness and anxiety around the home. Children may be prevented from visiting dying grandparents. But part of healing after a death is having the chance to say good-bye. Therefore, some psychologists suggest that trying to protect children by keeping them away from death may actually make it harder for them to cope with their grief.

Stages of Dying

Kübler-Ross (1969) worked with people who had terminal illnesses. An illness is terminal when it seems certain to lead to death. Some types of cancers are terminal illnesses. Kübler-Ross theorized that there are five stages through which many dying people pass. She believed that many older people have similar feelings when they suspect that death is near, even if they have not been diagnosed with a terminal illness. The stages are as follows:

1. *Denial.* For example, the dying person might think, "It can't be me. The doctor's diagnosis must be wrong."
2. *Anger.* People in this stage might think, "It's unfair. Why me?"
3. *Bargaining.* For instance, "I'll be kinder if I can just live to see my grandson graduate."
4. *Depression.* The person may despair and wonder, "What's the use of living another day?"
5. *Acceptance.* The person reasons, "I've had a good life. I'm ready to die."

Kübler-Ross's theory has met with considerable criticism. Some psychologists, such as Edwin Shneidman (1984), agree that many terminally ill people have the kinds of feelings described by Kübler-Ross. But Shneidman has not found that the feelings follow a particular sequence. Shneidman finds that people faced with approaching death show a variety of reactions. Some people have quickly shifting emotions that range from rage to surrender, from envying the young and healthy to yearning for the end. Some people accept death more easily; others feel despair. Still others feel terror. People's reactions to dying reflect their unique personalities and their philosophies of life.

Another problem with Kübler-Ross's theory is that it may tempt family members and health professionals to ignore the uniqueness of each individual's experiences at the end of life. If a dying person is angry or in despair, people may think that it is just a stage and not pay close attention to the dying person's feelings. In addition, people might try to encourage the dying person to work through the

An alternative to hospitals, hospices are homelike places where dying people and their families are given the physical and emotional support to help them cope with terminal illness. Here a patient receives hospice care at home.

sequence of stages in the belief that by doing so the dying person will reach the acceptance stage sooner. However, what a dying person may really need is to be treated as a living individual with hopes and feelings, not as someone undergoing predictable stages of behavior.

Dying with Dignity

Dying people, like other people, need security, self-confidence, and dignity. Dying people who are ill may also need relief from pain. One controversial issue surrounding death and dying is whether terminally ill individuals should be given painkilling drugs, such as narcotics, that are highly addictive. Physicians usually try to balance the patient's need for relief from severe and constant pain against the dangers of such drugs. However, some people feel that to worry about addiction does not make sense when a person is going to die soon.

Dying people, perhaps even more than other people, need to feel supported and cared for. Therefore, it is helpful for family members to encourage a dying person to talk about his or her feelings. Sometimes it is enough just to spend quiet time with the person—to let the person know that he or she is not alone. Family members and others also can help by assisting with the financial and legal arrangements to pay for medical care and distribution of property. The knowledge that one's final wishes will be carried out can help the dying person gain a sense of peace and completion.

Some dying people want to know all the details regarding their situation; others do not. Therefore, it is important for family members and health professionals to understand the extent of the person's need for details. It is also important to give the person accurate information about what she or he can expect to experience in terms of pain and loss of body functions and control. Old and dying people should not be treated like infants, but as adults who have dignity and a right to know what is going to happen to them.

The Hospice Alternative Linda mentioned that her grandmother had been in a hospice. A **hospice** is a homelike place where dying people and their families are given the physical and emotional support to help them cope with terminal illness. Unlike hospitals, hospices do not restrict visiting hours. Family members and friends work with trained staff to provide physical comfort and emotional support. Hospice care may be given in the patient's own home by visiting hospice workers.

In a hospital, rules determine a patient's treatment—usually the patient has little say in the matter. In a hospice, however, dying people are allowed more control over their lives. They are encouraged to make decisions about their diets, activities, and medication. Relatives and friends often remain in contact with the hospice staff to cope with their own feelings of grief after the person has died.

Euthanasia The term **euthanasia** comes from the Greek language and means "good death" (*eu* means "good"; *thanatos* means "death"). Euthanasia—also called mercy killing—is another controversial issue regarding death and dying.

Some physicians may consider euthanasia when they are absolutely convinced that there is no hope for a person's recovery, such as when a person has been in a coma for a long time or when the pain of a terminal illness is so severe and constant as to be unbearable. Euthanasia is illegal in most states.

Opponents of euthanasia argue that no one has the right to take—or to help another person take—a life, even one's own life. Opponents also maintain that new medications and therapies are continually being developed and that a person who feels today that death is the most desirable option may feel more optimistic tomorrow or next week. In other words, the pain and suffering may be temporary, but death is permanent.

The Living Will   Many people today write **living wills** to avoid being kept alive by artificial support systems (such as respirators) when there is no hope for recovery. The living will is a legal document.

A living will is intended to spare people the perceived indignity and cost of being kept alive when there is no hope of survival and to spare their families the misery of watching a loved one hooked up to an artificial life-support system. The idea is that once the person has died, the family members can grieve and move on with their lives. Of course, whether to have a living will is a choice that each individual must make.

The Funeral

The funeral is a traditional way for a community to acknowledge that one of its members has died. The rituals of the funeral also provide a framework for what to do and how to act when a family member or friend has died.

The specific kind of funeral chosen usually reflects religious beliefs and cultural customs. Some funeral services tie a person's death to the ongoing progression of time and the universe. Various professionals, such as undertakers and religious leaders, can be especially helpful when a family's grief adds to the difficulty of making decisions concerning the final arrangements for the deceased.

Funerals are a way of saying good-bye. But they accomplish much more. As the deceased is physically removed and prepared for burial or cremation, his or her body is both physically and symbolically separated from the living. In some religions and cultures, the transition is slow. Some customs provide periods of time during which mourners may view the body and meet with family members.

Funerals also provide a way to remember and celebrate the life of the deceased. Many funerals include a eulogy—a speech praising the person who has just died. Finally, there is the burial or the cremation of the body. This is when family and friends physically let go of the person who has died.

Bereavement

Linda was sad when her grandmother died, but she may also have felt a sense of relief that her suffering was finally over. Such feelings of relief often seem disturbing, but they are rather common. The people who are left behind are said to be **bereaved**, which means mourning

Different cultures deal with death in different ways. Most cultures have rituals to commemorate the life and passing of the deceased. Here, a New Orleans jazz band is featured in a funeral procession.

over something or someone precious who has been taken away. People who are bereaved may have feelings of sadness and loneliness, numbness, anger, and even relief. When the dying person suffers greatly, family members may feel they have reached the limits of their ability to be helpful. Therefore, it is normal for them to feel a certain amount of relief when death finally comes.

Some bereaved people may join support groups or seek professional help in dealing with their grief. With or without such help, most bereaved people eventually recover from their losses. They may never forget the person they have lost, but they usually become less preoccupied by the loss itself. They resume their lives at home and at work. They may always miss the person who died, but most of the time they are able to resume normal functioning. Sometimes the survivors grow in compassion because of their loss and gain a deeper appreciation of the value of life.

THINKING ABOUT PSYCHOLOGY

1. List the five stages of death and dying in Kübler-Ross's theory.

2. Identify three ways in which hospice care differs from hospital care.

3. **Critical Thinking**   List two or three ways that people tend to try to push aside death rather than face it. Do you think such techniques are useful in helping people cope? Why or why not?

12 REVIEW

SUMMARY

Human development continues throughout the three stages of adulthood: young adulthood, middle adulthood, and late adulthood.

I. Young Adulthood

A. Young adult men generally work toward independence from parental authority, while young adult women tend to be more interested in creating relationships.

B. Adults in their early 30s often reassess the life goals and plans they made in their 20s.

C. During their middle-to-late 30s, people become more interested in settling into a career and personal relationships.

D. One of the key tasks of young adulthood is establishing intimate relationships.
   1. Romantic love as a reason for marriage did not become widespread in Western society until the 1800s.
   2. People tend to choose spouses who are similar to themselves in characteristics such as ethnicity, level of education, social class, religion, age, and physical features.

E. Many marriages in the United States end in divorce.
   1. A variety of factors caused the divorce rate to rise through much of the 1900s.
   2. Divorce has many financial and emotional costs for the people involved.

II. Middle Adulthood

A. One of the key developmental tasks of middle age is generativity—the ability to create, originate, and produce.

B. During middle adulthood, many people experience a midlife transition.
   1. For some people the midlife transition can trigger a midlife crisis.
   2. Many people in middle adulthood go through "middlescence," a period in which they search for a new identity.

C. When grown-up children leave home to establish lives of their own, middle-aged parents must adjust to being alone.

D. Most women experience menopause during their late 40s or early 50s.

III. Late Adulthood

A. Despite the many physical changes that occur in late adulthood, older adults can do much to maintain their health, strength, and energy levels.

B. Theories as to why people age fall into two categories.
   1. Programmed theories maintain that aging is a result of genetics.
   2. Cellular damage theories maintain that aging occurs because the body's cells become worn out and damaged.

C. While most older people have no serious decline in intellectual skills, some older people do suffer from dementia.

D. Older adults must deal with many social changes, such as deciding how to spend their retirement, learning to balance their need for independence with their need to stay involved with their families, and working out living arrangements.

E. Ego integrity, a positive outlook, financial security, good health, and supportive relationships contribute to the likelihood of successful aging.

IV. Death and Dying

A. Psychiatrist Elisabeth Kübler-Ross theorized that dying people pass through five stages: denial, anger, bargaining, depression, and acceptance.

B. Hospice care and living wills seek to help terminally ill people die with dignity.

C. Euthanasia is a controversial issue.

D. Funerals help bereaved people, or people experiencing loss, to accept the death of a loved one.

TERM & CONCEPT REVIEW

1. What factors typically influence a young adult's choice of spouse?
2. What is a no-fault divorce?
3. In what way are middlescence and adolescence similar?
4. What is the empty-nest syndrome, and who is likely to be affected by it?
5. In what ways does a woman's body change during menopause?
6. What relationship do free radicals and cross-linking have with the aging process?
7. Why is maintaining ego integrity important for older adults?
8. What is senile dementia and what causes it?
9. List two ways in which family members and friends can help a dying person.
10. What is the purpose of a living will?

CRITICAL THINKING

1. You may recall from Chapter 11 that G. Stanley Hall described adolescence as a time of Sturm und Drang, or "storm and stress." How might this phrase also describe the three stages of adulthood? Which stage of adulthood might the term most accurately describe and why?
2. Why do you think large numbers of middle-aged adults enroll in classes and programs offered by community organizations, schools, and colleges?
3. How could the concept of free radicals be used in a campaign to discourage teenagers from using drugs and alcohol?
4. What strengths might workers in the different stages of adulthood bring to a business?
5. What could you, as a teenager, be doing to help ensure a successful old age for yourself?
6. What are the advantages and disadvantages of classifying adult development into stages?

APPLYING SKILLS IN PSYCHOLOGY

1. **COOPERATIVE LEARNING   Writing About Psychology**   Working with a partner, create a chart that summarizes the physical, mental, and social characteristics and issues of young adulthood, middle adulthood, and late adulthood. Start off by filling in the chart with information from the chapter. Then, interview people in each of the three stages to build on what you have already filled in. When your chart is completed, compare it with a chart prepared by another pair of students.

2. **Reading About Psychology**   Read about the marriage or funeral customs in a different culture or during a different time in history. As you read, look for answers to the following questions: What people play important roles in the customs? What is the basis of the customs? How have the customs changed over time, if at all, and what has led to the changes? Write a brief report summarizing your findings.

3. **Using Your Observation Skills**   Identify a middle-aged adult in your family, school, or community who demonstrates generativity. Be ready to tell your classmates about this person and give examples of his or her generativity to support your choice.

4. **Research in Psychology**   Look in newspapers and magazines or search the Internet for the latest information on and findings of research into Alzheimer's disease. You might locate reports on attempts to find the cause of the disease or research on medications to reverse or halt its symptoms. Share your findings with the class.

5. **Writing About Psychology**   Create a two-page dialogue between the following fictional characters: a 25-year-old, his or her 50-year-old parent, and his or her 75-year-old grandparent. In the dialogue, have the characters discuss some of the challenges each of them is facing and the methods each character is using to face the challenges.

UNIT 4
REVIEW

IDENTIFYING PEOPLE AND IDEAS

Explain the significance of each of the following people or terms to the study of psychology.

1. infancy
2. childhood
3. contact comfort
4. accommodation
5. Konrad Lorenz
6. concrete-operational stage
7. object permanence
8. postconventional moral reasoning
9. puberty
10. secondary sex characteristics
11. clique
12. Erik Erikson
13. identity moratorium
14. identity foreclosure
15. anorexia nervosa
16. generativity
17. midlife transition
18. programmed theories
19. free radical
20. senile dementia
21. ego integrity
22. euthanasia

HANDS-ON PSYCHOLOGY
Individual Project

Create a table highlighting the physical and mental changes the average person experiences during his or her life span. On the left-hand side of a sheet of paper, write down the stages of the life span: Infancy, Childhood, Adolescence, Young adulthood, Middle adulthood, and Late adulthood. To the right, draw two columns and label them Physical Changes and Mental Changes. Using the information you have learned in this unit, fill in the table with the key changes that occur during each stage. Once you have completed the table, prepare a written report in which you answer the following questions:

1. What do you think is the "ideal" age? Why? Use concepts discussed in the unit in completing your answer.

2. Give an example of a period of time when the mental or physical changes a person experiences at a particular stage might be different for men and women.

3. Pick two of the stages from your chart and explain how you think you would react to the physical and mental changes of these stages. Do you think the changes of one stage would be preferable to the changes of the other? Give examples to support your answer.

BUILDING YOUR PORTFOLIO

Individually or in a group, complete the following project to show your understanding of the psychology concepts involved.

Comparing Cultural Norms

The findings on human development presented in this unit are generally applicable to most human beings. Some elements of human development do, however, vary from culture to culture. (For example, as you read in Chapter 10, babies in Uganda start walking an average of two months earlier than their American counterparts.) Research the human development cycles of a culture other than that of the United States. Answer the following questions about the culture you choose:

1. Are there any physical developmental differences between infants and young children in the culture you researched and those in the United States? If so, what might account for those differences? How long does childhood last in this culture? What is an appropriate age for children to start working, if at all? If children do work, what type of labor do they engage in?

2. How long does adolescence last in this culture? Do you think James Marcia's categories of adolescent identity status apply in this culture? Why or why not? Do teenagers in this culture experience similar social problems to those of teenagers in the United States?

3. At what age are members of this culture considered adults? Does the age differ for boys and girls? Are the developmental tasks of young adulthood in this culture comparable to Erikson's list on page 276? What is the average age for marriage in this culture? Does it differ greatly from that in the United States? If so, what might account for the difference? What are the culture's attitudes toward aging and the elderly?

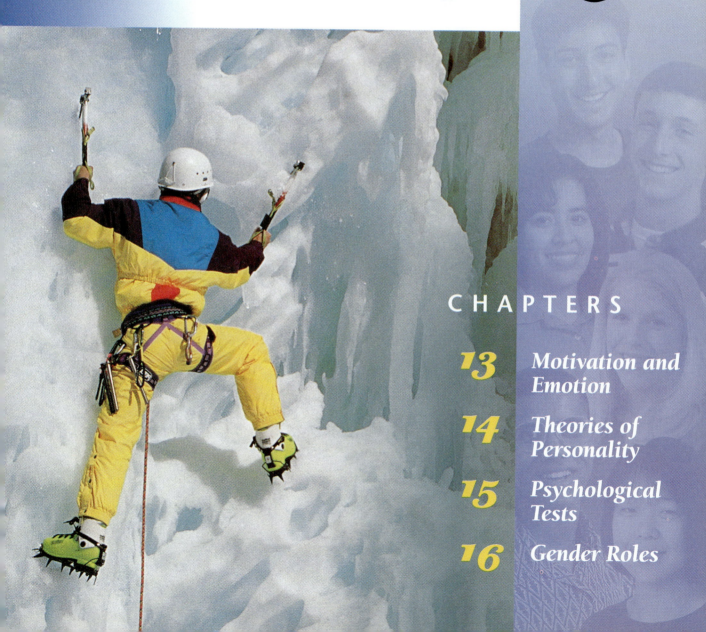

UNIT 5

PERSONALITY

Chapter 13

MOTIVATION AND EMOTION

Objectives

1 List and explain four theories of motivation.

2 Describe the hunger drive, and analyze the causes of obesity.

3 Explain stimulus motives, the balance theory, and achievement motivation.

4 Describe four theories of emotion.

A DAY IN THE LIFE

March 8

Hannah, Todd, and Dan were studying at Hannah's house after school today. Hannah was trying to work on her psychology assignment, but she could not seem to concentrate.

"Hannah, what are you thinking about?" Todd finally asked. "Every time I look at you, you're staring off into space and smiling."

"I'm sorry. I just can't stop thinking about my violin recital last night. I played better than I ever had in a recital before."

"I'm glad I was there to see it. You were great," Dan said.

"Thanks!" Hannah replied with enthusiasm. "At first, I was really nervous, but once I started playing, I was fine. Of course, it really helped that you, Marc, and Linda were all there with my parents. For some reason, I was so much more confident because I knew that all of you were in the audience."

"I really wish I could have been there," Todd commented, "but I had to study for that advanced biology test I had today."

Hannah knew how much Todd enjoyed studying science. "Don't worry about it," Hannah said. "You love science. And you need to do well in biology if you're going to get that scholarship."

"You'll have to try to go to the next recital, though, Todd. Hannah is really good," Dan added. "Hey, wasn't Janet going to study with us this afternoon?"

"She'll be here later," Hannah answered. "She wanted to stop by the recreation center after school. The youth group is planning a hiking trip and, knowing Janet, she'll probably be the first person to sign up. That is, of course, if she can fit it into her schedule."

Everyone laughed because they knew Hannah was right. Whenever Janet was not working at her part-time job or studying for her classes, she was outdoors playing basketball or riding her mountain bike.

Just then, Eddie, Hannah's three-year-old brother, came wandering into the room. "Hannah, I'm hungry," he announced as he walked over to sit with Dan.

Dan loved spending time with Eddie, so he welcomed the opportunity to take a study break. "You know what, Eddie?" Dan said. "I'm hungry too. Let's have a snack."

Why does Todd push himself to study advanced biology when he could be relaxing in front of the television set or outside playing ball? Why does Hannah spend hours, days, and weeks of her "free" time practicing the violin for a 40-minute recital? Is the elation Hannah feels after her recital worth the anxiety she felt on stage? The answers to these questions involve motivation (the elusive feelings that makes us do the things we do) and emotions (the responses generated by certain situations). In this chapter, we will examine the ways in which our emotions lead us to behave in certain ways.

Key Terms

- motive
- need
- drive
- instinct
- homeostasis
- self-actualization
- obesity
- stimulus motive
- sensory deprivation
- achievement motivation
- performance goal
- learning goal
- extrinsic reward
- intrinsic reward
- cognitive consistency
- balance theory
- imbalance
- nonbalance
- cognitive-dissonance theory
- affiliation
- emotion
- opponent-process theory

Read the following statements about psychology. Do you think they are true or false? You will learn whether each statement is true or false as you read the chapter.

- Robins and other birds have to learn the songs that are characteristic of their species.
- The major trigger of the hunger drive is hunger pangs in the stomach.
- Getting away from it all by going on a vacation from all sensory input is relaxing.
- When people feel anxious, they want to be alone.

1

The Psychology of Motivation

Why do many people like to travel to faraway places or to try new foods? The answer to this question—and other questions about why people do the things they do—relates to motivation. A **motive** is a stimulus that moves a person to behave in ways designed to accomplish a specific goal. Motives are considered theoretical states because they cannot be seen or measured directly. Psychologists assume that people and other organisms are "motivated" when they observe the people trying to reach their goals. The psychology of motivation deals with the *whys* of behavior.

Needs

When psychologists speak of motives, they also often speak of needs. A **need** is a condition in which we require something we lack. People have both biological and psychological needs. People fulfill biological needs to survive. Examples of biological needs include the need for oxygen and food. Some biological needs such as hunger and thirst occur because of physical deprivation. That is, people feel hungry or thirsty when they have not eaten or drunk for a while.

Achievement, self-esteem, a sense of belonging, and social approval are examples of psychological needs. Like biological needs, psychological needs motivate people to accomplish certain goals. However, psychological needs differ from biological

needs in two important ways. First, psychological needs are not necessarily based on deprivation. A person with a need to achieve an A on a test may already be an honor-roll student. Second, unlike biological needs, which are inborn, psychological needs may be learned. People possess common biological characteristics, thus they have similar physical needs. For example, all people must eat to survive, therefore all people need food. However, people have different psychological needs because they learn from a variety of experiences. Psychological needs are shaped by culture and learning, so people's psychological needs differ markedly. For example, some people prefer vegetarian diets because they believe it is morally wrong to kill animals for food.

Drives

Biological needs and psychological needs give rise to **drives**—the forces that motivate an organism to take action. The biological need for food gives rise to the hunger drive. The biological need for liquids gives rise to the thirst drive.

Although hunger and thirst are aroused by biological needs, the *experience* of them is psychological. The longer we are deprived of something such as food or water, the stronger our drive becomes. For example, our hunger drive is stronger six hours after eating than it is 20 minutes after eating.

Theories of Motivation

Psychologists agree that motives prompt behavior, but they are not in agreement about the nature of motivation. The leading theories of motivation are instinct theory, drive-reduction theory, humanistic theory, and sociocultural theory.

Instinct Theory   Behavior patterns that are genetically transmitted from generation to generation are known as **instincts**. Sometimes they are called fixed-action patterns. Researchers have discovered that many animals are born to act in certain ways in certain situations. Studies have shown that birds acquire the songs characteristic of their species largely by instinct (Marler, 1991).

Siamese fighting fish reared in isolation also display instinctive behavior. Males fan their fins and gills in the typical threatening posture when other males are introduced into their tanks. Similarly, bees perform an instinctive "dance" to relay the location of food to other bees (Moffett, 1990).

Certain behavior patterns are largely instinctive and do not have to be taught. Birds raised in isolation will build nests characteristic of their species, despite the fact that they were never taught how to do this by other members of the species.

Some drives, such as hunger, are caused by biological needs, which are inborn. Other drives, such as the drive for money, are learned from experience. According to drive-reduction theory, people will try to reduce these learned drives, just as they try to reduce biological drives.

Basic drives, such as hunger, motivate us to restore an internal state of equilibrium, or balance. The tendency to maintain this state of equilibrium in the body is called **homeostasis**. Homeostasis works like a thermostat. When room temperature drops below a certain point—called the set point—the heat comes on. The heat stays on until the set point is reached. Similarly, according to the theory, when people are hungry, they will eat until they reach a level at which they are no longer hungry.

Drive-reduction theory seems to apply to many biological drives, including hunger and thirst. Yet people sometimes eat when they are not hungry. They also often act to increase rather than decrease the tension they experience. For example, some people enjoy riding roller coasters and driving fast cars. Yet these activities *increase* rather than decrease the tension they experience. Clearly, drive-reduction theory does not explain all motivation.

TRUTH OR fiction

▪ REVISITED ▪

It is not true that robins and other birds have to learn the songs that are characteristic of their species. These songs are largely inborn, or instinctive, not learned.

At one time, psychologists believed that human behavior, like that of animals, is instinctive. In the late 1800s and early 1900s, psychologists William James (1890) and William McDougall (1908) argued that people have instincts that foster survival and social behavior. Today, however, most psychologists do not believe that human behavior is primarily motivated by instinct. If a behavior pattern is instinctive, they argue, it should be found throughout a species. However, there is so much variation in the way people behave that most human behavior seems unlikely to be instinctive.

Drive-Reduction Theory Psychologist Clark Hull formulated the drive-reduction theory in the 1930s. Drive-reduction theory is based on learning as well as motivation. According to this theory, people and animals experience a drive arising from a need as an unpleasant tension. They learn to do whatever will reduce that tension by reducing the drive, such as eating to reduce their hunger drive.

Humanistic Theory Humanistic psychologists argue that instinct theory and drive-reduction theory suggest that human behavior is mechanical and directed only toward surviving and reducing tension. According to humanistic psychologists, however, people are also motivated by the conscious desire for personal growth and artistic fulfillment. In fact, they argue, sometimes our drive to fulfill such needs outweighs our drive to fulfill more basic needs. For example, some people seek artistic or political goals, even though they may have difficulty affording food or have to give up a certain level of comfort or security to achieve their goals. Some artists, musicians, and writers commit themselves to their artistic goals even when they are unable to make a living by doing so.

Abraham Maslow, one of the pioneers of humanistic psychology, pointed out that some people are willing to tolerate pain, hunger, and other kinds of tension to achieve their artistic or political goals. Hannah undoubtably spent countless hours practicing the violin and learning new songs. Humanistic theory would suggest that her desire to achieve artistic fulfillment was worth sacrificing other desirable activities, such as spending time with her friends.

A DAY IN THE LIFE

Maslow claimed that people strive to fulfill their capacity for self-actualization. The term **self-actualization** refers to the need to become what one believes he or she is capable of being. The desire to fulfill oneself takes one past the point of just satisfying one's physical needs. Maslow believed that striving to become something or to do something meaningful in one's life is as essential to human well-being as food.

Maslow (1970) organized human needs into a hierarchy— a ranking of items in order of importance. (See Figure 13.1.) At the bottom of the hierarchy are biological needs. The need for self-actualization is at the top. Maslow believed that once a person's needs are satisfied at one level, the person will try to satisfy needs at the next higher level. For example, once food and drink have satisfied a person's biological needs, that person will then seek means to satisfy safety needs, such as the needs for shelter and security. Maslow believed that people rise naturally through the levels of this hierarchy as long as they do not encounter overwhelming obstacles along the way. Many people seek self-actualization through work, hobbies, and aesthetic experiences such as music, art, and poetry.

Critics of Maslow's hierarchy of needs argue that it does not apply to everyone (Neher, 1991). For example, some people show little interest in satisfying higher-level needs such as achievement and social recognition, even after their biological and safety needs have been met. But, one might ask, does their apparent lack of interest stem from not being motivated to seek achievement or from having met with overwhelming obstacles?

Sociocultural Theory Sociocultural theorists argue that even if basic drives such as hunger are inborn, cultural experiences and factors influence the behavior that people use to satisfy those drives. The foods people eat and the way they eat those foods are shaped by culture. Cultural experience affects whether people prefer hot dogs or tacos, coffee or tea, apples or pineapples. Cultural experiences also affect whether people prefer kissing lips or rubbing noses to express feelings of affection.

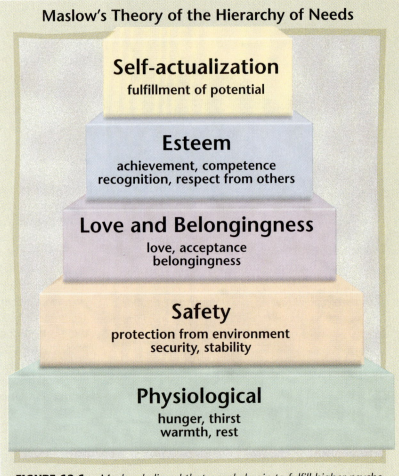

Maslow's Theory of the Hierarchy of Needs

Self-actualization
fulfillment of potential

Esteem
achievement, competence
recognition, respect from others

Love and Belongingness
love, acceptance
belongingness

Safety
protection from environment
security, stability

Physiological
hunger, thirst
warmth, rest

FIGURE 13.1 *Maslow believed that people begin to fulfill higher psychological needs (such as achievement) after their basic survival needs (such as hunger and thirst) have been met. Do you agree or disagree?*

THINKING ABOUT PSYCHOLOGY

1. Define the following terms: *motive, need,* and *drive.*

2. List and briefly summarize the four leading theories of motivation.

3. **Critical Thinking** Maslow believed that people seek to satisfy basic survival needs before they seek to satisfy higher psychological needs. Use specific examples to argue for or against Maslow's theory of the hierarchy of needs.

Biological Needs: Focus on Hunger

Biological needs are based mainly on body tissue needs, such as the needs for food, water, air, temperature regulation, and pain avoidance. However, even basic biological needs can be complex because they involve psychological as well as biological factors. People need food to survive, but food can mean much more than mere survival. Food can be a symbol of the closeness of the family, or it can be something to make a stranger feel welcome. Food

can also be part of a pleasurable social experience with others. For example, when Dan took time out from studying to share a snack with Hannah's little brother Eddie, it was an enjoyable break for both of them.

The Hunger Drive

Hunger is regulated by both biological and psychological factors. In this section, we will look at the mechanisms in the body that are involved in the hunger drive. We will also examine the psychological influences that are involved in hunger.

The Role of the Mouth   The acts of chewing and swallowing provide certain sensations that help satisfy the hunger drive, as shown by "sham feeding" research with dogs. In a classic research experiment, tubes were implanted in dogs' throats so that the food they swallowed was dropped out of their bodies instead of moving into their stomachs (Janowitz & Grossman, 1949). Nevertheless, the dogs stopped feeding after a brief period. Based on the finding of this and other studies, researchers have concluded that chewing and swallowing apparently help reduce feelings of hunger in animals as well as in people.

The hunger drive is usually satisfied when the body digests food and the nutrients in the food enter the bloodstream. However, this takes time. Chewing and swallowing help let the body know that its hunger drive is being satisfied, thus saving us from eating more than is needed. Still, it is wise to stop eating *before* feeling completely full because it takes time for the digestive tract to metabolize

Although food is a basic biological need, it can also be part of a pleasurable social experience with others.

food and provide signals to the brain that the need for food has been satisfied.

The Role of the Stomach   It was once believed that the growls and contractions (called *hunger pangs*) of an empty stomach were the cause of hunger. Researchers did, in fact, find that when a person is hungry, his or her stomach does contract. However, they also found that the stomach contracts at other times as well (Cannon, 1939). Furthermore, people who have surgery to remove their stomachs still experience hunger. Thus, the researchers concluded that hunger pangs felt in the stomach play a role in hunger but are not the main factor involved in signaling hunger.

The Hypothalamus   The level of sugar in the blood and the part of the brain known as the hypothalamus are key influences on feelings of hunger. When people have not eaten for a while, their blood sugar level drops. Information about the sugar level is then communicated to the hypothalamus, which is known to be involved in the regulation of body temperature and various aspects of psychological motivation and emotion.

Researchers have learned more about how the hypothalamus functions through research conducted with laboratory animals. In these studies, researchers implanted electrodes on the hypothalamus and observed their effects on the animals'

Researchers have discovered that a part of the hypothalamus, called the ventromedial hypothalamus (VMH), serves as a "stop-eating" center. When this portion of the hypothalamus is destroyed, the rat will continue to eat until it is several times its normal weight. Eventually, the rat's food intake will level off enough to simply maintain the rat's higher weight; that is, the rat will no longer continue to gain weight.

TRUTH
OR
fiction
■ R E V I S I T E D ■

It is not true that the major trigger of the hunger drive is hunger pangs in the stomach. The blood sugar level and the hypothalamus are actually more closely connected to the hunger drive than are hunger pangs, or contractions in the stomach.

Psychological Influences Many biological factors affect the hunger drive. However, this is only part of the story. In human beings, psychological as well as biological factors affect feelings of hunger. For example, we usually eat more when we are in the presence of other people than when we are alone (Zajonc, 1965). Dan did not realize he was hungry until Eddie mentioned that he was hungry. Eddie, therefore, acted as a psychological influence on Dan's hunger drive.

Learning that certain amounts of food or drink will produce a feeling of well-being and relaxation can cause people to eat and drink when they feel upset. For example, they may develop the habit of eating and drinking at the first sign of pressure or anxiety as a way to fend off feeling any negative emotions. People with a tendency to eat compulsively or drink alcohol excessively need to be alert to this tendency. Likewise, parents should consider whether it is wise to give children food as a reward for doing something good. Rewarding with food can cause a child to grow up associating food with parental approval, thus creating dietary problems in later life.

Obesity

About one out of every four American adults is obese. **Obesity** is defined as weighing more than 30 percent above one's recommended weight (Kuczmarski, 1992). In an effort to reduce excess weight, 25 percent to 50 percent of American adults are on a diet at any given moment (Bouchard, 1991). Yet the great majority of dieters eventually regain most or all of the weight they have lost (Wilson, 1993).

Obesity has both physical and social consequences. Studies have shown that obese people are more likely than others to come down with illnesses such as heart disease, diabetes, gout, respiratory

behavior. They found that the side of the hypothalamus, called the lateral hypothalamus (LH), appears to function as a "start-eating" center. If the LH is electrically stimulated, the rat will begin to eat, even if it has just finished eating a large meal (Miller, 1995). Conversely, if a lesion is made in the LH, the rat may stop eating altogether and eventually die of starvation if it is not force-fed.

The underside of the hypothalamus, called the ventromedial hypothalamus (VMH), apparently functions as a "stop-eating" center. When this center is electrically stimulated, the rat will stop eating. When this part of the hypothalamus is destroyed, the rat will continue to eat until it is several times its normal weight. The lesion to the VMH interferes with the rat's ability to recognize that its hunger has been fulfilled and the rat simply continues to nibble. Eventually, the rat's eating will level off and the rat will maintain the higher weight (Keesey, 1986).

EVERY MORNING I SAY THIS IS THE DAY I GO ON A DIET...

THEN SOMETHING ALWAYS HAPPENS...

LIKE BREAKFAST

CHRIS BROWNE 6-10

© 1996 by King Features Syndicate, Inc. World rights reserved.

Source: Reprinted with special permission of King Features Syndicate.

problems, and certain types of cancer (Manson et al., 1995). Research has also indicated that obese people tend to be less popular and successful than people who are not obese (Fitzgibbon et al., 1993; Stunkard & Sorensen, 1993).

Losing Weight   Psychologists have worked with other health professionals to devise strategies to help obese people lose weight. However, not everyone who is a few pounds overweight should be trying to slim down (Brownell, 1993; Brownell & Rodin, 1994).

Any teenager who considers going on a diet should proceed with caution. First of all, adolescents need a good deal of nourishment—perhaps more than any other age group. Second, adolescent girls are under extreme social pressure to conform to an unnaturally slender female ideal (Bordo, 1993; Wolf, 1991). Any young person thinking about dieting should first discuss it with his or her parents and with a health professional, such as a doctor or school nurse. Certainly, for most obese people, shedding extra pounds lowers the risks of many health problems, including diabetes and heart disease (Brody, 1992d). However, any diet needs to be sensible, realistic, and well planned.

Sound weight-control programs do not involve fasting or fad diets such as those that suggest eating just one type of food. Rather, healthy programs focus on changes in lifestyle that lead to gradual, healthful weight loss. These changes include reducing calorie intake, gaining better knowledge about nutrition, exercising, and modifying one's behavior (Brownell & Rodin, 1994; Brownell & Wadden, 1992). Research has shown that dieting plus exercise is more effective than dieting alone for shedding pounds and keeping them off (Epstein et al., 1995; Wood et al., 1991).

Nutrition   Knowledge of nutrition helps prevent people from depriving themselves of essential nutrients. It can also help people find ways to lose weight without feeling deprived. For example, eating foods that are low in saturated fats and cholesterol is not only good for the heart, but it is also a good, healthy way to lose weight.

Nutritional knowledge also helps people manage their food consumption in order to take in fewer calories—which is the most direct path to weight reduction for most people. Taking in fewer calories does not mean just eating smaller portions. It also means switching to lower-calorie foods, such as fruits and vegetables, preferably fresh and unsweetened (an apple is healthier than a piece of apple pie). In addition, caloric reduction means cutting down on butter, margarine, oils that are high in saturated fats, and sugar.

Foods that tend to be high in vitamins and fiber lower the risks of heart disease, cancer, and other health problems that are connected with high-fat, low-vitamin diets. Such foods also help people control their weight.

Causes of Obesity   Why are so many people obese? As with the hunger drive in general, both biological and psychological factors appear to contribute to obesity. Obesity seems to run in families. But does this mean that it is inherited? Not necessarily. For example, obese parents may simply encourage their children to overeat by having fattening foods around the house and setting an example. However, research suggests that heredity does play a role in obesity (Friedman & Brownell, 1995). One study showed that adopted children tend to more closely resemble their biological parents than their adoptive parents in terms of body weight (Stunkard et al., 1990).

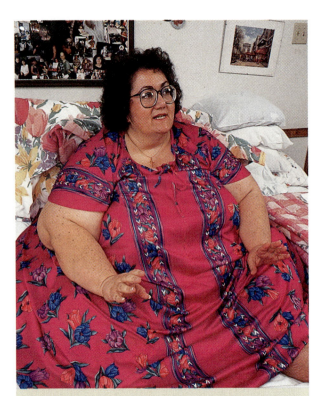

Obese people are more likely to suffer from such health problems as heart disease, diabetes, gout, poor respiratory systems, and some types of cancer than are their slimmer counterparts.

One of the ways in which heredity may contribute to obesity is that certain people with a particular gene may not receive the biological signal that they have eaten enough to sustain them (Lindpaintner, 1995). Thus, they end up eating more than they need to.

Genes also help determine the number of fat cells a person has. People with a greater number of fat cells feel hungry sooner than people with fewer fat cells, even if they are of the same weight. When overweight people take off extra pounds, they do not reduce the number of fat cells in their body. Instead, the fat cells shrink. As they shrink, they signal the brain, triggering the hunger drive. For this reason, many people who lose weight complain that they feel hungry all the time.

People metabolize food—or burn calories—at different rates and in accordance with the amount of muscle and fat in their bodies. Since fatty tissue converts food to energy more slowly than muscle does, people with more body fat metabolize food more slowly than people who weigh the same but have a lower percentage of body fat. Men tend to have more muscle and less fat in their bodies than women. The average man is approximately 40 percent muscle and 15 percent fat. The average woman is 23 percent muscle and 25 percent fat. Therefore, men tend to burn calories more quickly than women of the same weight. For this reason, men generally are able to lose weight more easily than women, and they can usually eat more than women can without putting on extra pounds.

Psychological factors also play a role in obesity. For example, people tend to eat more when they are under stress or experiencing certain negative emotions, such as anxiety (Cools et al., 1992; Greeno & Wing, 1994). Ironically, the stress of trying to diet can make some people want to eat even more.

Personal circumstances also affect people's ability to control their weight. For example, many people tend to overeat and ignore their diets when they are attending family gatherings, watching television, arguing, or experiencing tension at school or at work (Drapkin et al., 1995).

THINKING ABOUT PSYCHOLOGY

1. What is the role of the hypothalamus in the hunger drive?
2. What is the relationship between heredity and obesity?
3. **Critical Thinking** Explain how dieting may actually cause the body to resist efforts to lose weight.

3
Psychological Needs

Human beings and other organisms are motivated to reduce the tension or stimulation caused by biological needs such as hunger or thirst. The hungry person who "has a bite to eat" wants to reduce the feeling of being hungry. However, we experience psychological needs as well as biological needs. Some psychological needs motivate us to reduce tension or stimulation. Other psychological needs actually lead us to increase the amount of stimulation we experience.

Stimulus Motives

Desires for stimulation are called **stimulus motives**. Stimulus motives include sensory stimulation, activity, exploration, and manipulation of the environment. Some stimulus motives have clear survival value. Human beings and other organisms who are motivated to explore and manipulate their environment are more likely to survive (Keller & Boigs, 1991). Learning about one's surroundings increases usable information concerning resources and potential dangers. Manipulation allows people to change the environment in useful ways, thereby increasing and enhancing their chances of survival.

Sensory Deprivation

During the 1950s, several student volunteers at McGill University in Montreal were paid $20 a day for participating in an experiment in which they did nothing—literally nothing. They were blindfolded and placed in small rooms (Bexton et al., 1954). Their arms were bandaged so that they could feel no tactile sensations (sensations of touch), and they could hear nothing except the dull hum of the air-conditioning. The intention of the experiment was to see how people would react to an absence of stimulation, a state referred to as **sensory deprivation**.

With nothing to do, some of the students slept. Those who remained awake began to feel bored and irritable. As the hours passed, the students felt more and more uncomfortable. Some reported having hallucinations. The study was scheduled to last for several days, but many students quit during the first day despite the monetary incentive and the desire to help in the research. Most of those who completed the study felt they had been through a terrible ordeal and, for several days after the experiment, found it difficult to concentrate on even simple matters. They reported feeling extreme boredom and disorientation for some time. The experiment demonstrated the importance of sensory stimulation to human beings.

TRUTH OR fiction REVISITED *It is not true that getting away from it all by going on a vacation from all sensory input is relaxing.* The sensory deprivation experiments conducted at McGill University were shown to be very stressful to the participants.

Desire for Sensory Stimulation

All people seek sensory stimulation, but it is clear that some need it more than others. Some people like being couch potatoes. They enjoy sitting and relaxing in front of a television set whenever possible. Other people prefer to be more active. They are not happy unless they are out running or tossing a ball around.

 A DAY IN THE LIFE As Dan noted, Janet was always on the run. She seemed to be happiest when she was hiking or riding her mountain bike. Many psychologists would call Janet a sensation seeker. A sensation seeker is somebody who regularly seeks out thrilling activities such as riding mountain bikes, roller coasters, or even skydiving. They feel at their best when they are doing something active or adventurous.

It is not clear why some people seek high levels of sensation and others prefer relatively low levels. Inborn factors may play a role. So may learning experiences. For example, a child or adolescent whose parents ride motorcycles or skydive will be exposed to these activities at an early age. He or she may be more inclined to want to try these activities.

Exploration and Manipulation

Anybody who has ever had the experience of bringing home a new cat knows that the animal's first reaction to totally new surroundings is to show anxiety. The frightened cat may hide under a bed or in a closet. However, eventually, the cat will feel adventurous enough to take a few tentative steps out. Then it will begin exploring its new surroundings. Within a few days, the cat will probably have explored every corner of the house. In this respect,

Some people are more motivated to seek stimulation than others. These people are called sensation seekers.

Both animals and humans seem to have a need to explore objects in their environments.

cats and people appear to behave in similar ways. Most people are also motivated to explore their immediate surroundings.

Once people and animals become sufficiently comfortable with their environment, they seek novel stimulation. That is, they seek new and varied experiences. For example, researchers have shown that laboratory rats who are not terribly hungry usually choose to explore unfamiliar parts of mazes rather than head down familiar alleys directly to a food reward (Wilkie et al., 1992). Studies have also shown that monkeys learn to manipulate gadgets for the "reward" of being able to observe novel stimulation (Harlow et al., 1950).

Do people and animals explore and manipulate their environment because these activities help them meet their needs for food and safety? Or do they explore and manipulate these objects simply for the sake of novel stimulation? Many psychologists believe that exploration and manipulation are reinforcing in and of themselves. Monkeys appear to enjoy "monkeying around" with gadgets. If you leave mechanical devices in their presence, the monkeys will learn how to manipulate them without any reward other than the pleasure of manipulation (Harlow et al., 1950).

Many human infants will play endlessly with "busy boxes"—boards or boxes with pieces that move, honk, squeak, rattle, and buzz. Most children seem to find pleasure in playing with new gadgets and discovering interesting new activities. This seems to support the view of psychologists who see the desire for novel stimulation as natural to both people and animals.

Achievement Motivation

People who are driven to get ahead, to tackle challenging situations and to meet high personal standards of success are said to have high **achievement motivation**. For example, students who demonstrate high achievement motivation will work on difficult test items until they find the answer or run out of time. These students tend to earn higher grades than students with equal abilities but lower achievement motivation (Allen et al., 1992).

Adults with high achievement motivation may strive to move ahead in their careers. They may set challenging goals for themselves, broaden their skills, or simply recognize and take advantage of opportunities presented to them. Adults with high achievement motivation are more likely to be promoted and earn high salaries than less motivated people with similar opportunities. Research shows that people with high achievement motivation enjoy personal challenges and are willing to take moderate risks to achieve their goals (McClelland, 1965).

Types of Goals   Achievement motivation can be fueled by different sources (Dweck, 1990). For some students, performance goals may be the reason for their achievement motivation. **Performance goals** are specific goals such as gaining admission to college, earning the approval of parents or teachers, or even simply avoiding criticism. It was a performance goal—winning the science scholarship—that motivated Todd to study advanced biology.

A DAY IN THE LIFE

Other students are driven mainly by learning goals. For some students, learning for learning's sake is the most powerful motivator. We call such motivators **learning goals**. People who demonstrate high achievement motivation may be influenced by more than one type of goal. For example, in addition to striving to win the scholarship, Todd enjoyed studying science.

Performance goals are usually satisfied by external or extrinsic rewards. **Extrinsic rewards** include good grades, a good income, and respect from others. On the other hand, learning goals are usually satisfied by internal or **intrinsic rewards**, such as self-satisfaction.

Development of Achievement Motivation

Where does achievement motivation come from? Parents and caregivers certainly play a crucial role. Their attitude towards achievement is instrumental in developing a child's motivation.

Research suggests that children with learning goals often have parents who encourage them to be persistent, to enjoy schoolwork, and to find their own ways to solve problems whenever possible (Ginsburg & Bronstein, 1993; Gottfried et al., 1994). Such parents create opportunities to expose their children to new and stimulating experiences. Parents of children with performance goals, on the other hand, are often more likely to reward their children with toys or money for good grades and to punish them for poor grades.

Achievement motivation can come from a variety of sources. This graduate's motivation probably includes earning the approval of parents.

Research also shows that parents of children with high achievement motivation tend to be generous with their praise when their children do well. Such parents are also less critical of their children when they do poorly (Ginsburg & Bronstein, 1993; Gottfried et al., 1994). The children themselves set high personal standards and relate their feelings of self-worth to their achievements (Dweck, 1990; Ginsburg & Bronstein, 1993).

Making Things Fit

The stimulus motives we have been discussing are examples of psychological needs aimed at increasing our level of stimulation. However, many psychological needs are aimed at reducing stimulation or tension, especially in interactions with other people. These types of psychological needs are based on a person's need to maintain a balance between their personal beliefs, actions, and thoughts.

Cognitive Consistency Cognitive theorists, such as Leon Festinger (1957) and Sandra Bem (1993), maintain that people are motivated to achieve **cognitive consistency**. That is, they seek to think and behave in a way that fits what they believe and how others expect them to think and behave. According to Festinger, people are motivated to behave primarily according to their beliefs. Therefore, a person who is politically liberal would find it difficult to support a conservative candidate. According to Bem, most girls and boys try to behave in ways that are consistent with what people expect of females and males in their society.

Most people prefer that the "pieces" of their lives fit together. They seek out as friends those who have values and interests similar to their own. As they grow older, most people try to find a set of beliefs that will help them understand the world in which they live. Most people feel better when the important relationships in their lives are stable and orderly. Two theories that address this need to create cognitive consistency are balance theory and cognitive-dissonance theory.

Balance Theory According to **balance theory**, people need to organize their perceptions, opinions, and beliefs in a harmonious manner (Heider, 1958). They want to maintain a cognitive balance by holding consistent views and being with people who share their beliefs and values. When the people we like share our attitudes, there is a state of balance that gives us a feeling that all is well.

Hannah, Todd, Dan, Janet, Marc, and Linda are all very good friends. But why is this group of friends so close? According to balance theory, they have probably discovered that they share many of the same values, interests, and beliefs. Balance theory also suggests that, when we care about a person, we tend to share her or his interests. For example, prior to meeting Hannah, Dan may not have been very interested in attending a classical violin recital. However, because of his friendship with Hannah, he was introduced to, and developed positive feelings about, the things she liked.

Psychologists note that people who have strong feelings for each other, as Marc and Linda do, might be very upset to discover a major area of disagreement (Orive, 1988). Such a "disharmony" would place them in a state of **imbalance**. When someone we care about disagrees with us, an uncomfortable state of imbalance arises. We may attempt to end the uncomfortable state by trying to persuade the other person to change his or her attitude or by changing our feelings about the other person.

Relationships can usually survive disagreements about such things as different tastes in food or a difference of opinion about a movie. However, more basic conflicts such as religion, politics, or personal values can create a state of imbalance.

When we dislike certain people or have no feelings toward them one way or another, their attitudes are not of much interest to us. Because we do not care about them, we are not greatly affected by the disharmony between their views and ours. We can be said to be in a state of **nonbalance**. Unlike imbalance, which tends to upset people, nonbalance usually leaves people feeling indifferent (Newcomb, 1981).

Cognitive-Dissonance Theory   Why do people find a state of imbalance uncomfortable? The answer is that most people want their thoughts and attitudes (cognitions) to be consistent with their actions. Awareness that our cognitions are inconsistent (dissonant) with our behavior is unpleasant. It causes an inner tension, which can be uncomfortable. According to **cognitive-dissonance theory**, people are motivated to reduce this inconsistency (Festinger, 1957; Festinger & Carlsmith, 1959).

Classic research on cognitive dissonance was conducted by Leon Festinger and James Carlsmith (1959). Participants in their experiment were divided into two groups. The people in one group were paid $20 to tell another person that a boring task—such as turning pegs—was interesting. The people in the second group were paid $1 to say that it was interesting. Afterward, the participants were asked to express their own feelings about the task. The people who received $1 rated the task *more* interesting than the people who were paid $20.

According to cognitive-dissonance theory, this occured because the people who received $1 felt an inconsistency—a dissonance—between their cognition ("That was a boring task.") and their action ("I just told someone that task was interesting."). The people who received $20 could easily justify lying about how they really felt about the task because it was worthwhile, financially. The people who received just $1 could not use that excuse. Instead, they changed their attitude about the task. By convincing themselves that the task was more interesting than it really was, they were able to reduce the inconsistency between their cognition and their action.

What happens when two people in a relationship disagree about a key issue, such as religion? A strong disagreement about an important issue can injure or even end a relationship. Cognitive-dissonance theory suggests that people having such a basic disagreement may seek to reduce the dissonance by trying to pretend that the differences between them are unimportant or even by denying that the differences exist. They may avoid thinking about those differences and put off dealing with them as long as possible.

Affiliation

Of course, if we never dealt with other people we would not need to worry about balance or cognitive dissonance. However, humans are social beings who have a need to be with other people. The desire to join with others and be part of something larger than oneself is called **affiliation**. The desire to affiliate is what prompts people to make friends, join groups, and participate in activities with others rather than by oneself. During adolescence, the motive for affiliation with one's peers is particularly strong. It is a time of life when one discovers the extent to which peers provide emotional support, useful advice, and pleasurable company.

Affiliation motivation helps keep families, groups, and nations together. However, some people are so strongly motivated to affiliate that they find it painful to be by themselves. Sometimes a strong need to affiliate may be a sign of anxiety.

Psychologist Stanley Schachter (1959) showed how anxiety increases the desire to affiliate. In a classic study, he manipulated people's anxiety levels. He told one group of people that they would be given painful electric shocks. He told another group of people that they would be given mild electric shocks. All participants were then asked to wait for the shock apparatus to be set up. They were given the choice of waiting alone or waiting in a room with other participants.

The majority (63 percent) of those who expected the painful shock chose to wait with other participants. In contrast, only one third of those who expected the mild shock chose to wait with other participants. Schachter concluded that anxiety tends to cause people to want to affiliate with other people.

TRUTH OR fiction
■ REVISITED ■

It is not true that when people feel anxious, they want to be alone. A classic experiment by Stanley Schachter found that the more anxious the participants were, the more they wanted to be with other participants.

In general, individuals are motivated to make friends and participate in activities with others. This desire to join with others is known as affiliation motivation.

THINKING ABOUT PSYCHOLOGY

1. What are stimulus motives?
2. Define *balance, imbalance,* and *nonbalance* in terms of cognition.
3. **Critical Thinking** Why do you think anxiety increases the need for affiliation?

4 Emotions

Anxiety and elation are two commonly experienced emotions. Love, anger, and sadness are others. **Emotions** are states of feeling. For most people, positive emotions such as happiness and love make life worth living. Persistent negative emotions such as fear, anger, and sadness can make life difficult.

Some emotions are experienced in response to a person's situation. At her violin recital, Hannah was

A DAY IN THE LIFE

anxious because she was uncertain about her ability to perform. Emotions can also motivate behavior. When Hannah remembered that her friends and family were in the audience, she felt their love and support and played with great skill and confidence.

The Nature of Emotions

Emotions have biological, cognitive, and behavioral components (Carlson & Hatfield, 1992; Haaland, 1992). Strong emotions spark activity in the autonomic nervous system (LeDoux, 1994). For example, anxiety triggers activity of the sympathetic division of the autonomic nervous system. (See Chapter 3.) When people are anxious, their hearts race. They breathe rapidly, sweat heavily, and tense their muscles. The cognitive component of anxiety—the idea that something terrible might happen—may lead a person to try to escape from the situation. But where do emotions come from and how many does the average person experience?

The ancient Chinese believed that there are four inborn (instinctive) human emotions: happiness, anger, sorrow, and fear (Carlson & Hatfield, 1992). Behaviorist John B. Watson (1924) believed that there are three instinctive emotions: fear, rage, and love. In 1932, psychologist Katherine Bridges proposed that people are born with one basic emotion: general excitement. This excitement then divides into other emotions as children develop.

Psychologist Carroll Izard (1984, 1990, 1994) suggests that all the emotions that people experience are present and distinct at birth. However, they do not all show up at once. Instead, they emerge as the child develops.

Many psychologists support Izard's view. In fact, they have found that infants show many emotions at ages earlier than those suggested by Bridges. In one study, the mothers of three-month-old babies were interviewed (Johnson et al., 1982). Results of the study revealed that 99 percent of the mothers reported that their babies showed curiosity; 95 percent of the mothers reported that the babies displayed joy; 84 percent, anger; 74 percent, surprise; and 58 percent, fear.

Questions concerning how many emotions there are, how they develop, and how they affect our lives remain unanswered (Fischer et al., 1990). Two emotions of great importance to most people, however, are happiness and anger.

Happiness William James (1902) said that the motive behind everything that people do is "how to gain, how to keep, how to recover happiness." Certainly our state of happiness or unhappiness affects nearly everything we do, as well as our perception of our surroundings. People who are happy think the world is a happier, safer place (Johnson & Tversky, 1983), make decisions more readily (Isen & Means, 1983), and report greater satisfaction with their lives (Schwarz & Clore, 1983) than do people who are unhappy. When a person is unhappy, gloom seems to settle over everything he or she does. When the mood brightens, everything seems better—school, work, relationships, and self-image (Isen et al., 1987; Izard, 1989). It seems that happiness and unhappiness create their own momentum. When we feel good, the world looks good. But when we are feeling low, nothing seems to go right.

Moreover, many studies have found that the happier we are, the more likely we are to help others. When good things happen that lift our mood, we are more likely to volunteer our time to help other people (Khanna & Rathee, 1992).

Anger Anger is a common response to an insult or an attack. Anger can often make a person seem "out of control." Angry people may even seek revenge. The ancient Roman poet Horace called anger "a short madness."

What makes people angry? In one study, participants were asked to keep a record of their experiences with anger (Averill, 1983). Most of the participants reported becoming at least moderately angry several times a week, while others became angry several times a day. Usually the anger was directed against someone close—a friend or family member—and over some alleged offense, especially if the act seemed deliberate or thoughtless. However, small annoyances such as a loud noise, an unpleasant odor, or an accidental injury can also make a person angry.

What is an effective way to handle anger? Hold it in? Lash out at the offender? The participants in Averill's study reported that when they became angry they tended to react by being assertive rather than hostile. Their anger frequently prompted them to discuss the situation with the offending person, thus easing the unpleasant feelings. Such controlled reactions are almost always more effective at reducing anger than hostile outbursts or suppression of the angry feelings.

Facial Expressions

We often rely on the practice of "reading" people's faces. We can tell when people are happy from their smiles. We can see when they are fearful from their open mouths and eyes. We can read people's expressions and know when they are sad or surprised. Are these facial expressions of emotion instinctive, or do people learn to show these expressions to signify certain emotions on the basis of their cultural settings?

Cross-cultural evidence suggests that facial expressions are probably inborn. The ways in which many specific emotions are expressed appear to be the same around the world (Rinn, 1991). Certain facial expressions seem to suggest the same emotions in all people (Brown, 1991; Buss, 1992; Ekman, 1992, Izard, 1994). Smiling appears to be a universal sign of friendliness and approval. Baring the teeth may be a universal sign of anger. Charles Darwin, the evolution theorist, believed that the universal recognition of facial expressions had survival value by communicating motivation. For example, facial expressions could signal whether a group of approaching strangers were friendly or hostile.

In a classic study by Paul Ekman, people from around the world were asked to identify the emotions that were being expressed in a series of photographs. (The photos were of people showing anger, disgust, fear, happiness, sadness, and surprise.) Researchers interviewed people ranging

Do Lie Detectors Really Detect Lies?

The close connection between emotions and the nervous system has led to the creation of devices called polygraphs, or lie detectors. The assumption behind the lie detector is that when somebody tells a lie, his or her body reacts in a way that can be detected with specially designed sensitivity equipment.

A modern lie detector includes electrodes that measure the electrical resistance of the skin in order to detect sweating, a tube tied around the chest to measure breathing, and an inflatable cuff that measures heart rate and blood pressure. Polygraphs do not really detect lies as such. Rather, they record changes in the nervous system that occur in the test taker as he or she answers certain questions. These bodily changes include sudden shifts in breathing, blood pressure, heart rate, and perspiration.

The principle of the lie detector is based on an age-old assumption—namely, that when somebody tells a lie, it can be uncovered. The Bedouins of Arabia used to make parties involved in conflict lick a hot iron. They concluded that the one whose tongue was burned more was the one who was lying. The ancient Chinese had a somewhat similar lie-detection method. A person suspected of lying was forced to chew rice powder and then spit it out. If the powder was dry, the suspect was judged to be guilty.

Significantly, both the Bedouin and the Chinese methods for detecting lies depended on whether the person's mouth was dry or wet. The Bedouins knew that a liar's tongue would be drier and therefore more likely to burn. Similarly, the Chinese examined the chewed rice powder spit out by the suspect. If it was dry, that suggested that the suspect's mouth was dry and therefore that he was lying.

While these methods may seem primitive and strange to us today, they are consistent with modern psychological knowledge. People who lie are usually anxious and fearful that they will be discovered. The emotion of anxiety is linked to heightened activity of the sympathetic division of the autonomic nervous system. One of the signs of sympathetic arousal is a lack of saliva, or dryness in the mouth. Fear and guilt are also linked to sympathetic arousal. Hence, they also contribute to dryness in the mouth.

Many questions have been raised about the validity of the polygraph. The American Polygraph Association (1992) claims that the polygraph is 85 to 95 percent accurate. Critics, however, find that polygraphs are not this accurate and that they record more than just lying. For instance, the polygraph may simply measure the nervousness one might feel when taking a lie detector test, even if one is telling the truth. Therefore, it is difficult to be sure exactly what is being detected (Bashore & Rapp, 1993; Furedy, 1990; Saxe, 1991b; Steinbrook, 1992).

Studies also show that many people successfully fool polygraph interviewers by tensing their muscles or by using certain drugs. Previous experience with the polygraph also helps people evade being caught in lies (Steinbrook, 1992).

In one experiment on the accuracy of the polygraph, people were able to cut the lie-detection accuracy rate in half by biting their tongues (to produce pain) or by pressing their toes against the floor (to tense muscles) during the interview (Honts et al., 1985).

The U.S. Office of Technology Assessment (OTA) reviewed the research on the polygraph and concluded that the examination is not a reliable indicator of guilt or innocence. One problem is that no specific pattern of nervous system activity has been connected only with lying (Bashore & Rapp, 1993; Saxe, 1991b; Steinbrook, 1992). Because of this type of problem, results of polygraph examinations are no longer admitted as evidence in many courts.

Think About It

Do you think lie detector tests are an accurate way to determine whether someone is lying? Why or why not?

Many psychologists believe that all the emotions people experience are present at birth and that they emerge as the child develops.

from college students at a European university to tribal members in the remote highlands of New Guinea. All groups, including the New Guineans, who had had almost no contact with Americans or Europeans, agreed on the emotion that was being portrayed in each photograph (Ekman, 1982; Ekman & Friesen, 1984).

Theories of Emotion

As we have learned, emotions are states of feeling that influence thought and behavior. People respond emotionally to events and situations in a variety of ways. Psychologists have different theories about what emotions are, where they come from, and how they operate.

The Opponent-Process Theory   According to the **opponent-process theory**, originated by psychologist Richard Solomon, emotions often come in pairs, with one emotion being followed by its opposite. That is, one emotion—for example, extreme happiness—tends to be followed by feelings that are opposite—for example, extreme sadness—rather than by a neutral feeling (Kimble, 1994; Solomon, 1980). Solomon and his colleague J. D. Corbitt (1974) suggest that people are inclined to

maintain balance in their emotional lives. When this balance is upset by a strong emotional response to a particular situation, an opponent process, or opposite emotional response, occurs and eventually restores the balance.

Although Hannah had practiced in preparation for her recital, she was anxious when she went on stage. Once she began to play, however, and focused on the music, her anxiety disappeared and was replaced by tremendous relief, even elation. The first emotion (anxiety) was followed by its opposite (relief). At the end of the performance, when she drew her bow across the strings for the final time, she knew she had played the piece very well.

The Commonsense Approach   You and most of your classmates would probably agree with a "commonsense approach" to emotions. According to this view, when something happens to a person in a certain situation, the person quickly interprets the situation. The interpretation triggers body sensations that signal a feeling, or emotion. The emotion, in turn, triggers a behavior. For example, a person who is walking down the street and encounters a large stray dog may sense that he or she is in danger. That person then feels anxious (body sensation) and quickly turns down the nearest side street to avoid the dog (behavior).

Many psychologists agree that thoughts (appraisal of the situation) come before our feelings and behavior (Lazarus, 1991). They maintain that people's appraisals of their situations are the keys to emotional response. That is, people's thoughts, feelings, and behavior are strongly intertwined, and their thoughts to some degree determine their emotional and behavioral responses.

Other psychologists, however, believe that it is important to understand the biology of emotion. According to these psychologists, the activities of the nervous system and hormones play a more important role in determining emotion than what people are thinking about their situations (Izard, 1984; Zajonc, 1984). Some psychologists even believe that people's behavior determines their thoughts and feelings. Three important theories of emotion are the James-Lange theory, the Cannon-Bard theory, and the theory of cognitive appraisal.

The James-Lange Theory   About 100 years ago, William James suggested that people's emotions follow, rather than cause, their behavioral reactions to their situations. That is, people act first and then react emotionally according to the way they acted. For example, a person crossing the street who looks up and sees a truck bearing down acts first to get out of the way, then feels fright. James would say that the emotions of fear and panic are the *result* of jumping out of the way of the truck, not the cause of the action. This theory was also proposed by the Danish biologist Karl G. Lange at about the same time. Hence, it is called the James-Lange theory of emotion.

According to James and Lange, certain situations trigger reactions, called instinctive bodily response patterns. These patterns include specific feelings and behaviors. For example, a physical threat can trigger one of two instinctive response patterns: fighting or fleeing from the situation. According to this view, people who would meet the threat by fighting would experience the emotion of anger *because* (and only *after*) they acted aggressively. People who would meet the threat by fleeing would experience the emotion of fear *because* (and *after*) they ran away from the situation. In other words, their behavior would come first, followed by the emotion that fit the behavior.

The James-Lange theory suggests that people can change their feelings by changing their behavior. Changing one's behavior to change one's feelings is an approach used in behavior therapy, a method that has been employed to treat certain psychological disorders. (See Chapter 19.)

The James-Lange theory has been criticized, however, because it downplays the role of human cognition. This theory views the cognitive appraisal of a situation as having little or no role in determining human behavior. The James-Lange theory also minimizes the role of personal values and choice as factors in human behavior.

The Cannon-Bard Theory Walter Cannon (1927) and Philip Bard (1934) suggested that emotions *accompany* the bodily responses that are aroused by an external stimulus. According to the Cannon-Bard theory, a situation triggers an external stimulus that is processed by the brain. The brain then stimulates bodily changes and cognitive activity (the experience of the emotion) simultaneously. Emotions are not produced by the bodily responses.

The central question raised by the Cannon-Bard theory is whether bodily responses and emotions do in fact occur at the same time. In some cases, it seems they do not. For example, pain or a threat may trigger bodily responses (such as rapid heartbeat) in someone before that person begins to experience distress or fear. Also, people who manage a "narrow escape" from a dangerous situation often become quite upset and shaky afterward, when they have had a chance to consider what might have happened to them. In such situations it seems that a two-stage reaction is involved—the bodily response is followed by the emotional reaction.

The Theory of Cognitive Appraisal Other theoretical approaches to emotion have focused on cognitive factors. One such theory argues that all emotions have basically similar bodily response patterns (Schachter & Singer, 1962). That is, the body reacts in physically similar ways even though different emotions are being experienced. This theory, called the theory of cognitive appraisal, maintains that the way people label an emotion depends largely on their cognitive appraisal of the situation.

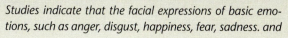

Studies indicate that the facial expressions of basic emotions, such as anger, disgust, happiness, fear, sadness, and surprise, are universally recognized. What emotions do you think are being expressed in these four photographs?

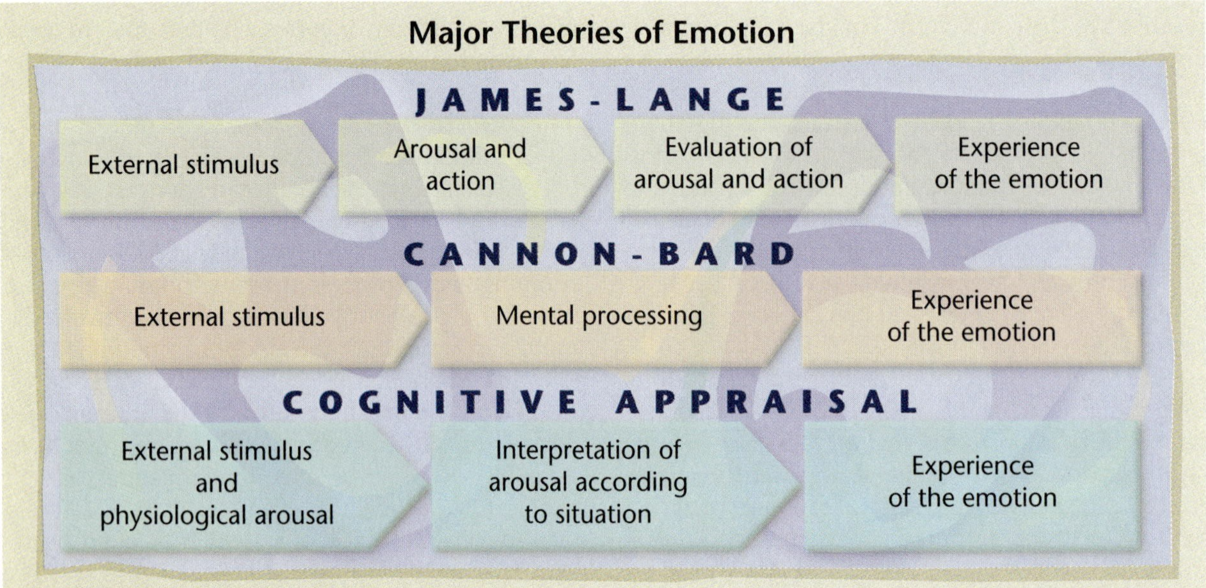

Major Theories of Emotion

JAMES-LANGE

| External stimulus | Arousal and action | Evaluation of arousal and action | Experience of the emotion |

CANNON-BARD

| External stimulus | Mental processing | Experience of the emotion |

COGNITIVE APPRAISAL

| External stimulus and physiological arousal | Interpretation of arousal according to situation | Experience of the emotion |

FIGURE 13.2 *According to the James-Lange theory, emotions follow the evaluation of a bodily response. The Cannon-Bard theory maintains that bodily response and emotion occur simultaneously. The cognitive appraisal theory states that emotion is the result of the individual's evaluation of a situation.*

The cognitive appraisal that occurs is based on many factors. These factors include the person's analysis of the situation and the ways other people are reacting in the same situation. When other people are involved in the same situation, an individual will look at the way they are reacting and then compare his or her reaction to theirs to arrive at what seems to be the right response.

Critics of the theory of cognitive appraisal point out that studies designed to support the theory often yield different results when repeated (Ekman, 1993). In science, research studies must be replicated with the same methods used and similar results obtained. Since several studies designed to prove cognitive appraisal theory produced different results, some psychologists have raised doubts about the theory's validity.

Evaluation of the Theories The theory of cognitive appraisal is quite different from the James-Lange theory. The James-Lange theory asserts that each emotion has distinct and easily recognized bodily sensations. The theory of cognitive appraisal asserts that all emotions are rooted in common bodily sensations but argues that we label these sensations differently according to the situation. The truth may lie somewhere in between.

In summary, it is possible that the bodily response patterns of different emotions are more distinct than Schachter and Singer suggested, but not as distinct as James and Lange suggested. In addition, research with PET scans suggests that different emotions involve different parts of the brain (Goleman, 1995). Furthermore, lack of control over our emotions and ignorance of what is happening to us appear to be distressing experiences (Zimbardo et al., 1993). Thus, it seems that our cognitive appraisals of our situations do affect our emotional responses but not to the extent envisioned by some cognitive-appraisal theorists.

People are complex, thinking beings who evaluate information both from their personal situations and from their bodily responses to their situations. Most likely, they process information from both sources to label their emotions and to decide what action to take. No one theory of emotion we have discussed applies to all people in all situations. That may not be a bad thing. People's emotions are not as easily understood or manipulated as some theorists have believed.

THINKING ABOUT PSYCHOLOGY

1. Identify the three theories of emotion, and describe how each one explains where emotions come from.

2. **Critical Thinking** How have photographs of faces been used to prove the universality of emotions?

CASE STUDIES
AND OTHER TRUE STORIES

The Schachter-Singer Experiment

A classic experiment by Stanley Schachter and Jerome Singer (1962) showed that similar bodily responses can be labeled differently, depending on a person's situation. Participants were told that the purpose of the study was to examine the effects of a particular vitamin on eyesight.

Half of the participants were given an injection of adrenaline, a hormone that activates the autonomic nervous system. The other half—the control group—was given an injection of an inactive solution that had no effect on behavior. None of the participants were aware of the type of injection they received.

The participants in the group who received adrenaline were organized into three smaller groups. Group 1 was told nothing about the side effects of the adrenaline. Group 2 was told that the substance would cause itching and numbness. Group 3 was told that the injection would increase the activity of their nervous systems.

After the participants were given their injections, they were taken to a reception room and asked to wait, in pairs, for their "vision test." The participants did not know that the person with whom they were paired was a confederate—someone who was "in" on the experiment. The participants believed that the confederates had received the same injection they had. The confederates exhibited behavior that the participants would believe was caused by the injection.

Some of the participants were paired with confederates who acted in a happy-go-lucky manner. They joked, danced around, and made paper airplanes out their questionnaires. Another set complained bitterly as they filled out their questionnaires. Some of them tore up the questionnaires and stormed out of the room. The researchers observed the reactions of the participants through a one-way mirror.

The participants in groups 1 and 2, who did not have accurate information about the effects of the injection, tended to imitate the behavior of the confederates. Those exposed to the happy-go-lucky confederates acted happy and relaxed. Those paired with the angry confederates also tended to be angry and upset. The participants in group 3 (who had been told the truth) and the members of the control group were relatively uninfluenced by the behavior of the confederates.

Schachter and Singer concluded that those in groups 1 and 2, who felt aroused by the adrenaline injection but had no accurate information with which to interpret their bodily reactions, looked to the confederates for behavioral cues to better understand their reactions. These participants then felt happy or angry, depending on how their confederates were behaving.

The participants in group 3, who were accurately informed about their adrenaline injection, expected arousal from the injection without any particular accompanying emotions. They watched as their confederates acted either happy or angry. They did not imitate the confederates because they had no reason to expect happiness or anger to be one of the consequences of receiving their adrenaline injection. Likewise, the participants in the control group were not inclined to imitate the behavior of the confederates. Since they had not been given adrenaline, they had no reactions that needed to be explained.

The experiment suggested those participants who had no way to interpret their reaction to the injection began feeling and acting the way they had been prompted. The experiment supports Schachter and Singer's theory that the body reacts in physically similar ways even though different emotions are being experienced. It also suggests that we interpret our emotions according to the behavior of those around us.

Think About It

Describe an incident in which your reaction was influenced by the behavior of people around you at the time.

13 REVIEW

SUMMARY

Biological and psychological needs, as well as emotions, help explain the reasons for human behavior.

I. The Psychology of Motivation

A. A motive is a stimulus that moves a person to exhibit behaviors designed to accomplish a specific goal.

B. A need is a condition in which one requires something one lacks; needs may be biological or psychological.

C. Drives are the forces associated with needs that motivate an organism to take action.

D. There are four main theories of motivation.

  1. The instinct theory proposes that behavior patterns are inborn.

  2. The drive-reduction theory suggests that people act to satisfy basic needs and to achieve a relaxation of tension.

  3. Humanistic theory states that the desire for personal growth and achievement motivates human behavior.

  4. Sociocultural theory proposes that cultural experiences affect behavior.

II. Biological Needs: Focus on Hunger

A. Biological needs are based on body-tissue needs, such as those for food, water, air, and temperature regulation.

B. The hunger drive is regulated by both biological and psychological factors.

  1. Hunger pangs are not the main factor that signals hunger.

  2. The hypothalamus signals an organism to start and stop eating.

  3. Psychological factors also affect the hunger drive.

C. Obesity is defined as weighing more than 30 percent above one's recommended weight.

  1. Sound weight-control programs focus on lifestyle changes that lead to gradual, healthful weight loss.

  2. Nutritional knowledge helps people lose weight without feeling deprived.

  3. Causes of obesity include a family history of obesity, stress and anxiety, and having an elevated number of fat cells.

III. Psychological Needs

A. Stimulus motives motivate organisms to manipulate their environment, thereby increasing their chances of survival.

B. People who tackle challenges and meet high personal standards for success are said to have high achievement motivation.

C. The desire for cognitive consistency also motivates human behavior.

  1. Balance theory asserts that people try to organize their perceptions, opinions, and beliefs in a harmonious manner.

  2. According to cognitive-dissonance theory, people act to reduce inconsistency between their thoughts and actions.

D. The need for affiliation prompts people to make friends, join groups, and participate in activities with others.

IV. Emotions

A. Emotions affect everything people do.

B. The exact number of human emotions and how they develop are not known.

C. Cross-cultural studies suggest that facial expressions, which are clues to human emotions, are probably inborn.

D. Four theories attempt to explain the nature of emotions.

  1. The opponent-process theory states that every emotion is followed by its opposite emotion.

  2. The James-Lange theory suggests that bodily responses produce emotions.

  3. The Cannon-Bard theory suggests that emotions accompany bodily responses.

  4. The theory of cognitive appraisal states that the way people view a situation determines their emotional response.

TERM & CONCEPT REVIEW

1. What is the difference between biological needs and psychological needs? Give an example of each and explain how these two basic needs are related to each other.
2. Define *self-actualization.* To which theory of motivation does this concept belong?
3. What is homeostasis? Give an example of a way you attempt to maintain a state of homeostasis in your daily life.
4. Why is knowledge of nutrition important as a strategy for weight loss? List three principles of nutrition that help ensure healthy weight loss.
5. What are two ways in which heredity may contribute to obesity?
6. Give two examples of stimulus motives. Why are stimulus motives important?
7. What is sensory deprivation? What often happens to people who suffer sensory deprivation?
8. What is the difference between imbalance and nonbalance in human relationships?
9. What is the difference between extrinsic rewards and intrinsic rewards? Give two examples of extrinsic rewards.
10. What term explains why we feel "on top of the world one day" and "down in the dumps" another day?

CRITICAL THINKING

1. Why is the instinct theory not used to explain human motivation?
2. How might the different theories of motivation explain why some people engage in high-risk behavior such as skydiving, stock-car racing, and bungee jumping while other people prefer to avoid any potentially dangerous situations?
3. What factors should a weight-loss counselor consider when counseling a client?
4. Why is sensory deprivation an important con-

cept in the study of human motivation and emotion? How do you think you would react to complete sensory deprivation?
5. Give an example to illustrate the James-Lange and Cannon-Bard theories of emotion. If possible, give examples from your own life.

APPLYING SKILLS IN PSYCHOLOGY

1. **Writing About Psychology** Imagine that a local school board is contemplating cutting all high school sports and extracurricular activities. Money, school officials say, should be spent on essentials, such as books and equipment, teachers' salaries, and building maintenance. Write a letter to the school board in which you argue in favor of retaining extracurricular activities. Use your knowledge of humanistic theory of motivation to support your point of view.
2. **Research in Psychology** Identify a person in your school or community who has worked hard to achieve a specific goal. Interview that person and try to determine the motivation behind his or her success. Also find out if the person gave up anything, or had to overcome obstacles, to achieve his or her goal. In a short speech to the class, nominate this person for an achievement award.
3. **COOPERATIVE LEARNING Research in Psychology** Working in small groups, prepare a debate about the four theories of motivation. Each student in your group should argue in support of one the four theories (Instinct Theory, Drive-Reduction Theory, Humanistic Theory, and Sociocultural Theory). You will need to be able to incorporate the various aspects of the theory you are advocating in order to persuade your opponents that your theory is the correct one. In addition, you should be able to challenge your debate opponents. To do so, you should be prepared to identify the weaknesses in your opponents' theories. Present your debate to the class.

14

THEORIES OF PERSONALITY

Objectives

1 Explain the history, main features, and limitations of the trait theory of personality.

2 Describe the impact of the psychoanalytic theory of personality and how the theory has been modified since Sigmund Freud.

3 Describe what learning theorists believe are the influences on and motivations for behavior.

4 Explain how the humanistic approach views the role of the self and free choice in shaping behavior.

5 Discuss how the sociocultural approach views the importance of ethnicity, gender, culture, and socioeconomic status in the development of personality.

A DAY IN THE LIFE

Janet and Todd were having lunch together, and Todd, as usual, kept joking around. "Hey, Janet, look! Over there," Todd said as he stole one of her pretzels.

"I can't believe you're still pulling that same joke," Janet laughed.

"Well, I can't believe you're still falling for it," joked Todd. "You are so gullible."

"I'm not gullible; I'm just trusting," Janet said laughing. Just then Hannah came running up.

"Janet, Todd—I'm so glad I found you both. I have the best news!" Hannah was talking so fast they could barely understand her.

"Hannah, calm down a second. What's going on?" Janet asked.

"Mr. Hochberg just called me into his office because he said he had some news for me. Remember my violin recital last week?" Hannah asked, still trying to talk slowly. "Well, there was an arts foundation representative there and she offered me a performing arts scholarship to almost any college I choose!"

"Hannah, that's great!" Janet exclaimed. "I always knew you could do it. Where do you think you'll go?"

"Well, I'm thinking about going to the same school where my brother goes. He loves it there. He said that there's a large Korean population. My parents have always raised us both to understand our heritage, but it will be really cool to meet lots of other people with the same background."

"Have you told your parents yet?" Todd asked.

"No, not yet. I want to tell them at the same time, and they're both at work right now," Hannah answered. "It would make them so happy if my brother and I were at the same school. It means a lot to them that we keep the family together as much as possible."

"Well, Hannah, congratulations," said Todd. "But you have to promise that you won't forget about us when you become a famous violinist!"

"Don't be silly," Hannah smiled. "Would I do a thing like that?"

Would Hannah do a thing like that? What influences the things people do and do not do? Some people might say that the answer is concerned with personality. But what exactly is personality? When people think of a person's personality, they usually think of the person's most striking characteristics, as in an "assertive personality" or an "artistic personality." Psychologists define **personality** as the patterns of feelings, motives, and behavior that set people apart from one another.

Psychologists seek to describe personality characteristics and to explain how personality develops. They try to predict how different people will respond to life's demands. In this chapter, we explore five approaches to the study of personality: trait theory, psychoanalytic theory, learning theory, humanistic theory, and sociocultural theory.

Key Terms

- personality
- trait
- surface trait
- source trait
- introvert
- extrovert
- id
- ego
- superego
- defense mechanism
- repression
- rationalization
- displacement
- regression
- projection
- reaction formation
- denial
- sublimation
- collective unconscious
- archetype
- inferiority complex
- socialization
- self-concept
- congruence
- acculturation

THEORIES OF PERSONALITY   321

1 The Trait Approach

A **trait** is an aspect of personality that is considered to be reasonably stable. We assume that a person has certain traits based on how the person behaves. If you describe a friend as "shy," it may be because you have seen your friend looking anxious and trying to escape social encounters. Traits are assumed to account for consistent behavior in different situations. You would probably expect your shy friend to act withdrawn in most social situations. Todd, on the other hand, was constantly making jokes with his friends. Therefore, we might conclude that outgoing and humorous are two of Todd's personality traits. But if Todd made jokes only around his friends, we would not consider him to have these traits.

Trait theorists have generally assumed that traits are somehow fixed or unchanging. However, the question of where traits come from has been pondered through the ages.

Hippocrates

An early answer to where traits come from was offered by the ancient Greek physician Hippocrates. The ancient Greeks believed that the body contains fluids called *humors*. Hippocrates suggested that traits are a result of different combinations of these bodily fluids.

Hippocrates believed that there are four basic fluids, or humors, in the body:

- yellow bile, which was associated with a choleric, or quick-tempered, disposition
- blood, which was connected with a sanguine, or warm and cheerful, temperament
- phlegm, which was linked with a phlegmatic, or sluggish and cool, disposition
- black bile, which was associated with a melancholic, thoughtful temperament

Certain diseases and disorders were believed to reflect a lack of balance in these humors. Methods such as bloodletting (the removal of blood from the body) and vomiting were recommended to restore the balance of fluids and one's health. Although there is no scientific evidence for Hippocrates' biological theory, the terms based on his ideas remain in use today. A cheerful person, for example, may still be called sanguine.

Gordon Allport

In the 1930s, psychologist Gordon Allport (1897–1967) searched through a dictionary to find every term that could describe a person (Allport & Odbert, 1936). He cataloged some 18,000 human traits from a search through lists of descriptive words. Some of the words, such as *short* and *brunette,* describe physical traits. Others, such as *shy* and *emotional,* describe behavioral traits. Still others, such as *honest,* concern morality.

Allport assumed that traits can be inherited and that they are fixed in the nervous system. He conducted thorough and detailed studies of individuals, noting their outstanding traits as well as their behavior. Allport's research led him to conclude that traits are the building blocks of personality. He believed that a person's behavior is a product of his or her particular combination of traits (Allport, 1937, 1961, 1965, 1966).

Raymond Cattell

Following on the heels of Allport, many psychologists have tried to determine the number of basic traits human personality can be boiled down to. Raymond Cattell (1905–) took the opposite approach from Allport, studying groups of people rather than individuals. Cattell began by identifying certain obvious personality traits such as integrity, friendliness, and tidiness (Cattell, 1965). He called these obvious traits **surface traits**.

Cattell noticed that clusters, or groups, of surface traits seemed to occur together. That is, if a person showed one trait in a cluster, he or she usually showed the others in the cluster as well. Cattell reasoned that a single, underlying trait gives rise to all the traits in each cluster. He called these underlying traits **source traits**.

Cattell finally settled on a list of 16 source traits. He believed that psychological measurement of these traits would enable us to predict people's behavior in various situations. Todd, for example, was able to predict that Janet would look away when he told her to because he had recognized her "trusting" nature before.

These 16 source traits are usually measured by means of Cattell's Sixteen Personality Factor Questionnaire, commonly known as the 16 PF. (See Figure 14.1.) The 16 PF is frequently used in psychological research that explores differences between groups of people and individuals. The 16 PF lists each source trait as part of a pair of opposites on a continuum—such as "reserved" versus "outgoing" and "trusting" versus "suspicious." Janet's past behavior would indicate that she would score on the "trusting" end of Cattell's "trusting" versus "suspicious" continuum.

Hans Eysenck

British psychologist Hans J. Eysenck (1916–) focused on the relationships between two personality dimensions: introversion-extroversion and emotional stability-instability. **Introverts** tend to be imaginative and to look inward rather than to other people for their ideas and energy. **Extroverts**, on the other hand, tend to be active and self-expressive and gain energy from interaction with other people. The contrast between introversion and extroversion was first proposed by Carl Jung, whom you will read about later in this chapter. Stable people are usually reliable, composed, and rational. Unstable people can be agitated and unpredictable.

Eysenck cataloged various personality traits according to where those traits appear within the dimensions of introversion-extroversion and emotional stability-instability. (See Figure 14.2 on page 324.) For instance, an anxious person might be highly introverted and emotionally unstable. A reckless or impulsive person might be highly extroverted and unstable (Eysenck, 1953).

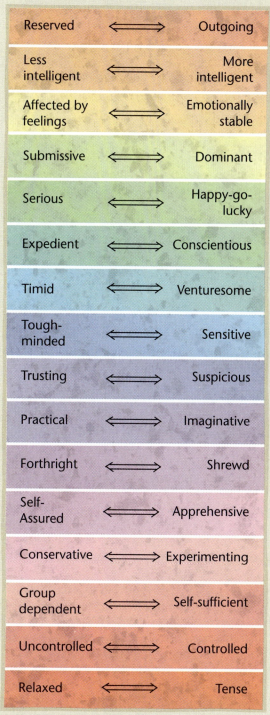

Raymond Cattell's Sixteen Personality Factor Questionnaire

Reserved	⟷	Outgoing
Less intelligent	⟷	More intelligent
Affected by feelings	⟷	Emotionally stable
Submissive	⟷	Dominant
Serious	⟷	Happy-go-lucky
Expedient	⟷	Conscientious
Timid	⟷	Venturesome
Tough-minded	⟷	Sensitive
Trusting	⟷	Suspicious
Practical	⟷	Imaginative
Forthright	⟷	Shrewd
Self-Assured	⟷	Apprehensive
Conservative	⟷	Experimenting
Group dependent	⟷	Self-sufficient
Uncontrolled	⟷	Controlled
Relaxed	⟷	Tense

FIGURE 14.1 *Cattell theorized that our surface personality traits are caused by 16 underlying traits, which he called source traits. He believed that through psychological measurement of these traits, we can predict people's behavior in various situations.*

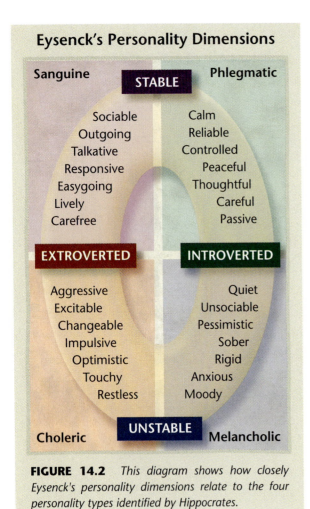

Eysenck's Personality Dimensions

STABLE

Sanguine
- Sociable
- Outgoing
- Talkative
- Responsive
- Easygoing
- Lively
- Carefree

Phlegmatic
- Calm
- Reliable
- Controlled
- Peaceful
- Thoughtful
- Careful
- Passive

EXTROVERTED   **INTROVERTED**

Choleric
- Aggressive
- Excitable
- Changeable
- Impulsive
- Optimistic
- Touchy
- Restless

Melancholic
- Quiet
- Unsociable
- Pessimistic
- Sober
- Rigid
- Anxious
- Moody

UNSTABLE

FIGURE 14.2 *This diagram shows how closely Eysenck's personality dimensions relate to the four personality types identified by Hippocrates.*

Eysenck's scheme is similar to the one suggested by Hippocrates. According to Eysenck's dimensions, the choleric type would be extroverted and unstable; the sanguine type, extroverted and stable; the phlegmatic type, introverted and stable; and the melancholic type, introverted and unstable.

The Big Five

The "big five" may sound like a description of a basketball team. In psychology, however, the term refers to recent research that suggests there may be five basic personality dimensions (Carson, 1989; Goldberg, 1993). These dimensions include the two found by Eysenck—introversion-extroversion and emotional stability-instability—and three others. They are conscientiousness-carelessness, agreeableness-disagreeableness, and openness to new experience-closed-mindedness.

Psychologists continue to disagree about which personality factors are the most basic (Digman &

Inouye, 1986; Eysenck, 1993). However, nearly all psychologists would agree that the "big five" personality dimensions are important in defining a person's psychological makeup. Moreover, a person's position along these dimensions tends to be established at an early age and then remains stable through life.

Evaluation of the Trait Approach

One shortcoming of the trait approach is that it describes personality but does not explain where traits come from. The efforts of Hippocrates, Allport, and other trait theorists to link our personality traits to biological factors have not been successful. Today, trait theory focuses on describing traits rather than tracing their origins or investigating how people with certain traits can change for the better.

The work of trait theorists has, however, had a number of practical applications. In suggesting that there are links between personalities, abilities, and interests, trait theorists have alerted us to the value of matching people to educational programs and jobs on the basis of their personality traits. For example, by identifying students' abilities and traits, guidance counselors help students make important schooling and employment decisions.

THINKING ABOUT PSYCHOLOGY

1. Explain the relationship between the personality traits described by Hippocrates and the personality dimensions that Eysenck focused on.
2. List the "big five" personality factors.
3. **Critical Thinking** Discuss the advantages and disadvantages of testing people to identify their personality traits.

2
The Psychoanalytic Approach

The psychoanalytic approach teaches that all people—even the most well-adjusted people—undergo inner struggles. According to this approach, people are born with certain biological drives such as aggression, sex, and the need for superiority. These drives, however, may come into conflict with laws, social rules, and moral codes that have previously been internalized. At any moment, a person's behavior, thoughts, and emotions represent the outcome of inner contests between the opposing forces of drives and rules.

Sigmund Freud

The "inner conflict" approach to personality theory owes its origin to Sigmund Freud (1856–1939). Freud was trained as a physician. Early in his practice in Vienna, Austria, he was astounded to find that some people had lost feeling in a hand or had become paralyzed in the legs even though nothing was medically wrong with them. When Freud interviewed these individuals, he found that many things in their lives were making them very angry or anxious. Yet they refused to recognize their emotional or social problems. They were at the mercy of very powerful inner emotions, yet, on the surface they seemed calm.

It is true that people can lose feeling in their hands or legs even though nothing is medically wrong with them. Sigmund Freud directly observed such ailments.

Freud concluded that conscious ideas and feelings occupy only a small part of the mind. Many of people's deepest thoughts, fears, and urges remain out of their awareness. These urges are pushed into an unconscious part of the mind.

One way in which Freud explored the unconscious is through psychoanalysis. In psychoanalysis, people are encouraged to talk about anything that pops into their minds. They do so in a comfortable and relaxed setting. The people Freud observed—those who had lost feeling in their hands or legs—regained much of their functioning when they talked about the things that were on their minds. For this reason, psychoanalysis has been called a "talking cure."

Freud also explored the unconscious through dream analysis. He believed that people experience unconscious wishes in their dreams—often in disguised form. For this reason, Freud asked people to record their dreams upon waking. He would then help them explore the dreams' hidden meanings.

In psychoanalysis, the client is made comfortable, usually on a couch similar to Freud's original couch, which is shown here.

Another technique that Freud used was hypnosis. He felt that people in a hypnotic state had better access to their unconscious thoughts. Freud eventually abandoned hypnosis, however, because many people later denied the things they said when they were in a hypnotic state.

Id, Ego, and Superego

Freud believed that the mind has three basic psychological structures: the id, the ego, and the superego. The id is like the stereotypical two-year-old: "I want what I want, and I want it now." The **id** represents basic drives such as hunger. It demands pleasure through instant gratification and pays no attention to laws, social customs, or the needs of others. It follows what Freud called the *pleasure principle*—the urge for an immediate release of energy or emotion that will bring personal gratification, relief, or pleasure.

According to Freud, the id is present at birth. The **ego**, however, develops because a child's demands for instant gratification cannot be met or because meeting these demands may be harmful. Freud wrote that the ego "stands for reason and good sense" (1964). It is guided by the *reality principle*—the understanding that in the real world we cannot always get what we want.

Calvin and Hobbes

by Bill Watterson

The ego seeks to satisfy the appetites of the id in ways that are consistent with reality. For example, the id lets you know that you are hungry, but the ego lets you know that certain ways of satisfying your hunger—such as cooking a hamburger—are more appropriate than others—such as eating raw hamburger. The ego also provides the conscious sense of self. Activities such as planning dinner and studying for a test are functions of the ego.

Although most of the ego is conscious, some of its business is carried out unconsciously. For instance, the ego acts as a censor that screens out the wild impulses of the id. When the ego senses that indecent or improper impulses are rising into awareness, it tries to repress them.

The third psychological structure Freud formulated is the **superego**. The superego develops throughout early childhood. It functions according to the *moral principle*. By incorporating the standards and values of parents and members of the community, the superego provides us with our moral sense. The superego acts as the conscience and floods the ego with feelings of guilt and shame when we think or do something that society defines as wrong.

The ego does not have an easy job. It is caught between the conflicting messages of the id and the superego. For example, the id may urge, "You want to go out with your friends. Don't study now!" while the superego warns, "You have to study or you will not pass the test." According to Freud, people with healthy egos—and thus healthy personalities—find ways to balance the id's demands and the superego's warnings. In this case, the healthy ego would probably conclude, "Study now, and after you do well on the test, you can spend time with your friends."

Defense Mechanisms

According to Freud, **defense mechanisms** are methods the ego uses to avoid recognizing ideas or emotions that may cause personal anxiety. These defenses operate unconsciously.

Repression One of the main defense mechanisms in psychoanalytic theory is repression. **Repression** removes anxiety-causing ideas from conscious awareness by pushing them into the unconscious. To explain repression, Freud compared people's personalities to teakettles. Primitive urges such as aggression, seek expression, just like steam tries to escape from a boiling kettle. But recognizing these urges would cause a person serious feelings of guilt, anxiety, and shame. Therefore, repression tries to keep the lid on the boiling kettle.

Repression, however, is not always successful. When enough steam builds up inside, the teakettle pops its lid. When people "pop their lids," the results are outbursts of anger and the development of other psychological and emotional problems.

Rationalization Other defense mechanisms protect us from unacceptable ideas in a different manner. They do not completely repress such ideas, but they distort them in one way or another. One such defense mechanism is **rationalization**—the use of self-deception to justify unacceptable behaviors or ideas. For instance, a student who cheats during a test may explain, "I only cheated on a couple of questions—I knew most of the material."

Displacement According to Freudian theorists, **displacement** is defined as the transfer of an idea or impulse from a threatening or unsuitable object to a less threatening object. For example, a football player who is yelled at by his coach may go home and yell at his little brother.

Regression   Freud believed that when an individual is under a great deal of stress he or she will return to behavior that is characteristic of an earlier stage of development. He termed this behavior **regression**. For example, an adolescent may pout and refuse to speak to her parents when forbidden to go out with friends. Similarly, an adult may become highly dependent on his parents following the breakup of his own marriage.

Projection   A motion picture projector thrusts an image outward onto a screen. Freud believed that people sometimes deal with unacceptable impulses by projecting these impulses outward onto other people. In other words, people see *their own* faults in other people. For example, hostile people, unable to think of *themselves* as hostile, may accuse other people of hostility. As a result of this **projection**, they may think of the world as a dangerous place.

Reaction Formation   People who use the defense of **reaction formation** act contrary to their genuine feelings in order to keep their true feelings hidden. A person who is angry with a coworker may behave in a "sickly sweet" manner toward that coworker. Someone who is unconsciously attracted to another person may keep the impulses out of mind by being mean to that person.

Denial   In the mechanism of **denial**, a person refuses to accept the reality of anything that is bad or upsetting. For example, people who smoke cigarettes may ignore the risks of lung cancer and heart disease from smoking because they think "it can't happen to me."

Sublimation   Freud also believed that individuals can channel their basic impulses into socially acceptable behavior through a process called **sublimation**. For example, a hostile student may channel aggressive impulses into contact sports.

Effects of Defense Mechanisms   According to Freud, when used in moderation, defense mechanisms may be normal and even useful to protect people from painful feelings such as anxiety, guilt, and shame. Such defense mechanisms become

unhealthy, he said, when they lead a person to ignore the underlying issues causing those feelings. However, Freud also noted that a person with a strong and healthy ego is able to balance the id and the superego without the use of such mechanisms. Therefore, the use of defense mechanisms may indicate the presence of inner conflict or personal anxiety.

Stages of Development

Freud believed that an individual's personality develops through a series of five stages. These stages of development begin at birth and continue to shape human personality through adolescence. He believed that people instinctively seek to preserve and extend life. He also thought that these instinctive efforts to survive are aided by a psychological energy he labeled libido. (*Libido* is the Latin word for "desire.")

Freud organized psychological development into five periods: oral, anal, phallic, latent, and genital. Children were said to encounter conflicts during each stage. If the conflicts were not resolved, Freud believed that the child might become fixated, or stuck, at an early stage of development. The child would then carry that stage's traits into adulthood. Thus, Freud believed that an adult's psychological problems might actually stem from unresolved childhood conflicts.

The Oral Stage   In Freud's theory, psychological development begins in the first year of life. He noted that infants are continually exploring their

During the oral stage of development, an infant's first reaction to many objects is often to suck on them.

CASE STUDIES
AND OTHER TRUE STORIES

The Case of Little Hans: A Mystery in Vienna

Five-year-old Hans lived in turn-of-the-century Vienna, a flourishing capital of music and the arts. But Hans was afraid—afraid that horses were biting people in the streets. He was terrified that he would be bitten himself if he left his house. In 1908, the boy's father, distressed about Hans' fears, turned to Sigmund Freud for advice. One year later, Freud set down a 140-page case history about Hans. It would become one of the most celebrated cases in psychology.

Freud came to believe that Hans did not fear horses because of anything the horses might do. Instead, Hans feared what horses symbolized, or represented, to him. According to Freud, horses represented Hans' father. As Freud studied Hans, he came to believe that Hans was hostile toward his father and that he *projected* this hostility onto the horses. Thus, he fantasized that his father—the horse—was hostile toward him. Hans' fear of being bitten by horses symbolized his unconscious fear of his father.

Why would Hans feel hostility and fear toward his father? Freud related these feelings to two aspects of the phallic stage: the strong desire a child has for the parent of the other sex and the jealousy the child has toward the parent of the same sex. In other words, little boys may expect to marry their mothers when they grow up, and little girls may expect to marry their fathers.

Such feelings toward parents would be difficult for children to handle if they were consciously aware of the feelings of aggression. For this reason, Freud believed that these feelings were repressed and would remain unconscious. Their influence would be felt, however, and the child would seek approval from the parent of the other sex and have hostility toward the parent of the same sex.

Freud labeled this conflict the *Oedipus complex* in boys. Oedipus was a legendary Greek king who unknowingly killed his father and married his mother. Freud said that similar feelings in girls give rise to the *Electra complex*. According to Greek legend, Electra was the daughter of the king Agamemnon. She longed for him after his death and sought revenge on his slayers—her mother and her mother's lover. Thus, the Oedipus and Electra complexes relate to feelings of desire for the parent of the other sex. They also both involve resentment toward the parent of the same sex.

Freud theorized that the Oedipus and Electra complexes are normally resolved by the time children are five or six years old. Hans overcame his fear of horses by age six. Freud believed that Hans had coped with his fear of his father by surrendering the wish to possess his mother. The father then ceased to be his rival in love, and Hans no longer had a reason to be hostile toward his father. Hans' projection of his hostile impulses was no longer necessary. Therefore, he no longer viewed horses, which represented his father, as being dangerous.

Hans not only repressed his hostility toward his father. He also started to identify with his father. He began to assume his father's behavior and attitudes. Freud believed that people try to become like the people they fear so that they will be accepted by them and will no longer need to fear them. Identification leads boys to assume the behavior of men and to bring inward, or internalize, their fathers' values. Similarly, identification leads girls to assume the behavior of women and to internalize their mothers' values. Identification is an indication that the Oedipus and Electra complexes have been resolved.

As celebrated as this case has been, Freud's theories on the matter have been widely criticized. Many psychologists believe that the Oedipus and Electra complexes do not really exist and that of all of Freud's theories, these are the weakest.

Think About It

According to Freudian theory, during which stages of development did Hans develop and resolve his personal conflict?

world by picking up objects and putting those objects into their mouths. Infants also receive their main source of pleasure—food—with their mouths. For these reasons, Freud termed the first stage of development the oral stage. He theorized that the infant's survival is dependent on the attention of adults. A child whose caretakers do not meet his or her needs during this stage may become fixated at the oral stage. Some examples of this fixation might include smoking, overeating, excessive talking, and nail biting. In addition, as an adult, such a person might be inclined to have clinging, dependent interpersonal relationships.

TRUTH
OR
fiction
■ R E V I S I T E D ■

It is true that, according to Freud's theory, biting one's fingernails and smoking cigarettes are signs of early childhood conflicts. Such behavior might reflect fixation at the oral stage of development.

The Anal Stage   According to Freud, the anal stage occurs between the ages of one and a half and two and a half. During this stage, children learn that they can control their own bodily functions, and the general issue of self-control becomes a vital issue to the children. Conflict during the anal stage can lead to two sets of adult personality traits. So-called anal-retentive traits involve an excessive use of self-control. They include perfectionism and strong needs for order and cleanliness. People with anal-expulsive traits, on the other hand, are less restrained and may be careless and messy.

The Phallic Stage   The third year of life marks the beginning of the phallic stage. Young girls and boys begin to discover the physical differences between the two sexes and become more focused on their own bodies. Children may also develop strong attachments to the parent of the opposite sex. At the same time, they may view the same-sex parent as a rival for the other parent's affections. Freud argued that the complex emotions of the phallic stage can lead to several psychological disorders later in life, including depression, excessive guilt, and anxiety.

The Latency Stage   By the age of five or six, Freud believed, children would have been in conflict with their parents for several years. At this

Pictured here is a mandala, the symbol Carl Jung used to represent the collective nature, or oneness, of human experience.

point, they would retreat from the conflict and repress all aggressive urges. In so doing, they would enter the latency stage. *Latent* means "hidden," and during the latency period, impulses and emotions remain hidden, or unconscious.

The Genital Stage   Freud wrote that people enter the final stage of psychological development, or the genital stage, at puberty. The adolescent does not generally encounter any new psychological conflicts during this period but does become more aware of his or her own gender identity. Instead, the conflicts of the early development stages resurface.

Carl Jung

Sigmund Freud had several intellectual heirs. The best known of these theorists was Carl Jung (1875–1961). Jung was a Swiss psychiatrist who had been a colleague of Freud's. He fell into disfavor with Freud, however, when he developed his own psychoanalytic theory—known as *analytic psychology*—which places a greater emphasis on the influences of mysticism and religion on human behavior.

Jung, like Freud, was intrigued by unconscious processes. But he dramatically altered Freud's theory of these processes. Jung believed that people

The deity is an example of an archetype. Although most cultures believe in deities, specific forms vary. Shown here are sculptures of the Aztec god Quetzalcóatl (left) and the Indonesian god Nusa Dua Beach (right).

have not only a *personal* unconscious that stores material that has been forgotten or repressed but also an inherited collective unconscious. According to Jung, the **collective unconscious** is a store of human concepts shared by all people across all cultures (Jung, 1917, 1936).

The structural components of the collective unconscious are basic, primitive concepts, called archetypes. **Archetypes** are ideas and images of the accumulated experience of all human beings. Examples of archetypes include the supreme being, the young hero, the fertile and nurturing mother, the wise old man, the hostile brother, and even fairy godmothers, wicked witches, and themes of rebirth or resurrection. Jung found that each of these concepts appears in some form across most cultures and religions (Jung, 1936).

Jung argued that although these images remain unconscious, they often appear to us as figures in our dreams. He declared that these images influence our thoughts and feelings and that they help form a foundation on which personality develops. Despite his interest in the collective unconscious, Jung granted more importance to conscious thoughts than Freud did. Jung believed that one archetype is the sense of self. According to Jung, the self is a unifying force of personality that gives people direction and provides a sense of completeness.

Jung believed that every person's conscious sense of self can be characterized by four functions of the mind—thinking, feeling, intuition, and sensation. He argued that all four of these elements exist in every individual's unconscious. However, an individual can be identified by the function that becomes his or her primary form of expression. He thought that people could form healthy personalities by bringing together, or integrating, these conscious elements with the collective unconscious archetypes. His name for this integrating process is *individuation.*

Many psychologists consider Jung's theory of the collective unconscious to be mystical and unscientific. But Jungian theory has a tremendous following among the general public. Many people enter Jungian analysis to examine their dreams and to work toward individuation. Scholars explore the use of archetypical symbols as they appear in literature and the arts. In addition, Jung's focus on myth has made him very popular with those interested in the study of religion.

Alfred Adler

Alfred Adler (1870–1937) was another follower of Freudian psychoanalysis. Adler believed that people are basically motivated by a need to overcome feelings of inferiority. To describe these feelings of inadequacy and insecurity, Adler coined the term **inferiority complex**.

In some people, Adler theorized, feelings of inferiority may be based on physical problems and the need to compensate for them (Adler, 1927). This theory may have developed in part from Adler's own attempts to overcome repeated bouts of illness. As a child, Adler was crippled by a disease called rickets and suffered from pneumonia.

Physical problems, however, are not the only source of feelings of inferiority, according to Adler. He believed that all of us have some feelings of inferiority because of our small size as children. He thought that these feelings give rise to a drive for superiority. Adler also introduced the term *sibling rivalry* to describe the jealousies that are often found among brothers and sisters.

Adler, like Jung, believed that self-awareness plays a major role in the formation of personality. Adler spoke of a creative self. The creative self is self-aware and strives to overcome obstacles and develop the individual's unique potential. President Theodore Roosevelt exemplified this theory. Roosevelt was a frail child who became not only president but also a strong and robust man. Similarly, football quarterback Boomer Esiason, who suffered from juvenile arthritis, overcame his disease to become a professional athlete.

Karen Horney

Karen Horney (HOR-neye), who lived from 1885 to 1952, agreed with Freud that childhood experiences play a major role in the development of adult personality. She believed that the greatest influences on personality are social relationships.

Horney, like Freud, saw parent-child relationships to be of paramount importance (Horney, 1937). Small children are completely dependent. When their parents treat them with indifference or harshness, children develop feelings of insecurity that Horney termed *basic anxiety*. Because children also resent neglectful parents, Horney theorized that feelings of hostility would accompany the anxiety. Horney agreed with Freud that children would repress rather than express feelings of hostility because they would fear driving their parents away. In contrast to Freud, however, she also believed that genuine and consistent love could temper the effects of even the most painful childhoods.

Erik Erikson

Like Horney, Erik Erikson (1902–1994) believed that social relationships are the most important factors in personality development (Erikson, 1950). He placed great emphasis on the general emotional climate of the mother-infant relationship. Erikson also granted more powers to the ego than Freud had allowed. According to Freud's theory, people may think that they are making choices, but they may only be rationalizing the compromises forced upon them by inner conflict. According to Erikson's theory, however, people are entirely capable of making real and meaningful choices.

Erikson, like Freud, devised a developmental theory of personality. Erikson, however, expanded on Freud's five stages of development and formulated a psychosocial theory of development consisting of eight stages. Whereas Freud's developmental theory ends with adolescence, Erikson's includes the changing concerns of adulthood.

Erikson named his stages after the traits people might develop during each of them. (See Figure 14.3 on page 332.) For example, the first stage of psychosocial development is named the stage of trust versus mistrust. A warm, loving relationship with the mother (and others) during infancy may lead to a sense of basic trust in people and in the world. Janet, for example, had always maintained a very close relationship with her mother. Erikson's theories would indicate that Janet's trusting personality may have been a result of that warm relationship.

A cold, unfulfilling relationship may generate a broad sense of mistrust, which could damage the formation of relationships for a lifetime unless it is resolved successfully. Erikson believed that most people maintain a blend of trust and mistrust.

Evaluation of the Psychoanalytic Approach

Although psychoanalytic concepts such as libido and id strike many psychologists as unscientific today, Freud was an important champion of the idea that human personality and behavior are subject to scientific analysis. In Freud's day, serious psychological problems were still commonly seen as signs of weakness or so-called craziness. Freud's thinking contributed greatly to the development of compassion for people with psychological disorders.

Psychoanalytic theory also focused the attention of scientists and therapists on the far-reaching effects of childhood events. Freud and Erikson suggested that early childhood traumas can affect us for a lifetime. Psychoanalytic theorists have heightened society's awareness of the emotional needs of children.

Freud also helped us recognize that sexual and aggressive urges are common. He pointed out that there is a difference between recognizing these urges and acting on them. He realized that our thinking may be distorted by our efforts to avoid anxiety and guilt. And he devised an influential method of psychotherapy, which is described in Chapter 19.

Erik Erikson's Stages of Psychosocial Development

Infancy (0-1)	Early childhood (2-3)	Preschool years (4-5)	Grammar school years (6-12)	
Trust versus mistrust	Autonomy versus shame and doubt	Initiative versus guilt	Industry versus inferiority	
Coming to trust the mother and the environment—to associate surroundings with feelings of inner goodness	Developing the wish to make choices and the self-control to exercise choice	Adding planning and "attacking" to choice; becoming active and on the move	Becoming eagerly absorbed in skills, tasks, and productivity; mastering the fundamentals of technology	

FIGURE 14.3 *Erik Erikson believed that social relationships are the most important factors in personality development. Shown here are the eight stages of Erikson's theory of psychosocial development.*

Psychoanalytic theories—particularly the views of Freud—have, however, been criticized on many counts. Even followers of Freud argued that he placed too much emphasis on unconscious motives and neglected the importance of social relationships. Opponents of Freud's theories also assert that people consciously seek self-enhancement and intellectual pleasures and do not merely try to gratify the dark demands of the id.

Critics have also questioned Freud's method of gathering evidence from clinical sessions (Robinson, 1993). Using this method, therapists may subtly influence clients to say what the therapists expect to hear. Also, Freud and many other psychoanalytic theorists gathered their evidence only from case studies of White, middle-class individuals who had sought help for their psychological problems. These individuals may not have provided the most representative sample of the general population. (See Chapter 2.)

THINKING ABOUT PSYCHOLOGY

1. Define the terms *id, ego,* and *superego.*
2. List the stages of development in Freud's theory, and describe the issues a child confronts at each stage.
3. How do the psychoanalytic theories of Jung and Horney disagree with the theories presented by Freud?
4. **Critical Thinking** In what ways do you think the trust that is developed during infancy might affect an individual's personality later in life?

3 The Learning Approach

A DAY IN THE LIFE

Some personality theorists might assume that Todd's sense of humor was largely a learned behavior. They might explain that Todd made jokes because he had learned that he would somehow be rewarded, or positively reinforced, for such behavior. Janet's laughter and obvious amusement would be examples of such positive reinforcement. Other theorists might suggest that Todd had learned to be comical by observing the behavior of other humorous people.

The two psychological approaches that might offer such explanations are, respectively, behaviorism and social-learning theory. Both are branches of a broader school of psychological thought called the learning approach.

Behaviorism

John B. Watson claimed that external forces or influences—not internal influences such as traits or inner conflict—largely shape people's preferences and behavior (Watson, 1924). In the 1930s, Watson's approach was taken up by B. F. Skinner. Skinner agreed that we should pay attention to how organisms behave and avoid trying to see within people's minds. Skinner also emphasized the effects of reinforcement on behavior (Skinner, 1938). (See Chapter 6.)

Adolescence (13-18)	Young adulthood (19-30)	Middle adulthood	Late adulthood
Identity versus role diffusion	Intimacy versus isolation	Generativity versus stagnation	Integrity versus despair
Connecting skills and social roles to formation of career objectives	Committing the self to another; engaging in sexual love	Needing to be needed; guiding and encouraging the younger generation; being creative	Accepting the timing and placing of one's own life cycle; achieving wisdom and dignity

Most of us assume that our wants originate within us. But Watson and Skinner largely discarded ideas of personal freedom, choice, and self-direction. Skinner suggested that environmental influences, such as parental approval and social custom, condition or shape us into wanting some things and not wanting others. **Socialization** is the process by which people learn the socially desirable behaviors of their particular culture and adopt them as part of their personalities.

In his 1948 novel, *Walden Two,* Skinner described a utopian (or ideal) society in which people are happy and content because every member of the society contributes to, and receives the benefits of, the society. They have been socialized from early childhood to help other people and society at large. Because of childhood socialization, people in the fictional community want to be decent, kind, and unselfish. They see their actions as a result of their own free will. According to Skinner, however, no one is really free. We may think of ourselves as being free because we can go after what we want and get it. But, Skinner said, society shapes us into wanting what is good for society at an early age.

It is not true that all psychologists believe that humans possess the free will to make their own choices in life. Behaviorists believe that a person's actions and choices are shaped by environmental influences and cultural factors, such as socialization.

Social-Learning Theory

Social-learning theory is a contemporary view of learning that is advocated by Albert Bandura and other psychologists. Social-learning theorists focus on the importance of learning by observation and on the role of the cognitive processes that produce individual differences (Bandura, 1986).

Unlike behaviorists, who believe that people are at the mercy of their environment, social-learning theorists argue that people can act intentionally to influence the environment. To behaviorists, learning is the mechanical result of reinforcement. To social-learning theorists, on the other hand, people engage in purposeful learning. Individuals seek to learn about their environment and have a certain degree of control over reinforcement. Observational learning extends to reading about others or watching them in media such as television and film.

According to social-learning theorists, behavior is not based solely on what is learned from observation. Internal variables also influence how we act in certain situations. These internal factors include the following:

- *Skills:* Skills include a person's physical and social abilities.
- *Values:* The value we put on the outcome of a certain behavior affects how we act. For example, if you value good grades, you will study.
- *Goals:* We regulate ourselves by setting goals. Once the goal is set, we plan the most effective way to achieve it.
- *Expectations:* Expectations are predictions of what will happen in certain situations.

Many behavior theorists believe that environmental factors, such as parental approval, condition us to exhibit certain behaviors and not others.

- *Self-efficacy expectations,* a term coined by Bandura (1989), refers to beliefs people have about themselves. For example, if you believe that you are a good public speaker, you will be motivated to speak before the class assembly. People with high self-efficacy expectations are also more likely to persist at difficult tasks.

Evaluation of the Learning Approach

Learning theorists—particularly behaviorists—believe that by emphasizing the importance of monitoring observable behaviors, psychology will be more accepted as a science. Learning theorists have also examined the conditions that promote learning. They have shown that we learn to do things because of reinforcements. We acquire many broad behavior patterns by observing others. Learning theorists have also devised methods for helping individuals solve psychological problems that probably would not have been derived from other theoretical approaches. (See Chapter 19.)

On the other hand, behaviorism and social-learning theory are limited in their ability to explain personality. Behaviorism does not acknowledge the richness of inner human experience, much less try to describe or explain it. Social-learning theory gives more weight to the importance of mental processes and feelings. But it has not been much more successful than behaviorism in explaining traits or personality types.

THINKING ABOUT PSYCHOLOGY

1. According to behaviorism, what is the main influence on how people act?

2. Many students strive to get good grades. How would social-learning theorists explain this behavior? Would behaviorists explain it differently?

3. **Critical Thinking**   Do you agree with the behaviorist view that true personal freedom does not exist? Why or why not?

4
The Humanistic Approach

Behaviorists argue that psychologists should not attempt to study self-awareness. Humanists, on the other hand, begin with the assumption that self-awareness is the very core of humanity. They focus on people's pursuits of self-fulfillment and ethical conduct. To humanistic psychologists, people are truly free to do as they choose with their lives. Moreover, because people are free to choose, they are responsible for the choices that they make.

Abraham Maslow

Humanistic psychologist Abraham Maslow (1908–1970) believed that humans are separated from lower animals because they recognize their desire to achieve self-actualization—to reach their full potential. (See Chapter 13.) He also believed that because people are unique, they must follow their own paths to self-actualization. However, accomplishing this requires taking risks. Maslow argued that people who stick to what is tried and true may find their lives boring and predictable. Although Hannah was very close with her friends, she realized that she possessed a unique musical ability. According to Maslow's theory, Hannah's willingness to pursue her talent and her courage to go away to college were factors in her search for self-actualization.

Carl Rogers

Carl Rogers (1902–1987), another advocate of the humanistic approach, believed that people are to some degree the conscious architects of their own personalities. In Rogers' view, people shape their personalities through free choice and action (Rogers, 1961, 1977). Because Rogers's theory revolves around people's sense of self, it is termed *self theory.*

Rogers placed great emphasis on the human ability to derive a **self-concept**, a view of oneself as an individual. He also believed that the self is concerned with recognizing one's values and establishing a sense of one's relationships to other people. The self is the center of each person's experience, an ongoing sense of who and what one is. It provides the experience of being human in the world and it is the guiding principle behind both personality and behavior.

The Self-Concept and Congruence

Our self-concepts are made up of our impressions of ourselves and our evaluations of our adequacy. Rogers believed that the key to happiness and healthy adjustment is **congruence**, or consistency between one's self-concept and one's experience. For example, if you consider yourself to be outgoing and friendly, this self-concept will be reinforced if you have good relationships with other people. This will probably lead to feelings of happiness and a sense that your self-concept is accurate. If, however, you have difficulty getting along with others, the inconsistency between your self-concept and your experience will probably cause you to feel anxious or troubled.

Self-Esteem and Positive Regard

Rogers assumed that we all develop a need for self-esteem. Self-esteem is belief in oneself, or self-respect. At first, self-esteem reflects the esteem in which others hold us. As discussed in Chapter 10, parents help children develop self-esteem when they show them unconditional positive regard. Parents show unconditional positive regard when they accept children as they are, regardless of the children's behavior at the moment.

Parents show children conditional positive regard if they accept children only when they behave in a desired manner. Conditional positive regard may lead children to think that they are worthwhile only if they behave in certain ways.

Humanistic psychologists believe that each of us has a unique potential. Therefore, children who think that they are worthwhile only if they behave in certain ways will end up being disappointed in themselves. Humanistic psychologists believe that we cannot fully live up to the wishes of others and also remain true to ourselves.

The expression of the self does not always have to lead to conflict. Rogers was optimistic about human nature. He believed that we hurt others or act in antisocial ways only when we are frustrated in our efforts to develop our potential. When parents and others are loving and tolerant of the ways in which we are different, we, too, are loving.

However, Rogers believed that children in some families learn that it is bad to have ideas of their own, especially about political, religious, or sexual matters. When they perceive their parents' disapproval, they may come to see themselves as rebels and label their feelings as selfish, wrong, or evil. If they wish to retain a consistent self-concept and self-esteem, they may have to deny many of their genuine feelings. They may, in a sense, have to disown parts of themselves.

According to Rogers' theory, the path to self-actualization requires getting in touch with our

Carl Rogers argued that people shape their personalities through free choice and action. He believed that it is important for individuals to recognize their personal values and to establish a sense of their relationships with other people.

PSYCHOLOGY

WATSON AND ROGERS:
At Opposite Ends of the Theory Spectrum

The theories of behaviorist John B. Watson and humanist Carl Rogers are at opposite ends of the theory spectrum. Consider Watson's challenge to the field of psychology in his influential 1924 book, *Behaviorism*:

> *Give me a dozen healthy infants, well-formed, and my own specified world to bring them up in and I'll guarantee to take any one at random and train him to become any type of specialist I might suggest—doctor, lawyer, merchant-chief and, yes, even beggar-man and thief, regardless of his talents, penchants, tendencies, abilities, vocations, and the race of his ancestors. (1924, p. 82)*

With these words, Watson stated the classic behaviorist belief: Regardless of who we think we really are inside, we can be totally molded, or "conditioned," by external pressures. Our belief in individual choice is just an illusion.

Carl Rogers had a very different view of the freedom and dignity of the individual human being. He summarized this view in a 1974 article:

> *My experience in therapy and in groups makes it impossible for me to deny the reality and significance of human choice. To me it is not an illusion that man is to some degree the architect of himself. (1974, p. 119)*

About 10 years before writing this article, Rogers described an experience he had had that helped him confirm his conviction that life is more than a reaction to environmental pressures:

> *During a vacation weekend some months ago I was standing on a headland [piece of ground jutting out over water] overlooking one of the rugged coves which dot the coastline of northern California. Several large rock outcroppings were at the mouth of the cove, and these received the full force of the great Pacific combers [waves] which, beating upon them, broke into mountains of spray before surging into the cliff-lined shore. As I watched the waves breaking over these large rocks in the distance, I noticed with surprise what appeared to be a tiny palm tree on the rocks, no more than two or three feet high, taking the pounding of the breakers. Through my binoculars I saw that these were some type of seaweed, with a slender "trunk" topped off with a head of leaves. . . . In the interval between the waves it seemed clear that this fragile, erect, top-heavy plant would be utterly crushed and broken by the next breaker. When the wave crunched down upon it, the trunk bent almost flat, the leaves were whipped into a straight line by the torrent of the water, yet the moment the wave had passed, here was the plant again, erect, tough, resilient. It seemed incredible that it was able to take this incessant [never-ending] pounding hour after hour, day after night, week after week, for all I know, year after year, and all the time nourishing itself, extending itself, reproducing itself; in short, maintaining and enhancing itself in this process which, in our shorthand, we call growth. Here in this palmlike seaweed was the tenacity of life, the forward thrust of life, the ability to push into an incredibly hostile environment and not only hold its own, but to adapt, develop, become itself. (1963, pp. 1–2)*

Rogers used this vivid metaphor to express the humanist belief that living things, including people, struggle on, attempting in the toughest of conditions to actualize themselves.

Think About It

1. Do you believe that anyone, regardless of ability, can be trained to become, say, a doctor, lawyer, or musician? Why or why not?
2. Do you believe, like Rogers, that each individual takes charge of his or her environment? Explain your answer.

genuine feelings and acting on them. This is the goal of person-centered therapy, Rogers' method of psychotherapy. (See Chapter 19.)

Evaluation of the Humanistic Approach

For most animals, to be alive is to move, to eat, to breathe, and to reproduce. However, humanistic psychologists feel that humans are not merely animals. They believe that for human beings, an essential aspect of life is conscious experience—the sense of one's self as progressing through space and time. Humanists grant consciousness a key role in our daily lives. This focus on conscious experience is one reason that humanistic theories have tremendous popular appeal.

Another reason for their popularity is that they stress human freedom. Psychoanalytic theories see us largely as products of our childhoods. Learning theories, to some degree, see us as products of circumstances. Both theories argue that our sense of freedom is merely an illusion. Humanistic theorists, however, say that our freedom is real.

Ironically, the primary strength of the humanistic theories—their focus on conscious experience—is also their main weakness. Conscious experience is private and subjective. Therefore, some psychologists question the soundness of framing theories in terms of consciousness (Liebert & Spiegler, 1982). Others, however, believe that the science of psychology can afford to relax its methods somewhat if loosening them will help it address the richness of human experience (Bevan & Kessel, 1994).

Critics also note that humanistic theories, like learning theories, have little to say about the development of traits and personality types. Humanistic theorists assume that we are all unique, but they do not predict the sorts of traits, abilities, and interests we will develop.

THINKING ABOUT PSYCHOLOGY

1. Summarize Rogers' concept of congruence, and explain how congruence is related to a person's self-concept.

2. Explain the difference between self-concept and self-esteem.

3. **Critical Thinking** Do you agree with the humanistic view that we cannot remain true to ourselves if we follow the wishes of others? Why or why not?

5
The Sociocultural Approach

A DAY IN THE LIFE
The sociocultural perspective focuses on the roles of ethnicity, gender, and culture in the formation of personality. Hannah was raised by parents who had grown up in Korea. She was also comfortable in an American school with her American friends. Sociocultural theorists would argue that her family and her environmental influences were key factors in the development of Hannah's personality.

Individualism Versus Collectivism

One aspect of culture that sociocultural theorists focus on is the level of individualism or collectivism in a society. Individualism is a trait valued by many people in the United States and in several European nations. Individualists tend to define themselves in terms of their personal identities. They usually give priority to their personal goals. When asked to complete the statement "I am," they are likely to respond in terms of their own personality traits or occupations. For example, they are likely to say, "I am outgoing" or "I am a nurse" (Triandis, 1990).

Collectivists, such as those pictured here, tend to define themselves in terms of the groups to which they belong. They often give priority to the goals of the group over their own individual needs.

The Self in Relation to Others from the Individualist and Collectivist Perspectives

Individualist

Collectivist

FIGURE 14.4 *An individualist sees the self as separate from other people. A collectivist, on the other hand, sees the self as complete only in terms of his or her relationships to other people.*

Based on Markus & Kitayama, 1991.

In contrast, many people from Africa, Asia, and Central and South America tend to be more collectivistic. (See Figure 14.4.) Collectivists tend to define themselves in terms of the groups to which they belong and often give priority to the goals of their group. They feel complete only in terms of their social relationships with others (Markus & Kitayama, 1991). When asked to complete the statement "I am," they are likely to respond in terms of their families, religion, or nation. For example, they are likely to say, "I am a father," "I am a Buddhist," or "I am Japanese" (Draguns, 1988; Triandis, 1994).

The Western capitalist system fosters individualism. It assumes that individuals are entitled to amass personal fortunes if they have the drive and ability to do so. The individualist perspective is found in the self-reliant heroes in Western entertainment—from Clint Eastwood's gritty cowboys to the character Belle in the Disney film *Beauty and the Beast.* The traditional writings of many non-Western cultures, on the other hand, have praised people who put the well-being of the group ahead of their personal ambitions.

There are, of course, conflicting ideals—as well as individual differences—within cultures. In the United States, for example, children are taught to share with other children as well as to be "Number

One." But on the whole, the contrast between the individualist Western world and the more collectivist nations of other parts of the world is a reliable measure of some general differences between individuals from these regions.

Sociocultural Factors and the Self

According to sociocultural theorists, sociocultural factors also affect the self-concept and self-esteem of the individual. Carl Rogers noted that our self-concepts tend to reflect how we believe other people see us. Members of ethnic groups who have been subjected to discrimination and poverty may have poorer self-concepts and lower self-esteem than people who have not experienced discrimination and poverty (Greene, 1993; Lewis-Fernández & Kleinman, 1994). Similarly, members of ethnic groups that have traditionally held power in society are likely to have a positive sense of self because they share in the expectations of personal achievement and respect that are typically given to members of such groups.

In some cases, however, things are not so simple. Many women in the United States, particularly White women, are unhappy with their appearance. This is because the current media ideal is found in female models who are on average 9 percent taller and 16 percent slimmer than the average woman in the United States (Williams, 1992). But a survey by the American Association of University Women (1992) found that African American girls are likely to be happier with their appearances than White girls are. Sixty-five percent of African American elementary schoolgirls said they were happy with the way they were, as compared with 55 percent of White girls. Among high school students, 58 percent of African American girls remained happy with the way they were, as compared with only 22 percent of White girls.

How do sociocultural theorists explain this difference? It appears that African American girls are taught that there is nothing wrong with them if they do not match the ideals of the majority culture. They come to believe that if the world treats them negatively, it is because of prejudice, not because of who they really are or what they do (Williams, 1992). White girls, on the other hand, may be more likely to look inward and blame themselves for not attaining the unreachable ideal.

Acculturation and Self-Esteem

Personalities are influenced by more than personal traits and learning experiences. They are also influenced by cultural settings. Hannah belonged to a traditional Korean family. At school, however, she was exposed daily to values that are in some ways unique to the United States.

Acculturation is the process of adapting to a new or different culture. People who immigrate to the United States undergo acculturation. If they come from Africa, Asia, or Latin America, they are likely to find that differences in language are only the tip of the iceberg of cultural differences.

Acculturation takes various patterns. Some immigrants become completely assimilated, or absorbed, into the culture of the area to which they move. They may stop using both the language and customs of their country of origin. Others choose to maintain separation. They retain the language and customs of their country of origin and never become completely comfortable with those of their adopted country. Still others become bicultural. That is, they successfully integrate both sets of customs and values.

Research suggests that people who are bicultural have the highest self-esteem (Phinney et al., 1992).

For example, Mexican Americans who are fluent in English are more likely to be emotionally stable than Mexican Americans who do not speak English as well (Salgado de Snyder et al., 1990). Adopting the ways of the new society without giving up a supportive cultural tradition and a sense of ethnic identity apparently helps people function most effectively. According to the sociocultural approach, Hannah's musical and educational success and her high self-esteem may have been results of her ability to balance her Korean heritage with her cultural surroundings in the United States.

TRUTH OR fiction ■ REVISITED ■ It is true that psychologists feel that culture, gender, and ethnicity are important in personality development. Sociocultural theorists believe that all of these factors contribute in some way to the development of personality.

Evaluation of the Sociocultural Approach

The sociocultural perspective provides valuable insights into the roles of ethnicity, gender, culture, and socioeconomic status in personality formation. Sociocultural factors are external forces that are internalized and affect all of us. They run through us deeply, touching many aspects of our personalities. Without reference to sociocultural factors, we may be able to understand generalities about behavior and mental processes. We cannot, however, understand how individuals think, behave, and feel about themselves within a given cultural setting. The sociocultural perspective also enhances our sensitivity to cultural differences and allows us to appreciate much of the richness of human behavior and mental processes.

THINKING ABOUT PSYCHOLOGY

1. Explain the difference between individualism and collectivism.

2. What is acculturation and how can it affect self-esteem?

3. **Critical Thinking** Why do you think some immigrants become completely assimilated while others retain many of their original customs and values?

SUMMARY

Psychologists use five approaches to explain the development of personality: trait, psychoanalytic, learning, humanistic, and sociocultural.

I. *The Trait Approach*

A. According to the trait approach, an individual's personality traits are fixed from an early age and account for consistent behavior in different situations.

B. Many trait theorists have been involved in identifying and cataloging human traits.
1. Hippocrates believed that personality traits result from combinations of humors, or fluids, in the body.
2. According to Gordon Allport, traits can be inherited and they are fixed in the nervous system.
3. Raymond Cattell identified 16 basic source traits for human personality.
4. Hans Eysenck proposed two personality dimensions: introversion-extroversion and emotional stability-instability.
5. Recent research suggests there may be five basic personality dimensions. These are known as the "big five."

II. *The Psychoanalytic Approach*

A. Sigmund Freud was the originator of the psychoanalytic approach.
1. According to Freud, personality development is influenced by inner conflict, unconscious processes, and defensive responses.
2. According to Freud, a person's inner conflict occurs among the three psychological structures of the mind—the id, ego, and superego. The id demands instant gratification. The superego demands morality. The ego tries to balance the other two structures.
3. Freud organized psychosexual development into five periods: the oral, anal, phallic, latent, and genital stages.

B. Several personality theorists were followers of Freud but emphasized different aspects of personality development than Freud did.
1. Carl Jung explained the collective unconscious and the sense of self.
2. Alfred Adler believed people are driven to overcome inferiority.
3. Karen Horney placed great emphasis on social relationships.
4. Erik Erikson devised an eight-stage theory of psychosocial development that covers the entire life span.

III. *The Learning Approach*

A. According to the learning approach, people's behaviors are learned responses.

B. Learning theories include behaviorism and social-learning theory.
1. Behaviorism teaches that environmental forces shape people's behavior.
2. Social-learning theory focuses on the importance of learning by observation and on the role of the cognitive processes that produce individual differences.

IV. *The Humanistic Approach*

A. According to the humanistic approach, people are free to make conscious choices and are responsible for their choices.

B. Abraham Maslow maintained that people wish to reach their full potential but must follow individual paths to do so.

C. Humanist Carl Rogers developed self theory, which asserts that people have a need for consistency between their self-concepts and their experiences.

V. *The Sociocultural Approach*

A. Sociocultural theory considers the effects of ethnicity, gender, culture, and socioeconomic status on personality development.

B. Sociocultural theorists believe that sociocultural factors affect an individual's self-concept and self-esteem.

TERM & CONCEPT REVIEW

1. Define the term *trait*. Give five examples of personality traits.
2. Explain why psychoanalysis has been called a "talking cure."
3. What is a defense mechanism? Name and give examples of three defense mechanisms.
4. Describe two traits an adult might have, according to the psychoanalytic theory of personality, if he or she experienced conflict during the anal stage of development.
5. According to Carl Jung, what is the difference between a personal unconscious and the collective unconscious? Give an example of each.
6. Explain Alfred Adler's concept of inferiority complex and Karen Horney's theory of basic anxiety.
7. How does Erik Erikson's view of the stages of development differ from that of Freud?
8. How are behaviorism and social learning theory similar? How are they different?
9. Give examples of behaviors that would indicate whether a person was more individualistic or collectivistic.
10. Define the term *acculturation*. Briefly describe the three basic patterns of acculturation.

CRITICAL THINKING

1. Describe situations in which an awareness of your own traits and abilities might help you make important decisions.
2. According to Freud, the mind has an id, an ego, and a superego. What do you think would happen to our society if people's minds had an id but not an ego or a superego?
3. Which do you think has a greater effect on people's behavior: the socialization we receive as children (nurture) or the natural instincts and feelings we are simply born with (nature)?

4. Do you agree with Rogers that people act in antisocial ways only when they are frustrated in trying to develop their potential? Give examples to illustrate your opinion.
5. Although people in the United States are generally considered to be individualists, they may also be collectivists at times. For example, we may think of ourselves as members of a team. Describe two positive and two negative aspects of individualism and of collectivism.

APPLYING SKILLS IN PSYCHOLOGY

1. **COOPERATIVE LEARNING** **Writing About Psychology** With a classmate, write a skit that shows someone using one of the defense mechanisms mentioned in the chapter. Act out your skit for the class, and have students guess which defense mechanism you are portraying. As a class, discuss situations in which defense mechanisms might be helpful and times when they might be harmful.
2. **Research in Psychology** List as many personality traits as you can think of. Include both positive and negative traits. Make five copies of your list. Give a copy to a parent, brother or sister, best friend, teacher, neighbor, or other person you feel knows you well. Have the five people circle the traits they think describe you. Compare the lists. Which traits are the same from list to list? Which traits are different? What might account for the differences? How can being aware of your personality traits help you? Write a summary of your findings.
3. **Using Your Observation Skills.** Visit a preschool or kindergarten classroom. Look for ways the teacher tries to instill self-esteem in the children. Write down examples of activities and routines, teacher-child interactions, and features of the classroom environment (bulletin boards, books). Share your examples with your classmates, and discuss the role of self-esteem in personality development.

15 PSYCHOLOGICAL TESTS

Objectives

1 List the purpose and characteristics of psychological tests.

2 Explain how achievement tests, aptitude tests, and interest inventories are used.

3 Identify the two kinds of personality tests, and discuss their uses.

4 Identify strategies for taking tests and ways to avoid test anxiety.

A DAY IN THE LIFE

Marc and Todd were meeting Dan in the library to study for a history test. When they found him, he was reading something intently.

"Hi, Dan. What are you reading?" Todd asked curiously.

"Oh, hi, guys," Dan answered. "I met with the guidance counselor, Mr. Hochberg, yesterday because I'm still having trouble figuring out what I want to do after high school. He asked me to take some tests, and now I'm trying to make sense of the results."

"Don't we take enough tests in school already?" Marc asked.

"These weren't *regular* school tests. Some tested my interests, and others looked at my aptitudes."

"I took some of those tests last year," Todd said. "I'd always known that I liked studying living things, but Mr. Hochberg showed me types of jobs I could pursue if I really took my biology courses seriously."

"So, Dan, what did your tests show?" Marc asked.

"Well, according to one of these tests, I have good communication skills and relate well to people. Both of those qualities are listed under guidance counselor and teacher."

"Guys, we really should start studying for this history test," Todd reminded them.

Suddenly Marc looked panicked. "I wish you hadn't reminded me."

"What's wrong?" Todd asked.

"I just don't like taking tests," Marc answered. "I get so nervous, and no matter how much I study, I always seem to draw a blank when I actually sit down to take the test."

"No one likes tests," Dan said.

"But I think I get more upset than most people. I know it's weird, but sometimes I get so nervous that I can't even think straight, even if I've studied enough."

Todd looked rather concerned about his friend. "Why don't you try talking to your teachers or maybe even to Mr. Hochberg? They might at least be able to give you some advice about how to study or how to concentrate during the actual test."

"I guess it's worth a try."

• • •

As Dan discovered, there are many different kinds of psychological tests. In Chapter 9, you learned about one kind of psychological test: intelligence tests. The psychological tests that will be discussed in this chapter are achievement tests, aptitude and interest tests, and personality tests.

Tests to determine how much students have learned are called achievement tests. Mr. Hochberg gave Dan a test for special aptitudes and interests to find out whether he is suited for certain occupations.

There are also tests that identify the psychological traits that make up a person's personality. Therefore, tests that measure psychological traits are also known as personality tests. Personality tests measure almost every known personality trait. Some tests measure a dozen or more traits at one time.

Key Terms

- behavior-rating scale
- self-report
- standardized test
- validity scale
- norm
- norm group
- achievement test
- aptitude test
- vocational interest inventories
- forced-choice format
- objective test
- projective test
- open-ended format
- cognitive restructuring

Read the following statements about psychology. Do you think they are true or false? You will learn whether each statement is true or false as you read the chapter.

- Psychologists can always tell whether a person has told the truth on a personality test.
- Some tests measure only aptitude.
- Psychologists agree that the Rorschach inkblot test is a reliable method for determining psychological health.
- You should always go with your first guess on a multiple-choice test.
- The longer your answer to an essay question, the better your score on that question is likely to be.

1
What Are Psychological Tests?

Psychological tests assess abilities, feelings, attitudes, and behaviors. The responses a person gives on test items help psychologists predict a person's future behavior.

Psychological tests are hardly a new invention. It appears that over 2,500 years ago, during the Golden Age of Greece, people were selected for government service on the basis of psychological tests (Matarazzo, 1990). Those early tests measured physical as well as mental abilities. Evidence also suggests that psychological tests were used to select civil service employees some 2,000 years ago in China (Bowman, 1989). The Chinese tests measured verbal and mathematical abilities as well as knowledge of law and geography.

Modern researchers have been using various types of psychological tests for about 100 years. Francis Galton, James Cattell, Alfred Binet, and other psychologists began constructing modern psychological tests in the late 1800s.

Uses of Psychological Tests

Psychological tests are used to help people make important decisions. Tests can help indicate whether a person is suited for a certain line of work, for a particular class in school, or for medication to

reduce agitation (Saccuzzo, 1994). Intelligence tests are often used to indicate whether children are likely to profit from special kinds of educational experiences. The Standard Assessment Test (SAT) is used to help determine whether students are likely to succeed in college. As part of their admissions process, college admissions personnel also often ask high school teachers and guidance counselors to rate applicants on scales that measure such traits as willingness to work hard and cooperativeness.

More specialized tests are used to measure students' prospects for success in graduate schools such as business schools, law schools, and medical schools. Law schools use the Law School Admissions Test (LSAT). Similarly, medical schools use the Medical College Admissions Test (MCAT).

Some psychological tests measure behavior directly. For example, **behavior-rating scales** are used to measure behavior in such places as classrooms and hospitals. With behavior-rating scales, trained observers may check off each occurrence of a specific behavior within a certain amount of time, say, 15 minutes. For example, an observer might count how many times a person gestures while talking to someone else. This might be a measure of how outgoing the person is.

Most psychological tests, however, rely on people's **self-reports**. That is, people are asked to report their attitudes, feelings, and behavior in interviews or on paper-and-pencil tests.

Features of Psychological Tests

Psychological tests are sometimes frightening for the test takers and sometimes misleading for the evaluators. Tests such as the SAT can be particularly frightening because the results on a test taken on one day can seem nearly as important as the grades earned over several years. The results can be misleading because a person may be ill or distracted on the day of the test and not perform as well as he or she might on another day.

For a psychological test to be useful and reasonably accurate, it has to have certain features, or characteristics. It has to be standardized, it has to show reliability and validity, and it has to have norms for scoring.

Standardization A **standardized test** is one that is administered and scored the same way every time. Psychologists and educators are trained in how to administer and score standardized tests accurately. For example, the two most widely used

Some psychological tests measure behavior directly by means of behavior-rating scales. With these scales, trained observers count the number of times a specific behavior occurs in a certain amount of time. For example, an observer might count how many times a person gestures during a conversation.

their problems on personality tests as a way to get attention. In addition, people may answer in the way they think is "correct," even if there are no objectively right or wrong answers. To avoid such distortion, some psychological tests have validity scales built into them.

Validity scales involve questions that, if answered in a certain way, let the psychologist know that the test taker is not answering the test questions honestly. Validity scales always depend on the answers to many interlinking questions. For example, there may be several test items on which a psychologist would expect to see a pattern of similar answers. If no such pattern is found, those answers, taken together, may indicate that the test taker is not answering the questions honestly. Validity scales are often quite helpful. However, they are not foolproof.

intelligence tests, the Stanford-Binet and Wechsler intelligence tests, are given individually. All test administrators are trained to ask the same questions in the same way. They also receive training in how to score the tests and interpret those scores.

Other tests, such as the SAT, are given to thousands of students at a time. All students receive the same instructions, and computers grade most of the answers. Essay questions on a standardized test are not graded by a computer. However, instructions for administrators on how to score essay questions are very clear and precise. This helps ensure that the same criteria will be used to score essay questions regardless of who is doing the scoring.

Reliability and Validity   In Chapter 9, you learned that the *reliability* of a measure is its consistency. That is, an individual's score on a test should be the same or very nearly the same every time the individual takes that test. Test-retest reliability is demonstrated when a person receives similar scores on the same test taken on different occasions. *Validity* refers to the extent to which a test measures what it is intended to measure and predicts what it is intended to predict.

Test results can be distorted when people answer in ways they think will please the interviewer. People have also been known to exaggerate

TRUTH OR fiction
■ R E V I S I T E D ■

It is not true that psychologists can always tell whether a person has told the truth on a personality test. Validity scales help, but they cannot indicate with certainty whether a test taker has answered questions honestly.

In general, the tests you take in your classes are not psychological tests, and most are not constructed scientifically. Still, these tests should also be reliable and valid. Generally speaking, the longer a test is, the more valid it is. (Would you rather have your grade on a math test depend on solving just one problem, or would you prefer it to be based on your solutions to 10 or 20 problems?) Marc

believes that the scores he receives on tests he takes in class are often not a valid measure of what he knows. He argues that the tests do not really measure what he has learned because his nervousness interferes with his ability to perform well.

Would You Tell Your Problems to a Computer?

Imagine you have been feeling tense lately and are wondering what is causing the tension. You decide to consult a psychologist. When you arrive at the psychologist's office, you are instructed to sit in a room with a computer that asks you several personal questions.

The fact is that computers have been "interviewing" people for more than 20 years. One computer program currently in use for this purpose is CASPER. CASPER stands for Computerized Assessment System for Psychotherapy Evaluation and Research. A CASPER interview lasts about 30 minutes. CASPER explores a wide variety of topics, including family relationships, social activities, overall life satisfaction, and specific behavior patterns that may be suggestive of physical and psychological disorders.

A CASPER interview

Questions and possible responses are displayed on the monitor. To answer a question, the test taker presses a number on the computer keyboard. CASPER then follows up with additional questions. For example, if you report difficulty sleeping, CASPER will inquire whether sleep has become a key problem. CASPER asks whether the sleep problem is "something causing you great personal distress or interfering with your daily functioning" (Farrell et al., 1987). If the answer is yes, the computer will explore further by asking more questions.

How well do people like being interviewed by a computer? Research shows that people find the computer program user-friendly. They also find that they are able to complete CASPER interviews with little difficulty. In fact, most people like the computerized interview (Bloom, 1992; Farrell et al., 1987). This is especially true for younger, better-educated people who are experienced with computers (Spinhoven et al., 1993).

People also seem to report more problems to CASPER than they do to a real, live psychologist. Why? Some people seem to prefer "speaking" with an impersonal computer to speaking with a person, who might disagree with or judge them.

Computer diagnostic programs apparently offer some advantages over human interviewers (Farrell et al., 1987):

- Standardization seems to be easier and more consistent. Computers can be programmed to ask specific questions in a prescribed sequence.
- People may be less embarrassed about reporting personal matters to a computer. Computers do not appear to respond to them emotionally or judgmentally.
- Use of the computer for purposes of diagnosis frees clinicians to spend more of their time doing psychotherapy.

As computer programs become able to handle larger amounts of information, they are also likely to become more accurate at diagnosis and better able to identify unusual problems. Because of its memory, a computer can also easily connect a person's complaints to similar cases and make the choice of treatment easier for the therapist.

A review of the research in computer diagnosis suggests that some computer programs are as capable of obtaining pertinent information from a client and arriving at an accurate diagnosis as trained clinicians (Bloom, 1992). Computer programs seem to be the wave of the future. As we enter the 21st century, sophisticated diagnostic and treatment programs are being developed.

Think About It

What possible problems do you think might occur with computer diagnosis and treatment?

Norms Psychological tests are usually scored by comparing an individual's score to the norm. **Norms** are established standards of performance. They are designed to tell test administrators which scores are average, high, or low.

Norms for a test are usually established by administering the test to a large group of people who are similar to those for whom the test is intended. This group of test takers is called the **norm group**.

Imagine you are asked to create a psychological test for elementary school students. Of course, such a test would not be the same as a test for adults. Tests for children need to ask questions appropriate to the age of the children. Once you had created the test, you would establish the norm by administering the test to thousands of elementary school students of the same age or grade level. This would be your norm group. The average score of the norm group would become the norm for that particular test, and the scores of all other children taking the test in the future would be compared to that norm.

THINKING ABOUT PSYCHOLOGY

1. What is a standardized test?
2. What is a norm group?
3. **Critical Thinking** Explain the importance of reliability and validity in standardized tests.

2
Measuring Achievement, Abilities, and Interests

Achievement tests, aptitude tests, and tests of interests are all closely related. Most of the tests that you have taken in your classes at school have probably been achievement tests. There are also tests that measure people's abilities, or aptitudes. Still other tests help people identify their interests. Dan and his friends had been taking achievement tests for many years. Then, when Dan was having difficulty deciding on a college major, Mr. Hochberg focused on testing Dan's abilities and interests.

Achievement Tests

Achievement tests measure people's skills and the knowledge they have in specific academic areas.

Achievement tests are given to most elementary and middle school students every year to assess basic skills such as reading and math.

A DAY IN THE LIFE

The history test Dan, Marc, and Todd were studying for was an achievement test. Throughout elementary and middle school, most students' basic skills are tested every year. They are tested in science, reading, math, and many other subject areas.

In high school, most students are tested repeatedly on their achievements in each of their courses. Factors such as intelligence and motivation play a role in achievement but so does learning. For example, it should come as no surprise that students taking Spanish will have higher scores on a Spanish achievement test than students who are not taking Spanish, even though they may be equal in intelligence and motivation.

College students who wish to go to graduate school may be required to take standardized achievement tests in their major field of study—Spanish, political science, math, or psychology, for example. The tests are designed to determine whether the students have enough knowledge in the specific area to succeed in graduate school.

Aptitude Tests

Achievement tests measure a narrow range of skills. Intelligence tests, on the other hand, measure overall learning ability. Aptitude tests fall somewhere in

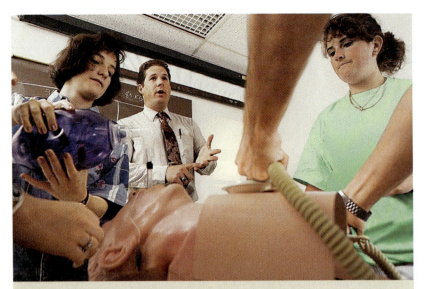

The Medical College Admissions Test (MCAT) is an aptitude test that can help predict how well students will do in medical school. Aptitude tests are broader than intelligence tests but narrower than achievement tests.

on achievements in English (or the language in which the individual takes the test).

Moreover, the SAT consists of verbal and quantitative parts. The verbal sections rely heavily on vocabulary—that is, knowledge of the meaning of words. The quantitative part relies heavily on mathematical knowledge. Skill in these areas—knowledge of vocabulary and mathematics—depends on the amount one has learned or achieved. However, because performance on the SAT does not depend on one specific course, the SAT used to be called the Scholastic *Aptitude* Test. Recently, however, in recognition of the role that achievement plays in the SAT, the test has been renamed the Standard *Assessment* Test.

It may be that there is no such thing as a "pure" aptitude test. All aptitude tests rely on some kind of prior achievement.

between. Aptitude tests measure more specific abilities or skills than intelligence tests but broader ones than achievement tests. **Aptitude tests** are generally used to determine whether a person is likely to do well in a given field of work or study.

The Standard Assessment Test is a general aptitude test. It is used to predict how well students are likely to do in college. The Law School Admissions Test and the Medical College Admissions Test are more specialized. They help predict how well students will do in law school and medical school, respectively. For example, success in medical school depends heavily on the ability to understand chemistry and biology. Therefore, the MCAT has many questions relating to these subjects.

Distinguishing Between Achievement and Aptitude

Sometimes it is difficult to distinguish between an achievement test and an aptitude test. Aptitude tests are intended to measure potential for learning in a specific area, such as algebra or a foreign language. An aptitude test is usually administered to a person before that person has had any training in a specific area. It is used to predict how well the person will do in that area after receiving training. However, current abilities and future success are often based on past achievements. For example, the SAT is intended to measure general ability to do well in college, but it is given in specific languages. Therefore, the ability to do well on the SAT depends

TRUTH OR fiction ▪ REVISITED ▪

It is not true that some tests measure only aptitude. All aptitude tests rely on some kind of achievement. In recognition of this fact, the Scholastic Aptitude Test has been renamed the Standard Assessment Test.

Vocational Interest Inventories

A DAY IN THE LIFE

When Dan was having difficulty deciding what to do after high school, Mr. Hochberg gave him some tests to help him figure out what his interests are. People usually perform better in jobs that interest them. Moreover, people who share interests with people who are successful in a given job are also more likely to succeed in that job. Thus, many psychologists and educators use **vocational interest inventories** to help people determine whether their interests are similar to those of people in various lines of work. Two widely used interest inventories are the Kuder Preference Record and the Strong-Campbell Interest Inventory.

Kuder Preference Record Mr. Hochberg may have given Dan a test called the Kuder Preference Record. This test has a **forced-choice format**, which means that the test taker is forced to choose one of the answers, even if none of them seems to fit his or her interests precisely. For example, test takers are asked to indicate which of a group of activities they like most, and which they like least. They are not allowed to answer "none of the above."

The Kuder asks test takers to choose between activities such as the following:
a. hiking in the forest
b. giving someone advice
c. playing a musical instrument
The results are scored to show how much the person appears to be interested in areas such as science, music, art, literature, outdoor work, mechanics, and so on.

Strong-Campbell Interest Inventory
People taking the Kuder test can see where their interests lie and which areas they might want to look into for employment opportunities. Obviously, a person who repeatedly indicates a preference for music-related activities is showing a definite interest in music. The Strong-Campbell Interest Inventory is not as obvious or direct. It includes many different kinds of items.

The Strong-Campbell compares the test taker's interests with the interests of people who enjoy and are successful in various kinds of work. For example, if most successful accountants enjoy reading and solving puzzles, then a test taker who indicates these same preferences might also be a successful accountant. Therefore, the content of the test question itself may not be as important as the combinations of interests the test taker shares with people in certain occupations.

Evaluation of Interest Inventories
Interest inventories are of great value to students such as Dan who do not have specific career goals. There are over 20,000 different occupations in the United States, and the task of trying to select one can be overwhelming to people who are unclear about their interests. Interest inventories can help point people in a direction they might find fulfilling.

On the other hand, interest in an area does not necessarily mean that one has the ability, or aptitude, to succeed in that area. Therefore, it is usually desirable to make vocational choices on the basis of one's abilities as well as one's interests.

No important life decisions should be made on the basis of a single psychological test. Tests provide only one source of information about an individual, and no test is perfectly reliable. Teachers' and counselors' personal knowledge of an individual should also be taken into account. People may also believe that the result of a single test may not be an accurate reflection of who they are.

Dan was pleased with the outcome of his interest test because it seemed to fit his own image of himself. If his test results had seemed wrong to him, it would be unwise for him to follow the directions suggested by the test results. For example, suppose the test showed that Dan likes outdoor activities, which suggests a career that includes working outdoors. Dan enjoys hiking and boating

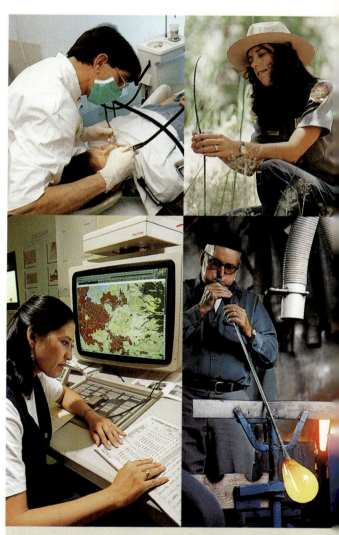

The vast number of occupations available in the United States can make it difficult to know which to pursue. Vocational interest inventories are often used to help people narrow down their career possibilities.

occasionally, but he also knows that he would dislike having to work outside all day and every day. He would have to carefully consider the test results in light of what he knows about himself. Taking additional interest tests might provide a clearer picture of the kind of career he would enjoy.

THINKING ABOUT PSYCHOLOGY

1. What is the difference between an achievement test and an aptitude test?
2. What is the purpose of vocational interest inventories?
3. **Critical Thinking** Why do you think vocational interest inventories use a forced-choice format rather than allow people to answer as they wish?

3
Personality Tests

An individual's personality consists of his or her characteristics, habits, preferences, and moods. Psychologists use personality tests to describe and measure various aspects of people's personalities. Sometimes, they also use personality tests to help diagnose psychological problems and disorders. There are two kinds of personality tests: objective tests and projective tests.

Objective Tests

Objective tests present test takers with a standardized group of test items in the form of a questionnaire. The Minnesota Multiphasic Personality Inventory (MMPI) and the California Psychological Inventory (CPI), discussed below, are examples of objective personality tests. Sometimes test takers are limited to a specific choice of answers—true or false, for example. Sometimes test takers are asked to select the preferred answer from groups of three. In either case, though, the test takers must choose from a list of answers provided for them.

Minnesota Multiphasic Personality Inventory
The MMPI is the psychological test most widely used in clinical work (Helmes & Reddon, 1993; Watkins et al., 1995) and in research that requires measurement of personality traits. First developed in the 1930s and 1940s, the MMPI was intended for

The results of the MMPI-2 can alert a psychologist to the possibility that the test taker may be suffering from a psychological disorder such as depression. Most psychologists believe that the MMPI-2 scores should be supplemented and confirmed by interviews and observation.

use by clinical and counseling psychologists to help diagnose psychological disorders. (See Chapter 18.) A revised version of the test (the MMPI-2) was released in 1989.

The MMPI-2 contains 567 items presented in a true-false format. Psychologists can score the MMPI-2 by hand, but they usually score it by computer. Computers generate reports by comparing the individual's score to group norms stored in the computer's memory. While the computer is certainly an objective (unbiased) scorer, most psychologists believe that the scores should be supplemented and confirmed by interviews and observation.

The MMPI-2 is organized into 10 clinical scales and 4 validity scales. The clinical scales reveal psychological problems. (Figure 15.1 describes the specific disorders the clinical scales of the MMPI-2 assess.) They also indicate whether people have stereotypical "masculine" or "feminine" interests and whether they are outgoing or shy.

To create the clinical scales of the MMPI, the designers interviewed people who had already been diagnosed with various psychological disorders. A test-item bank of several hundred items was derived from questions often asked in clinical interviews.

Commonly Used Validity and Clinical Scales of the Revised Minnesota Multiphasic Personality Inventory (MMPI-2)

	Scale	Abbreviation	Possible Interpretations
Validity Scales	Question	?	Corresponds to number of items left unanswered
	Lie	L	Lies or is highly conventional
	Frequency	F	Exaggerates complaints or answers items haphazardly
	Correction	K	Denies problems
Clinical Scales	Hypochondriasis	Hs	Has bodily concerns and complaints
	Depression	D	Is depressed, guilty; has feelings of guilt and helplessness
	Hysteria	Hy	Reacts to stress by developing physical symptoms; lacks insight
	Psychopathic deviate	Pd	Is immoral, in conflict with the law; has stormy relationships
	Masculinity/femininity	Mf	High scores suggest interests and behavior patterns considered stereotypical of the other gender
	Paranoia	Pa	Is suspicious and resentful, highly cynical about human nature
	Psychasthenia	Pt	Is anxious, worried, high-strung
	Schizophrenia	Sc	Is confused, disorganized, disoriented; has bizarre ideas
	Hypomania	Ma	Is energetic, restless, active, easily bored
	Social introversion	Si	Is introverted, timid, shy; lacks self-confidence

FIGURE 15.1 *The MMPI-2 is the most widely used psychological test in clinical work. Although originally intended for use by psychologists to diagnose psychological disorders, it has now become the most widely used instrument of personality measurement in psychological research. This list describes the specific disorders that the MMPI-2 typically assesses.*

Here are some of the true-false items:

My father was a good man. **T F**
I am seldom troubled by headaches. **T F**
My hands and feet are usually warm enough. **T F**
I have never done anything dangerous for the thrill of it. **T F**
I work under a great deal of tension. **T F**

People with various psychological disorders, such as depression or schizophrenia, will answer certain questions in predictable ways. For example, a person suffering from depression might answer "true" to such questions as "I often feel sad for no reason" or "Sometimes I think life simply isn't worth living." These test items are then placed on scales to measure the presence of psychological disorders in other people. If a person taking the test answers the questions in ways that are similar to people who are known to have a particular psychological disorder, the psychologist administering the test is alerted to the possible presence of that disorder.

The validity scales are designed to detect distorted answers, misunderstood items, or an uncooperative test taker. For example, people with high "T" scores may answer questions in a way that makes them seem excessively moral or well behaved. Such people might answer the item "I never get angry" with "true." People with high "F" scores have a tendency to exaggerate complaints, or they may be trying to get attention by giving seemingly bizarre answers. (See Figure 15.1.)

However, there are questions concerning the usefulness of the validity scales (Helmes & Reddon, 1993). For example, people with serious psychological disorders may indeed see the world in an unusual way. Therefore, if they obtain high F-scale scores, it may be because of their problems and not because they are exaggerating their situation.

California Psychological Inventory   Because the MMPI-2 was designed to diagnose and classify psychological disorders, some psychologists prefer not to use it to measure the personality traits of "normal" clients. Many of these psychologists instead use the California Psychological Inventory, or CPI. The format of the CPI is similar to that of the MMPI-2, but it is designed to measure 15 "normal" personality traits, such as dominance, sociability, responsibility, and tolerance.

In many ways, the CPI is a much more valid instrument than the MMPI-2, even though it is not as widely used. The norm group for the CPI (13,000 people) is much larger than that for the

MMPI (2,600 people), and greater care was taken in controlling for factors such as age, socioeconomic status, and geographical location. Furthermore, the CPI has a much higher test-retest reliability than the MMPI-2 and seems to be a better predictor of such things as school and job success, leadership, and reactions to stress (Ross, 1987).

Projective Tests

Projective tests, unlike objective tests, have no clearly specified answers. Such tests use an **open-ended format**. People are presented with ambiguous stimuli such as inkblots, drawings of vague shapes, or pictures of people engaged in various activities. The test takers are then asked to report what the stimuli represent to them. They might also be asked to tell stories about the stimuli. Since the inkblots or drawings are open to interpretation, it is thought that people's interpretations of the pictures reveal something about their personalities. The Rorschach (ROR-shahk) inkblot test and the Thematic Apperception Test (TAT) are two examples of widely used projective tests.

Rorschach Inkblot Test   Have you heard of a personality test that asks people to tell what a drawing or an inkblot looks like? There are actually a number of such personality tests. The Rorschach inkblot test is the best known of them. The Rorschach is named after its originator, Swiss psychiatrist Hermann Rorschach (1884–1922).

A Rorschach Inkblot

FIGURE 15.2   *While there is no "correct" response to a Rorschach inkblot, certain answers are more in keeping than others with the features of the blot. What do you see?*

CASE STUDIES
AND OTHER TRUE STORIES

What Personality Type Are You?

Have you ever wondered how you or someone else would classify your personality? Whether you are an extrovert or an introvert? Whether you are logical or emotional?

Many people like to find out about themselves—to identify their characteristics and personalities. One of the most popular tests for that purpose is the Myers-Briggs Type Indicator (MBTI). Isabel Briggs Myers and her mother, Katherine Cook Briggs, began designing a personality test in the 1940s. Their goal was to create an objective test to help employers hire the people who were best suited for particular jobs. Even today, the MBTI is popular in career and business counseling.

The MBTI is based on the personality theory of psychologist Carl Jung, who was one of Sigmund Freud's students. Jung believed that there are different personality types and that how a person acts in certain situations is based on the person's personality type. He also suggested that a person's personality preferences are present early in life and become more apparent as the person matures.

Each year, approximately 2 million people take the MBTI. The MBTI items are in forced-choice format. Typical questions include the following:

1. Which rules you more?
   (a) your head
   (b) your heart
2. At a party, do you
   (a) interact with many, including strangers?
   (b) interact with a few, known to you?

After choosing between (a) and (b) answers for 126 questions, the test taker's preferences are evaluated along four dimensions. The dimensions are extroversion versus introversion (E vs. I); sensation versus intuition (S vs. N) ; thinking versus feeling (T vs. F); and judging versus perceiving (J vs. P). Preferences may be classified as strong, moderate, or weak. The stronger one's preference along a dimension, the more one will exhibit the characteristics of that dimension.

Each preference is characterized by a particular way of seeing, or responding to, situations and other people. For example, extroverted people enjoy interacting with others, while introverted people prefer solitary activities. Intuitive people value creativity, while sensation people prefer practicality. Thinking people prefer to be logical and analytical when making decisions, while the decision-making process for feeling people relies more on interpersonal involvement and subjective values. Judgers typically prefer an environment that is ordered and structured, while perceivers tend to be more flexible and spontaneous.

The total possible combinations add up to 16 types, such as INTJ, ISFP, ESTJ, ENFP, and so on. In theory, each person is one of those 16 types. According to people who support the MBTI's results, how an individual sees the world and how he or she behaves can be predicted on the basis of the person's type.

The MBTI has had its share of criticism. One criticism has been that a person's type does not necessarily stay the same over time. Although Myers, Briggs, and Jung believed that an adult is one type and one type only, that appears to be untrue. The MBTI does not pass the test-retest standards for reliability.

Since the same test taker often obtains different results each time he or she takes the test, the MBTI cannot be considered an accurate predictor of behavior. In addition, the MBTI seems to "label" people in a prejudicial way.

For these and other reasons, a recent National Research Council Report has concluded that the Myers-Briggs Type Indicator is not useful in career counseling programs—at least not until further research proves otherwise.

Think About It

Imagine that you are an employer. Explain why you would or would not use the Myers-Briggs Type Indicator to select prospective employees.

Ironically, Rorschach's nickname as an adolescent was Klex, which means "inkblot" in German (Allison et al., 1988).

Figure 15.2 on page 352 shows a Rorschach inkblot. If you were taking the test, a psychologist would hand you a card with the inkblot and ask you what it looks like or what it could be. Because the Rorschach is a projective test, there is no list of clearly defined answers from which to choose. Instead, test takers provide their own responses to each inkblot. However, some answers are more in keeping than others with the features of the blot.

Look again at Figure 15.2. It could be a bat or a flying insect. It also could be an animal with a pointed face. It could be a jack-o'-lantern or many other things. But answers such as "diseased lungs" or "the devil in flames" are not readily suggested by the features of the blot. Therefore, a pattern of responses such as these is more likely than other patterns to suggest the presence of a personality disorder in the test taker.

Many attempts have been made to standardize the Rorschach. People's responses to the cards are usually interpreted according to factors such as location, determinants, content, and form level.

- The location is the part of the blot to which the person responds. Does he or she respond to the whole card or to a detail of the card?
- Determinants include features of the blot such as shading, texture, or color. People who are highly influenced by the texture and color are thought to be more emotional than those who do not focus on these aspects of the blot. Answers that incorporate many features of the blot are thought to reflect high intelligence.
- Content refers to the precise object the test taker reports seeing. Is he or she seeing a bat, a jack-o'-lantern, or a human figure?
- Form level indicates whether the answer is in keeping with the actual shape of the blot. Generally speaking, answers that fit the shape of the blot suggest that the individual sees the world the way most people do. (Some psychological disorders, such as schizophrenia, are characterized by bizarre perceptions.)

Supporters of the Rorschach test claim that it is a rich source of information about people's intelligence, interests, and backgrounds, as well as psychological health. Critics of the Rorschach test argue that no two professionals interpret Rorschach responses in exactly the same way. Therefore, the results are subjective (Sundberg, 1990; Walsh &

Betz, 1990). Questions have been raised about the reliability and validity of the test because of the differences in how the responses are interpreted.

■ ■ ■ ■ ■ ■ ■ ■ ■ ■ ■ ■ ■ ■ ■

TRUTH OR fiction ■ REVISITED ■

It is not true that psychologists agree that the Rorschach inkblot test is a reliable method for determining psychological health. Many psychologists are skeptical about the Rorschach. They argue that the test is not reliable because the results depend too much on the interpretation of the professional giving the test.

■ ■ ■ ■ ■ ■ ■ ■ ■ ■ ■ ■ ■ ■ ■

Thematic Apperception Test The Thematic Apperception Test, or TAT, was developed in the 1930s by psychologist Henry Murray at Harvard University. It is widely used in clinical practice and in motivation research (Watkins et al., 1995).

The TAT consists of drawings such as the one shown in Figure 15.3. These drawings, like the Rorschach inkblots, invite a variety of interpreta-

Thematic Apperception Test (TAT)

FIGURE 15.3 *Like the Rorschach inkblots, the TAT can invite a variety of interpretations. Test takers are asked to create a story for a variety of cards similar to the one pictured. From the responses, trained psychologists can derive achievement motivation scores.*

tions. As with the Rorschach, test takers are given the cards one at a time. They are then asked to create a story for each card. For example, people are asked what might have led to the scene depicted on the card, what the person (or people) in the picture is (are) doing, and how the story will end.

The idea behind the TAT is that people's needs and values emerge from the stories they tell. This can be especially true of attitudes toward other people, such as parents and romantic partners. The TAT is also used to measure achievement motivation. As you learned in Chapter 13, achievement motivation refers to the desire to do one's best and to realize one's goals.

For example, a TAT card may show an image of two women. However, it may be unclear exactly what their connection is. Are they mother and daughter? Do they have a close relationship? Are they friends? Here are two stories that could be told about this card:

Story 1 The mother and daughter are both annoyed. They dislike family gatherings. They have little in common and have nothing to say to one another, so they avoid even making eye contact. They are anxious for the awkward moment to be over.

Story 2 The mother and daughter are enjoying a quiet moment together. As they've gotten older, they don't have as much time to spend with one another. But they've remained close and have shared many special times. They feel lucky to have each other's support and love.

Psychologists are trained to derive attitudes and achievement motivation scores from stories such as these. As you might have guessed, the second story suggests a more positive attitude and achievement motivation than the first story.

THINKING ABOUT PSYCHOLOGY

1. What is the function of the validity scales in the MMPI-2?
2. List the four features of the inkblot that are used to score the Rorschach.
3. **Critical Thinking** Since there are no standardized criteria for scoring answers on projective tests such as the Rorschach and the TAT, how accurate do you think they are? Support your answer.

Studying in a group can often be helpful. Members of the study group can pool their knowledge and take turns quizzing each other.

4
Taking Tests

Many students think, "I know the material from my classes, but I just don't do well on tests." Sometimes they are right. But often they are wrong. When students are sure that they know something but cannot quite retrieve it—when it seems to be on the tip of their tongues—it may be that they did not learn it as well as they think they did. That is, some students have trouble on tests because they do not know the subject matter well enough, or they do not know it as well as they think they know it. For them, much of the cure lies in developing better study habits. (See Chapter 6.)

Some students, however, do know the material and yet they still perform poorly on tests. This section offers some general tips on taking tests, as well as specific ways of coping with certain types of test questions. Finally, the section analyzes the subject of test anxiety.

Tips for Taking Tests

Teachers generally determine the types of tests they give and when they give them. Midterm and final exams are usually a matter of school or department policy. And standardized tests, such as the SAT, are scheduled for certain dates throughout the year. You might think you have little control over the tests you take, but in reality there are many things students can do to help take charge of tests.

Gather Information   Learn where and when the next test will be given. Find out about the types of questions that will be asked and the topics you should study. Most teachers and other test administrators do not mind being asked questions. Some teachers may say that "everything" will be on the test, but others may offer specific information about what they consider important.

In addition, ask students who have already taken the course where test questions tend to come from. Do they tend to come from the textbook or from class notes?

Practice   Plan regular study periods. Use your reading assignments and class notes to create test questions that might be similar to those on the exam. Practice answering these test items with the members of your study group. Define key terms on your practice test. Outline the answers to possible essay questions. Try to answer all the questions and exercises in your textbook—even the ones that were not assigned as homework. Some of them may appear on the test. Even if they do not appear on it, they will provide useful practice.

Make the most of your study group. Pool your knowledge. Quiz one another, and read the answers to your essay questions aloud. This is a good way to prepare yourself for writing the essays on the actual test. In the process, you will probably discover the areas that need further study.

Be Test-Wise   Small oversights can cause you problems on a test. For example, be sure you read the directions carefully and follow them precisely.

Bring the right equipment to tests. Avoid asking your teacher for a pen or a pencil during a test. Doing so communicates a message that you are not prepared for the test and that you do not take the course seriously.

Be sure your pencils are sharpened or that your pens have blue or black ink. Have some loose-leaf paper available, if only to use as scrap paper. Ask your teacher if you may use a pocket dictionary to check your spelling on essays. Teachers may also let you bring calculators and formulas to science tests.

Multiple-Choice Questions

Multiple-choice items are commonly used on many types of tests. They are used in standardized tests such as the SAT, and they are also used in classroom quizzes and exams. Educators and psychologists often use multiple-choice questions because they encourage the student to focus on the right answer (and reject the wrong ones). They can also be graded quickly and objectively.

Below are two sample multiple-choice questions that might appear on a test for this chapter:

1. The Kuder Preference Record is a(n)
   (a) achievement test.
   (b) aptitude test.
   (c) vocational interest inventory.
   (d) personality test.
2. Which of the following tests is an objective personality test?
   (a) the Thematic Apperception Test
   (b) the Minnesota Multiphasic Personality Inventory
   (c) the Standard Assessment Test
   (d) the Rorschach inkblot test

Here are some hints for doing well on multiple-choice tests:

- *Try to answer the question before you look at the choices.* When you see "Kuder Preference Record," turn it into a question: "What is the Kuder Preference Record?" If you can describe the test to yourself, it will be easy to select the correct choice.

- *Consider every possible choice.* The last choice may read "All of the above." If you have time, find a coherent reason for eliminating each choice you reject.

- *Look for answers that are opposites.* When you see two answers that are opposite in meaning, one of them is likely to be the correct choice.

- *Look for the best choice listed.* It may be that no choice is perfect, but one choice is probably better than the others.

- *Mark difficult questions so that you can come back to them later.* Do not let a tough question eat up your time.

- *Guess only when the odds of gaining points outweigh the odds of losing points.* For example, always guess when there is no penalty for wrong answers. But if full credit is subtracted for wrong answers and you have no idea which is the correct choice, do not guess.

- *Change your answer if you think you have made a mistake.* It is only a myth that you should always go with your first hunch. Your first hunch could be wrong, and by looking at the question again, you may come up with the right answer.

For those who suffer from test anxiety, practicing cognitive restructuring can eventually result in better grades. Cognitive restructuring is a four-step process that involves replacing negative, self-defeating thoughts with positive ones.

True-False Questions

True-false questions can be tricky. After all, if half the questions are true and half are false, you could earn a grade of 50 percent simply by guessing. Below are two sample true-false questions that might appear on a test for this chapter:

1. The Minnesota Multiphasic Personality Inventory (MMPI-2) is a subjective personality test used in clinical work.
2. All psychologists consider the Rorschach inkblot test to be a valid measure for determining psychological health.

The following pointers can help you maximize your performance on true-false items:

- *For the item to be true, every part of it must be true.* If one part is false, then the entire item must be false. The question about the MMPI correctly identifies it as a personality test used in clinical work, but it is an objective test, not a subjective test. Therefore, the answer to this question would be "false."

- *Be wary of items that use absolutes such as all, always, or never.* These items are usually false. Since only some, not all, psychologists consider the Rorschach to be a valid measure of psychological health, the answer to the second question would be "false."

- *Items that provide more information and are longer than others tend to be true.*

Keep in mind that these are only rules of thumb, however. They are not foolproof instructions. Your best strategy is still to study thoroughly and know the answers on your own.

Short-Answer Questions

Short-answer items ask the test taker to give a brief response to a question. Here are some sample short-answer questions:

1. What is an achievement test?
2. What is the difference between an objective test and a projective test?

Here are some pointers for responding to short-answer questions:

- *Answer in brief but complete sentences.* For example, the answer to the first question might be phrased as follows: "An achievement test measures a person's skill or knowledge in a specific subject or field of study."

- *Include significant terms in your answer.* In the answer to question 1, the significant terms would include skill, knowledge, subject, and field of study.

- *Use detail if time and space allow.* A detail added to the answer might be the following: "An achievement test is used to determine how much knowledge a person has acquired in a particular subject."

Essay Questions

The first step in answering an essay question is making certain you have understood the question. When students do not understand the question, the answer may draw comments such as the following: "Strays from the question" or "Nicely written, but misses the point."

Guiding Words Found in Essay Questions

Analyze	Identify
Compare	Illustrate
Contrast	Interpret
Criticize	Justify
Define	List
Describe	Prove
Discuss	State
Enumerate	Support
Evaluate	Trace
Explain	

FIGURE 15.4 *The first step in answering an essay question is to make sure that you understand the question. Look for key words such as those in the list above to guide your answer.*

Read the directions carefully, and look for key words to guide your answer. Figure 15.4 lists some of these key words. Ignoring them increases the chances that you will omit important points from your answer.

Before beginning to write your essay, make a quick outline on a piece of scrap paper to help you organize your thoughts. The outline should help you keep track of the main points you wish to make in your answer. Mark where you will start and where you will end. Jot down key terms that represent ideas you wish to expand on in your essay. If you run out of time before you complete the essay, attach the outline to show where you were headed. It may help your grade (and it certainly will not hurt it).

Express your strongest ideas first. When you lead with the concepts you know best, you build a foundation for presenting a strong argument.

How long should your essay be? A good rule of thumb is "Don't count words; just answer the question." Teachers will reward you for being right on the mark as long as you have provided sufficient support for your argument.

It is not true that the longer your answer to an essay question, the better your score on that question is likely to be. Essay questions are graded on how completely and accurately you have covered the main points of the topic, regardless of how long the answer is.

Test Anxiety

Like Marc, some students become anxious before and during exams. The anxiety they experience consists of feelings of dread and foreboding. They may sense that something terrible—though they may not know what—is going to happen. Test anxiety ranges from increased tension to actual physical symptoms, such as rapid breathing, pounding heartbeat, lightheadedness or dizziness, nausea, and diarrhea.

Anxiety may be very uncomfortable, but it is not always a bad thing. It is normal to feel somewhat anxious as an important test approaches. Anxiety shows that we understand the importance of the occasion and that failure may have serious conse-

The test anxiety that many students feel before and during a test can often be overcome by being prepared and thinking positively.

Pulling an all-nighter is not the most effective way to learn. Instead, try studying a reasonable amount every day.

quences. Test anxiety reflects the thoughts of students before and during the test. Such thoughts might include the following:

- "I study as hard as I can, but my mind just blanks when the tests are distributed."
- "What's wrong with me? I know the material, but I just can't take tests."
- "I just know I'm going to flunk."
- "I wish I could get out of here. I wish the test was over."
- "I'm not going to have enough time to finish."

Test-anxious students allow these thoughts and self-doubts to distract them, preventing them from focusing on the test itself.

The good news, however, is that test anxiety can be overcome. The ways of handling test anxiety include being prepared, overlearning, and changing the way one thinks about tests. Changing the way one thinks about tests can also change the way in which one's body responds to test situations.

Be Prepared   One way to overcome test anxiety is to be prepared. Actors who have thoroughly memorized their lines may still be anxious when they hear their cue, but they are less likely to forget the line they have to speak. If you study carefully and review the material regularly, you can be confident that you will recall what you have learned.

Review the material regularly before a test, and avoid cramming. Learning takes time. Studying a reasonable amount every day is far more effective

than cramming suddenly the night before. You can begin to cope with possible test anxiety right from the beginning of the semester—by planning a regular study schedule and sticking to it.

Overlearn   Overlearning means reviewing the material over and over, even after you think you have mastered it. Overlearning accomplishes two objectives: remembering the subject matter longer and building confidence. Overlearning makes you realize, "I *really* know this stuff!"

Think Helpful Thoughts   What if you are well prepared for tests and still make yourself anxious with self-defeating thoughts? There are strategies for ending upsetting thoughts and focusing on the task at hand—the test.

What are the negative thoughts that occur to you at test-taking times? Write them on a sheet of paper. Once you are aware of these negative thoughts, you can replace them with positive ones. For example, replace "I'm probably going to fail this test" with "I'm prepared for this test, and I know I'll do well."

This method of coping is called cognitive restructuring. **Cognitive restructuring** means changing the thoughts one has in a particular situation. Cognitive restructuring consists of the following four steps:

1. Identify self-defeating thoughts, paying special attention to the ones that seem exaggerated.
2. Replace self-defeating thoughts with positive and encouraging messages to yourself.
3. Imagine yourself in the testing situation, and practice positive thinking.
4. Reward yourself for thinking positively.

If you consistently practice cognitive restructuring, chances are you will begin to see a change for the better. Eventually, you will become less anxious and more confident about taking tests. Your grades may reflect the changes.

THINKING ABOUT PSYCHOLOGY

1. How does making an outline help one answer an essay question more effectively?
2. List the four steps of cognitive restructuring to cope with test anxiety.
3. **Critical Thinking**   Write an essay agreeing or disagreeing with the following statement: Some people with test anxiety are their own worst enemies.

S U M M A R Y

Psychologists use different types of tests to evaluate a person's achievement, aptitudes, interests, and personality traits.

I. What Are Psychological Tests?

A. Psychological tests measure abilities, feelings, attitudes, and behaviors.
   1. Some psychological tests measure people's behavior directly.
   2. Most psychological tests rely on people's self-reports.
B. For a psychological test to be useful, it must be standardized, show reliability and validity, and have scoring norms.

II. Measuring Achievement, Abilities, and Interests

A. Achievement tests measure skills and the knowledge people have in certain areas.
B. Aptitude tests are generally used to determine whether a person is likely to do well in a given field of work or study.
C. Vocational interest inventories help people determine if their interests are similar to those of people in various occupations.
   1. The Kuder Preference Record is a vocational interest inventory with a forced-choice format.
   2. The Strong-Campbell Interest Inventory is used to assess combinations of interests the test taker shares with people in particular occupations.

III. Personality Tests

A. Objective personality tests present test takers with a standardized group of test items in the form of a questionnaire.
   1. The Minnesota Multiphasic Personality Inventory (MMPI-2) is an objective test widely used in clinical work and in research to help diagnose psychological disorders.

2. The California Psychological Inventory (CPI) is also an objective test but is considered a more valid and reliable instrument than the MMPI-2.
B. Projective personality tests require test takers to respond to ambiguous stimuli.
   1. The Rorschach inkblot test requires test takers to interpret a series of inkblots.
   2. The Thematic Apperception Test (TAT) requires test takers to create a story for a picture or a series of pictures.

IV. Taking Tests

A. Students may improve their test performance by gathering information, practicing with a study group, reading test directions carefully, and being prepared.
B. When answering multiple-choice questions, try to answer the question before you look at the choices; look for answers that are opposites; guess only when the odds of gaining points outweigh the odds of losing points; change your answer if you think you have made a mistake.
C. Tips for answering true-false items include the following: for the item to be true, every part of it must be true; be wary of items that use absolutes; items that provide more information than others tend to be true.
D. When answering short-answer questions, answer in brief but complete sentences; include significant terms in your answer; use detail if time and space allow.
E. When answering essay questions, make sure you understand the question; read the directions carefully; make an outline to help you organize your thoughts; express your strongest ideas first.
F. Some students suffer from test anxiety before and during exams. There are certain methods for controlling test anxiety.
   1. Be prepared.
   2. Overlearn the material.
   3. Think helpful thoughts.

TERM & CONCEPT REVIEW

1. List three types of psychological tests.
2. Explain what a behavior-rating scale is.
3. What three characteristics does a psychological test need to have in order to be useful and reasonably accurate?
4. What are validity scales?
5. What are aptitude tests generally used for? Give two examples of an aptitude test.
6. What are the two types of personality tests?
7. How were the clinical scales of the Minnesota Multiphasic Personality Inventory (MMPI) originally created?
8. What is a Rorschach inkblot test?
9. List three tips for doing well on multiple-choice questions.
10. Describe the physical symptoms of test anxiety. What steps might a student use to overcome test anxiety?

CRITICAL THINKING

1. In this chapter, you read that the longer a test is, the more valid and reliable it is. Why do you think this is true?
2. Why is it important not to depend too much on the results of interest inventories? Under what type of circumstances are interest inventories the most useful?
3. Do you think it is possible for psychologists to accurately measure a person's personality using only multiple-choice and true-false questions? Why or why not?
4. What do you think are the advantages and disadvantages of using self-reports to measure personality rather than observing behavior?
5. Why do you think people in the same occupation often share the same interests, even outside interests that do not directly relate to their actual jobs?

APPLYING SKILLS IN PSYCHOLOGY

1. **COOPERATIVE LEARNING** **Writing About Psychology** With a partner, review the tips on taking tests in this chapter. Decide on a format—such as a booklet, a poster, or a play—to give advice to other students on taking tests. Present the finished product to the class.
2. **Writing About Psychology** The importance and the validity of the Standard Assessment Test (SAT) have been a subject of debate for the past several years. Research some of the controversies surrounding the SAT. Write an essay stating your position on the use of the SAT as a part of the college admissions process. Be sure to include references to your research to support your position.
3. **Research in Psychology** Pick three professions that interest you and read about them. What do they have in common? In what ways are they different? On the basis of your reading, devise a 15-question interest inventory to predict which of the three professions would most likely interest a test taker. Give the test to two friends. What were the results? Did the test takers agree with your test's assessment of their level of interest in the specific professions? If they did not, how do you think your interest inventory could be adjusted to provide more accurate results? Prepare a report on your findings, and attach your questionnaire.
4. **Research in Psychology** Popular magazines often include tests or self-inventories that claim to measure such diverse qualities as one's ability to handle money or how happy one's marriage is. Look through magazines at home or in the library, and bring a copy of one of these tests to class. Briefly present your test to the class. What does it claim to measure? Do you think it has any scientific validity? Why or why not? As a class, discuss the kinds of issues the surveys seem to focus on. Why do you think these tests are so prevalent?

16

GENDER ROLES

Objectives

1 Define *gender roles* and *gender stereotypes,* and explain the difference between the two terms.

2 Describe gender differences in cognitive abilities, personality, and behavior.

3 Define *gender typing,* and discuss several theories that explain how it may occur.

4 Explain how gender roles have changed over time, and identify the ways in which they can vary from culture to culture.

A DAY IN THE LIFE

Marc, Janet, Dan, and Linda were at the recreation center after the annual career day at school. Suddenly they were all thinking about their futures.

"What's wrong, Dan?" Janet asked. She had noticed that Dan seemed exceptionally quiet.

"This career fair just made me realize that I still don't know for sure what I want to do after graduation. I'm afraid that if I don't make some decisions I may end up just like my uncle John," Dan said.

"Uncle John was laid off from his job, and my aunt Debbie had to go to work to support the family. Now she's making more money than Uncle John ever did."

"That's great, isn't it?" Linda said.

"It should be, but ever since Aunt Debbie went to work, my uncle is always upset. I think he can't accept that my aunt is making more money than he did. All I know is, when I'm older I want to have a good career so I can support my family."

"Are you saying you wouldn't want your wife to work outside the home?" Janet asked defensively.

"It's not that I wouldn't *want* her to work. I just feel that she shouldn't *have* to work. I should be able to support her and our family."

"I don't understand that attitude," Linda said. "My parents both work, and usually they both help around the house. But when my grandparents visit from Mexico, my dad won't be caught doing any housework. I guess he doesn't want his parents to see him doing work they still consider 'women's work.'"

"Some people don't realize that times change," Janet responded. "Ever since my parents' divorce, my mom has had to work nights and take care of the house during the day. She still manages to have time for me, though. She's been great."

"I plan to have a career," Linda said. "I've always wanted to do something with math—maybe engineering or architecture."

Grinning, Linda turned to Marc and asked, "So, Marc, what would you think about staying at home while your wife went to work?"

- gender
- gender role
- gender stereotype
- nurturance
- gender typing
- lateralization
- modeling
- gender schema

• • •

Dan's uncle was having a hard time accepting his wife's new role, but she also was having a difficult time. She worked all day at her job and then had to take care of the home. She also had to deal with her husband's feelings of frustration and depression. Her husband was normally a good and generous person, but he was feeling trapped by his beliefs about the kinds of behavior that are appropriate for men and for women.

Some people, such as Dan's uncle, believe that a woman's place is in the home with the children and that a man's place is on the job, working to support them. Other people believe that a wide range of behaviors are appropriate for men and women. This chapter explores these and other beliefs about what it means to be male and what it means to be female.

Read the following statements about psychology. Do you think they are true or false? You will learn whether each statement is true or false as you read the chapter.

- Men generally demonstrate more aggressive behavior than women.
- Women tend to be more talkative than men.
- The qualities men look for in a potential mate are different from the qualities women look for.
- Boys and girls are treated in much the same way until about age three.
- Much of the behavior we think of as typical male or female behavior we are not born with but learn from other members of our culture.

1

What Are Gender Roles?

We all have physical characteristics that make us different from other people. Height, hair color, eye color, and many other physical traits help to differentiate who we are. Possibly the most fundamental physical characteristic of any human being is his or her gender. **Gender** refers to the sex of an individual, either male or female. Like hair color and eye color, gender is a biological trait that is fixed by the genes before birth.

Gender Roles

Closely related to the concept of gender is the idea of **gender roles**—widely accepted societal expectations about how males and females should behave. Gender roles define what is considered to be appropriate masculine and feminine behavior in a particular culture.

A DAY IN THE LIFE

When Dan explained that he thought he should be able to support his wife and family, he was expressing his belief in the type of behavior that is considered appropriate for men in American society. That is, he was adhering to a gender role.

Unlike gender itself, gender roles are not genetically determined. Rather, gender roles appear to be a product of both biological and social factors.

Traditional Gender Stereotypes

Feminine	Masculine
Not aggressive	Aggressive
Dependent	Independent
Easily influenced	Not easily influenced
Submissive	Dominant
Passive	Active
Home-oriented	Worldly
Easily hurt emotionally	Not easily hurt emotionally
Indecisive	Decisive
Talkative	Not at all talkative
Gentle	Tough
Sensitive to the feelings of others	Less sensitive to the feelings of others
Very desirous of security	Not very desirous of security
Cries a lot	Rarely cries
Emotional	Logical
Verbal	Analytical
Kind	Cruel
Tactful	Blunt
Nurturing	Not nurturing

FIGURE 16.1 *Every culture has broad expectations about how males and females should behave. These gender roles are based primarily on gender stereotypes. Here is a partial list of gender stereotypes that exist in the United States.*

Source: Broverman, I.K., et al. (1972). Sex role stereotypes: a current appraisal. *Journal of Social Issues*, 28, 59–78.

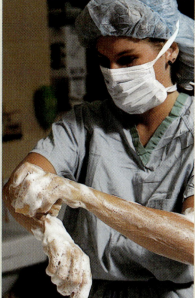

Many kinds of work that people do today can be done equally well by males and females. As an increased number of women have entered the workforce, gender roles have become less rigid. How might this affect future generations?

Although one speaks of "playing a role," people do not *play* gender roles in the same way that they play roles on the stage. That is to say, they do not usually see themselves as pretending to be someone they are not. Instead, for most people, gender roles are simply a part of who they are and how they see themselves.

Gender Stereotypes

Sometimes gender roles become so rigid that they develop into **gender stereotypes**, which are over-simplified and distorted beliefs about the way men and women should behave. In some societies, gender stereotypes are so widespread that they are held by almost everyone in the society. As a result, many behaviors that are considered acceptable for men in such societies are not considered acceptable for women and vice versa. Other societies recognize fewer differences between what is considered appropriate behavior for males and females. For example, although gender stereotypes exist in the United States, relatively few behaviors in this country are considered entirely unacceptable for one gender or the other.

Interestingly, many people who hold gender stereotypes about other people do not believe the stereotypes apply to themselves. One study asked male and female college students to judge how much certain traits, such as kindness or indepen-

dence, described themselves. The students were also asked how much those same traits described women and men in general. Males and females responded quite similarly when judging traits that described themselves. For instance, women and men rated themselves similar in terms of independence, hostility, helpfulness, and gentleness. At the same time, however, both women and men thought that males in general were more independent and hostile than females in general. Men and women alike also said that females in general were kinder and more helpful than males in general (Martin, 1987).

This and other studies emphasize that gender differences are much smaller than our stereotypes suggest (Hyde & Plant, 1995; Matlin, 1996). The fact that gender stereotypes exist, however, suggests that humans come to develop different ideas about how men and women should behave. As we shall see, this process begins early in life.

THINKING ABOUT PSYCHOLOGY

1. Define *gender, gender role,* and *gender stereotype.* How are these concepts related? How do they differ?

2. **Critical Thinking** What role does television and the media play in the development of gender stereotypes? Give several examples to support your answer.

Gender Differences 2

What kinds of differences actually exist between males and females? There are obvious physical differences between the sexes, but other, less obvious differences between males and females also seem to exist. These include differences in cognitive, or intellectual, abilities and differences in personality and behavior. As we shall see, psychologists disagree about whether these differences are biologically based or learned through experience.

It is important to note that *group* differences between males and females in certain traits and abilities says nothing about the differences among *individual* males and females. In fact, there is greater variation within each gender group than there is between the average male and the average female.

Physical Differences

Several physical differences between the sexes are usually readily apparent because males and females differ in both primary and secondary sex characteristics. Primary sex characteristics refer to the organs of the reproductive system. For example, women have ovaries and males have testes. Secondary sex characteristics include such traits as deeper voices and greater amounts of facial hair in males and smaller body size and wider hips in females. These traits are controlled by sex hormones, which, in turn, are determined by genes.

Differences in Cognitive Abilities

Males and females in the United States tend to show consistent differences in some basic cognitive abilities. In particular, girls appear to demonstrate somewhat greater verbal abilities, and boys seem to have somewhat greater visual-spatial abilities. Beginning in adolescence, boys also appear to be better at mathematics.

Verbal Abilities   Numerous studies have found that females outperform males in various verbal tasks (Beal, 1994; Golombok & Fivush, 1994), and that females in general have greater average verbal abilities than males (Hyde & Linn, 1988). In particular, these studies have found that females tend to talk and read at earlier ages, have fewer reading problems, and follow written instructions more easily than males (Golombok & Fivush, 1994; Hyde & Linn, 1988). Females also tend to be better spellers than males (Allred, 1990). The overall differences in verbal abilities appear in the first few years of life and continue throughout adolescence.

It is important to note, however, that these gender differences in verbal abilities are very small (Hyde & Plant, 1995). In addition, many other factors besides gender are known to influence verbal abilities, including differences in exposure to books and reading. Gender in and of itself can explain only a small fraction of the individual differences in verbal abilities (Hyde & Linn, 1988).

Mathematical Abilities   Research has also shown that males typically demonstrate greater mathematical ability than females. Although females tend to be better at computing numbers in elementary school, males tend to outdistance them in mathematical problem-solving ability in high school and college (Hyde et al., 1990). Boys, on average, score higher on the mathematics section of the Standard Assessment Test (SAT), for example, with twice as many males as females scoring above the average score of 500 (Byrnes & Takahira, 1993).

However, like gender differences in verbal abilities, the gender differences in mathematical abilities are extremely small—too small to be important in understanding most of the individual variation in mathematical achievement (Hyde et al., 1990). In addition, notable gender differences in mathematical achievement have been decreasing steadily over the past decade.

The gender gap in mathematical abilities seems to be closing, as more females are enrolling in advanced mathematics courses.

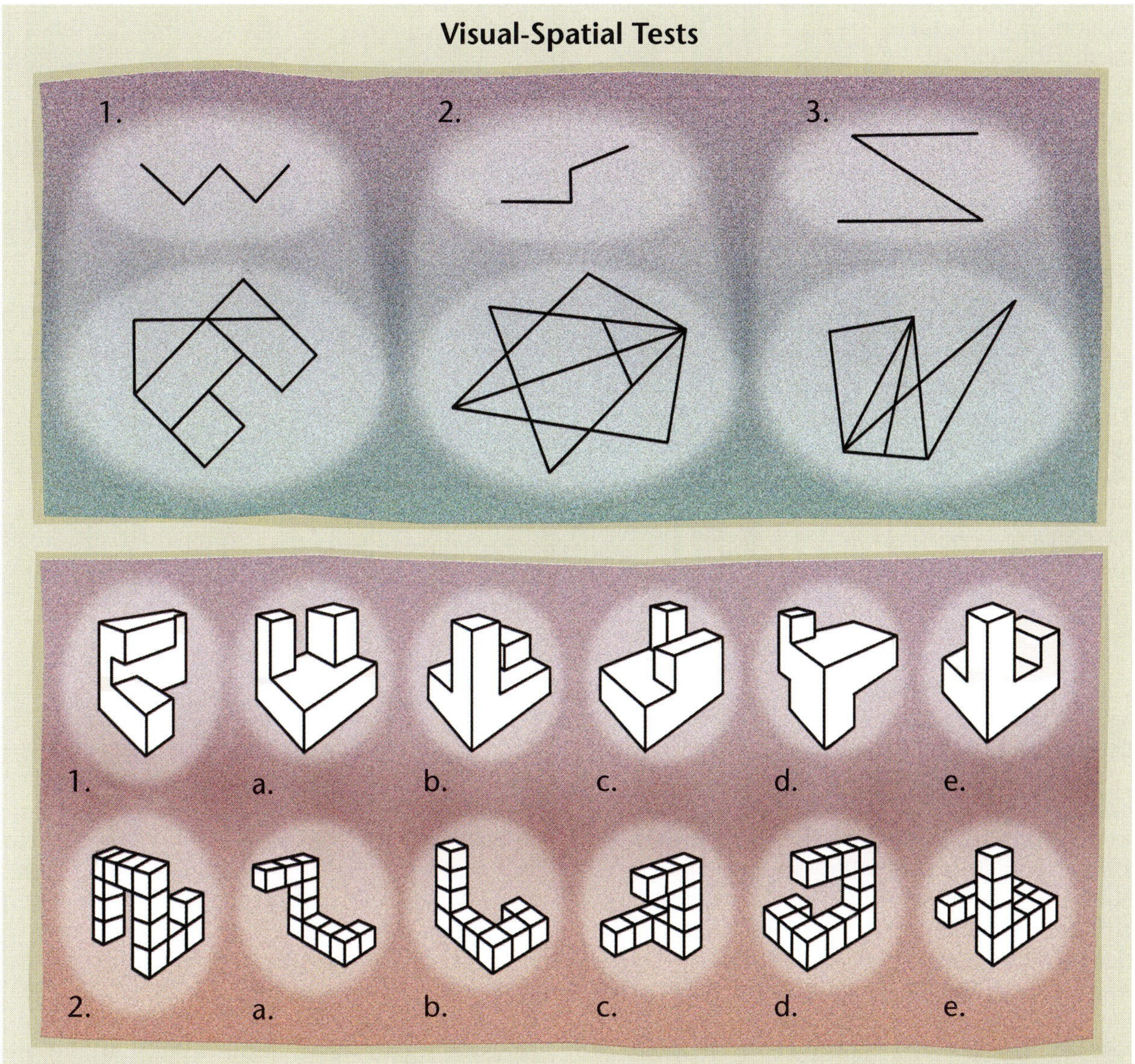

Visual-Spatial Tests

1.

2.

3.

1.   a.   b.   c.   d.   e.

2.   a.   b.   c.   d.   e.

FIGURE 16.2 *Two items commonly used to measure visual-spatial abilities are the embedded-figures test, which requires one to find a geometric shape embedded in a more complex design, and the mental rotation test, which requires one to imagine how a shape would change in appearance as it moved through space.*

Thus, it is likely that the differences between the sexes in mathematical abilities reflect the greater training and experience boys have in solving mathematical problems. As females take more mathematics courses and gain experience in solving problems, the gender differences in mathematical abilities seem to be shrinking (Hyde et al., 1990). More girls such as Linda are continuing to excel in mathematics. As Linda noted, her interest in mathematics could lead to a career in engineering or architecture—two professions previously dominated by men.

Visual-Spatial Abilities   Many studies have found that males generally do better than females in tasks requiring visual-spatial abilities, at least after about age 10 (Voyer et al., 1995). Visual-spatial abilities include spatial orientation and mental rotation skills. Examples of each type of visual-spatial skill are shown in Figure 16.2. Especially in mental rotation, males tend to show greater ability than females (Linn & Petersen, 1986).

Visual-spatial abilities help in understanding abstract concepts in geometry, trigonometry, and calculus. Thus, the relatively greater visual-spatial abilities of males may contribute to their apparent superiority in advanced mathematics (Golombok & Fivush, 1994). On a practical level, visual-spatial skills help in such activities as reading maps and assembling mechanical equipment and puzzles, tasks at which males have often shown greater skill than females.

There is some evidence that visual-spatial abilities may be influenced by the level of the male sex hormone testosterone. Thus, such abilities may be at least in part determined by biological factors (Halpern, 1992). However, it is likely that environmental influences also play a role. Adults tend to give boys more spatially complex toys, such as models and construction toys. Research has shown that these complex toys can help both males and females develop visual-spatial skills.

Recently, women's sports have become increasingly popular. In the past, however, sporting activities were primarily reserved for men. How might participation in sports help girls improve their visual-spatial skills?

When females are given the opportunity to develop visual-spatial skills, they often perform as well as males. In one study (Stericker & LeVesconte, 1982), female students who were given just three hours of training in rotating geometric figures did as well as male students at these tasks. Thus, gender differences in visual-spatial tasks seem to be the result of both small biological differences between the sexes and more significant differences in environment and learning experiences (Golombok & Fivush, 1994).

Differences in Personality and Behavior

Many notable gender differences are found in both personality and behavior. Females, for example, tend to exceed males in demonstrating trust and **nurturance**, or affectionate care and attention. Males, on the other hand, tend to exceed females in such traits as assertiveness and tough-mindedness. Other gender differences in personality and behavior include differences in levels of aggression, communication styles, and traits desired in a mate (Feingold, 1994).

Aggression   In most cultures, it is primarily the males who fight in war and compete in sports and games. This is, in part, because males tend to be physically larger and stronger than females, as previously mentioned. Yet males may be more suited to these activities for another reason as well—their generally higher level of aggression.

Most psychological studies of aggression have found that males tend to be more aggressive than females (Eagly & Wood, 1991; Knight et al., 1996). Not only are males more likely than females to act aggressively, particularly if provoked, but they are also more likely to use physical forms of aggression, such as hitting and shoving. Females act aggressively less often, and when they do, they tend to use indirect forms of aggression. For example, if provoked by a friend or an acquaintance, females are more likely to ignore or end their relationship with that person than to hit her or him (Bjorkqvist et al., 1992; Lagerspetz et al., 1988).

It is true that men generally demonstrate more aggressive behavior than women. According to several studies, men are also more likely than females to be physical in the expression of their aggression.

PSYCHOLOGY

GENDER DIFFERENCES IN INTIMACY AND INDEPENDENCE

In her book *You Just Don't Understand* (1990), psychologist Deborah Tannen discusses the human needs for intimacy and independence. Although males and females both need intimacy and independence, Tannen believes that women tend to focus on the former and men on the latter. The difference, Tannen argues, rests on how men and women interact with the world around them and view relationships. The difference also can lead to problems in communication between men and women.

According to Tannen, most women tend to live in a world of connection with others. They negotiate complex networks of friendship, try to reach consensus, minimize differences, and avoid the appearance of superiority because this tends to highlight differences. Intimacy with others is key for individuals with this view of relationships.

In contrast, Tannen sees the majority of men as living in a world of status, where they must establish their own place in a hierarchy of others. Here independence is key. This is because telling others what to do is a primary means of increasing status. Taking orders from others, on the other hand, is a mark of low status.

These differing perspectives of the two sexes can lead women and men to interpret and react to the same situation in very different ways. Tannen provides the example of a couple named Nancy and Josh to illustrate how these differing views of relationships create problems in communication.

Nancy and Josh   When Josh's old high school buddy called him at work and said he would be in town on business the following month, Josh invited him to stay for the weekend. That evening he informed Nancy that they were going to have a houseguest and that he and his buddy would be going out together like they did in high school.

When Josh told Nancy about the plans he had made, she was upset. Nancy reminded Josh that she was going to be away on business the week before his buddy's visit. The Friday night that Josh would be out with his buddy would be her first night home. What upset Nancy the most, however, was that Josh had made the plans on his own and only later informed her of them rather than discussing them with her first.

Nancy would never have made plans, even for an evening, let alone a whole weekend, without first checking with Josh. She could not understand why Josh did not show her the same courtesy and consideration that she would show him. When she protested, Josh responded, "I can't say to my friend, 'I have to ask my wife for permission!'"

To Josh, checking with his wife means seeking permission, and that, in turn, implies that he is not independent and free to act on his own. It would make him feel like a child. To Nancy, checking with her husband has nothing to do with permission. She thinks husbands and wives should discuss their plans with each other because their lives are connected and the actions of one have consequences for the other. Not only does Nancy not mind telling someone, "I have to check with Josh," but on the contrary, she likes it. It makes her feel good to know and to show that her life is connected with another's.

Conclusion   Nancy and Josh were more upset about the incidents described above, as well as by others like them, than seemed warranted. This is because the incident reflected basic gender differences in how they view the world of relationships. Nancy was upset because she sensed a failure of connectedness and intimacy in her relationship with Josh. Josh was upset because he felt as though Nancy was trying to control him and limit his independence.

Think About It

How, according to Tannen, do men and women place different emphases on intimacy and independence? How can this cause communication problems between them?

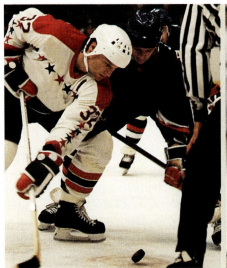

All of these predominantly male sports are based on aggressive behavior: hockey in Canada, judo in Japan, rugby in England, and boxing in the United States. Why do men tend to dominate aggressive sports?

Although it is clear that males tend to be more aggressive than females, the origins of this gender difference are not as clear. Some experts believe that gender differences in aggression are primarily due to biological differences between males and females (Baron & Richardson, 1994). For example, aggressive behavior has been linked with high levels of testosterone (Berman et al., 1993; Olweus, 1986). One theory suggests that, among early humans, more aggressive males were more successful at winning mates than were less aggressive males. According to this theory, the result was that genes for aggression were more likely to be passed on to following generations (Baron & Richardson, 1994).

Although biology may help explain gender differences in aggression, it is likely that the differences are also at least partly due to predominant male and female gender roles (Eagly & Steffen, 1986). In many societies, males are expected and socialized, or taught through the influence of social pressures, to be tougher, more assertive, and more aggressive than females (Eagly, 1987).

Communication Styles A common gender stereotype is that of the "strong, silent" male. Many people believe that women talk more than men do, but research shows that the opposite is actually true. Although girls tend to be more talkative than boys during early childhood, by the time they enter school, boys usually dominate classroom discussions (Sadker & Sadker, 1994). Indeed, as girls mature, they do less of the talking in most mixed-

sex groups. By adulthood, men spend more time talking than women do in many situations. Men are also more likely to introduce new topics and interrupt others (Etaugh & Rathus, 1995).

TRUTH OR fiction
▪ REVISITED ▪

It is not true that women tend to be more talkative than men. Girls may be more talkative when they are young, but as they mature, they generally talk less than men do.

Although males talk more in general, they tend to talk less than females do about their feelings and personal experiences (Dindia & Allen, 1992). Females often talk with other women—mothers, sisters, roommates, and friends—about intimate matters. Males talk about intimate matters much less often. When they do discuss personal matters, they generally do so with females rather than with other males, perhaps because females tend to be better at using and understanding nonverbal communication (Hall, 1978, 1984). Women are also more likely to offer understanding and support (Hall, 1984; Reisman, 1990). Dan, for example, was experiencing several issues that he was having difficulty working through. Rather than discuss these issues with Todd or Marc, he chose to confide in Janet.

A DAY IN THE LIFE

Whether these gender differences in communication styles are biologically based or socially learned is still unclear. Male and female children tend to be treated differently from birth in both the number and nature of verbal and nonverbal communications directed toward them.

Mate Selection   Many physical features are universally appealing to people of both sexes when they are forming a romantic relationship with a potential mate (Rathus et al., 1997). However, men tend to be more swayed than women by these aspects of physical appearance. Although women are also concerned with appearance, they tend to place greater emphasis on personal qualities, such as warmth, consideration, dependability, kindness, and fondness for children. Assertiveness, need for achievement, wit, and professional status are other traits many women reportedly find important in a mate (Nevid, 1984).

Some psychologists believe that males and females originally valued these different characteristics in potential mates because they are the traits that help assure successful reproduction (Buss, 1994; Feingold, 1992; Fisher, 1992). However, this explanation cannot be proved conclusively. Gender differences in socialization may also influence which traits males and females look for in a mate. Regardless of the cause, however, the differences between the sexes in the traits they consider important in a mate are real, and they can be found in many different cultures (Buss, 1989).

TRUTH OR fiction

■ REVISITED ■

It is true that the qualities men look for in a potential mate are different from the qualities women look for. Men tend to focus more on the physical attractiveness of potential mates, whereas females tend to place greater emphasis on personal qualities, such as kindness.

As discussed earlier, actual differences in cognitive abilities, personality, and behavior are quite small and appear to be diminishing (Hyde et al., 1990; Voyer et al., 1995). Furthermore, most differences between males and females appear to be due largely to environmental influences and cultural expectations and not to inborn biological differences between males and females.

THINKING ABOUT PSYCHOLOGY

1. What evidence suggests that gender differences in cognitive abilities are at least partly due to differences in boys' and girls' life experiences?

2. Identify the hormone that is linked to aggressive behavior.

3. **Critical Thinking**   Give three examples of ways that children might be socialized to be more or less aggressive.

3
Gender Typing

Subtle differences between the genders do exist. If these differences are not based solely on biological factors, however, how do they develop into gender roles? As in many areas of psychology, several different theories have been proposed to explain gender role development, which is also known as **gender typing**.

Research has shown that children as young as two and a half years of age have begun to develop ideas about traits and behaviors they consider characteristic of males and females (Etaugh & Rathus, 1995). These findings suggest that gender typing takes place at an early age. Exactly how and why gender roles develop, however, is a subject of debate among psychologists. Several theories have been proposed to explain gender typing. These theories fall into two general categories: those that explain gender typing as a biological process and those that explain it as a psychological process.

Biological Views

Biological views of gender typing focus on the impact of such factors as genes and hormones in the development of gender-related behavior.

Genetics   Most biologists believe that genes for traits that help individuals survive and reproduce tend to be passed on to future generations. Some psychologists have argued that the traits that assured the survival and reproductive success of early humans made early men successful hunters and warriors and early women successful child rearers (Kaplan & Hill, 1985). For males, these would have included such traits as good visual-spatial skills and aggression. For females, such traits would have included good nonverbal communication skills and nurturance. According to the theory, genes for these traits would have been passed on to future generations, and the traits would eventually come to characterize humans as a species.

The genetic view of gender role origins is highly controversial. Critics argue that a person's biological makeup does not predetermine how that person will behave. Instead, they point to cross-cultural research that suggests that gender roles are largely learned and not inherited (Mead, 1935). In their view, genes are important determinants of physical traits such as strength, but complex social behaviors such as aggression involve learning and cultural influences as well as heredity.

Hormones   Some psychologists believe that gender typing occurs because males and females differ in the organization and functioning of their brain. According to this view, sex hormones sculpt the brains of males and females differently before birth. To understand this theory, some background on brain structure and function is necessary.

The two hemispheres, or right and left sides, of the brain are somewhat specialized to carry out different functions. In most people, the right hemisphere tends to be better specialized to perform visual-spatial tasks, whereas the left hemisphere tends to be better specialized to perform verbal tasks. This does not imply a strict division of roles because neither hemisphere is solely responsible for any cognitive abilities. However, some cognitive tasks appear to be performed more quickly and efficiently by one hemisphere than by the other (Bradshaw et al., 1981). (See Chapter 3.)

This specialization of the two sides of the brain is called **lateralization**. Lateralization occurs during fetal development, and is apparently influenced by sex hormones. Thus, lateralization may occur somewhat differently in boys than in girls, resulting in some gender differences in brain organization and function (Collaer & Hines, 1995; Tan, 1994).

There is some evidence to suggest that testosterone leads to relatively greater growth of the right hemisphere as compared with the left hemisphere (Grimshaw et al., 1995). This evidence is consistent with research that indicates that females tend to show less lateralization than males (Witelson, 1991). Taken together, these studies could help explain why males seem to be better at visual-spatial tasks, which tend to be processed by the right hemisphere, and why females seem to be better at verbal tasks, which tend to be processed by the left hemisphere of the brain.

Some psychologists also believe that gender typing may be a result of subtle prenatal changes to the brain caused by sex hormones. These psychologists suggest that boys' inclinations toward aggression and rough-and-tumble play, for example, might also be due to the influence of testosterone on the brains of developing male fetuses (Collaer & Hines, 1995). The results of these and other ways that "masculine" and "feminine" brains in young children are thought to differ are shown in Figure 16.3.

Psychological Views

Although many psychologists believe that genes and sex hormones play some role in gender typing (Money, 1987), most believe that psychological processes play a more important role. Among the psychological theories that have been suggested to explain how gender typing comes about are psychoanalytic theory, social-learning theory, and gender-schema theory.

Psychoanalytic Theory Sigmund Freud's psychoanalytic theory argues that gender typing can be explained in terms of gender identification. According to Freud, boys come to identify with their fathers and girls with their mothers. This occurs between the ages of three and five.

At the beginning of this period, Freud argued, children seek the attention of the parent of the opposite sex and perceive the parent of the same sex as a rival for that attention. By the end of the period, however, children no longer feel this way and instead identify with the parent of the same sex. (See Chapter 14.)

According to Freud, it is through this process of identification with the same-sex parent that a child comes to develop the behaviors that are associated with his or her own sex. The child internalizes the standards of the same-sex parent, and eventually adopts that parent as a role model for behavior.

There are several problems with Freud's psychoanalytic theory, one of the most apparent being the age at which gender typing occurs. According to Freud, the complex feelings that children have for the parent of the opposite sex are not resolved until children reach age five. However, as noted above, children tend to display gender typing much earlier. Even in infancy, boys have been found in some studies to be more independent than girls. Also, between the ages of one and three, many girls appear to show preferences for dolls and soft toys, whereas many boys,

on the other hand, prefer hard transportation toys (Etaugh & Rathus, 1995).

Although Freud's theory has been criticized for this and other reasons, it laid the foundation for other theories that better fit the facts as we now know them. In particular, social-learning theory was influenced by Freud's emphasis on the importance of role models and learning by imitation (Beal, 1994).

Social-Learning Theory According to social-learning theory gender role behavior, like other behavior, is acquired through two different learning processes—reinforcement and modeling.

Reinforcement occurs when a behavior has favorable consequences. Because it is rewarded, the behavior is more likely to be repeated. In contrast, behaviors that are not rewarded and behaviors that are punished are less likely to be repeated because they are not reinforced. (See Chapter 6.)

Social-learning theorists argue that reinforcement of appropriate gender role behavior starts very early. Almost from the moment of birth, the way

Some Possible Differences Between Male and Female Preschoolers in Brain Organization and Function

Male preschoolers	Female preschoolers
Prefer blocks and building	Prefer playing with living things
Build high structures	Build long and low structures
Are indifferent to newcomers	Greet newcomers
Prefer stories of adventure	Prefer stories about relationships
Play more competitive games (e.g., tag)	Play less competitive games (e.g., hopscotch)
Are better visual-spatial learners	Are better auditory learners

FIGURE 16.3 *Some psychologists believe that the presence of prenatal sex hormones contributes to the development of male-differentiated brains and female-differentiated brains. This difference can affect the behavior of males and females, even those of preschool age.*

Source: Moir, A. & Jessel, D. (1991). *Brain Sex.* New York: Carol Publishing/Lyle Stuart.

Freud believed that children model gender-typed behaviors after their parent of the same sex. He termed this process identification.

appropriate for girls, such as dolls. They may frown, make sarcastic comments, and even physically separate the child from the toy (Langlois & Downs, 1980). Girls, however, are less likely to receive negative reactions from their fathers for playing with toys considered more appropriate for boys, such as trucks (Siegal, 1987).

From an early age, boys are also more likely to be given toy cars, toy guns, and athletic equipment. Girls, on the other hand, are more likely to receive dolls and other soft toys (Smith & Daglish, 1977). When playing with their children at home, parents also tend to reach first for toys considered appropriate for the child's sex, even when the child owns toys that are generally considered appropriate for both sexes (Eisenberg et al., 1985; Schau et al., 1980).

Aggression provides a good example of how behavior is learned through reinforcement. In one study (Fagot et al., 1985), one-year-old boys and girls were found to be equally likely to use aggressive actions, such as pushing or grabbing, in order to obtain what they wanted. They were also equally likely to use communication, such as whining or gesturing. However, adults' reactions to their efforts varied greatly, depending on the children's sex. The adults tended to respond positively when the girls tried to communicate and solve the dispute in a nonaggressive manner, but showed little response when the boys did. On the other hand, the adults tended to ignore aggression in the girls and respond positively to it in the boys.

Not surprisingly, by age two the girls in the study no longer acted aggressively. They had apparently learned through reinforcement to communicate their wants verbally. The boys had learned the opposite lesson, and their level of aggression remained high. As a result of such differences in reinforcement, girls tend to develop more anxiety about aggression and greater inhibitions against displaying it (Maccoby & Jacklin, 1974).

Even in the absence of reinforcement, social learning can occur through observation and imitation of others. This process is known as **modeling**. Children learn about both male and female gender

babies are treated may depend on their sex. When children are old enough to understand language, parents and others begin to instruct them about how they are expected to behave. Parents tend to talk and read more to baby girls, for example, and fathers often engage in more rough-and-tumble play with boys (Jacklin et al., 1984).

It is not true that boys and girls are treated in much the same way until about age three. Studies have shown that gender-typed treatment of children begins at a very early age. Thus, gender differences in the behavior of very young children are not necessarily due to biological differences between boys and girls.

Parents are also likely to reward children for behavior they consider appropriate for their gender and punish, or at least fail to reward, them for behavior they consider inappropriate. For example, studies have found that parents tend to react positively when their children play with toys considered appropriate for their gender. On the other hand, parents often react negatively when children play with toys considered inappropriate for their gender. Fathers especially are likely to react very negatively when their sons play with toys considered more

CASE STUDIES
AND OTHER TRUE STORIES
What Children Learn from Television

What do Masked Rider, Sonic the Hedgehog, Spiderman, and the Teenage Mutant Ninja Turtles have in common—aside from millions of young fans? The answer is that they are all male creatures. Almost every study in the past 20 years of children's television shows has found that many shows have all-male casts and that among shows with characters of both sexes, males outnumber females at least two or three to one (Comstock & Paik, 1991; Huston et al., 1992).

Children who watch television are learning more than how to rescue April O'Neil and fight Robotnik. Television—and other popular media, such as books, comics, magazines, radio, and film—often portray females and males in traditional gender roles (DeBell, 1993; Kortenhaus & Demarest, 1993; Signorielli, 1990). Female characters on television are portrayed as less active than males and more likely to follow the directions of others (especially male characters). The activities of female characters also have less impact on the outcome of stories than do those of males. Male characters are more likely to conceive and carry out plans and to be aggressive, dominant, and authoritative. These gender role images have not changed much over the past couple of decades (DeBell, 1993).

Television commercials also support gender role stereotypes. Even though men and women now appear equally often in prime-time commercials, women are more likely to be seen inside the home, advertising domestic products. Men continue to provide 90 percent of the narratives (known as voice-overs) in commercials, conveying the idea that men are more authoritative and knowledgeable (Bretl & Cantor, 1988; DeBell, 1993; Lovdal, 1989).

Not surprisingly, the more time children spend watching television, the more likely they are to hold stereotypical ideas about masculine and feminine behavior (Comstock & Paik, 1991; Huston et al., 1992). Davidson and others (1979), for example, found that children who watched cartoons in which characters adopted stereotypical gender roles were more likely than children who watched nonstereotyped gender role behavior to describe men and women according to the stereotypes. The same authors also found that children who were shown girls in nonstereotyped roles, such as building a clubhouse, held stereotypical attitudes less strongly afterward.

There is some evidence that the impact of television on children's stereotypes is lessened if children are raised by adults with more flexible views of gender roles. In one study, third graders were classified as either high, medium, or low stereotyped on the basis of their preferences for activities considered typically masculine or feminine (List et al., 1983). The children were then shown two films, one of a woman in traditional roles (those of wife and mother) and one of a woman in nontraditional roles (those of physician and army officer). Children low in gender role stereotyping later recalled details about both films equally, whereas children high in gender role stereotyping recalled more about the film showing the woman in traditional roles.

Television has a powerful potential to influence children's attitudes about appropriate gender role behaviors. Critics of gender stereotyping note that if producers can be encouraged to eliminate gender role stereotypes from television shows and commercials, sexism in American society could decrease substantially.

Think About It

Reread your favorite novel, magazine article, comic book, or cartoon series. Observe the action and events that take place and how each of the characters, both male and female, react to the same situations. What, if any, gender role stereotypes do the characters' behaviors reflect? How might the stories be changed to portray males and females in less stereotypical ways?

role behavior by observing the behavior of the males and females with whom they commonly interact. However, the children are more likely to model, or imitate, individuals, particularly parents, who are of the same sex as themselves. In addition, children are more likely to be positively reinforced for imitating the behavior of the parent of the same sex (Golombok & Fivush, 1994).

Observational learning and imitation were illustrated in a classic experiment by David Perry and Kay Bussey (1979). In their study, 8- and 9-year-old boys and girls watched adult models indicate their preferences for one of the items in each of 16 different pairs of items. The adults chose among such pairs as toy cows versus toy horses and oranges versus apples. The children in the study did not realize that the adults' preferences were purely arbitrary. When the children were asked to indicate their own preferences for the items in the pairs, the boys' choices matched the adult men's choices 14 out of 16 times, and the girls' choices matched the adult women's choices 13 out of 16 times. Thus, both boys and girls tended to model their behavior after role models of their own sex, even though the behavior was arbitrary and unrelated to gender.

If gender roles are learned, as social-learning theory suggests, then they should be flexible, or capable of changing. Indeed, there are indications that this is the case. Today, as more women are working outside the home, gender roles seem to be changing. Janet's mother is a good example. After Janet's parents divorced, her mother took on the role of wage earner in addition to her roles as parent and homemaker. Another indication of gender role change is that parents are more likely now than in the past to encourage their daughters to play sports and follow careers. They are also more likely to encourage their sons to be nurturing and cooperative.

Gender-Schema Theory   Social-learning theory has made important contributions to our understanding of how reinforcement and modeling promote gender-typed behavior. A related but somewhat different view of gender typing is provided by gender-schema theory. According to this theory, children themselves play an active role in developing gender-appropriate behavior. Children form their own concepts about gender and then shape their behavior so that it conforms to their gender concepts.

Specifically, children develop a gender schema in order to organize their perceptions of the world (Bem, 1993; Martin & Halverson, 1981). A **gender schema** is a cluster of physical qualities, behaviors, and personality traits associated with one sex or the other. It is argued that because society places so much emphasis on gender, children organize their perceptions along gender lines.

Gender-schema theorists suggest that as soon as children learn whether they are boys or girls, they begin to seek information concerning gender-typed traits. Even very young children start to mentally group people of the same sex according to the traits they believe are representative of that gender.

Once their gender schema is formed, children strive to live up to it. They begin to judge themselves according to the traits they believe are relevant to their sex, using their gender schema as a standard for comparison. In so doing, children blend their developing self-concepts with the prominent gender schema of their culture. For example, boys may react aggressively when provoked because they perceive that is what society expects males to

Children may be less likely to adopt traditional gender behaviors if they are allowed to play freely with both masculine and feminine toys.

do. Girls, on the other hand, may try to cooperate because they perceive that society expects such behavior from females.

Across both genders, children's self-esteem depends in part on how similar their own personalities, behaviors, and physical appearances are to those of the prominent gender schema of their culture. In other words, boys who see themselves as fitting their culture's idea of masculinity are more likely to develop higher self-esteem than boys who do not. Similarly, girls who see themselves as fitting their culture's idea of femininity are more likely to develop higher self-esteem than girls who do not (Bem, 1993).

Children's gender schema also determines how important particular traits are to them. Consider the dimensions of strength-weakness and kindness-cruelty. Children are likely to learn that the strength-weakness dimension is more important to males, whereas the kindness-cruelty dimension is more important to females. Thus, a boy is more likely to be concerned about how strong he is, whereas a girl is more likely to be concerned about being kind.

In summary, both biological and psychological views of gender typing can help us understand why males and females behave as they do. This is because differences in gender roles are likely to be influenced by differences in biology, life experiences, and cultural expectations. All of these factors appear to play some role in determining how individual males and females behave.

Regardless of how gender typing occurs, it should not be viewed as an inevitable process. In early human societies, it may have seemed appropriate for males and females to have very different roles. Today, however, many people believe that these strict gender roles no longer suit our contemporary way of life.

Source: Ziggy copyright 1995 Ziggy & Friends, INC. Dist. by UNIVERSAL PRESS SYNDICATE. Reprinted with permission. All rights reserved.

THINKING ABOUT PSYCHOLOGY

1. Why do some theorists believe that brain lateralization leads to gender-typed behaviors and abilities?

2. Give an example to show how reinforcement could influence the types of toys children choose to play with.

3. **Critical Thinking** What role do you think television might play in the development of a child's gender schema? Give examples to support your answer.

4
Variation in Gender Roles

Both social-learning theory and gender-schema theory support the idea that learning plays a key part in gender role development. This suggests that gender roles are not inborn or fixed at birth and may vary from person to person. Indeed, the increasing participation of women in activities long considered appropriate only for men—business, sports, and politics, to name a few—demonstrates that gender roles have changed dramatically over time. Research has also shown that gender roles can vary greatly from culture to culture. In other words, what is considered gender-appropriate behavior in one society may be viewed very differently in another cultural setting.

Variation Through Time

In the past, gender roles were more distinct and rigid than they are today. There were distinct female and male worlds that were clearly set apart from each other. Throughout most of history, women in many parts of the world were expected to be the

In the 1950s, most families lived on one income. It was typical then for the husband to work outside the home and the wife to stay home and care for the house and family.

and raising a family was not very widespread. According to the dominant ideas of the time concerning gender roles, the ideal woman was the devoted wife who kept a clean house and had dinner waiting when her husband returned from work.

Over the past several decades, women in the United States have entered the workforce in increasing numbers. Today, many women work outside the home because they enjoy the financial rewards and the social and intellectual stimulation their jobs provide. In other instances, economic conditions have led women into the workplace. Many working women are single mothers; others work because their families cannot afford to live on the husband's income alone. In some families, the wife works to support the family while the husband remains at home, either by choice or because he is unable to find a job.

Not surprisingly, male and female gender roles in the United States are much more flexible today than they were just a few decades ago. In many marriages, for example, husbands and wives share household chores, child rearing, and wage earning equally (Goodnow & Bowes, 1994). This is the case

with Linda's parents. As Linda noted, her father, like an increasing number of men in American society, is willing to take on at least some of the tasks that were once performed almost solely by women.

homemakers and child rearers, and men were expected to be the providers for and protectors of women and children.

These differences in gender roles were based in part on the different biological characteristics of the two sexes. Females were more restricted in their activity and mobility by childbearing and the need to nurse their young children. In the earliest human societies, women typically stayed home and assumed responsibility for the homemaking and child rearing chores. Males, being larger, stronger, and biologically less tied to childbearing and rearing, were considered better suited for hunting and similar activities. These roles remained largely unchanged until quite recently.

Just a generation or two ago, the accepted pattern was for a woman to marry, stay at home, and care for the house and children. She was expected to put the needs of her husband and children ahead of her own. The idea that a woman should put her own career or personal ambitions ahead of marriage

In contemporary society, women often balance two full-time jobs—their careers and motherhood.

Both men and women of Arapesh society were taught from birth that aggressive behavior is unacceptable.

However, most women who work outside the home are still expected to retain traditional feminine gender roles in the household (Crosby & Jaskar, 1993; Deaux & Lewis, 1983). Dan's aunt Debbie is a good example. In addition to her outside work, she is expected to maintain the household and care for the children.

Cultural Variation

Gender roles not only vary through time, but they also vary from culture to culture. A classic study by anthropologist Margaret Mead (1935) makes this point very clearly. In the 1930s, Mead studied three different groups of people—the Mundugumor, the Arapesh, and the Tchambuli—on the South Pacific island of New Guinea.

According to Mead, the Mundugumor were a warlike people, and both men and women were very aggressive. Mundugumor women looked down on bearing and rearing children because this interfered with their ability to go to battle. In contrast, the neighboring Arapesh were a gentle and peaceful culture. In this group, both men and women played an equal role in caring for the children and maintaining the land.

The Tchambuli differed from both the Mundugumor and Arapesh in their gender roles. Interestingly, they exhibited behavior that was the opposite of traditional gender roles in the United States. Tchambuli men spent most of their time caring for children, gossiping, bickering, primping, and haggling over prices. Tchambuli women, on the other hand, spent most of their time catching the fish that made up the bulk of the Tchambuli diet. Tchambuli women also kept their heads shaved, disliked wearing ornaments, and were more aggressive than the men.

Margaret Mead's interpretation of her New Guinea study has been criticized as being too subjective, or biased by her personal views concerning gender roles (Errington & Gewertz, 1987). However, the data Mead collected does show that what is considered to be appropriate behavior for men and women can differ from one culture to another. Thus, the data support the claim that many gender differences are learned, not inborn.

TRUTH OR fiction
■ REVISITED ■

It is true that much of the behavior we think of as typical male or female behavior we are not born with but learn from other members of our culture. Because gender roles differ from culture to culture, it is likely that they are learned and not the result of inborn traits.

A DAY IN THE LIFE

Linda's father grew up in a culture in which the roles of men and women were strictly defined. His parents supported these roles. In his own marriage, however, he adopted a less stereotypical role. Clearly, gender roles are not only learned but can be unlearned as well.

THINKING ABOUT PSYCHOLOGY

1. What biological factors have been suggested to explain the historic division between male and female gender roles?

2. How have gender roles in the United States changed in the past few decades?

3. **Critical Thinking** If gender roles were inborn, what might anthropologist Margaret Mead have found when she studied men and women in New Guinea?

16 Chapter REVIEW

SUMMARY

Gender roles reflect a culture's ideas about the differing natures of males and females. Gender differences appear to be due at least as much to the different cultural expectations and life experiences of males and females as they are to basic biological differences between the sexes.

I. What Are Gender Roles?

A. Gender refers to the sex of a person, either male or female.

B. Gender is a biological trait that is fixed by the genes before birth.

C. Gender roles are broad cultural expectations about how males and females should behave in society and in the home.

D. Gender roles seem to be determined by the interaction of both biological and environmental influences.

E. Gender stereotypes are oversimplified and distorted ideas about appropriate behavior for males and for females.

II. Gender Differences

A. Males and females differ in primary and secondary sex characteristics.

B. Males and females also tend to differ in some aspects of cognitive abilities, personality, and behavior.
1. Girls seem to have somewhat greater verbal abilities than boys. Boys tend to display somewhat greater visual-spatial abilities.
2. Males tend to be more aggressive than females. They also talk more than females (but less about intimate matters, and they are less skilled at nonverbal communication).
3. Gender differences are very small and growing smaller. There is greater variation within each gender group than between the average male and the average female.

III. Gender Typing

A. Gender typing is the process whereby individuals learn to behave in accordance with the gender roles of their culture.

B. Both biological and psychological theories have been proposed to explain how gender typing occurs.
1. Some psychologists believe that males and females developed different traits that helped our ancestors survive and reproduce and have been passed on to successive generations.
2. Other psychologists believe that gender typing occurs because males and females differ in the organization and functioning of their brains due to the influence of prenatal sex hormones.
3. Freud believed that gender typing occurs as children resolve the complex feelings they have for the parent of the opposite sex and begin to identify with the same-sex parent.
4. Social-learning theorists believe that gender typing occurs through two different learning processes: reinforcement and modeling. There is evidence that both types of learning can occur very early in a person's life.
5. According to gender-schema theory, children form their own concepts about gender and then shape their behavior so that it conforms to those concepts.
6. The concepts children adopt tend to reflect the predominant gender schema of their culture.

IV. Variation in Gender Roles

A. Gender roles vary both over time and from culture to culture.

B. Gender roles in the United States have changed greatly over the past few decades.

C. Margaret Mead's study of gender roles in New Guinea showed that gender roles can vary dramatically from culture to culture.

TERM & CONCEPT REVIEW

1. Define *gender role,* and give examples of how gender roles in the United States have changed over the past few decades.
2. Define each of the following terms: *nurturance, gender typing,* and *lateralization.*
3. Identify the roles reinforcement and modeling play in gender typing.
4. How do children use gender schemas to organize their perceptions of the world?
5. Give examples of one secondary sex characteristic in males and one in females.
6. How do the average verbal and mathematical abilities of girls differ from those of boys?
7. Give examples of spatial orientation and mental rotation skills.
8. Provide one possible explanation of why boys seem to outperform girls in tasks requiring visual-spatial skills.
9. Identify two differences in the typical communication styles of men and women.
10. How has the entrance of large numbers of women into the workforce affected current expectations concerning women's roles?

CRITICAL THINKING

1. Provide evidence that suggests that gender roles are in a state of transition.
2. Explain why biological theories of gender differences tend to support the current unequal status of men and women in society.
3. How might male children be socialized to become more nurturant?
4. Why do you think the increase in the number of women in the workplace has helped change gender stereotypes in the United States?
5. What advantages and disadvantages do you think there would be for girls to be educated in female-only classes?

APPLYING SKILLS IN PSYCHOLOGY

1. **COOPERATIVE LEARNING Research in Psychology** With several of your classmates, undertake a survey to assess currently held gender stereotypes in your community. First, work together as a group to brainstorm a list of questions and develop a questionnaire that will reveal how people think about males and females and what behaviors they think are appropriate for each. Then work individually to interview at least three or four different people. Overall, both males and females from a wide range of ages should be included in the survey. Then, again as a group, analyze the survey findings and summarize them in an oral report to the rest of the class. On the basis of the results of your survey, do you think gender stereotypes have changed over time?

2. **Using Your Observational Skills** Visit a preschool classroom or go to a playground and observe children aged three to five at play. Take notes on your observations. In particular, note ways in which the style of play and the toys selected for play by boys and girls are different or the same. Based on your observations, what conclusions would you draw about gender similarities and differences in this age group? Share your conclusions with the rest of the class.

3. **Research in Psychology** Cut out or copy several advertisements from magazines and newspapers. Divide the advertisements into two groups: those that reflect gender stereotypes and those that do not. Select one advertisement from each group to share with the rest of the class. Point out how each advertisement does or does not reinforce particular gender stereotypes. Try to identify other differences between the two groups of advertisements, such as the types of products or services they are selling or the audiences they seem to be targeting. If there are differences, how would you explain them?

REVIEW

IDENTIFYING PEOPLE AND IDEAS

Explain the significance of each of the following people or terms to the study of psychology.

1. drive
2. homeostasis
3. Abraham Maslow
4. performance goals
5. cognitive consistency
6. opponent-process theory
7. trait
8. Gordon Allport
9. id
10. collective unconscious
11. Carl Jung
12. self-concept
13. standardized test
14. validity scale
15. aptitude test
16. vocational interest inventories
17. cognitive restructuring
18. gender role
19. lateralization
20. modeling
21. gender schema
22. socialized

HANDS-ON PSYCHOLOGY

Individual Project

Psychological tests can be valuable tools and provide useful information about a person. Some qualities, however, are difficult to measure. For each of the following traits, achievements, or aptitudes, design a "minitest" of five questions. You may want to do additional research for some of the qualities. In conducting any additional research, you should formulate an understanding of the traits themselves, as well as the types of tests that are generally used to assess them.

a. honesty
b. creativity
c. sense of humor
d. knowledge of American history
e. aptitude to be a firefighter

Once you have created the tests, prepare a brief written report in which you answer the following questions.

1. What was your reasoning behind the types of questions you wrote for each minitest? Were you basing your questions on the qualities themselves, or did you focus on the individuals who would be taking the test?
2. Which qualities were the easiest to test for? Which were the most difficult? Why do you think it is more difficult to test for certain qualities?
3. Do you think there are characteristics, abilities, or traits that psychological tests cannot measure accurately? If a test cannot be constructed to test for these traits, how else can they be assessed?

BUILDING YOUR PORTFOLIO

Individually or in a group, complete the following project to show your understanding of the basic psychology concepts involved.

Observing Behavior

Find a public setting in which you can observe the behavior of children and their parents. A playground, park, or fast-food restaurant would be ideal. Choose two individual children for your "case studies," and take notes on their actions. When writing a report on your case studies, answer the following questions about each child:

1. Review Maslow's hierarchy of needs on page 302. What physiological and/or safety needs did the child exhibit? (For instance, was the child acting tired?) What love and belongingness and/or self-esteem needs did the child exhibit? (For example, was the child clinging to his or her parent?)
2. What personality traits did the child exhibit? According to Freud's theory, what developmental stage is the child in? What stage, according to Erikson? How would a behaviorist view the child's behavior? How would a humanist view it?
3. Did the child attempt to explore his or her environment or seek stimulation? What emotions did the child exhibit? What facial expressions or body language did you use as clues to the child's emotional state?
4. Did the child exhibit any behavior that is stereotypical of his or her sex? Did the parent (or parents) say or do anything to reinforce behavior that is generally considered "appropriate" for the child's sex?

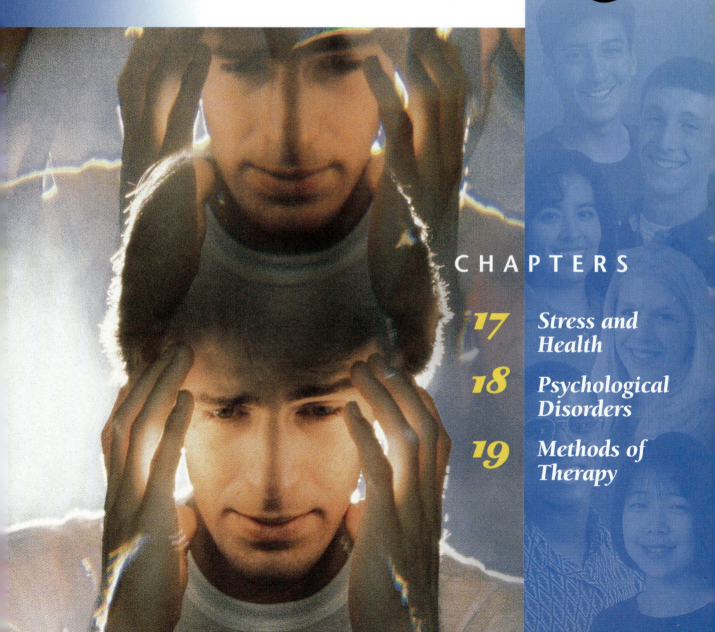

UNIT 6

HEALTH AND ADJUSTMENT

17

STRESS AND HEALTH

Objectives

1 Define *stress* and explain some of its main causes.

2 Identify the factors that determine one's responses to stress.

3 Explain the general adaptation syndrome, and describe the effects of stress on the immune system.

4 Identify the ways in which psychological factors contribute to headaches, heart disease, and cancer.

5 Describe some ways in which people cope with stress.

A DAY IN THE LIFE

Hannah, Marc, and Janet were relaxing after a frantic day at school when they saw Todd rush by. Until recently, Todd was the one person they knew who never seemed to be "stressed out."

"Hey, Todd," Marc called out. "Slow down a second. Why are you in such a hurry?"

"Sorry, guys. I really can't talk," Todd answered. "I have to get this scholarship application to Mr. Hochberg, then I have to finish my biology project. Then my dad and I are going to sit down and decide what college I should go to."

"Stay and talk with us for a second," Janet suggested. "You have time to get the application to Mr. Hochberg. And, Todd, you really shouldn't be so stressed. You've already been accepted by almost every college you applied to."

"I know I was accepted by colleges, but now I have to decide which one I want to go to. And what if I don't get this scholarship. . . ? Oh, my headache's coming back again."

"Todd, you're going to make yourself sick if you don't calm down a little," Linda warned.

"Thanks for worrying, but I'll be fine," Todd insisted.

"Don't you remember when my dad got sick last year?" Marc reminded Todd. "My dad always seemed like the healthiest guy in the world. Then he got so stressed over work that he started having serious heart problems."

"He's right, Todd," Janet added. "I don't want you to get sick."

"I know, but I have to decide what school to attend, I have to finish my homework, and I'm still working at my part-time job. These aren't things I can just ignore."

"We just want you to find a way to take it easy. We're worried about you," Linda told him.

"Well, I'm open to suggestions if you have any ideas," he said as he tried to smile.

"Okay, then," Janet said suddenly. "Why don't you and I play a little basketball tonight? It'll take your mind off things, and the exercise will make you feel better."

"Okay, you're on," said Todd smiling. "Now may I go to Mr. Hochberg's office?"

"Sure," laughed Janet, "but I hope it won't add to your stress when I beat you at basketball."

* * *

With some help from his friends, Todd recognized that he was stressed out and needed to ease up on himself. Many young people and adults alike experience a great deal of stress. This chapter is about the relationship between stress and health. We will explore the many sources of stress and some specific behavior patterns that contribute to stress. We then will look at the psychological factors associated with stress, the body's response to stress, and the effect of stress on one's health. Finally, we will examine the various ways in which people cope with stress.

Key Terms

- stress
- eustress
- distress
- stressor
- approach-approach conflict
- avoidance-avoidance conflict
- approach-avoidance conflict
- multiple approach-avoidance conflict
- self-efficacy expectation
- general adaptation syndrome
- defensive coping
- active coping

1

What Is Stress?

In physics, stress is defined as pressure, or a force. Examples of physical stress include tons of rock crushing the earth, water pressing against a dam, and a rubber band stretching. Psychological forces, or stresses, can "crush," "press," and "stretch" people. People may feel crushed by the burden of making an important decision. They may feel pressed by a lack of time in which to complete a major task, or they may feel stretched to the point of snapping.

In psychology, **stress** is the arousal of one's mind and body in response to demands made upon them. Stress forces an organism to adapt, to cope, to adjust. There are different kinds of stress, including frustration, daily hassles, life changes, and conflict. Furthermore, the word *stress* is used differently by different psychologists. Some psychologists describe stress as an event that causes tension. Others describe stress as a person's response to a disturbing event. Still others define stress as a person's perception of an event.

Not all stress is bad. Stress can increase sharpness and motivation and can keep people alert and involved. This kind of positive stress is called **eustress**. Positive stress can be a sign that a person is taking on a challenge or trying to reach a goal.

Negative stress—called **distress**—is linked to intense pressure or anxiety that can have severe psychological and physical effects. When stress becomes too severe or prolonged, it can strain people's ability to adjust to various situations. Negative stress can dampen people's moods and impair their

Students' Reasons for Seeking Counseling

REASON REPORTED	PERCENT REPORTING REASON
Stress, anxiety, nervousness	51
Romantic relationships	47
Low self-esteem, self-confidence	42
Depression	41
Family relationships	37
Academic problems, grades	29
Transition to the career world	25
Loneliness	25
Financial problems	24

FIGURE 17.1 *This table lists some of the reasons college students give for seeking counseling.*

Source: Data are from "College Youth Haunted by Increased Pressures" by B. Murray, 1996, *APA Monitor*, 26 (4), 47.

ability to experience pleasure. Negative stress can even harm the body.

High school and college students often experience stress that is related to family problems, relationships, pressures at school, loneliness, and general nervousness. In fact, a recent study shows that stress is one of the main reasons that college students seek help at college counseling centers (Murray, 1996). Figure 17.1 lists some of the reasons students give for seeking counseling.

Sources of Stress

The event or situation that produces stress is called a **stressor**. However, what is a stressor for one person may not be a stressor for another. For example, two people might react to a long bus trip quite differently. For one it might be a relaxing vacation, while for another person it could be stressful and unpleasant. However, some stressors are common to most people. For example, a loud, continuous drilling noise outside one's window would be irritating to just about everyone.

When stressors and stresses pile up on each other, we can reach a point where we have difficulty coping. To avoid reaching that point, it is important to recognize some of the causes of stress.

Frustration One of the most common sources of stress is frustration, being blocked from obtaining a goal. Examples include being delayed from keeping an appointment, lacking enough money to buy an item we want, or forgetting something important. Sometimes life seems full of frustrations. Although many frustrations are minor, the more serious ones can be extremely stressful—for example, working for weeks on an important project, only to lose it and have to create it all over again.

Daily Hassles The everyday frustrations we all experience are called daily hassles. They come in different shapes and sizes, but they have one thing in common—they all create stress. When daily hassles become severe or frequent enough, they can threaten a person's well-being. Psychologist Richard Lazarus and his colleagues (1985) found that there are eight main types of hassles:

- household hassles, including preparing meals, cleaning, shopping, and mowing the lawn;
- health hassles, including illness, anxiety about medical or dental treatment, and the side effects of medications;
- time-pressure hassles, including the feeling that there are too many things to do, too many responsibilities, and not enough time to do what needs to be done;
- inner-concern hassles, including feelings of low self-esteem and loneliness;
- environmental hassles, including noise, crowding, pollution, traffic, and crime;
- financial hassles, including concerns about paying current bills, repaying loans, and saving for the future;
- work hassles, including unhappiness with one's job and problems with coworkers;
- future-security hassles, including concerns about job security, taxes, investments, and retirement income.

These hassles can result in feelings of tension, nervousness, worry, and sadness.

Life Changes British writer Samuel Johnson wrote, "Change is not made without inconvenience, even from worse to better." Next year, when Todd goes to college, he will be living away from home for the first time. Right now, he may not know where he is going or even where he wants to go. He is, however, undergoing a major life change.

Life changes—such as moving, serious illness, or a death in the family—are another source of stress. Life changes differ from daily hassles in two important ways: (1) All hassles are annoying or irritating, but many life changes go "from worse to better." That is, they are positive and desirable changes. (2) Hassles occur regularly, often on a daily basis; life changes tend to happen less frequently, often after a long, stable period of little or no change.

Even new and positive events in a person's life can cause stress. For example, a high school senior who is looking forward to enlisting in the armed forces, joining the workforce, or attending college

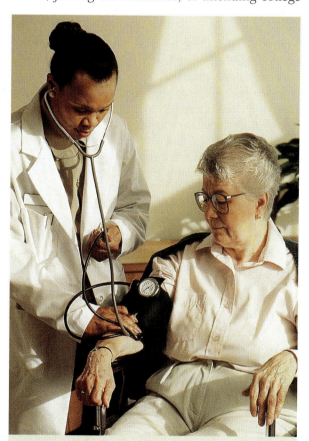

Daily hassles, such as anxiety about medical tests, can create stress. When daily hassles become severe enough, they may threaten a person's well-being.

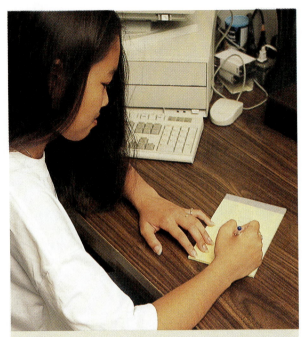

Some people cope with the stress and confusion of making decisions by listing the pros and cons of each possible alternative.

disease (Kanner et al., 1981; Smith et al., 1990; Stewart et al., 1994). Holmes and Rahe found that people who experienced many life changes within a year's time were much more likely to develop medical problems than those who did not.

TRUTH *It is true that changes are stressful, even when those changes are for the better.* **fiction** Changes that improve one's situation can cause stress because, like negative stressors and life changes, they also require adjustment.

Conflict Another source of stress is conflict, being pulled in two or more directions by opposing forces or motives. Conflict can be frustrating, especially when a person is facing a difficult decision.

For example, Todd had been accepted by several colleges, and he had to decide which college he wanted to attend. The pressure to make the right choice only adds to the stress involved in making such a major decision.

A person thinking about going to college or entering the service may feel conflicting emotions. He or she may be excited about the prospect of learning new information and developing new skills for the future. However, college is expensive, and a person who plans to attend college must think about how to pay for it. A young person may be reluctant to accumulate a large debt through college loans that will take many years to repay. The person may also have mixed feelings about leaving his or her home and friends.

Psychologists have identified four types of conflicts. (Moir & Jessel, 1991). These are approach-approach conflicts, avoidance-avoidance conflicts, approach-avoidance conflicts, and multiple approach-avoidance conflicts. (See Figure 17.3 on page 390.)

An **approach-approach conflict** is the least stressful type of conflict because the choices are positive. In this situation, each of the goals is both desirable and within reach. Since Todd was accepted by several colleges, he was faced with an approach-approach conflict because he had to choose which college to attend.

An approach-approach conflict is usually resolved by making a decision. However, after the decision is made, the person may still have

may experience stress when preparation for such life changes is combined with schoolwork, a part-time job, social life, or other responsibilities.

Researchers Thomas Holmes and Richard Rahe (1967) attempted to rank the effects of various life changes according to the amount of stress each produced. These life changes ranged from the death of a spouse to less upsetting events, such as a change in sleeping or eating habits and going on a vacation. The researchers asked people to rate each of the life changes on a scale of 1 to 100 in terms of how much stress they experienced and how much adjustment they needed to make. They used the figures they collected to create the Social Readjustment Rating Scale. (See Figure 17.2.)

Even life changes that are enjoyable are stressful because they require a certain amount of adjustment. According to Holmes and Rahe, too much of a good thing can even make a person ill. Also, too many life changes, even good ones, can cause stress that leads to headaches, high blood pressure, accidents, and other health problems.

Daily hassles and life changes—especially unpleasant ones—influence the quality of a person's life. They can cause a person to worry excessively and can dampen his or her spirits. Stressors can also lead to health problems that range from minor athletic injuries to serious illnesses such as heart

Social Readjustment Rating Scale

Rank	Life Event	Mean Value	Rank	Life Event	Mean Value
1	Death of spouse	100	22	Change in responsibilities at work	29
2	Divorce	73	23	Son or daughter leaving home	29
3	Marital separation	65	24	Trouble with in-laws	29
4	Jail term	63	25	Outstanding personal achievement	28
5	Death of close family member	63	26	Wife begin or stop work	26
6	Personal injury or illness	53	27	Beginning or ending school	26
7	Marriage	50	28	Change in living conditions	24
8	Fired at work	47	29	Revision of personal habits	24
9	Marital reconciliation	45	30	Trouble with boss	23
10	Retirement	45	31	Change in work conditions	20
11	Change in health of family member	44	32	Change in residence	20
12	Pregnancy	40	33	Change in schools	20
13	Sex difficulties	39	34	Change in recreation	19
14	Gain of new family member	39	35	Change in church activities	19
15	Business readjustment	39	36	Change in social activities	18
16	Change in financial state	38	37	Mortgage or loans less than $10,000	17
17	Death of close friend	37	38	Change in sleeping habits	16
18	Change to different line of work	36	39	Change in number of family get-togethers	15
19	Change in number of arguments with spouse	35	40	Change in eating habits	15
20	Mortgage over $10,000	31	41	Vacation	13
21	Foreclosure of mortgage or loan	30	42	Christmas	12
			43	Minor violations of the law	11

FIGURE 17.2 *Researchers Thomas Holmes and Richard Rahe created the Social Readjustment Rating Scale to rank the effects of various life changes according to the amount of stress each produces. Since its creation in 1967, it has been revised and expanded by several other researchers.*

Reprinted with permission from T. H. Holmes and R. H. Rahe (1967). The social readjustment rating scale. *Journal of Psychosomatic Research,* 11, 213-218.

The Four Types of Conflict

Type of Conflict	Definition	Example
Approach-approach	A choice between two equally attractive alternatives	Choosing between cake and ice cream for dessert
Avoidance-avoidance	A choice between two equally unattractive alternatives	Going to the dentist or letting a toothache get worse
Approach-avoidance	A choice of whether or not to do something when part of the situation is attractive but the other is not	Deciding whether or not to buy a new CD player because it will cost a lot of money
Multiple approach-avoidance	A choice between alternatives that have both good and bad aspects	Deciding to stay at home to study for a test or to go out to the movies with friends

FIGURE 17.3 *Conflict, the feeling that you are being pulled in two or more directions by opposing forces or motives, can be a source of stress. Psychologists have identified four types of conflict.*

persistent self-doubts about whether he or she has made the right decision. The decision maker may not feel settled until he or she is in the new situation and knows that things are working out. For example, even after Todd talks with his father and decides which college he will attend, he may still feel uncertain until he settles into his dorm, meets his roommates, and begins classes.

A DAY IN THE LIFE

An **avoidance-avoidance conflict** is more stressful. People in this type of conflict are forced to choose "the lesser of two evils," that is, to choose between two unsatisfactory alternatives. People are motivated to avoid each of two negative goals, but the problem is that avoiding one requires approaching the other. For example, a student may be faced with the choice of dropping a course in which he or she is doing poorly and may receive a failing grade. However, by dropping the course, the student will not have enough credits to graduate. Both alternatives have a negative side.

A single goal can produce both approach and avoidance motives. This is called an **approach-avoidance conflict**. People face an approach-avoidance conflict when a choice is both good and bad at the same time. For Todd, it might be a college that has an excellent reputation and exactly the program he is looking for, but the college is very far away and visiting home will be difficult and costly.

The most complex form of conflict is a **multiple approach-avoidance conflict**. In this kind of conflict, each of several alternative courses of action has its advantages and disadvantages. Todd may face this type of conflict when he has to decide which college courses to take. The factors he will consider may include his level of interest in the subject, the reputation of the teacher, the usefulness of the course to his overall plan, and the difficulty of the course (does he have the educational background necessary to succeed).

When making a decision about what to eat in a restaurant, you might have to decide between food that is healthful but not very tasty, tasty food that is not very healthful, and food that is both tasty and healthful but is too expensive. In such a situation, you would be faced with a multiple approach-avoidance conflict.

When conflicting motives are strong, people may encounter high levels of stress and confusion about what course of action to choose. They need to make a decision to reduce the stress, yet decision making itself can be quite stressful, especially when there is no clear right choice. Some people cope with such difficult decisions by making a two-column list, jotting down all the reasons for and against a particular choice. The thought that goes into making the list sometimes helps people decide what to do.

CASE STUDIES

AND OTHER TRUE STORIES

Ten Doorways to Distress

According to psychologist Albert Ellis (1977, 1993), people's beliefs about events, as well as the events themselves, can be stressful. For example, a student who suddenly finds out she must move with her family to another state may feel a great deal of stress as she wonders how her life will change. Although the move itself may be stressful, anticipating the change and worrying about possible consequences may prove even more stressful.

Ellis uses an A-B-C approach when looking at each situation. For example, moving to another state is an activating event (A). The consequence (C) is stress. Between the activating event (A) and the consequence (C) lie beliefs (B). These beliefs may include such thoughts as "I may not be able to make friends in my new school." Anxieties about the future are normal and to be expected. However, according to Ellis, people tend to have irrational beliefs that can lead to both depression and stress. He calls these beliefs "personal doorways to distress" because they create problems themselves and, at the same time, aggravate problems from other sources.

Ellis has identified some of these unrealistic expectations and beliefs, which are described below.

Irrational Belief 1: I must have sincere love and approval just about all the time from the people who are important to me.

Irrational Belief 2: I must prove myself to be thoroughly adept at something important. (This belief is called perfectionism.)

Irrational Belief 3: Things have to go the way I want them to go. Life is awful when I can't have my first choice in everything.

Irrational Belief 4: Other people must treat me fairly and justly. When people act unfairly or unethically, they are bad.

Irrational Belief 5: When I see something that is dangerous or makes me afraid, I must concentrate on it and become upset.

Irrational Belief 6: People and things should turn out better than they do. It is terrible when I don't find quick solutions to life's hassles.

Irrational Belief 7: My emotional misery stems from outside pressures that I have little or no ability to control. Unless these pressures change, I'm going to have to stay stressed out.

Irrational Belief 8: It is easier to evade life's responsibilities and problems than to face them and try to work them out.

Irrational Belief 9: My past influenced me immensely and must therefore continue to determine the way I feel and act today.

Irrational Belief 10: I can achieve happiness by staying on my present path or by just enjoying myself from day to day.

In the case of the first irrational belief, for example, Ellis finds it understandable that people want the approval of others. However, he thinks it is irrational for them to believe that they cannot survive without it. The belief invites disappointment since it is unrealistic to expect approval all the time. Ellis allows that childhood experiences often explain where such beliefs come from. He also notes, however, that to retain those beliefs can cause much unhappiness. Challenging and changing irrational beliefs is an effective way to reduce stress.

Think About It

Select one of the irrational beliefs described above, and suggest ways to change it in order to avoid the stress it is likely to create.

Here is a classic example of a type A personality—highly driven, intense, and impatient.

Personality Types

Some people actually create their own stress. Psychologists have classified people into two basic personality types: type A (intense) and type B (laid-back). Type A people are always on the go; they put pressure on themselves and are constantly under stress. They are highly driven, competitive, and impatient. Type A people always feel rushed and pressured because they operate at full speed and become annoyed when there is even the slightest delay. They are irritable when they have to wait in line. Type A people never seem to have enough time, especially since they often try to do several things at once. They walk, eat, and talk faster than other people, and they are generally quick to become angry.

Type B people, in contrast, are more relaxed. They are more patient, do not become angry as easily, and are typically less driven than type A people. While type A people often earn more money than type B people do, type A people pay a high price for their "success." They must live with the heightened stress they create for themselves. Research shows that type A personalities run a much greater health risk than type B people. If they do not loosen up and relax, but instead continue their type A behavior, they are also in greater danger of suffering coronary heart disease.

THINKING ABOUT PSYCHOLOGY

1. What are the differences between daily hassles and life changes?
2. List the four types of conflict and give an example of each.
3. **Critical Thinking** Do you agree that some people create their own stress through type A behavior?

2 Responses to Stress

Psychological factors play an important role in people's responses to stress. People with different types of personalities respond to stress in different ways (Vaillant, 1994). People who are more relaxed and free of conflict are less likely than others to become sick when they do experience prolonged stress (Holahan & Moos, 1990).

A DAY IN THE LIFE

The stress of an event depends largely on what the event means to the person involved (Whitehead, 1994). Going to college is important to Todd, but leaving home and being away from his family and friends also means a great deal to him. Moving can be a positive or a negative event, depending on whether one moves to where one wants to be and on the difficulties of packing, unpacking, and paying for the move. Even

In contrast to type A individuals, those with type B personalities tend to be more relaxed, less ambitious, and more patient.

a positive move, such as moving to a larger house, creates some stress. However, a negative move, such as an eviction, is much more stressful because of the fear, anxiety, anger, and depression it can trigger.

Biological factors also account for some of the differences in people's responses to stress. Research suggests that some people inherit the tendency to develop certain health problems under stress. Yet most people can do things to influence or reduce the effects of their stress. Factors that influence the effects of stress include self-efficacy expectations, psychological hardiness, a sense of humor, predictability, and social support.

Self-Efficacy Expectations

Do you remember the story "The Little Engine That Could"? In an effort to pull a heavy load up a great hill, the engine repeated to itself, "I think I can, I think I can. . . ." The engine succeeded because of its self-efficacy expectations. **Self-efficacy expectations** are the beliefs people have that they can accomplish goals that they set for themselves. The goal might be to write a persuasive essay, dunk a basketball, or learn to solve math problems. Believing one can do it helps one reach the goal.

Self-efficacy expectations are closely related to self-confidence. Self-confidence affects people's abilities to withstand stress (Bandura, 1991; Basic Behavioral Science Task Force, 1996). For example, when people are in frightening situations, self-confidence reduces the level of adrenaline in the bloodstream (Bandura et al., 1985). As a result, people are less likely to experience panic and nervousness. People with more self-confidence—a strong belief that they can handle difficult situations—are also less likely than those with less self-confidence to be upset by stress. In other words, a self-confident person is more likely to keep cool under pressure.

Psychological Hardiness

Psychological hardiness is a personality characteristic that helps people withstand stress. The research on psychological hardiness is based on the pioneering work of Suzanne Kobasa and her colleagues (1982). They studied business executives who were able to resist illness despite heavy workloads and stress. The researchers found that these psychologically hardy executives differed from other executives in three important ways:

- Commitment. The hardy executives were highly committed to their jobs; they believed

A child who develops strong self-efficacy expectations will probably have a greater sense of self-confidence as an adult.

that their work was meaningful even though it was demanding and stressful; they regarded their stress as a source of motivation rather than as something that was victimizing them.

- Challenge. The hardy executives sought out challenges; they preferred change to stability, even though change required adjustment; they regarded change as interesting rather than threatening.

- Control. The hardy executives viewed themselves as being in control of their lives and able to influence and control the rewards and punishments they received; they did not feel helpless in the face of the forces that were involved in shaping their lives.

Other researchers have also found that believing that one is in control of one's situation tends to enhance one's feeling of self-confidence in the face of stress (Alloy & Clements, 1992).

Sense of Humor

When Janet jokingly hinted that she would beat Todd at basketball, she instinctively knew that humor was what the situation needed. Do you remember the old saying "Laughter is the best medicine"? The idea that

Both scientific studies and anecdotal evidence suggest that humor has positive effects on one's health.

Predictability

The ability to predict a stressor seems to reduce the amount of stress it causes. Predictability allows people to brace themselves for an event and, in many cases, to plan various ways to cope with it. Since having control of the situation helps reduce stress, having prior information about the expected stressor gives people a feeling that they will be able to deal with it. For example, ill people who ask about the medical procedures they will undergo and the pain they will experience tend to cope with the stress better than ill people who do not know what to expect (Ludwick-Rosenthal & Neufeld, 1993).

Social Support

The presence and interest of other people provide the social support that helps people cope with stress. Todd's friends realized he was under stress and tried to find ways to help him cope with it. Like psychological hardiness, social support helps insulate people from the effects of stress (Burman & Margolin, 1992; Coyne & Downey, 1991; Holahan & Moos, 1990). People who lack social skills and spend most of their time alone seem more likely to develop infectious diseases when they are under stress (Cohen & Williamson, 1991).

There are several ways to provide social support to people who are under stress.

- Express your concern by listening to people's problems and offering sympathy, understanding, and reassurance.
- Provide physical relief by offering the material support and services that help people adjust to stress—for example, financial assistance, food, and temporary shelter.
- Offer information, including advice, that helps people cope with stress.
- Provide feedback to help people understand or make sense of what they have experienced.
- Socialize, which includes talking, playing, or just being with the people who are under stress. While this may not directly solve people's problems, it helps them feel less isolated.

Research clearly suggests the value of social support. For example, older people who have social support recover more rapidly from physical problems than older people who have no support (Wilcox et al., 1994). People who have "buddies" who help them begin an exercise program are more

humor lightens the burdens of life is one that dates back to ancient times (Lefcourt & Martin, 1986). One study found that students who had a sense of humor and saw humor in difficult situations experienced less stress than students who were not able to find humor in the same situations (Martin & Lefcourt, 1983).

Research suggests that emotional responses such as happiness and even anger may have beneficial effects on the immune system as well (Kemeny, 1993). Since humor and laughter are connected with feelings of happiness, they probably really are good medicine for the body. In *Anatomy of an Illness*, Norman Cousins (1979) reported his experience with a painful illness that is similar to arthritis. He found that laughing at Marx Brothers movies reduced his pain. Laughter also helped him sleep better. He believed that it even reduced the painful inflammation in his joints.

TRUTH **OR** **fiction** ▪ R E V I S I T E D ▪

It is true that laughter can help people cope with stress. Research studies and the personal experiences of many people suggest that laughter is healthy and can actually reduce certain physical symptoms.

likely than others to stay with the activity (Gruder et al., 1993; Nides et al., 1995). Social support also appears to shield people and help them recover from feelings of depression (Holahan et al., 1995; Lewinsohn et al., 1994; McLeod et al., 1992).

People who receive social support may even live longer than those who do not. Two independent studies (Berkman & Breslow, 1983; House et al., 1982) found that the mortality rate was lower for married men than for single men. The mortality rate was lowest for married men who also regularly attended meetings of voluntary associations and who regularly engaged in social leisure activities.

THINKING ABOUT PSYCHOLOGY

1. What is psychological hardiness?
2. Describe five kinds of social support.
3. **Critical Thinking**   Explain how the predictability of a stressor can affect the impact of stress in a positive way.

When an animal is confronted by a stressor, it prepares itself for defensive action. During which stage of the GAS does this occur?

3
Physical Effects of Stress

How is it that daily hassles, life changes, conflict, and other sources of stress often make people ill? Stress researcher Hans Selye (1976) suggested that the body under stress is like a clock with an alarm that does not shut off.

The General Adaptation Syndrome

Selye observed that different stressful situations each produced similar responses by the body. Whether the source of stress was a financial problem, a physical threat, or a bacterial invasion, the body's response was the same. Selye labeled this response the **general adaptation syndrome** (GAS). The GAS has three stages: an alarm reaction, a resistance stage, and an exhaustion stage.

The Alarm Reaction   The alarm reaction is initiated when a stressor is perceived. This reaction alerts and mobilizes the body for defensive action. In the early 1900s, physiologist Walter Cannon described this internal alarm system as the "fight-or-flight" reaction.

Animals and human beings experience this fight-or-flight reaction in similar ways. Consider an animal's reaction when a stranger approaches or when the animal notices some other change in its environment that signals possible danger. You might react the same way. Imagine that, as you are about to go to sleep, you hear a loud noise in another room. Like the animal, you also become alert to your environment and sensitive to any sight, sound, or other stimulus around you that might indicate danger. Your body is in a state of high alert. Your heart is beating faster, your breathing is quicker, and your muscles are tense. Your body is in the fight-or-flight mode that occurs whenever danger is present.

During the alarm reaction, the sympathetic nervous system is activated (Gallucci et al., 1993). (See Chapter 3.) This produces a flood of stress hormones, including adrenaline, noradrenaline, adrenocorticotropic hormone (ACTH), and corticosteroids. These hormones act in different ways to prepare the body to deal with the stressor.

Adrenaline and noradrenaline arouse the body to help it cope with threats and stress. They do this by speeding up the heart rate and causing the liver to release glucose (sugar), which provides energy for the body under stress. Corticosteroids and ACTH protect the body from allergic reactions (such as difficulty breathing). They also produce an inflammation that increases circulation to the part of the body that may be injured. Finally, they send

The "Fight-or-Flight" Response

- Air passages widen to allow more air intake
- Hair stands on end
- Level of blood sugar increases
- Heart rate increases
- Muscles tighten up
- Blood pressure rises
- Senses sharpen and become more alert
- Steroids and adrenaline are secreted

GRRRR!

FIGURE 17.4 *When a person first perceives a stressor, the body initiates an alarm reaction, which mobilizes the body for defensive action. This reaction is known as the fight-or-flight response.*

white blood cells to the injury to fight off invading germs. Some of the changes that occur as a result of the alarm reaction are shown in Figure 17.4. Once the stressor or threat is removed, the body returns to its previous state.

The Resistance Stage   If the alarm reaction mobilizes the body and the stressor is not removed, people enter the resistance stage of the GAS. During this stage, people find a way to cope with the stressor to avoid being overwhelmed by their negative reactions to the stressor. Hormones are still being released but at lower levels than in the alarm reaction stage. The body tries to regain its lost energy, repair damage, and restore balance. However, at this stage, people may still feel enough of a strain to continue to experience some physical symptoms.

The Exhaustion Stage   If the stressor is still not removed, people may enter the exhaustion stage of the GAS. The capacity to resist stress varies from person to person, but everyone eventually becomes exhausted when severe stressors persist. At this

stage, the adrenal and other glands activated by the fight-or-flight reaction can no longer continue to secrete hormones. People's muscles become worn out. Their heart and breathing rates slow down.

As the resources available to combat stress become depleted, people reach a breaking point. Continued stress during the exhaustion stage may cause people to develop severe health problems ranging from allergies and hives to ulcers and heart disease—and even death.

Effects of Stress on the Immune System

Stress also affects the body's ability to cope with disease. Research shows that chronic stress suppresses the activity of the body's immune system (Coe, 1993; Delahanty et al., 1996; O'Leary, 1990).

The Immune System   You might think that some people, luckily, are not exposed to the kinds of organisms that cause serious health problems. Actually, that is not true. Most people are exposed

This marathon runner has probably entered the exhaustion stage, during which the adrenal gland and other glands that were activated by the alarm reaction can no longer continue to secrete hormones and the runner's muscles become worn out.

Stress and the Immune System One of the reasons that stress eventually exhausts people is that it stimulates their bodies to produce steroids, which suppress the functioning of the immune system. Persistent secretion of steroids interferes with the formation of antibodies, which are so crucial in fighting germs.

In the case of some serious diseases, such as cancer, the added stress that results from having a life-threatening disease contributes to the suppression of the immune system, thus leading to further health problems (Andersen et al., 1994).

A study of dental students showed the effects of stress on the immune system (Jemmott et al., 1983). To test the functioning of each student's immune system, researchers measured the level of antibodies in the students' saliva at different times during the school year. The lower the level of antibodies, the lower a person's immune-system functioning.

Students showed lower immune-system functioning during more stressful school periods than during the periods immediately after vacations. The study also showed that students with many friends had healthier immune systems than students with fewer friends. The study suggests that social support may have been a factor in insulating some students from the detrimental effects of stress.

Other studies have found that the stress of examinations weakens the capacity of the immune system to combat certain viruses, such as the Epstein-Barr virus, which causes fatigue and other health problems (Glaser et al., 1991, 1993). In yet another study—this one with older people—researchers found that training aimed at improving coping skills and relaxation techniques improved the functioning of the immune systems of the participants (Glaser et al., 1991).

These studies prove that stress causes the immune system to function less effectively. They also indicate that social support, which reduces stress, makes the immune system function better.

to a great variety of disease-carrying organisms. However, an intact immune system manages to fight off most of them.

How does the immune system fight against disease? The immune system prevents disease by producing white blood cells that destroy disease-causing microorganisms (bacteria, fungi, and viruses), worn-out body cells, and cells that have become malignant (cancerous). White blood cells engage in search-and-destroy missions. They first recognize and then destroy foreign bodies and unhealthy cells.

Some white blood cells produce antibodies—chemicals that attach to harmful cells and microorganisms, marking them for destruction. Other white blood cells destroy the foreign bodies by surrounding and digesting them. The immune system "remembers" these invaders and maintains antibodies in the bloodstream to fight them, often for years.

TRUTH
OR
fiction
■ R E V I S I T E D ■

It is not true that few people are exposed to the microorganisms that cause disease. Most people are continuously exposed to a great variety of disease-causing microorganisms. However, a healthy immune system produces white blood cells that fight off most of them.

THINKING ABOUT PSYCHOLOGY

1. List and describe the three stages of the general adaptation syndrome.

2. How does the immune system protect people against disease?

3. **Critical Thinking** What advice for maintaining his or her immune system would you give to a student who was in a high-pressure situation?

4
Psychological Factors and Health

Why do some people develop cancer or have heart attacks? Why do others seem immune to these health problems? Why do some people seem to fall prey to just about everything that is going around, while others ride out the longest winters with hardly a sniffle?

Biological factors play an important role in physical illness. For example, family history of a certain disease can certainly increase a person's susceptibility to that disease. Other biological factors that are involved in the development of illness include exposure to disease-causing microorganisms, inoculations against certain diseases, accidents and injuries, and age.

A family history of health problems, such as heart disease and cancer, tempts some people to assume there is little they can do to influence their health. But one's family history (or genetic inheritance) merely suggests a potential for developing an illness. Health writer Jane Brody (1995) noted that a bad family medical history should not be considered a sign of doom. She noted that, instead, it should be welcomed as an opportunity to keep the harmful genes from expressing themselves.

 Prolonged stesss may have caused Marc's father to develop heart problems. This does not necessarily mean, however, that Marc will develop similar health problems. Instead, it has helped Marc recognize how harmful stress can be and take steps to manage the stress in his own life—and advise his friend Todd to do the same.

While biological factors are important, many health problems are affected by psychological factors, such as one's attitudes and patterns of behavior (Ader, 1993; Angell, 1993; Farley, 1993). Psychological states of anxiety and depression can impair the functioning of the immune system and make people all the more vulnerable to health problems (Esterling et al., 1993; Herbert & Cohen, 1993; Kemeny et al., 1994).

Health psychology is concerned with the relationship between psychological factors and the prevention and treatment of physical illness (Taylor,

1990). In recent years, health psychologists have been exploring the various ways in which states of mind influence physical well-being. Because of the growing recognition of the link between psychological factors and health, an estimated 3,500 psychologists are now on the faculties of medical schools (Matarazzo, 1993; Wiggins, 1994).

This section examines the interrelationship of biological and psychological factors in the development and treatment of three fairly common health problems: headaches, heart disease, and cancer. Health psychologists have made important contributions to the understanding and treatment of all three of these medical problems.

Headaches

Among the most common stress-related health problems are headaches. People under stress will sometimes get a headache as a direct result of feeling tense. Todd felt a headache developing as he was trying to deal with the stress of getting his scholarship application in on time. It is estimated that 20 percent of Americans experience intense stress-induced headaches such as the one Todd suffered.

Headaches are among the most common stress-related health problems. They can be treated with medicine and various behavioral methods, such as progressive relaxation and biofeedback.

Types of Headaches There are several types of headaches. The single most frequent kind is the muscle-tension headache. When people are under stress, the muscles in their shoulders, neck, forehead, and scalp tend to tighten up. Prolonged stress can lead to prolonged muscle contraction, which causes muscle-tension headaches. Such headaches usually come on gradually. They are characterized by dull, steady pain on both sides of the head and by feelings of tightness or pressure.

Most other types of headaches, including the severe migraine headaches, stem from changes in the blood supply to the head (Welch, 1993). Migraine headaches are intensely painful. They are caused by a two-stage process that begins with the constriction, or narrowing, of the arteries that supply blood to the brain. This constriction of the arteries often produces warning signals that a migraine headache is coming. These signals include dizziness, a flushed feeling, visual problems, and sometimes a sense of unusual odors. Little or no pain may be felt at this stage.

In the second stage of migraine headaches, the arteries dilate, or expand. The expanding arteries press on nerve endings that surround the arteries, producing the great pain associated with migraine headaches. The migraines themselves often include sensitivity to light, loss of appetite, nausea, vomiting, loss of balance, and significant changes in mood. Migraine headaches tend to come on suddenly and are characterized by intense throbbing on one side of the head. They can occur at any age but usually begin when people are between the ages of 10 and 30.

Migraine headaches may be caused by a change in air pressure (such as the change in atmospheric pressure that occurs before a thunderstorm), pollen, hormonal changes connected with menstruation, certain drugs, the flavor-enhancing chemical monosodium glutamate (MSG), chocolate, and aged cheeses (Brody, 1992). Type A behavior may also contribute to migraine headaches. One study found that 53 percent of people who experience migraine headaches had type A personalities (Rappaport et al., 1988).

People who suffer from headaches can become caught in a vicious cycle. The reason is that headache pain is itself a stressor that increases muscle tension in the neck, shoulders, scalp, and face. That tension makes the headaches worse.

Treatment Aspirin, acetaminophen, and ibuprofen are frequently used to reduce pain, including headache pain. These drugs work by inhibiting the production of certain chemical compounds that transmit pain messages to the brain. Other medications that affect the blood flow in the brain can also help people who suffer from migraine headaches (Welch, 1993).

Behavioral methods are another means of helping reduce the pain of headaches. Progressive relaxation is one way of decreasing muscle tension and has been shown to be effective in relieving muscle-tension headaches (Blanchard, 1992b; Blanchard et al., 1990a, 1991). Biofeedback training that alters the flow of blood to the head has helped many people with migraine headaches (Blanchard et al., 1990b; Gauthier et al., 1994). However, these methods, like other forms of treatment, should be attempted only under the supervision of a trained professional. (See Chapter 5.)

Heart Disease

Nearly half the deaths in the United States are caused by heart disease (U.S. Department of Health and Human Services, 1991), making it a major national health problem. Marc's father is just one of the people who have developed heart disease. There are many risk factors associated with heart disease.

A DAY IN THE LIFE

- Family history (genetics). People with a family history of heart disease are more likely than others to develop heart disease themselves (Marenberg et al., 1994).

- Physical conditions. Obesity, high serum cholesterol levels, and hypertension all contribute to heart disease. About one American in five has hypertension, or abnormally high blood pressure (Leary, 1991). Although there appears to be a genetic component to hypertension (Caulfield et al., 1994), many other factors are also involved. These factors include smoking, obesity, and excessive salt in one's diet. Blood pressure also rises when people become angry or are on guard against threats (Suls et al., 1995).

- Patterns of consumption. Heavy drinking, smoking, overeating, and eating food high in cholesterol can also contribute to heart disease (Castelli, 1994; Keil, 1993). Smoking, for example, raises the level of cholesterol in the blood and weakens the walls of blood vessels (Bartecchi et al., 1994).

EXPLORING
DIVERSITY

Cultural Differences in Diet and Health

How important is an individual's diet to his or her health? In their search for evidence about the relationship between diet and health, researchers often look at Asian countries, where rates for cancer, heart disease, and other degenerative diseases are notably lower than in Western nations.

Research indicates that death rates from cancer and heart disease are relatively high in Western nations such as the Netherlands, Denmark, England, Canada, and the United States, where people eat foods with a high fat content (Cohen, 1987). Death rates from cancer, heart disease, and other serious conditions are lower in Asian nations such as Thailand, the Philippines, Japan, and China, where the consumption of fat is also lower.

Studies have shown that the difference has more to do with diet than with race. For example, the diets of Japanese Americans are similar in fat content to those of other Americans—and so are their death rates from cancer. Because of dietary differences, Japanese American men living in California and Hawaii are also much more likely to become overweight than Japanese men who live in Japan (Curb & Marcus, 1991).

One of the most extensive nutrition research projects ever undertaken was conducted by Dr. T. Colin Campbell, professor of nutritional biochemistry at Cornell University, and colleagues from China and Oxford University. Begun in 1983, the China Diet and Health Study used the vast population of China to study the relationship between

The low-fat diet in many Asian countries has been linked to lower rates of cancer, heart disease, and other degenerative diseases than the rates in Western countries.

dietary intake and health. Beginning in 1983, the study collected information about the eating habits and health records of thousands of people in 65 Chinese provinces. The researchers studied the kinds of foods eaten, examined medical records, took blood samples, and made other tests on thousands of people living in rural China.

In 1991, Dr. Campbell's team published an 896-page report containing their initial findings, which they are continuing to analyze and add to as the study progresses. So far, the researchers have found that the Chinese consume far greater amounts of rice and other grains, vegetables, and legumes (beans and peas) than Americans do. They also found that Asian diets are much lower in protein than the average American diet. On average, Asians eat far less meat and dairy products than Americans do. The Chinese plant-based diets are much more healthful because they consist of significantly less fat and animal protein.

The preliminary conclusion of this ongoing study is that the Chinese diet of good-quality plant foods is preventing a wide range of degenerative diseases. "Our study suggests," says Dr. Campbell, "that the closer one approaches a total plant food diet, the greater the health benefits."

Think About It

Suggest some positive dietary changes that Americans could make to ensure longer and healthier lives.

- Type A behavior. People who exhibit type A behavior are more likely than people who exhibit type B behavior to develop heart disease (Thoresen & Powell, 1992).

- Anger and hostility. A constant need to control angry and hostile impulses increases the risk of developing heart disease (Kneip et al., 1993; Suarez et al., 1993).

- Job strain. Overtime work, assembly line labor, and exposure to conflicting demands on the job can all contribute to heart disease (Jenkins, 1988).

- Lack of exercise. People who do not get regular exercise are more likely to suffer from coronary heart disease than those who do exercise regularly (Dubbert, 1992; Lakka et al., 1994).

Once heart disease has been diagnosed, various medical treatments, such as surgery and medication, are available. However, people can also benefit from behavioral changes that reduce the risks of heart disease. Among these behavioral changes are the following:

- Quitting smoking. The links between smoking and heart disease (and lung cancer) make quitting smoking one of the best ways to reduce the risks of serious health problems.

- Controlling weight. Maintaining a healthy weight appropriate to one's body proportions, not being either overweight or underweight, can help reduce the risk of heart disease.

- Reducing hypertension. Relaxation training, meditation, exercise, weight control, and a reduction in the intake of salt all help control blood pressure.

- Lowering serum cholesterol levels. Behavioral methods for lowering cholesterol include cutting down on foods high in cholesterol and saturated fats and exercising regularly (Castelli, 1994; Shepherd et al., 1995).

- Changing type A behavior patterns. Learning to slow down and relax can decrease the risk of heart attacks. This is especially true for people who exhibit type A behavior and who have had previous heart attacks (Friedman & Ulmer, 1984; Roskies et al., 1986).

- Exercising regularly. A sustained program of exercise protects people from heart disease (Castelli, 1994; Curfman, 1993b). (People should consult their physicians before beginning an exercise program.)

Cancer

Cancer is a disease that involves the rapid and abnormal growth of malignant cells. Cancerous cells can take root anywhere—for example, in the blood, skin, bones, digestive tract, lungs, or reproductive organs. If not controlled early, cancer cells can spread and establish masses, or tumors, elsewhere in the body. People actually develop cancer cells frequently, but the immune system normally succeeds in destroying them. Individuals whose immune systems are weakened by physical or psychological problems appear to be more likely candidates than others for getting cancer (Antoni, 1987; Greenberg, 1987).

TRUTH OR **fiction** ■ R E V I S I T E D ■ *It is true that many people develop cancerous cells but do not become ill from them. A strong immune system regularly rids the body of such cells. A weakened immune system has a more difficult time destroying them.*

Risk Factors People may inherit a tendency to develop certain kinds of cancer. The genes involved may remove the normal controls on cell division, allowing cancer cells to multiply wildly ("Damaged Gene," 1996). Certain kinds of behavior also increase the risk of cancer. These behaviors include smoking, sunbathing (ultraviolet light can cause skin cancer), and eating animal fats (Bartecchi et al., 1994; Willett et al., 1990). Substances in cigarette smoke may damage the genes that would otherwise block the development of many types of cancers. Psychological problems such as prolonged anxiety and depression may also heighten the risk of cancer (Antoni, 1987).

Research suggests that stress may be an additional risk factor for the development of cancer. In one study, researchers separated mice into one of two groups. One group was regularly subjected to stressful conditions, while the other group was not. The immune systems of the mice in the group that was exposed to stressful conditions showed a reduced ability to kill tumor cells compared to the mice that were not exposed to stressful conditions (Kandil & Borysenko, 1987). Other experiments with animals have suggested that once cancer has taken root, stress can affect the course of its development (Visintainer et al., 1982).

In one study, researcher V. Riley (1981) examined the effects of a cancer-causing virus that can be passed from female mice to their nursing offspring. The virus usually produces breast cancer in 80 percent of the female offspring by the time they have reached the age of 400 days.

Riley placed one group of female offspring that had been infected with the virus into a stressful environment with loud noises and unpleasant odors. She placed another group in a less stressful environment. By the age of 400 days, 92 percent of the female mice in the stressful environment had developed breast cancer, as compared with 7 percent of those in the other group. The mice that underwent stress also had increased levels of steroids that suppress the functioning of the immune system.

However, by the time another 200 days had elapsed, the mice that had been placed in the non-stressful environment showed about the same incidence of cancer as those that had experienced the stressful environment. Exposure to stress seemed to hasten the development of cancer in the mice infected with the cancer-causing virus. Nevertheless, the absence of stress did not prevent mice placed in a less stressful atmosphere from ultimately developing cancer as well.

Psychological Aspects People with cancer must cope with the many biological aspects of their illness, ranging from possible weakness and pain to the side effects of their medications. They also face many psychological effects of cancer. Anxiety about the medical treatment itself and about the possible approach of death are common psychological effects of cancer. Additionally, severe depression and feelings of vulnerability often accompany the diagnosis of cancer (Jacox et al., 1994).

Many people who are diagnosed with cancer are also burdened by the necessity of dealing with the insensitivity of others. Other people may actually criticize the person with the illness for feeling sorry for himself or herself or for "giving up" the fight against the disease (Andersen et al., 1994; Rosenthal, 1993).

Painful side effects sometimes accompany the treatment for certain types of cancer. For example, nausea frequently accompanies chemotherapy. People receiving chemotherapy are sometimes taught relaxation and guided imagery techniques, which have been shown to significantly reduce the nausea and vomiting associated with chemotherapy (Burish et al., 1987).

Studies with children and adolescents who have cancer have found that playing video games also reduces the discomfort of chemotherapy (Kolko & Rickard-Figueroa, 1985; Redd et al., 1987). By allowing the children to focus their attention on battling computer-generated enemies, such games help keep the children distracted from the chemicals being injected into their bodies.

Cancer requires medical treatment, and in some cases there are too few available treatment options. However, the attitudes people have about their cancer do seem to make a difference. A 10-year follow-up of women with breast cancer found a significantly higher survival rate among women who met their diagnosis with a "fighting spirit" rather than with acceptance or resignation (Pettingale et al., 1985). A desire to fight the illness is apparently a key component of successful treatment. Social support also increases the survival rate of people who have cancer (Sleek, 1995).

Psychologists have found that the feelings of hopelessness that sometimes accompany the diagnosis of cancer may hinder recovery because they can suppress the person's immune system (Brody, 1994; Levy et al., 1985). Hospitalization itself is stressful because it removes people from the familiar surroundings of home and the sources of social support. Furthermore, being in the hospital and subject to hospital routines—for any reason—reduces one's sense of control.

In some cases, there may not be a great deal that a person with cancer can do to affect the eventual outcome of the disease. However, there are numerous ways to reduce the risk of developing cancer. The most effective way is to avoid behavioral risk factors for cancer by reducing the intake of fats and increasing the intake of fruits and vegetables (Mevkens, 1990; Willett et al., 1990). Controlling the amount of stress one is exposed to and having regular medical checkups are also vital factors in the reduction of the risk of developing cancer.

THINKING ABOUT PSYCHOLOGY

1. What psychological factors contribute to headaches, heart disease, and cancer?

2. Explain how stress might affect the progression of cancer.

3. **Critical Thinking** Explain how psychological methods can be used to help people prevent or deal effectively with health problems.

Ways of Coping with Stress

5

Because stress harms people's physical and psychological well-being, it is important to know how to cope with or reduce the stress in one's life. In this section we consider various ways of handling stress, including defensive coping and active coping.

Defensive Coping

Defensive coping is one way to reduce the immediate effects of a stressor, but it is probably not the most desirable way. Defensive coping may involve socially unacceptable behavior (substance abuse or aggression), running away from one's problems (withdrawal), or self-deception (use of defense mechanisms).

Defensive coping may give people time to gather their resources, but it does not eliminate the source of stress or improve the effectiveness of one's response to stress. In fact, in the long run, defensive methods are self-defeating and usually harmful.

Some people use aggression to cope with stressful situations. However, aggressive behavior can often increase conflict rather than resolve it.

Substance Abuse   Some adolescents and adults use alcohol, tranquilizers, and other drugs to try to reduce feelings of stress (Wills et al., 1996). People may become psychologically dependent on these substances as they try to decrease their awareness of stress or to disguise what has become, for them, an unpleasant reality. That dependence only makes a problem worse because it makes people less able and less willing to deal with it.

Aggression   Some people use aggression and violence to cope with stressful situations, such as those that involve feelings of frustration or a difference of opinion with another person. However, violence rarely, if ever, provides solutions to people's problems. In fact, aggressive behavior often heightens social conflict because it may motivate a person to seek revenge.

Withdrawal   Some people withdraw from a stressful situation because they are frightened, feel helpless, or believe that any decision they make will be a mistake. Withdrawal can be emotional (loss of interest in life, turning away from friends and family), or it can be physical (moving to a new location to avoid dealing with an old problem).

Suicide   Suicide is the ultimate form of withdrawal. Some people experience so much stress and feel so hopeless about solving their problems that they believe the only way out is to commit suicide. Of course, suicide never solves or reduces problems. It usually only increases the pain of those who are left to deal with its aftermath.

Defense Mechanisms   Sigmund Freud believed that defense mechanisms protect the ego from anxiety that may be produced by an awareness of unacceptable ideas or impulses. (See Chapter 14.) Defense mechanisms become problematic when they are the only means used to cope with stress.

Active Coping

Active coping involves changing the environment or situation (in socially acceptable ways) to remove stressors or changing one's response to stress so that stressors are no longer harmful. Todd was actively coping with the stressors in his life by submitting his scholarship application, talking with his father about his college selection, and completing his biology project.

Changing Stressful Thoughts

Stressful Thoughts	Calming Thoughts
"I feel like I'm losing control."	"This is painful and upsetting, but I don't have to go to pieces."
"This will never end."	"This will come to an end even if it's hard to see it right now."
"How can I go out there? I'll look like a fool."	"So you're not perfect. That doesn't mean that you're going to look stupid. And so what if someone thinks you look stupid? You can live with that too. Just stop worrying and have some fun."
"My heart is beating so fast. I feel like it's about to leap out of my chest."	"Calm down—hearts don't leap out of chests. Stop and think! Distract yourself. Breathe slowly, in and out."
"There's nothing I can do!"	"Stop and think—just because you can't come up with a solution right now doesn't mean there's nothing you can do. Take it a minute at a time. Breathe easy."

FIGURE 17.5 *Some people think stressful thoughts—thoughts that increase the stress they experience. People can actively cope with stress by becoming aware of these thoughts and changing them.*

Sometimes stressors cannot be reduced, eliminated, or changed. In such cases, active coping involves adjusting to the stressors by reducing their impact. When Janet suggested playing basketball with Todd, she was trying to help him soften the effect of the stressors he was experiencing. Some methods of active coping include changing stressful thoughts, relaxing, and strengthening one's ability to withstand stress through exercise.

Changing Stressful Thoughts   Have you ever had any of these thoughts?

"I feel like I'm losing control."

"This will never end."

"How can I go out there? I'll look like a fool."

"My heart is beating so fast. I feel like it's about to leap out of my chest."

"There's nothing I can do!"

Each of these thoughts increases the amount of stress people experience. However, people who have stressful thoughts can learn to recognize and change them before becoming overwhelmed by them. Through careful study, people can learn to identify self-defeating thoughts. Whenever a person feels tense or anxious, he or she should pay close attention to the thoughts and transform them into calming ones. (See Figure 17.5.) A sign that this is working is evident when the person begins to automatically have calming thoughts rather than stressful ones.

Relaxation   Stress can cause strong bodily reactions, such as muscle tension, rapid breathing, high blood pressure, sweating, and a rapid heart rate. These reactions are signs that something is wrong. They prompt people to survey the situation and try to make things right. Psychologists and other researchers have developed a number of methods for reducing the bodily changes that are brought on by stress. These include meditation, biofeedback, and progressive relaxation. (See Chapter 5.)

Progressive relaxation helps lower stress in the body by reducing muscle tension. Reducing tension also affects the heart and breathing rates. Progressive relaxation teaches people how to relax by having them purposely tense a specific muscle group and then relax it. This process of tensing and then relaxing helps people (1) develop awareness of muscle tension and (2) distinguish between feelings of tension and feelings of relaxation. For example, a person can experience muscle relaxation in the arms while leaning back in a reclining chair by first tightening one fist, then the other, and gradually increasing the pressure (Wolpe & Lazarus, 1966).

Changing stressful thoughts and lowering the level of bodily reactions to stress reduce the effects of stressors and give the person more time to develop a plan for effective action. When there is no way to reduce or eliminate the stressors, thinking calming thoughts and relaxing the body will increase the ability to endure stress.

Exercise Exercise fosters physical health, enhances people's psychological well-being, and helps people cope with stress (Berger, 1993; Hays, 1995). Janet knew that. That's why she suggested to Todd that they play basketball. Other kinds of stress-reducing exercise include activities such as running and jogging, running in place, brisk walking, swimming, bicycle riding, jumping rope, and playing team sports.

Sustained physical activity reduces the incidence of heart attacks (Castelli, 1994; Curfman, 1993a). In one long-term research project, Paffenbarger and his colleagues (1993) studied

Exercise is one of the most effective ways to control stress and maintain physical and psychological well-being.

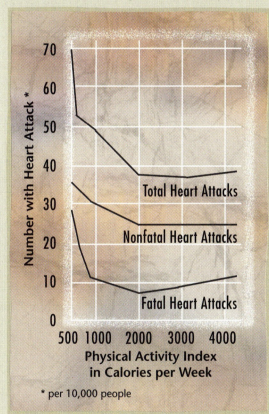

Incidence of Heart Attacks and Level of Physical Activity

Number with Heart Attack *

Total Heart Attacks

Nonfatal Heart Attacks

Fatal Heart Attacks

500 1000 2000 3000 4000

Physical Activity Index in Calories per Week

* per 10,000 people

FIGURE 17.6 *Research suggests that sustained physical activity reduces the incidence of heart attacks. In one study, researchers (1993) correlated the incidence of heart attacks with the level of physical activity. Their results showed a decline in the incidence of heart attacks as the activity level rose. The decline seemed to level off at the activity level of burning approximately 2,000 calories a week.*

Source: Paffenbarger et al. (1993). *New England Journal of Medicine. 328,* 538–545.

17,000 people. They examined the relationship between the incidence of heart attacks and the levels of physical activity in the people they studied. As shown in Figure 17.6, the incidence of heart attacks began declining when the physical activity level rose to that of burning as few as 500 calories a week.

Inactive people run the highest risk of heart attacks. People who burn at least 2,000 calories a week through physical activity live two years longer, on average, than less active people. Sustained exercise also appears to strengthen the functioning of the immune system (Antoni et al., 1991; Laperriere et al., 1991).

THINKING ABOUT PSYCHOLOGY

1. What is the difference between defensive coping and active coping?

2. How do people's thoughts affect the amount of stress they experience?

3. **Critical Thinking** Explain how methods of defensive coping become harmful rather than helpful.

17 REVIEW

Chapter

SUMMARY

Stress has many sources and can contribute to health problems ranging from headaches to cancer. People have different ways of coping with stress.

I. What Is Stress?

A. Stress is the demand made on an organism to adapt, to cope, and to adjust.

B. Positive stress is called eustress; negative stress is called distress.

C. An event or situation that produces stress is called a stressor; stressors include frustration, daily hassles, life changes, and conflict.

D. There are four types of conflict.
1. Approach-approach (both goals are desirable and attainable).
2. Avoidance-avoidance (neither option is desirable).
3. Approach-avoidance (the option is both good and bad at the same time).
4. Multiple approach-avoidance (several options exist and each has many advantages and disadvantages).

E. Psychologists have classified people into two basic personality types: type A (intense) and type B (laid-back).

II. Responses to Stress

A. People's responses to stress vary, depending on what an event means to them.

B. Psychological factors, such as personality type, play an important role in a person's reaction to stress. Biological factors also account for some of the variability in people's responses to stress.

C. Self-efficacy expectations are the beliefs that people have that they can accomplish what they set out to do; self-efficacy is related to self-confidence and the ability to withstand stress.

D. Psychological hardiness helps people withstand stress.

E. Humor may be beneficial in combating illness and reducing stress.

F. The ability to predict a stressor seems to reduce its effects.

G. Social support often helps people deal with stress.

III. Physical Effects of Stress

A. Hans Selye observed that although stressful situations differ, the body's responses to various stressors are similar. The general adaptation syndrome (GAS) has three stages: the alarm reaction, the resistance stage, and the exhaustion stage.

B. Stress affects the body's ability to cope with disease by weakening the immune system.

IV. Psychological Factors and Health

A. Health psychology is concerned with the relationship between psychological factors and physical health.

B. Headaches are among the most common stress-related health problems.

C. Heart disease is the leading cause of death in the United States. Factors that contribute to heart disease include family history of heart disease, physical condition, patterns of consumption, type A behavior, anger and hostility, and job pressures.

D. People whose immune systems are weakened by physical or psychological problems appear to develop cancer more readily than those without such problems.

V. Ways of Coping with Stress

A. Defensive coping may involve socially unacceptable behavior, social withdrawal, or self-deception.

B. Active coping involves changing the environment or situation in socially acceptable ways to remove stressors or changing one's response to stress so that stressors are no longer harmful.

TERM & CONCEPT
REVIEW

1. What is eustress? What are its benefits?
2. What are daily hassles? List two examples of daily hassles.
3. Identify the four types of conflict. Which type is the least stressful?
4. List the two basic personality types and their characteristics.
5. How does predictability reduce the harmful effects of stress?
6. What is the general adaptation syndrome (GAS)? What are its three stages?
7. What is health psychology?
8. What are some behavioral methods for reducing the pain of headaches?
9. List three behavioral changes that help reduce the risk of heart disease.
10. List two defensive coping methods and two active coping methods.

CRITICAL
THINKING

1. Which of the following reactions to stress are defensive coping and which are active coping: overeating, leaving for work early to avoid rush hour traffic, lying down and listening to music?
2. Using examples not in the text, create a situation to illustrate each of the four types of conflict: approach-approach, avoidance-avoidance, approach-avoidance, and multiple approach-avoidance.
3. Think of a stressful experience you have encountered in the past few months. Explain how you coped with it, positively or negatively.
4. Insurance companies often charge higher rates for people with higher health risks, such as smokers and people with high blood pressure. Knowing that high levels of stress can be a health risk, do you think insurance companies should charge higher rates to people under high levels of stress? Why or why not? Do you think it would be possible for an insurance company to determine who is highly stressed? Explain your answer.
5. Describe a time when eustress helped you perform better.
6. Describe a time when distress hindered your performance.

APPLYING SKILLS
IN PSYCHOLOGY

1. **Using Your Observation Skills** Observe your family and friends for a week. Record situations they encountered in which the fight-or-flight response was triggered. Did they experience the three stages of GAS?
2. **Writing About Psychology** Reread the section in the chapter on type A and type B personalities. Think of famous people (present or past) or fictional characters that exemplify either type of personality. Write a paragraph to explain each choice.
3. **Research in Psychology** High levels of stress on the job, as with other kinds of stress, can greatly affect a person's health and well-being. Do some research on stress in the workplace. What kinds of situations contribute to job stress? Briefly explain how employers attempt to deal with job stress? Write a 500-word report on your findings.
4. **COOPERATIVE LEARNING** **Writing About Psychology** The Social Readjustment Rating Scale created by Holmes and Rahe (shown on page 389) focuses primarily on life changes experienced by adults. In small groups, create a social readjustment rating scale for teens. Make a list of 20 events, and assign a rating to each item on the basis of a consensus of group members. Post the completed scales in the classroom so others can see them. As a class, discuss the similarities and differences between the scales and whether or not you agree with the events and the ratings the other groups listed.

18 PSYCHOLOGICAL DISORDERS

Objectives

1 Explain the basis for classifying psychological disorders.

2 Distinguish among the anxiety disorders, and outline the theories that explain them.

3 Define *dissociation,* and describe the dissociative disorders.

4 Explain somatization, and list the symptoms of two somatoform disorders.

5 Identify several theories that attempt to explain mood disorders.

6 Describe subtypes and causes of schizophrenia.

7 Distinguish personality disorders from other psychological disorders.

A DAY IN THE LIFE

May 16

Janet was studying in her room when the telephone rang. "Hello?" she answered.

"Hey, Janet, it's me—Dan. Can you talk for a minute?"

Janet and Dan had been friends for years, and she could always tell when he sounded depressed. "Of course I can. What's up?" Janet answered, trying to sound positive.

"It's Michelle again," Dan said.

About a year ago, Dan's older sister, Michelle, had been diagnosed with a serious psychological disorder called schizophrenia. Michelle was 23 years old and lived with her husband, Jeff, in a small house in the country. Accepting the fact that Michelle had a psychological disorder had been difficult for Dan. At first, he didn't talk about it with anyone outside his family. Then, after a while, he began confiding in Janet.

"It's so hard sometimes," Dan said sadly. "I really thought she was going to be okay after the doctors finally diagnosed and started treating her last year."

"Did something happen?" Janet asked, genuinely concerned.

"Well, I hadn't seen her in weeks because Jeff was the only person she would talk to. I finally saw her tonight, and I could tell that something was happening again. She always seems so distracted. It's like she's listening to something only she can hear."

"Has she been taking the medicine that the doctor prescribed?" Janet asked.

"I don't know for sure," Dan answered. "I asked her about it tonight, but she got really defensive. She kept saying that I was trying to confuse her, and then she insisted that Jeff take her home."

"I'm sorry, Dan. I wish there were something I could do," Janet responded sympathetically.

"Thanks," Dan said. "It really helps to be able to talk to someone. At least I'm handling it a lot better than my parents are. My mom thinks that somehow it's her fault—like it is hereditary or Michelle caught it as a baby."

"Do the doctors have any idea how she *did* get it?" Janet asked.

"Not really," Dan said. "They have a bunch of different theories, but I don't think they know for sure. I'm just hoping that somehow they'll figure out exactly what's wrong so they'll be able to really help her."

"Me, too," Janet replied softly.

Key Terms

- psychological disorder
- culture-bound syndrome
- anxiety
- phobia
- simple phobia
- social phobia
- panic attack
- agoraphobia
- obsession
- compulsion
- post-traumatic stress disorder
- dissociation
- depersonalization
- somatization
- depression
- bipolar disorder
- mania
- schizophrenia
- catatonic stupor

Dan's sister, Michelle, has schizophrenia, a serious psychological disorder that causes her to hear things that others cannot hear and, in general, often to lose touch with reality. Most psychological disorders are less serious than schizophrenia, but they still may cause great distress for affected individuals and their families and friends. This chapter describes several types of psychological disorders, including schizophrenia. The treatment of psychological disorders is the focus of Chapter 19.

Estimates suggest that about one out of every three people in the United States will have a psychological disorder at some point in life.

What Are Psychological Disorders?

Psychology is the scientific study of behavior and mental processes. **Psychological disorders** are behavior patterns or mental processes that cause serious personal suffering or interfere with a person's ability to cope with everyday life.

Many people believe that psychological disorders are uncommon, affecting relatively few individuals. It is true that the great majority of people are never admitted to mental hospitals, and most people never seek the help of psychologists or psychiatrists. And although many people have relatives they consider eccentric, few people have family members they consider to be truly abnormal.

Estimates suggest, however, that almost one third of the adults in the United States have experienced some type of psychological disorder (Goldstein et al., 1986). In addition to the many people with substance abuse disorders, 23 percent of people in the United States experience some type of psychological disorder in their lifetime. In any given month, the figure is appoximately 13 percent (Regier, 1993). As Dan's family discovered, psychological disorders can affect almost anyone.

Identifying Psychological Disorders

Deciding whether particular behaviors, thoughts, or feelings are "normal" or "abnormal" can be difficult. What is "normal" is often equated with what is average for the majority of people. Using this definition of normality, deviation from the majority becomes the primary criterion for abnormality.

People with psychological disorders usually do not differ much from "normal" people. In fact, the primary difference is the simple exaggeration of certain behaviors or mental processes. For example, laughing is a normal and healthy response to humorous situations. However, someone who laughs all the time, even in very inappropriate situations, might be considered abnormal.

Symptoms of Psychological Disorders

Several behavior patterns and mental processes may suggest that an individual has a psychological disorder. The word *suggest* is important here because diagnosing an individual with a psychological disorder is often difficult, and diagnoses are not always simple or straightforward.

However, psychologists generally use several criteria to determine whether a person's behavior indicates the presence of a psychological disorder. These criteria include how typical the behavior is of people in general, whether the behavior is maladaptive, whether the behavior causes the individual emotional discomfort, and whether the behavior is socially unacceptable.

Typicality As previously noted, the normality of a behavior or mental process is often determined by the degree to which it is average, or typical, of the behavior or mental processes of the majority of people. There are, however, problems with defining normality in terms of what is typical of most people. The fact that a behavior is not typical of most people does not mean it is abnormal. Scientific and artistic geniuses, such as Marie Curie and Pablo Picasso, certainly are not "typical" of humans in general. That does not mean, however, that such people are abnormal.

Maladaptivity Many psychologists believe that what makes a behavior abnormal is the fact that it is maladaptive (Coleman et al., 1984). That is, the behavior impairs an individual's ability to function adequately in everyday life. Behavior that causes misery and distress rather than happiness and fulfillment may be considered maladaptive. Alcohol abuse is one such behavior. Alcohol abuse often has strong negative effects on the drinker's health, job, and family life. Abuse of alcohol may discourage the drinker from seeking healthier solutions to the problem of anxiety as well as create additional problems of its own.

Behavior that is hazardous to oneself or to others may also be considered maladaptive. This type of maladaptive behavior may include threatening or attempting suicide as well as threatening or attacking other people.

It is important to note that most people who commit violent crimes do not have psychological disorders. This is because most criminals are fully aware of what they are doing. That is, they know that their behavior is illegal and that they can be held responsible for it. Equally important, the majority of people with psychological disorders, even severe psychological disorders, are not necessarily violent or dangerous.

Emotional Discomfort Psychological disorders such as anxiety and depression cause most people great emotional discomfort. For example, people who are depressed often suffer feelings of helplessness, hopelessness, worthlessness, guilt, and extreme sadness. They may lose interest in virtually everything they once enjoyed and believe that life is no longer worth living. Such feelings are so stressful that they may lead the affected individual to consider suicide. Thus, severe emotional discomfort may be a sign of a psychological disorder.

Socially Unacceptable Behavior Behavior that violates a society's accepted norms may also be an indication of a psychological disorder. However, whether a behavior is socially unacceptable may depend on the particular society or culture in which it occurs. What is considered normal behavior in one culture may be considered abnormal in another. Therefore, the cultural context of a behavior must be taken into account before deciding that the behavior indicates a psychological disorder.

The importance of culture is demonstrated by **culture-bound syndromes**, clusters of symptoms that define or describe an illness. Many behaviors associated with culture-bound syndromes would be considered abnormal by people who are unaware of the syndrome's cultural context. For example, many people in Middle Eastern cultures believe that certain inappropriate behaviors, such as banging one's head, are due to possession of the body by a spirit. In the United States, such a belief would likely be considered a sign of a serious psychological disorder. However, in the cultural context of the Middle East, spirit possession is considered to be a rational explanation for certain types of behavior, and the "possessed" individual is not thought to have a psychological disorder. There are many examples of culture-bound syndromes, some of which are listed in Figure 18.1 on page 413.

Classifying Psychological Disorders

Most psychologists believe that it is important to have a widely agreed upon classification of psychological disorders. Unless there is agreement about how to classify psychological disorders, it is difficult to know how many people have a given disorder or what other factors, such as socioeconomic status, heredity, or gender differences, may be associated with it. It is also important to classify psychological disorders so that individuals can be correctly diagnosed and treated.

CASE STUDIES

AND OTHER TRUE STORIES

Not Guilty by Reason of Insanity

The vast majority of people with mental illnesses are not dangerous to others. Some, however, do commit crimes. Many people have been found not guilty of serious crimes—even murder— "by reason of insanity." Typically, they are sent to psychiatric institutions instead of prison. They may be released when they are judged no longer to be a threat to others.

A well-known example of the insanity plea occurred in the case of John Hinckley, the man who attempted to assassinate President Ronald Reagan. Not only did Hinckley attempt to murder the president, but he did so in front of millions of television witnesses. Nevertheless, Hinckley was found not guilty by reason of insanity after expert witnesses testified that he had schizophrenia. Rather than being sent to prison, Hinckley was committed to a psychiatric institution.

In using an insanity defense, lawyers apply a modified version of the M'Naghten Rule, which states that if it can be proved that, at the time of committing a criminal act, a person either did not understand the nature of the act or did not know that it was wrong, then the person is insane and not responsible for the act.

The M'Naghten Rule goes back to 1843, when a Scotsman named Daniel M'Naghten was found not guilty of murder by reason of insanity. M'Naghten had tried to kill the British prime minister, Sir Robert Peel, because he had delusions that Peel was persecuting him. In the assassination attempt, Peel's secretary was killed. However, the court found M'Naghten not guilty of murder, arguing that he was insane and thus not responsible for his criminal act.

Typically, when an accused person pleads insanity, prosecuting attorneys try to demonstrate

John Hinckley's lawyers used the insanity defense at his trial.

that the accused was sane at the time of the crime, while the defense tries to prove that the accused was not sane. Both rely on the testimony of expert witnesses, usually psychologists, who have interviewed the accused since the crime or who have previous knowledge of the accused.

Many people are worried about all the criminals who are literally "getting away with murder" because of the insanity defense— even though it is actually used in just 1 percent of felony cases and is successful in only three-fourths of those. Recent legal reforms have made it more difficult to use the insanity plea successfully. For example:

- In many states, to be considered insane the accused now must be diagnosed with a severe psychological disorder.

- The burden of proof has been shifted from the prosecution to the defense. It is now up to the defense to prove the accused was insane.

- Some states have gone even further and abolished the insanity plea altogether.

Insanity is a legal concept, not a psychological one, and to be legally useful, it must be all or nothing—one is either sane or insane. In reality, most psychological disorders are a matter of degree. The distinction is important. One can be just a little depressed, for example, but according to the law, one cannot be just a little insane. Because of its all-or-nothing nature, deciding on someone's sanity can be a very difficult decision to make.

Think About It

If the insanity appeal were abolished, how should society deal with mentally ill individuals who commit serious crimes?

The most widely used classification system for psychological disorders is the DSM, or *Diagnostic and Statistical Manual of Mental Disorders,* published by the American Psychiatric Association. The most recent version of the manual, the DSM-IV, which was published in 1994, recognizes 18 different categories of psychological disorders, most of which are shown in Figure 18.2 on page 414.

It is important to note that the classification of psychological disorders shown in Figure 18.2 is significantly different from earlier classifications. Until 1980, when the third edition of the DSM was published, psychological disorders were classified on the basis of their presumed causes. For many decades, the most widely accepted causes were those suggested by Freud's psychoanalytic theory.

Many psychologists criticized early versions of the DSM because very diverse psychological disorders were grouped together under the labels "neuroses" and "psychoses." As a result, beginning with the DSM-III in 1980, psychological disorders have been categorized on the basis of observable signs and symptoms rather than presumed causes.

The DSM is subject to ongoing revision. New categories are added and old ones deleted as knowledge of psychological disorders increases. For example, the category of post-traumatic stress disorder was added to the DSM only after the Vietnam War, when large numbers of returning soldiers were found to suffer from the disorder.

The remainder of this chapter focuses on six major types of psychological disorders as classified by the DSM-IV: anxiety disorders, dissociative disorders, somatoform disorders, mood disorders, schizophrenia, and personality disorders. Many symptoms are simply exaggerations of normal thoughts, feelings, or behaviors. They do not necessarily indicate a psychological disorder. Psychological disorders can only be diagnosed by a skilled professional after careful evaluation.

Some Culture-Bound Syndromes

Latah

Malaysia and elsewhere:
hypersensitivity to sudden fright, often with nonsense mimicking of others; trance-like behavior

Hwa-byung

Korea:
panic, depression, or other symptoms believed to be due to the suppression of anger

Zar

Middle East:
shouting, laughing, head banging, or other inappropriate behavior that is believed to be caused by possession of the body by a spirit

Susto

Latin groups in the United States and the Caribbean:
unhappiness and illness following a frightening event that is believed to cause the soul to leave the body

Ghost sickness

Native Americans in the United States:
bad dreams, hallucinations, fainting, and other symptoms belived to be due to preoccupation with death and the dead

Mal de ojo

Mediterranean and elsewhere:
sufferers, mostly children, are believed to be under the influence of an "evil eye," causing fitful sleep, crying, and sickness

FIGURE 18.1 *Several patterns of abnormal behavior are recognized in specific cultures and may or may not be linked to an official category of psychological disorder.*

Listed here are a few of these culture-bound syndromes. Why is it important to consider the cultural context of a behavior before classifying it as a psychological disorder?

Source: Adapted from the DSM-IV, 1994.

Categories of Psychological Disorders in the DSM-IV

Disorder	Examples	Disorder	Examples
Disorders Usually First Diagnosed in Infancy, Childhood, or Adolescence	Mental Retardation, Reading Disorder, Autistic Disorder	Factitious Disorders	With Predominantly Psychological Signs, with Predominantly Physical Signs
Delirium, Dementia, and Amnesic and Other Cognitive Disorders	Substance Intoxication, Delirium, Alzheimer's Disease	Sexual and Gender Identity Disorders	Sexual Dysfunctions, Paraphilias, Gender Identity Disorders
Mental Disorders Due to a General Medical Condition Not Elsewhere Classified	Catatonic Disorder, Personality Change	Sleep Disorders	Primary Insomnia, Sleepwalking Disorder
Substance-Related Disorders	Caffeine-Related Disorders, Hallucinogen-Related Disorders, Nicotine-Related Disorders	Impulsive-Control Disorders Not Elsewhere Classified	Kleptomania, Pyromania
		Adjustment Disorders	With Depressed Mood, with Anxiety
Schizophrenia and Other Psychotic Disorders	Delusional Disorder, Shared Psychotic Disorder	Personality Disorders	Paranoid Personality Disorder, Schizoid Personality Disorder, Dependent Personality Disorder
Mood Disorders	Major Depressive Disorder, Bipolar II Disorder	Eating Disorders	Bulimia, Anorexia Nervosa
Anxiety Disorders	Panic Disorder, Social Phobia, Obsessive-Compulsive Disorder	Conditions That May Be a Focus of Clinical Attention	Non-compliance with Treatment, Malingering, Academic or Occupational Problem
Somatoform Disorders	Conversion Disorder, Hypochondriasis	Additional Codes	Unspecified Mental Disorder (nonpsychotic disorders)
Dissociative Disorders	Dissociative Amnesia, Dissociative Identity Disorder		

FIGURE 18.2 *The most widely used classification system for psychological disorders is found in the* Diagnostic and Statistical Manual of Mental Disorders *(DSM). The most recent version is called the DSM-IV.*

Source: Adapted from the DSM-IV, 1994.

2
Anxiety Disorders

Anxiety refers to a general state of dread or uneasiness that occurs in response to a vague or imagined danger. It differs from fear, which is a response to a real danger or threat. Anxiety is typically characterized by nervousness, inability to relax, and concern about losing control. Physical signs and symptoms of anxiety may include trembling, sweating, rapid heart rate, shortness of breath, increased blood pressure, flushed face, and feelings of faintness or light-headedness. All are the result of overactivity of the sympathetic branch of the autonomic nervous system. (See Chapter 3.)

Everyone feels anxious at times—for example, before a big game or an important test. In such situations, feeling anxious or worried is an appropriate response that does not indicate a psychological disorder. However, some people feel anxious all or most of the time, or their anxiety is out of proportion to the situation provoking it. Such anxiety may interfere with effective living, the achievement of desired goals, life satisfaction, and emotional comfort. When these problems occur, anxiety is considered a sign of a psychological disorder. Anxiety-based disorders are among the most common of all psychological disorders in the United States (Gorman et al., 1989).

Types of Anxiety Disorders

Anxiety disorders classified in the DSM-IV include phobic disorder, panic disorder, generalized anxiety disorder, obsessive-compulsive disorder, and stress disorders. A description of each follows.

Phobic Disorder The word **phobia** derives from the Greek root *phobos,* which means "fear." **Simple phobia,** which is the most common of all the anxiety disorders, refers to a persistent excessive or irrational fear of a particular object or situation. To be diagnosed as a phobic disorder, the fear must lead to avoidance behavior that interferes with the affected person's normal life.

Almost any object or situation may lead to a phobic reaction. Several phobias, however, are especially common. The most common include:

- zoophobia: a fear of animals
- claustrophobia: a fear of enclosed spaces
- acrophobia: a fear of heights
- arachnophobia: a fear of spiders

Other relatively common phobias include fear of storms, blood, snakes, dental procedures, driving, and air travel.

When people with simple phobias are confronted with the object or situation they fear, they are likely to feel extremely anxious. As a result, they tend to avoid what they fear. For example, someone with hematophobia (a fear of blood) might avoid needed medical treatment. Someone with aviaphobia (a fear of air travel) might turn down a job

This person is waiting anxiously to be interviewed for a job. What situations make you feel anxious?

Someone with agoraphobia or panic disorder would be likely to avoid this crowded shopping mall. Why do the two disorders lead to similar avoidance behaviors?

"going crazy." Not surprisingly, they usually have persistent fears of another attack.

For most people who suffer panic disorder, attacks have no apparent cause. However, many people with panic disorder also have agoraphobia. **Agoraphobia** is a fear of being in places or situations in which escape may be difficult or impossible. People with agoraphobia may be especially afraid of crowded public places such as movie theaters, shopping malls, buses, or trains.

Agoraphobia is a common phobia among phobic adults. In fact, people with one or both disorders make up about 50 to 80 percent of the phobic individuals seen in clinical practice (American Psychiatric Association, 1994).

Most people with agoraphobia respond with panic attacks when they cannot avoid the situations they fear. They are afraid they will have a panic attack in a public place, where they will be humiliated or unable to obtain help. Panic disorder and agoraphobia both lead to avoidance behaviors. These behaviors can range from avoiding crowded places to never leaving home at all. Thus, these phobias can be very serious.

promotion because the new position involves air travel. Thus, although most people with simple phobias never seek treatment for their disorders, a simple phobia can seriously disrupt a person's life.

Social phobia is characterized by persistent fear of social situations in which one might be exposed to the close scrutiny of others and thus be observed doing something embarrassing or humiliating. Some people with social phobias fear all social situations; others fear specific situations, such as public speaking, eating in public, or dating.

People with social phobias generally try to avoid the situations they fear. They may invent excuses to avoid going to parties or other social gatherings, for example. If avoidance is impossible, the situations are likely to cause great anxiety. In addition, the avoidance behavior itself may greatly interfere with work and social life.

Panic Disorder and Agoraphobia   People with panic disorder have recurring and unexpected panic attacks. A **panic attack** is a relatively short period of intense fear or discomfort, characterized by shortness of breath, dizziness, rapid heart rate, trembling or shaking, sweating, choking, nausea, and/or other distressing physical symptoms. It may last from a few minutes to a few hours. People having a panic attack may believe they are dying or

Generalized Anxiety Disorder   According to the DSM-IV, generalized anxiety disorder (GAD) is an excessive or unrealistic worry about life circumstances that lasts for at least six months. The worries must be present during most of that time in order to warrant a diagnosis of GAD. Typically, the worries focus on finances, work, interpersonal problems, accidents, or illness.

GAD is one of the most common anxiety disorders, yet few people seek psychological treatment for it because it does not differ, except in intensity and duration, from the "normal" anxiety of everyday life. It is difficult to distinguish GAD from other anxiety disorders, and many people with GAD have other anxiety disorders as well, most often phobic disorders (Barlow et al., 1986).

Obsessive-Compulsive Disorder   Among the most acute of the anxiety disorders is obsessive-compulsive disorder (OCD). **Obsessions** are unwanted thoughts, ideas, or mental images that occur over and over again. They are often senseless or repulsive, and most people with obsessions try to ignore or suppress them. The majority of people with obsessions also practice compulsions, which may reduce the anxiety their obsessions produce. **Compulsions** are repetitive ritual behaviors, often involving checking or cleaning.

The following examples are typical of people with OCD. One person is obsessed every night with doubts that he has locked the doors and windows before going to bed. He feels driven to compulsively check and recheck every door and window in the house, perhaps dozens of times. Only then can he relax and go to sleep. In another example, a team of researchers reported the case of a woman who was obsessed with the idea that she would pick up germs from nearly everything she touched. She compulsively washed her hands over and over again, sometimes as many as 500 times a day (Davison & Neale, 1990).

People who experience obsessions are usually aware that the obsessions are unjustified (March et al., 1989; Rapoport, 1989; Swedo et al., 1989). This distinguishes obsessions from delusions. Although obsessions are a sign of a less serious psychological disorder than delusions, they still can make people feel extremely anxious, and they can seriously interfere with daily life. Compulsions may alleviate some of the anxiety associated with obsessions, but the compulsions themselves are time-consuming and usually create additional interference with daily life.

Constantly organizing and cleaning are common compulsions in people who experience obsessive-compulsive disorder.

Stress Disorders   Stress disorders include post-traumatic stress disorder (PTSD) and acute stress disorder. The two disorders have similar symptoms, but they differ in how quickly they occur after the traumatic event that triggers the disorder. They also differ in how long they last.

Post-traumatic stress disorder refers to intense, persistent feelings of anxiety that are caused by an experience so traumatic that it would produce stress in almost anyone. Experiences that may produce PTSD include rape, severe child abuse, assault, severe accident, airplane crash, natural disasters, and war atrocities. It appears to be a common syndrome in people who have experienced extensive trauma. For example, more than one third of the victims of Hurricane Andrew in 1992 developed PTSD (Ironson, 1993).

People who suffer from PTSD may exhibit any or all of the following symptoms (American Psychiatric Association, 1993):

- flashbacks, which are reexperiences of the actual trauma

- nightmares or other unwelcome thoughts about the trauma

- numbness of feelings

- avoidance of stimuli associated with the trauma

- increased tension, which may lead to sleep disturbances, irritability, poor concentration, and similar problems

The symptoms may occur six months or more after the traumatic event, and they may last for years or even decades. The more severe the trauma, the worse the symptoms tend to be.

Acute stress disorder is a short-term disorder with symptoms similar to those of PTSD. Also like PTSD, acute stress disorder follows a traumatic event. However, unlike with PTSD, the symptoms occur immediately or at most within a month of the event. The anxiety also lasts a shorter time—from a few days to a few weeks. Not everyone who experiences a trauma, however, will develop PTSD or acute stress disorder.

Explaining Anxiety Disorders

Several different explanations for anxiety disorders have been suggested. As is true for most of the psychological disorders discussed in this chapter, the explanations fall into two general categories: psychological views and biological views.

THE BOY WHO COULDN'T STOP WASHING

Each morning for one hour, 18-year-old Morris washes his hands and arms with either Top Job or Mr. Clean. He scrubs his hands so hard that they become raw; they sometimes bleed from the intense scrubbing.

Morris can remember exactly how it started, even though he was only three. He was nervous, in a new house his family had just moved into. Pulling a chair up to the sink, he climbed onto it, turned on the spigot and washed his hands. For two years it just made him feel better. He did this over and over again (Rapoport, 1989).

Morris is just one of many people, most of them children and teens, psychiatrist Judith Rapoport has treated and writes about in her book *The Boy Who Couldn't Stop Washing.* Morris, like Rapoport's other patients, experiences obsessive-compulsive disorder (OCD). Also like many of her other patients, Morris' first symptoms showed up at a very early age.

In her fascinating best-seller, Rapoport convinces the reader that these "weird" people with their "bizarre" behaviors are really just normal people with a strange twist—the need to wash, clean, count, check, or hoard, a need that is compulsive and abnormal.

Unlike people with schizophrenia, who have lost touch with reality, individuals with OCD know their behavior is strange, and they usually want more than anything else to be free of it. Instead, they are prisoners of their own compulsions, no more able to fight them than they are able to fight the need to eat or sleep.

In fact, according to Rapoport, the compulsions of OCD may be basic urges much like the urges to eat or sleep. As she documents, the compulsions of people with the disorder are remarkably similar. Thousands of people all over the world, people who have never met, report almost identical compulsions. Rapoport argues convincingly that these similarities reflect an underlying biological cause for the disorder.

Recent evidence of brain abnormalities in people with OCD supports this claim. So do studies of behavior patterns in nonhuman animals. Many other animal species have similar rituals—controlled by genes and thus "wired" into their brains—rituals that are associated with important life functions. Grooming rituals are by far the most common of all obsessive-compulsive behaviors.

Rats, like many other animals, spend a good deal of their waking time in grooming rituals that have an elaborate, fixed pattern. In times of stress, rats groom even more. In the lab, their grooming behavior can be turned on or off by the administration of drugs.

The washing and other cleaning behaviors of individuals with OCD are like the exaggerated grooming behaviors of laboratory rats—"a compunction for cleanliness run wild," as Rapoport suggests. For people such as Morris, washing is a ritualized behavior, just as it is in rats. Indeed, each individual with OCD has a specific routine that is followed in exactly the same way in each washing episode. The case of a boy named Brendan demonstrates this clearly.

In the shower, Brendan strokes the right side of his head eight times, applies shampoo, then strokes another eight times, rinses eight times, and strokes eight times more. He repeats this for the top of his head, the left side, and the back, in that order.

It appears, then, that brain abnormalities lead some people to perform ritualized behaviors that are similar to the ritualized behaviors of nonhuman animals. This is good news for the millions of people who experience OCD. It means that medication to treat the brain abnormality may be able to cure them of their compulsive behaviors. In fact, as Rapoport reports, at least a third of people with OCD are cured with medication, and many more are helped significantly by it.

Think About It

What evidence suggests that OCD may be caused by biological factors? Why is this promising news for people who suffer from OCD?

Psychological Views   For anxiety disorders, as well as the other disorders discussed later in this chapter, psychoanalytic views are presented even though they may no longer be widely accepted. These views are included because they influenced later theories and had a major impact on the classification of psychological disorders until recently, as discussed earlier.

According to psychoanalytic theory, anxiety is the result of forbidden childhood urges that have been repressed, or hidden from consciousness (Freud, 1936). If repressed urges do surface, psychoanalysts argue, they may do so as obsessions and eventually lead to compulsive behaviors. For example, if one is trying to repress "dirty" sexual thoughts, then repetitive hand washing may help relieve some of the anxiety.

Learning theorists believe that phobias are conditioned, or learned, in childhood. This may occur when a child experiences a traumatic event—such as being lost in a crowd or frightened by a bad storm—or when a child observes phobic behavior in other people (Bandura, 1986). If a parent screams or faints when a child picks up a spider, for example, the child may learn that spiders are things to be feared and develop a fear of them. Learning theorists argue that such conditioned phobias may remain long after the experiences that produced them have been forgotten.

Learning theorists also believe that people will learn to reduce their anxiety by avoiding the situations that make them anxious (Gorman et al., 1989). For example, a student who feels anxious speaking in front of others in class may learn to keep quiet because it reduces his or her feelings of anxiety. However, by intentionally avoiding the anxiety-producing behavior, the student has no chance to learn other ways of coping with or unlearning the anxiety. As a result, the anxiety may worsen or be generalized to other situations that involve speaking in front of others.

Cognitive theorists, on the other hand, believe that people make themselves feel anxious by responding negatively to most situations and coming to believe they are helpless to control what happens to them. This creates great anxiety.

Biological Views   Research indicates that heredity may play a role in most psychological disorders, including anxiety disorders. For example, one study showed that, if one of a pair of identical twins exhibited an anxiety disorder, there was a 45 percent chance that the other twin would also exhibit

the disorder. This was true even of twins raised in different families. By contrast, the chances of fraternal twins both developing anxiety disorders was only about 15 percent (Torgersen, 1983). Similarly, adopted children are more likely to have an anxiety disorder if a biological parent has one than if an adoptive parent does. Both types of studies suggest that genes play at least some role in the development of anxiety disorders.

How did genes get involved? Some psychologists believe that people are genetically inclined to fear things that were threats to their ancestors (Mineka, 1991). These psychologists argue that people who rapidly acquired strong fears of real dangers—such as large animals, snakes, heights, and sharp objects—would be more likely to survive and reproduce. To the extent that the tendency to develop such fears is controlled by genes, they conclude, the tendency would be passed on to future generations and explain why the disorders are relatively common today.

Interaction of Factors   Some cases of anxiety disorder may reflect the interaction of biological and psychological factors. People with panic disorder, for example, may have a biologically based tendency to overreact psychologically to physical sensations (Ciesielski et al., 1981; Turner et al., 1985). The initial physical symptoms of panic—such as rapid heart rate and shortness of breath—cause these people to react with fear, leading to even worse panic symptoms. They may think they are having a heart attack and experience severe psychological stress. Anxiety about having another panic attack becomes a psychological disorder itself—one that originated in a biological reaction.

Regardless of their cause, anxiety disorders are both common and disabling. In serious cases, they lead to tremendous restrictions and limitations in lifestyle, relationships, and work. They can also lead to great personal distress. Fortunately, most people who suffer from anxiety disorder respond well to treatment, which is covered in Chapter 19.

THINKING ABOUT PSYCHOLOGY

1. How does anxiety differ from fear?

2. Describe the relationship between panic disorder and agoraphobia.

3. **Critical Thinking**   Explain why studies of twins are important for determining whether a disorder has a biological basis.

Dissociative Disorders 3

Dissociation refers to the separation of certain personality components or mental processes from conscious thought. In some situations, dissociation is normal. Someone may be so engrossed in reading a book or watching a television program, for example, that he is unaware that his name is being called. Someone else may become so involved in watching the road that she misses the sign for her exit on the highway. Perhaps the most common form of normal dissociation is daydreaming, in which the person's thoughts may be "a million miles away." In each of these cases, dissociation probably does not indicate a psychological disorder.

However, when dissociation occurs as a way to avoid stressful events or feelings, it is considered to be a sign of a psychological disorder. People with dissociative disorders may lose their memory of a particular event or even forget their identity. It is believed that dissociation occurs when individuals are faced with urges or experiences that are very stressful. By dissociating, they are able to remove themselves from the source of stress and lessen their feelings of anxiety.

There are no current statistics on the prevalence of dissociative disorders. In part, this is because the DSM-IV classifies them somewhat differently than they were classified in the past. However, dissociation is a common psychological symptom.

Types of Dissociative Disorders

In the DSM-IV, the dissociative disorders are classified as dissociative amnesia, dissociative fugue, dissociative identity disorder, and depersonalization disorder. These disorders are described next.

Dissociative Amnesia   Formerly called psychogenic amnesia, dissociative amnesia is characterized by a sudden loss of memory, usually following a particularly stressful or traumatic event. A person experiencing dissociative amnesia typically cannot remember any events that occurred for a certain period of time surrounding the traumatic event. Less commonly, a person may forget all prior experiences and may be unable to remember his or her name, recognize friends and family, or recall important personal information. Dissociative amnesia may last for just a few hours, or it may persist for

years. Memory is likely to return just as suddenly as it was lost, and the amnesia rarely recurs.

The term *psychogenic* means "psychological in origin." Thus, dissociative amnesia cannot be explained biologically—as the result of a head injury, for example. Most often, a traumatic event, such as witnessing a serious accident, precedes the amnesia. Not surprisingly, the incidence of dissociative amnesia rises markedly during wartime and civilian crises, such as natural disasters.

TRUTH OR fiction ■ REVISITED ■   *It is true that people sometimes forget a very traumatic event as a way of coping with the psychological stress of the trauma.* This occurrence is called dissociative amnesia.

Dissociative Fugue   Dissociative fugue—previously called psychogenic fugue—is characterized not only by forgetting personal information and past events but also by suddenly relocating from home or work and taking on a new identity. Like dissociative amnesia, dissociative fugue usually follows a traumatic event that is psychologically very stressful. It is reported most frequently during wartime and natural disasters.

When individuals with dissociative fugue travel away from their home or workplace, they may take on a new name, residence, and occupation. They may become socially active in their new identity and not appear to be ill in any way. When the fugue comes to an end, they no longer remember what happened during the fugue state.

Dissociative Identity Disorder   Formerly called multiple personality disorder, dissociative identity disorder involves the existence of two or more personalities within a single individual. The various personalities may or may not be aware of the others, and at least two of the personalities take turns controlling the individual's behavior.

Each personality is likely to be different from the others in several ways, including in such observable traits as voice, facial expressions, and handedness, as well as self-perceived age, gender, and physical characteristics. The personalities may even have different allergies and eyeglass prescriptions. They may also behave very differently from one another.

People who are diagnosed with dissociative identity disorder usually were severely abused in childhood. They typically suffered severe physical, sexual, and/or psychological abuse (Spanos, 1994). Less often, dissociative identity disorder is preceded by other types of trauma.

Depersonalization Disorder   Depersonalization refers to feelings of detachment from one's mental processes or body. People with this disorder describe feeling as though they are outside their bodies, observing themselves at a distance.

Depersonalization is a common symptom of other psychological disorders in addition to being a disorder in its own right. After depression and anxiety, it is the most common complaint among psychiatric patients. Like the other dissociative disorders, depersonalization disorder is likely to be preceded by a stressful event.

Explaining Dissociative Disorders

Dissociative disorders have been explained primarily by psychological views. According to psychoanalytic theory, people dissociate in order to repress unacceptable urges. In dissociative amnesia or fugue, for example, the person forgets the disturbing urges. In dissociative identity disorder, the person expresses undesirable urges by developing other personalities that can take responsibility for them. In depersonalization, the person goes outside the self, away from the turmoil within.

According to learning theorists, individuals with dissociative disorders have learned not to think about disturbing events in order to avoid feelings of guilt, shame, or pain. They dissociate themselves from the stressful events by selectively forgetting them. This is reinforced by the reduced anxiety they feel when the trauma is forgotten.

Neither cognitive nor biological theorists have offered a complete explanation for dissociative disorders. At present, there is no convincing evidence that either biological or genetic factors play a role in the development of dissociative disorders.

THINKING ABOUT PSYCHOLOGY

1. Explain how dissociative fugue differs from dissociative amnesia.
2. **Critical Thinking**   In some cultures, people are encouraged to go into trance-like states. Should this type of dissociation be considered a sign of a psychological disorder? Why or why not?

4
Somatoform Disorders

Somatization refers to the expression of psychological distress through physical symptoms. People with somatoform disorders have psychological problems (such as depression or anxiety) but experience inexplicable physical symptoms (such as paralysis or pain).

It is important to distinguish between somatoform disorders and malingering, or the conscious attempt to "fake" an illness in order to avoid work, school, or other responsibilities. People with somatoform disorders do not intentionally fake their illnesses. They honestly feel pain or believe they cannot move their limbs.

TRUTH OR fiction ▪ R E V I S I T E D ▪   *It is not true that people whose illnesses are "all in their heads" do not really have symptoms of the disease.* Although psychological in origin, the physical symptoms of somatoform disorders are very real to the people who experience them.

Reliable statistics on the prevalence of somatoform disorders are not available. Many diagnoses of somatoform illness later prove to be incorrect when patients are found to have medical illnesses that account for their symptoms. On the other hand, many cases of somatoform disorders probably go undiagnosed because of the focus on physical, as opposed to psychological, symptoms.

Types of Somatoform Disorders

The DSM-IV identifies six types of somatoform disorders. The two most common are conversion disorder and hypochondriasis. The symptoms of these two disorders are described below and summarized in Figure 18.3 on page 422.

Conversion Disorder   People with conversion disorder experience a change in or loss of physical functioning in a major part of the body for which there is no medical explanation. For example, they may suddenly develop the inability to see at night or to move their legs, even though no medical explanation exists for their sudden disability. These behaviors are not, however, intentionally produced. That is, the person is not faking it.

Conversion disorder is further complicated because many people who experience conversion disorder show little concern about their symptoms, no matter how serious or unusual those symptoms may be. This lack of concern about the symptoms may help in the diagnosis of conversion disorder, although it is not present in all cases.

Hypochondriasis Also called hypochondria, hypochondriasis is defined as a person's unrealistic preoccupation with the fear that he or she has a serious disease. People with hypochondriasis become absorbed by minor physical symptoms and sensations, convinced that the symptoms indicate a serious medical illness. These people maintain their erroneous beliefs despite reassurances from doctors that there is nothing physically wrong with them. Some people with hypochondriasis visit doctor after doctor, seeking the one physician who will find the cause of their symptoms.

Explaining Somatoform Disorders

Explanations for somatoform disorders in general, and conversion disorder or hypochondriasis specifically, are primarily psychological views. According to psychoanalytic theory, somatoform disorders occur when individuals repress emotions associated with forbidden urges and instead express them symbolically in physical symptoms. The physical symptoms thus represent a compromise between the unconscious need to express feelings and the fear of actually expressing them.

More recently, other psychologists have argued that people with conversion disorder "convert" psychological stress into actual medical problems. For example, a fighter pilot may lose the ability to see at night as a response to the great anxiety he feels

Two Examples of Somatoform Disorders

Type	Characteristics
Conversion Disorder	Sudden and severe loss of physical functioning despite the fact that no medical explanation exists for the physical symptoms; usually characterized by the person's apparent lack of concern about his or her physical symptoms
Hypochondriasis	An unhealthy fear of having, or the unsubstantiated belief that one has, a serious disease; characterized by the person's misinterpretation of his or her normal bodily symptoms or functions

FIGURE 18.3 *People with somatoform disorders have psychological problems that express themselves in physical symptoms. There is, however, no medical basis for the physical symptoms. The two most prevalent of the somatoform disorders are conversion disorder and hypochondriasis, the symptoms of which are described here.*

Source: Adapted from the DSM-IV, 1994.

about flying nighttime bombing missions. Another individual may suffer paralysis of the legs after nearly being run over by a car.

Some behavioral theorists have suggested that somatoform symptoms can serve as a reinforcer if they successfully allow a person to escape from anxiety. There are also some indications that biological or genetic factors may play a role in the development of somatoform disorders (Kellner, 1990).

THINKING ABOUT PSYCHOLOGY

1. Define malingering. How does somatization differ from malingering?

2. How do conversion disorder and hypochondriasis differ?

3. **Critical Thinking** How do you think learning theorists might explain somatoform disorders? Do you agree with this type of explanation? Why or why not?

FRANK & ERNEST® by Bob Thaves

NEUROSIS CLINIC

PHOBIA CLINIC

HYPO-CHONDRIA CLINIC
CLOSED DUE TO POSSIBLE ILLNESS

Source: FRANK & ERNEST reprinted by permission of Newspaper Enterprise Association, Inc.

5
Mood Disorders

Most people have mood changes that reflect the normal ups and downs of daily life. They feel "down" when things go wrong, such as failing an important test, and they feel "up" when good things happen, such as when their team wins a championship. Dan felt down when his sister's condition worsened. Janet noted that Dan was depressed, but she also realized that Dan's mood was a normal reaction to his situation.

A DAY IN THE LIFE

Some people, however, experience mood changes that seem inappropriate for or inconsistent with the situations to which they are responding. These people feel sad when things are going well, or they feel elated for no apparent reason. People who have abnormal moods such as these may have a mood disorder.

Mood disorders fall into two general categories: **depression** (which typically involves feelings of helplessness, hopelessness, worthlessness, guilt, and great sadness) and **bipolar disorder** (which involves a cycle of mood changes from depression to wild elation and back again).

Mood disorders—particularly depression—are very common psychological disorders. In any six-month period, about 8 percent of women and 4 percent of men are likely to be diagnosed with some form of depression (Myers et al., 1984).

Types of Mood Disorders

The DSM-IV classifies mood disorders into several different types of depressive and bipolar disorders. These are summarized in Figure 18.4 on page 424.

Major Depression Depression is by far the most common of all the psychological disorders. It has been estimated that depression affects more than 100 million people worldwide and that between 8 and 18 percent of the general population will experience depression in their lifetime (Boyd & Weissman, 1982).

TRUTH OR fiction
■ R E V I S I T E D ■

It is true that depression is the most common type of psychological disorder. At least 8 percent of the general population will experience depression.

Major depression is diagnosed when an individual experiences at least five of the following nine symptoms of depression (American Psychiatric Association, 1994):

- persistent depressed mood for most of the day
- loss of interest or pleasure in all, or almost all, activities
- significant weight loss or gain due to changes in appetite
- sleeping more or less than usual
- speeding up or slowing down of physical and emotional reactions
- fatigue or loss of energy
- feelings of worthlessness or unfounded guilt
- reduced ability to concentrate or make meaningful decisions
- recurrent thoughts of death or suicide

For a diagnosis of major depression to be made, at least one of the individual's five symptoms must be one of the first two symptoms in the list. Additionally, the symptoms must be present for at least two weeks, and occur nearly every day during that period (American Psychiatric Association, 1994).

Severely depressed individuals may become consumed by feelings of worthlessness or guilt. Severe depression calls for immediate treatment—as many as 15 percent of severely depressed individuals eventually kill themselves (Hirschfield & Goodwin, 1988).

Bipolar Disorder Formerly called manic depression, bipolar disorder is characterized by dramatic ups and downs in mood. Periods of **mania** (extreme excitement characterized by hyperactivity and chaotic behavior) can change into depression very quickly and for no apparent reason.

The manic phase is characterized by a mood that is persistently and abnormally elevated. In some people, however, this phase may be characterized by irritability instead of elation. Manic moods are also characterized by at least some of the following traits:

- inflated self-esteem
- inability to sit still or sleep restfully
- pressure to keep talking and switching from topic to topic
- racing thoughts (referred to as "flight of ideas")
- difficulty concentrating

Individuals in the manic phase may appear highly excited and act silly or argumentative. In severe cases, they may have delusions (beliefs that have no basis in reality) about their own superior abilities or about others being jealous of them. They may also experience hallucinations (sensory perceptions that occur in the absence of sensory stimuli) such as hearing imaginary voices or seeing things that are not really there. These individuals may also engage in impulsive behaviors, such as going on wild spending sprees, quitting their jobs to pursue wild dreams, or making foolish business

Types of Mood Disorders and Their Characteristics

Type	Characteristics
Major Depressive Disorder	At least two weeks of depressed mood or loss of interest accompanied by at least four additional symptoms of depression
Dysthymic Disorder	At least two years of depressed mood for more days than not, accompanied by additional depressive symptoms
Bipolar I Disorder	One or more manic episodes, usually accompanied by major depressive episodes
Bipolar II Disorder	One or more major depressive episodes accompanied by at least one mild manic episode
Cyclothymic Disorder	At least two years of numerous periods of mild manic symptoms

FIGURE 18.4 *The DSM-IV classifies mood disorders into two types: depressive and bipolar disorders. Listed here are some of the major types of depressive and bipolar disorders and their characteristics.*

Source: Adapted from the DSM-IV, 1994.

investments. Thus, the manic phase of bipolar disorder can be very disruptive to an individual's life.

Explaining Mood Disorders

Psychological and biological theories have been proposed to explain why such a large number of people experience mood disorders, particularly depression. These theories are explained here.

Psychological Views The psychoanalytic view of depression is that some people are prone to depression because they suffered a real or imagined loss of a loved object or person in childhood. According to this view, the child feels anger toward the lost object or person but, instead of expressing the anger, internalizes it and directs it toward himself or herself. This leads to feelings of guilt and loss of self-esteem, which in turn lead to depression.

Learning theorists have suggested other explanations for depression. Some believe that *learned helplessness* makes people prone to depression. Psychologist Martin Seligman (1975) demonstrated the concept of learned helplessness in a classic study in which he taught dogs that they were helpless to escape from electric shock. First, he placed a barrier in the dogs' cage to prevent them from leaving when shocks were administered. Later the barrier was removed. However, when shocks were again administered, the dogs made no effort to escape. They had apparently learned they were helpless to do anything to prevent the pain.

This helpless behavior has been compared to the helplessness often seen in people who are depressed. Learning theorists argue that people prone to depression have learned through experience to believe that previous events in their lives were out of their control. This leads them to expect that future events will be out of their control as well. As a result, whenever a negative event occurs, these people feel helpless, and this leads to depression.

In contrast, cognitive theorists have suggested that some people are prone to depression because of their habitual style of explaining life events. According to this view, people assign different types of explanations to most events—internal or external, stable or unstable, and global or specific. Suppose, for example, that someone goes on a date that does not work out. Different ways to explain this might include the following:

- "I really messed up" (internal explanation, places blame on self).
- "Some people just don't get along" (external explanation, places the blame elsewhere).
- "It's my personality" (stable explanation, suggests problem cannot be changed).
- "It was my head cold" (unstable explanation, suggests problem is temporary).
- "I have no idea what to do when I'm with other people" (global explanation, suggests problem is too large to deal with).
- "I have difficulty making small talk" (specific explanation, suggests problem is small enough to be manageable).

Research shows that people who are depressed are more likely than other people to explain their failures on internal, stable, and global causes—causes they feel helpless to change (Abramson et al., 1989; Alloy, 1988; Peterson & Seligman, 1985). Cognitive theorists argue that such explanations give rise to feelings of helplessness, which in turn lead to depression. Dan's hope that the doctors would find a treatable (unstable, specific) cause for Michelle's disorder would be considered a healthy outlook.

Another cognitive theory was proposed by psychologist Aaron Beck (1976), who suggested that people who are depressed have a negative view of themselves, their experiences, and their future. According to Beck, this is because people who are depressed have negative self-schemas, developed from negative experiences in early childhood. This leads them to filter out positive information and perceive negative information as more negative than it really is. Such negativity, Beck argued, makes people prone to depression.

Biological Views   Other researchers have investigated biological factors in mood disorders. Mood disorders, like anxiety disorders, tend to occur more often in the close relatives of affected individuals than they do in the general population (Rose, 1995; Wachtel, 1994). Between 20 and 25 percent of people with mood disorders have a family member who is affected by a similar disorder (Hirschfeld & Goodwin, 1988). Moreover, identical twins of affected individuals are more likely to be affected than fraternal twins (Goodwin & Jamison, 1990). These studies seem to indicate that mood disorders have a genetic basis.

Scientists believe that two neurotransmitters, or chemical messengers, in the brain—serotonin and noradrenaline—may at least partly explain the connection between genes and mood. Serotonin and noradrenaline both play a role in mood regulation (Cooper et al., 1991; Michels & Marzuk, 1993). Low levels, or deficiencies, of serotonin may create a tendency toward mood disorders in general. Deficiencies of serotonin *combined* with deficiencies of noradrenaline, however, may be linked to depression specifically. These findings have been important in the development of drug therapy for the treatment of mood disorders. (See Chapter 19.)

Biological and Psychological Factors   Many cases of depression may reflect the interaction of biological factors such as neurotransmitter levels and psychological factors such as learned helplessness. This has been demonstrated with laboratory animals. Seligman (1975) and Weiss (1982) found that dogs that learned they were helpless to escape electric shocks also had less noradrenaline activity in their brains. Helplessness is thus linked to specific neurotransmitter deficiencies. The relationship may result in a vicious cycle: a depressing situation may slow down the activity of noradrenaline in the brain; the chemical changes may then worsen the depression.

THINKING ABOUT PSYCHOLOGY

1. What is the difference between depression and bipolar disorder?

2. List five symptoms of major depression.

3. **Critical Thinking** Give examples of external, unstable, and specific explanations for a disappointing event.

6

Schizophrenia

Schizophrenia, usually considered the most serious of the psychological disorders, is characterized by loss of contact with reality. Schizophrenia is very disabling, often leading to the affected person's inability to function independently. Typically, schizophrenia first appears in young adulthood, but it may occur at other ages. Although it usually develops gradually, it can also appear quite suddenly. Schizophrenia is extremely difficult to treat, and it frequently worsens over time.

The most obvious symptoms of schizophrenia include hallucinations, delusions, and thought disorders. In most cases, the hallucinations are auditory—voices may tell the individual what to do or comment on the individual's behavior. This is what Dan's sister Michelle experienced. Sometimes the voices may tell the individual to harm herself or himself or others.

Individuals with schizophrenia may experience delusions of grandeur—beliefs that they are superior to others. For example, such individuals may believe that they are famous or on a special mission to save the world. Sometimes the delusions are of persecution. A person with schizophrenia may believe that he or she is being pursued by the CIA or the FBI. Other delusions may include beliefs that one has committed unpardonable sins or even that one does not really exist.

Thought disorders involve problems in the organization or the content of mental processes. Thoughts of a person with schizophrenia may skip from topic to topic in an apparently illogical way. This is reflected in the person's speech, which sounds disorganized and confused. A person with schizophrenia may also repeat the same word or phrase over and over, repeat words or phrases that another person has spoken, or invent new words.

People with schizophrenia experience other symptoms that result in a decreased ability to function. These symptoms include social withdrawal, loss of social skills, and loss of normal emotional responsiveness. Some people with schizophrenia may even go into a **catatonic stupor**, an immobile, expressionless, comalike state.

Understandably, these symptoms cause tremendous stress to individuals with schizophrenia and their families. It has been estimated that as many as 20 percent of people with schizophrenia attempt suicide and that 10 percent actually do kill themselves (Caldwell & Gottesman, 1990).

Schizophrenia is found in all cultures and has been recognized for several thousand years. Fortunately, it is a relatively rare psychological disorder, affecting between 0.5 and 1 percent of the world's population. Nonetheless, a large number of people have schizophrenia—an estimated 2 million in the United States alone (Regier, 1993).

Types of Schizophrenia

Individuals with schizophrenia vary greatly in the symptoms they exhibit, although virtually all have thought disorders. Most people with schizophrenia exhibit a combination of symptoms.

The disturbed thoughts of people with schizophrenia are obvious in their artwork as well as in their speech.

The DSM-IV classification of schizophrenia and other psychotic disorders, shown in Figure 18.5, is based primarily on the duration and recurrence of symptoms. The types of schizophrenia include paranoid, disorganized, and catatonic schizophrenia.

Paranoid Schizophrenia

People with paranoid schizophrenia have delusions or frequent auditory hallucinations, all relating to a single theme. These people may have delusions of grandeur, persecution, or jealousy. For example, an individual with paranoid schizophrenia may be convinced that people have been plotting against him or her even when there is no evidence for it.

Dan's sister, Michelle, was distrustful of everyone except her husband. She even accused Dan of trying to confuse her when he asked how she was feeling. Although people with this type of schizophrenia tend to have less disordered thoughts and bizarre behavior than do people with other types of schizophrenia, they may be agitated, confused, and afraid.

Disorganized Schizophrenia

People with disorganized schizophrenia are incoherent in their thought and speech and disorganized in their behavior. They usually have delusions or hallucinations as well, but these tend to be fragmentary and unconnected, unlike the organized, systematic delusions of those with paranoid schizophrenia.

People with disorganized schizophrenia also are either emotionless or show inappropriate emotions. Typically, they act silly and giddy, and they tend to giggle and speak nonsense. They may neglect their appearance and hygiene and even lose control of their bladders and bowels.

The following case description (adapted from Spitzer et al., 1988, pp.137–138) illustrates several symptoms of disorganized schizophrenia. A 40-year-old man was brought to the hospital by his mother, who reported that she was afraid of him. It was his twelfth hospitalization. The man was dressed in a tattered overcoat, a baseball cap, and house slippers. He spoke with a childlike quality and walked with exaggerated movements. His emotions ranged from anger (hurling obscenities) to silliness (giggling for no apparent reason).

Since stopping his medication about a month prior to his hospitalization, the man had been hearing voices and looking and acting more bizarre. He told the interviewer that he had been "eating wires and lighting fires." His speech was generally incoherent and frequently fell into rhyme.

Catatonic Schizophrenia

The most obvious symptom of catatonic schizophrenia is disturbance of movement. Activity may slow to a stupor and then suddenly switch to agitation. Individuals with this disorder may hold unusual, uncomfortable body positions for long periods of time, even after

Characteristics of Schizophrenia and Other Psychotic Disorders

Disorder	Characteristics
Schizophrenia	Lasts at least six months and includes one month of symptoms such as delusions, hallucinations, and disorganized speech
Schizophreniform Disorder	Similar to schizophrenia but shorter in duration
Schizoaffective Disorder	A depressive or manic episode along with symptoms of schizophrenia
Delusional Disorder	At least one month of nonbizarre delusions without other symptoms of schizophrenia
Brief Psychotic Disorder	Lasts more than one day and ends by one month
Shared Psychotic Disorder	Involves the influence of one individual with an established delusion on another individual exhibiting similar symptoms

FIGURE 18.5 *Schizophrenia is the most serious psychological disorder. Listed here are the characteristics of schizophrenia and other psychotic disorders.*

Source: Adapted from the DSM-IV, 1994.

Individuals with catatonic schizophrenia may hold unusual positions for hours. Many of these people alternate between periods of immobility and periods of frenzied physical activity.

their arms and legs swell and stiffen. They may also exhibit waxy flexibility, a condition in which other people can mold them into strange poses that they continue to hold for hours.

Explaining Schizophrenia

As Dan noted, many different theories have been proposed to explain schizophrenia. These include both psychological and biological views.

Psychological Views   According to the psychoanalytic perspective, schizophrenia is the result of the overwhelming of the ego by urges from the id. The urges threaten the ego and cause intense conflict. In response, the individual regresses to an early phase of the oral stage of development in which the infant has not yet learned that it is separate from the mother. (See Chapter 14.) In this condition, fantasies become confused with reality, leading to hallucinations and delusions. Like many psychoanalytic theories, this one has fallen into disfavor over the years.

Other psychological views focus on the family environment as the root of schizophrenia. One such theory suggests that a family environment in which

a parent frequently expresses intense emotions and has a pushy, critical attitude puts children at risk of developing schizophrenia (Leff & Vaughn, 1985). It is possible, however, that such a family environment may only increase the chances of relapse in individuals who have schizophrenia. That is to say the family environment may not actually *produce* schizophrenia.

Biological Views   Genetic factors appear to play a role in schizophrenia, a view to which Dan's mother had alluded. The risk of developing the disorder is higher among relatives of people with schizophrenia. The closer the relationship, the higher the risk. For example, the likelihood of developing schizophrenia if a sibling has the disorder is about 8 percent, as compared with 1 percent or less for the general population (Gotteman & Shields, 1982; Plomin, 1989). If the sibling is an identical twin, the risk rises to 44 percent (Gotteman & Shields, 1982). Similarly, if one parent has schizophrenia, a child has about a 10 percent chance of having it, but if both parents have the disorder, a child has a 35 to 40 percent chance (Baron et al., 1985; Kendler et al., 1985; Loehlin et al., 1988).

Adoption studies also suggest that genes play a role in schizophrenia. Adopted children whose biological mothers have schizophrenia, but whose adoptive mothers do not, are more likely to develop the disorder than children whose biological mothers do not have schizophrenia (Moldin, 1994).

Other factors associated with increased risk of developing schizophrenia are listed below.

- People with schizophrenia are more likely than others to have suffered an injury or other trauma around the time of their birth.

- People with schizophrenia are more likely to be born during the winter than during other seasons, which may increase their risk of trauma at birth, possibly due to viral infection.

- Years in which large numbers of individuals with schizophrenia were born were also years with high rates of viral illness.

All of these factors suggest that complications around the time of birth may play a role in the development of schizophrenia, at least in individuals with a genetic risk of the disorder.

How biological factors, such as injury at birth, could lead to the symptoms of schizophrenia has also been investigated. Research has shown that some people with schizophrenia have structural brain abnormalities, including enlargement of the ventricles, or cavities, within the brain; a decrease in the size of the frontal lobes; and changes in brain cells (Andreasen et al., 1990; Johnstone et al., 1989; Kaplan et al., 1990).

The brains of some people with schizophrenia show functional differences from the brains of people who do not have the disorder, particularly in the frontal region (Andreasen, 1988; Posner, 1988; Suddath et al., 1989). In particular, the brains of people with schizophrenia appear to be more responsive to the neurotransmitter dopamine, perhaps causing nerve cells to fire too rapidly, leading to thought and speech confusion (Barnes, 1987; Grey et al., 1991; Wong et al., 1986).

A Multifactorial Model of Schizophrenia

The multifactorial (marked by many factors) model of schizophrenia, shown in Figure 18.6, illustrates how several biological and psychological factors may interact in the development of the disorder. In this model, genetic factors are seen as creating a vulnerability, or susceptibility, to schizophrenia. Among people who are genetically vulnerable, other factors, such as trauma during birth, may lead to brain injury and the subsequent development of schizophrenia. Once the disorder develops, its course may be negatively affected by the family environment.

The model also suggests that environmental factors alone are not enough to lead to the development of schizophrenia. Thus, people who are not genetically vulnerable are unlikely to develop the disorder, regardless of the environmental risk factors to which they are exposed.

7
Personality Disorders

Personality disorders are patterns of inflexible traits that disrupt social life or work and/or distress the affected individual. They usually show up by late adolescence and affect all aspects of the individual's personality, including thought processes, emotions, and behavior.

It is important to note the distinction between personality disorders and other psychological disorders that they may resemble. Psychological disorders, such as schizophrenia or phobic disorder, for example, are episodes of illness that an individual experiences. They can be distinguished from the individual's personality. In contrast, personality disorders are enduring traits that are major components of the individual's personality.

Antisocial personality disorder, described in detail below, is the only personality disorder for which there are data on prevalence. The estimates as to the number of affected individuals vary widely—from less than 1 percent to almost 10 percent of the population (Robins, 1987).

Types of Personality Disorders

Figure 18.7 on page 430 shows the DSM-IV classification of personality disorders. Four of these personality disorders—paranoid, schizoid, antisocial, and avoidant—are described next.

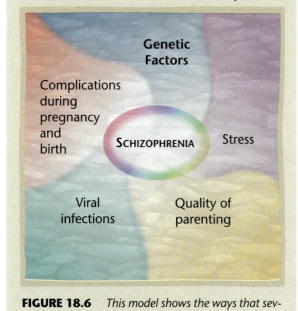

Multifactorial Model of Schizophrenia

Genetic Factors

Complications during pregnancy and birth

SCHIZOPHRENIA

Stress

Viral infections

Quality of parenting

FIGURE 18.6   *This model shows the ways that several biological and psychological factors may interact in the development of schizophrenia.*

Source: Adapted from the DSM-IV, 1994.

Paranoid Personality Disorder   People with paranoid personality disorder tend to be distrustful and suspicious of others and to interpret others' motives as harmful or evil. They tend to perceive other peoples' behavior as threatening or insulting even when it is not. They are difficult to get along with—argumentative, yet cold and aloof. Not surprisingly, these people often lead isolated lives.

Unlike individuals with paranoid schizophrenia, people with paranoid personality disorder are not confused about reality. However, their view of reality is distorted, and they are unlikely to see their mistrust and suspicions as unfounded or abnormal.

Schizoid Personality Disorder   People with schizoid personality disorder have no interest in relationships with other people. They also lack normal emotional responsiveness. They do not have tender feelings for, or become attached to, other people. Thus, people with schizoid personalities tend to be loners, with few if any friends.

These symptoms are similar to some of the symptoms of schizophrenia. Unlike people with schizophrenia, however, people with schizoid personality disorder do not have delusions or hallucinations. They stay in touch with reality.

Antisocial Personality Disorder   People with antisocial personality disorder show a persistent behavior pattern of disregard for, and violation of, the rights of others. Typically, they do not feel guilt or remorse for their antisocial behaviors, and they continue the behaviors despite the threat of social rejection and punishment.

It is true that some people never feel guilty, even when they have committed serious crimes. Such people are likely to experience antisocial personality disorder.

In childhood and early adolescence, a person with antisocial personality disorder may skip school, run away from home, hurt other people or animals, lie, or steal. In adulthood, the person may be aggressive and reckless, have a hard time holding a job, fail to pay bills and debts, or break the law.

Avoidant Personality Disorder   People with avoidant personality disorder desire relationships with other people, but they are prevented from forming these relationships by tremendous fear of the disapproval of others. Thus, they act shy and withdrawn in social situations, always afraid they will say or do something foolish or embarrassing.

Personality Disorders and Their Characteristics

Type	Characteristics
Paranoid	Suspiciousness and distrust about others' motives
Schizoid	Detachment from social relationships
Schizotypal	Acute discomfort in close relationships, eccentricities of behavior
Antisocial	Disregard of the rights of others
Borderline	Instability in interpersonal relationships and self-image
Histrionic	Excessive emotionality, need for attention
Narcissistic	Grandiosity, need for admiration, lack of empathy
Avoidant	Social inhibition, feelings of inadequacy
Dependent	Submissive, clinging
Obsessive-Compulsive	Obsession with orderliness, perfectionism, and control

FIGURE 18.7   *Personality disorders are inflexible and lasting patterns of behavior that hamper social functioning. Listed here are the 10 specific personality disorders and their main characteristics.*

Source: Adapted from the DSM-IV, 1994.

This teen wants to join the fun but holds back out of fear of looking foolish. If he had a personality disorder, how could you tell if it was avoidant personality disorder or social phobia? What difference do you think it would make?

The symptoms of avoidant personality disorder are similar to those of social phobia, and people with avoidant personality disorder virtually always have social phobias as well. However, not all people who have social phobias have avoidant personality disorder. The latter seems to be a more severe and all-encompassing condition.

Explaining Personality Disorders

Most personality disorders were not classified until 1980, with the publication of the third edition of the DSM. However, the concept of personality disorder is not new, and both psychological and biological theories have been suggested to explain certain types of personality disorders.

Psychological Views Freud's psychoanalytic theory regarding the antisocial personality type states that a lack of guilt underlies the antisocial personality. This is due to a problem in the development of the conscience, or superego.

In support of the Freudian view, research has found that children who are rejected by adults and harshly punished rather than treated with affection tend to lack a sense of guilt. According to the findings, women are more likely to feel guilty about perceived immoral behavior, whereas men are more likely to fear being caught (Baumeister et al., 1994).

Some learning theorists have suggested that childhood experiences "teach" children how to relate to other people. If children are not reinforced for good behavior and only receive attention when they behave badly, they may learn antisocial behaviors. Such behaviors may persist into adulthood. Other learning theorists maintain that antisocial personality disorder develops when a child lacks appropriate role models and when the role models they encounter act aggressively (Millon, 1981).

Cognitive theorists have argued that antisocial adolescents tend to see other peoples' behavior as threatening, even when it is not. They use this faulty interpretation of other people's words and actions to justify their own antisocial behavior (Lochman & Dodge, 1994).

Biological Views Heredity may be another factor involved in antisocial personality disorder (Nigg & Goldsmith, 1994). For example, adoption studies show a higher incidence of antisocial behavior among the biological relatives than the adoptive relatives of people diagnosed with antisocial personality disorder (DiLalla & Gottesman, 1991). The exact link between genes and antisocial behavior is still under investigation.

Although the origins of antisocial and other personality disorders are still unresolved, treatment of these disorders is more straightforward. Methods of treatment for personality disorders—as well as for the other psychological disorders discussed in this chapter—are the focus of Chapter 19.

THINKING ABOUT PSYCHOLOGY

1. What is the major difference between personality disorders and other psychological disorders they may resemble?

2. Describe three behaviors of an individual with avoidant personality disorder.

3. **Critical Thinking** People with antisocial personality disorder are often more difficult to treat than people with other types of personality disorders. Why do you think this is so?

SUMMARY

Psychological disorders cause distress and interfere with normal functioning. They are classified into many different types on the basis of their symptoms. Both psychological and biological theories attempt to explain psychological disorders.

I. What Are Psychological Disorders?

A. Psychological disorders are persistent behaviors or mental processes that cause emotional pain or interfere with daily life.

B. Psychological disorders are very common, affecting millions of people.

C. It is important to classify psychological disorders to understand them better and to diagnose and treat affected individuals.

II. Anxiety Disorders

A. Anxiety refers to a general state of dread or uneasiness that occurs in response to a vague or imagined danger.

B. Types of anxiety disorders include phobic disorder, panic disorder, generalized anxiety disorder, obsessive-compulsive disorder, and stress disorders.

C. Both psychological and biological theories have been proposed to explain the occurrence of anxiety disorders.

   1. Psychological explanations include the following: anxiety is the result of repressed urges; phobias are learned in childhood.

   2. Biological explanations include the following: most anxiety disorders have a genetic basis, and certain genetically based fears were adaptive to human ancestors and thus passed on to successive generations.

III. Dissociative Disorders

A. Dissociation refers to the separation of some personality components or mental processes from conscious thought.

B. Types of dissociative disorders include dissociative amnesia, dissociative fugue, dissociative identity disorder, and depersonalization disorder.

C. Primarily psychological views have been proposed to account for the various dissociative disorders.

IV. Somatoform Disorders

A. Somatization refers to the expression of psychological distress through physical symptoms. There is, however, no medical explanation for the symptoms.

B. The two primary types of somatoform disorders are conversion disorder and hypochondriasis.

C. Somatoform disorders have been explained primarily by psychological theories.

V. Mood Disorders

A. The DSM-IV classifies mood disorders into several different types of depressive and bipolar disorders.

B. Many mood disorders, especially severe depression, may be linked to various biological factors.

VI. Schizophrenia

A. Schizophrenia is characterized by loss of contact with reality.

B. Subtypes of schizophrenia differ in their primary symptoms.

C. Many theories, both psychological and biological, have been proposed to explain schizophrenia. A multifactorial model is needed to account for all the factors believed to influence schizophrenia.

VII. Personality Disorders

A. Personality disorders are patterns of inflexible traits that disrupt social life or work and/or distress the affected individual.

B. Types of personality disorders include, among others, paranoid, schizoid, antisocial, and avoidant personality disorders.

TERM & CONCEPT
REVIEW

1. Define each of the following terms: *phobia, dissociation, depersonalization,* and *mania.*
2. Give examples of delusions of grandeur and delusions of persecution.
3. What are obsessions and compulsions, and how are they related?
4. What fears are associated with each of the following phobias: agoraphobia, claustrophobia, and zoophobia?
5. Describe a typical panic attack. Which psychological disorder are they associated with?
6. What must occur before a psychologist will make a diagnosis of major depression?
7. What role does culture play in the diagnosis of psychological disorders?
8. What did Seligman mean by learned helplessness? How is it related to depression?
9. How does acute stress disorder differ from post-traumatic stress disorder?
10. How do learning theorists explain dissociative disorders?

CRITICAL
THINKING

1. Explain why compulsions might be considered self-defeating behaviors.
2. Why might bipolar disorder be confused with schizophrenia?
3. What do dissociative disorders have in common with stress disorders?
4. What are the similarities and differences between schizoid personality disorder and avoidant personality disorder?
5. Like psychological disorders, physical disorders can be classified on the basis of their causes or their symptoms. Use examples of physical disorders, such as the common cold and hay fever, to demonstrate these two approaches to classifying disease.

APPLYING SKILLS
IN PSYCHOLOGY

1. **COOPERATIVE LEARNING** **Research in Psychology** Work with a small group of other students to research psychological theories that attempt to explain depression, including psychoanalytic, learning, and cognitive theories. Summarize arguments for and against each of the theories. Then select one student to represent each of the theories in a debate in front of the rest of the class. After the debate, ask volunteers from the class to state which theory they agree with and why.
2. **Writing About Psychology** Learn more about a psychological disorder that is not covered in this chapter, such as histrionic personality disorder, alcohol abuse disorder, anorexia nervosa, or conduct disorder. Make sure the information is up-to-date and based on the DSM-IV classification of the disorder. Then write a thorough report on the disorder. Your report should include a description of symptoms, estimates of how common the disorder is, and an overview of theories that have been proposed to explain the disorder.
3. **COOPERATIVE LEARNING** **Reading About Psychology** Working with a few other students, first read about the history of schizophrenia, from Hippocrates to the mid-20th century. Then summarize your most important findings in an illustrated time line that shows how schizophrenia has been perceived at different times in the past. Share your time line with the rest of the class, and explain how changing perceptions of schizophrenia influenced the way affected individuals were treated by society.
4. **Research in Psychology** Research mental illness in another culture. Try to find out how mental illness is defined, what types of behavior are considered abnormal, and how people with mental illness are treated. How does that culture's treatment of psychological disorders differ from that of the United States?

19 METHODS OF THERAPY

Objectives

1 Define *psychotherapy*, and list the advantages of each method of psychotherapy.

2 Describe the aims and major techniques of psychoanalysis.

3 Identify the primary goals and methods of humanistic therapy.

4 State the goals of cognitive therapy and behavior therapy, and describe the techniques used by cognitive and behavior therapists.

5 Describe the three major biological treatments for psychological disorders and possible side effects of these treatments.

A DAY IN THE LIFE

"Hey, Janet, what's up?" Dan asked.

"Not much. I'm on my way to the library to study with Marc and Linda for Friday's history test," Janet replied.

"Marc is studying for a test that's three days away?" Dan joked. "I thought he always waited until the last minute."

"That's what I thought too," Janet laughed. "Marc said that he talked to his mom and to one of his teachers because he used to get so nervous when he took tests. Whatever they said seems to be working. He still doesn't enjoy studying, but he isn't dreading tests like he used to. So, what are you up to?"

" I'm just looking over the college brochures that Mr. Hochberg gave me. I asked him what I should major in in college, but he keeps telling me that I have to decide for myself."

"Any ideas?" Janet asked.

"I'm still leaning toward counseling. Especially lately." Dan said.

"Why lately?" Janet asked.

"I guess it has something to do with everything my family has been going through with Michelle." [Michelle, Dan's sister, had been diagnosed with schizophrenia.]

"How is she doing?" Janet asked.

"Better," Dan said. "She's taking her medication and she started seeing the psychiatrist again."

"That's good. You seem to be feeling better too," Janet noted.

"I really am. Can I tell you something, just between us?" Dan asked.

"Of course you can," Janet assured him. "What's up?"

"Well, my parents and I started going to therapy too. The psychologist we're seeing is trying to help us deal with Michelle's disorder."

"That's great," Janet said. "But Dan, you really don't have to worry about people finding out that you're seeing a therapist. You know, my mom and I went to talk with someone after she and my dad got divorced. It was good just to talk to someone about what I was feeling."

"I guess you're right," Dan agreed. "Thanks, Janet."

• • •

Chapter 18 explored the many different types of psychological problems, from anxiety, such as Marc suffered before tests, to the symptoms of schizophrenia that afflict Dan's sister, Michelle. In this chapter, we will look at the various treatments, or therapies, for such problems.

Methods for treating psychological problems and disorders fall into two general categories: psychological methods, or methods of psychotherapy, and biological methods. The methods of psychotherapy aim to change the thought processes, feelings, or behavior of the individual. They are based on psychological principles. In contrast, biological therapies attempt to alleviate psychological problems by affecting the nervous system in some way. This chapter examines several different methods of therapy for psychological problems, including both psychological and biological methods.

Key Terms

- psychotherapy
- self-help group
- encounter group
- free association
- resistance
- dream analysis
- manifest content
- latent content
- transference
- humanistic therapy
- person-centered therapy
- nondirective therapy
- active listening
- rational-emotive therapy
- aversive conditioning
- token economy
- successive approximations
- antianxiety drug
- antidepressant drug
- lithium
- antipsychotic drug
- electroconvulsive therapy
- psychosurgery
- prefrontal lobotomy

TRUTH OR fiction ?

Read the following statements about psychology. Do you think they are true or false? You will learn whether each statement is true or false as you read the chapter.

- Just believing they will improve helps some people recover from psychological disorders.
- It is always preferable to see a therapist alone rather than in a group.
- Some therapists analyze people's dreams.
- People should avoid relating to their therapist as a parent or other authority figure.
- People's reactions to life events are based not on the events themselves but on people's ways of thinking about the events.
- Severe depression is sometimes treated by passing an electric current through the brain.

The development of a trusting relationship between client and therapist is one way that psychotherapy helps people with psychological problems.

What Is Therapy?

Therapy is a general term for the variety of approaches that mental health professionals use to treat psychological problems and disorders. Although there are many types of therapy, all approaches fall into two basic categories: psychologically based therapy and biologically based therapy. Psychologically based therapy, known as **psychotherapy**, involves verbal interactions between a trained professional and a person—usually called the client or patient—who is seeking help for a psychological problem. Biologically based therapy involves the use of drugs and other medical procedures to treat psychological disorders.

Achieving the Goals of Psychotherapy

Although the various methods of psychotherapy use different approaches, they all seek to help troubled individuals They do this by giving individuals hope for recovery; helping individuals gain new perspectives on their problems; and providing the individual with a caring, trusting relationship with a mental health professional.

Giving people hope for recovery is important because most people who seek therapy have prob-lems they believe they cannot handle alone. They may have low self-esteem and lack the confidence to recognize that their situation can improve. Just the belief that therapy will make them better is enough to put many people on the road to recovery. This is called the placebo effect.

TRUTH OR fiction ▪ REVISITED ▪

It is true that just believing they will improve helps some people recover from psychological disorders. This is called the placebo effect. Belief in recovery increases their confidence and gives people the motivation they need to become well.

Helping the individual gain a new perspective is important because many psychological problems are the result of negative outlooks and misinterpretations. For example, someone who is depressed is likely to have poor self-esteem. This person may be able to see only the negative side of every situation and may feel responsible for that negativity. Changing this individual's outlook and perceptions may help to relieve the depressed mood and to improve his or her self-esteem.

Providing a caring, trusting relationship is important because people with psychological problems often feel isolated, afraid, and distrustful of others. Psychotherapy encourages individuals to talk freely about their uncomfortable feelings and problems. Therefore, a trusting relationship with the therapist is essential to the process. Establishing such a relationship between client and therapist is a key goal of psychotherapy.

In addition to providing hope, a new perspective, and a trusting relationship, all psychotherapy methods share the goal of bringing about changes in the individuals who are seeking help. In the case of an individual who is depressed, for example, the psychotherapist tries to help the client develop a more positive outlook and higher self-esteem. In the case of a person experiencing a phobia, the psychotherapist helps the individual become desensitized, or less likely to react, to the object of fear.

The most commonly used methods of psychotherapy are psychoanalysis, humanistic therapy, cognitive therapy, and behavior therapy. Figure 19.1 summarizes the main features of these methods.

Each method of psychotherapy has a different goal and different ways of achieving that goal. Some psychotherapists use just one method. Others use an eclectic approach; that is, they choose from a variety of methods, depending on what works best for the individual client. Which method is the most effective often depends on the nature of the psychological problem (Beutler, 1991; Shoham-Salomon, 1991; Snow, 1991).

This raises the issue of the effectiveness of psychotherapy in general. Although some people find that psychotherapy does not help them, many people seem to benefit from it. However, it is difficult to know how those who benefit would have done in the absence of treatment. Some people feel better about themselves as time goes on, even without treatment; others find solutions to problems on their own. Nonetheless, research on the effectiveness of psychotherapy is encouraging (Barlow, 1994; Lipsey & Wilson, 1993).

Psychotherapy in Practice

Many types of professionals are involved in the treatment of psychological problems and disorders. (See Figure 19.2 on page 438.) However, it is primarily psychologists, psychiatrists, and social workers who practice psychotherapy.

Types of Mental Health Professionals

Counseling psychologists generally treat people with less serious psychological problems, such as adjustment problems. These psychologists often work in schools and other educational institutions, where they counsel people about their personal problems. Clinical psychologists help people with psychological problems adjust to the demands of life. Their clients' problems may range from anxiety to loss of motivation. Many clinical psychologists work in hospitals or clinics, while others work in private practice.

Commonly Used Psychotherapy Methods

Method	Main Goal	How Goal Is Achieved	Main Techniques
Psychoanalysis	To reduce anxiety and guilt over unconscious urges	Verbal processes	Free association, dream analysis, transference
Humanistic therapy	To help clients realize their full potential	Verbal processes	Active listening, acceptance and support
Cognitive therapy	To change assumptions or thought processes	Cognitive training	Rational-emotive therapy, Beck's cognitive therapy
Behavior therapy	To eliminate undesirable behaviors or acquire desirable behaviors	Behavioral training	Counterconditioning, operant conditioning

FIGURE 19.1   *The main features of the most commonly used methods of psychotherapy are listed here.*

Psychiatrists are medical doctors and many have private practices. As medical doctors, psychiatrists are the only mental health professionals who can prescribe medication and administer other types of biological therapy.

Other professionals who help people with psychological problems include psychiatric social workers and psychiatric nurses. Both have special training in psychology and usually work with other medical or mental health professionals. Psychiatric social workers may also practice psychotherapy.

Teachers, guidance counselors, clergy, and family doctors may also help individuals with psycho-logical problems. Although such professionals may have little formal training in psychology, they are often the people troubled individuals turn to first for help. Marc, for example, went to his teacher for advice on dealing with his test anxiety, and Dan asked his guidance counselor for help in making a career decision.

Selecting the Right Professional   Those seeking help for a psychological problem should familiarize themselves with the various practitioners and the type of treatment each offers. One way that people can gain that type of information is to ask the following questions:

- What is the professional's field? For example, people with psychological problems should see people who belong to a recognized profession, such as psychology, medicine, social work, or nursing.

- What degrees does the professional hold? Psychiatrists have medical degrees; psychologists usually have doctoral degrees; and social workers usually have master's degrees. The

Professionals Involved in the Treatment of Psychological Problems and Disorders

Type of Professional	Typical Education/Training	Usual Role
Counseling psychologist	Master's degree or Ph.D. (Doctor of Philosophy) in counseling psychology	Works in educational institutions, such as colleges and high schools, or in businesses; usually refers clients with serious problems to a clinical psychologist
Clinical psychologist	Ph.D. in psychology	Works in hospitals and clinics; assists and treats people with psychological problems
Psychiatrist	M.D. with a specialization in psychiatry and postgraduate training in abnormal behavior	Able to prescribe medicine and perform operations
Psychiatric social worker	Master's degree in social work with additional practical training and two years of graduate-level courses in psychology	Counsels people with everyday personal and family problems
Psychiatric nurse	Standard nursing license with advanced training in psychology	Dispenses medicine and acts as a contact person between counseling sessions

FIGURE 19.2   *Several types of professionals practice psychotherapy. A few of the various kinds of therapists are listed here along with the training they receive and descriptions of the work they do.*

appropriate degrees help ensure that the professional is properly trained.

- Is the professional licensed by the state? All states require licensing of psychologists and psychiatrists. Some states also require the licensing of social workers and nurses. To be issued a state license, professionals must pass exams or demonstrate expertise and knowledge in other ways.

People in group therapy usually sit in a circle as they share their thoughts and feelings. A therapist is usually present to guide and facilitate the discussion.

- What are the therapist's plans with treatment, and how long will treatment likely take? There is considerable variation in the nature and duration of treatment for different psychotherapy methods. For example, traditional psychoanalysis tends to take longer than other psychotherapy methods. The individual should know in advance what to expect from the treatment method.
- What is the estimated cost of treatment? Psychotherapy can be expensive, and it is not always covered by health insurance plans. Although cost should not have to be the deciding factor in choosing a therapist, for some people, it must be.

Individual Versus Group Therapy

Methods of psychotherapy are practiced either with individuals or in groups. Frequently, people who seek help for psychological problems have a choice between individual and group therapy. To make the best choice, it is important to be aware of the advantages of each type.

Advantages of Individual Therapy Some people do better with individual therapy because they need more personal attention than they would receive as part of a group. Moreover, some people feel uncomfortable talking about their problems in front of other people. These individuals are likely to talk more openly and freely if they are alone with their therapist.

Advantages of Group Therapy Group therapy can, however, have certain advantages over individual therapy. In fact, many people who begin seeing a therapist individually eventually switch to group therapy.

One advantage of group therapy is that it helps individuals realize that they are not alone. People can see other group members struggling with problems similar to their own. Members of the group can often benefit from the insights gained by other group members who have gone through similar struggles. Group members can support each other because they all have had similar experiences—they have "been there" themselves. Group therapy also gives individuals a chance to practice their new coping skills in a supportive environment.

One of the most significant advantages of group therapy is that it shows individuals that therapy can work. People see other members of the group recovering, and this gives them hope of recovery for themselves.

From a practical standpoint, group therapy enables the therapist to work with several people at once. In addition, it often allows a therapist to immediately see people who might otherwise have to be placed on a waiting list to receive help. It is also more affordable for clients because they share the cost of the therapist's time.

TRUTH **OR** **fiction** • REVISITED • *It is not true that it is always preferable to see a therapist alone rather than in a group.* In group therapy, members of the group can provide support and understanding and serve as role models for each other.

In family therapy, the therapist often can help family members see their problems more clearly.

Types of Group Therapy There are several types of group therapy. These include couples therapy, family therapy, and therapy for people who are dealing with similar problems, such as an eating disorder or the loss of a loved one.

Couples therapy tries to help two people improve or find more satisfaction in their relationship with each other. In particular, it helps them communicate more effectively by helping them learn new ways to listen to each other and to express their feelings (Markman et al., 1993). Such therapy also helps couples discover healthy ways to resolve conflicts and handle intense emotions.

Family therapy aims to help troubled families by improving communications and relations among family members. It also seeks to promote the family's emotional growth (Annunziata & Jacobson-Kram, 1995; Mikesell et al., 1995). Family therapy is based on the assumption that the lives of family members are so intertwined that the family as a whole is likely to suffer when one member has a problem. A parent may be addicted to alcohol, for example, and become abusive when intoxicated. The abuse may lead to low self-esteem, anxiety, and depression in other family members. Dan's family provides another example. They sought family therapy to help them cope with Michelle's schizophrenia. Janet and her mother also sought family therapy to help them adjust to the divorce.

Self-help groups are composed of people who share the same problem, such as overeating, drug addiction, or compulsive gambling. Members of a self-help group meet regularly—often without a therapist—to discuss their problem, share solutions, and give and receive support. One of the best-known self-help groups is Alcoholics Anonymous (AA). AA has served as a developmental model for many other self-help programs.

Encounter groups differ from these other kinds of groups. They are composed of strangers who do not necessarily share a common problem. In fact, encounter group members do not necessarily have psychological problems at all. Encounter groups are sometimes comprised of people who simply desire emotional growth.

Encounter groups promote emotional growth by helping group members become more aware of their own feelings and the feelings of others. Under the guidance of a leader, group members share their feelings through role-playing and other group techniques. The fact that group members are strangers makes it easier for some people to reveal their private feelings in an encounter group. However, other people are often unprepared for the intense emotions they experience in encounter therapy. For this and other reasons, encounter groups are somewhat controversial and less popular today than they were in the past.

THINKING ABOUT PSYCHOLOGY

1. Explain why psychotherapy has been referred to as "the talking cure."

2. What questions should one ask when selecting a psychotherapist?

3. **Critical Thinking** What do you think are the advantages and disadvantages of group therapy for someone with a social phobia? Explain your answer.

A DAY IN THE LIFE

The Psychoanalytic Approach

Psychoanalysis, the model of therapy developed by Sigmund Freud, literally means "analysis of the psyche (mind)." Psychoanalysis was the first formal method of psychotherapy used in Western countries. For many years, it was the only method used. In recent decades, however, it has become less popular (Arlow, 1989).

As you may recall from Chapter 14, Freud believed that most of people's problems originate in early childhood experiences and inner conflicts. These conflicts can cause people to develop unconscious sexual and aggressive urges that, in turn, cause anxiety. According to Freud, guilt occurs when the urges enter conscious thought or the individual acts upon them. Guilt also leads to more anxiety. For example, someone may experience feelings of anxiety and guilt caused by repressed rage toward a parent.

Psychoanalysts try to reduce anxiety and guilt by helping clients become aware of the unconscious thoughts and feelings that are at the root of their problems. Psychoanalysts call this self-awareness *insight*. Once insight has been gained, clients can use the knowledge to resolve the problems that arise in their daily lives. Some of the techniques psychoanalysts use to help clients gain insight include free association, dream analysis, and transference.

Free Association   The primary technique of psychoanalysis is **free association**. In free association, the analyst asks the client to relax and then to say whatever comes to mind. Free association developed from Freud's early use of hypnosis to tap into his clients' unconscious thoughts and feelings. The use of free association instead of hypnosis enables the client to participate more actively in the analysis.

The topic of the free association might be a memory, dream, fantasy, or recent event. The analyst may say nothing, occasionally ask a question, or attempt to lead the client in a particular direction. The assumption is that, as long as the client associates freely, unconscious thoughts and feelings will "break through" and show up in what the client says. The client is encouraged to say whatever comes to mind, no matter how trivial, embarrassing, or painful the ideas may seem. In fact, psychoanalysts believe that the more hesitant the patient is to say something, the more likely it is that the hesitancy reflects an unconscious thought or feeling.

Resistance is the term psychoanalysts use to refer to a client's hesitancy or unwillingness to discuss issues raised during free association. An experienced psychoanalyst can recognize a client's resistance. It may occur when the client makes a joking remark about a serious subject, for example, or when the client changes the subject entirely. Resistance is believed to reflect a defense mechanism, such as the repression or denial of painful feelings. (See Chapter 14.)

The role of the analyst in free association is to point out the types of things the client is saying—or resisting saying—and to help the client interpret the meaning of the utterances or lack of utterances. Psychoanalysts believe that free association allows the client to express troubling, unconscious thoughts and feelings in a safe environment, where those thoughts and feelings may be explored. Through such means, clients are thought to gain insight into their problems.

Dream Analysis   Freud believed that dreams express unconscious thoughts and feelings. He called them the "royal road into the unconscious." In a technique called **dream analysis**, the analyst interprets the content of clients' dreams to unlock these unconscious thoughts and feelings.

Freud also distinguished between the manifest and latent content of dreams (Freud, 1952). **Manifest content** refers to the actual content of the dream as it is remembered by the client. **Latent content** refers to the hidden meaning in the dream that the therapist interprets from the manifest content. For example, a client may dream about falling from a mountain and being unable to grab anything to break his fall (manifest content). The therapist might interpret the dream to mean that the client has repressed feelings that his life is out of control (latent content).

It is true that some therapists analyze people's dreams. Most psychoanalysts believe that dreams are an expression of unconscious thoughts and feelings.

Traditionally, psychoanalysis was conducted with the patient lying on a couch and the analyst sitting out of the patient's line of vision in order to be less of a distraction. Today, psychoanalysis is often conducted with patient and analyst sitting face-to-face.

Transference As analysis proceeds, many clients begin having relationships with their analyst that are similar to those they have or had with another important person in their lives, often a parent. They experience similar feelings toward the analyst and expect the analyst to feel and behave as the other person did. In other words, the client is transferring feelings and expectations from one person to another. This process is called **transference**.

Psychoanalysts make use of transference to help the client express and analyze unconscious feelings he or she has toward that other important person. In fact, establishing a transference relationship is a major goal of psychoanalysis. Transference exposes unresolved problems in earlier relationships that the client can then work through, with the help of the analyst, in order to solve similar problems in current relationships.

TRUTH OR **fiction** ▪ REVISITED ▪

It is not true that people should avoid relating to their therapist as a parent or other authority figure. People in psychoanalysis are often encouraged to relate to their therapist in this way.

The following example makes the concept of transference easier to understand. Consider a client who has repressed feelings of anger toward her mother because of her mother's cold, critical attitude toward her throughout her childhood. During the course of psychoanalysis, the client transfers the unconscious anger at her mother to the therapist. She falls into patterns of interaction with the therapist that are characteristic of her relationship with her mother.

The therapist, however, does not react as the client's mother would. Instead, he or she remains neutral and helps the patient examine her feelings. Through this process, the client gains insight into her relationship with her mother and how it affects her current relationships. The client begins to understand, for example, that problems with her boss at work may stem from unconscious and unresolved feelings of anger toward her mother.

Evaluation of Psychoanalysis Many psychologists believe that Freud placed too much emphasis on sexual and aggressive urges. Some argue that he underestimated the importance of conscious ideas and changes in behavior. Despite these criticisms, however, a classic review of dozens of studies concluded that people who had received psychoanalysis showed greater well-being than 70 to 75 percent of those who had not received treatment (Smith & Glass, 1977). Psychoanalysis has proved especially useful in the treatment of anxiety, mild depression, and difficulty in handling social relationships. However, it is generally not useful for the treatment of major depression, bipolar disorder, or schizophrenia (Melle & Friis, 1991).

The techniques of traditional psychoanalysis often require clients to meet with their analyst four or five times a week, for as long as three to six years. For some clients, this provides a supportive, long-term relationship that fosters emotional growth and insight. For others, however, the cost of therapy in time, money, and emotional distress is too great to make psychoanalysis a real option.

Psychoanalysis does not work for everyone. For example, it is not the most effective type of psychotherapy for individuals who are less verbal or who have limited educational background. Psychoanalysis also is not useful for people who are too seriously disturbed to gain insight into their problems. For example, a person with schizophrenia may lose touch with reality. Such an individual is unlikely to be able to gain the insight needed for effective psychoanalytic treatment.

CASE STUDIES
AND OTHER TRUE STORIES

The Transference Relationship

To develop and resolve a transference relationship between client and analyst may take years. The following excerpt (Silverman, 1984) from a therapy session shows how an analyst focuses on the client's feelings for him. The analyst is thus encouraging the development of a transference relationship.

Client: I have been feeling weak and tired. I saw my doctor yesterday and he said there's nothing . . . wrong.

Analyst: Does anything come to mind in relation to weak and tired feelings?

Client: I'm thinking of the way you looked last year after you came out of the hospital. [The client was referring to a hospitalization (of the analyst) during which treatment sessions were suspended.]

Analyst: Do you recall how you felt when you saw me looking that way?

Client: It made me upset, even guilty.

Analyst: But why guilty?

Client: I'm not sure why I said that. There was nothing to feel guilty about.

Analyst: Perhaps you had other feelings.

Client: Well, it's true that at one point I felt faintly pleased that I was young and vigorous and you seemed to be going downhill. . . .

Analyst: Perhaps . . . you imagined I felt bad because you were going uphill while I was going down.

BiZarro   by Dan Piraro

TELL ME ABOUT YOUR FATHER...

COULDN'T WE TALK ABOUT *ME* FOR ONCE, DAD?

Client: That feels correct. . . . [The client looks distressed and then goes off on another topic.]

Analyst: Clearly you're not very comfortable when you contrast your state with mine. . . .

Client: Well, you know I've never felt comfortable when thinking of myself outdoing you in any way. And when it comes to our states of health, the idea is particularly distressing.

Analyst: I wonder now if the weak and tired feelings that you spoke about earlier in the session aren't related to what we're discussing now. . . . Perhaps you felt that you were making me ill again with your wishes and thus you had to punish yourself by making yourself ill.

By the end of the excerpt, the analyst is interpreting the client's feelings in typical Freudian terms: hidden urges (wishing the father were sick and weak) are transferred to the analyst; these urges lead in turn to guilt and anxiety ("you had to punish yourself by making yourself ill"). In this way, the transference relationship helps the client gain an awareness of his unconscious feelings of rivalry toward his father.

Think About It

Suppose a student has a troubled relationship with a parent and develops a transference relationship with a teacher. How might this affect the student's performance in that teacher's class?

Brief Psychoanalysis Over the past several decades, shorter terms of psychoanalysis have become increasingly popular. In traditional psychoanalysis, a client and therapist may meet daily over the course of several years. By contrast, in brief psychoanalysis, client and analyst typically meet just 10 to 20 times over the course of a few months to a year. The shorter duration of treatment makes brief psychoanalysis available to a wider range of people (Strupp, 1992).

The techniques used in brief psychoanalysis are generally the same techniques that are used in traditional psychoanalysis. The primary difference between the two approaches is that brief psychoanalysis has a more limited focus. Whereas traditional psychoanalysis examines the client's entire personality, brief psychoanalysis concentrates on fixing a specific problem. For brief psychoanalysis to be effective, clients usually must be highly motivated and actively involved in applying the insights gained in therapy to the events in their lives.

THINKING ABOUT PSYCHOLOGY

1. Identify and describe the three techniques used in traditional psychoanalysis.
2. **Critical Thinking** According to psychoanalytic theory, what effect do unconscious thoughts and feelings have on a person's ability to form meaningful personal relationships?

3
The Humanistic Approach

The primary goal of **humanistic therapy** is to help individuals reach their full potential. It does this by helping individuals develop self-awareness and self-acceptance. The method assumes that most people are basically good and have a natural tendency to strive for self-actualization, that is, to become all that they are capable of being. (See Chapter 13.) The method also assumes that people with psychological problems merely need help tapping their inner resources so that they can grow and reach their full potential. Among the several types of humanistic therapy, person-centered therapy is the most widely used.

Person-Centered Therapy **Person-centered therapy** was developed in the early 1950s by psychologist Carl Rogers. According to Rogers, psychological problems arise when people stop being true to themselves and instead act as others want or expect them to act (Rogers, 1986). The role of therapy is to help clients find their true selves and realize their unique potential.

Person-centered therapy is also called client-centered therapy. The use of the term *client* instead of *patient* reflects the status given to individuals seeking help. Clients are seen as equals in a working relationship with the therapist rather than as inferiors who are ill. Clients are encouraged to take the lead in therapy, talking openly about whatever may be troubling them. This method is called **nondirective therapy** because it is not directed by the therapist. The therapist's role is to act as a mirror, reflecting clients' thoughts and feelings back so that they can see themselves more clearly.

Techniques of Person-Centered Therapy **Active listening** is a widely used communication technique in which the listener repeats, rephrases, and asks for clarification of the statements made by the speaker. Facial expressions and body language are also important. The goal is to convey to the speaker that his or her words are being heard and that his or her thoughts and feelings are being understood.

The therapist also must remain nonjudgmental, accepting, and supportive, regardless of what the client says, providing what Rogers calls *unconditional positive regard*. The acceptance and support of the therapist help the client accept himself or herself and his or her true feelings. Self-esteem also rises, giving the client the confidence to make his or her own choices, take responsibility for those decisions, and form healthy relationships.

Other Applications Person-centered therapy is practiced widely by school and college counselors. It not only helps students deal with anxiety, depression, and other psychological problems but also helps students make decisions. Counselors try to provide a supportive atmosphere in which students feel free to explore alternatives and make their own choices. Dan's school counselor, Mr. Hochberg, is not a psychologist, but he took a person-centered approach in helping Dan decide on a career. He helped Dan identify choices, but he did not make a decision for him.

A DAY IN THE LIFE

EXPLORING
DIVERSITY

Therapy and Culture

Increasingly in the United States, people who seek help for psychological disorders come from a wide range of cultures. This has led to a growing awareness on the part of therapists that culture is a significant factor in the diagnosis and treatment of psychological disorders. People differ in how they describe or even experience universal problems such as anxiety and depression. Their ideas about psychological disorders—and in some cases even the disorders themselves—are influenced by their culture.

The relevance of culture to the diagnosis and treatment of psychological disorders is illustrated by the case of a woman, originally from Ecuador, who was taken to a psychiatric hospital in the United States by her relatives. The woman seemed to be seriously disturbed. She was listless and withdrawn, complaining only that she had "lost her soul" (Goleman, 1995c).

Most therapists probably would have diagnosed the woman with schizophrenia and labeled as a delusion her belief that she had lost her soul. However, the psychiatrist who interviewed the woman at the hospital was familiar with her cultural background. He recognized the woman's "soul loss" as a symptom of *susto*.

Susto is a term used only in Latin American cultures. The condition is believed to occur when a person's soul is captured by spirits and taken from the body. The condition often develops after a frightening or stressful event, such as a serious injury or the death of a loved one. The symptoms of *susto* include loss of appetite, loss of weight, listlessness, apathy, and withdrawal from normal activities. Do these symptoms sound familiar?

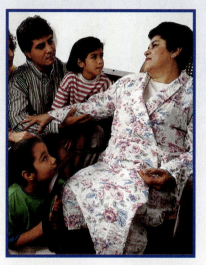

The symptoms of susto *include loss of appetite, listlessness, and depression.*

They should—they are also the symptoms of what Western psychiatrists call depression.

In the case of the Ecuadoran woman, the psychiatrist determined that her problem had started when a close relative in Ecuador had died unexpectedly. In her grief, the woman had developed all the typical symptoms of *susto*. In Western psychiatric terms, the woman was depressed. However, the psychiatrist did not prescribe antidepressants, as he might have for some other depressed patients. Instead, he decided on a form of therapy that was culturally more relevant.

In Ecuador, a mourning ceremony would have been held to help family members adjust to the loss of the loved one. Therefore, with the help of the woman's family, the therapist arranged a mourning ceremony to help the woman confront and accept the death of her relative. Openly mourning the death in a supportive circle of family and friends was apparently what the woman needed to begin healing from her loss and recovering from her depression. Within a few weeks her symptoms had improved and she was functioning normally again.

This example illustrates the relevance of culture to therapy. Clearly, both the diagnosis and the treatment of psychological disorders should take into account a person's cultural background.

Think About It

What do you think might have happened to the woman from Ecuador if she had been diagnosed incorrectly with schizophrenia?

Evaluation of Humanistic Therapy In a review of several studies, nearly three fourths of people obtaining person-centered therapy showed greater well-being, on average, than people who did not receive therapy (Smith & Glass, 1977). Like psychoanalysis, person-centered therapy seems to be most helpful for well-educated, motivated people. Humanistic therapy in general works best for people who experience anxiety, mild depression, or problems in their social relationships. However, it is ineffective for people who have major depression, bipolar disorder, or schizophrenia.

THINKING ABOUT PSYCHOLOGY

1. What assumptions about human nature form the basis of humanistic therapy?
2. What is the goal of active listening?
3. **Critical Thinking**   Discuss the role of the therapist in person-centered therapy.

4
Cognitive Therapy and Behavior Therapy

Cognitive therapy and behavior therapy are considered together because both methods share the same goal—to help clients develop new ways of thinking and behaving. Both cognitive and behavior therapists encourage the clients to focus on their thoughts and actions. Advocates of these two theories contend that only by modifying self-defeating thoughts and behavior patterns will the client truly be able to solve his or her own problems. Thus, the aim of these therapies is to eliminate troubling emotions or behaviors rather than to help patients gain insight into the underlying cause of their problems, which is a key goal of psychoanalysis and humanistic therapy.

Cognitive Model of Depression

FIGURE 19.3 *Cognitive psychologists believe that some people develop ways of thinking that can lead to emotional and behavioral problems. In this example, we will call the person on the left Person A and the person on the right Person B. A's positive thinking gives him the motivation to keep practicing and to try to make the team. B's negative thinking leads to depression, feelings of worthlessness, and a reluctance to try again.*

Cognitive Therapy

The aim of cognitive therapy is to help people learn to think about their problems in more productive ways. Cognitive psychologists focus on the beliefs, attitudes, and thought processes that create and compound their clients' problems (Beck, 1993; Ellis, 1995). They believe that some people develop ways of thinking that are illogical or based on faulty assumptions. Such ways of thinking can lead to emotional and behavioral problems. This idea is illustrated in Figure 19.3 on page 446.

Figure 19.3 shows how two different individuals, whom we will call Person A and Person B, react to the same event—being rejected for the swim team. Person A has a positive, logical way of thinking. His ability to look forward gives him the motivation to continue practicing and to try again next year. Person B's negative way of thinking, on the other hand, leads to feelings of worthlessness and depression. It is highly unlikely that Person B will continue practicing, let alone try out for the team again next year.

 *It is true that people's reactions to life events are based not on the events themselves but on people's ways of thinking about the events.* This is why cognitive therapists try to help people who are having emotional problems change the ways that they think.

Cognitive therapists help people change their ways of thinking by showing them that their thinking is based on faulty assumptions or that their thought processes are illogical. These therapists also try to help people develop more realistic and logical ways of thinking. Cognitive psychologists argue that once people have changed their ways of thinking, they become more capable of solving their emotional and behavioral problems.

The two most widely used cognitive therapy methods are rational-emotive therapy and psychiatrist Aaron Beck's model of therapy, simply called cognitive therapy. Both methods aim at modifying people's ways of thinking as a means of improving their emotional health. However, the methods differ somewhat in the aspects of thinking they maintain must be changed and in the approach they take to bring about those changes.

Rational-Emotive Therapy   Developed by psychologist Albert Ellis in the 1950s, **rational-emotive therapy** (RET) is based on Ellis' belief that people are basically logical in their thinking and actions. However, the assumptions upon which they base their thinking or actions are sometimes incorrect. According to Ellis, people may develop emotional problems when they base their behavior on these faulty assumptions (Ellis, 1984).

An example of a commonly held false assumption that leads to emotional problems is "I must do everything perfectly." People who believe they must do everything perfectly in order to be happy must also believe that if they are unhappy, it is because they did something imperfectly. Thus, their unhappiness is their own fault. In addition, no matter how hard these people try, they are unlikely to be able to live up to their own unrealistically high standard of perfection. It is easy to see why belief in this false assumption could lead a person to experience anxiety or severe depression.

People are often unaware of their faulty assumptions even though the assumptions influence their conscious thoughts and actions. The role of the therapist in RET is first to identify and then to challenge the false assumptions. To teach individuals to think more realistically, RET therapists use techniques such as role-playing and modeling. Role-playing helps individuals see how their assumptions affect their relationships. Modeling is used to show individuals other, more realistic assumptions they might adopt.

Individuals in rational-emotive therapy may also receive homework assignments. For example, they may be asked to read relevant literature, listen to tapes of psychotherapy sessions, or carry out experiments designed to test their assumptions. The more faithfully patients complete their homework, the more likely it is that their therapy will succeed (Maultsby, 1971).

Beck's Cognitive Therapy   Another form of cognitive therapy was introduced in the 1960s by psychiatrist Aaron Beck. In contrast to RET's focus on faulty assumptions, the focus of Beck's method of cognitive therapy is on illogical thought processes. Beck (1963) has noted several types of illogical thought processes that may lead to emotional problems, particularly depression. Some of these illogical thoughts include the following:

- *Arbitrary inference,* or drawing conclusions for which there is no evidence. For example, when a teacher passes a student in the hall and does not smile, the student may arbitrarily conclude that the teacher is planning to fail her.

- *Selective abstraction,* or drawing conclusions about a situation or event on the basis of a single detail and misinterpreting or ignoring other details that would lead to a different conclusion. For example, a person may look at his reflection in a mirror, but instead of feeling happy about his good features—say, a handsome smile and a muscular build—all he notices is the small blemish on his chin.

- *Overgeneralization,* or drawing a general conclusion from a single experience. For example, a person may conclude that she is worthless because she failed one test.

Instead of confronting and challenging clients about the errors in their way of thinking, as the RET therapist does, the therapist using Beck's approach gently guides clients in testing the logic of their own thought processes and developing more logical ways of thinking. One technique for doing this is to train clients to observe and record their thoughts in response to the events of daily life. Therapists can later review events with clients and help them see the illogical thought processes that are causing them emotional problems.

Evaluation of Cognitive Therapy   Cognitive therapy tends to be a short-term method, making it a realistic option for more people than traditional psychoanalysis. Clients generally meet with their therapist once a week for 15 to 25 weeks.

Studies show that cognitive therapy is especially helpful for treating depression. People with anxiety often benefit from cognitive therapy as well (Engels et al., 1993; Haaga & Davison, 1993; Robins & Hayes, 1993; Whisman et al., 1991). Even people with major depression, for whom only medication was once thought could be helpful, appear to respond well to cognitive therapy (Hollon et al., 1991; Jacobson & Hollon, 1996; Simons et al., 1995). Cognitive therapy has also been particularly effective in helping people with personality disorders (Beck & Freeman, 1990).

On the other hand, people with severe psychological disorders, such as schizophrenia, usually are not good candidates for cognitive therapy unless they are also receiving drug therapy to help control their delusions (Chadwick & Lowe, 1990). Otherwise, they may be too agitated and out of touch with reality to see that their ways of thinking are illogical.

A person who has a phobia of snakes may seek behavior therapy as a means of confronting and overcoming the phobia. According to behavior theorists, a client who fears snakes can be counterconditioned to react to snakes in a relaxed manner.

Behavior Therapy

The goal of behavior therapy, which is also called *behavior modification,* is to help people develop more adaptive behavior. Some people seek behavior therapy to eliminate undesirable behaviors, such as overeating or smoking. Others seek behavior therapy to acquire desirable behaviors, such as the skills needed to develop healthy social relationships or confront phobias.

Behaviorists believe that both desirable and undesirable behaviors are largely learned and that people with psychological problems have learned unhealthy ways of behaving. The aim of behavior therapy is to teach people more desirable (or healthier) ways of behaving. To behaviorists, the reasons for the undesirable behavior are unimportant.

Changing the behavior is what matters. For example, in Marc's case, changing his study habits led to a decrease in his test anxiety, but it did not help him understand why he had test anxiety in the first place.

Many behavioral techniques fall into two categories: counterconditioning, which helps in the unlearning of undesirable behaviors, and operant conditioning, which helps in the learning of desirable behaviors. The choice of behavioral techniques for an individual client depends largely on the nature of the individual's psychological disorder.

Counterconditioning If undesirable behaviors are conditioned, or learned through reinforcement, then presumably they can be unlearned, or counterconditioned. Counterconditioning pairs the stimulus that triggers an unwanted behavior (such as fear of spiders) with a new, more desirable behavior. (See Chapter 6.) For example, a client who reacts with fear to spiders can be counterconditioned to respond to spiders in a relaxed manner instead. Counterconditioning techniques include systematic desensitization, modeling, and aversive conditioning.

Systematic desensitization was developed by psychiatrist Joseph Wolpe in the 1950s as a treatment for phobias and other anxiety disorders. The assumption underlying systematic desensitization is that a person cannot feel anxious and relaxed at the same time. The therapist therefore trains the client to relax in the presence of an anxiety-producing situation (Wolpe, 1990).

This is done in a systematic way. First, the therapist teaches the client how to relax completely. Once this has been accomplished, the therapist gradually exposes the client to the object or situation that causes the phobic response. For a person who fears spiders, the therapist might first ask the person to simply imagine a spider. If the thought of a spider makes the client feel anxious, the client is told to stop thinking about the spider and relax again. This is done repeatedly until the thought of a spider no longer causes anxiety.

Gradually, the stimulus is increased—the person might be shown pictures of spiders, asked to hold a toy spider, and eventually asked to handle a real spider. In each case, the person is trained to respond with relaxation until the stimulus no longer provokes anxiety.

Systematic desensitization may be combined with other counterconditioning measures, such as modeling and aversive conditioning. Modeling involves observational learning. The client observes and then imitates the therapist or another person coping with the feared object or situation. For the person with a fear of spiders, the therapist might ask the person to observe someone calmly watching a spider make a web. The client would then be encouraged to behave in the same way.

Aversive conditioning is, in a sense, the opposite of systematic desensitization. In aversive condi-

Someone who has a fear of water may gradually lose that fear through the behavior-therapy technique of systematic desensitization. Once a person has overcome the fear of water, she may actually enjoy the experience of swimming. What other fears might be overcome through systematic desensitization?

tioning, the therapist replaces a positive response to a stimulus with a negative response. For example, for a person who wants to stop smoking, the therapist might replace the pleasant feelings associated with smoking with unpleasant ones. The person might be asked to smoke several cigarettes at once through a device that holds two or more cigarettes. This overexposure to cigarette smoke makes smoking an unpleasant experience. With repetition, the person may come to avoid smoking.

People who learn more desirable behaviors through counterconditioning often experience a boost in their self-esteem as well. Furthermore, by confronting, challenging, and overcoming their fears, such people will increase their opportunity to lead less restrictive lives.

Operant Conditioning   The behavioral technique of operant conditioning is based on the assumption that behavior that is reinforced tends to be repeated, whereas behavior that is not reinforced tends to be extinguished. Behavioral therapists reinforce desirable behaviors with rewards and at the same time withhold reinforcement for undesirable behaviors. The rewards for desirable behavior might be praise or treats, for example, depending on the client and the setting. For Marc, reducing his test anxiety may be all the reward he needs to motivate him to continue his new study habits.

Operant conditioning has sometimes proved effective in more severe cases, such as schizophrenia and childhood autism, that have previously been resistant to other types of treatment. In addition, operant conditioning is often used in institutional settings, such as mental hospitals and prisons. In such settings, the therapist may set up a system of rewards, called a **token economy**. When people in these settings begin to demonstrate appropriate behavior, they are rewarded with a plastic coin or token. The tokens can be accumulated and exchanged for real rewards, such as snacks, extra television time, a trip to town, or a private room.

The staff at one mental hospital used operant conditioning to convince withdrawn schizophrenic patients to eat their meals (Ayllon & Haughton, 1962). The more the staff coaxed the patients to eat—sometimes even hand-feeding them—the worse the problem became. The extra attention from the staff was apparently reinforcing the patients' lack of cooperation: the greater the refusal to eat, the more attention the patients received.

The solution was to stop reinforcing the uncooperative behavior and instead reinforce cooperative behavior. Patients who arrived late at the dining hall were locked out, and hospital staff were prevented from helping patients at mealtime. Thus, uncooperative behavior was no longer rewarded with extra attention. Only those who cooperated received food. As a result, the uncooperative patients quickly changed their eating habits.

Sometimes people find it difficult to adopt a new behavior all at once, finding it easier to change their behavior gradually. Another method of operant conditioning, called successive approximations, is useful in such situations. The term **successive approximations** refers to a series of behaviors that gradually become more similar to a target behavior. Through reinforcement of behaviors at each stage, the target behavior is finally achieved.

The technique of successive approximations is best understood by considering an example. Suppose a student wants to increase his studying

Aversive Versus Operant Conditioning		
	Aversive	**Operant**
Goal	Extinguish an undesirable behavior.	Encourage a desirable behavior.
Technique	Replace the positive response to the behavior with a negative response.	Reward the behavior with a form of positive reinforcement.
Rationale	When the behavior is no longer enjoyable, it will be extinguished.	Behavior that is positively reinforced tends to be repeated.

FIGURE 19.4   *Behavior therapy is based largely on the idea that all behavior is learned. Listed here are two types of conditioning behavior therapists use to teach people healthy ways of behaving.*

time to two hours a day. However, he is not used to studying that long and cannot maintain his concentration for more than half an hour at a time. Instead of trying to study for two hours the first day, he studies for half an hour and then gives himself a small reward, such as shooting baskets for 15 minutes. Each night he adds five minutes to his study time, and each time he meets his new goal he reinforces his behavior with a small reward. Within a few weeks, through successive approximations, he reaches his goal of studying for two hours a day.

Yet another method of operant conditioning is social skills training. People with severe psychological problems may lack social skills because of isolation and social withdrawal. In fact, lacking the social skills needed for independent living is one of the major symptoms of schizophrenia. Helping people with schizophrenia and other psychological disorders develop better social skills can improve their relationships and make them better able to function independently.

Behavior therapists help people build their social skills by advising clients on their behavior, modeling effective behaviors, and encouraging clients to practice effective behaviors. Such techniques have proved successful in helping students build social relationships. They have also been used to help people with severe psychological disorders. With social skills training, a person who otherwise would be dependent on others might be able to hold a job and live on her or his own.

Evaluation of Behavior Therapy   Behavior therapy tends to be somewhat more effective overall than psychoanalysis or person-centered therapy. It is also a short-term therapy, sometimes bringing about lasting results in just a few months.

Behavior therapy is especially effective for well-defined problems such as phobias, post-traumatic stress disorder, and compulsions (Borkovec & Costello, 1993; Bowers & Clum, 1988). It has also helped many people overcome depression, social problems, and problems with self-control (as in quitting smoking or drinking). In addition, behavior therapy has proved very useful for managing the care of people living in institutions, including people with schizophrenia and people with mental retardation (Spreat & Behar, 1994).

Behavior therapy is less useful for some other disorders. For example, it is not usually effective for treating the thought disorder of schizophrenia (Wolpe, 1990), and it is less effective than cognitive therapy for treating depression.

THINKING ABOUT PSYCHOLOGY

1. How does Ellis' rational-emotive therapy differ from Beck's cognitive therapy?
2. What is aversive conditioning?
3. **Critical Thinking**   How might systematic desensitization be used to treat a person with a social phobia?

5 Biological Therapy

The methods of psychotherapy described so far rely on verbal interactions between the psychotherapist and the individual seeking help. As you have seen, psychotherapists may give their clients emotional support, advice, and help in understanding and changing their thoughts and behaviors.

Biological therapy, on the other hand, relies on methods such as medication, electric shock, and even surgery to help people with psychological disorders. All of these biological methods affect the brain in some way.

Because these treatments are medical in nature, they must be administered or prescribed by psychiatrists or other physicians. Psychologists do not prescribe drugs or administer biological treatments, but they may help decide whether a certain kind of biological therapy is appropriate for the treatment of a particular individual.

Drug Therapy

Drug therapy is the most widely used biological treatment for psychological disorders. It works well for several different problems. Four major types of medication are commonly used: antianxiety drugs, antidepressant drugs, lithium, and antipsychotic drugs. All of these medications can be obtained only with a prescription.

Antianxiety Drugs   Also called minor tranquilizers, **antianxiety drugs** are used as an outpatient treatment to help people with anxiety disorders or panic attacks. (See Chapter 18.) They are also prescribed for people who are experiencing serious distress or tension in their lives.

Antianxiety drugs work by depressing the activity of the nervous system. They lower the heart rate and respiration rate. They also decrease feelings of nervousness and tension. Although antianxiety medications help control the symptoms of anxiety, they are not a permanent cure for anxiety disorders. Thus, most people use them for a short period of time (Shader & Greenblatt, 1993). The longer a person takes an antianxiety medication, the less effective the drug may become. Higher doses may be needed in order to achieve the same effect.

The major side effects of antianxiety medications are feelings of fatigue (Shader & Greenblatt, 1993). It is also possible to become dependent on antianxiety drugs. People who are dependent on these drugs may lose the ability to face the stresses and strains of everyday life without them.

Antidepressant Drugs   People who suffer from major depression are often treated with **antidepressant drugs**. Antidepressant drugs are also sometimes used in the treatment of eating disorders and panic disorder (Craighead & Agras, 1991).

Antidepressants work by increasing the amount of one or both of the neurotransmitters noradrenaline and serotonin. They tend to be most helpful in reducing the physical symptoms of depression. They increase activity levels and reduce the severity of eating and sleeping problems.

In order to work effectively, antidepressant medications must build up in the body to a certain level. This may take anywhere from several days to a few weeks. Severely depressed people who are at risk of suicide are sometimes hospitalized until the medication reaches the level required to improve their depressed mood. This is to prevent them from taking an overdose, which could be lethal.

Some studies, however, have found antidepressant drugs to be no more effective than cognitive therapy for treating depression (Antonuccio, 1995; Jacobson & Hollon, 1996; Munoz et al., 1994). In fact, cognitive therapy actually offers some advantages over drug therapy. For example, cognitive therapy can help improve a person's coping skills. This, in turn, can reduce the risk of depression returning after treatment ends (Hollon et al., 1993). In addition, antidepressants sometimes have negative side effects, such as escalated heart rate and excessive weight gain (Sleek, 1996). For these and other reasons, some experts believe that antidepressant medications should be reserved for people who fail to respond to psychotherapy.

Lithium   The ancient Greeks and Romans may have been the first people to use the metal **lithium** to treat psychological disorders. They discovered that mineral water helped many people with what is now called bipolar disorder. (See Chapter 18.) It has been speculated that the mineral water may have contained lithium.

Today lithium carbonate, a salt of the metal lithium, is given in tablet form to help people with bipolar disorder. Lithium seems to flatten out their cycles of mania and depression. How lithium does this is not completely understood, although it is known to affect the functioning of several neurotransmitters (Price & Heninger, 1994).

Lithium may have side effects such as shakiness, memory impairment, and excessive thirst (Price & Heninger, 1994). Memory problems are reported to be the major reason that people stop using the drug.

Antipsychotic Drugs   People with schizophrenia, such as Dan's sister, are likely to be prescribed **antipsychotic drugs**, also called major tranquilizers.

Antipsychotic medications are effective for reducing agitation, delusions, and hallucinations (Kane, 1996). Their use has enabled many thousands of people with schizophrenia to live outside of mental hospitals and even to hold jobs.

Schizophrenia is associated with high levels of dopamine activity. (See Chapter 18.) Antipsychotic medications are thought to work by blocking the activity of dopamine in the brain. Unfortunately, prolonged use of these medications can lead to problems in balance and coordination and produce tremors and twitches (Kane, 1996).

Electroconvulsive Therapy

Electroconvulsive therapy (ECT), commonly called electric-shock therapy, was introduced as a treatment for psychological disorders in the 1930s by Italian psychiatrist Ugo Cerletti. Before ECT is given, anesthesia is administered to render the person unconscious throughout the procedure. Then an electric current is passed through the person's brain. The electric current produces convulsions (violent involuntary contractions of muscles) throughout the body. In some cases, muscle relaxant drugs are given to prevent injury during the convulsions.

When ECT was first introduced, it was used for many psychological disorders, including schizophrenia. However, once antipsychotic drugs became available, ECT was used much less often. In fact, in 1990, the American Psychiatric Association recommended that ECT be used primarily for people with major depression who do not respond to antidepressant drugs. ECT does appear to help many severely depressed people for whom antidepressants have failed to bring relief (Janicak et al., 1985; National Institute of Mental Health, 1985).

TRUTH OR fiction
■ R E V I S I T E D ■

It is true that severe depression is sometimes treated by passing an electric current through the brain. This is called electroconvulsive therapy. It is a biological treatment used primarily for patients with severe depression who do not respond to antidepressants.

ECT remains a highly controversial treatment. Many professionals believe the treatment is too drastic, especially given the fact that they do not know exactly how the procedure works. ECT also has serious side effects, including the disruption of memory of recent events. Although memory usually improves over time, some people seem to develop permanent memory problems after receiving ECT (Coleman, 1990).

Psychosurgery

Psychosurgery is brain surgery that is performed to treat psychological disorders. The best-known technique, **prefrontal lobotomy**, has been used to reduce the agitation and violence of people with severe psychological disorders.

The method was developed by Portuguese neurologist Antonio Egas Moniz in the 1930s. The procedure involves cutting nerve pathways in the brain between the prefrontal lobes and the thalamus. (See Chapter 3.) However, the treatment produces several serious side effects, including distractibility, reduced learning ability, overeating, apathy, social withdrawal, seizures, reduced creativity, and occasionally even death.

Not surprisingly, prefrontal lobotomy is an even more controversial procedure than ECT. The original rationale behind the surgery has been challenged, and early success rates are now known to have been exaggerated (Valenstein, 1986). Because of the side effects of the surgery and the availability of antipsychotic drugs, prefrontal lobotomies are now performed only rarely.

Drug therapies, and to a limited extent ECT,

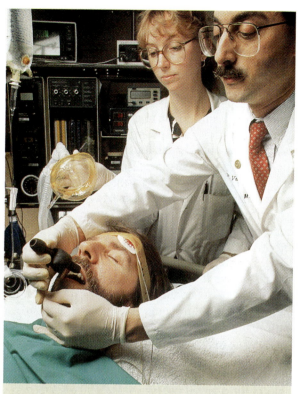

When a person with severe depression fails to respond to medications, electroconvulsive therapy may be considered. It is a drastic treatment that is used only in extreme cases.

seem to be effective for some psychological disorders that do not respond to psychotherapy. It is important to realize, however, that medications and electric shocks cannot help a person develop more logical ways of thinking or solve relationship problems. Changes such as these are likely to require psychotherapy. In some cases, medications may only dull the pain and postpone the day when people seek psychotherapy for their problems.

THINKING ABOUT PSYCHOLOGY

1. Why do some experts believe that antidepressant drugs should be reserved for people who fail to respond to psychotherapy?

2. Explain why electroconvulsive therapy is a controversial treatment for psychological disorders.

3. **Critical Thinking** What type of biological therapy might be prescribed for each of the following: panic disorder, bipolar disorder, schizophrenia, and severe depression?

Chapter 19 REVIEW

SUMMARY

Methods for treating psychological problems and disorders fall into two general categories: psychological therapies and biological therapies.

I. What Is Therapy?

A. Psychotherapy helps people by giving them hope for recovery, a new perspective, and a trusting relationship.

B. Most methods of psychotherapy are practiced either with individuals or in groups. Both individual and group therapy have several advantages.

II. The Psychoanalytic Approach

A. Freudian psychoanalysis was the only method of psychotherapy used in Western nations for many years.

B. Psychoanalysts use several techniques to help clients expose and resolve their unconscious thoughts and beliefs. These techniques include:
   1. Free association, in which clients say whatever comes to mind and analysts interpret the responses.
   2. Dream analysis, in which the analyst interprets the content of client's dreams.
   3. Transference, which can help clients understand troubling past relationships.

C. Brief psychoanalysis uses the same methods as traditional psychoanalysis but has a more specific focus.

III. The Humanistic Approach

A. Humanistic psychology assumes that people with psychological problems merely need help to reach self-actualization.

B. Person-centered therapy is the most widely used technique of humanistic psychology.

C. Person-centered therapy uses active listening and unconditional positive regard to help clients reach self-actualization and realize their unique potentials.

IV. Cognitive Therapy and Behavior Therapy

A. The aim of cognitive therapy is to change false or illogical ways of thinking that are creating emotional or behavioral problems.

B. The goal of behavior therapy is to help people eliminate undesirable behaviors or acquire desirable ones.
   1. Counterconditioning techniques include systematic desensitization, modeling, and aversive conditioning.
   2. Forms of operant conditioning include token economies, successive approximations, and social skills training.
   3. Behavior therapy is effective for treating phobias, post-traumatic stress disorder, compulsions, social problems, and substance addiction. It is also used for managing the care of people living in institutions.

V. Biological Therapy

A. Drug therapy is the most widely used biological treatment and works well for several different problems.
   1. Antianxiety medications are prescribed to control the symptoms of anxiety disorders and to reduce stress due to temporary life circumstances.
   2. Antidepressants are prescribed to help people with major depression and sometimes to help people with eating disorders and panic disorder.
   3. Antipsychotic drugs are prescribed to control the disordered thoughts, delusions, and hallucinations of people with schizophrenia.

B. Electroconvulsive therapy has limited usefulness as a treatment for people with severe depression who do not respond to other types of therapy.

C. Psychosurgery is rarely performed anymore because of severe side effects and questionable usefulness.

TERM & CONCEPT
REVIEW

1. Define and identify the significance of each of the following terms: *resistance, nondirective therapy,* and *successive approximations.*
2. In what three ways do all methods of psychotherapy help troubled individuals?
3. What types of professionals can practice psychotherapy? Can these individuals also administer biological therapy? Explain your answer.
4. List the advantages of group therapy.
5. What is the difference between the manifest content and the latent content of dreams?
6. Give an example of a transference relationship. Why might a therapist encourage the formation of such a relationship?
7. What is the goal of humanistic therapy?
8. List and describe two counterconditioning techniques.
9. What is a token economy?
10. Why is psychosurgery only rarely used? Under what circumstances might it be used?

CRITICAL
THINKING

1. What type of psychotherapist do you think would be most appropriate to treat each of the following psychological disorders: major depression, schizophrenia, and simple phobia? Explain your answers.
2. Why did Freud think that free association can reveal unconscious thoughts and feelings?
3. How could belief in the assumption "I must be loved by everyone to be happy" lead to unreasonable thoughts and feelings of depression?
4. Describe an example of the use of systematic desensitization that is different from the examples given in the text.
5. What are the advantages of treating depression with cognitive therapy instead of with antidepressant drugs?

APPLYING SKILLS
IN PSYCHOLOGY

1. **Reading About Psychology** Read more about the antidepressant drug Prozac, which has been prescribed for millions of people since the early 1990s. As you read the material, consider the following questions: What is the drug prescribed for? What claims do people who support the use of Prozac make about the benefits of the drug? What claims do critics of Prozac make? Why is the drug such a controversial method of therapy?

2. **Research in Psychology** Scientists are influenced by the social and cultural conditions of their time. Research how the social and cultural conditions of Sigmund Freud's time influenced his ideas about the causes of psychological problems. How did Freud's era differ from the present? How did conditions then influence Freud's ideas? Summarize your findings in a short, written report.

3. **Reading About Psychology** In addition to person-centered therapy, there are other types of humanistic therapy. Three of these are existential therapy, Gestalt therapy, and transactional analysis. Read more about these other types of humanistic therapy. Then write a brief summary of their similarities and differences.

4. **COOPERATIVE LEARNING** **Writing About Psychology** With a partner, write a skit showing how a client and a person-centered therapist might interact. First, select a problem suited for person-centered therapy, based on your reading of the text. Then prepare the skit, writing dialogue and descriptions for body language and facial expressions that illustrate active listening and unconditional positive regard. Rehearse the skit, and then arrange to present it to the rest of the class. After the skit has been performed, ask the class to identify examples of active listening and unconditional positive regard from the skit. Point out any examples they miss.

UNIT 6
R E V I E W

IDENTIFYING PEOPLE AND IDEAS

Explain the significance of each of the following people or terms to the study of psychology.

1. stress
2. eustress
3. approach-avoidance conflict
4. self-efficacy expectation
5. Hans Selye
6. general adaptation syndrome
7. defensive coping
8. anxiety
9. phobia
10. obsession
11. compulsion
12. depersonalization
13. somatization
14. bipolar disorder
15. mania
16. psychotherapy
17. manifest content
18. active listening
19. aversive conditioning
20. successive approximation
21. antidepressant drug
22. electroconvulsive therapy

HANDS-ON PSYCHOLOGY

Cooperative Project

You learned from the table on page 386 that stress and depression are two of the most common reasons for students to seek counseling. Working with two of your classmates, create a questionnaire to find out the following information: the most common causes of mild depression and stress in teens; the methods (both healthy and unhealthy) that teens use to cope with these problems; the frequency with which teens experience stress and mild depression; and teens' attitudes toward seeking counseling for these problems. Remember that these are sensitive and private issues for many teens. To protect the privacy of your participants, allow them to respond anonymously, and assure them that their responses will be kept confidential.

Decide on an appropriate sample size and method for distributing the questionnaires. One student should be responsible for typing, formatting, and copying the questionnaire; another for distributing the questionnaires to the sample group and collecting the completed questionnaires; and the third for compiling the data. As a group, analyze the data and write up your findings in a written report. In the report, include your group's general analysis of the data and answers to the following questions: Were you surprised by the results? Why or why not?

BUILDING YOUR PORTFOLIO

Individually or in a group, complete the following project to show your understanding of the psychology concepts involved.

Understanding Concepts

Below are two fictional "cases" that depict two individuals with symptoms that seem to indicate psychological problems or disorders. Review the symptoms covered in the unit. Then read the case histories, thinking of a possible diagnosis for both cases. Keep in mind that more than one diagnosis may be possible or that further information may be needed in order to narrow the possibilities. After you have read the case histories, complete the questions that follow.

> Miguel is a 24-year-old law student. Lately, he has had repeated bouts of illness. He also suffers from frequent headaches during which he feels nauseous and dizzy. His classmate, Sylvia, is usually extremely happy, almost euphoric. Sometimes, however, she has problems concentrating in school because her mind always seems to be wandering from one topic to the next. Both Miguel and Sylvia go through periods in which their ill health or lack of concentration make them very depressed.

1. How could the law school environment be a cause of both Miguel's and Sylvia's health problems. Does one case seem to be more related to stress than the other? If so, what symptoms indicate that the individual is having an adverse reaction to stress?

2. Do the symptoms of either individual seem extreme enough to indicate the presence of a psychological disorder? If so, what are these symptoms and what disorder might they indicate?

3. Given the diagnosis you have arrived at, decide whether or not treatment is necessary for each case. If treatment is necessary, what type of therapy would be appropriate?

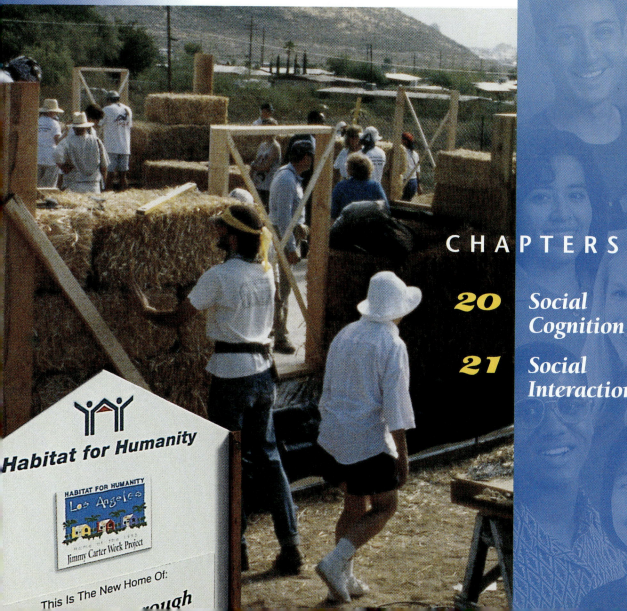

UNIT 7

SOCIAL PSYCHOLOGY

Habitat for Humanity

HABITAT FOR HUMANITY
Los Angeles

Home of the 1995
Jimmy Carter Work Project

This Is The New Home Of:

20 SOCIAL COGNITION

Chapter

Objectives

1 Define *attitudes,* and explain how they develop and how they are related to behavior.

2 Describe the influence of persuasion on people's attitudes and behavior.

3 Identify causes of prejudice and ways in which it can be overcome.

4 List factors that influence our perceptions of other people, and explain how people use various forms of nonverbal communication.

5 Describe the role of attraction in friendships and love relationships.

A DAY IN THE LIFE

Saturday morning Marc was in a complete panic when he called Linda at home. That night, Marc was to have dinner with Linda's entire family—grandparents and all—and he was really nervous.

"Why are you so nervous?" Linda asked with a smile. "You know how much my parents like you."

"I know," Marc said, "but have you forgotten their attitude toward me at first? They didn't like me very much. I finally convinced your parents that I'm a good guy—now I have to go through the same thing with your grandparents."

"Marc, my parents first met you when we were six years old. When we started dating this year, they only remembered you from when we were little kids. Now that they know you better, they really like you," Linda tried to assure him.

"But what about your grandparents?" Marc said. "I really want them to like me the first time I meet them. What if I still come across as that same clumsy kid?"

"You'll be fine," Linda said. "Just try to relax, and I'll see you at six o'clock. I really have to go now—

I promised Hannah I'd help her out this afternoon."

"Okay," Marc sighed. Somehow Linda had managed to calm his fears. "What are you and Hannah doing today?" he asked. For the first time all morning, he was able to think about something other than the upcoming dinner.

"Remember how that representative from the performing arts foundation offered her a scholarship? Well, she has to pass an interview before they'll give her the scholarship, and I promised her that I'd help her prepare for it," Linda said.

"What are you going to help her with?" Marc asked.

"Well, she's been practicing the types of things she wants to say in the interview, and she wants to try them out on me first. She also wants me to help her decide what she should wear for the interview," Linda explained.

"Oh no!" Marc suddenly exclaimed in panic.

"What's wrong?" Linda asked.

"What am I going to wear to dinner tonight?"

Linda just laughed. "Really, Marc, I think you're taking this first impression thing a little too seriously."

· · ·

Both Marc and Hannah want to make a good impression on other people. Their concern about how other people see them is one of the major aspects of the field of social psychology referred to as social cognition, which is the subject of this chapter.

Social cognition refers to the way people think and act in social situations. It is concerned not only with first impressions but also with attitudes, persuasion, attraction, and love. These and other aspects of social cognition are the focus of this chapter.

1
Attitudes

Attitudes are beliefs and feelings about objects, people, and events that lead people to behave in certain ways. A person's attitude about strangers, for example, can influence how that person feels and behaves around people he or she does not know. If a person believes that strangers are dangerous, that person is likely to feel afraid around strangers and may try to avoid situations where he or she is likely to meet new people. On the other hand, if a person believes that strangers are just people like him or her, that person is more likely to feel open toward strangers and try to know them better.

Attitudes are a major aspect of social cognition. In fact, our attitudes may be the primary motivator for how we behave and how we view the world.

Attitudes are such an important aspect of our psychological lives because they foster strong emotions, such as love or hate (Shavitt, 1990; Snyder & DeBono, 1989). Attitudes can also vary greatly. Negative attitudes, such as prejudice, can lead people to harm others. Positive attitudes, such as attraction, can encourage people to help others.

Under certain circumstances, a person's attitudes can change. They tend to remain stable, however, unless that person is strongly encouraged to change them. This section examines several aspects of attitudes—how they develop, how they affect behavior, and how behavior affects them.

How Attitudes Develop

People often have attitudes about things they have never experienced directly. People may be opposed to war or capital punishment, for example, even though they have no personal experience of either event. Where do such attitudes come from?

Attitudes develop in a variety of ways. Conditioning, observational learning, cognitive evaluation, and the use of cognitive anchors all play roles in the development of attitudes.

Conditioning   Learning through conditioning plays an important role in acquiring attitudes. Children are often reinforced for saying and doing things that are consistent with the attitudes held by their parents, teachers, and other authority figures. For example, parents who believe that it is important to share with others may praise, or reinforce, a child who shares a toy with a friend. Through such conditioning, the child acquires an attitude about the importance of sharing.

Observational Learning   People also acquire attitudes by observing other people. For example, teens may observe that classmates who dress, talk, or act in certain ways seem to be admired by their peers. These teens may adopt the same ways of dressing, talking, or acting because they have learned through observation that doing so might lead to acceptance and approval.

People who act with kindness and generosity toward others—such as the teens pictured here—may come to like other people better.

Cognitive Evaluation People often evaluate evidence and form beliefs on the basis of their evaluations. This process, which is known as **cognitive evaluation**, also plays a role in the development of attitudes. For example, a person may develop the attitude that using seat belts is important—and then always buckle up—after hearing about someone who would have survived a car crash if he or she had been wearing a seat belt.

People are especially likely to evaluate evidence if they think they will have to justify their attitudes to other people (Tetlock, 1983). For example, a teen who wants a part-time job after school may evaluate the evidence about working if he knows he will have to justify it to his parents. He may ask friends who have part-time jobs how they handle the extra responsibility and still do their schoolwork.

Cognitive evaluation was involved in Linda's parents' change in attitude toward Marc. At first, Linda's parents did not especially like Marc, an attitude that was based on their knowledge of him as a six-year-old child who misbehaved. Once they came to know the teenage Marc, however, they formed a new, more positive attitude toward him.

Cognitive Anchors A person's earliest attitudes tend to serve as **cognitive anchors**, or persistent beliefs that shape the ways in which he or she sees the world and interprets events. Cognitive anchors tend to keep a person's attitudes from changing. Attitudes that emerge later in life may be rejected if they differ greatly from a person's cognitive anchors (Quattrone, 1982).

Attitudes and Behavior

The definition of *attitudes* suggests that people's behavior is always consistent with their attitudes. However, the link between attitudes and behavior is not always strong (Eagly & Chaiken, 1993). In fact, people often behave in ways that contradict their attitudes. For example, many people know that smoking cigarettes and drinking alcohol excessively are harmful to their health, yet they still smoke and drink excessively. Likewise, some people realize that it is dangerous and illegal to drink and drive, yet they do it just the same (Stacy et al., 1994).

When Behavior Follows Attitudes People are more likely to behave in accordance with their attitudes if the attitudes are specifically tied to the

These children are learning an attitude of patriotism, which may serve as a cognitive anchor later in life.

behaviors. For example, someone who believes that aerobic exercise is necessary to prevent heart disease is more likely to exercise regularly than someone who believes that only a healthy lifestyle is important for good health. Similarly, strong attitudes are better predictors of behavior than weak attitudes (Fazio, 1990). Students who believe strongly in the value of hard work, for example, may be more likely to study than students who believe less strongly in hard work.

People are also more likely to behave in accordance with their attitudes when they have a vested interest, or a personal stake, in the outcome of a behavior (Johnson & Eagly, 1989). People are more likely to go to the polls and vote on an issue, for example, if the issue affects them directly. That is one reason why issues such as tax reform often have high voter turnouts.

Attitudes are more likely to guide behavior when people are aware of them, particularly if the attitudes are put into words and spoken (Fazio, 1990; Krosnick, 1989). Verbalizing and repeating an attitude make it come to mind quickly, and attitudes that come to mind quickly are more likely to influence how people act (Fazio, 1990). People are also more likely to be aware of attitudes that affect them emotionally (Wu & Shaffer, 1987). Someone who loves animals is likely to be aware of his attitude about animal rights, for example. Likewise, someone who is angered by destruction of the environment is likely to be aware of her attitudes about recycling and conservation.

When Attitudes Follow Behavior   Most psychologists agree that attitudes usually come first and that behavior follows (Breckler & Wiggins, 1989; Eagly & Chaiken, 1993; Petty & Cacioppo, 1986). However, sometimes the reverse is true. In some situations, attitudes follow behavior.

Attitudes are especially likely to follow behavior when people are encouraged to behave in ways that go against their attitudes. In such situations, people may suffer cognitive dissonance, an uncomfortable feeling of tension due to a contradiction between attitudes and behaviors (Festinger, 1957). In order to reduce the tension they feel, people may try to justify their behavior and gradually change their attitudes to fit their acts.

As an example, in one experiment, people were asked to argue in favor of something they did not believe in. Doing so made them feel very uncomfortable, and they eventually modified their attitudes to bring them more in line with their arguments (Cialdini, 1993).

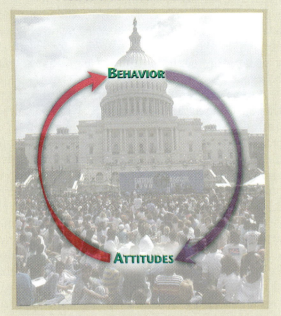

The Relationship Between Attitudes and Behavior

FIGURE 20.1   *Behavior usually follows attitudes, but attitudes can follow behavior when people behave in ways that go against their attitudes.*

Although the patterns may change, one thing is certain—attitudes and behavior influence each other. As Figure 20.1 shows, people tend to act as they believe, but they may also come to believe as they act.

THINKING ABOUT PSYCHOLOGY

1. What are attitudes?
2. How do attitudes develop?
3. **Critical Thinking**   Why might telling a lie lead to cognitive dissonance? What might be done to reduce the dissonance?

2
Persuasion

Attitudes tend to remain constant unless people are strongly motivated to change them. People may change their attitudes because they are persuaded to do so. **Persuasion** is a direct attempt to influence other people's attitudes. Parents, for example, may try to persuade their children to adopt the parents' own values. Children, on the other hand, may try to persuade their parents to allow them more freedoms and privileges.

 A DAY IN THE LIFE   Both Marc and Hannah want to persuade others to have a favorable impression of them. Both are hoping to influence people by the way they will dress for two important occasions— Hannah's interview with the performing arts foundation and Marc's first meeting with Linda's grandparents.

Methods of Persuasion

There are two basic ways to persuade people: via the central route and via the peripheral route (Petty & Cacioppo, 1986). The most persuasive messages use both routes.

The **central route** uses evidence and logical arguments to persuade people (Eagly & Chaiken, 1993). Advertisements might point out the superior quality of a product or a service—the superior taste and nutritional content of a breakfast cereal, for example. Similarly, a parent might use statistics on bicycle accidents and injuries to persuade a child to wear a safety helmet.

The **peripheral route** is indirect. It attempts to associate objects, people, or events with positive or negative cues. For example, an advertisement for athletic shoes might feature a famous athlete. A public service announcement for staying in school might feature an admired actor. The aim is to influence people to associate their positive feelings for the famous individual with the product or the message that is being endorsed.

In the central route, the message itself is most important. In the peripheral route, other factors, including the messenger, the situation, and the nature of the audience, are also important. Each of these aspects of persuasion is considered in turn.

The Message

Research shows that repeated exposure to a stimulus eventually results in a more favorable attitude toward that stimulus. For example, studies have found that people respond more favorably to abstract art (Heingartner & Hall, 1974) or classical music (Smith & Dorfman, 1975) after being repeatedly exposed to it.

Advertisers, political candidates, and others who want to persuade people use repetition to encourage people to adopt a favorable attitude toward their product or idea. Many television commercials are repeated over and over so that potential consumers will react favorably to the products—and buy them—when they see these items in the store. One might think that such repetition would offend or annoy viewers (and to some extent it does), but research suggests that commercials are more effective when they are repeated regularly (Haugtvedt et al., 1994). Similarly, political candidates who appear regularly in television commercials tend to receive more votes than candidates who appear less often in commercials (Grush, 1980).

TRUTH OR fiction ▪ REVISITED ▪ *It is not true that showing television commercials over and over reduces their effectiveness.* In fact, studies have shown that the more often a commercial is repeated, the more likely it is to be persuasive.

In addition to being presented frequently, the persuasive message can be presented in ways that are especially effective. Two-sided arguments tend to be more effective than one-sided arguments, especially when the audience is uncertain about its position on the issue (Sorrentino et al., 1988). Emotional appeals are also very effective.

Two-Sided Arguments One of the most persuasive types of messages is the **two-sided argument**, in which people present not only their side of the argument but also the opposition's side. The purpose is to discredit the opposition's views. For example, a cereal advertiser admits that its brand of cereal is not as sweet as competing brands and then explains how the less sweet taste is evidence that the product is more nutritious. Admitting weaknesses in this way also makes the message seem more honest (Bridgwater, 1982).

Emotional Appeals Another effective way to present a persuasive message is to appeal to the audience's emotions. **Emotional appeals** persuade

Politicians try to persuade people to vote for them. Yet it is not always clear which route a politician is using—the central route or the peripheral route. Which route do you think politicians use most often?

by arousing such feelings as loyalty, desire, or fear rather than by convincing through evidence and logic. Thus, an emotional appeal is a peripheral route in persuasion.

Arousing fear is a particularly effective method of persuasion. Smokers are more likely to be convinced to quit smoking, for example, when they are presented with frightening photos of blackened lungs rather than dry, unemotional statistics on lung cancer. In general, appeals based on fear tend to be most effective when they are strong, when the audience believes them, and when the audience believes it can avoid the danger by changing its behavior (Eagly & Chaiken, 1993).

The Messenger

Some people are more persuasive than others. Research (Hennigan et al., 1982; Mackie et al., 1990; Wilder, 1990) shows that people are persuasive if they are

- experts. (This makes the audience more likely to follow their advice.)
- trustworthy. (This makes the audience more likely to believe what they say.)
- physically attractive. (This makes the audience more likely to pay attention to them.)
- similar to their audience in ethnicity, age, and other physical characteristics. (People are more likely to imitate others who appear similar to themselves.)

Messengers who stand to gain from their persuasive efforts are less likely than others to be effective. For example, if the president of a company says his or her company's product is the best one on the market, people are generally less likely to be persuaded by his or her arguments.

The Situation

When a person is in a good mood, he or she is less likely to evaluate messages carefully (Petty et al., 1991; Schwarz et al., 1991). As a result, people tend to be more receptive to persuasion when they are feeling good. Thus, putting people in a good mood—with a compliment, for example—tends to boost the acceptance of persuasive messages.

The Audience

Most messages are aimed at a specific audience. A political candidate is trying to reach the voters in his

A child's prayer:
"Ala Ka Barika Di N'Ma, N'Ka Dinyè Tò Lahan Ni Hèrè Ye."

Translation:
Give me the strength to live another day in this world.

Advertisements such as this one are meant to appeal to the emotions of the audience rather than to convince through logic.

or her district, for example. Differences in age, sex, and other characteristics of the intended audience influence how the message should be delivered to be most persuasive. Emotional appeals may work better with children, for example, whereas logic may be more effective with adults (Kunkel & Roberts, 1991).

Saying No to Persuasive Messages

Some people are less easily persuaded than others. For example, some people have **sales resistance**. People with sales resistance have no trouble turning down requests to buy products or services or make donations. Other people have little or no sales resistance. They find it difficult to refuse a sales pitch or other types of requests.

Research suggests that two personality factors may be involved in sales resistance—self-esteem and social anxiety (Rhodes & Wood, 1992; Santee & Maslach, 1982). People who find it easy to refuse requests tend to have high self-esteem and low social anxiety. They believe in themselves, stand up for what they want, and are not overly concerned about what other people think of them.

People who find it difficult to say no, on the other hand, are likely to have lower self-esteem and greater social anxiety. They may worry what salespeople will think of them, for example, or be concerned that the people requesting donations will be insulted if they refused to give. Such people may also believe they should help others rather than act self-centered (Schwartz & Gottman, 1976).

People with low self-esteem and high social anxiety are likely to be easily persuaded in situations other than sales and donations. For example, they may be more easily persuaded to engage in activities that go against their attitudes, beliefs, and values, such as using alcohol or other drugs.

THINKING ABOUT PSYCHOLOGY

1. Explain the difference between central and peripheral routes of persuasion.
2. What characteristics would you expect to find in an individual with sales resistance?
3. **Critical Thinking**   Give examples of ways an advertiser might use persuasion to sell a car.

For decades, Blacks in South Africa were discriminated against by the ruling White minority. A series of political reforms in the early 1990s, however, brought about the official end of apartheid. By mid 1994, Blacks were able for the first time to vote in South African elections.

3
Prejudice

A type of attitude that causes a great deal of harm is prejudice. **Prejudice**—a generalized attitude toward a specific group of people—literally means "prejudgment." People who are prejudiced judge other people on the basis of their group membership rather than as individuals. People who are prejudiced may decide, for example, that one person is deceitful because he or she belongs to a particular ethnic group or that another person is highly intelligent because that individual belongs to another ethnic group. Prejudicial attitudes such as these are based on stereotypes.

Stereotypes

Stereotypes are unchanging, oversimplified, and usually distorted beliefs about groups of people. People tend to develop or adopt stereotypes as a way to organize information about their social world (Bodenhausen, 1988; Devine, 1989; Dovidio et al., 1986; Fiske, 1989). Stereotypes make it easier for people to interpret the behavior of others, even though the interpretations are often wrong. For example, if we expect an older man to be sexist because a sexist attitude is part of our stereotype of older males, then we are more likely to interpret his words and deeds as sexist.

Another reason people tend to develop stereotypes is because they assume that those who are different from themselves are similar to each other in many ways (Judd & Park, 1988; Wilder, 1986). Traits seen in some members of a group are incorrectly assumed to characterize all members of the group. An Asian American may think, for example, that all European Americans or all African Americans have similar personality traits, behavior patterns, or attitudes.

Stereotypes are harmful because they ignore people's individual natures and assign traits to them on the basis of the groups to which they belong. One of the many problems with stereotyping is that the traits assigned are usually negative. However, stereotypes can also include positive traits—such as the belief that members of a particular group are hard workers.

Stereotypes limit possibilities by discouraging the expression of the full range of an individual's talents, interests, and feelings. Even positive stereotypes can be harmful because they may put pressure on people to live up to unrealistic expectations.

Discrimination

Prejudice often leads to negative behavior in the form of discrimination. **Discrimination** refers to the unfair treatment of individuals because they are members of a particular group. For example, people may be denied jobs, housing, voting privileges, or other rights because of their skin color, sex, or religion. Victims of discrimination may begin to see themselves as inferior. Thus, they are likely to have low self-esteem (Bohon et al., 1993). People with low self-esteem tend to have low expectations for themselves, thus reducing their chances for success.

Causes of Prejudice

Why are some people prejudiced and others are not? Psychologists and other researchers have studied the origins of prejudice and have found many potential causes.

Exaggerating Differences
One reason some people are prejudiced is that they exaggerate how different others are from themselves. People tend to prefer (as friends and acquaintances) those who are similar to themselves and who share their attitudes. People who differ in one or several ways—in skin color or religion, for example—are often assumed to have attitudes and customs that are more different than they really are.

Justifying Economic Status
People also tend to develop prejudice against those who are not in the same economic group. Those in higher socioeconomic groups often justify their own economic superiority by assuming that people who have a lower economic status are inferior to them. They may believe that people who are worse off than themselves work less hard or are less motivated to succeed. Such beliefs may be used as an excuse for—and thus help maintain—existing injustices.

Social Learning
Children, like adults, acquire many attitudes from other people. They are especially likely to acquire the attitudes of their parents. Children tend to imitate their parents, and parents reinforce their children when they do. In this way, parents who are prejudiced often pass along their prejudicial attitudes to the next generation.

Victimization
Sometimes people who are the victims of prejudice feel empathy for others who are discriminated against. However, this is not always the case. In fact, some victims of prejudice try to gain a sense of power and pride by asserting their superiority over groups that are even worse off than themselves (Van Brunt, 1994). Thus, victimization may lead to further prejudice.

Scapegoating
A **scapegoat** is an individual or group that is blamed for the problems of others because the real cause of the problems is too complex, powerful, or remote to be addressed. The term *scapegoating* refers to aggression against the group that has been identified as the scapegoat.

The scapegoat group is likely to have certain characteristics that make it a safe and highly visible target. Typically, scapegoats are people who are too weak to defend themselves or who choose not to return the attack. They are also likely to stand out because they look different from the majority.

Probably the best-known and most extreme example of scapegoating is the victimization of European Jews in the 1930s and 1940s. Nazi dictator Adolf Hitler blamed Jewish people for Germany's serious financial troubles. Under Hitler's leadership, approximately 6 million Jews were killed.

Intergroup contact can reduce feelings of prejudice by giving people the opportunity to work together and come to know each other as individuals.

CASE STUDIES
AND OTHER TRUE STORIES
Being Black in America

W. E. B. Du Bois was one of the most influential educators, writers, and social leaders in American history. A child of mixed European and African ancestry, he was born in Massachusetts in 1868, just five years after President Abraham Lincoln issued the Emancipation Proclamation.

After earning a Ph.D. from Harvard University, he became active in the movement to gain equality for African Americans and became a prominent member of the National Association for the Advancement of Colored People (NAACP). He died in 1963 at the height of the civil rights movement—a movement he helped to foster and one that inspired millions of Americans to call for equality and freedom.

In 1903, Du Bois published a classic work titled *The Souls of Black Folk.* The book is partly autobiographical, and in the following excerpt, Du Bois reveals how he felt when he first learned, as a schoolboy, that he was "different from the others" and "shut out from their world." The incident may seem trivial, but it had a profound effect on him for the rest of his life.

W.E.B. Du Bois

It is in the early days of rollicking boyhood that the revelation first bursts upon one, all in a day, as it were. I remember well when the shadow swept across me. I was a little thing, away up in the hills of New England. . . . In a wee wooden schoolhouse, something put it into the boys' and girls' heads to buy gorgeous visiting-cards—ten cents a package—and exchange. The exchange was merry, till one girl, a tall newcomer, refused my card. . . . Then it dawned upon me with a certain suddenness that I was different from the others; or like, mayhap, in heart and life and longing, but shut out from their world by

a vast veil. I had thereafter no desire to tear down that veil, to creep through; I held all beyond it in common contempt, and lived above it in a region of blue sky and great wandering shadows. That sky was bluest when I could beat my mates at examination-time, or beat them at a foot-race. . . . Alas, with the years all this fine contempt began how to fade; for the words I longed for, and all their dazzling opportunities, were theirs, not mine. But they should not keep these prizes, I said; some, all, I would wrest from them. Just how I would do it I could never decide: by reading law, by healing the sick, by telling the wonderful tales that swam in my head—some way. With other black boys the strife was not so fiercely sunny: their youth shrank into tasteless sycophancy [fawning], or into silent hatred of the pale world about them and mocking distrust of everything white; or wasted itself in a bitter cry, Why did God make me an outcast and a stranger in mine own house?

Despite legislation against discrimination, the "worlds" of European Americans and African Americans remain for many as far apart as they were in Du Bois' childhood. This is because attitudes of racial prejudice still exist. For many African American youths today, as for Du Bois a century ago, the "pale world" and its "dazzling opportunities" are still beyond their grasp.

Think About It

Why did the incident described above affect Du Bois so deeply? How was Du Bois' reaction to racial inequality the same as and different from that of other African American youths of his time?

Overcoming Prejudice

Although prejudice is difficult to overcome, it can be done. Increased contact among members of different groups is one of the best ways for people to develop less prejudicial attitudes toward others. For example, when people work together to achieve common goals, they are likely to learn about one another as individuals, and this may weaken the stereotypes (Smith et al., 1993).

On an individual level, one can reduce prejudice by speaking up when other people act or talk in ways that reflect prejudicial attitudes. Individuals can also set an example of tolerance and understanding for others by their own words and actions.

Finally, prejudicial attitudes do not have to lead to discriminatory behavior. A person who is prejudiced can make a conscious effort to treat other people courteously and fairly, regardless of the groups to which they belong. This, in turn, may help reduce the person's own prejudicial attitudes.

THINKING ABOUT PSYCHOLOGY

1. Explain the difference between prejudice and discrimination.
2. Identify several causes of prejudice.
3. **Critical Thinking** Identify three ways people can help reduce prejudice in their communities.

4
Social Perception

Social perception refers to the ways in which people perceive one another. Social perception affects the attitudes people form toward others. For example, Marc believed that if he made a negative first impression on Linda's grandparents, it would be difficult to change their opinion of him later. He assumed that first impressions have a lasting effect on people's attitudes toward others. As you will see in this section, Marc was right.

Primacy and Recency Effects

People often wear their best clothes to job interviews. Likewise, defense attorneys encourage their clients to be well dressed when they are in the courtroom and within view of the jury. The reason? People think that their first impressions of other people are accurate (Burnstein & Schul, 1982; Wyer, 1988), and first impressions are often based on how a person looks. The tendency for people to form opinions of others on the basis of first impressions is called the **primacy effect**.

First impressions are important because they may have lasting effects on our relationships with others. If our first impression of a new acquaintance is negative because the person appears to be self-centered, for example, then we are unlikely to want to know the person better. However, if our first impression is positive—the person seems friendly and interesting—then we are more likely to want to develop a relationship with that person.

How people interpret the future behavior of others is also influenced by their first impressions. For example, someone who impresses us as intelligent and well educated is more likely to be taken seriously in future encounters than someone who comes across as superficial and silly.

TRUTH OR fiction ■ R E V I S I T E D ■ *It is true that our first impressions of other people tend to have lasting effects on our relationships with them.* This is because people often interpret another person's future behavior in light of their first impressions.

The **recency effect** occurs when people change their opinions of others on the basis of recent interactions instead of holding on to their first impressions. This is what happened with Linda's parents and Marc. Linda's parents' first impression of him was of a rude and misbehaving six-year-old. After they got to know Marc as a teen, however, they saw him in a more positive light and changed their attitude toward him.

Attribution Theory

People often explain the behavior of others differently from the ways in which they explain their own behavior. According to **attribution theory**, people tend to explain the behavior of others in terms of either dispositional, or personality, factors or in terms of situational, or external, factors. For example, suppose you meet someone at a party who

PSYCHOLOGY
IN THE WORLD TODAY

What Can Be Done About Prejudice?

Prejudice is not just an abstract concept that affects people other than ourselves. Prejudice dwells within us. In fact, people are often unaware of their own prejudices because such attitudes tend to be deep-seated. Thus, overcoming prejudice can be difficult. What can you do to help reduce prejudice?

Speak Out Against Prejudice Even people who do not have feelings of prejudice themselves often do little to counter the prejudice of others. They may say nothing when they hear another person make a sexist joke or an ethnic slur. They may do nothing when their club or other organization denies admission to people of other racial or religious groups. By saying and doing nothing when they encounter prejudice, people appear to be condoning, or excusing, it. Therefore, it is important to speak out against prejudice in others as well as to show an attitude of tolerance in one's own words and actions.

Break Down Stereotypes Prejudice is based on stereotypes. Thus, one of the best ways to combat prejudice is to break down stereotypes. The more contact we have with people of other races, ethnic groups, or religions, the more aware we become that these groups are made up of individuals who are not only different from one another but also similar to ourselves in many ways. Through intergroup contact, we are likely to learn that people of the same skin color, for example, differ from one another in ways such as language, values, abilities, religious beliefs, and interests.

Intergroup contact is especially effective at breaking down stereotypes and reducing prejudicial attitudes when individuals work cooperatively to achieve common goals. Playing together on the same sports team, working together on a class project, or working side by side on the school yearbook are examples of cooperative efforts that can foster increased understanding and tolerance of others.

If individuals share similar backgrounds, intergroup contact is even more effective at breaking down stereotypes and reducing prejudice. People who have the same socioeconomic background, religious beliefs, or level of education, for example, are more likely to have the same values. Shared values, in turn, promote liking and openness toward others.

Intergroup contact is generally more effective when it is informal. Informal contacts, such as sitting together in the school cafeteria or hanging out together at the mall, encourage people to get to know one another as individuals. In contrast, more formal contacts, such as participating in the same class debate or attending the same religious service, allow people to maintain their distance from one another.

Brief contacts are also less likely to produce lasting changes in stereotypes and prejudicial attitudes than contacts that are longer lasting. Chatting with a stranger on a bus, for example, is not likely to bring about a permanent change in attitudes toward the group the stranger represents. However, working in chemistry lab throughout the school year with a lab partner who belongs to a different group may well break down stereotypes and reduce prejudice.

Combat Discrimination Even when people's attitudes of prejudice cannot be changed, it is still possible to combat discrimination. Discrimination on the basis of sex, religion, race, or disability is against the law. Thus, when people are discriminated against, they can seek legal remedies. Similarly, when students believe that they have been denied access to organizations or opportunities at school because of prejudice, they should report the discrimination to their guidance counselor or school administration.

Think About It

Give examples of ways not mentioned in the feature that students might work together in or out of school to break down their own stereotypes and reduce their prejudices toward others.

The same man is shown in both of these photographs, but he looks very different in each. If you were the taxi driver, whom would you be more likely to pick up? How does this relate to the concept of social perception?

seems reluctant to talk to other people. You may assume that this person is either shy or conceited. This would be a dispositional attribution. On the other hand, you may assume that this person is usually friendly but simply does not know anyone at the party. This would be a situational attribution.

Actor-Observer Bias   For the most part, people tend to attribute the behavior of others to dispositional, or internal, factors and to attribute their own behavior to situational, or external, factors. This tendency is called the **actor-observer bias** (Jellison & Green, 1981). Actor-observer bias occurs because we tend to judge others only by the behavior we witness, and people's behavior may not always be a true reflection of their personalities.

Suppose you observe a stranger acting in a rude manner. If this is your only encounter with the person, you are likely to assume that the stranger has a rude disposition—that is, that he or she is a rude person. In most other situations, however, the same person might behave in a very polite fashion. Observing the stranger in most other situations, then, would lead to the assumption that he or she has a polite, respectful disposition. This may in fact be the case. The person might have acted rudely only because of the circumstances. For example, perhaps the person was provoked.

Fundamental Attribution Error   The tendency to overestimate the effect of dispositional causes for another person's behavior, and to underestimate the effect of situational causes, is referred to as the **fundamental attribution error**. It is a common mistake that affects many of our interactions with other people. To further understand this concept, look at the photographs on page 471. If you observed this teenager in only one situation you might assume that she was either an extremely helpful person or a very rude person. That is, you might commit a fundamental attribution error and overlook or misinterpret the true causes of her behavior.

Self-Serving Bias   People are more likely to attribute their own successes to dispositional, or personality, factors. They are also more likely to attribute their failures to situational factors (Baumgardner et al., 1986; Van der Plight & Eiser, 1983). This is called a **self-serving bias**. The self-serving bias allows individuals to place the blame for their failures on circumstances outside their control. At the same time, however, it enables them to take full credit for their successes.

If Hannah's scholarship interview is a success, for example, she may

A DAY IN THE LIFE

attribute it to the fact that she is talented and motivated. If, on the other hand, the interview goes badly, she may attribute it to circumstances beyond her control—perhaps she had a headache that day, or the interviewer was in a bad mood.

Nonverbal Communication

It is not only what people say and do but how they say and do it that influences our perceptions of them. Forms of nonverbal, or unspoken, communication include facial expressions, gestures, posture, and the distance we keep from others. These and other forms of nonverbal communication affect our perceptions of people, largely because they often indicate feelings. Feelings of sympathy or anger, for example, may be inferred from a concerned look or frown.

Nonverbal forms of communication are learned early. Even young children can "read" a tone of voice, a facial expression, or other forms of nonverbal communication. Thus, before they understand all the words their parents are speaking, they can tell from nonverbal communication how their parents are feeling (Saarni, 1990).

Without necessarily being aware of it, people use nonverbal communication to send messages to other people (Patterson, 1991). They may even use nonverbal communication to mask their true feelings (DePaulo, 1992). For example, a parent who wishes to hide his fear or worry from his child might use nonverbal forms of communication, such as smiles and a relaxed bearing, to convince the child that all is well.

Physical Contact   Touching is one way in which people communicate nonverbally. However, not all people use physical contact to communicate with others. For example, American women are more likely than American men to touch the people with whom they are interacting (Stier & Hall, 1984). There is also considerable cultural variation in the use of touch to communicate with others.

Touching can be an effective means of communication. In one experiment, college students who had filled out several personality questionnaires were asked by the experimenter to stay and help in another study. Students who were touched during the request were more likely to help in the subsequent study (Powell et al., 1984). In another study, waitresses received larger tips when they touched customers on the hand or shoulder while making change (Crusco & Wetzel, 1984).

A study in a nursing home found that the ways in which people respond to touch depend on many factors. In the study, whether touching was responded to favorably or unfavorably depended on the status of the staff member doing the touching, the type of touch, and the part of the body that was touched. Touching was not appreciated when it was inappropriate or forceful (Hollinger & Buschmann, 1993).

How do you think first impressions of this teen might vary from one situation to another?

Eye Contact   People can learn a great deal about the feelings of others from eye contact. When someone who is talking looks directly into the eyes of the listener, for example, the talker is usually telling the truth. Avoidance of eye contact, on the other hand, may indicate that the talker is lying. This is why a message is more believable and persuasive when the messenger makes eye contact with the audience.

One type of eye contact is gazing, or looking at someone with a steady, intent look that conveys eagerness or attention. Gazing usually is interpreted as a sign of liking or friendliness, and it may greatly influence relationships (Kleinke, 1986).

Another type of eye contact is staring, or looking fixedly with wide-open eyes. Staring is usually interpreted as a sign of anger. Being the object of staring makes most people uncomfortable, and they may try to avoid the stare. For example, one study found that drivers who were stared at by other drivers at an intersection crossed the intersection faster when the light changed (Ellsworth et al., 1972).

Whether or not they are aware of it, most people send unspoken messages that can greatly influence how other people see them. Thus, becoming more aware of nonverbal communication can increase our understanding of others.

THINKING ABOUT PSYCHOLOGY

1. Explain the difference between primacy and recency effects.

2. Define *fundamental attribution error.*

3. **Critical Thinking**   Think about a recent interaction you had with another person. What forms of nonverbal communication did you, or the other person, use to convey thoughts or feelings?

5
Interpersonal Attraction

Attraction is a kind of attitude—an attitude of liking. Attraction to others often leads to friendship or love. Factors that attract us to particular people as potential friends or partners include physical appearance, similarity to ourselves, and evidence that our attraction is returned.

Physical Appearance

Physical appearance tends to influence our choice of friends and partners. What qualities make someone physically attractive? There is no single answer. Some people find blond hair most attractive; others may prefer black hair. Some people may find a slim body build most attractive, while others may prefer a more muscular build. Clearly, people's ideas of attractiveness differ.

Universals of Beauty   Although there is variation among people in the types of traits they consider attractive, some aspects of attractiveness appear to be widely shared or even universal. For example, a smiling person is generally perceived to be more attractive than a person who is frowning (Reis et al., 1990).

Studies have also found that certain types of facial features are attractive to most people. In one study, both British and Japanese people were asked to identify the types of features they found most attractive in women. People from both cultures identified large eyes, high cheekbones, and narrow jaws as the most attractive types of facial features (Perret et al., 1994).

Another study investigated the kinds of faces that infants find most attractive (Langlois, 1994). This was judged by the amount of time the infants spent looking at the faces of strangers—the longer the gaze, the greater the presumed attraction. As early as the age of two months, infants in the study seemed to prefer faces that were also rated by adults as most attractive. This evidence suggests that we do not "learn" what is attractive by being socialized in a particular culture. Instead, we may be born with a predisposition to find certain types of physical features attractive.

Differences in Body Shape Preference

Although preferences for certain facial features may be universal, preferences for body shape vary greatly (Etcoff, 1994). There is, in fact, a great deal of variation in people's standard for attractiveness of body shape—both in the shape we prefer in others and the shape we perceive ourselves as having.

This was demonstrated in a study of college men and women (Fallon & Rozin, 1985). The men in the study tended to believe their own body shape closely approached the "ideal" shape that women find attractive. However, the women tended to believe that they were heavier than the "ideal" shape men find attractive.

The results of this study are important. They suggest that females are more likely than males to incorrectly think they are too heavy to be attractive. Not surprisingly, women are more likely than men to go on weight-loss diets, and they have far higher rates of eating disorders. (See Chapter 11.)

Evidence suggests that in the United States, many men prefer their partners to be shorter than themselves, whereas many women prefer their partners to be taller (Gillis & Avis, 1980). On the job as well as in relationships, tallness tends to be perceived as an asset for men, whereas height in women tends to have less impact on their jobs (Sheppard & Strathman, 1989).

This is not to say, however, that physical appearance will determine an individual's ability to succeed on the job or in relationships. The initial attraction one feels for another person may be based on the person's physical appearance. However, other traits usually become more important as people get to know one another better. Traits such as honesty, loyalty, warmth, and sensitivity tend to be more important than physical appearance in forming and maintaining long-term relationships.

Similarity and Reciprocity

You may be familiar with the saying "Birds of a feather flock together." This saying suggests that we are usually attracted to people who are like us. On the other hand, another popular saying asserts "Opposites attract." Which of these two contradictory statements is true? Generally speaking, the answer is that we are more attracted to people who are like us.

Similarity in Physical Attractiveness

According to the **matching hypothesis**, people tend to choose as friends and partners those who are similar to themselves in attractiveness (Feingold, 1988b). One reason for this may be the fear of rejection—the belief that someone more attractive will not be interested in them (Bernstein et al., 1983).

Although conceptions of beauty vary from culture to culture, studies have shown that certain aspects of attractiveness appear to be widely shared or even universal.

People are more likely to form relationships with people who are similar to themselves than with those who differ in terms of level of attractiveness, age, and level of education.

Similarity in Other Characteristics   People's friends and partners also tend to be similar to them in race, ethnicity, age, level of education, and religion (Michael et al., 1994). One reason we choose friends and partners with backgrounds that are similar to our own is that we tend to live among people who are similar to ourselves. Thus, these are the people we are most likely to meet, to know, to date, and possibly to marry (Michael et al., 1994).

Another reason people tend to choose friends and partners with similar backgrounds is that such people often have similar attitudes as well—and people tend to be attracted to others with attitudes similar to their own. In fact, similarity of attitudes is a key contributor to attraction in both friendships and romantic relationships (Cappella & Palmer, 1990; Laumann et al., 1994). Attitudes toward religion and children tend to be the most important factors in people's attraction to potential partners (Buss & Barnes, 1986; Howard et al., 1987).

TRUTH OR fiction
■ R E V I S I T E D ■

It is not true that when it comes to choosing a partner or friend, "opposites attract." People are more likely to choose as partners—and also as friends—people who are similar to themselves in many ways.

Reciprocity   When we have feelings of attraction or affection for another person, we want that person to return those feelings. **Reciprocity** is the mutual exchange of feelings or attitudes. It applies to situations in which the person we like likes us back. In other words, our feelings are returned, or reciprocated. Like similarity, reciprocity is a powerful contributor to feelings of attraction (Condon & Crano, 1988).

Reciprocity of feelings is a major factor in forming romantic relationships, but it may also apply to casual encounters. Research shows that people are more open, warm, and helpful when they are talking with strangers who seem to like them (Clark et al., 1989; Curtis & Miller, 1986).

Friendship

Friends are people for whom one has affection, respect, and trust. Most people value friends because of the rewards that friendship offers. For example, friends are concerned about one another and help and support one another when they can. As friendships develop, people may evaluate, consciously or unconsciously, how well the relationship is providing the rewards they seek in the friendship.

The people we choose as friends tend to be people with whom we have frequent contact—a next-door neighbor or a student who sits beside us in class. The people we find attractive and the people who approve of us are the people we are likely to choose as friends. In addition, they are likely to be similar to us in important ways, such as in attitudes, in values, and often in their selection of other friends (Gonzales et al., 1983).

Love

The word *love* is used in everyday life in numerous ways. Love refers to the feelings of attachment that exist between children and their parents. Love also refers to feelings of patriotism for one's country or to feelings of passion about strongly held values such as freedom. Most commonly, however, love refers to the feelings of mutual attraction, affection, and attachment shared by people who are "in love."

To better understand the relationships of people in love, psychologist Robert Sternberg (1988) developed the **triangular model of love**, shown in Figure 20.2. As defined in the figure, Sternberg identifies seven types of love relationships, each of which is characterized by at least one of three components: intimacy, passion, or commitment.

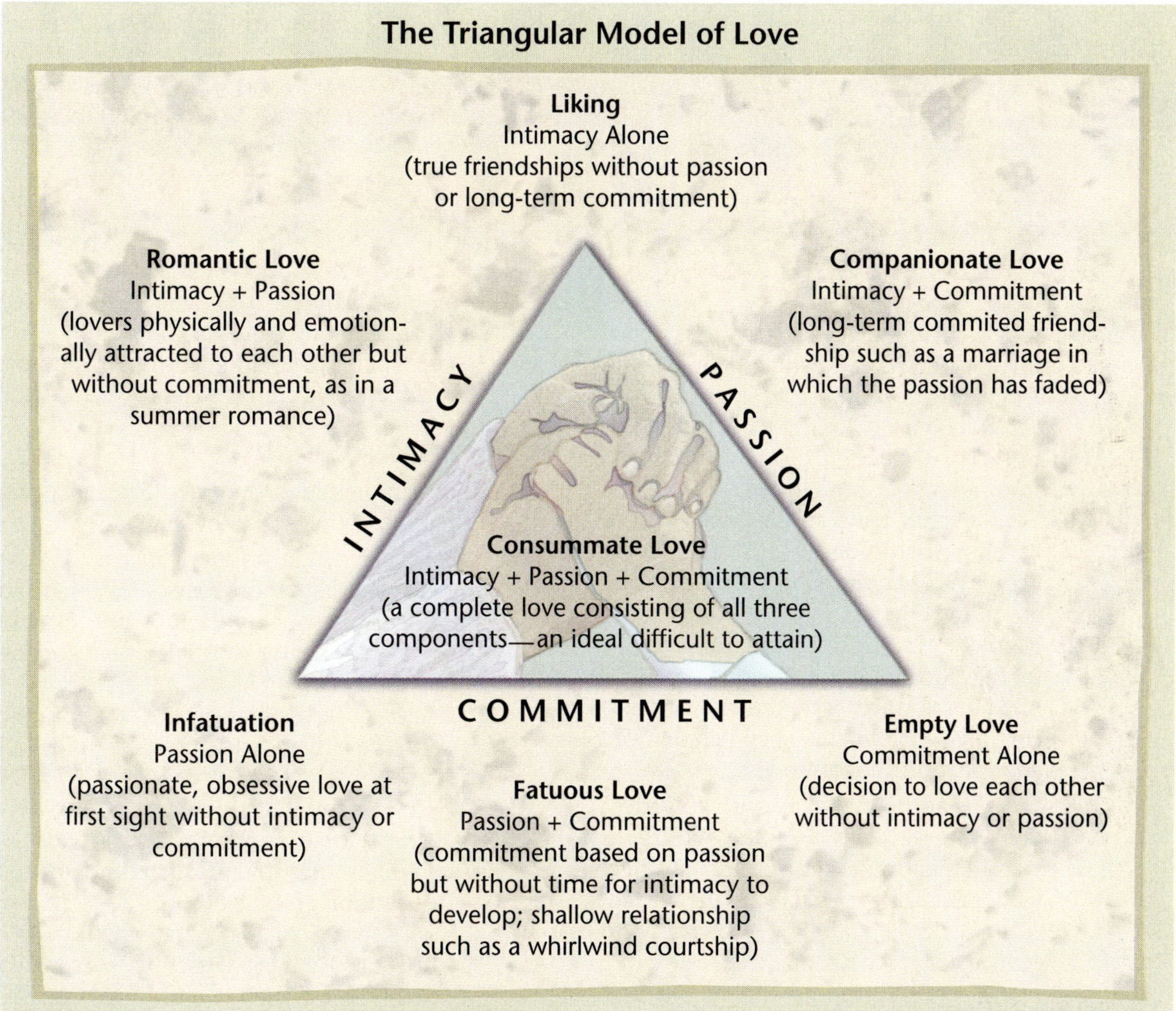

The Triangular Model of Love

Liking
Intimacy Alone
(true friendships without passion
or long-term commitment)

Romantic Love
Intimacy + Passion
(lovers physically and emotionally attracted to each other but
without commitment, as in a
summer romance)

Companionate Love
Intimacy + Commitment
(long-term commited friendship such as a marriage in
which the passion has faded)

INTIMACY

PASSION

Consummate Love
Intimacy + Passion + Commitment
(a complete love consisting of all three
components—an ideal difficult to attain)

COMMITMENT

Infatuation
Passion Alone
(passionate, obsessive love at
first sight without intimacy or
commitment)

Fatuous Love
Passion + Commitment
(commitment based on passion
but without time for intimacy to
develop; shallow relationship
such as a whirlwind courtship)

Empty Love
Commitment Alone
(decision to love each other
without intimacy or passion)

FIGURE 20.2 *Robert Sternberg believes that love rela-tionships are characterized by at least one of three components: intimacy, passion, or commitment. Consummate love combines all three components.*

Intimacy refers to closeness and caring. It is reflected by mutual concern and by the sharing of feelings and resources. **Passion** refers to feelings of romantic and sexual attraction. In addition to ver-bal expressions of love, passion is reflected by many types of nonverbal communication, such as gazing, hugging, and kissing. **Commitment** refers to a cou-ple's recognition that they are "in love" and want to be together, "for better or worse." According to Sternberg (1988), consummate (or complete) love is an ideal that is difficult to attain and that is char-acterized by all three components.

Most couples start out with feelings of physical attraction that may develop into passion. If they are compatible, their intimacy and passion may grow. Eventually, they may decide to make a commitment to each other. Thus, from dating, to a steady rela-tionship, to marriage, love changes as our relation-ships endure, deepen, and become a more impor-tant part of our lives.

THINKING ABOUT PSYCHOLOGY

1. How does physical attractiveness influ-ence one's choice of friends and partners?

2. Why are most people attracted to people who are similar to themselves?

3. **Critical Thinking** If you were to create a triangular model of friendship similar to the triangular model of love, shown in Figure 20.2, what components of friend-ship would you think should make up the three corners of the triangle?

SUMMARY

The field of social psychology referred to as social cognition addresses the ways in which people think and act in certain situations.

I. Attitudes

A. Attitudes develop through experience.
   1. Conditioning plays an important role in developing attitudes.
   2. People often develop attitudes by observing others.
   3. People form attitudes on the basis of their evaluation of information.
   4. Attitudes formed early tend to serve as cognitive anchors that keep people from adopting different attitudes.
B. Behavior tends to be linked with attitudes.
   1. Behavior is likely to follow attitudes when the attitudes are specific, strongly held, personally relevant, and verbalized.
   2. Attitudes often follow behavior to reduce cognitive dissonance.

II. Persuasion

A. Attempts to persuade others may follow a central route or a peripheral route.
B. Two-sided arguments tend to be more persuasive than one-sided arguments; emotional appeals are especially persuasive because they arouse feelings such as loyalty.
C. People who appear knowledgeable, trustworthy, and attractive are most persuasive.
D. People are more receptive to persuasion when they are in a good mood.
E. Differences in the age, sex, and other characteristics of an audience influence how a persuasive message should be delivered.
F. Some people are less receptive to persuasion because they have sales resistance.

III. Prejudice

A. Prejudice is often based on stereotypes.
B. Prejudice can lead to discrimination.
C. Prejudice has many potential causes.
D. Prejudice can be overcome by increased contact among groups, speaking out against prejudice, and setting an example of tolerance with one's words and actions.

IV. Social Perception

A. First impressions tend to have a lasting effect on people's relationships.
B. According to attribution theory, people tend to explain the behavior of others in terms of personality factors but explain their own behavior in terms of situational, or external, factors.
   1. Actor-observer bias occurs when people observe others in a limited number of situations.
   2. When people attribute the wrong personality traits to others because of actor-observer bias, this is called fundamental attribution error.
   3. Self-serving bias occurs when people attribute their successes to personality factors and their failures to circumstances beyond their control.
C. Nonverbal communication, such as touching and eye contact, affect people's perceptions of other people.

V. Interpersonal Attraction

A. Physical attractiveness tends to be an important influence on people's choice of friends and partners.
   1. Some aspects of facial attractiveness appear to be universal.
   2. Preferences for body shape vary greatly.
B. People tend to be more attracted to other people who are like them than to people who are different.
C. Affection, respect, and trust are important factors in a friendship.
D. Love relationships are characterized by intimacy, passion, and/or commitment to the other person.

TERM & CONCEPT REVIEW

1. What are cognitive anchors?
2. Summarize the relationship between attitudes and behavior.
3. Why are two-sided arguments generally more persuasive than one-sided arguments?
4. Identify the characteristics that make people persuasive messengers.
5. What is the relationship between prejudice and stereotyping?
6. What is a scapegoat?
7. Give an example of actor-observer bias.
8. What is the difference between gazing and staring?
9. What is the matching hypothesis?
10. Define *reciprocity*.

CRITICAL THINKING

1. Give an example of a slogan used by an advertiser to sell a product or a service. Why do you think this particular slogan might be an effective way to reinforce or change people's attitudes about this product or service?
2. Assume you want to persuade a friend to join you in a walk-a-thon to raise money for a good cause. Explain how you would try to persuade your friend, first using a central route and then using a peripheral route.
3. Most people are aware of racism and sexism but less aware of ageism (prejudice against people of a certain age group, often the elderly). What are some common negative stereotypes associated with specific age groups? How might these stereotypes be eliminated?
4. Explain why interpreting events with a self-serving bias might lead to higher self-esteem.
5. There is a saying that states, "Beauty is in the eye of the beholder." Do you think it is true? Why or why not?

APPLYING SKILLS IN PSYCHOLOGY

1. **COOPERATIVE LEARNING Research in Psychology** With a partner, watch several television commercials for a variety of products. Discuss with your partner the ways in which the advertisers are trying to sell their products. For example, do they take a central or a peripheral route? Whom do they use for a messenger? What, if anything, makes the messenger persuasive? Also, identify the audience the advertisers are trying to reach. With your partner, decide which two commercials you think are likely to be the most effective for their intended audience. Describe the two commercials to the rest of the class, and explain why you think they are effective.

2. **Writing About Psychology** Write a brief description of a hypothetical incident in which someone acts aggressively, such as pushing through a crowd to get to the head of a line, interrupting someone else who is talking, or swearing at another driver on the road. Be careful to word the description so that the sex of the rude individual is not revealed by the use of masculine or feminine pronouns. Read the description to several different people, such as classmates and friends. Ask each person to guess whether the aggressive individual is male or female. In a brief written report, describe how the responses are related to common gender stereotypes.

3. **Using Your Observation Skills** Over the next few days, collect examples of nonverbal communication you observe in other people. For each example, write a brief description of the feelings that were communicated and how they were expressed. Also note whether the feelings were consistent with the people's words and whether it was the spoken or the unspoken message that seemed to make a greater impact on the recipient of the message. Share what you learn from your observations in a brief report.

21 SOCIAL INTERACTION

Chapter 21

Objectives

1 Identify the ways in which membership in a group can influence individual behavior, and describe styles of group leadership.

2 Define *social norms,* and list the factors that lead people to conform to social norms.

3 Describe Milgram's studies of obedience, and explain why most people tend to obey authority figures.

4 Define *aggression,* and summarize the various views on the causes of aggressive behavior.

5 Define *altruism,* and identify the factors that promote and the factors that inhibit altruistic behavior.

A DAY IN THE LIFE

"I can't believe we are graduating in four days," Janet said excitedly.

Janet and Linda were still setting up the picnic table when Marc, Hannah, Todd, and Dan arrived. They had decided to meet for a picnic lunch this weekend, and all they were able to talk about was memories of high school and the fact that it was almost over.

"Todd, remember when we first met?" Linda asked. "We were in introductory biology together. You really helped me a lot in that class—not to mention the fact that you always kept me laughing."

"I remember," Todd said. "I had just moved here and you introduced me to your friends."

"I'd forgotten all about that," Dan replied. "Marc and I were at Janet's track meet that day."

"Hey, I made it to district finals that day," Janet reminded them.

"Of course you did," Hannah chimed in. "The track meet was at home, and all your friends were cheering you on."

They all sat quietly for a while, eating their lunch and thinking about their futures, their pasts, and their friends. Suddenly, Todd started laughing. "Do you remember the time we went to the amusement park, and we all decided to take the shortcut back to the gate? We ended up missing our bus home."

"Wait a minute, Todd!" Hannah exclaimed. "If I remember correctly, you were the one who insisted on that 'shortcut.' We just went along with you."

"Hey, it seemed like a good idea. Besides, it's not my fault that you all listened to me," Todd joked.

"Listening to you isn't always a bad idea," Dan said. "If it weren't for you, I would have fought that guy at the basketball game. Remember that? He bumped into me by accident, but I thought he shoved me on purpose. You were the only person who could calm me down."

"Who knows what any of us would be doing if we didn't have each other," Hannah added. "I'm excited about college, but I'm going to miss seeing all of you every day."

* * *

Todd often influenced his friends—to take a shortcut and to avoid a fight, for example—because they respected his opinions. Having an audience helped Janet run faster and play better. These are just two examples of social influence, or the way other people affect what we say and do. Other people can also influence us by giving us orders or pressuring us to adapt to their standards of behavior.

People behave differently when they are around other people than they do when they are by themselves. How people behave toward others depends on many factors. Sometimes people behave aggressively toward others; sometimes they help others. In this chapter, you will learn more about all of these aspects of social interaction.

Key Terms

- social facilitation
- evaluation apprehension
- social loafing
- diffusion of responsibility
- risky shift
- social decision scheme
- majority-wins scheme
- truth-wins scheme
- two-thirds–majority scheme
- first-shift scheme
- polarization
- authoritarian leader
- democratic leader
- laissez-faire leader
- conform
- social norm
- explicit norm
- implicit norm
- foot-in-the-door effect
- sociobiology
- catharsis
- altruism
- bystander effect

TRUTH OR fiction ?

Read the following statements about psychology. Do you think they are true or false? You will learn whether each statement is true or false as you read the chapter.

- People tend to take greater risks as part of a group than they would if they were acting alone.
- When there is no right or wrong choice, people often go along with the majority.
- Most people try to act as individuals and not simply "go along with the crowd."
- People seldom obey orders to do things that conflict with their own attitudes.
- It is "just human nature" to be aggressive.
- People are more likely to help someone in trouble when no one else is present to help.

Playing on their home court with fans cheering them on usually motivates players to compete harder. What concept of social psychology does this illustrate?

1

Group Behavior

How people behave as part of a group often differs from how they behave as individuals. People may try harder, take greater risks, or make different decisions when they are with others than they would if they were alone. The ways in which groups affect individual behavior are discussed in this section.

Social Facilitation

Social facilitation refers to the concept that people often perform better when other people are watching than they do when they are alone. In other words, the presence of other people seems to facilitate and encourage their performance. Hannah, for example, was not at all surprised that Janet had done so well at the track meet. She had witnessed before that Janet competed harder when her friends cheered her on.

Social facilitation is not limited to people. Psychologist Robert Zajonc (1980) found that dogs and cats—and even cockroaches—do things faster when they are in a group than when they are alone. This suggests that social facilitation may be a basic animal response. Zajonc believes that animals, including humans, respond in this way because the presence of others increases their level of arousal.

Evaluation apprehension, or the concern about the opinion of others, is another reason that the presence of other people may improve an individual's performance (Bray & Sugarman, 1980; Sanna & Shotland, 1990). Evaluation apprehension may motivate people to try harder so that others will think more highly of them.

Social Loafing

Being a member of a group does not always improve one's performance. When people are working together toward a common goal rather than working on individual tasks, they may "slack off" and not try as hard. This is referred to as **social loafing**. Social loafing is especially likely to occur when people see that other members of the group are not pulling their share of the load.

Social loafing may occur because of **diffusion of responsibility**—the tendency for people to feel less responsible for accomplishing a task when the effort is shared among members of a group. As part of a group, individuals are likely to feel less accountable for their actions. Therefore, they are less likely to worry about what others think of them (that is, to have less evaluation apprehension). They may even feel that their contribution to the group's effort is not very important (Harkins & Szymanski, 1989; Kerr & Bruun, 1983). When Todd said, "you all listened to me [about the shortcut]," he was diffusing, or spreading out, his own responsibility for an unwise decision to the other members of the group.

Risky Shift

A related social phenomenon is the **risky shift**—the tendency for people to take greater risks as part of a group than they would as individuals acting on their own. People may feel more powerful (or less vulnerable) as part of a group. This is because the responsibilty for a particular situation or action is shared with the other group members (Myers, 1996; Smith and Mackie, 1995). The risky shift may help explain such events as prison riots and mob attacks.

It is true that people tend to take greater risks as part of a group than they would if they were acting alone. This is because individuals can share responsibility for a decision.

Group Decision Making

Many important decisions are made by groups rather than by individuals. Committees, for example, are often appointed to study and make decisions about specific issues. Juries of 12 decide on the guilt or innocence of people accused of crimes. Similarly, a group of friends may make a joint decision about which movie to see. These are examples of group decision making.

Because many decisions are made by groups, psychologists have studied how being part of a group affects the decision-making process. They have identified a number of **social decision schemes**, or rules that govern group decision making (Davis et al., 1984; Kerr & MacCoun, 1985; Stasser et al., 1989). These include the majority-wins scheme, the truth-wins scheme, the two-thirds–majority scheme, and the first-shift scheme.

Majority-Wins Scheme   In the **majority-wins scheme**, the group comes to agreement on a deci-

sion that was initially supported by a majority of group members. For example, a group of five friends might be trying to decide what to do on the weekend—say, whether to go to a movie or to a video arcade. At first, three of the five friends might opt for the movie and the other two friends for the arcade. However, after discussing the two choices, all five friends might agree to go to the movie, the option that was initially supported by the majority.

The majority-wins scheme applies most often to situations in which there are no right or wrong choices. In the example just given, both the movie and the arcade were acceptable options—neither one was right or wrong. Rather, the preference of the majority guided the decisions of the others.

It is true that when there is no right or wrong choice, people often go along with the majority. This is called the majority-wins scheme of group decision making.

Truth-Wins Scheme   Often, the members of a group come to realize that one option is better than others after they learn more about the different choices available. This is referred to as the **truth-wins scheme**. Suppose that in the example just given, the five friends learn that the movie they hoped to see has been canceled and that another movie is being shown, one that interests them less. After gathering and sharing the information, the group might decide to go to the arcade instead, a decision that is based on a clearly better choice between their two options.

Two-Thirds–Majority Scheme   Some groups concur with a decision after two thirds of their members come to an agreement about the correct choice. This is called the **two-thirds–majority scheme**. It often applies to decisions made by juries. When two thirds of a jury initially vote for conviction, the remaining third may go along with the decision of the others.

First-Shift Scheme   The **first-shift scheme** applies to groups that are deadlocked, or split 50-50, about a decision. If just one person changes his or her mind, or shifts from one side to the other, others may follow and shift to the opposite side as well. For example, a jury might be deadlocked, with half believing the defendant is guilty and half believing the defendant is innocent. Those jurors who initially thought the defendant was guilty might follow the lead of the first juror who changes his or her vote from guilty to not guilty, even in the absence of additional information about the case.

Polarization

Members of a group usually share similar attitudes. Indeed, shared attitudes are often what attracts people to particular groups in the first place. For example, teens who are concerned about cruelty to animals might join an organization that has the goal of ending laboratory experimentation on animal subjects. Teens who are not as concerned about animal rights, on the other hand, are unlikely to join such a group.

The shared attitudes that group members hold are likely to grow stronger through time. This strengthening of a group's shared attitudes is called **polarization**. It occurs as group members discuss and act upon the attitudes they share.

Polarization can be positive or negative. If group members are prejudiced against people of other races or religions, for example, then polarization is likely to increase their prejudice. If, on the other hand, group members are tolerant of people who are different, then polarization may make them even more so (Myers & Bishop, 1970; Zuber et al., 1992). Such polarization in group attitudes is illustrated in Figure 21.1.

Group Leadership

All groups, regardless of their nature, have leaders who serve several important functions in their groups. Leaders help group members identify the group's goals and establish and implement plans for reaching them. Leaders may also offer emotional support to group members.

Some leaders are appointed by outsiders; others are chosen by a vote of group members. The president of an organization might be elected by a vote of group members, for example. The president, in turn, might appoint a member of the group to head a committee to study a particular issue or complete a particular task.

Organizations such as businesses, schools, and the military usually have clear chains of command, or leadership. Group members know to whom to report and whose directions to follow.

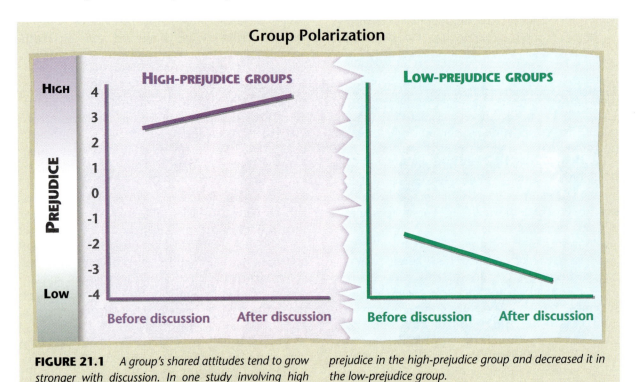

FIGURE 21.1 *A group's shared attitudes tend to grow stronger with discussion. In one study involving high school students, a discussion of racial issues increased prejudice in the high-prejudice group and decreased it in the low-prejudice group.*

Source: "Discussion Effects on Racial Attitudes" (1970) by D. G. Myers and G. D. Bishop, *Science, 169,* 778–779.

CASE STUDIES
AND OTHER TRUE STORIES

Dr. Martin Luther King, Jr., and Nonviolent Action

People are usually influenced by the views of the majority. In some cases, however, the opinion of a single individual has influenced the behavior of the majority; and that minority influence has changed the course of history.

Researchers have investigated factors that enable a minority to influence the majority. They have found that the most influential individuals are those who hold steadfastly to

Dr. Martin Luther King, Jr.

their views and never waver, in words or actions, from what they believe. One of the best examples of such unyielding commitment is provided by Dr. Martin Luther King, Jr. His belief in nonviolent action shaped the course of the civil rights movement throughout the 1960s and beyond.

Dr. King believed that the only way African Americans could achieve racial equality in the United States was through nonviolent action. Even as a boy, Dr. King reacted to racial insults and violence with nonviolence. When a school bully attacked him, he did not fight back. When a White woman in a store slapped him, he said nothing (Osborne, 1968).

Dr. King's extraordinary leadership qualities and his strong belief in nonviolent action changed the course of the civil rights movement. In 1955, inspired by Rosa Parks, Dr. King led a boycott of Montgomery city buses that eventually resulted in an integrated bus system in Montgomery and in nearly every other city in the South as well.

Dr. King continued to lead nonviolent protests against racial inequality in the United States. He led lunch-counter sit-ins to desegregate eating facilities and organized prayer vigils to focus the nation's attention on the need to desegregate public parks and rest rooms. But he is probably best known for the 1963 March on Washington.

During this historic event, more than 200,000 people gathered at the Lincoln Memorial in Washington, D.C., to hear Dr. King deliver his famous speech, "I Have a Dream."

At these and other events Dr. King remained steadfast in his belief in nonviolence. Despite repeated arrests and physical violence against himself and his family, King never wavered in his belief that nonviolence was the only real solution to the problem of racial inequality.

Dr. King was feared and attacked by some White people because his methods were so effective. He was also criticized by other African Americans because they saw his nonviolence as weakness. When one civil rights activist was shot soon after the start of a freedom march, some members of the movement questioned the wisdom of King's nonviolent approach. Dr. King, however, patiently urged his followers to remain true to the nonviolent movement. He was persuasive, and the march continued peacefully.

Dr. King's influence on the civil rights movement was vast. Nonviolence continually proved to be the most effective means of bringing about change. In 1964, Dr. Martin Luther King, Jr., received the Nobel Peace Prize for his struggle to achieve racial equality through peaceful means. By 1965, because of his influence, civil rights organizations across the country had adopted nonviolent action as their primary method of addressing racial inequality.

Think About It

What evidence shows that Martin Luther King, Jr., was deeply committed to nonviolent action? How did he express his views and influence others to adopt them?

Informal groups, such as groups of friends, may not have official leaders. However, some members are likely to have more influence over the group than others. This was true of Todd and his circle of friends. Todd tended to be the leader of the group and to influence the others because of his intelligence and leadership abilities. He influenced his friends to take a shortcut at the amusement park, for example, and he influenced Dan not to fight.

Like Todd, group leaders often have certain personality traits and social skills that enable them to influence the decisions and behavior of others. For example, leaders tend to be more self-confident, outgoing, and intelligent than other group members (Smith & Mackie, 1995). Despite these similarities, leaders may differ in how they operate. In other words, they may have different styles of leadership. Leaders may be authoritarian, democratic, or laissez-faire.

Authoritarian Leaders   **Authoritarian leaders** exert absolute control over all decisions for the group. They tell other group members what to do, and demand that group members obey their orders. Military leaders, for example, are usually authoritarian. They give orders to those of lesser rank and expect their orders to be carried out immediately and without question.

Democratic Leaders   Although military leaders tend to be authoritarian to those below them in the chain of command, they are more democratic when they are planning strategies with other officers. **Democratic leaders** encourage group members to express and discuss their ideas and to make their own decisions. Such leaders may try to build a consensus—that is, to encourage unanimous agreement on a decision. Alternatively, they may request that group members take a vote and follow the decision of the majority.

Laissez-Faire Leaders   The term *laissez-faire* is French for "to allow to do (as one chooses)." Like democratic leaders, **laissez-faire leaders** encourage group members to express and explore their own ideas. However, laissez-faire leaders tend to take a less active role in the decision-making process. They tend to stand back from the group and allow group members to move in whatever direction they wish, even if the group seems to be making false starts or poor choices.

Comparing Leadership Styles   No one style of leadership is best for every group or situation. In times of crisis, authoritarian leaders may be more effective because they can make decisions quickly and know that those decisions will be carried out promptly. This is one reason nations often prefer authoritarian leaders when the country is having serious problems.

In other situations, democratic or laissez-faire leaders may be more effective. Their styles of leadership allow group members to express themselves and grow as individuals. This may be important when the group is searching for new ways to solve a problem or trying to help group members meet challenges in their lives.

THINKING ABOUT PSYCHOLOGY

1. Explain the difference between social facilitation and social loafing.
2. List four social decision schemes.
3. **Critical Thinking**   Give an example of a group or situation that might benefit from a laissez-faire style of leadership. Explain your choice.

2
Conformity

The least direct social influence on behavior is the pressure to **conform**, or to modify one's attitudes and behavior to make them consistent with those of other people. People who conform bring their behavior into line with that of a group. The group may be a formal organization, such as a school club, or a loose collection of people, such as several friends who always hang out together. Linda, Marc, Todd, and the others in their circle of friends are an example of such a group.

Importance of Groups

Being accepted by a group can be important because groups help people satisfy many needs. Groups can fulfill an individual's needs for belonging, affection, and attention. Meeting such needs is one reason why many teens join clubs at school, sports teams, academic clubs, and other social organizations.

Social norms vary from one group to another. People of different ages and occupations tend to have different standards of dress, for example. How might this be an example of both explicit and implicit norms?

Groups are also important because they offer support to individuals when they are facing difficult problems. People who are grieving the loss of a loved one, for example, may benefit by joining a support group. (See Chapter 19.) Groups may also help people accomplish things they could not accomplish on their own. For instance, workers may join together to form a labor union in order to fight for better working conditions or higher wages.

Social Norms

Belonging to a group usually means following, or conforming to, the group's social norms. **Social norms** are the standards that people share. They serve as guidelines for what people should and should not do or say in a given situation. For example, social norms tell people what to eat, what to wear, and when and where to make a joke.

Social norms can be explicit or implicit. **Explicit norms** are spoken or written rules. Examples include traffic rules and school dress codes. **Implicit norms** are unspoken, unwritten rules. Examples include modes of dress or ways of greeting that are unique to a particular group. Although implicit norms are unstated, they nonetheless guide people's words and actions.

Social norms can be useful or harmful. They are useful if they help promote the safety and well-being of individuals or groups. Bathing regularly and not talking in a theater during a movie are examples of useful social norms. Social norms are harmful when they promote risky behavior. Smoking cigarettes and drinking alcohol excessively are examples of harmful social norms.

Asch's Studies of Conformity

To what extent will people conform to social norms? Psychologist Solomon Asch (1955) addressed this question in a series of well-known experiments. Asch wanted to determine whether people would go along with group opinion even when the group opinion differed from their own.

Procedure   Asch asked participants in the study to look at three lines of varying length and to compare them with a standard line, as shown in Figure 21.2 on page 486. The participants were asked to indicate which of the three lines was the same length as the standard line. Each participant was tested in a group of several other people. However, the other group members were really Asch's associates, who were simply posing as study participants.

For the first few comparisons, all of Asch's associates gave the correct answer. However, for many of the remaining comparisons, all of the associates gave the same *wrong* answer. For example, they might have said that line 1 was the same length as the standard line.

Results   When Asch's associates gave an answer that was obviously wrong, many study participants conformed to the group opinion and gave the same wrong answer. About three fourths of study participants went along with group opinion at least once, one third went along with the group at least half the time, and one fourth went along with the group virtually all the time. Study participants who conformed to group opinion later admitted that they knew the answers they gave were incorrect, but they went along with the group so as not to appear different from the others.

TRUTH OR fiction ■ REVISITED ■

It is not true that most people try to act as individuals and not just "go along with the crowd." Asch's studies of conformity revealed that most people conform to those around them so as not to appear different.

Why Do People Conform?

"Going along with the crowd" is probably at least as common in everyday life as it was in Asch's experiments. Most people avoid talking, acting, or dressing differently from other members of the groups to which they belong. Why is conformity so common?

Asch's Conformity Experiment

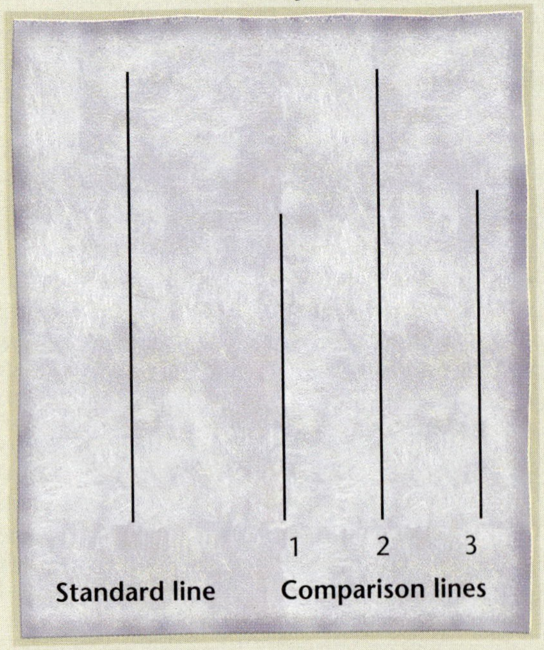

Standard line   Comparison lines
1   2   3

FIGURE 21.2   *In this example from Asch's studies, line 2 is clearly the same length as the standard line.*

Several factors may contribute to the tendency to conform to social norms (Bond & Smith, 1996; Myers, 1996; Smith & Mackie, 1995).

Cultural Influences   Some cultures are collectivistic, which means that they place greater emphasis on the group than on its individual members. In many Asian cultures, for example, the person is seen as part of the family and society rather than as an individual. (See Chapter 14.) In such cultures, individuals show a greater tendency to conform to the group, and they may feel extremely uncomfortable if they are singled out as different from the others in the group.

Need for Acceptance   Some people conform to social norms in order to be liked and accepted by others. This need to conform stems from the belief that people who dress, talk, or act differently from other people stand out from the crowd and thus draw negative attention to themselves. In actuality, however, this is not always true.

People who depend the most on the acceptance and approval of others tend to be those with low self-esteem and high social anxiety (Singh & Sharma, 1989). They may value being liked more than they value being right. They may also be very self-conscious about standing out from others, fearing that others will ridicule or reject them if they appear different.

Other Factors   Several other factors contribute to the tendency to conform to social norms. For example, the chances of conforming to a group's norms increase as the group grows in size—at least up to about eight members. Further increases in size (past eight members) seem to have little effect on the tendency to conform.

Individuals are more likely to conform to the group when all other members of the group are unanimous in their words and actions. However, if even one person disagrees with the rest of the group, others in the group also are less likely to conform.

THINKING ABOUT PSYCHOLOGY

1. What is the difference between explicit norms and implicit norms?

2. What factors influence people to conform to social norms?

3. **Critical Thinking**   How did Asch show that people tend to conform to others?

3
Obedience

One of the most obvious and direct social influences on people's attitudes and behavior is the power of people in positions of authority. Parents often order their children to clean their rooms or do their homework. Judges often order lawbreakers to pay fines or perform community service. Most children obey their parents, teachers, and other adults. Most adults obey police officers, judges, and other authority figures. Such obedience is necessary to protect the safety and well-being of the community and its people.

Throughout history, however, many people have also obeyed orders to commit immoral acts, such as killing innocent people. In the 20th century alone, Nazis killed Jews in Europe, Serbs killed Muslims in Bosnia, and Turks killed Armenians. In each case, those who did the killing justified their acts by saying they were "just following orders."

Milgram's Studies of Obedience

Are people who commit immoral acts unusual or abnormal? Or would most people be obedient in a similar situation? Yale University psychologist Stanley Milgram, who was influenced by the atrocities of World War II, investigated this question in a series of studies conducted in the 1960s and 1970s. The purpose of Milgram's research was to determine whether the average person would obey the commands of authority figures.

Procedure In the first phase of his research, Milgram (1963) placed advertisements in local newspapers seeking male volunteers to participate in a study of learning. In response, 40 men, ranging in age from 20 to 50, volunteered for the study. The volunteers represented a wide range of educational levels—from people who had not completed elementary school to others who had earned graduate degrees. Study participants also represented a variety of occupations, including teachers, engineers, laborers, and salespeople.

Instead of revealing the true nature of the study, Milgram told participants that its purpose was to investigate the effects of punishment on memory. Some participants, Milgram explained, would be "teachers" and others would be "learners." In reality, all the volunteers who answered the advertisement

Scenes such as this may come to mind when we hear the phrase "obedience to authority," but obedience characterizes many of our interactions in daily life. Can you think of other examples of obedience?

were assigned to the teacher group, whereas those in the learner group were Milgram's associates.

Study participants were told that learners were expected to learn word pairs that would be read to them from a list. After the learners had heard the entire list, the teachers read the words one at a time. Each learner was then asked to provide the word that was paired with the word read by the teacher. If a learner made the correct choice, nothing happened, and teacher and learner went on to the next test item. However, if a learner made an incorrect choice, the teacher was to deliver an electric shock. With each mistake a learner made, the teacher was to increase the amount of voltage.

As shown in the second photograph in the series on page 488, learners were strapped into chairs and electrodes were attached to their wrists. The teachers sat at a console in an adjacent room. On the console were levers labeled with the voltage they controlled (from 15 to 450 volts) and the seriousness of the shocks they delivered (from slight to severe). Although the teachers were led to believe that the learners received shocks for each incorrect answer, the equipment did not really deliver shocks, and the learners were never hurt or put at risk in any way.

Teachers were first given a sample shock of 45 volts so they would have some idea of what learners supposedly would be experiencing. A shock of 45 volts is not harmful, but it was unpleasant enough to convince teachers that high-voltage shocks would be painful, even dangerous. Teachers were told that

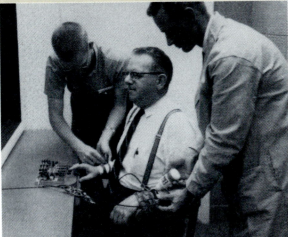

The machine and the procedure used in Stanley Milgram's classic study on obedience are pictured here. The third photograph in the series shows one of the few participants who refused to continue with the experiment.

they could quit at any time. However, if they hesitated to deliver a shock, or to go on with the experiment, they were urged by repeated commands from the researcher to continue. The researcher also offered reassurances that the shocks, though painful, would cause no permanent damage.

Results As learners made errors, teachers delivered greater and greater voltage in each shock. At 300 volts, learners pounded on the other side of the wall, even screamed in make-believe pain—yet 35 of the 40 participants continued with the experiment. Nine participants refused to continue somewhere between the 300-volt and the 450-volt level. However, the rest, almost two thirds of the participants, obeyed instructions to give shocks throughout the entire range of voltage, up to 450 volts, even though these participants later said they had been afraid of harming the people receiving the shocks (Milgram, 1971).

Were the people who volunteered for Milgram's study abnormally insensitive, even cruel? Apparently not. They showed signs of great distress as the shocks they delivered increased in voltage. They sweated, bit their lips, trembled, stuttered, groaned, and dug their fingernails into their palms. Some even had fits of nervous laughter. Many also told the researcher that they wanted to stop. Nonetheless, most continued to deliver shocks of increasing voltage to the learners in the study.

Milgram repeated the experiment with other participants, including women and college students, and in other settings, including a storefront on a city street. In each phase of the research, at least half the participants obeyed the researcher and administered the entire series of electric shocks.

TRUTH OR fiction · R E V I S I T E D · *It is not true that people seldom obey orders to do things that conflict with their own attitudes.* Milgram's studies of obedience showed that the majority of people will obey such orders, even though doing so may cause them great emotional distress.

Why Do People Obey?

Why did the participants in Milgram's studies obey the researcher? What causes people, in general, to obey? Several causes have been identified.

Socialization One reason people tend to be obedient is that they have been socialized from childhood to obey authority figures, such as parents, teachers, and police officers. Study participants saw the researchers in Milgram's studies as authority figures so they obeyed orders to give shocks to the learners. To do otherwise would have conflicted with deeply held attitudes about correct behavior (Blass, 1991).

Foot-in-the-Door Effect Another reason that people tend to be obedient to authority figures is the **foot-in-the-door effect**. This is the tendency for people to give in to major demands once they have given in to minor ones (Gilbert, 1981). The foot-in-the-door effect is an example of how people may gradually change their attitudes to justify their behavior. (See Chapter 20.)

After participants in Milgram's studies had delivered small shocks to learners, it was easier for them to deliver increasingly larger shocks. In a similar way, soldiers become accustomed to obeying commands concerning relatively unimportant matters, such as how to dress, when and where to eat, and how to perform routine drills. Later on, they are more likely to obey commands relating to much more important matters that may involve risking their lives or taking the lives of other people.

Confusion About Attitudes People who are aware of their attitudes are more likely to behave in accordance with those attitudes (Fazio, 1990; Krosnick, 1989). As people become disturbed by what is happening around them—by the learners' screams and wall pounding in Milgram's studies, for example—they are likely to become less aware of, or at least more confused about, their own beliefs. Thus, they may be more likely to behave in ways that are in conflict with their attitudes.

Buffers When people are buffered, or protected, from observing the consequences of their actions, they are more likely to follow orders, even immoral ones. In the first phase of Milgram's research, for

Obedience—even to immoral commands, as in the Milgram studies—may be an offshoot of socially desirable respect for authority figures that most people learn in childhood.

example, teachers and learners were placed in separate rooms. Thus, teachers could not see how their actions were affecting others. In later phases of the research, teachers and learners were placed in the same room so that teachers could see the pain they were inflicting on the learners. Without the buffer of a wall to separate them from the people they thought they were hurting, compliance with the researcher's demands dropped from 65 percent to about 40 percent (Miller, 1986).

Today, many soldiers are similarly buffered from their enemies. Their only contact with opposing forces may be a blip on a radar screen. Attacking their enemies may involve little more than pressing a button that launches a missile. The results of Milgram's studies suggest that obeying orders to kill enemies in this way may be easier than obeying orders to kill other human beings at close range.

THINKING ABOUT PSYCHOLOGY

1. What did Milgram's studies reveal about obedience to authority?
2. Identify some of the reasons that explain why people tend to obey the orders of those in authority.
3. **Critical Thinking** Give examples of situations in which obedience to authority is considered socially acceptable.

4
Aggression

Aggression refers to words or actions that are meant to hurt other people. It is a serious and widespread social problem. For example, murder is the second-leading cause of death in the United States among young people between the ages of 15 and 24 (Lore & Schultz, 1993), and more than a million children each year are victims of abuse. Children not only suffer from the results of aggression; they seem to be fascinated by it as well. For example, children are drawn to video games in which they can manipulate figures to kill or torture others.

Why are people aggressive? Several reasons have been suggested. They include biological, psychoanalytic, cognitive, learning, and sociocultural views.

Biological View

The best-known biological explanation of aggression comes from **sociobiology**, the subfield of biology that is concerned with the social behavior of humans and other animals. The term *sociobiology* was coined by Harvard professor E. O. Wilson (1975), an expert on the social behavior of ants and other insects.

Children's games often involve make-believe aggression.

According to Wilson and other sociobiologists, much of social behavior (including aggression) is controlled by genes. Sociobiologists believe that humans and many other animal species tend to be aggressive because aggression helps individuals survive and reproduce. Those who fight successfully for territory, food, or mates are likely to live longer and have more offspring than those who are less aggressive. Thus, the genes that are connected with aggression are more likely to be passed on to succeeding generations and influence the behavior of the entire species.

The sociobiological view has been criticized for several reasons. For one, it underplays the importance of cooperation in human survival. In many situations, people who work together may be more likely to survive to maturity and have offspring than those who are aggressive toward others. In addition, a clear-cut genetic basis for aggressive behavior has not been found. Biologists know of no single gene—or group of genes—that directly controls aggressive behavior. Many scientists also agree that the tendency toward aggression varies too widely from culture to culture and person to person to be under direct genetic control.

Thus, many experts believe that genetics does not explain aggression. This is not to say, however, that aggression has no biological basis. Certain areas of the brain, when stimulated, have been shown to produce aggressive behavior (Moyer, 1983). (See Chapter 3.) However, aggression is a complex behavior that is influenced by many external factors. The brain is involved in producing aggressive behavior, but outside stimuli are needed to provoke most people to act aggressively.

TRUTH OR fiction ■ REVISITED ■ *It is not true that it is "just human nature" to be aggressive. While aggression may be a part of the biological makeup of our species, it is unlikely that all aggressive behavior is caused by genetic or biological factors.*

Psychoanalytic View

Sigmund Freud believed that aggressive urges are unavoidable reactions to the frustrations of daily life. According to this view, it is normal for people to have urges to hurt other people who do not meet their wishes or demands. Such urges tend to be repressed, however, because people fear hurting others (especially their parents) and, in turn, being rejected by them.

Freud also believed that repressed aggressive urges are likely to find other outlets. The urges might be expressed indirectly—for example, by the aggressive individual destroying other people's possessions or disobeying their orders. Alternatively, the urges might be expressed directly but toward strangers later in life.

Freud believed that the best way to reduce the tension caused by repressed aggressive urges and to prevent harmful aggression toward other people is to allow, or even encourage, less harmful expressions of aggression. For example, verbal aggression in the form of sarcasm or the expression of angry feelings might vent some of the aggressive feelings in the unconscious without causing bodily harm to other people. So might cheering on one's team or watching aggressive sports such as boxing or wrestling. Psychologists refer to such venting of aggressive impulses as **catharsis**.

Does catharsis really act as a safety valve, reducing feelings of tension and lowering the chances of harmful aggression toward others? Some studies have found that catharsis does seem to play this role (Doob & Wood, 1972). Other studies, however, have found that "letting off steam," either verbally or by watching aggressive sports, seems to encourage people to be more, not less, aggressive (Bennett, 1991; Geen et al., 1975). Thus, it is unclear whether catharsis increases or decreases aggressive behavior.

Cognitive View

Cognitive psychologists believe that people's behavior, including aggressive behavior, is not influenced by inherited tendencies or repressed urges. Instead, they maintain, aggressive behavior is influenced by people's values, the ways in which they perceive events, and the choices they make. According to this view, people choose to act aggressively because they believe that aggression is justified and necessary—either in general or in particular situations (Feshbach, 1994).

Some cognitive psychologists have suggested that frustration and suffering trigger feelings of anger and that these feelings in turn cause people to act aggressively (Rule et al., 1987). However, they also argue that people do not act aggressively automatically and without thought. Rather, people decide whether they will act aggressively on the basis of such factors as their previous experiences

These sports fans are obviously excited by the soccer match they are watching. Some psychologists believe that watching the aggressive play of a sports team is a harmless way to vent aggressive urges.

with aggression and their interpretation of other people's behavior (Berkowitz, 1994).

How people interpret the behavior of others may be especially important in this regard. Some people tend to interpret other people's behavior as intentionally insulting or cruel even when it is not (Akhtar & Bradley, 1991; Crick & Dodge, 1994; Dodge et al., 1990). This interpretation may stir up feelings of anger that in turn lead to aggression (Lochman, 1992; Lochman & Dodge, 1994). That is what happened to Dan. When someone accidentally bumped into him at a basketball game, he thought he had been shoved on purpose. It made him so angry that he almost started a fight.

A DAY IN THE LIFE

Learning View

Learning theorists believe that people learn to repeat behaviors that are reinforced. Thus, when aggressive behavior is reinforced, people learn to behave aggressively.

One reason that aggression may be reinforced is that it helps people have their own way. For example, teens who bully other people may be able to control others with force or threats of force. Although other people may stay out of their way, bullies are also likely to be rejected as friends by most of their peers. Thus, it is questionable whether such behavior is really reinforced.

However, there is little question that other types of aggressive behavior are reinforced. In many sports, aggression helps players win games. Winning, in turn, gains them the admiration of fans and often, at least in professional sports, large paychecks.

Learning theorists also believe that people learn many behaviors by observing others. People observe aggressive behavior on television, in the movies, and in video games (Fling et al., 1992; Wood et al., 1991). Many people also observe aggressive behavior in their own homes and neighborhoods. Thus, most people have ample opportunity to observe aggression and learn from their observations.

The role that television violence plays in teaching children aggressive behavior has received a considerable amount of attention. This is because most children spend a great deal of time watching television—more time, in fact, than they spend in school. Evidence suggests that by the time the average child reaches middle school, he or she has viewed more than 8,000 murders and 100,000 other acts of violence on television (Huston et al., 1992).

Most experts agree that watching violence on television leads people to act more aggressively (American Psychological Association Commission on Violence and Youth, 1992). Figure 21.3 shows some of the data that support this conclusion. It shows how the seriousness of criminal acts committed by age 30 corresponds to the amount of television watched before age 8.

Watching violence on television may influence people to become more aggressive because television may reinforce an individual's ideas about violence and thus lessen his or her inhibitions against aggression. Children may also learn to imitate the acts of violence they see on television.

Sociocultural View

Sociocultural theorists argue that some cultures encourage independence and competitiveness and that this, in turn, promotes aggression. The United

Television Viewing and Aggression

Seriousness of criminal acts by age 30

males

females

Low Medium High   Low Medium High

Frequency of television viewing

* The seriousness of crimes refers to a score assigned to each crime by the New York State Criminal Justice Division in which each type of offense is assigned a specific score (Rossi et al., 1974).

FIGURE 21.3 *This chart illustrates the results of a study that measured the seriousness of criminal acts by age 30 as a function of the frequency of television viewing at age 8.*

Huesmann, L. R., Eron, L. D., Dubow, E. F., & Seebauer, E. (1988). Television viewing habits in childhood and adult aggression. *Child Development.*

States is a good example. Most Americans place a high value on individual rights and freedoms. They also emphasize competition. When so much importance is attached to the individual, getting along with others becomes less important. When one person is strongly encouraged to win over others, hostility and aggression may result.

Other cultures place greater value on the welfare of the group and encourage people to cooperate. This may reduce levels of aggression. Children in cultures such as Thailand and Jamaica, for example, where courtesy, respect, and cooperation are encouraged, tend to be less aggressive than children in the United States (Tharp, 1991).

THINKING ABOUT PSYCHOLOGY

1. How do sociobiologists explain human aggression?

2. According to learning theorists, how do children learn aggressive behavior?

3. **Critical Thinking**   Explain why it is important to understand the causes of aggression in order to find solutions to the problem of violence in society.

PSYCHOLOGY

CONFORMITY AND INDIVIDUAL CHOICE

How far will an individual deviate from his or her own beliefs to conform to the beliefs and actions of the majority? Could the power of social conformity influence an average man to commit murder? In the most extreme cases, the answer seems to be yes.

The following excerpts are from American historian Christopher R. Browning's book, *Ordinary Men: Reserve Police Battalion 101 and the Final Solution in Poland* (1992). The book is a reconstruction of the events and motives that led 500 middle-aged, middle-class German men of Reserve Police Battalion 101 to launch a reign of terror against Jews in Poland in July 1942. By November 1943, these ordinary civilians had brutally killed at least 85,000 Jewish people.

It is important to note that the commanding officer, Major Trapp, explicitly offered to "excuse" any man who did not want to participate in the impending mass murder. Trapp's offer thrust responsibility onto each man individually. Unlike regular soldiers, these policemen bore the burden of choice. They were not "just following orders." The pressure to conform to their peers' expectations, however, was paramount.

> Only the very exceptional remained indifferent to taunts of 'weakling' from their comrades and could live with the fact that they were considered to be 'no man.'. . . Killing was seen as a collective obligation, so not killing was asocial vis-à-vis one's comrades. Those who did not shoot risked isolation [and] rejection . . . —a very uncomfortable prospect within the framework of a tight-knit unit stationed abroad among a hostile population, so that the individual had virtually nowhere else to turn for support and social contact. (pp.184–185)

Browning notes that no member of Reserve Police Battalion 101 was physically harmed or officially punished for refusing to shoot. Instead, outright refusal—total nonconformity—brought other, more subtle, consequences.

> There is the threat of isolation. . . . Stepping out could have been seen as a moral reproach of one's comrades: the nonshooter was potentially indicating that he was 'too good' to do such things. . . . Most nonshooters intuitively tried to diffuse the criticism of their comrades. . . . They pleaded not that they were 'too good' but rather that they were 'too weak' to kill. (p.185)

> . . . most of those who did not shoot only reaffirmed the 'macho' values of the majority—according to which it was a positive quality to be 'tough' enough to kill unarmed, noncombatant men, women, and children—and tried not to rupture the bonds of comradeship that constituted their social world.

> What, then, is one to conclude? . . . The reserve policemen faced choices, and most of them committed terrible deeds. But those who killed cannot be absolved by the notion that anyone in the same situation would have done as they did. For even among them, some refused to kill and others stopped killing. (p.188)

> Yet 80 to 90 percent of the men proceeded to kill, though all of them—at least initially—were horrified and disgusted by what they were doing. To break ranks and step out, to adopt overtly nonconformist behavior, was simply beyond most of the men. It was easier for them to shoot. (p.184)

> . . . Within virtually every social collective, the peer group exerts tremendous pressures on behavior and sets moral norms. If the men of Reserve Police Battalion 101 could become killers under such circumstances, what group of men cannot? (p.189)

Think About It

What factors may have led more men to refuse to conform to the murderous actions of the rest of the group?

5
Altruism

Altruism is an unselfish concern for the welfare of other people. Altruistic people sacrifice their own well-being to help others in need. For example, an altruistic person might jump into the water to save someone who is drowning, even though doing so could put the would-be rescuer's own life in danger.

Explaining Altruism

Sociobiologists believe that altruism, like aggression, is linked to genetics (Guisinger & Blatt, 1994; Rushton, 1989). Although altruistic behavior benefits other people, sociobiologists believe it can also help people pass on their genes to future generations. At least it can do so if the altruistic behavior is directed toward relatives—that is, toward people who have many of the same genes as the altruist.

By helping our relatives survive and reproduce, sociobiologists argue, we are indirectly passing on our own genes to the next generation. In this way, genes for altruism have come to be part of the human gene pool. Thus, according to the sociobiological view, humans are altruistic by nature (Simon, 1990).

The sociobiological explanation of altruism has been criticized for many of the same reasons that the sociobiological explanation of aggression has been criticized: no clear-cut genetic basis for altruistic behavior has been found, and the tendency to act altruistically varies too widely to be under genetic control. The sociobiological view of altruism has also been criticized for failing to explain why people act altruistically toward those who are not related to themselves.

Factors Promoting Altruism

Research has shown that several factors influence whether a person will help others in particular situations. One factor is the person's state of mind. Many studies have found that people are more likely to help others when they are in a good mood (Berkowitz, 1987; Manucia et al., 1984). Being in a good mood seems to make people feel more generous and eager to help others (Carlson et al., 1988). It also may make people feel more powerful and thus better able to provide aid to those in need (Cunningham et al., 1990).

Altruism is just part of the job for the firefighter pictured here. Can you think of other professions that require altruistic behavior?

People who have problems themselves may also be more likely to act altruistically, perhaps because their own problems make them sensitive to the troubles of others (Thompson et al., 1980). People who are empathic, that is, able to put themselves in another's place, may be more likely to be altruistic for the same reason (Batson et al., 1989a).

Being competent to help others seems to increase the chances that people will act altruistically. For example, registered nurses are more likely than people with no medical training to come to the aid of accident victims (Cramer et al., 1988). Similarly, police officers, who are trained to intervene in violent and dangerous situations, are more likely than the average person to help people in trouble. Being a good student himself, Todd felt competent to help others with their schoolwork and did so for Linda when they first met in biology class.

People with a strong need for approval also may be more likely to act altruistically. By doing so, they hope to gain the approval of others. In addition, a sense of personal responsibility may increase the chances of altruistic behavior (Maruyama et al., 1982). Teachers and camp counselors, for example, are responsible for those in their care, and they are more likely to act altruistically toward them than others would.

Factors Inhibiting Altruism

There are also several factors that seem to make people reluctant to help others in distress. In some cases, people may not be aware that another person is in trouble. In fact, the less sure they are that another person needs help, the less likely they are to offer assistance (Shotland & Heinold, 1985).

Some people may fail to act altruistically because they think there is nothing they can do to help. Others may be afraid of making a social blunder and being ridiculed (Pantin & Carver, 1982). For example, someone who sees an individual with a disability struggling with a door may fear offending the person by offering help. Finally, people may fail to act altruistically, particularly in dangerous situations, because they fear injuring themselves in the attempt.

Bystander Effect

The chances of people helping someone in need also depend on how many other people are present to help. Research has shown that people are less likely to give aid when other bystanders are present. This is called the **bystander effect**.

A classic experiment by psychologists Darley and Latané (1968) is one of many studies that have documented the bystander effect. In one phase of the study, participants were placed in separate cubicles and asked to talk with one another over an intercom. One of the participants was actually an associate of the researchers. When his turn came to talk, he called for help and then made sounds that suggested he was having an epileptic seizure.

Some study participants had been led to believe that they alone could hear the person having the seizure. Others had been led to believe that from one to four other participants could hear him as well. About 85 percent of participants who thought that no one else could hear the person came to his aid. However, when participants thought that others could also hear the individual in trouble, fewer of them tried to help. In fact, the more people who were presumed to be able to hear him, the less likely participants were to become involved. Only 31 percent of participants made an effort to help when they thought that four other people could hear the person in need.

As with other types of social interaction, it seems that diffusion of responsibility limits altruistic behavior. When people are members of a group, they are likely to stand back and wait for others to help the person in need. However, when others are not around, they are more likely to act altruistically.

THINKING ABOUT PSYCHOLOGY

1. Define *altruism*.
2. What factors promote altruistic behavior? What factors inhibit it?
3. **Critical Thinking** Describe two situations, one in which bystanders are likely to help a person in trouble and one in which bystanders are less likely to help. Explain your answer.

Whether we act altruistically to help others in need depends on many factors, including the presence of other bystanders who could also offer assistance.

SUMMARY

One of the most important aspects of social interaction is social influence—the ways in which other people affect what we say and do.

I. *Group Behavior*

A. Social facilitation refers to the tendency of people to perform at a higher level when others are watching.

B. Social loafing refers to the tendency for people to slack off when they are working with others toward a common goal.

C. The risky shift is the tendency to take greater risks as part of a group than as an individual acting alone.

D. The rules that govern group decision making are the majority-wins scheme; the truth-wins scheme; the two-thirds–majority scheme; and the first-shift scheme.

E. The strengthening of a group's shared attitudes, as group members discuss and act upon them, is referred to as polarization.

F. Styles of leadership vary greatly. Group leaders may be authoritarian, democratic, or laissez-faire.

II. *Conformity*

A. Being accepted by a group is important because groups help people satisfy many psychological needs.

B. Belonging to a group usually means conforming to the group's explicit and implicit social norms.

C. Psychologist Solomon Asch conducted experiments to determine why most people conform to social norms.

D. Several factors contribute to the tendency to conform to social norms. These factors include being a member of a collectivistic culture, the need to be liked and accepted by other people, and the size and unanimity of the group.

III. *Obedience*

A. Psychologist Stanley Milgram conducted experiments to see if people would obey the commands of authority figures even when those commands conflicted with their own attitudes.

B. Obedience to authority is influenced by socialization, the foot-in-the-door effect, confusion about attitudes, and buffers.

IV. *Aggression*

A. Sociobiologists believe that aggression helps people survive, reproduce, and transmit their genes to the next generation.

B. Freud believed that aggressive urges are natural but that they tend to be repressed and only expressed indirectly or toward strangers later in life.

C. Cognitive psychologists believe that people choose to exhibit aggressive behavior because they think that aggression is justified and necessary.

D. Learning theorists believe that people learn to be aggressive through reinforcement and observational learning.

E. Sociocultural theorists believe that some cultures encourage independence and competitiveness and that this, in turn, promotes aggression.

V. *Altruism*

A. The factors that promote altruistic behavior are being in a good mood, being sensitive to the problems of others, being empathic, being competent to help, needing social approval, and having a sense of responsibility for others.

B. Factors that inhibit altruism include being unsure that another person needs help, believing there is nothing one can do to help, being afraid of making a social blunder, and being afraid of getting hurt.

C. The bystander effect inhibits altruism.

TERM & CONCEPT REVIEW

1. What is the difference between obedience and conformity? Give an example of each.
2. Define *foot-in-the-door effect.*
3. What is the difference between explicit and implicit social norms?
4. Why are people in collectivistic cultures more likely to conform to social norms?
5. How does evaluation apprehension contribute to social facilitation?
6. Explain the relationship between diffusion of responsibility and the risky shift.
7. Give an example of polarization, and explain how it occurs.
8. *Define aggression,* and give examples of aggressive behavior.
9. Why do some psychologists believe that catharsis can help prevent aggression?
10. What is the bystander effect?

CRITICAL THINKING

1. How do you think a sociobiologist and a learning theorist would explain the tendency for people to obey authority figures?
2. Think of a group to which a typical teen might belong. What needs do you think the group is likely to fulfill?
3. Imagine that a high school Spanish club is trying to decide how to raise money for a trip to Spain. Describe how group members might come to a decision using the truth-wins social decision scheme.
4. Both sociobiologists and psychoanalysts have explanations for human aggression. What are the similarities and differences between the two explanations?
5. Explain how the bystander effect is related to evaluation apprehension. Give examples to illustrate this relationship.

APPLYING SKILLS IN PSYCHOLOGY

1. **Research in Psychology** Over the next week, take a survey of several television programs that are aimed at young children. As you watch each program, make note of all verbal and physical aggressive behaviors that occur. Calculate how many times aggression occurs per hour of viewing time. What effect do you think this amount of television violence has on viewers? Summarize your observations and analysis in a brief written report.

2. **Using Your Observation Skills** Request permission to attend a meeting of a school or community organization. During the meeting, take notes on how the group's leader conducts the meeting. Afterward, review your notes and decide what style of leadership was used. How might the meeting have been conducted if another style of leadership had been used instead? Summarize your observations in an oral report to the rest of the class.

3. **Reading About Psychology** Read more about the sociobiological explanation for human aggression or altruism. What types of evidence and arguments are used to back the claims that the behavior helps individuals survive, reproduce, and contribute their genes to the next generation? What evidence and arguments have been presented to refute the claims? Summarize both the pros and the cons in a short written report, ending with a statement of your own position on the subject.

4. **COOPERATIVE LEARNING** **Writing About Psychology** With several other classmates, work together to write and perform a skit that shows how teens are pressured to conform to their peers in words and actions. After presenting the skit, ask the class to identify the ways in which individuals in the skit conformed to group norms. Help your group lead the class in a discussion of what might have happened if the individuals had decided not to conform.

REVIEW

IDENTIFYING PEOPLE AND IDEAS

Explain the significance of each of the following people or terms to the study of psychology.

1. attitudes
2. cognitive dissonance
3. central route
4. peripheral route
5. scapegoat
6. primacy effect
7. attribution theory
8. fundamental attribution error
9. matching hypothesis
10. reciprocity
11. Robert Sternberg
12. Stanley Milgram
13. social norms
14. social facilitation
15. evaluation apprehension
16. diffusion of responsibility
17. first-shift scheme
18. polarization
19. aggression
20. sociobiology
21. altruism
22. bystander effect

HANDS-ON PSYCHOLOGY

Individual Project

At any given time, we all belong to a group, whether it be a formal group (such as student council) or an informal group (of friends). Most people are members of several different groups. Identify eight different groups of people to which you or others belong. Try to include a wide range of groups—for example, social cliques, clubs, political parties, and sports teams. Next, divide a sheet of paper into five columns with the following headings: Group, Attitudes, Norms, Leader, and Leader's Style. Fill in the table with the appropriate information for each group. Then answer the following questions:

1. What were the most difficult items to identify about each group? Why?

2. For the groups in which you participate, do you think that an outsider would identify the same norms, attitudes, and leaders as you did? Why or why not?

BUILDING YOUR PORTFOLIO

Individually or in a group, complete the following project to show your understanding of the psychology concepts involved.

Television and Observational Learning

According to many psychologists, television is not simply entertaining children—it is also teaching them social behavioral patterns that may last a lifetime. For instance, many studies have shown that there is a correlation between the amount of violence a child watches on television and his or her

level of aggression. Although the belief that television can influence children's behavior and values is now widely accepted, many children's shows, particularly cartoons, persist in showing graphic violence and negative stereotypes of women and ethnic minorities.

Imagine that you are a concerned parent trying to find out what messages your child has been absorbing from television programs. Choose two programs aimed at children—one that is considered to be educational (such as *Sesame Street*) and one that is more entertainment oriented (such as *The Mighty Morphin Power Rangers*). You may choose from the local television listings or ask children or their parents to recommend popular programs. Watch two or three episodes of each program. Then answer the following questions:

1. Does the program portray any stereotypes, either positive or negative? If so, what are they? Does it depict characters of different cultural and ethnic backgrounds? If so, are these depictions positive or negative? Is the ratio of men to women roughly even? Does the program show characters encountering and dealing with prejudice or discrimination?

2. What is the average number of violent occurrences per episode? Is violence or aggression routinely used to address problems, or do characters use other methods to resolve conflicts? In general, is violence glorified, tolerated, or rejected in the program?

Once you have completed the questions above, organize your data into a brief report. The report should include your answers to the questions as well as a brief analysis of how these shows might affect human behavior in society.

APPENDIX

STATISTICS

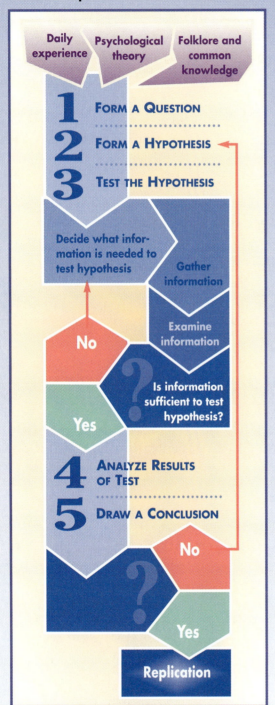

The Steps of Scientific Research

Daily experience | Psychological theory | Folklore and common knowledge

1 FORM A QUESTION

2 FORM A HYPOTHESIS

3 TEST THE HYPOTHESIS

Decide what information is needed to test hypothesis

Gather information

Examine information

No

Is information sufficient to test hypothesis?

Yes

4 ANALYZE RESULTS OF TEST

5 DRAW A CONCLUSION

No

Yes

Replication

A flow chart is used to illustrate a sequence of events or the steps in a process. This flowchart demonstrates the steps a researcher generally follows.

Reading Charts and Graphs

Charts and graphs are used to organize and present information visually. They categorize and display data in a variety of ways, depending on the type of chart or graph being used and the subject matter of the data.

Using Charts

There are several type of charts. This textbook uses the following types of charts to illustrate various concepts: flow charts, Venn diagrams, organization charts, and tables.

A *flowchart* illustrates a sequence of events or the steps in a process. "The Steps of Scientific Research," shown to the left, is an example of a flowchart. Cause-and-effect relationships are also frequently depicted in flowcharts.

Venn diagrams use circles to represent simple relationships among sets. Overlapping regions in the Venn diagram represent the intersection of information. The Venn diagram shown on page 501, for example, demonstrates that Seoul is located within South Korea and South Korea is in Asia. Therefore, it follows that Seoul is located in Asia.

An organization chart, such as the one on page 501 titled "Divisions of the Nervous System," displays the structure of a particular organization or concept. It illustrates the ranking or function of the organization's internal parts and the relationship between those parts.

A *table* is generally a multi-column chart that presents data in categories that are easy to understand and compare. This textbook frequently uses tables to organize data and concepts. For an example, see page 430.

Using Graphs

There are also several types of graphs used in this textbook. Each has certain advantages in displaying data for a particular emphasis.

A *line graph,* for example, plots changes in quantities over time. It consists of a horizontal and a vertical axis. One axis generally lists numbers or percentages, while the other axis usually marks off periods of time. A line is created by plotting data on the grid formed by the intersecting axes and then connecting the dots. "Average Growth Rates for Boys and Girls from Childhood Through Adolescence" is an example of a line graph.

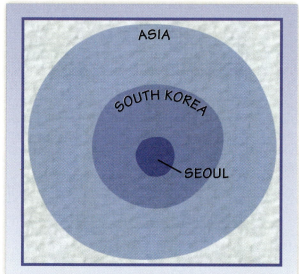

ASIA

SOUTH KOREA

SEOUL

Venn diagrams represent the intersection of information. For example, Seoul is in South Korea, which is in Asia. Therefore, Seoul is in Asia.

ber of pain receptors and sensitivity to pain and pressure in different parts of the human body.

A *pie graph*, or *circle graph*, displays proportions at a glance by showing sections of a whole, like slices of a pie, with the whole equaling 100 percent. "United States Population by Group" is an example of a pie graph.

How to Read Charts and Graphs

1. **Read the title.** Read the title to identify the focus of the chart or graph, remembering what each kind is designed to emphasize.
2. **Study the parts.** To identify the type of information presented, read the headings, subheadings, and labels that define each axis, bar, or section of the graph. Study the categories used and the specific data given for each category in a chart.
3. **Analyze the details.** Note increases or decreases in quantities. When reading dates, note intervals of time. When viewing a flowchart, follow directional arrows or lines. When reading graphs, look for trends, relationships, and changes in the data.
4. **Put the data to use.** Formulate generalizations or draw conclusions based on the data presented.

A *bar graph* can also be used to display changes in quantities over time. More often, however, bar graphs are used to compare quantities within the same category, and to summarize the differences succinctly. For example, the bar graph on page 502, "Distribution of Pain Receptors" compares the num-

Divisions of the Nervous System

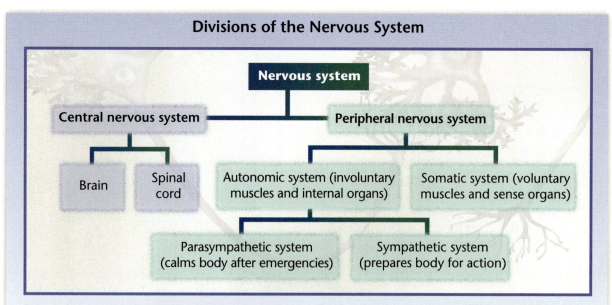

Nervous system

Central nervous system

Peripheral nervous system

Brain

Spinal cord

Autonomic system (involuntary muscles and internal organs)

Somatic system (voluntary muscles and sense organs)

Parasympathetic system (calms body after emergencies)

Sympathetic system (prepares body for action)

In an organization chart, the structure of a particular concept or organization is illustrated graphically. This organization chart, for example, shows the divisions of the human nervous system, the parts of those divisions, and the relationship between each of those parts.

Average Growth Rate for Boys and Girls from Childhood Through Adolescence

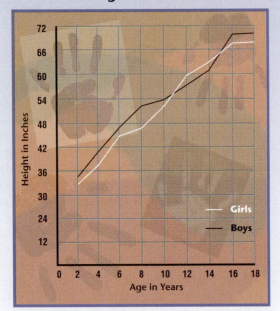

Line graphs are effective tools for illustrating the changes in a particular quantity over time. For example, this line graph demonstrates the change in height of boys and girls throughout the years of adolescence.

Source: Tanner, J.M. (1978). *Fetus into man: Physical growth from conception to maturity.* Cambridge, MA: Harvard University Press. (p. 118)

Practicing Your Skills

Use the flowchart, "The Steps of Scientific Research," on the previous page to answer questions 1 and 2. Then complete questions 3 and 4 using the bar graph an page 502.

1. Write a detailed description of the steps illustrated in the chart, but do not use numbers or refer to the chart.
2. Decide whether the information is more easily understood in chart form or in a prose description. Give reasons for your opinion.
3. Which part of the body has the most pain receptors? The fewest?
4. Assuming that the information presented in this graph is valid, do you believe that individuals differ in their sensitivities to pain? How could you account for someone claiming to have a "high pain threshold"?

Analyzing Observations

Conducting a research study is actually only a small part of the research process. Imagine that you decide to conduct a survey about the amount of television teenagers watch daily. After you conducted interviews and received dozens of completed questionnaires you would probably feel overwhelmed by the amount of data you had collected. What is the next step?

When faced with this situation, psychologists use mathematical procedures, called *statistics*, to organize, analyze, and interpret the data. Psychologists then use the statistical analyses to construct charts and graphs. In short, statistics help psychologists make sense of their research findings.

Distribution of Pain Receptors

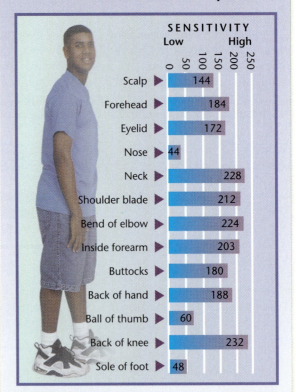

Bar graphs are a common method of comparing quantities within the same category. This bar graph compares the levels of sensitivity to pain in the various parts of the human body.

Source: Strughold, H. (1924). On the density and thresholds in the areas of pain on the epidermis in the various regions of the body. 2. Biol, 80, 367-380 (in German)

United States Population by Group

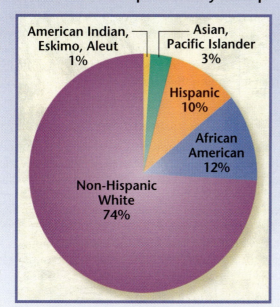

American Indian, Eskimo, Aleut 1%

Asian, Pacific Islander 3%

Hispanic 10%

African American 12%

Non-Hispanic White 74%

Pie graphs are effective tools for illustrating the proportional divisions of a central concept. This pie graph, for example, demonstrates the proportions of the various ethnic groups as a percentage of the U.S. population as a whole. Hypothetically, if the U.S. population were one million, how many African Americans would you expect there to be?

Source: Statistical Abstract of the United States 1995. Figures have been rounded.

Understanding Frequency Distributions

One of the most common forms of statistical analysis researchers use to organize their data is the *frequency distribution*. A frequency distribution is a way of arranging data to determine how often a certain piece of data—such as a score, salary, or age—occurs. In setting up a frequency distribution, researchers arrange the data from highest to lowest, and enter a mark when a piece of data occurs. The sum of each group's marks determines the frequency.

If there are too many different pieces of data to list individually, as is sometimes true for class scores, a researcher may substitute specific numerical spans, called *class intervals,* for individual scores. Again, the data are arranged from highest to lowest. A frequency distribution would allow a teacher to see at a glance how well a group of students did on a test, for instance, but it does not provide any information about individual performance.

Understanding Bell Curves

One of the most useful statistical concepts for psychologists is the *bell curve*, or *normal curve*. The bell curve is an ideal, a hypothetical standard against which actual categories of people or things (such as scores) can be measured and compared.

Usually, bell curves are used to categorize characteristics of people in large groups. The closer the group comes to the center of the curve, where the most "normal" traits congregate, the more validity the study appears to have.

For example, the bell curve, "Distribution of IQ Scores," shown on page 504, illustrates a hypothetical standard against which actual IQ scores can be compared. This curve is a model of an ideal. It shows what would happen if the largest number of scores fell exactly in the middle of a range of scores. A comparison of the actual scores against this bell curve tells psychologists how representative the IQ test really is.

A bell curve is a normal frequency distribution. This means that after counting the occurrence, or *frequency*, of specific data (scores, for instance), researchers can create an arrangement, or *distribution*, that is concentrated on or near the curve's center, which represents the norm. The fewest entries of data should appear at the far ends of the distribution—away from the highly concentrated norm.

It follows then, that when the graphed results of an experiment come close to matching a bell curve, the results are assumed to be highly representative of that experiment. If most scores or data cluster toward the ends of the curve, however, the experiment or test is assumed to be unrepresentative of the group.

Bell curves and frequency distributions seem very complicated. However, they are simply ways to condense information and put it in a visual form. Within moments of glancing at a real plotted curve and the bell curve beside it, researchers can judge approximately how far from the norm their experimental group was, and how closely their results conform to what is "perfectly" normal.

Practicing Your Skills

1. Define *frequency distribution*, and identify a situation in which you have applied this concept.
2. Look at the bell curve on page 504. What percentage of students would be expected to score between 90 and 110? Between 70 and 130?
3. What problems can you identify with basing assumptions on a bell curve?

Distribution of IQ Scores

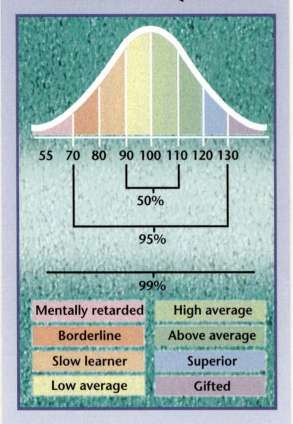

Bell curves, or normal curves, represent a hypothetical standard against which actual categories of people or things can be measured and compared. This bell curve illustrates a hypothetical standard against which actual IQ scores could be compared. If the actual scores closely represent this standard, the IQ test is considered to be valid.

Mode, Mean, and Median: Measures of Central Tendency

Three other measures are used to compare data that fall within the central points of a distribution: the *mode*, the *mean*, and the *median*.

Mode

Simply, the *mode* is the piece of data (or the score) that occurs most often in a given set of numbers. To find the mode, examine any frequency distribution and choose the number that appears most often. The mode is of limited use to researchers because "occurring most often" in a distribution may mean,

for instance, that this number occurred only twice among fifty different test scores.

Mean

The *mean* is an average. The mean is found by adding all the scores or data together and then dividing that sum by the number of scores. The formula for finding the mean is:

$$\text{mean} = \frac{\text{sum of the scores}}{\text{number of scores}}$$

A significant disadvantage of using the mean is that any extreme score, whether high or low, distorts a researcher's results. For instance, if five waiters earn $300, $350, $325, $390, and $600 per week respectively, the mean—or average—weekly salary for this group would be $393. Yet three of the five waiters earn less than the average amount. In this circumstance, using the mean would not necessarily be representative of the waiters' wages.

Median

The *median* is the score or piece of data that falls precisely in the middle of all the scores when they are arranged in descending order. Exactly half of the students score above the median, and exactly half score below it. In the previous example of waiters' salaries, the median would be $350, because two waiters earned more and two earned less than $350.

The median, unlike the mean, is usually an actual number or score. To find the median of an even number of scores, you would find the median of the two numbers that fall in the middle, and then take the mean of those two central numbers in the distribution.

One major advantage of the median is that extreme scores, high or low, will not affect it. For example, examine the following two distributions:

> **Group X:** 4, 10, 16, 18, 22
> **Group Y:** 4, 10, 16, 18, 97

The median for each group is 16, because that number falls precisely in the middle of all the scores. However, the mean for Group X is 14 (4 + 10 + 16 + 18 + 22 = 70; 70 ÷ 5 = 14), while the mean for Group Y is 29 (4 + 10 + 16 + 18 + 97 = 145; 145 ÷ 5 = 29). The mean changes dramatically simply by introducing one extreme score. The median, however, remains the same.

The kind of central point that researchers choose to use in any given situation depends on what they are trying to find out. The median is not the best choice in all instances. Actually, in a bell curve—the idealized norm—the mode, the mean, and the median are identical.

Variability

Knowing what the mode, the mean, and the median are tells a researcher a great deal but not everything about the data. Researchers also need to know how much *variability* there is among the scores in a group of numbers. That is, researchers must discover how far apart the numbers or scores are in relation to the mean. For this purpose, psychologists use two measures: the range and the standard deviation.

Range

The *range* is the mathematical difference between the highest and lowest scores in a frequency distribution. If the highest grade in a class is 100 and the lowest is 60, the range is 40 (100 – 60 = 40).

Two groups of numbers may have the same mean but different ranges. For example, consider the batting averages of two baseball teams:

> **Team A:** 210 250 285 300 340
> **Team B:** 270 270 275 285 285

The mean for each team is 277. However, the range for Team A is 130 points, whereas the range for Team B is 15 points. This would tell a researcher that Team B is more alike in its batting abilities than is Team A.

The range tells psychologists how similar the subjects in each group are to one another in terms of what is being measured. This information could not be obtained from the mode, the mean, or the median alone, since each is just one number and not a comparison.

The disadvantage of the range, though, is that it takes only the lowest and highest scores of a frequency distribution into account. The middle numbers may be substantially different in two groups that have the same range. For example, here are two distributions:

> **Group A:** 5, 8, 12, 14, 15
> **Group B:** 5, 6, 7, 8, 15

Each group has the same range of 10. But the scores in Group A differ greatly from the scores in Group B.

For this reason, psychologists often use the standard deviation.

Standard Deviation

Psychologists sometimes want to know how much any particular score is likely to vary from the mean, or how spread out the scores are around the mean. To derive these measures, researchers calculate the standard deviation. The closer the standard deviation is to zero, the more reliable that data tends to be.

Let's say that the standard deviation of Team A's batting average is about 44.2, and the standard deviation of Team B's batting average is 6.8. From this information we know that the typical score of Team A will fall within 44.2 points of the mean, and the typical score of Team B will be within 6.8 points of the mean. This tells us that the quality of batting is more consistent on Team B than on Team A.

Two bell curves can have the same mode, mean, and median, but different standard deviations. If you were plotting two bell curves on a line graph, and one curve had a much larger standard deviation than the other, the curve with the larger standard deviation would show a more pronounced bell shape on the graph.

Correlation

Correlation is a measure of the relationship between two variables. A *variable* is any behavior or condition that can change in quantity or quality. Examples of variables that people frequently encounter are age, hair color, weight, and height.

Correlation and causation are two types of relationships between variables that have great importance for psychologists.

When two variables are related, they are said to have a *correlation*. Changes in variables often occur together. Sometimes, an increase or decrease in one is accompanied by a corresponding increase or decrease in the other. For example, a decrease in someone's caloric intake is accompanied by a decrease in that person's weight. Such variables are said to be *positively correlated*.

Sometimes, when one variable increases, the other decreases, or vice-versa. These variables are said to be *negatively correlated*. Examples of positive and negative correlations are illustrated in the chart on page 506.

STATISTICS

Correlation Coefficient

The *correlation coefficient* describes the degree of relationship between variables. The concept of correlation allows researchers to predict the value of one variable if they know the value of the other and the way that the variables are correlated. A perfect positive correlation would have a coefficient of +1.00; a perfect negative correlation has a coefficient of –1.00. A correlation coefficient of zero indicates that there is no correlation between two variables.

Perfect positive correlations (+ 1.00 coefficient), when graphed, form a straight line that leans to the right; a perfect negative correlation (–1.00 coefficient), shown on a line graph, would form a straight line to the left. In reality, few correlations are perfect. While one variable may increase or decrease in relation to the other, both variables probably will not change to the same degree.

The following is an example of a strong negative correlation with predictive potential: The more hours Tracy spends commuting to work, the less she enjoys driving. We can predict that if Tracy shortens her commute, her enjoyment of driving will increase.

Causation

Although correlation is an important concept in statistics, it does not explain everything about relationships between variables. For one thing, correlation does not speak to the concept of causation. No correlation, of any degree, in itself proves that one variable causes another.

It is difficult to determine whether one variable actually causes another. Researchers determine causal relationships scientifically rather than relying on the intuitive sense of causality that may be implied in a correlation. They compare the differences between an experimental group—the group that displays the condition that is being studied—and a control group, in which this condition is not present. The *independent variable* is the variable being manipulated by the researcher.

If Group A is exposed to a virus and gets sick, and Group B is exposed to the same virus but has been vaccinated and does not become ill, there appears to be a causal relationship at work. It seems that the vaccine protected Group B from the virus, and therefore from illness. But researchers probably would want to examine how the vaccine actually worked—if it did. It may have been coincidental that Group B remained well.

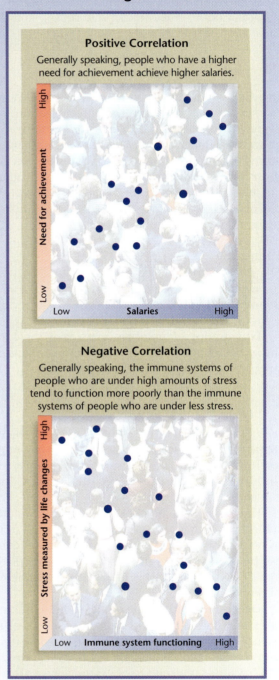

Positive and Negative Correlations

Positive Correlation

Generally speaking, people who have a higher need for achievement achieve higher salaries.

Negative Correlation

Generally speaking, the immune systems of people who are under high amounts of stress tend to function more poorly than the immune systems of people who are under less stress.

Correlations represent the relationship between two variables. When two variables show a positive correlation, one rises as the other rises. If the two variables are negatively correlated, one of the variables rises as the other falls.

CAREERS IN PSYCHOLOGY

Overview

A career in psychology is bound to be fascinating, for the fundamental subject matter is, after all, us. That so many people decide to study human behavior, in all its diversity, should come as no surprise. The range of specializations and kinds of jobs available within the broad area of psychology are so varied that there may well be a career in psychology to suit almost everyone's interests.

But how can you start narrowing the field for yourself? What educational training and personality characteristics are required for each psychology-related career? How do you decide on a specialization and actually become a psychologist?

Career opportunities in the field abound on every educational level. If you are most interested in relating to people directly, and helping them deal with serious mental or emotional problems in therapy, perhaps you will consider becoming a clinical psychologist. This is the area that most people think of when they hear the word "psychologist." Many clinical psychologists specialize in treating one or more specific problems, such as substance abuse, eating disorders, or phobias. Others specialize in group treatment settings, working as family therapists or couples therapists, for instance. But clinical psychology is just one of numerous possibilities.

Other careers in psychology do not necessarily involve working directly with people or doing therapy at all. If you enjoy working in a laboratory and conducting basic scientific research, you may be attracted to the exacting field of experimental psychology. Some fields offer a combination of research- and people-oriented work. As an industrial or organizational psychologist, for example, you might apply psychological techniques to work-oriented issues in a business environment.

The first step to pursuing a career in psychology is usually a four-year university degree, consisting of specific core courses. In addition, today's student is well-advised to take a course in computer science, which is mandatory for conducting research.

Not all careers related to psychology require graduate study. Options in psychological careers with a four-year bachelor's degree (B.A. or B.S.) alone do exist, although they tend to be somewhat limited in scope. Examples include working as an aide or a social worker in a mental hospital, hospice, nursing home, residential treatment center for disturbed youth, or

government agency. These same settings, among others, offer psychology-related careers in administration, human resources, and customer service.

Most careers in psychology, however, now require at least a master of arts or master of science degree (M.A. or M.S.), and often a doctoral degree (Ph.D. or Ed.Psy.). It takes about two years of study in a graduate program to earn a master's degree, and about four to six years above that to earn a doctoral degree.

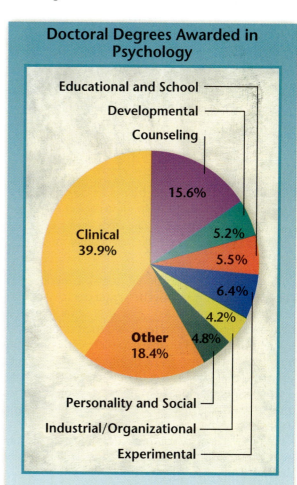

Doctoral Degrees Awarded in Psychology

- Educational and School
- Developmental
- Counseling — 15.6%
- 5.2%
- 5.5%
- 6.4%
- 4.2%
- Clinical 39.9%
- Other 18.4% — 4.8%
- Personality and Social
- Industrial/Organizational
- Experimental

Career opportunities in the field of psychology are both numerous and diverse. Preparation for these careers generally begins with a doctoral degree. This graph illustrates the percentage of doctoral degrees awarded in the various areas of psychological specialization.

Source: *Summary Report Doctorate Recipients from United States Universities* (Table W04846), Office of Demographic, Employment, and Educational Research, 1994, Washington, DC: American Psychological Association.

Clinical psychologists are trained to diagnose and treat individuals with various psychological disorders such as this woman suffering from depression—as well as other social and adjustment problems.

severe behavioral or adjustment problems. In the course of their work, clinical psychologists may deal with such diverse problems as severe depression and other psychological disorders, juvenile delinquency, drug abuse, marital problems, or eating disorders.

People often confuse clinical psychologists with psychiatrists. The distinction is a significant one, however. In treating their patients, clinical psychologists conduct interviews, practice methods of psychotherapy, and administer and interpret psychological tests. They are not, however, able to prescribe medication or administer other kinds of biological therapy. Psychiatrists, on the other hand, are medical doctors who specialize in the treatment of psychological disorders. By law, only psychiatrists have the right and responsibility to prescribe medication to their clients.

Many clinical psychologists with doctoral degrees maintain a private practice, where they see clients who voluntarily come to them for treatment. Others, however, work in veteran's hospitals, mental health clinics, schools for the mentally retarded, or correctional institutions, where they are generally assigned to a specific number of patients.

Many clinical psychologists teach—primarily in colleges, universities, or medical schools—where they pass on their experience and knowledge to others, rather than apply their skills directly. Still others conduct workshops on specific topics, and engage in the training of business professionals or other psychologists. Those with literary talents often write scholarly or popular books and articles.

Clinical psychologists may be self-employed, or hired by government, business, schools, universities, hospitals, prisons, or nonprofit organizations, as consultants or full-time employees. The field is extremely flexible, thus it is also becoming more competitive, as is admission to strong graduate programs. Clinical psychologists also must be licensed by the state in which they live and work.

For careers in educational, social, experimental, clinical, or counseling psychology, a doctoral degree is highly recommended. However, many people take some time off after receiving their undergraduate degree to gain valuable experience in laboratory or clinical work instead of plunging into years and years of schooling. In fact, if you intend to become a school or educational psychologist, your state may require that you first gain a few years of teaching experience.

Whatever career you ultimately select, it should be rewarding for you, personally. Rewarding opportunities in psychology exist on all levels.

Clinical Psychologist

About half of all graduate degrees in psychology are awarded in the demanding field of clinical psychology. In this sense, clinical psychology is the most popular branch of psychology. Some clinical psychologists work with individuals who suffer from severe psychological disorders, while others prefer to limit their practices to treating people with less

Counseling Psychologist

Like clinical psychologists, counseling psychologists work with people experiencing personal distress. Counseling psychologists, however, tend to treat people who are confronted with stressful or highly emotional situations, rather than people who have more severe mental disorders. For example, a cou-

CAREERS

ple having marital difficulties might go to a counseling psychologist in the hopes of avoiding a divorce. The suicide of a family member may prompt a person to seek out a counseling psychologist's support and perspective for a few months.

People with a chronic physical disease or a catastrophic illness often look to counselors for help in coping with difficulties of various magnitudes that feel overwhelming. It may be that a high school students feels anxious because she believes that her parents expect too much of her, for instance, or that a formerly happy young man experiences depression after a job loss.

Differences between clinical and counseling psychologists are growing fainte. Both the work itself and the educational requirements in most graduate schools, are nearly identical. Also, the same types of employers that hire clinical psychologists are likely to hire counseling psychologists of the same educational level for the same positions. The final choice to become a clinical or a counseling psychologist ultimately may be determined by the specific graduate program that you find most appealing.

Counseling psychologists tend to work with patients who are faced with stressful or emotional situations. They help people to confront and overcome their fears or other disturbing emotions.

Both clinical and counseling psychologists use the techniques and theories with which they personally agree. They must be careful, however, not to impose their views on their clients. Both types of psychologist might use psychological assessments or tests to evaluate their clients. Graduate programs in counseling psychology, however, tend not to emphasize research as much as do programs that train clinical psychologists.

Subspecialties in Counseling Psychology

Career counselors (also known as vocational counselors) administer interest-inventory and other psychological tests to help people make appropriate and gratifying career choices. They may work with university students, with adult career-changers, or in private businesses or corporations. Career counselors may lead workshops on job-searching skills, facilitate discussion and support groups, and sometimes work with motivated clients on a one-to-one basis. Some career counselors also function as intermediaries between industry and colleges, helping to place new graduates in jobs, or directing them to other resources. This career invites outgoing people who love helping others and who thrive in a relatively fast-paced, upbeat environment that addresses a rather limited range of problems in a practical manner.

Rehabilitation counselors work with physically challenged individuals, helping them adapt to their disabilities and become self-sufficient and self-supporting. They work with people of all ages, whether disabled after an accident, an illness, or from birth. Their primary job is a tough one: helping people face the hard reality of having physical challenges while remaining realistic, yet hopeful, about the client's potential.

Rehabilitation (or occupational) counselors help prepare clients for jobs that they are capable of doing. In some cases, they also arrange for additional training. Part of their job may entail soliciting potential employers for their clients while also acting as morale coaches in an individual's physical and emotional rehabilitative process.

A master's degree in rehabilitative counseling (often offered within university departments of education or health/kinesthesiology) is recommended, but a bachelor's degree in psychology, especially with volunteer experience, may be an acceptable substitute. This can be an extremely rewarding career, though also a frustrating one, as in the case of any career that requires frequent contact with bureaucratic agencies. Rehabilitation counselors must demonstrate persistence, dedication, patience, and stamina.

Teachers of special education face similar tasks and issues as rehabilitation counselors (or therapists, as they are sometimes known). The objective of both special education teachers and rehabilitation counselors is the same: helping people with disabilities achieve their full potential.

School counselors (or school psychologists) work with students, teachers, and administrators to make the school the best possible environment for learning. One of their primary tasks is to help students who are having problems that interfere with learning. These problems may involve peers, families, teachers, coursework, or a combination of these and other factors. Such counselors must be observant and knowledgeable enough to identify and diagnose a student's problems, devise possible solutions, and make recommendations regarding a student's placement in special education or gifted classes.

Like other counseling psychologists, school counselors make use of a range of intelligence, interest, and psychological tests. A routine part of the job

The primary tasks of a school counselor are to administer, score, and interpret the results of standardized tests.

is administering and scoring standardized tests. More importantly, the school psychologist interprets these test results. This interpretation is then used to identify and address the special needs of individual students.

In some cases, school psychologists are also called in to resolve conflicts, either between students and teachers, students and parents, or students and other students. The psychologist will generally listen to both sides of the dispute and try to resolve the conflict with an amicable compromise.

Some states require school counselors to obtain a teaching credential and gain practical experience in the classroom. Training for school counselors usually takes place through a college's department of education, not necessarily within the psychology department. If you are tactful yet assertive, and flourish in the challenging school environment, this rewarding career may be high on your list of considerations.

Educational Psychologist

Should classrooms consist of one age student only, or should students be grouped according to skill levels, regardless of age? Should a school district revise its curriculum and teaching methods to meet the changing needs of students? How can computers facilitate learning in the classroom?

Educational psychologists study how people learn. They perform research—both in and out of the classroom—geared to facilitating the learning process and improving education as a whole. Although educational psychologists typically work for school districts, they are frequently employed by universities, where they engage in research and assist in training teachers and school counselors.

Unlike school psychologists, educational psychologists are more involved with theoretical issues that affect learning rather than with individual students. Their research often involves measuring a group's abilities and achievements by administering, and sometimes creating, standardized tests. Educational psychologists then use the results of these tests to help place students in specific programs and to develop curricula in schools.

Educational psychologists may focus on several other issues. They may, for example, study the psychological factors that affect a student's test-taking

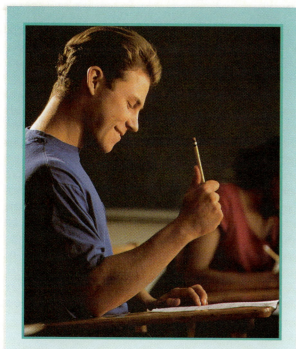

Educational psychologists do not generally work with individual students. They do, however, develop curriculum standards and teaching methods. Thus, indirectly, they have a profound effect on the individual student's education.

ability or school performance in general. They may research the effects that cultural and gender differences have on learning.

Educational psychologists also analyze the range of instructional methods available to teachers in the classroom. Then they use their research discoveries to expand or refine these instructional options.

Work for educational psychologists is not necessarily limited to the academic environment, however. Large corporations and government agencies often hire educational psychologists to devise staff training programs.

A bachelor's degree in psychology is the first step of the long, complex process of becoming an educational psychologist. Candidates are urged to gain teaching experience on the elementary, middle school, or high school levels before pursuing a doctoral program within a university's education or psychology department. Since the work of educational psychologists involves evaluating and interpreting research data, the training requires proficiency in mathematics, statistics, and computer science.

Depending on the graduate program, the final degree earned will be a Doctor of Education (Ed.D.) or a Doctor of Philosophy (Ph.D.). Although educational psychology is a difficult profession to break into, it is an attractive career for those who wish to affect the course of the educational system itself.

Developmental Psychologist

At what age do children develop the ability to think abstractly? Does isolation reduce short-term memory in elderly people? Why do infants need more sleep than older children? If questions related to stages of life intrigue you, perhaps you would want to become a developmental psychologist.

Developmental psychologists study the behavioral changes that occur at various stages in a person's life. In the past, developmental psychology was limited to the study of changes in the developmental stages in children. For this reason, it was called *child psychology.* Recently, however, researchers have become aware that people experience complex and interconnected physical, psychological, intellectual, and social changes throughout the entire life span.

Among the contemporary issues developmental psychologists are concerned with is the question of how our ability to perform certain tasks changes throughout our lifetime. Developmental psychologists also investigate language acquisition, changes in perception, creativity, sensory acuity, intellectual abilities, and emotions at different stages of life.

Most developmental psychologists focus on a certain period in the life span, such as infancy, childhood, adolescence, middle age, or old age. This last category, called *gerontology*, promises to be particularly important in the future, as the country's population ages and life spans increase.

Another topic of interest to developmental psychologists includes the changing roles of men and women in society. They study the impact of gender stereotyping and the implications of that stereotyping on a child's development.

Developmental psychologists usually work for universities, teaching and conducting research. Many combine academic careers with a secondary career in writing, as a natural outgrowth of their interests. Some developmental psychologists also work in clinical settings such as hospitals, prisons, nursing homes, schools, group homes, nursery schools, or hospices.

Developmental psychologists no longer limit their research to children only. The field has expanded to address the behavioral changes that occur throughout the lifespan.

As our society changes, new and exciting issues will be raised. Developmental psychologists are likely to lead the way in answering these questions. The more we learn, the more we will understand about human development and behavior.

Social Psychologist

How do individuals behave in social and group situations? Do boys and girls play differently, and if so, why? Do people's styles of interacting change in the workplace?

Social psychologists study the effects of group membership on individual behavior. Their primary focus is, generally, how behavior in social situations affects individuals. However, social psychologists tend to focus on external influences and environments. They focus on such issues as attitudes, influence, and social cognition and interaction.

Social psychologists are often confused with social workers. Both focus on social behavior. Social workers, however, are more involved with individuals. Their work is more practical and less research oriented than the work of the social psychologist.

There is a distinct overlap with the field of anthropology as well. Anthropologists also study social behavior, but they are more concerned with the social customs, rituals, and interaction of various groups of people.

Finally, social psychology is also closely related to sociology. There is, however, a distinct difference between the two. Social psychologists focus on the effects of group membership on the behavior of an individual person. Sociologists, on the other hand are more concerned with the group as a whole—its structure and characteristics.

Some issues that social psychologists explore may involve gender studies, conformity, or peer

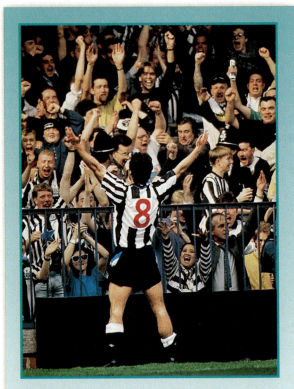

Social psychologists study the effects of group membership on individual behavior. They may be interested to study how this aggressive crowd as a whole affects the thoughts and behavior of any single individual in the crowd.

pressure. They may study more specific issues as well—such as the effects of prejudice and discrimination on self-esteem.

Many social psychologists prefer to conduct their research in a naturalistic environment rather than in a laboratory. In a naturalistic observation they have less control of the variables in the study, but the results are based on "real-life" factors.

Preparation for this multi-dimensional career is by no means uniform. Social psychologists usually first obtain a bachelor's degree in psychology, anthropology, or sociology. A doctoral degree in social psychology or anthropology offers the most flexibility and career advancement in research.

Many social psychologists are employed in dedicated research facilities or in universities. They may work in industry, where they can study consumer spending habits. They may work for the newspaper where they write articles on the causes and possible prevention of riots. The options in this field are vast and rewarding. People who enjoy observing others, gathering and synthesizing information, and being associated with academic settings are most likely to be happy in this stimulating field.

Experimental Psychologist

Why do people need sleep? What biological processes contribute to the feelings of happiness and sadness? Where in the brain does the ability to recognize faces reside?

Generally considered the most scientific of psychological disciplines, experimental psychologists conduct research into the basic biological processes related to behavior, thoughts, and emotions. They follow a set of strictly controlled scientific procedures to learn about the relationship between two or more variables. Their research usually emphasizes physiological studies of the nervous system, the brain itself, and the basic processes of thinking, feeling, remembering, and perceiving external stimuli.

Experimental psychologists lay the groundwork for more practical kinds of psychological research and counseling. This basic research, which may seem to have no practical value at the time it is conducted, has led other researchers to develop useful techniques for reducing stress, increasing motivation, enhancing memory, and encouraging longer attention spans, for example.

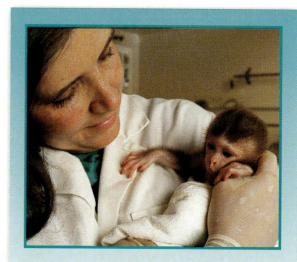

Experimental psychologists often work with animals. They try, however, to ensure that the animals are handled in a humane manner.

Experimental psychologists do not necessarily try to apply the knowledge they acquire. That is, they do not try to use their research to solve practical problems. They generally leave the actual application of research findings for psychologists from other fields to implement.

In conducting their research, experimental psychologists often work with animals. They may compare the behavior of one species with that of another. In many cases, experimental psychologists use primates because their behavior is so similar to that of humans. The use of animals in research procedures is a matter of continual ethical debate. The benefits from using them, however, generally outweigh the potential harms. Also, experimental psychologists are extremely careful to make sure the animals receive humane treatment.

Temperament may be one of the most important factors when considering a career in experimental psychology because it takes a certain type of person to think in these process-oriented terms. Like those in other basic research fields, experimental psychologists tend to be highly detail-oriented, patient individuals who easily become absorbed in their work, and do not require regular, close contact with other people. They tend to be independent, abstract thinkers who prefer working in laboratory settings. A doctoral degree is mandatory for the most engrossing work in experimental psychology. Candidates must have strong preparation in the hard sciences, with a concentration on courses in neuroanatomy, physiology, biology and molecular biology, and genetics. Undergraduates often major in psychology, but a degree in any biological science, accompanied with appropriate courses in psychology, is usually an acceptable start.

Most graduate programs prefer candidates who have already demonstrated some competency in research and laboratory skills before entering the doctoral program. If a career in experimental psychology appeals to you, it would be wise to gain some exposure to research science as an undergraduate, or even while still in high school.

Industrial/Organizational Psychologist

What color package most attracts the eyes of shoppers? How can a company arrange cubicles to maximize space without isolating employees from each other? How would a department lay-off affect the company's morale, as a whole?

Psychology enters the workplace with industrial or organizational psychologists. Organizational psychologists are usually employed by business or government to figure out ways of increasing productivity, improving working conditions, and saving money in the process. Organizational psychologists generally consult with various divisions of one or more companies.

They are often consulted by the marketing divisions of companies. Here, they conduct surveys and focus groups to help marketing divisions determine their advertising campaigns based on the psychological profile of their intended audience. They may also be called upon by the human resource department to create a new series of questions for interviewers, or to suggest ways to improve employee morale. They may also be called upon by the administrative department to assess the company's time-management program.

The more the workplace changes, the more need there will be for organizational/industrial psychologists to smooth things out. And so far, there is no sign that the workplace will cease changing.

Like counselors, organizational/industrial psychologists assume the titles indicated by the specific work they perform. If working for an oil company or a conservation organization, they may be called

environmental psychologists. If they work for an advertising firm, perhaps they'll be called *consumer psychologists.* Working for a hospital, a health maintenance organization, or for government health agency on issues of preventive health and health promotion awareness, they may be called *health psychologists.*

As is the case throughout the psychological profession, a master's degree is usually the basic educational requirement for more challenging positions, with doctorates becoming more prevalent. Although industrial/organizational psychology is one of the less visible careers in psychology, it is one of the most far-reaching in terms of the work's impact on the public. The career choices available to those individuals qualified for industrial/organizational psychology are quite extensive. There are no fewer choices than there types of industries. Industrial/Organizational psychology, thus, offers some of the most varied of career opportunities. The field is most appealing to people who have a knack for spotting trends, are relatively outgoing, and who get along well with a variety of individuals and groups.

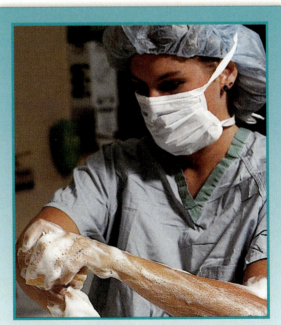

An organizational/industrial psychologist may be interested in studying how stressful work environments—such as that experienced by surgeons—affects a person's psychological health.

Aaronson, B. S. (1972). Color perception and effect. *American Journal of Clinical Hypnosis, 14,* 38–43.

Aber, J. L., & Allen, J. P. (1987). Effects of maltreatment of young children on young children's socioemotional development: An attachment theory perspective. *Developmental Psychology, 23,* 406–414.

Abramson, M. Y., Metalsky, G. I., & Alloy, L. B. (1989). Hopelessness-depression: A theory-based subtype of depression. *Psychological Review, 9,* 358–372.

Abramson, L. Y., Seligman, M. E. P., & Teasdale, J. D. (1978). Learned helplessness in humans: Critique and reformulation. *Journal of Abnormal Psychology, 87,* 49–74.

Ackerman, G. L. (1993). A congressional view of youth suicide. *American Psychologist, 48,* 183–184.

Adams, D. M., Overholser, J. C., & Spirito, A. (1992, August). *Life stress related to adolescent suicide attempts.* Paper presented at the meeting of the American Psychological Association, Washington, DC.

Ader, D. N., & Johnson, S. B. (1994). Sample description, reporting, and analysis of sex in psychological research: A look at APA and APA division journals in 1990. *American Psychologist, 49,* 216–218.

Ader, R. (1993). Conditioned responses. In B. Moyers (Ed.), *Healing and the mind.* New York: Doubleday.

Adler, A. (1927). *Understanding human nature.* Greenwich, CT: Fawcett.

Adler, T. (1993a). Shy, bold temperament? It's mostly in the genes. *APA Monitor, 24*(1), 7–8.

Adler, T. (1993b). Sleep loss impairs attention—and more. *APA Monitor, 24*(9), 22–23.

Agras, W. S., & Kirkley, B. G. (1986). Bulimia: Theories of etiology. In K. D. Brownell & J. P. Foreyt (Eds.), *Handbook of eating disorders.* New York: Basic Books.

Ainsworth, M. D. S. (1973). The development of infant-mother attachment. In B. Caldwell & H. Ricciuti (Eds.), *Review of child development research* (Vol. 3). Chicago: University of Chicago Press.

Ainsworth, M. D. S. (1979). Infant-mother attachment. *American Psychologist, 34,* 932–937.

Ainsworth, M. D. S., Blehar, M. L., Waters, E., & Wall, S. (1978). *Patterns of attachment.* Hillsdale, NJ: Erlbaum.

Ainsworth, M. D. S., & Bowlby, J. (1991). An ethological approach to personality development. *American Psychologist, 46,* 333–341.

Akhtar, N., & Bradley, E. J. (1991). Social information processing deficits of aggressive children: Present findings and implications for social skills training. *Clinical Psychology Review, 11,* 621–644.

Allen, J., Blanton, P., Johnson-Greene, D., Murphy-Farmer, C., et al. (1992). Need for achievement and performance on measures of behavioral fluency. *Psychological Reports, 71,* 471–478.

Allison, J., Blatt, S. J., & Zimet, C. N. (1988). *The interpretation of psychological tests.* Washington, DC: Hemisphere.

Allison, K. W., Crawford, I., Echemendia, R., Robinson, L. V., & Knepp, D. (1994). Human diveristy and professional competence. *American Psychologist, 49,* 792–796.

Alloy, L. B. (1988). *Cognitive processes in depression.* New York: Guilford Press.

Alloy, L. B., & Clements, C. M. (1992). Illusion of control: Invulnerability to negative affect and depressive symptoms after laboratory and natural stressors. *Journal of Abnormal Psychology, 101,* 234–245.

Allport, G. (1937). *Personality: A psychological interpretation.* New York: Holt, Rinehart and Winston.

Allport, G. (1961). *Pattern and growth in personality.* New York: Holt, Rinehart and Winston.

Allport, G. (1965). *Letters from Jenny.* New York: Harcourt Brace Jovanovich.

Allport, G. (1966). Traits revisited. *American Psychologist, 21,* 1–10.

Allport, G., & Odbert, H. S. (1936). Trait names: A psycho-lexical study. *Psychological Monographs, 47*(211), 1–171.

Allread, R. A. (1990). Gender differences in spelling achievement in grades 1 through 6. *Journal of Educational Research, 83,* 187–193.

Alsaker, F. D. (1992). Pubertal timing, overweight, and psychological adjustment. *Journal of Early Adolescence, 12,* 396–419.

Amaro, H. (1995). Love, sex, and power: Considering women's realities in HIV prevention. *American Psychologist, 50,* 437–447.

Amato, P. R., & Keith, B. (1991). Parental divorce and the well-being of children: A meta-analysis. *Psychological Bulletin, 110,* 26–46.

American Association of University Women. (1992). *How schools shortchange women: The A.A.U.W. report.* Washington, DC: A.A.U.W. Educational Foundation.

American Polygraph Association. (1992). Cited in Bashore, T. R., & Rapp, P. E. (1993). Are there alternatives to traditional polygraph procedures? *Psychological Bulletin, 113,* 3–22.

American Psychiatric Association. (1987). *Diagnostic and Statistical Manual of Mental Disorders* (3rd ed.). Washington DC: Author.

American Psychiatric Association. (1994). *Diagnostic and Statistical Manual of Mental Disorders* (4th ed.). Washington DC: Author.

American Psychological Association. (1990). *The practice of electroconvulsive therapy.* Washington, DC: Author.

American Psychological Association. (1993a). American Psychological Association Commission on Violence and Youth. *American Psychologist, 48,* 89.

American Psychological Association. (1993b). Guidelines for providers of psychological services to ethnic, linguistic, and culturally diverse populations. *American Psychologist, 48,* 45–48.

American Psychological Association. (1994a). *Ethical principles of psychologists and code of conduct.* Washington, DC: Author.

American Psychological Association. (1994b). *Publication manual of the American Psychological Association* (4th ed.). Washington, DC: Author.

Andersen, B. L., Kiecolt-Glaser, J. K., & Glaser, R. (1994). A biobehavioral model of cancer stress and disease course. *American Psychologist, 49,* 389–404.

Andersson, T., & Magnusson, D. (1990). Biological maturation in adolescence and the development of drinking habits and alcohol abuse among young males: A prospective longitudinal study. *Journal of Youth and Adolescence, 19*(1), 33–41.

Andreasen, N. C. (1988). Brain imaging: Applications in psychiatry. *Science, 239,* 1381–1388.

Andreasen, N., Ehrhardt, J., Sayze, V., Alliger, R., Yuh, W., Cohen, G., & Ziebell, S. (1990). Magnetic resonance imaging of the brain in schizophrenia. *Archives of General Psychiatry, 47,* 35–44.

Angell, M. (1993). Privilege and health—What is the connection? *New England Journal of Medicine, 329,* 126–127.

Angier, N. (1994). Factor in female sexuality. *The New York Times,* p. C13.

Annunziata, J., & Jacobson-Kram, P. (1995). *Solving your problems together: Family therapy for the whole family.* Washington, DC: American Psychological Association.

Antoni, M. H. (1987). Neuroendocrine influences in psychoimmunology and neoplasia: A review. *Psychology and Health, 1,* 3–24.

Antoni, M. H., et al. (1991). Cognitive-behavioral stress management intervention buffers distress responses and immunologic changes following notification of HIV-1 seropositivity. *Journal of Consulting and Clinical Psychology, 59,* 906–915.

Antonuccio, D. (1995). Psychotherapy for depression: No stronger medicine. *American Psychologist, 50,* 452–454.

Apter, T. (1995). *Secret paths: Women in the new midlife.* New York: Norton.

Archer, R. P., & Cash, T. F. (1985). Physical attractiveness and maladjustment among psychiatric patients. *Journal of Social and Clinical Psychology, 3,* 170–180.

Archer, S. L. (1991). Gender differences in identity development. In J. Brooks-Gunn, R. Lerner, & A. C. Petersen (Eds.), *Encyclopedia of adolescence, II.* New York: Garland.

Archer, S. L. (1992). A feminist's approach to identity research. In G. R. Adams, T. P. Gullotta, & R. Montemayor (Eds.), *Adolescent identity formation.* Newbury Park, CA: Sage.

Archer, S. L., & Waterman, A. S. (1990). Varieties of identity diffusions and foreclosures: An exploration of subcategories of the identity statuses. *Journal of Adolescent Research, 5,* 96–111.

Arlow, J. A. (1989). Psychoanalysis. In R. J. Corsini & D. Wedding (Eds.), *Current psychotherapies* (4th ed., pp. 19–62). Itasca, IL: Peacock.

Arnold, D. H., Lonigan, C. J., Whitehurst, G. J., & Epstein, J. N. (1994). Accelerating language development through picture book reading: Replication and extension to a videotape training format. *Journal of Educational Psychology, 86,* 235–243.

Asch, S. E. (1955). Opinions and social pressure. *Scientific American, 193,* 31–35.

Atchley, R. C. (1991). *Social forces and aging* (6th ed.). Belmont, CA: Wadsworth.

Atkinson, R. C. (1975). Mnemotechnics in second-language learning. *American Psychologist, 30,* 821–828.

Atkinson, R. L., Atkinson, R. C., Smith, E. E., Bem, D. J., & Nolen-Hoeksema, S. (1996). *Hilgard's introduction to psychology* (12th ed.). Fort Worth, TX: Harcourt Brace College Publishers.

Attie, I., Brooks-Gunn, J., & Petersen, A. C. (1990). A developmental perspective on eating disorders and eating problems. In M. Lewis & S. M. Miller (Eds.), *Handbook of developmental psychopathology.* New York: Plenum Press.

Audrain, J. E., Klesges, R. C., & Klesges, L. M. (1995). Relationship between obesity status and the metabolic effects of smoking in women. *Health Psychology, 14,* 116–123.

Averill, J. R. (1993). Autonomic response patterns during sadness and mirth. *Psychophysiology, 5,* 399–414.

Ayllon, T., & Haughton, E. (1962). Control of the behavior of schizophrenic patients by food. *Journal of the Experimental Analysis of Behavior, 5,* 343–352.

Azar, B. (1995). Breaking through barriers to creativity. *APA Monitor, 26*(8), 1, 20.

Baddeley, A. D. (1982). *Your memory: A user's guide.* New York: Macmillan.

Bahrick, H. P., Bahrick, P. O., & Wittlinger, R. P. (1975). Fifty years of memory for names and faces: A cross-sectional approach. *Journal of Experimental Psychology: General, 104,* 54–75.

Baker, L. A., DeFries, J. C., & Fulker, D. W. (1983). Longitudinal stability of cognitive ability in the Colorado adoption project. *Child Development, 54,* 290–297.

Baltes, P., & Baltes, M. (1995). Cited in Margoshes, P. (1995). For many, old age is the prime of life. *APA Monitor, 26*(5), 36–37.

Bandura, A. (1986). *Social foundations of thought and action: A social-cognitive theory.* Englewood Cliffs, NJ: Prentice-Hall.

Bandura, A. (1991). Human agency: The rhetoric and the reality. *American Psychologist, 46,* 157–162.

Bandura, A., Blanchard, E. B., & Ritter, B. (1969). The relative efficacy of desensitization and modeling approaches for inducing behavioral, affective, and cognitive changes. *Journal of Personality and Social Psychology, 13,* 173–199.

Bandura, A., & McDonald, F. J. (1963). Influence of social reinforcement and the behavior of models in shaping children's moral judgments. *Journal of Abnormal and Social Psychology, 67,* 274–281.

Bandura, A., Ross, S. A., & Ross, D. (1963). Imitation of film-mediated aggressive models. *Journal of Abnormal and Social Psychology, 66,* 3–11.

Bandura, A., Taylor, C. B., Williams, S. I., Medford, I. N., & Barchas, J. D. (1985). Catecholamine secretion as a function of perceived coping self-efficacy. *Journal of Consulting and Clinical Psychology, 53,* 406–414.

Banks, S. M., et al. (1995). The effects of message framing on mammography utilization. *Health Psychology, 14,* 178–184.

Bard, P. (1934). The neurohumoral basis of emotional reactions. In C. A. Murchison (Ed.), *Handbook of general experimental psychology.* Worcester, MA: Clark University Press.

Barlow, D. H. (1994). Cited in Howard, K., Barlow, D., Christiensen, A., & Frank, E. (1994). *Evaluating outcomes of psychological interventions: Evaluating the effectiveness of psychotherapy.* Symposium conducted at the meeting of the American Psychological Association, Los Angeles.

Barlow, D. H., Adler, C. M., Craske, M. G., & Kirshenbaum, S. (1989). "Fear of panic": An investigation of its role in panic occurrence, phobic avoidance, and treatment outcome. *Behaviour Research and Therapy, 27*(4), 391–396.

Barnes, D. (1987). Biological issues in schizophrenia. *Science, 235,* 430–433.

Barnett, W. S., & Escobar, C. M. (1990). Economic costs and benefits of early intervention. In S. J. Meisels & J. P. Shonkoff (Eds.), *Handbook of early childhood intervention.* New York: Cambridge University Press.

Baron, M., Gruen, R., Ranier, J., Kane, J., & Asnis, L. (1985). A family study of schizophrenia and normal control probands: Implications for the spectrum concept of schizophrenia. *American Journal of Psychiatry, 142,* 447–455.

Baron, R. A., & Richardson, D. R. (1994). *Human aggression* (2nd ed.). New York: Plenum Press.

Barringer, F. (1993, April 25). Polling on sexual issues has its drawbacks. *The New York Times,* p. A23.

Bart, P. (1970). Mother Portnoy's complaints. *Trans-action, 8,* 69–74.

Bartecchi, C. E., MacKenzie, T. D., & Schrier, R. W. (1994). The human cost of tobacco use. *New England Journal of Medicine, 330,* 907–912.

Bashore, T. R., & Rapp, P. E. (1993). Are there alternatives to traditional polygraph procedures? *Psychological Bulletin, 113,* 3–22.

Basic Behavioral Science Task Force of the National Advisory Mental Health Council. (1996). Basic behavioral science research for mental health: Vulnerability and resilience. *American Psychologist, 51,* 22–28.

Batson, C. D., et al. (1989). Negative state relief and the empathy-altruism hypothesis. *Journal of Personality and Social Psychology, 56,* 922–933.

Baumeister, R. F., Stillwell, A. M., & Heatherton, T. F. (1994). Guilt: An interpersonal approach. *Psychologial Bulletin, 115,* 243–267.

Baumgardner, A. H., Heppner, P. P., & Arkin, R. M. (1986). Role of causal attribution in personal problem solving. *Journal of Personality and Social Psychology, 50,* 636–643.

Baumrind, D. (1989). Rearing competent children. In W. Damon (Ed.), *Child development today and tomorrow.* San Francisco: Jossey-Bass.

Baumrind, D. (1991a). The influence of parenting style on adolescent competence and substance abuse. *Journal of Early Adolescence, 11,* 56–95.

Baumrind, D. (1991b). Parenting styles and adolescent development. In J. Brooks-Gunn, R. Lerner, & A. C. Petersen, (Eds.), *Encyclopedia of adolescence, II.* New York: Garland.

Baumrind, D. (1993). The average expectable environment is not good enough. A response to Scarr. *Child Development, 64,* 129–1317.

Beal, C. R. (1994). *Boys and girls: The development of gender roles.* New York: McGraw-Hill.

Beck, A. T. (1963). Thinking and depression: I. Idiosyncratic content and cognitive distortions. *Archives of General Psychiatry, 9,* 324–333.

Beck, A. T. (1976). *Cognitive therapy and the emotional disorders.* New York: International Universities Press.

Beck, A. T. (1991). Cognitive therapy: A 30-year retrospective. *American Psychologist, 46,* 368–375.

Beck, A. T. (1993). Cognitive therapy: Past, present, and future. *Journal of Consulting and Clinical Psychology, 61,* 194–198.

Beck, A. T., & Freeman, A. (1990). *Cognitive therapy of personality disorders.* New York: Guilford Press.

Belsky, J. (1993). Etiology of child maltreatment: A developmental-ecological analysis. *Psychological Bulletin, 114,* 413–434.

Belsky, J., Fish, M., & Isabella, R. (1991). Continuity and discontinuity in infant negative and positive emotionality: Family attachments and attachment consequences. *Developmental Psychology, 27,* 421–431.

Bem, D. J., & Honorton, C. (1994). Does psi exist? Replicable evidence for an anomalous process of information transfer. *Psychological Bulletin, 115,* 4–18.

Bem, S. L. (1993). *The lenses of gender.* New Haven, CT: Yale University Press.

Bennett, J. C. (1991). The irrationality of the catharsis theory of aggression as justification for educators' support of interscholastic football. *Perceptual and Motor Skills, 72,* 415–418.

Benson, F. (1995). Cited in Margoshes, P. (1995). For many, old age is the prime of life. *APA Monitor, 26*(5), 36–37.

Benson, H., Manzetta, B. R., & Rosner, B. (1973). Decreased systolic blood pressure in hypertensive subjects who practiced meditation. *Journal of Clinical Investigation, 52,* 8.

Berger, B. D. (1993). Drinking to cope with stress: The effect of self-efficacy and alcohol expectancy on alcohol consumption. *Dissertation Abstracts International, 53,* 12-B. (6539)

Berger, K. S. (1994). *The developing person through the life span* (3rd ed.). New York: Worth.

Berkman, L. F., & Breslow, L. (1983). *Health and ways of living: The Alameda County study.* New York: Oxford University Press.

Berkowitz, L. (1987). Mood, self-awareness, and willingness to help. *Journal of Personality and Social Psychology, 52,* 721–729.

Berkowitz, L. (1994). Is something missing? Some observations prompted by the cognitive-neoassociationist view of anger and emotional aggression. In L. R. Huesmann (Ed.), *Aggressive behavior: current perspectives.* New York: Plenum Press.

Berman, A. L., & Jobes, D. A. (1991). *Adolescent suicide: Assessment and intervention.* Washington, DC: American Psychological Association.

Berman, M., Gladue, B., & Taylor, S. (1993). The effects of hormones, type A behavior pattern, and provocation on aggression in men. *Motivation and Emotion, 17,* 125–138.

Bernal, M. E., & Castro, F. G. (1994). Are clinical psychologists prepared for service and research with ethnic minorities? *American Psychologist, 49,* 797–805.

Berndt, T. J., & Perry, T. B. (1990). Distinctive features and effects of early adolescent friendships. In R. Montemayor, G. R. Adams, & T. P. Gullotta (Eds.), *From childhood to adolescence: A transitional period?* Newbury Park, CA: Sage.

Berne, E. (1976). *Beyond games and scripts.* New York: Grove Press.

Bernstein, W. M., Stephenson, B. O., Snyder, M. L., & Wicklund, R. A. (1983). Causal ambiguity and heterosexual affiliation. *Journal of Experimental Social Psychology, 19,* 78–92.

Bersoff, D. (1994). Cited in DeAngelis, T. (1994). Experts see little impact from insanity plea ruling. *APA Monitor, 25*(6), 28.

Berzonsky, M. C., Kuk, L. S., & Storer, C. J. (1993, March). *Identity development, autonomy, and personal effectiveness.* Paper presented at the meeting of the Society for Research in Child Development, New Orleans, LA.

Bettencourt, B. A., Brewer, M. B., Croak, M. R., & Miller, N. (1992). Cooperation and the reduction of intergroup bias: The role of reward structure and social orientation. *Journal of Experimental Social Psychology, 28,* 301–319.

Beutler, L. E. (1991). Have all won and must all have prizes? *Journal of Consulting and Clinical Psychology, 59,* 226–232.

Bevan, W., & Kessel, F. (1994). Plain truths and home cooking: Thoughts on the making and remaking of psychology. *American Psychologist, 49,* 505–509.

Bexton, W. H., Heron, W., & Scott, T. H. (1954). Effects of decreased variation in the sensory environment. *Canadian Journal of Psychology, 8,* 70–76.

Bjorkqvist, K., Lagerspetz, K. M., & Kaukiainen, A. (1992). Do girls manipulate and boys fight? Developmental trends in regard to direct and indirect aggression. *Aggressive Behavior, 18,* 117–127.

Blakeslee, S. (1992, January 7). Scientists unraveling chemistry of dreams. *The New York Times,* pp. C1, C10.

Blakeslee, S. (1995, May 16). The mystery of music: How it works in the brain. *The New York Times,* pp. C1, C10.

Blanchard, E. B. (1992a). Psychological treatment of benign headache disorders. *Journal of Consulting and Clinical Psychology, 60,* 537–551.

Blanchard, E. B. (1992b). Introduction to the special issue on behavioral medicine: An update for the 1990s. *Journal of Consulting and Clinical Psychology, 60,* 491–492.

Blanchard, E. B., et al. (1990a). A controlled evaluation of thermal biofeedback and thermal feedback combined with cognitive therapy in the treatment of vascular headache. *Journal of Consulting and Clinical Psychology, 58,* 216–224.

Blanchard, E. B., et al. (1990b). Placebo-controlled evaluation of abbreviated progressive muscle relaxation and of relaxation combined with cognitive therapy in the treatment of tension headache. *Journal of Consulting and Clinical Psychology, 58,* 210–215.

Blanchard, E. B., et al. (1991). The role of regular home practice in the relaxation treatment of tension headache. *Journal of Consulting and Clinical Psychology, 59,* 467–470.

Blanck, P. D., Bellack, A. S., Rosnow, R. L., Rotheram-Borus, M. J., & Schooler, N. R. (1992). Scientific rewards and conflicts in ethical choices in human subjects research. *American Psychologist, 47,* 959–965.

Blass, T. (1991). Understanding behavior in the Milgram obedience experiment: The roles of personality, situations, and their interactions. *Journal of Personality and Social Psychology, 60,* 398–413.

Bloom, B. L. (1992). Computer assisted psychological intervention: A review and commentary. *Clinical Psychology Review, 12,* 169–197.

Blum, R. W., Harmon, B., Harris, L., Bergeisen, L., & Resnick, M. D. (1992). American Indian-Alaska native youth health. *Journal of the American Medical Association, 267,* 1637–1644.

Boccia, M., & Campos, J. J. (1989). Maternal emotional signals, social referencing, and infants' reactions to strangers. In N. Eisenberg (Ed.), *Empathy and related emotional responses.* New Directions for Child Development, no. 44. San Francisco: Jossey-Bass.

Bodenhausen, G. V. (1988). Stereotypic biases in social decision making and memory. *Journal of Personality and Social Psychology, 55,* 726–737.

Bohon, L. M., Singer, R. D., & Santos, S. J. (1993). The effects of real-world status and manipulated status on the self-esteem and social competition of Anglo-Americans and Mexican-Americans. *Hispanic Journal of Behavioral Sciences, 15,* 63–79.

Bond, R., & Smith, P. B. (1996). Culture and conformity: A meta-analysis of studies using Asch's line judgment task. *Psychological Bulletin, 119,* 111–137.

Bordo, S. (1993). *Unbearable weight: Feminism, Western culture, and the body.* Berkeley: University of California Press.

Borkovec, T. D., & Costello, E. (1993). Efficacy of applied relaxation and cognitive-behavioral therapy in the treatment of generalized anxiety disorder. *Journal of Consulting and Clinical Psychology, 61,* 611–619.

Borod, C. (1992). Interhemispheric and intrahemispheric control of emotion: A focus on unilateral brain damage. *Journal of Consulting and Clinical Psychology, 60,* 339–348.

Bouchard, C. (1991). Is weight fluctuation a risk factor? *New England Journal of Medicine, 324,* 1887–1889.

Bouchard, T. J., Jr., Lykken, D. T., McGue, M., Segal, N. L., & Tellegren, A. (1990). Sources of human psychological differences: The Minnesota study of twins reared apart. *Science, 250,* 223–228.

Bower, G. H. (1981). Mood and memory. *American Psychologist, 36,* 129–148.

Bowers, T. G., & Clum, G. Z. (1988). Relative contribution of specific and nonspecific treatment effects: Meta-analysis of placebo-controlled behavior therapy research. *Psychological Bulletin, 103,* 315–323.

Bowman, M. L. (1989). Testing individual differences in ancient China. *American Psychologist, 44,* 576–578.

Boyd, J. H., & Weissman, M. M. (1984). Epidemiology of affective disorders: A reexamination and future directions. *Archives of General Psychiatry, 38,* 1039–1045.

Boyd, J. H., Weissman, M. M., Thompson, W. D., & Myers, J. K. (1982). Screening for depression in a community sample: Understanding the discrepancies between depression syndrome and diagnostic scales. *Archives of General Psychiatry, 39,* 1195–1200.

Bradley, R. H., et al. (1989). Home environment and cognitive development in the first three years of life: A collaborative study involving six sites and three ethnic groups in North America. *Developmental Psychology, 25,* 217–235.

Bradshaw, J. L., Nettleton, N. C., & Taylor, M. J. (1981). Right hemisphere language and cognitive deficit in sinistrals. *Neuropsychologia, 19,* 113–132.

Bray, R. M., & Sugarman, R. (1980). Social facilitation among interaction groups: Evidence for the evaluation-apprehension hypothesis. *Personality and Social Psychology Bulletin, 6,* 137–142.

Breckler, S. J., & Wiggins, E. C. (1989). Affect versus evaluation in the structure of attitudes. *Journal of Experimental Social Psychology, 25,* 253–271.

Brenner, J. (1992). Cited in Williams, L. (1992, February 6). Woman's image in a mirror: Who defines what she sees? *The New Times,* pp. A1, B7.

Bretl, D. J., & Cantor, J. (1988). The portrayal of men and women in U.S. television commercials: A recent content analysis and trends over 15 years. *Sex Roles, 18,* 595–609.

Bridges, K. (1932). Emotional development in early infancy. *Child Development, 3,* 324–341.

Bridgewater, C. A. (1982). What candor can do. *Psychology Today, 16*(5), 16.

Brigham, J. C. (1980). Limiting conditions of the "physical attractiveness stereotype": Attributions about divorce. *Journal of Research in Personality, 14,* 365–375.

Bril, B. (1986). Motor development and cultural attitudes. In H. T. A. Whiting & M. G. Wade (Eds.), *Themes in motor development.* Dordrecht, Netherlands: Martinus Nijhoff.

Brody, J. E. (1990, January 19). High cholesterol poses heart risk in older men. *The New York Times,* p. A19.

Brody, J. E. (1992, January 8). Migraines and the estrogen connection. *The New York Times,* p. C12.

Brody, J. E. (1992b, June 16). Suicide myths cloud efforts to save children. *The New York Times,* pp. A1, B7.

Brody, J. E. (1992c, December 30). How weight loss changes risk. *The New York Times,* p. C6.

Brody, J. E. (1994, March 16). Cancer pain is beatable, but too few know it. *The New York Times,* p. C12.

Brody, J. E. (1995a). Cited in DeAngelis, T. (1995). Eat well, keep fit, and let go of stress. *APA Monitor, 26*(10), 20.

Brody, J. E. (1995b, August 30). Hormone replacement therapy for men: When does it help? *The New York Times,* p. C8.

Brook, J. S., Whiteman, M. M., & Finch, S. (1993). Childhood aggression, adolescent delinquency, and drug use: A longitudinal study. *Journal of Genetic Psychology, 153,* 369–383.

Brooks-Gunn, J., & Furstenberg, F. F. (1989). Adolescent sexual behavior. *American Psychologist, 44,* 249–257.

Broverman, I. K., Vogel, S. R., Broverman, D. M., Clarkson, F. E., & Rosenkrantz, P. S. (1972). Sex-role stereotypes: A current appraisal. *Journal of Social Issues, 28,* 59–78.

Brown, B. B., Mounts, N., Lamborn, S. D., & Steinberg, L. (1993). Parenting practices and peer group affiliation in adolescence. *Child Development, 64,* 467–482.

Brown, D. E. (1991). *Human universals.* Philadelphia: Temple University Press.

Brownell, K. D. (1993). Whether obesity should be treated. *Health Psychology, 12,* 339–341.

Brownell, K. D., & Rodin, J. (1994). The dieting maelstrom: Is it possible and advisable to lose weight? *American Psychologist, 49,* 781–791.

Brownell, K. D., & Wadden, T. A. (1992). Obesity: Understanding a serious, prevalent, and refactory disorder. *Journal of Consulting and Clinical Psychology, 60,* 505–517.

Browning, C. (1992). *Ordinary men: Reserve Police Battalion 101 and the Final Solution in Poland.* New York: HarperCollins.

Buchanan, C. M., Eccles, J. S., & Becker, J. B. (1992). Are adolescents the victims of raging hormones? Evidence for activational effects of hormones on moods and behavior at adolescence. *Psychological Bulletin, 111,* 62–107.

Budzynski, T. H., & Stoyra, J. M. (1984). Biofeedback methods in the treatment of anxiety and stress. In R. I. Woolfolk & P. M. Lehrer (Eds.), *Principles and practice of stress management.* New York: Guilford Press.

Burish, T. G., Carey, M. P., Krozely, M. G., & Greco, F. A. (1987). Conditioned side effects induced by cancer chemotherapy: Prevention through behavioral treatment. *Journal of Consulting and Clinical Psychology, 55,* 42–48.

Burkett, S. (1980). Religiosity, beliefs and normative standards and adolescent drinking. *Journal of Studies on Alcohol, 41,* 662–671.

Burman, B., & Margolin, G. (1992). Analysis of the association between marital relationships and health problems: An interactional perspective. *Psychological Bulletin, 112,* 39–63.

Burns, G. L., & Farina, A. (1987). Physical attractiveness and self-perception of mental disorder. *Journal of Abnormal Psychology, 96,* 161–163.

Burnstein, E., & Schul, Y. (1982). The informational basis of social judgments: Operations in forming an impression of another person. *Journal of Experimental Social Psychology, 18,* 217–234.

Buss, D. M. (1989). Sex differences in human mate preferences: Evolutionary hypotheses tested in 37 cultures. *Behavioral and Brain Sciences, 12,* 1–49.

Buss, D. M. (1992). Is there a universal human nature? *Contemporary Psychology, 37,* 1262–1263.

Buss, D. M. (1994). *The evolution of desire: Strategies of human mating.* New York: Basic Books.

Buss, D. M. (1995). Psychological sex differences: Origins through sexual selection. *American Psychologist, 50,* 164–168.

Buss, D. M., & Barnes, M. (1986). Preferences in human mate selection. *Journal of Personality and Social Psychology, 50,* 559–570.

Butterfield, F. (1992, January 1). Studies find a family link to criminality. *The New York Times,* pp. A1, A8.

Byrnes, J., & Takahira, S. (1993). Explaining gender differences on SAT-math items. *Developmental Psychology, 29,* 805–810.

Caldwell, C. B., & Gotteman, I. I. (1990). Schizophrenics kill themselves too: A review of the risk factors for suicide. *Schizophrenia Bulletin, 16,* 571–589.

Califano, J. A. (1995). The wrong way to stay slim. *New England Journal of Medicine, 333,* 1214–1216.

Camarena, P. M. (1991). Conformity in adolescence. In R. M. Lerner, A. C. Petersen, & J. Brooks-Gunn (Eds.), *Encyclopedia of adolescence.* New York: Garland.

Campos, J. J., Langer, A., & Krowitz, A. (1970). Cardiac responses on the visual cliff in prelocomotor infants. *Science, 170,* 196–197.

Cannon, W. B. (1927). The James-Lange theory of emotions: A critical examination and an alternative theory. *American Journal of Psychology, 39,* 106–124.

Cannon, W. B. (1939). *The wisdom of the body.* New York: Norton.

Cappella, J. N., & Palmer, M. T. (1990). Attitude similarity, relational history, and attraction: The mediating effects of kinesic and vocal behaviors. *Communication Monographs, 5,* 161–183.

Carey, G. (1992). Twin imitation for antisocial behavior: Implications for genetic and family environment research. *Journal of Abnormal Psychology, 101,* 18–25.

Carey, G., & DiLalla, D. L. (1994). Personality and psychopathology: Genetic perspectives. *Journal of Abnormal Psychology, 103,* 32–43.

Carlson, J. G., & Hatfield, E. (1992). *Psychology of emotion.* Fort Worth, TX: Harcourt Brace Jovanovich.

Carlson, M., Charlin, V., & Miller, N. (1988). Positive mood and helping behavior: A test of six hypotheses. *Journal of Personality and Social Psychology, 55,* 211–229.

Carmichael, L. L., Hogan, H. O., & Walter, A. A. (1932). An experimental study of the effect of language on the reproduction of visually perceived form. *Journal of Experimental Psychology, 15,* 73–86.

Carroll, K. M., Rounsaville, B. J., & Nich, C. (1994). Blind man's bluff: Effectiveness and significance of psychotherapy and pharmacotherapy blinding procedures in a clinical trial. *Journal of Consulting and Clinical Psychology, 62,* 276–280.

Carson, R. C. (1989). Personality. *Annual Review of Psychology, 40,* 227–248.

Carstensen, L. (1995). Cited in Margoshes, P. (1995). For many, old age is the prime of life. *APA Monitor, 26*(5), 36–37.

Caspi, A., Lynam, D., Moffitt, T. E., & Silva, P. A. (1993). Unraveling girls' delinquency: Biological, dispositional, and contextual contributions to adolescent misbehavior. *Developmental Psychology, 29,* 19–30.

Cassidy, J. (1988). Child-mother attachment and the self in six-year-olds. *Child Development, 39*(1), 121–134.

Castelli, W. (1994). Cited in Brody, J. E. (1994, February 8). Scientist at work—William Castelli: Preaching the gospel of healthy hearts. *The New York Times,* pp. C1, C10.

Cattell, R. (1965). *The scientific analysis of personality.* Baltimore: Penguin Books.

Caulfield, M., et al. (1994). Linkage of the angiotensinogen gene to essential hypertension. *New England Journal of Medicine, 330,* 1629–1633.

Centers for Disease Control and Prevention. (1993). Infant mortality—United States, 1990. *Morbidity and Mortality Weekly Report, 42,* 161–165.

Centers for Disease Control and Prevention. (1993, October). *HIV/AIDS surveillance: Third quarter edition. U.S. AIDS cases reported through September 1993.* Atlanta, GA: U.S. Department of Health and Human Services.

Chadwick, P. D. J., & Lowe, C. F. (1990). Measurement and modification of delusional beliefs. *Journal of Consulting and Clinical Psychology, 58,* 225–232.

Chase, J., Jessor, R., & Donovan, J. (1980). Psychological correlates of marijuana use and drinking in a national sample of adolescents. *American Journal of Public Health, 70,* 604–612.

Cherlin, J. (1992). *Marriage, divorce, remarriage: Social trends in the United States.* Cambridge, MA: Harvard University Press.

Chira, S. (1992, February 12). Bias against girls found rife in schools, with lasting damage. *The New York Times,* pp. A1, A23.

Chomsky, N. (1980). Rules and representations. *Behavioral and Brain Sciences, 3,* 1–16.

Chomsky, N. (1991). Linguistics and cognitive science: Problems and mysteries. In A. Kasher (Ed.), *The Chomskyan turn.* Cambridge, MA: Blackwell.

Cialdini, R. B. (1993). *Influence: Science and practice* (3rd ed.). New York: HarperCollins.

Cicchetti, D., & Olson, K. (1990). The developmental psychopathology of child maltreatment. In M. Lewis & S. M. Miller (Eds.), *Handbook of developmental psychopathology* (pp. 261–279). New York: Plenum Press.

Ciesielski, K., Beech, H., & Gordon, P. (1981). Some electrophysical observations in obessional states. *British Journal of Psychiatry, 138,* 479–484.

Clark, K. B. (1955/1988). *Prejudice and your child.* Middletown, CT: Wesleyan University Press.

Clark, K. B., and Clark, M. P. (1947). Racial identification and preference in Negro children. In T. M. Newcomb & E. L. Hartley (Eds.), *Readings in Social Psychology.* New York: Holt, Rinehart and Winston.

Clark, L. A., Watson, D., & Mineka, S. M., (1994). Temperament, personality, and the mood and anxiety disorders. *Journal of Abnormal Psychology, 103,* 103–116.

Clark, M. S., Mills, J. R., & Corcoran, D. M. (1989). Keeping track of needs and inputs of friends and strangers. *Personality and Social Psychology Bulletin, 15,* 533–542.

Clarke-Stewart, K. A. (1978). And daddy makes three: The father's impact on mother and young child. *Child Development, 49,* 466–478.

Clarke-Stewart, K. A. (1989). Infant day care: Maligned or malignant? *American Psychologist, 44,* 266–273.

Clarke-Stewart, K. A. (1991). A home is not a school: The effects of child care on children's development. *Journal of Social Issues, 47,* 105–123.

Coe, C. (1993). Cited in Adler, T. (1993). Men and women affected by stress, but differently. *APA Monitor, 24*(7), 8–9.

Cohen, L. A. (1987, November). Diet and cancer. *Scientific American,* pp. 42–48, 53–54.

Cohen, S., Tyrrell, D. A. J., & Smith, A. P. (1993). Negative life events, perceived stress, negative affect, and susceptibility to the common cold. *Journal of Personality and Social Psychology, 64,* 131–140.

Cohen, S., & Williamson, G. M. (1991). Stress and infectious disease in humans. *Psychological Bulletin, 109,* 5–24.

Coleman, J., Butcher, J., & Carson, R. (1984). *Abnormal psychology and modern life* (7th ed.). Glenview, IL: Scott, Foresman.

Coleman, L. (1990). Cited in Goleman, G. (1990, August 2). The quiet comeback of electroshock therapy. *The New York Times,* p. B5.

Collaer, M. L., & Hines, M. (1995). Human behavioral sex differences: A role for gonadal hormones during early development? *Psychological Bulletin, 118,* 55–107.

Collier, G. (1994). *Social origins of mental ability.* New York: Wiley.

Collins, W. A. (1990). Parent-child relationships in the transition of adolescence: Continuity and change in interaction, affect, and cognition. In R. Montemayor, G. R. Adams, & T. P. Gullotta (Eds.), *From childhood to adolescence: A transitional period.* Newbury Park, CA: Sage.

Collins, W. A., & Russell, G. (1991). Mother-child and father-child relationships in middle childhood and adolescence: A developmental analysis. *Developmental Review, 11,* 99–136.

Comas-Diaz, L. (1994, February). Race and gender in psychotherapy with women of color. *Winter roundtable on cross-cultural counseling and psychotherapy: Race and gender.* New York: Teachers College, Columbia University.

Comstock, G., & Paik, H. (1991). *Television and the American child.* San Diego, CA: Academic Press.

Condon, J. W., & Crano, W. D. (1988). Inferred evaluation and the relation between attitude similarity and interpersonal attraction. *Journal of Personality and Social Psychology, 54,* 789–797.

Conger, J. J. (1978). Adolescence: A time for becoming. In M. Lamb (Ed.), *Social and personality development.* New York: Holt, Rinehart and Winston.

Cools, J., Schotte, D. E., & McNally, R. J. (1992). Emotional arousal and overeating in restrained eaters. *Journal of Abnormal Psychology, 101,* 348–351.

Coon, H., Fulker, D. W., DeFries, J. C., & Plomin, R. (1990). Home environment and cognitive ability of 7-year-old children in the Colorado Adoption Project: Genetic and environmental etiologies. *Developmental Psychology, 26,* 459–468.

Cooper, J. R., Bloom, F. E., & Roth, R. H. (1991). *The biochemical basis of neuropharmacology.* New York: Oxford University Press.

Corkin, S., et al. (1985). Analyses of global memory impairments of different etiologies. In D. S. Olton, E. Gamzu, & S. Corkin (Eds.), *Memory dysfunction.* New York: New York Academy of Sciences.

Cousins, N. (1979). *Anatomy of an illness as perceived by the patient: Reflections on healing and regeneration.* New York: Norton.

Cox, M. J., Owen, M. T., Henderson, V. K., & Margand, N. A. (1992). Prediction of infant-father and infant-mother attachment. *Developmental Psychology, 28,* 474–483.

Coyne, J. C., & Downey, G. (1991). Social factors and psychopathology: Stress, social support, and coping processes. *Annual Review of Psychology, 42,* 401–425.

Craighead, L. W., & Agras, W. S. (1991). Mechanisms of action in cognitive-behavioral and pharmacological interventions for obesity and bulimia nervosa. *Journal of Consulting and Clinical Psychology, 59,* 115–125.

Crain, W. C. (1992). *Theories of development: Concepts and applications* (3rd ed.). Englewood Cliffs, NJ: Prentice-Hall.

Cramer, R. E., McMaster, M. R., Bartell, P. A., & Dragna, M. (1988). Subject competence and minimization of the bystander effect. *Journal of Applied Social Psychology, 18,* 1133–1148.

Crews, D. (1994). Animal sexuality. *Scientific American, 270*(1), 108–114.

Crick, N. R., & Dodge, K. A. (1994). A review and reformulation of social information-processing mechanisms in children's social adjustment. *Psychological Bulletin, 115,* 74–101.

Crosby, F. J., & Jaskar, K. L. (1993). Women and men at home and at work: Realities and illusions. In S. Oskamp & M. Costanzo (Eds.), *Gender issues in contemporary society.* Newbury Park, CA: Sage.

Cross, W. (1991). *Shades of identity.* Philadelphia: Temple University Press.

Crusco, A. H., & Wetzel, C. G. (1984). The Midas touch: The effects of interpersonal touch on restaurant tipping. *Personality and Social Psychology Bulletin, 10,* 512–517.

Cummings, J. L. (1995, June 10). Dementia: the failing brain. *Lancet,* p. 772.

Cunningham, M. R., Shaffer, D. R., Barbee, A. P., Wolff, P. L., & Kelley, D. J. (1990). Separate processes in the relation of elation and depression to helping: Social versus personal concerns. *Journal of Experimental Social Psychology, 26,* 13–33.

Curb, J. D., & Marcus, E. B. (1991). Body fat and obesity in Japanese Americans. *American Journal of Clinical Nutrition, 53,* 1552S–1555S.

Curfman, G. D. (1993a). The health benefits of exercise: A critical reappraisal. *New England Journal of Medicine, 328,* 574–576.

Curfman, G. D. (1993b). Is exercise beneficial—or hazardous—to your heart? *New England Journal of Medicine, 329,* 1730–1731.

Curtis, R. C., & Miller, K. (1986). Believing another likes or dislikes you: Behavior making the beliefs come true. *Journal of Personality and Social Psychology, 51,* 284–290.

Damaged gene is linked to lung cancer. (1996, April 6). *The New York Times,* p. A24.

Damasio, H., & Damasio, A. (1992, September). Brain and language. *Scientific American,* pp. 89–95.

Darwin, C. (1872). *The expression of the emotions in man and animals.* London: J. Murray.

Davey, L. F. (1993, March). *Developmental implications of shared and divergent perceptions in the parent-adolescent relationship.* Paper presented at the biennial meeting of the Society for Research in Child Development, New Orleans, LA.

Davidson, E. S., Yasuna, A., & Tower, A. (1979). The effects of television cartoons on sex-role stereotyping in young girls. *Child Development, 50,* 597–600.

Davidson, J. E. (1986). The role of insight in giftedness. In R. J. Sternberg & J. E. Davidson (Eds.), *Conceptions of giftedness.* New York: Cambridge University Press.

Davies, P. T., & Cummings, E. M. (1994). Marital conflict and child adjustment. *Psychological Bulletin, 116,* 387–411.

Davis, J. H. (1975). The design processes of 6- and 12-person mock juries assigned unanimous and two-thirds majority rules. *Journal of Personality and Social Psychology, 32,* 1–14.

Davis, J. H., Tindale, R. S., Nagao, D. H., Hinsz, V. B., & Robertson, B. (1984). Order effects in multiple decisions by groups: A demonstration with mock juries and trial procedures. *Journal of Personality and Social Psychology, 47,* 1003–1012.

Davison, G., & Neale, J. (1990). *Abnormal psychology* (5th ed.). New York: Wiley.

DeAngelis, T. (1993a). It's baaack: TV violence, concern for kid viewers. *APA Monitor, 24*(8), 16.

DeAngelis, T. (1993b). Law helps American Indians enter field. *APA Monitor, 24*(3), 26–27.

DeAngelis, T. (1995). Mental health care is elusive for Hispanic. *APA Monitor, 26*(7), 49.

Deaux, K., & Lewis, L. L. (1983). Assessment of gender stereotypes: Methodology and components. *Psychological Documents, 13*(25, Ms. No. 2583).

DeBell, C. (1993, August). *Occupational gender-role stereotyping in television commercials: A nine-year longitudinal study.* Paper presented at the meeting of the American Psychological Association, Toronto.

DeFries, J. C., Plomin, R., & LaBudam, M. C. (1987). Genetic stability of cognitive development from childhood to adulthood. *Developmental Psychology, 23,* 4–12.

DeGree, C. E., & Snyder, C. R. (1995). Adler's psychology (of use) today: Personal history of traumatic life events as a self-handicapping strategy. *Journal of Personality and Social Psychology, 48,* 1512–1519.

DeKovic, M., & Janssens, J. (1992). Parents' child-rearing style and child's sociometric status. *Developmental Psychology, 28,* 925–932.

Delhanty, D. L., et al. (1996). Time course of natural killer cell activity and lymphocyte proliferation in response to two acute stressors in healthy men. *Health Psychology, 15,* 48–55.

Delgado, J. M. R. (1969). *Physical control of the mind.* New York: Harper & Row.

DePaulo, B. M. (1992). Nonverbal behavior and self-presentation. *Psychological Bulletin, 111,* 203–243.

Desmond, A. M. (1994). Adolescent pregnancy in the United States: Not a minority issue. *Health Care for Women International, 15*(4), 325–331.

Deutsch, M., & Collins, M. (1951). *Interracial housing: A psychological evaluation of a social experiment.* Minneapolis: University of Minnesota Press.

Devine, P. G. (1989). Stereotypes and prejudice: Their automatic and controlled components. *Journal of Personality and Social Psychology, 56,* 5–18.

Diaz, R. M. (1985). Bilingual cognitive development: Addressing three gaps in current research. *Child Development, 56,* 1376–1388.

Digman, J. M., & Inouye, J. (1986). Specification of the five robust factors of personality. *Journal of Personality and Social Psychology, 50,* 116–123.

DiLalla, L. F., & Gottesman, I. I. (1991). Biological and genetic contributors to violence—Widom's untold tale. *Psychological Bulletin, 109,* 125–129.

Dill, C. A., Gilden, E. R., Hill, P. C., & Hanselka, L. L. (1982). Federal human subjects regulations: A methodological artifact. *Personality and Social Psychology Bulletin, 8,* 417–425.

Dindia, K., & Allen, M. (1992). Sex differences in self-disclosure: A meta-analysis. *Psychological Bulletin, 112,* 106–124.

Dix, T. (1991). The affective organization of parenting: Adaptive and maladaptive processes. *Psychological Bulletin, 110,* 3–25.

Doctors tie male mentality to shorter life span. (1995, June 14). *The New York Times,* p. C14.

Dodge, K. A., Price, J. M., Bachorowski, J., & Newman, J. P. (1990). Hostile attributional biases in severely aggressive adolescents. *Journal of Abnormal Psychology, 99,* 385–392.

Doob, A. N., & Wood, L. (1972). Catharsis and aggression: The effects of annoyance and retaliation on aggressive behavior. *Journal of Personality and Social Psychology, 22,* 236–245.

BOOKSHELF

Dovidio, J. H., Evans, N., & Tyler, R. B. (1986). Racial stereotypes: The contents of their cognitive representations. *Journal of Experimental Social Psychology, 22,* 22–37.

Draguns, J. G. (1988). Personality and culture: Are they relevant for the enhancement of quality of mental life? In P. R. Dasen, J. W. Berry, & N. Sartorius (Eds.), *Health and cross-cultural psychology: Toward applications.* Newbury Park, CA: Sage.

Drapkin, R. G., Wing, R. R., & Shiffman, S. (1995). Responses to hypothetical high risk situations: Do they predict weight loss in a behavioral treatment program or the context of dietary lapses? *Health Psychology, 14,* 427–434.

Dubbert, P. M. (1992). Exercise in behavioral medicine. *Journal of Consulting and Clinical Psychology, 60,* 613–618.

DuBois, D. L., & Hirsh, B. J. (1990). School and neighborhood friendship patterns of Blacks and Whites in adolescence. *Child Development, 61,* 524–536.

Du Bois, W. E. B. (1903/1990). *The souls of black folk.* New York: Random House.

Duckitt, J. (1992). Psychology and prejudice: A historical analysis and integrative framework. *American Psychologist, 47,* 1182–1193.

Dumas, J. E., & LaFreniere, P. J. (1993). Mother-child relationships as a support of support or stress: A comparison of competent, average, aggressive, and anxious dyads. *Child Development, 64.*

Duncker, K. (1945). On problem solving. *Psychological Monographs, 58.* (Whole No. 270)

Dunphy, D. C. (1963). The social structure of urban adolescent peer groups. *Sociometry, 26,* 230–246.

Dweck, C. S. (1990). Toward a theory of goals: Their role in motivation in personality. In R. A. Dienstbier (Ed.), *Nebraska symposium on motivation, 38.* Lincoln: University of Nebraska Press.

Eagly, A. H. (1987). *Sex differences in social behavior: A social-role interpretation.* Hillsdale, NJ: Erlbaum.

Eagly, A. H., Ashmore, R. D., Makhijani, M. G., & Longo, L. C. (1991). What is beautiful is good, but . . . : A meta-analytic review of research on the physical attractiveness stereotype. *Psychological Bulletin, 110,* 109–128.

Eagly, A. H., & Chaiken, S. (1993). *The psychology of attitudes.* Fort Worth, TX: Harcourt Brace Jovanovich.

Eagly, A. H., & Steffen, V. J. (1986). Gender and aggressive behavior: A meta-analytic review of the social psychological literature. *Psychological Bulletin, 100,* 309–330.

Eagly, A. H., & Wood, W. (1991). Explaining sex differences in social behavior: A meta-analytic perspective. *Personality and Social Psychology Bulletin, 17,* 306–315.

Ebbinghaus, H. (1913/1885). *Memory: A contribution to experimental psychology* (H. A. Roger & C. E. Bussenius, Trans.). New York: Columbia University Press.

Eccles, J. S. (1993). *Parents as gender-role socializers during middle childhood and adolescence.* Paper presented at the meeting of the Society for Research on Child Development, New Orleans, LA.

Eccles, J. S., Wigfield, A., Harold, R. D., & Blumenfeld, P. (1993). Age and gender differences in children's self- and task perceptions during elementary school. *Child Development, 64,* 830–847.

Egeland, B., Jacobvitz, D., & Sroufe, L. A. (1988). Breaking the cycle of abuse. *Child Development, 59,* 1080–1088.

Egeth, H. E. (1993). What do we not know about eyewitness identification? *American Psychologist, 48,* 577–580.

Eisenberg, N., Wolchik, S. A., Hernandez, R., & Pasternack, J. F. (1985). Parental socialization of young children's play: A short-term longitudinal study. *Child Development, 56,* 1506–1513.

Ekman, P. (1980). *The face of man.* New York: Garland.

Ekman, P. (1982). *Emotion and the human face* (2nd. ed.). New York: Cambridge University Press.

Ekman, P. (1992). Are there basic emotions? *Psychological Review, 99,* 550–553.

Ekman, P. (1993). Facial expression and emotion. *American Psychologist, 48,* 384–392.

Ekman, P. (1994). Strong evidence for universals in facial expression. *Psychological Bulletin, 115,* 268–287.

Ekman, P., et al. (1995). Universals and cultural differences in the judgments of facial expressions of emotion. *Journal of Personality and Social Psychology, 14,* 109–115.

Ekman, P., & Friesen, W. (1984). *Unmasking the face* (2nd ed.). Palo Alto, CA: Consulting Psychologists Press.

Ekvall, S. W. (Ed.). (1993). *Pediatric nutrition in chronic diseases and developmental disorders: Prevention, assessment, and treatment.* New York: Oxford University Press.

Ellis, A. (1977). The basic clinical theory of rational-emotive therapy. In A. Ellis & R. Grieger (Eds.), *Handbook of rational-emotive therapy.* New York: Springer.

Ellis, A. (1984). Rational-emotive therapy. In R. J. Corsini (Ed.), *Current psychotherapies.* Itasca, IL: Peacock.

Ellis, A. (1993). Reflections on rational-emotive therapy. *Journal of Consulting and Clinical Pscyhology, 61,* 199–201.

Ellis, A. (1995). Thinking processes involved in irrational beliefs and their disturbed consequences. *Journal of Cognitive Psychotherapy: An International Quarterly, 9*(2), 105–116.

Ellis, A., & Dryden, W. (1987). *The practice of rational emotional therapy.* New York: Springer-Verlag.

Ellsworth, P. C., Carlsmith, J. M., & Henson, A. (1972). The stare as a stimulus to flight in human subjects. *Journal of Personality and Social Psychology, 21,* 302–311.

Emde, R. (1993). Cited in Adler, T. (1993). Shy, bold temperament? It's mostly in the genes. *APA Monitor, 24*(1), 7, 8.

Engels, G. I., Garnefski, N., & Diekstra, R. F. W. (1993). Efficacy of rational-emotive therapy: A quantitative analysis. *Journal of Consulting and Clinical Psychology, 61,* 1083–1090.

Epstein, L. H., et al. (1995). Effects of decreasing sedentary behavior and increasing activity on weight change in obese children. *Health Psychology, 14,* 109–115.

Erel, O., & Burman, B. (1995). Interrelatedness of marital relations and parent-child relations: A meta-analytic review. *Psychological Bulletin, 118,* 108–132.

Erikson, E. H. (1950). *Childhood and society* (1st ed.). New York: Norton.

Erikson, E. H. (1963). *Childhood and society* (2nd ed.). New York: Norton.

Erikson, E. H. (1968). *Identity: Youth and crisis.* New York: Norton.

Eron, L. D. (1993). Cited in DeAngelis, T. (1993a). It's baaack: TV violence, concern for kid viewers. *APA Monitor, 24*(8), 16.

Errington, D., & Gewertz, D. (1987). *Cultural alternatives and a feminist anthropology: An analysis of culturally constructed gender interest in Papua, New Guinea.* New York: Cambridge University Press.

Esterling, B. A., Antoni, M. H., Kumar, M., & Schneiderman, N. (1993). Defensiveness, trait anxiety, and Epstein-Barr viral capsid antigen antibody titers in healthy college students. *Health Psychology, 12,* 132–139.

Etaugh, C., & Rathus, S. A. (1995). *The world of children.* Fort Worth, TX: Harcourt Brace College Publishers.

Etcoff, N. L. (1994). Cited in Brody, J. E. (1994, March 21). Notions of beauty transcend culture, new study suggests. *The New York Times,* p. A14.

Eysenck, H. J. (1953). *The structure of human personality.* London: Meuthen.

Eyesenck, H. J. (1993). Comment on Goldberg. *American Psychologist, 48,* 1299–1300.

Facts on File. (1994, October 20), p. 772.

Fagot, B. I. (1978). The influence of sex of child on parental reactions to toddler children. *Child Development, 49,* 459–465.

Fagot, B. I., Hagan, R., Leinbach, M. D., & Kronsberg, S. (1985). Differential reactions to assertive and communicative acts of toddler boys and girls. *Child Development, 56,* 1499–1505.

Fallon, A. E., & Rozin, P. (1985). Sex differences in perceptions of desirable body shape. *Journal of Abnormal Psychology, 94,* 102–105.

Fantz, R. L. (1961). The origin of form perception. *Scientific American, 204*(5), 66–72.

Farina, A., Burns, G. L., Austad, C., Bugglin, C. S., & Fischer, E. H. (1986). The role of physical attractiveness in the readjustment of discharged psychiatric patients. *Journal of Abnormal Psychology, 95,* 139–143.

Farley, F. (1993). Cited in Michaelson, R. (1993). Farley calls for more money for health, behavior research. *APA Monitor, 24*(4), 3.

Farrell, A. D., Camplair, P. S., & McCullough, L. (1987). Identification of target complaints by computer interview: Evaluation of the Computerized Assessment System for Psychotherapy Evaluation and Research. *Journal of Consulting and Clinical Psychology, 55,* 691–700.

Fazio, R. H. (1990). Multiple processes by which attitudes guide behavior: The MODE model as an integrative framework. In M. P. Zanna (Ed.), *Advances in experimental social psychology.* San Diego, CA: Academic Press.

Feingold, A. (1988). Matching for attractiveness in romantic partners and same-sex friends: A meta-analysis and theoretical critique. *Psychological Bulletin, 104,* 226–235.

Feingold, A. (1992a). Gender differences in mate selection preferences: A test of the parental investment model. *Psychological Bulletin, 112,* 125–139.

Feingold, A. (1992b). Good-looking people are not what we think. *Psychological Bulletin, 111,* 304–341.

Feingold, A. (1992c). Sex differences in the effects of similarity and physical attractiveness on opposite-sex attraction. *Basic and Applied Social Psychology, 12,* 357–367.

Feingold, A. (1994). Gender differences in personality: A meta-analysis. *Psychological Bulletin, 116,* 429–456.

Feiring, C. (1993, March). *Developing concepts of romance from 15 to 18 years.* Paper presented at the meeting of the Society for Research in Child Development, New Orleans, LA.

Feshbach, S. (1994). Nationalism, patriotism, and aggression: A clarification of functional differences. In L. R. Huesmann (Ed.), *Aggressive behavior: Current perspectives.* New York: Plenum Press.

Festinger, L. (1957). *A theory of cognitive dissonance.* Stanford, CA: Stanford University Press.

Festinger, L., & Carlsmith, J. M. (1959). Cognitive consequences of forced compliance. *Journal of Abnormal and Social Psychology, 58,* 203–210.

Field, T. M. (1991). Young children's adaptations to repeated separations from their mothers. *Child Development, 62,* 539–547.

Field, T. M., Schanberg, S. M., Scafidi, F., Bauer, C. R., Vega-Lahr, N., Garcia, R., Nystrom, J., & Kuhn, C. M. (1986). Tactile/kinesthetic stimulation effects on preterm neonates. *Pediatrics, 77,* 654–658.

Finkelhor, D., & Dziuba-Leatherman, J. (1994). Victimization of children. *American Psychologist, 49,* 173–183.

Fischer, K. W., Shavber, P. R., & Carochan, P. (1990). How emotions develop and how they organize development. *Cognition and Emotion, 4,* 81–127.

Fisher, C. B., & Fyrberg, D. (1994). Participant partners: College students weigh the costs and benefits of deceptive research. *American Psychologist, 49,* 417–427.

Fisher, H. E. (1992). *Anatomy of love: The natural history of monogamy, adultery and divorce.* New York: Norton.

Fisher-Thompson, D. (1990). Adult sex typing of children's toys. *Sex Roles, 23,* 291–303.

Fiske, S. T. (1989). *Interdependence and stereotyping: From the laboratory to the Supreme Court (and back).* Paper presented to the meeting of the American Psychological Association, New Orleans, LA.

Fiske, S. T. (1993). Controlling other people: The impact of power on stereotyping. *American Psychologist, 48,* 621–628.

Fiske, S. T., & Taylor, S. E. (1984). *Social cognition.* Reading, MA: Addison-Wesley.

BOOKSHELF

Fitzgibbon, M. L., Stolley, M. R., & Kirschenbaum, D. S. (1993). Obese people who seek treatment have different characteristics than those who do not seek treatment. *Health Psychology, 12,* 342–345.

Flannery, D. J., Rowe, D. C., & Gulley, B. L. (1993). Impact of pubertal status, timing, and age on adolescent sexual experience and delinquency. *Journal of Adolescent Research, 8,* 21–40.

Flavell, J. H., Miller, P. H., & Miller, S. A. (1993). *Cognitive development* (3rd ed.). Englewood Cliffs, NJ: Prentice-Hall.

Fling, S., Smith, L., Rodriguez, T., Thornton, D., et al. (1992). Videogames, aggression, and self-esteem: A survey. *Social Behavior & Personality, 20,* 39–45.

Foster-Clark, F. S., & Blyth, D. A. (1991). Peer relations and influences. In R. M. Lerner, A. C. Petersen, & J. Brooks-Gunn (Eds.), *Encyclopedia of adolescence.* New York: Garland.

Fowler, R. D. (1992). Solid support needed for animal research. *APA Monitor, 23*(6), 2.

Frankenberg, W., Dodds, J., Archer, P., Shapiro, H., & Bresnick, B. (1992). The Denver II: A major revision and restandardization of the Denver Developmental Screening Test. *Pediatrics, 89,* 91–97.

Franzoi, S. L., & Herzog, M. E. (1987). Judging physical attractiveness: What body aspects do we use? *Personality and Social Psychology Bulletin, 13,* 19–33.

Freud, S. (1936). *The problem of anxiety.* New York: Norton.

Freud, S. (1952). *A general introduction to psychoanalysis.* New York: Washington Square Press. (Original work published 1920)

Freud, S. (1933/1964). New introductory lectures. In J. Strachey (Ed. and Trans.), *The standard edition of the complete psychological works of Sigmund Freud* (Vol. 22). London: Hogarth.

Friedman, M. A., & Brownell, K. D. (1995). Psychological correlates of obesity: Moving to the next research generation. *Psychological Bulletin, 117,* 3–20.

Friedman, M., & Ulmer, D. (1984). *Treating type A behavior and your heart.* New York: Fawcett Crest.

Frodi, A. M., Macauley, J., & Thome, P. R. (1977). Are women always less aggressive than men? A review of the experimental literature. *Psychological Bulletin, 84,* 634–660.

Fromm-Reichmann, F. (1948). Notes on the development of treatment of schizophrenics by psychoanalytic psychotherapy. *Psychiatry, 11,* 263–273.

Furedy, J. J. (1990, July). *Experimental psychophysiology and pseudoscientific polygraphy: Conceptual concerns and practical problems.* Symposium at the 5th International Congress of Psychophysiology, Budapest, Hungary.

Furman, W., & Buhrmester, D. (1992). Age and sex differences in perceptions of networks of personal relationships. *Child Development, 63,* 103–115.

Galambos, N. L. (1992). Parent-adolescent relations. *Current Directions in Psychological Science, 1,* 146–149.

Galambos, N. L., & Almeida, D. M. (1992). Does parent-adolescent conflict increase in early adolescence? *Journal of Marriage and the Family, 54,* 737–747.

Galanter, E. (1962). Contemporary psychophysics. In R. Brown et al. (Eds.), *New directions in psychology.* New York: Holt, Rinehart and Winston.

Galassi, J. P. (1988). Four cognitive-behavioral approaches: Additional considerations. *Counseling Psychologist, 16*(1), 102–105.

Gallagher, R. (1996). Cited in Murray, B. (1996). College youth haunted by increased pressures. *APA Monitor, 26*(4), 47.

Gallucci, W. T., et al. (1993). Sex differences in sensitivity of the hypothalamic-pituitary-adrenal axis. *Health Psychology, 12,* 420–425.

Gardner, B., & Gardner, G. (1980). Object permanence in child and chimpanzee. *Animal Learning and Behavior, 8*(1), 3–9.

Gardner, H. (1983). *Frames of mind: The theory of multiple intelligences.* New York: Basic Books.

Gardner, H. (1993). *Creating minds: An anatomy of creativity seen through the lives of Freud, Einstein, Picasso, Stravinsky, Eliot, Graham and Gandhi.* New York: Basic Books.

Gardner, H. (1995, November). Reflections on multiple intelligences: Myths and messages. *Phi Delta Kappan, 77,* 200–208.

Gardner, H., & Hatch, T. (1989). Multiple intelligences go to school: Educational implications of the theory of multiple intelligences. *Educational Researcher, 18*(8), 4–10.

Garfinkel, R. (1995). Cited in Margoshes, P. (1995). For many, old age is the prime of life. *APA Monitor, 26*(5), 36–37.

Garland, A. F., & Zigler, E. (1993). Adolescent suicide prevention. *American Psychologist, 48,* 169–182.

Gauthier, J., Côte, G., & French, D. (1994). The role of home practice in the thermal biofeedback treatment of migraine headache. *Journal of Consulting and Clinical Psychology, 62,* 180–184.

Gazziniga, M. S. (1992). *Nature's mind.* New York: Basic Books.

Geen, R. G., Stonner, D., & Shope, G. L. (1975). The facilitation of aggression by aggression: Evidence against the catharsis hypothesis. *Journal of Personality and Social Psychology, 31,* 721–726.

Gelernter, D. (1994). *The muse in the machine: Computerizing the poetry of human thought.* New York: Free Press.

Gentry, J., & Eron, L. D. (1993). American Psychological Association Commission on Violence and Youth. *American Psychologist, 48,* 89.

Geschwind, N. (1979, September). Specializations of the human brain. *Scientific American,* pp. 180–199.

Gibbs, J. T. (1992). Negotiating ethnic identity: Issues for Black-White biracial adolescents. In M. P. P. Root (Ed.), *Racially mixed people in America.* Newbury Park, CA: Sage.

Gibson, M., & Ogbu, J. (Eds.). (1991). *Minority status and schooling: A comparative study of immigrant and involuntary minorities.* New York: Garland.

Gick, M. L., & Holyoak, K. J. (1980). Analogical problem solving. *Cognitive Psychology, 12,* 306–355.

Gigerenzer, G., Hoffrage, U., & Kleinböting, H. (1991). Probabilistic mental models: A Brunswikian theory of confidence. *Psychological Review, 98,* 506–528.

Gilbert, S. J. (1981). Another look at the Milgram obedience studies: The role of the gradated series of shocks. *Personality and Social Psychology Bulletin, 7,* 690–695.

Gilligan, C. (1982). *In a different voice.* Cambridge, MA: Harvard University Press.

Gilligan, C., Lyons, P., & Hanmer, T. J. (Eds.). (1990). *Making connections.* Cambridge, MA: Harvard University Press.

Gilligan, C., Rogers, A. G., & Tolman, D. L. (Eds.). (1991). *Women, girls, and psychotherapy.* New York: Haworth Press.

Gilligan, C., Ward, J. V., & Taylor, J. M. (1989). *Mapping the moral domain: A contribution of women's thinking to psychological theory and education.* Cambridge, MA: Harvard University Press.

Gillin, J. C. (1991). The long and short of sleeping pills. *New England Journal of Medicine, 324,* 1735–1736.

Gillis, J. S., & Avis, W. E. (1980). The male-taller norm in mate selection. *Personality and Social Psychology Bulletin, 6,* 396–401.

Gingerich, W. J. (1990). Expert systems: New tools for professional decision-making. *Computers in Human Services, 6,* 219–230.

Ginsburg, G., & Bronstein, P. (1993). Family factors related to children's intrinsic/extrinsic motivational orientation and academic performance. *Child Development, 64,* 1461–1474.

Glaser, R., et al. (1991). Stress-related activation of Epstein-Barr virus. *Brain, Behavior, and Immunity, 5,* 219–232.

Glaser, R., et al. (1993). Stress and the memory T-cell response to the Epstein-Barr virus. *Health Psychology, 12,* 435–442.

Gleason, J. B., & Ratner, N. B. (1993). Language development in children. In J. B. Gleason & N. B. Ratner (Eds.), *Psycholinguistics.* Fort Worth, TX: Harcourt Brace Jovanovich.

Gleaves, D. H., Williamson, D. A., & Barker, S. E. (1993). Confirmatory factor analysis of a multidimensional model of bulimia nervosa. *Journal of Abnormal Psychology, 102,* 173–176.

Godden, D. R., & Baddeley, A. D. (1975). Context-dependent memory in two natural environments: On land and underwater. *British Journal of Psychology, 66,* 325–331.

Goldberg, L. R. (1993). The structure of phenotypic personality traits. *American Psychologist, 48,* 26–34.

Goldfried, M. R., & Padawer, W. (1982). Current status and future directions in psychotherapy. In M. R. Goldfried (Ed.), *Converging themes in psychotherapy: Trends in psychodynamic, humanistic, and behavioral practice.* New York: Springer.

Goldman, K. (1993, June 1). Jordan & Co. play ball on Madison Avenue. *The Wall Street Journal,* p. B9.

Goldman-Rakic, P. S. (1995). Cited in Goleman, D. (1995b, May 2). Biologists find site of working memory. *The New York Times,* pp. C1, C9.

Goldsmith, H. H. (1993). Cited in Adler, T. (1993a). Shy, bold temperament? It's mostly in the genes. *APA Monitor, 24*(1), 7–8.

Goldstein, M., Baker, B., & Jamison, K. (1986). *Abnormal Psychology* (2nd ed.). Boston: Little, Brown.

Goleman, D. (1995a, March 28). The brain manages happiness and sadness in different centers. *The New York Times,* pp. C1, C9.

Goleman, D. (1995b, May 2). Biologists find site of working memory. *The New York Times,* pp. C1, C9.

Goleman, D. (1995c, December 5). Making room on the couch for culture. *The New York Times,* pp. B5, B10.

Goleman, D. J. (1995d). *Emotional intelligence.* New York: Bantam Books.

Golombok, S., & Fivesh, R. (1994). *Gender development.* New York: Cambridge University Press.

Gonzales, M. H., et al. (1983). Interactional approach to interpersonal attraction. *Journal of Personality and Social Psychology, 44,* 1192–1197.

Goodnow, J. J., & Bowes, J. M. (1994). *Men, women, and household work.* Melbourne: Oxford University Press.

Goodwin, F. K., & Jamison, K. R. (1990). *Manic-depressive illness.* New York: Oxford University Press.

Gorman, J., Liebowitz, M., Fyer, A., & Stein, J. (1989). A neuroanatomical hypothesis for panic disorder. *The American Journal of Psychiatry, 146,* 148–161.

Gotlib, I. H., Lewinsohn, P. M., Seeley, J. R., Rohde, P., & Redner, J. E. (1993). Negative cognitions and attributional style in depressed adolescents: An examination of stability and specificity. *Journal of Abnormal Psychology, 102,* 607–615.

Gottesman, I., & Shileds, J. (1982). *Schizophrenia: The epigenetic puzzle.* Cambridge, MA: Cambridge University Press.

Gottfried, A. E., Fleming, J. S., & Gottfried, A. W. (1994). Role of parental motivational practices in children's academic intrinsic motivation and achievement. *Journal of Educational Psychology, 86,* 104–113.

Green, S. K., Buchanan, D. R., & Heuer, S. K. (1984). Winners, losers, and choosers: A field investigation of dating initiation. *Personality and Social Psychology Bulletin, 10,* 502–511.

Greenberg, P. D. (1987). Tumor immunology. In D. P. Stites et al. (Eds.), *Basic and clinical immunology* (6th ed.). Norwalk, CT: Appleton & Lange.

Greenberger, E., & Steinberg, L. (1986). *When teenagers work: The psychological and social costs of adolescent employment.* New York: Basic Books.

Greene, A. L., & Grimsley, M. D. (1990). Age and gender differences in adolescents' preferences for parental advice: Mum's the word. *Journal of Adolescent Research, 5,* 396–413.

Greene, A. S., & Saxe, L. (1990). *Tall tales told to teachers.* Unpublished manuscript, Brandeis University.

Greene, B. A. (1992). Still here: A perspective on psychotherapy with African American women. In J. Chrisler & D. Howard (Eds.), *New directions in feminist psychology.* New York: Springer.

BOOKSHELF

Greene, B. A. (1993). African American women. In L. Comas-Diaz & B. A. Greene (Eds.), *Women of color and mental health.* New York: Guilford Press.

Greeno, C. G., & Wing, R. R. (1994). Stress-induced eating. *Psychological Bulletin, 115,* 444–464.

Grey, J., Feldon, J., Rawlins, J., Hemsley, D., & Smith, A. (1991). The neuropsychology of schizophrenia. *Behavioral and Brain Sciences, 14,* 1–84.

Griffin, E., & Sparks, G. G. (1990). Friends forever: A longitudinal exploration of intimacy in same-sex friends and platonic pairs. *Journal of Social and Personal Relationships, 7,* 29–46.

Grimshaw, G. M., Bryden, M. P., & Finegan, J. K. (1995). Relations between prenatal testosterone and cerebral lateralization in children. *Neuropsychology, 9*(1), 68–79.

Grogger, J., & Bronars, S. (1993). The socioeconomic consequences of teenage childbearing: Findings from a natural experiment. *Family Planning Perspectives, 25,* 156–161.

Gruder, C. L., et al. (1993). Effects of social support and relapse prevention training as adjuncts to a televised smoking-cessation intervention. *Journal of Consulting and Clinical Psychology, 61,* 113–120.

Grush, J. E. (1980). The impact of candidate expenditures, regionality, and prior outcomes on the 1976 Democratic presidential primaries. *Journal of Personality and Social Psychology, 38,* 337–347.

Grych, J. H., & Fincham, F. D. (1993). Children's appraisals of marital conflict. *Child Development, 64,* 215–230.

Guilford, J. P. (1967). *The nature of human intelligence.* New York: McGraw-Hill.

Guisinger, S., & Blatt, S. J. (1994). Individuality and relatedness: Evolution of a fundamental dialectic. *American Psychologist, 49,* 104–111.

Gulevich, G., Dement, W., & Johnson, L. (1966). Psychiatric and EEG observations on a case of prolonged (264 hours) wakefulness. *Archives of General Psychiatry, 15,* 29–35.

Haaf, R. A., Smith, P. H., & Smitley, S. (1983). Infant response to facelike patterns under fixed trial and infant-control procedures. *Child Development, 54,* 172–177.

Haaga, D. A. F., & Davison, G. C. (1993). An appraisal of rational-emotive therapy. *Journal of Consulting and Clinical Psychology, 61,* 215–220.

Haaland, K. Y. (1992). Introduction to the special section on the emotional concomitants of brain damage. *Journal of Consulting and Clinical Psychology, 50,* 327–328.

Haber, R. N. (1980). Eidetic images are not just imaginary. *Psychology Today, 14*(11), 72–82.

Hall, J. A. (1978). Gender effects in decoding nonverbal cures. *Psychological Bulletin, 85,* 845–875.

Hall, J. A. (1984). *Nonverbal sex differences: Communication accuracy and expressive style.* Baltimore, MD: Johns Hopkins University Press.

Halpern, D. F. (1992). *Sex differences in cognitive abilities* (2nd ed.). Hillsdale, NJ: Erlbaum.

Harkins, S. (1987). Social loafing and social facilitation. *Journal of Experimental Social Psychology, 23,* 1–18.

Harlow, H. F. (1959). Love in infant monkeys. *Scientific American, 200,* 68–86.

Harlow, H. F., Harlow, M. K., & Meyer, D. R. (1950). Learning motivated by a manipulation drive. *Journal of Experimental Psychology, 40,* 228–234.

Harlow, H. F., & Zimmermann, R. R. (1959). Affectional responses in the infant monkey. *Science, 130,* 421–432.

Harris, L., & Associates (1995). Cited in Mom the provider. (1995, May 14). *The New York Times,* p. A14.

Harter, S. (1990a). Issues in the assessment of the self-concept of children and adolescents. In A. LaGrea (Ed.), *Through the eyes of a child.* Boston: Allyn & Bacon.

Hartup, W. W. (1993). Adolescents and their friends. In B. Laursen (Ed.), *Close friendships in adolescence.* New Directions in Child Development, no. 60. San Francisco: Jossey-Bass.

Hasselhorn, M. (1992). Task dependency and the role of typicality and metamemory in the development of an organizational strategy. *Child Development, 63,* 202–214.

Haugtvedt, C. P., Schumann, D. W., Schneier, W. L., & Warren, W. L. (1994). Advertising repetition and variation strategies: Implications for understanding attitude strength. *Journal of Consumer Research, 21,* 176–189.

Hauser-Cram, P., Pierson, D. E., Walker, D. K., & Tivnan, T. (1991). *Early education in the public schools.* San Francisco: Josey-Bass.

Hawkins, J. D., Catalano, R. F., & Miller, J. Y. (1992). Risk and protective factors for alcohol and other drug problems in adolescence and early adulthood: Implications for substance abuse prevention. *Psychological Bulletin, 112,* 64–105.

Hayes, K. J., & Hayes, C. (1951). The intellectual development of a home-raised chimpanzee. *Proceedings of the American Philosophical Society, 95,* 105–109.

Hayflick, L. (1977). The cellular basis for biological aging. In C. E. Finch & L. Hayflick (Eds.), *Handbook of the biology of aging.* New York: Van Nostrand Reinhold.

Hayflick, L. (1994). *How and why we age.* New York: Ballantine Books.

Hays, K. F. (1995). Putting sport psychology into (your) practice. *Professional Psychology: Research and Practice, 26,* 33–40.

Heckler, M. (1985). The fight against Alzheimer's disease. *American Psychologist, 40,* 1240–1244.

Heider, F. (1958). *The psychology of interpersonal relations.* New York: Wiley.

Heingartner, A., & Hall, J. V. (1974). Affective consequences in adults and children of repeated exposure to auditory stimuli. *Journal of Personality and Social Psychology, 29,* 719–723.

Hellige, J. B. (1990). Hemispheric asymmetry. *Annual Review of Psychology, 41,* 55–80.

Helmes, E., & Reddon, J. R. (1993). A perspective on developments in assessing psychopathology: A critical review of the MMPI and MMPI-2. *Psychological Bulletin, 113,* 453–471.

Helms, J. E. (1992). Why is there no study of cultural equivalence of standardized cognitive ability testing? *American Psychologist, 47,* 1083–1101.

Helson, R., & Moane, G. (1987). Personality change in women from college to midlife. *Journal of Personality and Social Psychology, 53,* 176–186.

Hendrick, C. D., Wells, K. S., & Faletti, M. V. (1982). Social and emotional effects of geographical relocation on elderly retirees. *Journal of Personality and Social Psychology, 42,* 951–962.

Hennigan, K. M., Cook, T. D., & Gruder, C. L. (1982). Cognitive tuning set, source credibility, and the temporal persistence of attitude change. *Journal of Personality and Social Psychology, 42,* 412–425.

Hepworth, J. T., & West, S. G. (1988). Lynchings and the economy: A time-series reanalysis of Hovland and Sears (1940). *Journal of Personality and Social Psychology, 55,* 239–247.

Herbert, T. B., & Cohen, S. (1993). Depression and immunity: A meta-analytic review. *Psychological Bulletin, 113,* 472–486.

Herek, G. M. (1993). Sexual orientation and military service: A social science perspective. *American Psychologist, 48,* 538–549.

Herrmann, D. J. (1991). *Super memory.* Emmaus, PA: Rodale Press.

Herzog, D. B., Keller, M. B., & Lavori, P. W. (1988). Outcome in anorexia and bulimia nervosa: A review of the literature. *Journal of Nervous and Mental Disease, 176,* 131–143.

Heston, L. L. (1966). Psychiatric disorders in foster home reared children of schizophrenic mothers. *British Journal of Psychiatry, 112,* 819–825.

Hinshaw, S. P. (1992). Externalizing behavior problems and academic underachievement in childhood and adolescence: Causal relationships and underlying mechanisms. *Psychological Bulletin, 111,* 127–155.

Hirschfeld, R. M. A., & Goodwin, F. K. (1988). Mood disorders. In J. A. Talbott, R. E. Hales, & S. C. Yudofsky (Eds.), *Textbook of psychiatry.* Washington, DC: American Psychiatric Press.

Hobfoll, S. E., Ritter, C., Lavin, J., Hulsizer, M. R., & Cameron, R. P. (1995). Depression prevalence and incidence among inner-city pregnant and postpartum women. *Journal of Consulting and Clinical Psychology, 63,* 445–453.

Hoffman, C., & Hurst, N. (1990). Gender stereotypes: Perception or rationalization? *Journal of Personality and Social Psychology, 58,* 197–208.

Hogrebe, M. C., Nist, S. L., & Newman, I. (1985). Are there gender differences in reading achievement? An investigation using the high school and beyond data. *Journal of Educational Psychology, 77,* 716–724.

Holahan, C. J., & Moos, R. H. (1990). Life stressors, resistance factors, and psychological health: An extension of the stress-resistance paradigm. *Journal of Personality and Social Psychology, 58,* 909–917.

Holahan, C. J., Moos, R. H., Holahan, C. K., & Brennan, P. L. (1995). Social support, coping, and depressive symptoms in a late-middle-aged sample of patients reporting cardiac illness. *Health Psychology, 14,* 152–163.

Holden, C. (1980). Identical twins reared apart. *Science, 207,* 1323–1325.

Holden, G. W., & Ritchie, K. L. (1991). Linking extreme marital discord, child rearing, and child behavior problems. *Child Development, 62,* 311–327.

Hollinger, L. M., & Buschmann, M. B. (1993). Factors influencing the perception of touch by elderly nursing home residents and their health caregivers. *International Journal of Nursing Studies, 30,* 445–461.

Hollon, S. D., Shelton, R. C., & Loosen, P. T. (1991). Cognitive therapy and pharmacotherapy for depression. *Journal of Consulting and Clinical Psychology, 59,* 88–99.

Holmbeck, G. N., & Hill, J. P. (1991). Conflictive engagement, positive affect, and menarche in families with seventh-grade girls. *Child Development, 62,* 1030–1048.

Holmes, S. A. (1996, October 5). U.S. reports drop in rate of births to unwed women. *The New York Times,* pp. A1, A9.

Holmes, T. H., & Rahe, R. H. (1967). The social readjustment scale. *Journal of Psychosomatic Research, 11,* 213–218.

Honan, W. H. (1966, April 11). Male professors keep 30% lead in pay over women, study says. *The New York Times,* p. B9.

Honorton, C., et al. (1990). Psi communication in the Ganzfield: Experiments with an automated testing system and a comparison with a meta-analysis of earlier studies. *Journal of Parapsychology, 54,* 99–139.

Honts, C., Hodes, R., & Raskin, D. (1985). *Journal of Applied Psychology, 70*(1).

Hopper, J. L., & Seeman, E. (1994). The bone density of female twins discordant for tobacco use. *New England Journal of Medicine, 330,* 387–392.

Horn, J. M. (1983). The Texas adoption project: Adopted children and their intellectual resemblance to biological and adoptive parents. *Child Development, 54,* 268–275.

Horney, K. (1937). *The neurotic personality of our time.* New York: Norton.

House, J. S., Robbins, C., & Metzner, H. L. (1982). The association of social relationships and activities with mortality: Prospective evidence from the Tecumseh Community Health Study. *American Journal of Epidemiology, 116,* 123–140.

Howard, J. A., Blumstein, P., & Schwartz, P. (1987). Social or evolutionary theories: Some observations on preferences in mate selection. *Journal of Personality and Social Psychology, 53,* 194–200.

Hudson, J. (1993). Cited in Goleman, D. J. (1993, April 6). Studying the secrets of childhood memory. *The New York Times,* pp. C1, C11.

Huesmann, L. R. (1993). Cited in DeAngelis, T. (1993a). It's baaack: TV violence, concern for kid viewers. *APA Monitor, 24*(8), 16.

Huesmann, L. R., & Miller, L. S. (1994). Long-term effects of repeated exposure to media violence in childhood. In L. R. Huesmann (Ed.), *Aggressive behavior: Current perspectives.* New York: Plenum Press.

Hultquist, C. M., et al. (1995). The effect of smoking and light activity on metabolism in men. *Health Psychology, 14,* 124–131.

Humphrey, L. L. (1986). Family dynamics in bulimia. In S. C. Feinstein et al. (Eds.), *Adolescent psychiatry.* Chicago: University of Chicago Press.

Hussong, A. M., & Chassin, L. (1993, March). *The stress-negative affect model of adolescent alcohol use: Disaggregating negative affect.* Paper presented at the meeting of the Society for Research in Child Development, New Orleans, LA.

Huston, A. C., Donnerstein, E., Fairchild, H., Feshbach, N. D., Katz, P. A., Murray, J. P., Rubenstien, E. A., Wilcox, B. L., & Zuckerman, D. (1992). *Big world, small screen: The role of television in American society.* Lincoln: University of Nebraska Press.

Hyde, J. S., & Linn, M. C. (1988). Gender differences in verbal ability: A meta-analysis. *Psychological Bulletin, 104,* 53–69.

Hyde, J. S., Fennema, E., & Lamon, S. J. (1990). Gender differences in mathematics performance: A meta-analysis. *Psychological Bulletin, 107,* 139–155.

Hyde, J. S., & Plant, E. A. (1995). Magnitude of psychological gender differences: Another side to the story. *American Psychologist, 50,* 159–161.

Hyman, R. (1994). Anomaly or artifact? Comments on Bem and Honorton. *Psychological Bulletin, 115,* 19–24.

Ironson, G. (1993). Cited in Adler, T. (1993). Men and women affected by stress, but differently. *APA Monitor, 24*(7), 8–9.

Isen, A. M., Daubman, K. A., & Gorgoglione, J. M. (1987). The influence of positive affect on cognitive organization: Implications for education. In R. E. Snow & M. J. Farr (Eds.), *Aptitude, learning, and instruction* (Vol. 3, pp. 143–164). Hillsdale, NJ: Erlbaum.

Isen, A. M., & Means, B. (1983). The influence of positive affect on decision-making strategy. *Social Cognition, 2,* 28–31.

Izard, C. E. (1984). Emotion-cognition relationships and human development. In C. E. Izard, J. Kagan, & R. B. Zajonc (Eds.), *Emotions, cognition, and behavior.* New York: Cambridge University Press.

Izard, C. E. (1989). The structure and function of emotions: Implications for cognition, motivation, and personality. In I. S. Cohen (Ed.), *The G. Stanley Hall Lecture Series* (Vol. 9, pp. 37–73). Washington, DC: American Psychological Association.

Izard, C. E. (1990). Facial expression and the regulation of emotions. *Journal of Personality and Social Psychology, 58,* 487–498.

Izard, C. E. (1994). Basic emotions, relations among emotions, and emotion-cognition relations. *Psychological Bulletin, 115,* 561–565.

Jacklin, C. N., DiPietro, J. A., & Maccoby, E. E. (1984). Sex-typing behavior and sex-typing pressure in child-parent interaction. *Archives of Sexual Behavior, 13,* 413–425.

Jacklin, C. N., Maccoby, E. E., & Dick, A. E. (1973). Barrier behavior and toy preference: Sex differences (and their absence) in the year-old child. *Child Development, 44,* 196–200.

Jackson, J. F. (1993). Human behavioral genetics, Scarr's theory, and her views on interventions: A critical review and commentary on their implications for African American children. *Child Development, 64,* 1318–1332.

Jacobson, N. S., & Addis, M. E. (1993). Research on couples and couples therapy: What do we know? Where are we going? *Journal of Consulting and Clinical Psychology, 61,* 85–93.

Jacobson, N. S., & Hollon, S. D. (1996). Cognitive-behavior therapy versus pharmocotherapy: Now that the jury's returned its verdict, it's time to present the rest of the evidence. *Journal of Consulting and Clinical Psychology, 64,* 74–80.

Jacobson, N. S., et al. (1985). Efficacy of ECT: A meta-analysis. *American Journal of Psychiatry, 142,* 297–302.

Jacox, A., Carr, D. B., & Payne, R. (1994). New clinical-practice guidelines for the management of pain in patients with cancer. *New England Journal of Medicine, 330,* 651–655.

James, W. (1890). *The principles of psychology* (Vols. 1 and 2). New York: Henry Holt and Company.

James, W. (1902/1958). *Varieties of religious experience.* New York: Mentor Books.

Janicak, P. G., et al. (1985). Efficacy of ECT: A meta-analysis. *American Journal of Psychiatry, 142,* 297–302.

Janowitz, H. D., & Grossman, M. I. (1949). Effects of variations in nutritive density on intake of food in cats and dogs. *American Journal of Physiology, 158,* 184–193.

Jellison, J. M., & Green, J. (1981). A self-presentation approach to the fundamental attribution error: The norm of internality. *Journal of Personality and Social Psychology, 40,* 643–649.

Jenkins, C. D. (1988). Epidemiology of cardiovascular diseases. *Journal of Consulting and Clinical Psychology, 56,* 324–332.

Johnson, B. T., & Eagly, A. H. (1989). Effects of involvement on persuasion: A meta-analysis. *Psychological Bulletin, 106,* 290–314.

Johnson, D. J. (1992). Developmental pathways: Toward an ecological theoretical formulation of race identity in Black-White biracial children. In M. P. P. Root (Ed.), *Racially mixed people in America.* Newbury Park, CA: Sage.

Johnson, E. J., & Tversky, A. (1983). Affect, generalization, and the perception of risk. *Journal of Personality and Social Psychology, 45,* 20–31.

Johnson, W., Emde, R. N., Pannabecker, B., Stenberg, C., & Davis, M. (1982). Maternal perception of infant emotion from birth to 18 months. *Infant Behavior and Development, 5,* 313–322.

Johnston, L. D., O'Malley, P. M., & Bachman, J. G. (1995, December). The Monitoring the Future Study. The University of Michigan Institute for Social Research; National Institute on Drug Abuse, 5600 Fishers Lane, Rockville, MD 20957; USDHHS, Public Health Service, National Institutes of Health.

Johnstone, E., Owens, D., Bydder, G., Colter, N., Crow, T., & Frith, C. (1989). The spectrum of structural brain changes in schizophrenia: Age of onset as a predictor of cognitive and clinical impairments and their cerebral correlates. *Psychological Medicine, 19,* 91–103.

Jones, E. E. (1990). *Interpersonal perception.* New York: W. H. Freeman.

Jones, J. L., & Leary, M. R. (1994). Effects of appearance-based admonitions against sun exposure on tanning intentions in young adults. *Health Psychology, 13,* 86–90.

Jones, M. C. (1924). Elimination of children's fears. *Journal of Experimental Psychology, 7,* 381–390.

Jones, S. R. G. (1992). Was there a Hawthorne Effect? *American Journal of Sociology, 98,* 451–468.

Jordan, J. V., Kaplan, A. G., Miller, J. B., Stiver, L. P., & Stiver, J. L. (Eds.). (1991). *Women's growth in connection.* New York: Guilford Press.

Judd, C. M., & Park, B. (1988). Out-group homogeneity: Judgments of variability at the individual and group levels. *Journal of Personality and Social Psychology, 54,* 778–788.

Jung, C. G. (1917/1966). *The collected works of C. G. Jung No. 7: Two essays on analytical psychology.* Princeton, NJ: Princeton University Press.

Jung, C. J. (1936/1968). *The collected works of C. G. Jung No. 9, Pt. 1: The archetypes and the collective unconcious.* Princeton, NJ: Princeton University Press.

Kahlbaugh, P., & Haviland, J. M. (1991). Formal operational thinking and identity. In R. M. Lerner, A. C. Petersen, & J. Brooks-Gunn (Eds.), *Encyclopedia of adolescence.* New York: Garland.

Kandil, O., & Borysenko, M. (1987). Decline of natural killer cell target binding and lytic activity in mice exposed to rotation stress. *Health Psychology, 6,* 89–99.

Kane, J. M. (1996). Schizophrenia. *New England Journal of Medicine, 334,* 34–41.

Kanner, A. D., Coyne, J. C., Schaefer, C., & Lazarus, R. S. (1981). Comparison of two modes of stress measurement: Daily hassles and uplifts versus major life events. *Journal of Behavioral Medicine, 4,* 1–39.

Kantrowitz, B. (1992, August 3). Teenagers and AIDS. *Newsweek,* 45–50.

Kaplan, H., & Hill, K. (1985). Hunting ability and reproductive success among male Ache foragers: Preliminary results. *Current Anthropology, 26*(1), 131–133.

Kaplan, M., Lazoff, M., Kelly, K., Lukin, R., & Garver, D. (1990). Enlargements of cerebral third ventricle in psychotic patients with delayed response to neuroleptics. *Biological Psychiatry, 27,* 205–214.

Kaplan, S. J. (1991). Physical abuse and neglect. In M. Lewis (Ed.), *Child and adolescent psychiatry: A comprehensive textbook* (pp. 1010–1019). Baltimore, MD: Williams & Wilkins.

Karney, B. R., & Bradbury, T. N. (1995). The longitudinal course of marital quality and stability: A review of theory, method, and research. *Psychological Bulletin, 118,* 3–34.

Katzman, M., Wolchik, S., & Braver, S. (1984). The prevalence of frequent binge eating and bulimia in nonclinical sample. *International Journal of Eating Disorders, 3,* 53–62.

Kaufman, J., & Zigler, E. (1989). The intergenerational transmission of child abuse. In D. Cichetti & V. Carlson (Eds.), *Child maltreatment: Theory and research on the causes and consequences of child abuse and neglect* (pp. 129–150). Cambridge, England: Cambridge University Press.

Kazdin, A. E. (1993). Adolescent mental health: Prevention and treatment programs. *American Pscyhologist, 48,* 127–141.

Keesey, R. E. (1986). A set-point theory of obesity. In K. D. Brownell & J. P. Foreyt (Eds.), *Handbook of eating disorders: Physiology, psychology, and treatment of obesity, anorexia, and bulimia.* New York: Basic Books.

Keil, J., et al. (1993). Mortality rates and risk factors for coronary disease in Black as compared with White men and women. *New England Journal of Medicine, 329,* 73–78.

Keller, H., & Boigs, R. (1991). The development of exploratory behavior. In M. E. Lamb & H. Keller (Eds.), *Infant development: Perspectives from German-speaking countries* (pp. 275–297). Hillsdale, NJ: Erlbaum.

Kellerman, J., Lewis, J., & Laird, J. D. (1989). Looking and loving: The effects of mutual gaze on feelings of romantic love. *Journal of Research in Personality, 23,* 145–161.

Kellner, R. (1990). Somatization: Theories and research. *Journal of Nervous and Mental Disease, 178,* 150–160.

Kemeny, M. E. (1993). Emotions and the immune system. In B. Moyers (Ed.), *Healing and the mind.* New York: Doubleday.

Kemeny, M. E., Weiner, H., Taylor, S. E., Schneider, S., Visscher, B., & Fahey, J. L. (1994). Repeated bereavement, depressed mood, and immune parameters in HIV seropositive and seronegative gay men. *Health Psychology, 13,* 14–24.

Kemper, P., & Murtaugh, C. M. (1991). Lifetime use of nursing home care. *New England Journal of Medicine, 324,* 595–600.

Kendler, K., Gruenberg, A., & Tsuang, M. (1985). Psychiatric illness in first-degree relatives of schizophrenics and surgical control patients: A family study using DSM-III criteria. *Archivesof General Psychiatry, 42,* 770–779.

Kerr, N. L., & Bruun, S. E. (1983). Dispensability of member effort and group motivation losses: Free-rider effects. *Journal of Personality and Social Psychology, 44,* 78–94.

Kerr, N. L., & MacCoun, R. J. (1985). The effects of jury size and polling method on the process and product of jury deliberation. *Journal of Personality and Social Psychology, 48,* 349–363.

Kershner, J. R., & Ledger, G. (1985). Effect of sex, intelligence, and style of thinking on creativity: A comparison of gifted and average IQ children. *Journal of Personality and Social Psychology, 48,* 1033–1040.

Kevorkian found not guilty. (1996, March 8). Reuters. America Online.

Khanna, R., & Rathee, R. (1992). Altruism, mood, and help to drug addicts. Special Series I: Alcohol and drug use. *Journal of Personality and Clinical Studies, 8,* 23–26.

Kihlstrom, J. F., Glisky, M. L., & Angiulo, M. J. (1994). Dissociative tendencies and dissociative disorders. *Journal of Abnormal Psychology, 103,* 117–124.

Kilborn, P. T. (1995, March 16). Women and minorities still face "glass ceilings." *The New York Times,* p. A22.

Kimble, D. P. (1992). *Biological psychology* (2nd ed.). Fort Worth, TX: Harcourt Brace Jovanovich.

Kimble, G. A. (1994). A frame of reference for psychology. *American Psychologist, 49,* 510–519.

Kinnunen, T., Zamansky, H. S., & Block, M. L. (1994). Is the hypnotized patient lying? *Journal of Abnormal Psychology, 103,* 184–191.

Kirchler, E., Pombeni, M. L., & Palmonari, A. (1991). Sweet sixteen . . . : Adolescents' problems and the peer group as a source of support. *European Journal of Psychology of Education, 6,* 393–410.

Kleinke, C. L. (1977). Compliance to requests made by gazing and touching experimenters in field settings. *Journal of Experimental Social Psychology, 13,* 218–223.

Kleinke, C. L. (1986). Gaze and eye contact: A research review. *Psychological Review, 100,* 78–100.

Kleinmuntz, B., & Szucko, J. J. (1984). Lie detection in ancient and modern times: A call for contemporary scientific study. *American Psychologist, 39,* 766–776.

Kneip, R. C., et al. (1993). Self- and spouse ratings of anger and hostility as predictors of coronary heart disease. *Health Psychology, 12,* 301–307.

Knight, G. P., Fabes, R. A., & Higgins, D. A. (1996). Concerns about drawing causal inferences from meta-analyses: An example in the study of gender differences in aggression. *Psychological Bulletin, 119,* 410–421.

Kobasa, S. C., Maddi, S. R., & Kahn, S. (1982). Hardiness and health: A prospective study. *Journal of Personality and Social Psychology, 42,* 168–177.

Koestner, R., Franz, C., & Weinberger, J. (1990). The family origins of empathic concern: A 26-year longitudinal study. *Journal of Personality and Social Psychology, 58,* 709–717.

Kohlberg, L. (1963). Moral development and identification. In H. W. Stevenson (Ed.), *Yearbook of the national survey for the study of education: 1. Child psychology.* Chicago: University of Chicago Press.

Kohlberg, L. (1969). *Stages in the development of moral thought and action.* New York: Holt, Rinehart and Winston.

Kolb, B., & Taylor, L. (1981). Affective behavior in patients with localized cortical excisions: Role of lesion site and side. *Science, 214,* 89–91.

Kolko, D. J., & Richard-Figueroa, J. L. (1985). Effects of video games on the adverse corollaries of chemotherapy in pediatric oncology patients: A single-case analysis. *Journal of Consulting and Clinical Psychology, 53,* 223–228.

Kopera-Frye, K., Ager, J., Saltz, E., Poindexter, J., & Lee, S. (1993, March). *Predictors of adolescent delinquency.* Paper presented at the meeting of the Society for Research in Child Development, New Orleans, LA.

Kornblum, W. (1994). *Sociology in a changing world* (3rd ed.). Fort Worth, TX: Harcourt Brace Jovanovich.

Kortenhaus, C. M., & Demarest, J. (1993). Gender role stereotyping in children's literature: An update. *Sex Roles, 28,* 219–231.

Krosnick, J. A. (1989). Attitude importance and attitude accessibility. *Personality and Social Psychology Bulletin, 15,* 297–308.

Krueger, R. F., Schmutte, P. S., Caspi, A., Moffitt, T. E., Campbell, K., & Silva, P. A. (1993, May). *Delinquency affect and constraint: Personality and illegal behavior in late adolescence.* Paper presented at the meeting of the Midwestern Psychological Association, Chicago.

Kübler-Ross, E. (1969). *On death and dying.* New York: Macmillan.

Kuczaj, S. A., II. (1982). On the nature of syntactic development. In S. A. Kuczaj, II (Ed.), *Language development, Vol. 1.: Syntax and semantics.* Hillsdale, NJ: Erlbaum.

Kuczmarski, R. J. (1992). Prevalence of overweight and weight gain in the United States. *American Journal of Clinical Nutrition, 55*(Suppl.), 495S–502S.

Kuhn, D., et al. (1978). Sex-role concepts of two- and three-year-olds. *Child Development, 49,* 445–451.

Kunkel, D., & Roberts, D. (1991). Young minds and marketplace values: Issues in children's television advertising. *Journal of Social Issues, 47,* 57–72.

Kutner, L. (1993, February 4). For both boys and girls, early or late puberty can lead to social or emotional problems. *The New York Times,* p. B6.

LaFramboise, T. (1994). Cited in DeAngelis, T. (1994). History, culture affect treatment for Indians. *APA Monitor, 27*(10), 36.

Lagerspetz, K. M., Bjorkqvist, K., & Peltonen, T. (1988). Is indirect aggression typical of females? Gender differences in aggressiveness in 11- to 12-year-old children. *Aggressive Behavior, 14,* 403–414.

Lakka, T. A., et al. (1994). Relation of leisure-time physical activity and cardiorespiratory fitness to the risk of acute myocardial infarction in men. *New England Journal of Medicine, 330,* 1549–1554.

Lamb, L. E. (1993). Aging: the cross-linking link. *Muscle and Fitness, 54*(4), 166–167.

Lamb, M. E. (1977). Father-infant and mother-infant interaction in the first year of life. *Child Development, 48,* 167–181.

Lamb, M. E., Sternberg, K. J., & Prodomidis, M. (1992). Nonmaternal care and the security of infant-mother attachment: A reanalysis of the data. *Infant Behavior and Development, 15,* 71–83.

Lambert, W. E., Genesee, F., Holobow, N., & Chartrand, L. (1991). *Bilingual education for majority English-speaking children.* Montreal: McGill University.

Langlois, J. H. (1994). Cited in Brody, J. E. (1994, March 21). Notions of beauty transcend culture, new study suggests. *The New York Times,* p. A14.

Langlois, J. H., & Downs, C. (1980). Mothers, fathers and peers as socialization agents of sex-typed play behavior in young children. *Child Development, 51,* 1217–1247.

LaPerriere, A. R., et al. (1991). Aerobic exercise training in an AIDS risk group. *International Journal of Sports Medicine, 12,* S53–S57.

Larson, R., & Richards, M. H. (1991). Daily companionship in late childhood and early adolescence: Changing development contexts. *Child Development, 62,* 284–300.

Laumann, E. O., Gagnon, J. H., Michael, R. T., & Michaels, S. (1994). *The social organization of sexuality: Sexual practices in the United States.* Chicago: University of Chicago Press.

Lazarus, A. A. (1990). If this be research . . . *American Psychologist, 45,* 670–671.

Lazarus, R. S. (1991). Cognition and motivation in emotion. *American Psychologist, 46,* 352–367.

Lazarus, R. S., DeLongis, A., Folkman, S., & Gruen, R. (1985). Stress and adaptational outcomes: The problem of confounded measures. *American Psychologist, 40,* 770–779.

Leary, W. E. (1991, October 22). Black hypertension may reflect other ills. *The New York Times,* p. C3.

Leary, W. E. (1995, May 2). Billions suffering needlessly, study says. *The New York Times,* p. C5.

LeDoux, J. E. (1994, June). Emotion, memory, and the brain. *Scientific American,* pp. 50–57.

Lefcourt, H. M., & Martin, R. A. (1986). *Humor and life stress: Antidote to adversity.* New York: Springer-Verlag.

Leff, J., & Vaughn, C. (1985). *Expressed emotion in families.* New York: Guilford Press.

Lehrman, S. (1995, January). Can the clock be slowed? *Harvard Health Letter, 20*(3), 1–3.

Leibel, R. L., Rosenbaum, M., & Hirsch, J. (1995). Changes in energy expenditure resulting from altered body weight. *New England Journal of Medicine, 332,* 621–628.

Leippe, M. R. (1985). The influence of eye-witness non-identifications on mock-jurors' judgments of a court case. *Journal of Applied Social Psychology, 15,* 656–672.

Lenneberg, E. H. (1967). *Biological foundations of language.* New York: Wiley.

Leon, G. R., & Dinklage, D. (1989). Obesity and anorexia nervosa. In T. H. Ollendick & M. Hersen (Eds.), *Handbook of child psychopathology* (2nd ed., pp. 247–263). New York: Plenum Press.

Leslie, C. (1993, August 2). Girls will be girls. *Newsweek,* p. 44.

Lesnik-Oberstein, M., & Cohen, L. (1984). Cognitive style, sensation seeking, and assortive mating. *Journal of Personality and Social Psychology, 46,* 57–66.

Levinson, D. J. (1996). *The seasons of a woman's life.* New York: Knopf.

Levinson, D. J., Darrow, C. N., Klein, E. B., Levinson, M. H., & McKee, B. (1978). *The seasons of a man's life.* New York: Knopf.

Levy, S. M., Herberman, R. B., Maluish, A. M., Schlien, B., & Lippman, M. (1985). Prognostic risk assessment in the primary breast cancer by behavioral and immunological parameters. *Health Psychology, 4,* 99–113.

Lewin, T. (1995, September 18). Women are becoming equal providers. *The New York Times,* p. A27.

Lewin, T. (1995, December 7). Parents poll shows higher incidence of child abuse. *The New York Times,* p. B16.

Lewinsohn, P. M., et al. (1994). Adolescent psychopathology: II. Psychosocial risk factors for depression. *Journal of Abnormal Psychology, 103,* 302–315.

Lewis-Fernández, R., & Kleinman, A. (1994). Culture, personality, and psychopathology. *Journal of Abnormal Psychology, 103,* 67–71.

Lichtenstein, E., & Glasgow, R. E. (1992). Smoking cessation: What have we learned in the past decade? *Journal of Consulting and Clinical Psychology, 60,* 518–527.

Liebert, R., & Spiegler, M. (1982). *Personality: Strategies and issues.* Homewood, IL: Dorsey Press.

Liebert, R. M., Sprafkin, J. N., & Davidson, E. S. (1989). *The early window: Effects of television on children and youth* (3rd ed.). New York, Pergamon Press.

Lillydahl, J. (1995). Cited in Pantiel, M. (1995, September). Should your teenager work? *Better Homes and Gardens,* p. 226.

Lindpaintner, K. (1995). Finding an obesity gene—A tale of mice and man. *New England Journal of Medicine, 332,* 679–680.

Lindsay, R. C. L., Lim, R., Marando, L., & Culley, D. (1986). Mock-juror evaluations of eyewitness testimony: A test of metamemory hypotheses. *Journal of Applied Social Psychology, 16,* 447–459.

Linn, M. C., & Petersen, A. C. (1986). A meta-analysis of gender differences in spatial ability: Implications for mathematics and science achievement. In J. S. Hyde & M. C. Linn (Eds.), *The psychology of gender: Advances through meta-analysis* (pp. 67–101). Baltimore, MD: Johns Hopkins University Press.

Linville, P. W., Fischer, G. W., & Salovey, P. (1989). Perceived distribution of the characteristics of in-group and out-group members. *Journal of Personality and Social Psychology, 57,* 165–188.

Lips, H. (1993). *Sex and gender: An introduction* (2nd ed.). Mountain View, CA: Mayfield.

Lipsey, M. W., & Wilson, D. B. (1993). The efficacy of psychological, educational, and behavioral treatment: Confirmation from meta-analysis. *American Psychologist, 48,* 1181–1209.

List, J. A., Collins, W. A., & Westby, S. D. (1983). Comprehension and inferences from traditional and non-traditional sex-role portrayals on television. *Child Development, 54,* 1579–1587.

Livson, N., & Peskin, H. (1972). Pre- and postpubertal personality and adult psychological functioning. *Seminars in Psychiatry, 4*(4), 343–353.

Lochman, J. E. (1992). Cognitive-behavioral intervention with aggressive boys: Three-year follow-up and preventive effects. *Journal of Consulting and Clinical Psychology, 60,* 426–432.

Lochman, J. E., & Dodge, K. A. (1994). Social-cognitive processes of severely violent, moderately aggressive, and nonagressive boys. *Journal of Consulting and Clinical Psychology, 62,* 366–374.

Loehlin, J. C., Willerman, L., & Horn, J. M. (1988). Human behavior genetics. *Annual Review of Psychology, 39,* 101–133.

Loftus, E. F. (1983). Silence is not golden. *American Psychologist, 38,* 564–572.

Loftus, E. F. (1994). Conference on memory. Harvard Medical School. Cited in Goleman, D. (1994, May 31). Miscoding is seen as the root of false memories. *The New York Times,* pp. C1, C8.

Loftus, E. F., & Loftus, G. R. (1980). On the permanence of stored information in the brain. *American Psychologist, 35,* 409–420.

Loftus, E. F., & Palmer, J. C. (1974). Reconstruction of automobile destruction: An example of interaction between language and memory. *Journal of Verbal Learning and Verbal Behavior, 13,* 585–589.

Lore, R. K., & Schultz, L. A. (1993). Control of human aggression: A comparative perspective. *American Psychologist, 48,* 16–25.

Lorenz, K. (1937). The companion in the bird's world. *Auk, 54,* 245–273.

Lovdal, L. T. (1989). Sex role messages in television commercials: An update. *Sex Roles, 21,* 715–724.

Lown, J., & Dolan, E. (1988). Financial challenges in remarriage. *Lifestyles: Family and Economic Issues, 9,* 73–88.

Luchins, A. S., & Luchins, E. H. (1959). *Rigidity of behavior.* Eugene: University of Oregon Press.

Ludwick-Rosenthal, R., & Neufeld, R. W. J. (1993). Preparation for undergoing an invasive medical procedure: Interacting effects of information and coping style. *Journal of Consulting and Clinical Psychology, 61,* 156–164.

Lundeberg, M. A., Fox, P. W., & Puncochar, J. (1994). Highly confident but wrong: Gender differences and similarities in confidence of judgments. *Journal of Educational Psychology, 86,* 114–121.

Lykken, D. T., McGue, M., Tellegen, A., & Bouchard, T. J., Jr. (1992). Emergencies: Genetic traits that may not run in families. *American Psychologist, 47,* 1565–1577.

Lyons-Ruth, K., Alpern, L., & Repacholi, B. (1993). Disorganized infant attachment classification and maternal psychosocial problems as predictors of hostile-aggressive behavior in the preschool classroom. *Child Development, 64,* 575–585.

Maccoby, E. E., & Jacklin, C. N. (1974). *The psychology of sex differences.* Stanford, CA: Stanford University Press.

Maccoby, E., & Martin, J. A. (1983). Socialization in the context of the family: Parent-child interaction. In E. M. Hetherington (Ed.), *Handbook of child psychology* (Vol. 4). New York: Wiley.

MacDonald, K. (1992). Warmth as a developmental construct: An evolutionary analysis. *Child Development, 63,* 753–773.

MacDonald, K., & Parke, R. D. (1984). Cited in Bridges, L., Connell, J. P., & Belsky, J. (1988). Similarities and differences in infant-mother and infant-father interaction in the strange situation: A component process analysis. *Developmental Psychology, 24*(1), 92–100.

Mackie, D. M., Worth, L. T., & Asuncion, A. G. (1990). Processing of persuasive in-group messages. *Journal of Personality and Social Psychology, 58,* 812–822.

Maier, N. R. F. (1931). Reasoning in human beings: II. The solution of a problem and its appearance in consciousness. *Journal of Comparative Psychology, 12,* 181–194.

Malina, R. M. (1978). Adolescent growth and maturation: Selected aspects of current research. *Yearbook of Physical Anthropology, 21,* 63–94.

Malinosky-Rummell, R., & Hansen, D. H. (1993). Long-term consequences of childhood physical abuse. *Psychological Bulletin, 114,* 68–79.

Manke, B. (1993, March). *Dimensions of intimacy during adolescence: Correlates and antecedents.* Paper presented at the meeting of the Society for Research in Child Development, New Orleans, LA.

Manson, J. E., et al. (1995). Body weight and mortality among women. *New England Journal of Medicine, 333,* 677–685.

Manucia, G. K., Baumann, D. J., & Cialdini, R. B. (1984). Mood influences on helping: Direct effects or side effects? *Journal of Personality and Social Psychology, 46,* 357–364.

March, J., Johnston, H., & Greist, J. (1989). Obsessive-compulsive disorder. *American Family Practice, 39,* 175–182.

Marcia, J. E. (1966). Development and validation of ego identity status. *Journal of Personality and Social Psychology, 3,* 551–558.

Marcia, J. E. (1991). Identity and self-development. In R. M. Lerner, A. C. Petersen, & J. Brooks-Gunn (Eds.), *Encyclopedia of adolescence.* New York: Garland.

Marcia, J. E., Waterman, A. S., Matteson, D. R., Archer, S. L., & Orlofsky, J. L. (1993). *Ego identity: A handbook for psychosocial research.* New York: Springer-Verlag.

Marenberg, M. E., et al. (1994). Genetic susceptability to death from coronary heart disease in women. *New England Journal of Medicine, 330,* 1041–1046.

Margoshes, P. (1995). For many, old age is the prime of life. *APA Monitor, 26*(5), 36–37.

Margules, D. L., & Olds, J. (1962). Identical "feeding" and "rewarding" systems in the lateral hypothalmus of rats. *Science, 135,* 374–375.

Markman, H. J., Renick, M. J., Floyd, F. J., Stanley, S. M., & Clements, M. (1993). Preventing marital distress through communication and conflict management training: A 4- and 5-year follow-up. *Journal of Consulting and Clinical Psychology, 61,* 70–77.

Marks, C. (1984). *World artists, 1950–1980* (pp. 664–675). New York: H. W. Wilson.

Markstrom-Adams, C. (1992). A consideration of intervening factors in adolescent identity formation. In G. R. Adams, T. P. Gullotta, & R. Montemayor (Eds.), *Adolescent identity formation.* Newbury Park, CA: Sage.

Markus, H., & Kitayama, S. (1991). Culture and the self: Implications for cognition, emotion, and motivation. *Psychological Review, 98*(2), 224–253.

Marler, P. (1991). The instinct for vocal learning: Songbirds. In S. E. Brauth, W. S. Hall, & R. J. Dooling (Eds.), *Plasticity of development* (pp. 107–125). Cambridge, MA: MIT Press.

Marriott, M. (1991, June 5). Beyond "yuck" for girls in science. *The New York Times,* p. A26.

Marsh, H. W., Craven, R. G., & Debus, R. (1991). Self-concepts of young children 5 to 8 years of age: Measurement and multidimensional structure. *Journal of Educational Psychology, 83,* 377–392.

Martin, C. L. (1987). A ratio measure of sex stereotyping. *Journal of Personality and Social Psychology, 52,* 489–499.

Martin, C. L., & Halverson, C. F., Jr. (1981). A schematic processing model of sex typing and stereotyping in children. *Child Development, 54,* 1119–1134.

Martin, R. A., & Lefcourt, H. M. (1983). Sense of humor as a moderator of the relation between stressors and moods. *Journal of Personality and Social Psychology, 45,* 1313–1324.

Martin, S. (1994). Music lessons enhance spatial reasoning skills, *APA Monitor, 27*(10), 5.

Maruyama, G., Fraser, S. C., & Miller, N. (1982). Personal responsibility and altruism in children. *Journal of Personality and Social Psychology, 42,* 658–664.

Maslow, A. H. (1970). *Motivation and personality* (2nd ed.). New York: Harper & Row.

Matarazzo, J. D. (1990). Psychological assessment versus psychological testing. *American Psychologist, 45,* 999–1017.

Matarazzo, J. D. (1993). Cited in Michaelson, R. (1993). Behavior gets big billing in medical schools today. *APA Monitor, 24*(8), 56.

Matlin, M. (1996). *The psychology of women* (3rd ed.). Fort Worth, TX: Harcourt Brace Jovanovich.

Maultsby, M. C. (1971). Systematic written homework in psychotherapy. *Psychotherapy, Theory, Research, and Practice, 8,* 195–198.

Maybury-Lewis, D. (1992). *Millennium: Tribal wisdom and the modern world.* New York: Viking.

McCall, R. B. (1977). Children's IQs as predictors of adult educational and occupational status. *Science, 297,* 482–483.

McCarley, R. W. (1992). Cited in Blakeslee, S. (1992, January 7). Scientists unraveling chemistry of dreams. *The New York Times,* pp. C1, C10.

McCarthy, K. (1993). Research on women's health doesn't show whole picture. *APA Monitor, 24*(7), 14–15.

McClelland, D. C. (1965). Achievement and entrepreneurship: A longitudinal study. *Journal of Personality and Social Psychology, 1,* 389–392.

McDougall, W. (1908). *An introduction to social psychology.* London: Meuthen.

McGowan, R. J., & Johnson, D. K. (1984). The mother-child relationship and other antecedents of childhood intelligence: A casual analysis. *Child Development, 55,* 810–820.

McLeod, J. D., Kessler, R. C., & Landis, K. R. (1992). Speed of recovery from major depressive episodes in a community sample of married men and women. *Journal of Abnormal Psychology, 101,* 277–286.

Mead, M. (1935). *Sex and temperament in three primitive societies.* New York: Dell.

Meehan, P. J., Lamb, J. A., Saltzman, L. E., & O'Carroll, P. W. (1992). Attempted suicide among young adults: Progress toward a meaningful estimate of prevalence. *American Journal of Psychiatry, 149,* 41–44.

Meichenbaum, D. (1993). Changing conceptions of cognitive behavior modification: Retrospect and prospect. *Journal of Consulting and Clinical Psychology, 61,* 202–204.

Melle, I., & Friis, S. (1991). Psychosocial treatment of schizophrenia. *Nordisk Psykiatrisk Tidsskrift, 45,* 97–108.

Metalsky, G. I., Joiner, T. E., Jr., Hardin, T. S., & Abramson, L. Y. (1993). Depressive reactions to failure in naturalistic setting: A test of the hopelessness and self-esteem theories of depression. *Journal of Abnormal Psychology, 102,* 101–109.

Mevkens, F. L. (1990). Coming of age—The chemoprevention of cancer. *New England Journal of Medicine, 323,* 825–827.

Michael, R. T., Gagnon, J. H., Laumann, E. O., & Kolata, G. (1994). *Sex in America: A definitive survey.* Boston: Little, Brown.

Michaelson, R. (1993). Tug-of-war is developing over defining retardation. *APA Monitor, 24*(5), 34–35.

Michels, R., & Marzuk, P. M. (1993). Progress in psychiatry: II. *New England Journal of Medicine, 329,* 628–638.

Mikesell, R. H., Lusterman, D., & McDaniel, S. (Eds.). (1995). *Family psychology and systems therapy.* Washington, DC: American Psychological Association.

Milgram, S. (1963). Behavioral study of obedience. *Journal of Abnormal and Social Psychology, 67,* 371–378.

Miller, A. (1992, June 29). Baby makers, Inc. *Newsweek,* pp. 38–39.

Miller, B. C., McCoy, J. K, & Olson, T. D. (1986). Dating age and stage as correlates of adolescent sexual attitudes and behavior. *Journal of Adolescent Research, 1,* 361–371.

Miller, G. A. (1956). The magical number seven, plus or minus two: Some limits on our capacity for processing information. *Psychological Review, 63,* 81–97.

Miller, J. L. (1992). Trouble in mind. *Scientific American, 267*(3), 180.

Miller, N. B., Cowan, P. A., Cowan, C. P., Hetherington, E. M., & Clingempeel, W. G. (1993). Externalizing in preschoolers and early adolescents: A cross-study replication of a family model. *Developmental Psychology, 29,* 3–18.

Miller, N. E. (1995). Clinical-experimental interactions in the development of neuroscience. *American Psychologist, 50,* 901–911.

Millon, T. (1981). *Disorders of personality.* New York: Wiley.

Mineka, S. (1991, August). Paper presented to the annual meeting of the American Psychological Association, San Francisco, CA. Cited in Turkington, C. (1991). Evolutionary memories may have phobia role. *APA Monitor, 22*(11), 14.

Mintz, L. B., Bartels, K. M., & Rideout, C. A. (1995). Training in counseling ethnic minorities and race-based availability of graduate school resources. *Professional Psychology: Research in Practice, 26,* 316–321.

Mitchell, J. E., & Eckert, E. D. (1987). Scope and significance of eating disorders. *Journal of Consulting and Clinical Psychology, 55,* 628–634.

Moffet, M. (1990). The dance of the electric honeybee. *National Geographic, 177,* 134–140.

Moir, A., & Jessel, D. (1991). *Brain sex.* New York: Carol Publishing/Lyle Stuart.

Moldin, S. O. (1994). Indicators of liability to schizophrenia: Perspectives from genetic epidemiology. *Schizophrenia Bulletin, 20*(1), 169–184.

Mom, Dad, I want a job. (1993, May 17). *U.S. News & World Report,* pp. 68–72.

Money, J. (1987). Sin, sickness or status—Homosexual gender identity and psychoneuroendocrinology. *American Psychologist, 42,* 384–399.

Money, J. (1994). The concept of gender identity disorder in childhood and adolescence after 39 years. *Journal of Sex and Marital Therapy, 20*(3), 163–177.

Montemayor, R., & Flannery, D. J. (1991). Parent-adolescent relations in middle and late adolescence. In R. M. Lerner, A. C. Petersen, & J. Brooks-Gunn (Eds.), *Encyclopedia of adolescence.* New York: Garland.

Moore, K. A., & Stief, T. M. (1992). Changes in marriage and fertility behavior: Behavior versus attitudes of young adults. *Youth and Society, 22,* 362–386.

Morrison, A. M., & Von Glinow, M. A. (1990). Women and minorities in management. *American Psychologist, 45,* 200–209.

Moyer, K. E. (1983). The physiology of motivation: Aggression as a model. In C. J. Scheier & A. M. Rogers (Eds.), *G. Stanley Hall Lecture Series* (Vol. 3). Washington, DC: American Psychological Association.

Muñoz, R. F., Hollon, S. D., McGarth, E., Rehm, L. P., & VandenBos, G. R. (1994). On the AHCPR *Depression in Primary Care* guidelines: Further consideration for practitioners. *American Psychologist, 49,* 42–61.

Murray, B. (1996). College youth haunted by increased pressures. *APA Monitor, 26*(4), 47.

Myers, D. G. (1996). *Social psychology* (5th ed.). New York: McGraw-Hill.

Myers, D. G., & Bishop, G. D. (1970). Discussion effects on racial attitudes. *Science, 169,* 778–779.

Myers, J. K., Weissman, M. M., Tischler, G. L., Holzer, C. E., Leaf, P. J., Orvaschel, H. A., Anthony, J. C., Boyd, J. H., Burke, J. D., Kramer, M., & Stoltzman, R. (1984). Six-month prevalence of psychiatric disorders in three communities: 1980–1982. *Archives of General Psychiatry, 41,* 959–967.

National Center for Health Statistics (1982). *Monthly Vital Statistics Report, Advance Report of Final Natality Statistics, 33*(6), supplement.

National Institute of Child Health and Human Development. (1996). Infant child care and attachment security: Results of the NICHD study of early child care. Cited in Chira, D. J. (1996, April 21). Study says babies in child care keep secure bonds to mothers. *The New York Times,* pp. C10, C32.

National Institute of Mental Health. (1985). *Electroconvulsive therapy: Consensus Development Conference statement.* Bethesda, MD: U.S. Department of Health and Human Services.

Neher, A. (1991). Maslow's theory of motivation: A critique. *Journal of Humanistic Psychology, 31,* 89–112.

Neisser, U. (1993). Cited in Goleman, D. J. (1993, April 6). Studying the secrets of childhood memory. *The New York Times,* pp. C1, C11.

Neisser, U., Bouchard, T. J., Jr., & Boyin, A. W. (1996). Intelligence: Knowns and unknowns. *American Psychologist, 51*(2), 77–101.

Nevid, J. S. (1984). Sex differences in factors of romantic attraction. *Sex Roles, 11,* 401–411.

Nevid, J. S., Rathus, S. A., & Greene, B. A. (1997). *Abnormal psychology in a changing world* (3rd ed.). Englewood Cliffs, NJ: Prentice-Hall.

Newcomb, M. D., & Bentler, P. M. (1992, August). *Substance abuse and gender: Accounting for the differences.* Paper presented at the meeting of the American Psychological Association, Washington, DC.

Newcomb, T. M. (1981). Heiderian balance as a group phenomenon. *Journal of Personality and Social Psychology, 40,* 862–867.

Nides, M. A., et al. (1995). Predictors of initial smoking cessation and relapse through the first 2 years of the lung health study. *Journal of Consulting and Clinical Psychology, 63,* 60–69.

Nigg, J. T., & Goldsmith, H. H. (1994). Genetics of personality disorders: Perspectives from personality and psychopathology research. *Psychological Bulletin, 115,* 346–380.

Noller, P., & Callan, V. J. (1990). Adolescents' perceptions of the nature of their communication with parents. *Journal of Youth and Adolescence, 19,* 349–362.

Norton, A., & Moorman, J. (1987). Current trends in marriage and divorce among American women. *Journal of Marriage and the Family, 49,* 3–14.

BOOKSHELF

Novacek, J., Raskin, R., & Hogan, R. (1991). Why do adolescents use drugs? Age, sex, and user differences. *Journal of Youth and Adolescence, 20,* 475–492.

Ogbu, J. U. (1993). Differences in cultural frame of reference. *International Journal of Behavioral Development, 16,* 483–506.

Olds, J. (1969) The central nervous system and the reinforcement of behavior. *American Psychologist, 24,* 114–132.

O'Leary, A. (1990). Stress, emotion, and human immune function. *Psychological Bulletin, 108,* 363–382.

Olson, S. L., Bates, J. E., & Kaskie, B. (1992). Caregiver-infant interaction antecedents of children's school-age cognitive ability. *Merrill-Palmer Quarterly, 38,* 309–330.

Olweus, D. (1986). Aggression and hormones: Behavioral relationship with testosterone and adrenaline. In D. Olweus, J. Block, & M. Radke-Yarrow (Eds.), *Development of antisocial and prosocial behavior* (pp. 51–72). New York: Academic Press.

Orive, R. (1988). Social projective and social comparison of opinion. *Journal of Personality and Social Psychology, 54,* 953–964.

Osborne, C. (Ed.). (1968). *I have a dream: The story of Martin Luther King in text and pictures.* New York: Time-Life Books.

Osofsky, J. D., Osofsky, H. J., & Diamond, M. O. (1988). The transition to parenthood: Special tasks and risk factors for adolescent parents. In G. Y. Michaels & W. A. Goldberg (Eds.), *The transition to parenthood: Current theory and research.* New York: Cambridge University Press.

Padgham, J. J., & Blyth, D. A. (1991). Dating during adolescence. In R. M. Lerner, A. C. Petersen, & J. Brooks-Gunn (Eds.), *Encyclopedia of adolescence.* New York: Garland.

Paffenbarger, R. S., Jr., et al. (1993). The association of changes in physical-activity level and other lifestyle characteristics with mortality among men. *New England Journal of Medicine, 328,* 538–545.

Paikoff, R. L., & Collins, A. C. (1991). Editor's notes: Shared views in the family during adolescence. In R. L. Paikoff & A. C. Collins (Eds.), New Directions for Child Development, no. 51. San Francisco: Josey-Bass.

Pantiel, M. (1995, September). Should your teenager work? *Better Homes and Gardens,* p. 226.

Pantin, H. M., & Carver, C. S. (1982). Induced competence and the bystander effect. *Journal of Applied Social Psychology, 12,* 100–111.

Papini, D. R., & Roggman, L. A. (1992). Adolescent perceived attachment to parents in relation to competence, depression, and anxiety: A longitudinal study. *Journal of Early Adolecence, 12,* 420–440.

Papousek, M., Papousek, H., & Symmes, D. (1991). The meanings of melodies in motherese in tone and stress languages. *Infant Behavior and Development, 14,* 415–440.

Pardes, H., et al. (1991). Physicians and the animal-rights movement. *New England Journal of Medicine, 324,* 1640–1643.

Parke, R. D. (1981). *Fathers.* Cambridge, MA: Harvard University Press.

Patterson, M. L. (1991). Functions of nonverbal behavior in interpersonal interaction. In R. S. Feldman & B. Rime (Eds.), *Fundamentals of nonverbal behavior.* Cambridge, England: Cambridge University Press.

Patterson, S. J., Sochting, I., & Marcia, J. E. (1992). The inner space and beyond: Women and identity. In G. R. Adams, T. P. Gullotta, & R. Montemayor (Eds.), *Adolescent identity formation.* Newbury Park, CA: Sage.

Pearlman, C. (1994, January). Pets can be great friends: Research shows animal owners have less stress and live longer lives. *Safety & Health,* pp. 80–81.

Pena, N., & Bricklin, M. (1990). The future of fitness. *Prevention, 42*(1), 41–43.

Penfield, W. (1969). Consciousness, memory, and man's conditioned reflexes. In K. H. Pribram (Ed.), *On the biology of learning.* New York: Harcourt Brace Jovanovich.

Penn, N. E., Kar, S., Kramer, J., Skinner, J., & Zambrana, R. E. (1995). Panel IV. Ethnic minorities, health care systems, and behavior. *Health Psychology, 14,* 641–648.

Perils of part-time work for teens. (1991, March 30). *Science News,* p. 205.

Perrett, D. I. (1994). Cited in Brody, J. E. (1994, March 21). Notions of beauty transcend culture, new study suggests. *The New York Times,* p. A14.

Perry, C. L. (1991). Programs for smoking prevention with early adolescents. In R. M. Lerner, A. C. Petersen, & J. Brooks-Gunn (Eds.), *Encyclopedia of adolescence.* New York: Garland.

Perry, D. G., & Bussey, K. (1979). The social learning theory of sex differences: Imitation is alive and well. *Journal of Personality and Social Psychology, 37,* 1699–1712.

Petersen, A. C. (1987, September). Those gangly years. *Psychology Today,* pp. 28–34.

Peterson, C., & Seligman, M. E. P. (1985). The learned helplessness model of depression: Current status of theory and research. In E. E. Beckham & W. R. Leber (Eds.), *Handbook of depression* (pp. 914–939). Homewood, IL: Dorsey.

Peterson, L. R., & Peterson, M. J. (1959). Short-term retention of individual verbal items. *Journal of Experimental Psychology, 58,* 193–198.

Pettingale, K. W., et al. (1985). Mental attitudes to cancer: An additional prognostic factor. *Lancet, 1,* 750.

Petty, R. E., & Cacioppo, J. T. (1986). The elaboration-likelihood model of persuasion. In L. Berkowitz (Ed.), *Advances in experimental social psychology* (Vol. 19). New York: Academic Press.

Petty, R. E., Gleicher, F., & Baker, S. M. (1991). Multiple roles for affect in persuasion. In J. Forgas (Ed.), *Emotion and social judgments.* London: Pergamon Press.

Phinney, J. S., Chavira, V., & Williamson, L. (1992). Acculturation attitudes and self-esteem among high school and college students. *Youth and society, 23*(3), 299–312.

Phinney, J. S., & Rosenthal, D. A. (1992). Ethnic identity in adolescence. In G. R. Adams, T. P. Gullotta, & R. Montemayor (Eds.), *Adolescent identity formation.* Newbury Park, CA: Sage.

Piaget, J. (1932, 1965). *The moral judgment of the child.* New York: Free Press.

Pike, K. M., & Rodin, J. (1991). Mothers, daughters, and disordered eating. *Journal of Abnormal Psychology, 100,* 198–204.

Pinker, S. (1990). Language acquisition. In D. N. Osherson & H. Lasnik (Eds.), *An invitation to cognitive science: Language* (Vol. 1). Cambridge, MA: MIT Press.

Pinker, S. (1994a, June 19). Building a better brain. *The New York Times Book Review,* pp. 13–14.

Pinker, S. (1994b). *The language instinct: How the mind creates language.* New York: William Morrow.

Plomin, R. (1989). Enviornment and genes: Determinants of behavior. *American Psychologist, 44,* 105–111.

Plomin, R., & Rende, R. (1991). Human behavioral genetics. *Annual Review of Psychology, 43,* 161–190.

Plutchik, R. (1984). A general psychoevolutionary theory. In K. Scherer & P. Ekman (Eds.), *Approaches to emotion.* Hillsdale, NJ: Erlbaum.

Pombeni, M. L., Kirchler, E., & Palmonari, A. (1990). Identification with peers as a strategy to muddle through the troubles of the adolescent years. *Journal of Adolescence, 13,* 351–369.

Pomerantz, E. M., Frey, K., Greulich, F., & Ruble, D. N. (1993, March). *Explaining the decrease in perceived competence: Grade and gender differences in perceptions of ability as stable.* Paper presented at the meeting of the Society for Research in Child Development. New Orleans, LA.

Pope-Davis, D. B., Reynolds, A. L., Dings, J. G., & Nielson, D. (1995). Examining multicultural counseling competencies of graduate students in psychology. *Professional Psychology: Research and Practice, 26,* 322–329.

Posner, M. I. (1988). Structures and functions of selective attention. In T. Boll & B. Bryant (Eds.), *Clinical neuropsychology and brain function* (pp. 169–202). Washington, DC: American Psychological Association.

Posner, M. I., & Raichle, M. E. (1994). *Images of mind.* New York: W. H. Freeman.

Powell, J. L., Meil, W., Patterson, M. L., Chouinard, E. F., et al. (1994). Effects of timing of touch on compliance to a request. *Journal of Social Behavior and Personality, 9,* 153–162.

Price, L. H., & Heninger, G. R. (1994). Lithium in the treatment of mood disorders. *New England Journal of Medicine, 331,* 591–598.

Putallaz, M., & Heflin, A. H. (1990). Parent-child interaction. In S. R. Asher & J. D. Coie (Eds.), *Peer rejection in childhood.* New York: Cambridge University Press.

Putnam, F., Guroff, J., Silberman, E., Barban, L., & Post, R. (1986). The clinical phenomenology of multiple personality disorder: Review of 100 recent cases. *Journal of Clinical Psychiatry, 47,* 285–293.

Quattrone, G. A. (1982). Overattribution and unit formation: When behavior engulfs the person. *Journal of Personality and Social Psychology, 42,* 593–607.

Quinn, S. (1987). *A mind of her own: The life of Karen Horney.* New York: Summit Books.

Radin, N. (1981). The role of the father in cognitive, academic, and intellectual development. In M. E. Lamb (Ed.), *The role of the father in child development.* New York: Wiley.

Raichle, M. E. (1994). Visualizing the mind. *Scientific American, 270*(4), 58–64.

Rakowski, W. (1995). Cited in Margoshes, P. (1995). For many, old age is the prime of life. *APA Monitor, 26*(5), 36–37.

Rapoport, J. (1989a, March). The biology of obsessions and compulsions. *Scientific American,* pp. 83–89.

Rapoport, J. L. (1989b). *The boy who couldn't stop washing.* New York: Penguin Books USA.

Rappaport, N. B., McAnulty, D. P., & Brantley, P. J. (1988). Exploration of the type A behavior pattern in chronic headache sufferers. *Journal of Consulting and Clinical Psychology, 56,* 621–623.

Rathus, S. A., Nevid, J. S., & Fichner-Rathus, L. (1997). *Human sexuality in a world of diversity* (3rd ed.). Boston: Allyn & Bacon.

Rauscher, F., Shaw, G., & Ky, K. (1993, October). Music training and spatial-relations skills. *Nature.*

Rauscher, F., Shaw, G., Levine, L., Ky, K., & Wright, E. (1994, August). *Music and spatial task performance: A causal relationship.* Paper presented to the meeting of the American Psychological Association.

Raynor, J. (1970). Relationships between achievement-related motives, future orientation, and academic performance. *Journal of Personality and Social Psychology, 15,* 28–33.

Redd, W. H., et al. (1987). Cognitive/attentional distraction in the control of conditioned nausea in pediatric cancer patients receiving chemotherapy. *Journal of Consulting and Clinical Psychology, 55,* 391–395.

Regier, D. A., Narrow, W. E., Rae, D. S. Manderscheid, R. W., Locke, B. Z., & Goodwin, F. K. (1993). The de facto U.S. mental and addictive disorders service system: Epidemiologic catchment area prospective 1-year prevalence rates of disorders and services. *Archives of General Psychiatry, 50,* 85–94.

Reinke, B. J., Holmes, D. S., & Harris, R. L. (1985). The timing of psychosocial changes in women's lives. *Journal of Personality and Social Psychology, 48,* 1353–1364.

Reis, H. T., et al. (1990). What is smiling is beautiful and good. *European Journal of Social Psychology, 20,* 259–267.

Reisman, J. M. (1990). Intimacy in same-sex friendships. *Sex Roles, 23,* 65–72.

Remafedi, G. (1990). Study group report on impact of television portrayals of gender roles on youth. *Journal of Adolescent Health Care, 11*(1), 59–61.

Renzulli, J. S. (1986). The three ring conception of giftedness: A developmental model for creative productivity. In R. J. Sternberg & J. E. Davidson (Eds.), *Conceptions of giftedness.* New York: Cambridge University Press.

Rhodes, N., & Wood, W. (1992). Self-esteem and intelligence affect influenceability: The mediating role of message reception. *Psychological Bulletin, 111,* 156–171.

Riley, V. (1981). Psychoneuroendocrine influences on immuno-competence and neoplasia. *Science, 212,* 1100–1109.

Rinn, W. E. (1991). Neuropsychology of facial expression. In R. S. Feldman & B. Rime (Eds.), *Fundamentals of nonverbal behavior.* Cambridge, England: Cambridge University Press.

Ritvo, E. R., Freeman, B. J., Mason-Brothers, A., Mo, A., & Ritvo, A. M. (1985). Concordance for the syndrome of autism in 40 pairs of afflicted twins. *American Journal of Psychiatry, 142,* 74–77.

Robbins, C., & Ehri, L. C. (1994). Reading storybooks to kindergartners helps them to learn new vocabulary words. *Journal of Educational Psychology, 86,* 54–64.

Robins, C. J., & Hayes, A. M. (1993). An appraisal of cognitive therapy. *Journal of Consulting and Clinical Psychology, 61,* 205–214.

Robins, L. (1987). The epidemiology of antisocial personality. In J. Cavenar (Ed.), *Psychiatry.* Philadelphia: Lippincott.

Robinson, P. (1993). *Freud and his critics.* Berkeley: University of California Press.

Roche, A. F. (1979). Structural trends in stature, weight, and maturation. In A. F. Roche (Ed.), Secular trends in growth, maturation, and development of children. *Monographs of the Society for Research in Child Development, 44,* 3–27.

Rogers, C. R. (1951). *Client-centered therapy.* Boston: Houghton Mifflin.

Rogers, C. (1961). *On becoming a person: A therapist's view of psychotherapy.* Boston: Houghton Mifflin.

Rogers, C. (1963). The actualizing tendency in relation to "motives" and to consciousness. In M. R. Jones (Ed.), *Nebraska Symposium on Motivation* (pp. 1–24). Lincoln: University of Nebraska Press.

Rogers, C. (1974). In retrospect: 46 years. *American Psychologist, 29,* 115–123.

Rogers, C. (1977). *On personal power: Inner strength and its revolutionary impact.* New York: Delacorte.

Rogers, C. (1986). Client-centered therapy. In I. Kutash & A. Wolf (Eds.), *Psychotherapist's casebook.* San Francisco: Jossey-Bass.

Rose, R. J. (1995). Genes and human behavior. *Annual Review of Psychology, 46,* 625–654.

Rosenberg, J., Perlstadt, H., & Phillips, W. R. (1993). Now that we are here: Discrimination, disparagement, and harassment at work and the experience of women lawyers. *Gender & Society, 7,* 415–433.

Rosenthal, E. (1993, July 20). Listening to the emotional needs of cancer patients. *The New York Times,* pp. C1, C7.

Roskies, E., et al. (1986). The Montreal Type A Intervention Project: Major findings. *Health Psychology, 5,* 45–69.

Ross, A. (1987). *Personality: The scientific study of complex human behavior.* New York: Holt, Rinehart and Winston.

Rothbart, M. K., & Ahadi, S. A. (1994). Temperament and the development of personality. *Journal of Abnormal Psychology, 103,* 55–66.

Ruble, D. N., & Ruble, T. L. (1982). Sex stereotypes. In A. G. Miller (Ed.), *In the eye of the beholder: Contemporary issues in stereotyping.* New York: Praeger.

Rule, B. G., Taylor, B. R., & Dobbs, A. R. (1987). Priming effects of heat on aggressive thoughts. *Social cognition, 5,* 131–143.

Rymer, R. (1993). *Genie: An abused child's flight from silence.* New York: HarperCollins.

Saarni, C. (1990). Emotional competence: How emotions and relationships become integrated. In R. Thompson (Ed.), *Nebraska Symposium on Motivation: Vol. 36. Socioemotional development.* Lincoln: University of Nebraska Press.

Saccuzzo, D. (1994, August). *Coping with the complexities of contemporary psychological testing: Negotiating shifting sands.* G. Stanley Hall Lecture presented at the meeting of the American Psychological Association, Los Angeles.

Sadker, M., & Sadker, D. (1994). *How America's schools cheat girls.* New York: Scribners.

Salgado de Snyder, V. N., Cervantes, R. C., & Padilla, A. M. (1990). Gender and ethnic differences in psychosocial stress and generalized distress among Hispanics. *Sex roles, 22,* 441–453.

Sanders, G. S. (1984). Effects of context cues on eyewitness identification responses. *Journal of Applied Social Psychology, 14,* 386–397.

Sanders, G. S., & Chiu, W. (1988). Eyewitness errors in free recall of actions. *Journal of Applied Social Psychology, 18,* 1241–1259.

Sandman, C., & Crinella, F. (1995). Cited in Margoshes, P. (1995). For many, old age is the prime of life. *APA Monitor, 26*(5), 36–37.

Sanna, L. J., & Shotland, R. L. (1990). Valence of anticipated evaluation and social facilitation. *Journal of Experimental Social Psychology, 26,* 82–92.

Santee, R. T., & Maslach, C. (1982). To agree or not to agree: Personal dissent amid social pressure to conform. *Journal of Personality and Social Psychology, 42,* 690–700.

Sattler, J. M. (1988). *Assessment of children.* San Diego, CA: Jerome M. Sattler.

Savage-Rumbaugh, E. S., Murphy, J., Sevcik, R. A., Brakke, K. E., Williams, S. L., & Rumbaugh, D. M., with commentary by Bates, E. (1993). Language comprehension in ape and child. *Monographs of the Society for Research in Child Development, 58*(233), 1–254.

Savin-Williams, R. C., & Berndt, T. (1990). Friendship and peer relations. In S. S. Feldman & G. R. Elliott (Eds.), *At the threshold: The developing adolescent.* Cambridge, MA: Harvard University Press.

Saxe, L. (1991a). Lying. *American Psychologist, 46,* 409–415.

Saxe, L. (1991b). Science and the CQT polygraph: A theoretical critique. *Integration of Physiological and Behavioral Sciences, 26,* 223–231.

Scarr, S., & Weinberg, R. A. (1983). The Minnesota adoption studies: Genetic differences and malleability. *Child Development, 54,* 260–267.

Schachter, S. (1959). *The psychology of affiliation.* Stanford, CA: Stanford University Press.

Schachter, S., & Singer, J. E. (1962). Cognitive, social, and physiological determinants of emotional state. *Psychological Review, 69,* 379–399.

Schafer, R. B., & Keith, P. M. (1990). Matching by weight in married couples: A life cycle perspective. *Journal of Social Psychology, 130,* 657–664.

Schaie, K. W. (1993). The Seattle longitudinal studies of adult intelligence. *Current Directions, 2,* 171–175.

Schaie, K. W. (1994). The course of adult intellectual development. *American Psychologist, 49,* 304–313.

Schaie, K. W., & Willis, S. L. (1991). Adult personality and psychomotor performance. Cross-sectional and longitudinal analyses. *Journal of Gerontology: Psychological Sciences, 46,* 275–284.

Schau, C. G., Kahn, L., Diepold, J. H., & Cherry, F. (1980). The relationship to parental expectations and preschool children's verbal sex-typing to their sex-typed toy play behavior. *Child Development, 51,* 607–609.

Schneider, W., & Bjorklund, D. (1992). Expertise, aptitude, and strategic remembering. *Child Development, 63,* 461–473.

Schwartz, R. M., & Gottman, J. M. (1976). Toward a task analysis of assertive behavior. *Journal of Consulting and Clinical Psychology, 44,* 910–920.

Schwarz, N., Bless, H., & Bohner, G. (1991). Mood and persuasion: Affective states influence the processing of persuasive communications. In M. Zanna (Ed.), *Advances in experimental social psychology* (Vol. 24). New York: Academic Press.

Schwarz, N., & Clore, G. L. (1983). Mood, misattribution, and judgments of well-being: Informative and directive functions of affective states. *Journal of Personality and Social Psychology, 45,* 513–523.

Schweinhart, L. J., & Weikart, D. P. (Eds.). (1993). *Significant benefits: The High/Scope Perry Preschool Study through age 27.* Ypsilanti, MI: High/Scope Press.

Segal, N. (1993). Twin, sibling, and adoption methods. *American Psychologist, 48,* 943–956.

Segall, M. H., Campbell, D. T., & Herskovits, M. J. (1966). *The influence of culture on visual perception.* New York: Bobbs-Merrill.

Selfe, L. (1978). Cited in Bootzin, R. R., & Acocella, J. R. (1984). *Abnormal pscyhology: Current perspectives* (4th ed.). New York: Random House.

Seligman, M. E. P. (1975). *Helplessness: On depression, development, and death.* New York: W. H. Freeman.

Seligman, M. E. P. (1996, August). *Predicting and preventing depression.* Master lecture presented to the meeting of the American Psychological Association, Toronto.

Selkoe, D. J. (1992). Aging brain, aging mind. *Scientific American, 267*(3), 134–142.

Selye, H. (1976). *The stress of life* (rev. ed.). New York: McGraw-Hill.

Shader, R. I., & Greenblatt, D. J. (1993). Drug therapy: Use of benzodiazepines in anxiety disorders. *New England Journal of Medicine, 328,* 1398–1405.

Shah, M., & Jeffery, R. W. (1991). Is obesity due to overeating and inactivity or to a defective metabolic rate? A review. *Annals of Behavioral Medicine, 13,* 73–81.

Shavitt, S. (1990). The role of attitude objects in attitude functions. *Journal of Experimental Social Psychology, 26,* 124–148.

Sheehy, G. (1976). *Passages: Predictable crises of adult life.* New York: Dutton.

Sheehy, G. (1995). *New passages: Mapping your life across time.* New York: Random House.

Shepherd, J., et al. (1995). Prevention of coronary heart disease with pravastatin in men with hypercholesterolemia. *New England Journal of Medicine, 333,* 1301–1307.

Sheppard, J. A., & Strathman, A. J. (1989). Attractiveness and height: The role of stature in dating preference, frequency of dating, and perceptions of attractiveness. *Personality and Social Psychology Bulletin, 15,* 617–627.

Sher, K. J., & Trull, T. J. (1994). Personality and disinhibitory psychopathology: Alcoholism and antisocial personality disorder. *Journal of Abnormal Psychology, 103,* 92–102.

Shneidman, E. S. (Ed.). (1984). *Death: Current perspectives* (3rd ed.) Mountain View, CA: Mayfield.

Shoham-Salomon, V. (1991). Introduction to special section on client-therapy interaction research. *Journal of Consulting and Clinical Psychology, 59,* 203–204.

Shotland, R. L., & Heinold, W. D. (1985). Bystander response to arterial bleeding: Helping skills, the decision-making process, and differentiating the helping response. *Journal of Personality and Social Psychology, 49,* 347–356.

Shusterman, G., & Saxe, L. (1990). *Deception in romantic relationships.* Unpublished manuscript.

Siegal, M. (1987). Are sons and daughters treated more differently by fathers than by mothers? *Developmental Review, 7,* 183–209.

Siegel, L. J., & Senna, J. J. (1994). *Juvenile delinquency: Theory, practice and law.* St. Paul, MN: West.

Signorielli, N. (1990). Children, television, and gender roles: Messages and impact. *Journal of Adolescent Health Care, 11,* 50–58.

Silver, E., Cirincione, C., & Steadman, H. J. (1994, February). *Law and Human Behavior.* Cited in DeAngelis, T. (1994). Public's view of insanity plea quite inaccurate, study finds. *APA Monitor, 25*(6), 28.

Silverman, L. H. (1984). Beyond insight: An additional necessary step in redressing intrapsychic conflict. *Psychoanalytic Psychology, 1,* 215–234.

Silverstein, L. B. (1991). Transforming the debate about child care and maternal employment. *American Psychologist, 46,* 1025–1032.

Simmons, R. G., & Blyth, D. A. (1987). *Moving into adolescence: The impact of pubertal change and school context.* New York: Aldine de Gruyter.

Simon, H. A. (1990). A mechanism for social selection and successful altruism. *Science, 250,* 1665–1668.

Simons, A. D., Gordon, J. S., Monroe, S. M., & Thase, M. E. (1995). Toward an integration of psychologic, social, and biologic factors in depression: Effects on outcome and course of cognitive therapy. *Journal of Consulting and Clinical Psychology, 63,* 369–377.

Simons, R. K., Whitbeck, L. B., Conger, R. D., & Chyi-In, W. (1991). Intergenerational transmission of harsh parenting. *Developmental Psychology, 27,* 159–171.

Simonton, D. (1988). Age and outstanding achievement: What do we know after a century of research? *Psychological Bulletin, 104,* 251–267.

Singh, R. B., & Sharma, S. K. (1989). Anxiety and conformity behavior. *Indian Journal of Current Psychological Research, 42,* 98–102.

Skinner, B. F. (1948). *Walden Two.* New York: Macmillan.

Skinner, B. F. (1961). Teaching machines. *Scientific American, 205,* 90–102.

Skinner, B. F. (1938/1966). *The behavior of organisms.* New York: Appleton Century Crofts.

Skinner, B. F. (1971). *Beyond Freedom and Dignity.* New York: Knopf.

Skinner, B. F. (1987). Whatever happened to psychology as the science of behavior? *American Psychologist, 42,* 780–786.

Sleek, S. (1995a). Group therapy: Tapping the power of teamwork. *APA Monitor, 26*(7), 1, 38–39.

Sleek, S. (1995b). Rallying the troops inside our bodies. *APA Monitor, 26*(12), 1, 24–25.

Sleek, S. (1996). Side effects undermine drug compliance. *APA Monitor, 26*(3), 32.

Slobin, D. I. (1983, April). *Crosslinguistic evidence of basic child grammar.* Paper presented at the biennial meeting of the Society for Research in Child Development, Detroit, MI.

Smetana, J. G., Killen, M., & Turiel, E. (1991). Children's reasoning about interpersonal and moral conflicts. *Child Development, 62,* 629–644.

Smetana, J. G., Yau, J., Restrepo, A., & Braeges, J. L. (1991). Conflict and adaptation in adolescence: Adolescent-parent conflict. In M. E. Colten & S. Gore (Eds.), *Adolescent stress: Causes and consequences.* New York: Aldine de Gruyter.

Smith, E. R., & Mackie, D. M. (1995). *Social psychology.* New York: Worth.

Smith, G. F., & Dorfman, D. (1975). The effect of stimulus uncertainty on the relationship between frequency of exposure and liking. *Journal of Personality and Social Psychology, 31,* 150–155.

Smith, M. L., & Glass, G. V. (1977). Meta-analysis of psychotherapy outcome studies. *American Psychologist, 32,* 752–760.

Smith, P. K., Boulton, M. J., & Cowie, H. (1993). The impact of cooperative group work on ethnic relations in middle school. *Social Psychology International, 14,* 21–42.

Smith, P. K., & Daglish, L. (1977). Sex differences in parent and infant behavior in the home. *Child Development, 48,* 1250–1254.

Smith, R. E., Smoll, F. L., & Ptacek, J. T. (1990). Conjunctive moderator variables in vulnerability and resiliency research: Life stress, social support and coping skills, and adolescent sport injuries. *Journal of Personality and Social Psychology, 58,* 360–370.

Smith, S. M., Glenberg, A. M., & Bjork, R. A. (1978). Environmental context and human memory. *Memory and Cognition, 6,* 342–355.

Snow, C. E., (1993). Bilingualism and second language acquisition. In J. Berko-Gleason & N. B. Ratner (Eds.), *Psycholinguistics.* Fort Worth, TX: Harcourt Brace Jovanovich.

Snow, R. E. (1991). Aptitude-treatment interaction as a framework for research on individual differences in psychotherapy. *Journal of Consulting and Clinical Psychology, 59,* 205–216.

Snyder, M., & DeBono, G. (1989). Understanding the functions of attitudes. In A. R. Pratkanis et al. (Eds.), *Attitude structure and function.* Hillsdale, NJ: Erlbaum.

Snyderman, M., & Rothman, S. (1987). Survey of expert opinion on intelligence and aptitude testing. *American Psychologist, 43,* 137–144.

Snyderman, M., & Rothman, S. (1990). *The I.Q. controversy.* New Brunswick, NJ: Transaction.

Solomon, R. L. (1980). The opponent-process theory of acquired motivation: The costs of pleasure and the benefits of pain. *American Psychologist, 35,* 691–712.

Solomon, R., & Corbitt, J. (1974). An opponent-process theory of motivation. *Psychological Review, 81,* 119–145.

Sorenson, S. B., & Rutter, C. M. (1991). Transgenerational patterns of suicide attempt. *Journal of Consulting and Clinical Psychology, 59,* 861–866.

Sorrentino, R. M., et al. (1988). Uncertainty orientation and persuasion. *Journal of Personality and Social Psychology, 55,* 371–375.

Spanos, N. O. (1994). Multiple identity enactments and multiple personality disorder: A sociocultural perspective. *Psychological Bulletin, 116*(1), 143–165.

Spencer, M. B., Dornbusch, S. M., & Mont-Reynaud, R. (1990). Challenges in studying minority youth. In S. S. Feldman & G. R. Elliott (Eds.), *At the threshold: The developing adolescent.* Cambridge, MA: Harvard University Press.

Spencer, M. B., & Markstrom-Adams, C. (1990). Identity processes among racial and ethnic minority children in America. *Child Development, 61,* 290–310.

Sperry, R. W. (1993). The impact and promise of the cognitive revolution. *American Psychologist, 48,* 878–885.

Spinhoven, P., Labbe, M. R., & Rombouts, R. (1993). Feasibility of computerized psychological testing with psychiatric outpatients. *Journal of Clinical Psychology, 49,* 440–447.

Spitzer, R. L., Gibbon, M., Skodol, A. E., Williams, J. B. W., & First, M. B. (1989). *DSM-III-R casebook.* Washington, DC: American Psychiatric Press.

Spreat, S., & Behar, D. (1994). Trends in the residential (inpatient) treatment of individuals with a dual diagnosis. *Journal of Consulting and Clinical Psychology, 61,* 43–48.

Squire, L. R., Cohen, N. J., & Nadel, L. (1984). The medical temporal region and memory consolidations: A new hypothesis. In H. Weingartner & E. Parker (Eds.), *Memory consolidation.* Hillsdale, NJ: Erlbaum.

Stacy, A. W., Bentler, P. M., & Flay, B. R. (1994). Attitudes and health behavior in diverse populations: Drunk driving, alcohol use, binge eating, marijuana use, and cigarette use. *Health Psychology, 13,* 73–85.

Stasser, G., Taylor, L. A., & Hanna, C. (1989). Information sampling in structured and unstructured discussion of three- and six-person groups. *Journal of Personality and Social Psychology, 57,* 67–78.

Steinberg, L. (1991). Parent-adolescent relations. In R. M. Lerner, A. C. Petersen, & J. Brooks-Gunn (Eds.), *Encyclopedia of adolescence.* New York: Garland.

Steinberg, L. (1993). Cited in Perils of part-time work for teens. (1991, March 30). *Science News,* p. 205.

Steinberg, L., Lamborn, S. F., Dornbusch, S. M., & Darling, N. (1992). Impact of parenting practices on adolescent achievement: Authoritative parenting, school involvement, and encouragement to succeed. *Child Development, 63,* 1266–1281.

Steinbrook, R. (1992). The polygraph test—A flawed diagnostic method. *New England Journal of Medicine, 327,* 122–123.

Steinhauer, J. (1995, July 6). No marriage, no apologies. *The New York Times,* pp. C1, C7.

Stericker, A., & LeVesconte, S. (1982). Effect of brief training on sex-related differences in visual-spatial skill. *Journal of Personality and Social Psychology, 43,* 1018–1029.

Sternberg, R. J. (1988). Triangulating love. In R. J. Sternberg & M. J. Barnes (Eds.), *The psychology of love.* New Haven, CT: Yale University Press.

Sternberg, R. J. (1990). Wisdom and its relations to intelligence and creativity. In R. J. Sternberg (Ed.), *Wisdom: Its nature, origins, and development.* New York: Cambridge University Press.

Sternberg, R. J. (1995). *In search of the human mind.* Fort Worth, TX: Harcourt Brace.

Sternberg, R. J. (1996). Love stories. *Personal Relationships, 3,* 59–79.

Sternberg, R. J., Wagner, R. K., Williams, W. M., & Horvath, J. A. (1995). Testing common sense. *American Psychologist, 50,* 912–927.

Stewart, M. W., Knight, R. G., Palmer, D. G., & Highton, J. (1994). Differential relationships between stress and disease activity for immunologically distinct subgroups of people with rheumatoid arthritis. *Journal of Abnormal Psychology, 103,* 251–258.

Stier, D. S., & Hall, J. A. (1984). Gender differences in touch: An empirical and theoretical review. *Journal of Personality and Social Psychology, 47,* 440–459.

Stock, R. (1995, June 1). Wrongheaded views persist about the old. *The New York Times,* p. C8.

Stone, N. M. (1993). Parental abuse as a precursor to childhood onset depression and suicidality. *Child Psychiatry and Human Development, 24,* 13–24.

Strughold, H. (1924). On the density and thresholds in the areas of pain on the epidermis in the various regions of the body. *Z. Biol, 80,* (in German), 367–380.

Strupp, H. H. (1992). The future of psychodynamic psychotherapy. *Psychotherapy, 29,* 21–27.

Study finds smaller pay gap for male and female doctors. (1996, April 11). *The New York Times,* p. B9.

Stunkard, A. J., Harris, J. R., Pedersen, N. L., & McLearn, G. E. (1990). A separated twin study of the body mass index. *New England Journal of Medicine, 322,* 1483–1487.

Stunkard, A. J., & Sørensen, T. I. A. (1993). Obesity and socioeconomic status—A complex relation. *New England Journal of Medicine, 329,* 1036–1037.

Suarez, E. C., Harlan, E., Peoples, M. C., & Williams, R. B., Jr. (1993). Cardiovascular and emotional responses in women: The role of hostility and harassment. *Health Psychology, 12,* 459–468.

Suddath, R., Casanova, M., Goldberg, T., Daniel, D., Kelsoe, J., & Weinberger, D. (1989). Temporal lobe pathology in schizophrenia: A quantitative magnetic resonance imaging study. *American Journal of Psychiatry, 146,* 464–472.

Suls, J., Wan, C. K., & Costa, P. T., Jr. (1995). Relationship of trait anger to resting high blood pressure: A meta-analysis. *Health Psychology, 14,* 444–456.

Sundberg, N. D. (1990). *Assessment of persons* (2nd ed.). Englewood Cliffs, NJ: Prentice-Hall.

Swedo, S., Rapoport, J., Chelow, D., Leonard, H., Ayoub, E., Hosier, D., & Wald, E. (1989). High prevalence of obsessive-compulsive symptoms in patients with Sydenham's chorea. *American Journal of Psychiatry, 146,* 246–249.

Tahka, S., Wood, M., & Loewenthal, K. (1981). Age changes in the ability to replicate foreign pronunciation and intonation. *Language and Speech, 24,* 363–372.

Tanfer, K. (1987). Patterns of premarital cohabitation among never married women. *Journal of Marriage and the Family, 49,* 483–497.

Tannen, D. (1990). *You just don't understand.* New York: Ballantine Books.

Tanner, J. M. (1978). *Fetus into man: Physical growth from conception to maturity* (p. 118). Cambridge, MA: Harvard University Press.

Tanner, J. M. (1991). Adolescent growth spurt. In R. M. Lerner, A. C. Petersen, & J. Brooks-Gunn (Eds.), *Encyclopedia of adolescence.* New York: Garland.

Tanzi, R. E. (1995). A promising animal model of Alzheimer's disease. *New England Journal of Medicine, 332,* 1512–1513.

Taylor, I., & Taylor, M. M. (1990). *Psycholinguistics: Learning and using language.* Englewood Cliffs, NJ: Prentice-Hall.

Taylor, S. E. (1990). Health psychology: The science and the field. *American Psychologist, 45,* 40–50.

Teri, L., & Wagner, A. (1992). Alzheimer's disease and depression. *Journal of Consulting and Clinical Psychology, 60,* 379–391.

Tetlock, P. E. (1983). Accountability and complexity of thought. *Journal of Personality and Social Psychology, 45,* 74–83.

Tharp, R. G. (1991). Cultural diversity and treatment of children. *Journal of Consulting and Clinical Psychology, 59,* 799–812.

Thompson, R. A. (1991a). Attachment theory and research. In M. Lewis (Ed.), *Child and adolescent psychiatry: A comprehensive textbook.* Baltimore, MD: Williams & Wilkins.

Thompson, R. A. (1991b). Infant daycare: Concerns, controversies, choices. In J. V. Lerner & N. L. Galambos (Eds.), *Employed mothers and their children* (pp. 9–36). New York: Garland.

Thompson, R. A., & Limber, S. P. (1990). "Social anxiety" in infancy: Stranger and separation reaction. In H. Leitenberg (Ed.), *Handbook of social and evaluation anxiety.* New York: Plenum Press.

Thompson, W. C., Cowan, C. L., & Rosenhan, D. L. (1980). Focus of attention mediates the impact of negative affect on altruism. *Journal of Personality and Social Psychology, 38,* 291–300.

Thoresen, C., & Powell, L. H. (1992). Type A behavior pattern: New perspectives on theory, assessment, and intervention. *Journal of Consulting and Clinical Psychology, 60,* 595–604.

Thurstone, L. L., & Thurstone, T. G. (1963). *SRA primary abilities.* Chicago: SRA.

Togersen, S. (1983). Gentic factors in anxiety disorders. *Archives of General Psychiatry, 40,* 1085–1089.

Tolman, E. C., & Honzik, C. H. (1930). Introduction and removal of reward, and maze performance in rats. *University of California Publications in Psychology, 4,* 257–275.

Tomes, H. (1995). Minorities' access to care is top priority. *APA Monitor, 26*(7), 52.

Triandis, H. C. (1990). Cross-cultural studies of individualism and collectivisim. In J. J. Berman (Ed.), *Nebraska symposium on motivation, 1989. Cross-cultural perspectives.* Lincoln: University of Nebraska Press.

Triandis, H. C. (1994). *Culture and social behavior.* New York: McGraw-Hill.

Trickett, P. K., Aber, J. L., Carlson, V., & Cicchetti, D. (1991). Relationship of socioeconomic status to etiology and developmental sequence of physical child abuse. *Developmental Psychology, 27,* 148–158.

Turnbull, C. (1961). Some observations regarding the experiences and behavior of the Bambuti Pygmies. *American Journal of Psychology, 74,* 301–308.

Turner, S., Beidel, D., & Nathan, R. (1985). Biological factors in obsessive-compulsive disorders. *Psychological Bulletin, 97,* 430–450.

United States Bureau of the Census. (1993). *Statistical abstract of the United States* (113th ed.). Washington, DC: U.S. Government Printing Office.

United States Bureau of the Census. (1995). *Statistical abstract of the United States* (115th ed.). Washington, DC: U.S. Government Printing Office.

United States Bureau of the Census. (annual). *Current population reports.* Washington, DC: U.S. Government Printing Office.

United States National Center for Health Statistics. (annual). *Vital statistics of the United States* and *Monthly vital statistics reports.*

United States Public Health Service (1967). *Vital statistics of the United States, 1900–1967.*

Vaillant, G. E. (1994). Ego mechanisms of defense and personality psychopathology. *Journal of Abnormal Psychology, 103,* 44–50.

Valenstein, E. S. (1986). *Great and desperate cures: The rise and decline of psychosurgery and other radical treatments for mental illness.* New York: Basic Books.

Van Brunt, L. (1994, March 27). About men: Whites without money. *The New York Times Magazine,* p. 38.

Vandell, D. L., & Corasaniti, M. A. (1990). Child care and the family: Complex contributors to child development. In K. McCartney (Ed.), *New Directions for Child Development,* no. 49, pp. 23–37. San Francisco: Josey-Bass.

Van der Pligt, J., & Eiser, J. R. (1983). Actors' and observers' attributions, self-serving bias, and positivity bias. *European Journal of Social Psychology, 13,* 95–104.

Visitainer, M. A., Volpicelli, J. R., & Seligman, M. E. P. (1982). Tumor rejection in rats after inescapable or escapable shock. *Science, 216,* 437–439.

Vitousek, K., & Manke, F. (1994). Personality variables and disorders in anorexia nervosa and bulimia nervosa. *Journal of Abnormal Psychology, 103,* 137–147.

Voyer, D., Voyer, S., & Bryden, M. P. (1995). Magnitude of sex differences in spatial abilities: A meta-analysis and consideration of critical variables. *Psychological Bulletin, 117,* 250–270.

Wachtel, P. L. (1994). Cyclical processes in personality and psychopathology. *Journal of Abnormal Psychology, 103,* 51–54.

Walk, R. D., & Gibson, E. J. (1961). A comparative and analytical study of visual depth perception. *Psychology Monographs, 75,* 15. (Whole No. 519)

Wallerstein, J. S., & Blakeslee, S. (1989). *Second chances: Women and children a decade after divorce.* New York: Ticknor & Fields.

Walsh, M. R. (1993, August). *Teaching the psychology of women and gender for undergraduate and graduate faculty.* Workshop of the Psychology of Women Institute presented at the meeting of the American Psychological Association, Toronto.

Walsh, W. B., & Betz, N. E. (1990). *Tests and assessment* (2nd ed.). Englewood Cliffs, NJ: Prentice-Hall.

Waterman, A. S. (1992). Identity as an aspect of optimal psychological functioning. In G. R. Adams, T. P. Gullotta, & R. Montemayor (Eds.), *Adolescent identity formulation.* Newbury Park, CA: Sage.

Watkins, C. E., Jr., Campbell, V. L., Nieberding, R., & Hallmark, R. (1995). Contemporary practice of psychological assessment by clinical psychologists. *Professional Psychology: Research and Practice, 26,* 54–60.

Watson, J. B. (1924). *Behaviorism.* New York: Norton.

Weiss, J. M (1982, August). *A model for the neurochemical study of depression.* Paper presented at the meeting of the American Psychological Association, Washington, DC.

Welch, K. M. A. (1993). Drug therapy of migraine. *New England Journal of Medicine, 329,* 1476–1483.

Wells, G. L. (1993). What do we know about eyewitness identification? *American Psychologist, 48,* 553–571.

Wentzel, K. R. (1994). Relations of social goal pursuit to social acceptance, classroom behavior, and perceived social support. *Journal of Educational Psychology, 86,* 173–182.

Westerman, M. A. (1990). Coordination of maternal directives with preschoolers' behavior in compliance-problem and healthy dyads. *Developmental Psychology, 26,* 621–630.

Wetzler, S. E., & Sweeney, J. A. (1986). Childhood amnesia. In D. C. Rubin (Ed.), *Autobiographical memory.* New York: Cambridge University Press.

Whisman, M. A., Miller, I. W., Norman, W. H., & Keitner, G. I. (1991). Cognitive therapy with depressed inpatients: Specific effects on dysfunctional cognitions. *Journal of Consulting and Clinical Psychology, 61,* 261–269.

White, S. D., & DeBlassie, R. R. (1992). Adolescent sexual behavior. *Adolescence, 27,* 183–191.

Whitehead, W. E. (1994). Assessing the effects of stress on physical symptoms. *Health Psychology, 13,* 99–102.

Wiggins, J. G., Jr. (1994). Would you want your child to be a psychologist? *American Psychologist, 49,* 485–492.

Wilcox, V. L., Kasl, S. V., & Berkman, L. F. (1994). Social support and physical disability in older people after hospitalization. *Health Psychology, 13,* 170–179.

Wilder, D. A. (1986). Social categorization: Implications for creation and reduction of intergroup bias. In L. Berkowitz (Ed.), *Advances in experimental social psychology.* New York: Academic Press.

Wilder, D. A. (1990). Some determinants of the persuasive power of in-groups and out-groups: Organization of information and attribution of independence. *Journal of Personality and Social Psychology, 59,* 1202–1213.

Wilkie, D. M., Mumby, D. G., Needham, G., & Smeele, M. (1992). Sustained arm visiting by nondeprived, nonrewarded rats in a radial maze. *Bulletin of the Psychonomic Society, 30,* 314–316.

Willett, W. C., et al. (1990). Relation of meat, fat, and fiber intake to the risk of colon cancer in a prospective study among women. *New England Journal of Medicine, 323,* 1664–1672.

Williams, L. (1992, February 6). Woman's image in a mirror: Who defines what she sees? *The New York Times,* pp. A1, B7.

Williamson, D. A., Cubic, B. A., & Gleaves, D. H. (1993). Equivalence of body image disturbances in anorexia and bulimia nervosa. *Journal of Abnormal Psychology, 102,* 177–180.

Willoughby, T., Wood, E., & Khan, M. (1994). Isolating variables that impact on or detract from the effectiveness of elaboration strategies. *Journal of Educational Research, 86,* 279–289.

Wills, T. A., McNamara, G., Vaccaro, D., & Hirky, A. E. (1996). Escalated substance abuse: A longitudinal grouping analysis from early to middle adolescence. *Journal of Abnormal Psychology, 195,* 166–180.

Wilson, E. O. (1975). *Sociobiology: The new synthesis.* Cambridge, MA: Harvard University Press.

Wilson, G. T. (1993). Cited in O'Neill, M. (1993, September 29). Diet sabotage: The new battle of the sexes. *The New York Times,* pp. C1, C6.

Winson, J. (1992). Cited in Blakeslee, S. (1992, January 7). Scientists unraveling chemistry of dreams. *The New York Times,* pp. C1, C10.

Witelson, S. F. (1991). Neural sexual mosaicism: Sexual differentiation of the human temporo-parietal region for functional asymmetry. *Psychoneuroendocrinology, 16,* 131–153.

Wolf, N. (1991). *The beauty myth: How images of beauty are used against women.* New York: William Morrow.

Wolock, I., & Horowitz, B. (1984). Child maltreatment as a social problem: The neglect of neglect. *American Journal of Orthopsychiatry, 54,* 530–545.

Woloshyn, V. E., Paivio, A., & Pressley, M. (1994). Use of elaborative interrogation to help students acquire information consistent with prior knowledge and information inconsistent with prior knowledge. *Journal of Educational Psychology, 86,* 78–89.

Wolpe, J. (1990). *The practice of behavior therapy* (4th ed.). New York: Pergamon Press.

Wolpe, J., & Lazarus, A. A. (1966). *Behavior therapy techniques: A guide to the treatment of neurosis.* Elmsford, NY: Pergamon Press.

Wong, D., Wagner, H., Tune, L., Dannals, R., Pearson, G., Links, J., Tamminga, C., Broussolle, E., Ravert, H., Wilson, A., Tuong, J., Malat, J., Williams, J., O'Tuama, L., Snyder, S., Kuhar, M., & Gjedde, A. (1986). Positron emission tomography reveals elevated D_2 dopamine receptors in drug-naive schizophrenics. *Science, 234,* 1558–1563.

Wood, J. M., & Bootzin, R. R. (1990). The prevalence of nightmares and their independence from anxiety. *Journal of Abnormal Psychology, 99,* 64–68.

Wood, J. M., Bootzin, R. R., Rosenhan, D., Nolen-Hoeksema, S., & Jourden, F. (1992). Effects of the 1989 San Francisco earthquake on frequency and content of nightmares. *Journal of Abnormal Psychology, 101,* 219–224.

Wood, P. D., et al. (1991). The effects on plasma lipoproteins of a prudent weight-reducing diet, with or without exercise, in overweight men and women. *New England Journal of Medicine, 325,* 461–466.

Wood, W., Wong, F. Y., & Chachere, J. G. (1991). Effects of media violence on viewers' aggression in unconstrained social interaction. *Psychological Bulletin, 109,* 371–383.

Wren, C. S. (1996, February 20). Marijuana use by youths continues to rise. *The New York Times,* p. A11.

Wu, C., & Shaffer, C. R. (1987). Susceptibility to persuasive appeals as a function of source credibility and prior experience with the attitude object. *Journal of Personality and Social Psychology, 52,* 677–688.

WuDunn, S. (1995, July 9). Many Japanese women are resisting servility. *The New York Times,* p. A10.

Yoder, J. D., & Kahn, A. S. (1993). Working toward an inclusive psychology of women. *American Psychologist, 48,* 846–850.

Youngblade, L. M., & Belsky, J. (1992). Parent-child antecedents of 5-year-olds' close friendships: A longitudinal analysis. *Developmental Psychology, 28,* 700–713.

Youniss, J., & Haynie, D. L. (1992). Friendship in adolescence. *Developmental and Behavioral Pediatrics, 13,* 59–66.

Yutrzenka, B. A. (1995). Making a case for training in ethnic and cultural diversity in increasing treatment efficacy. *Journal of Consulting and Clinical Psychology, 63,* 197–206.

Zajonc, R. B. (1965). Social facilitation. *Science, 149,* 269–275.

Zajonc, R. B. (1980). Compresence. In P. Paulus (Ed.), *The psychology of group influence.* Hillsdale, NJ: Erlbaum.

Zajonc, R. B. (1984). On the primacy of affect. *American Psychologist, 39,* 117–123.

Zigler, E. (1995). *Modernizing early childhood intervention to better serve children and families in poverty.* Master lecture delivered at the meeting of the American Psychological Association, New York.

Zigler, E., Taussig, C., & Black, K. (1992). Early childhood intervention: A promising preventative for juvenile delinquency. *American Psychologist, 47,* 997–1006.

Zimbardo, P. G., LaBerge, S., & Butler, L. D. (1993). Psychophysiological consequences of unexplained arousal: A posthypnotic suggestion paradigm. *Journal of Abnormal Psychology, 102,* 466–473.

Ziv, T. A., & Lo, B. (1995). Denial of care to illegal immigrants—Proposition 187 in California. *New England Journal of Medicine, 332,* 1095–1098.

Zuber, J. A., Crott, H. W., & Werner, J. (1992). Choice shift and group polarization: An analysis of the status of arguments and social decision schemes. *Journal of Personality and Social Psychology, 62,* 50–61.

ETHICAL PRINCIPLES

OF PSYCHOLOGISTS

PREAMBLE

Psychologists work to develop a valid and reliable body of scientific knowledge based on research. They may apply that knowledge to human behavior in a variety of contexts. In doing so, they perform many roles, such as researcher, educator, diagnostician, therapist, supervisor, consultant, administrator, social interventionist, and expert witness. Their goal is to broaden knowledge of behavior and, where appropriate, to apply it pragmatically to improve the condition of both the individual and society. Psychologists respect the central importance of freedom of inquiry and expression in research, teaching, and publication. They also strive to help the public in developing informed judgments and choices concerning human behavior. This Ethics Code provides a common set of values upon which psychologists build their professional and scientific work.

This Code is intended to provide both the general principles and the decision rules to cover most situations encountered by psychologists. It has as its primary goal the welfare and protection of the individuals and groups with whom psychologists work. It is the individual responsibility of each psychologist to aspire to the highest possible standards of conduct. Psychologists respect and protect human and civil rights, and do not knowingly participate in or condone unfair discriminatory practices.

The development of a dynamic set of ethical standards for a psychologist's work-related conduct requires a personal commitment to a lifelong effort to act ethically; to encourage ethical behavior by students, supervisees, employees, and colleagues, as appropriate; and to consult with others, as needed, concerning ethical problems. Each psychologist supplements, but does not violate, the Ethics Code's values and rules on the basis of guidance drawn from personal values, culture, and experience.

GENERAL PRINCIPLES

PRINCIPLE A: COMPETENCE

Psychologists strive to maintain high standards of competence in their work. They recognize the boundaries of their particular competencies and the limitations of their expertise. They provide only those services and use only those techniques for which they are qualified by education, training, or experience. Psychologists are cognizant of the fact that the competencies required in serving, teaching, and/or studying groups of people vary with the distinctive characteristics of those groups. In those areas in which recognized professional standards do not yet exist, psychologists exercise careful judgment and take appropriate precautions to protect the welfare of those with whom they work. They maintain knowledge of relevant scientific and professional information related to the services they render, and they recognize the need for ongoing education. Psychologists make appropriate use of scientific, professional, technical, and administrative resources.

PRINCIPLE B: INTEGRITY

Psychologists seek to promote integrity in the science, teaching, and practice of psychology. In these activities psychologists are honest, fair, and respectful of others. In describing or reporting their qualifications, services, products, fees, research, or teaching, they do not make statements that are false, misleading, or deceptive. Psychologists strive to be aware of their own belief systems, values, needs, and limitations and the effect of these on their work. To the extent feasible, they attempt to clarify for relevant parties the roles they are performing and to function appropriately in accordance with those roles. Psychologists avoid improper and potentially harmful dual relationships.

PRINCIPLE C: PROFESSIONAL AND SCIENTIFIC RESPONSIBILITY

Psychologists uphold professional standards of conduct, clarify their professional roles and obligations, accept appropriate responsibility for their behavior, and adapt their methods to the needs of different populations. Psychologists consult with, refer to, or cooperate with other professionals and institutions to the extent needed to serve the best interests of their patients, clients, or other recipients of their services. Psychologists' moral standards and conduct are personal matters to the same degree as is true for any other person, except as psychologists' conduct may compromise their professional responsibilities or reduce the public's trust in psychology and psychologists. Psychologists are concerned about the ethical compliance of their colleagues' scientific and professional conduct. When appropriate, they consult with colleagues in order to prevent or avoid unethical conduct.

PRINCIPLE D: RESPECT FOR PEOPLE'S RIGHTS AND DIGNITY

Psychologists accord appropriate respect to the fundamental rights, dignity, and worth of all people. They respect the rights of individuals to privacy, confidentiality, self-determination, and autonomy, mindful that legal and other obligations may lead to inconsistency and conflict with the exercise of these rights. Psychologists are aware of cultural, individual, and role differences, including those due to age, gender, race, ethnicity, national origin, religion, sexual orientation, disability, language, and socioeconomic status. Psychologists try to eliminate the effect on their work of biases based on those factors, and they do not knowingly participate in or condone unfair discriminatory practices.

PRINCIPLE E: CONCERN FOR OTHERS' WELFARE

Psychologists seek to contribute to the welfare of those with whom they interact professionally. In their professional actions, psychologists weigh the welfare and rights of their patients or clients, students, supervisees, human research participants, and other affected persons, and the welfare of animal subjects of re- search. When conflicts occur among psychologists' obligations or concerns, they attempt to resolve these conflicts and to perform their roles in a responsible fashion that avoids or minimizes harm. Psychologists are sensitive to real and ascribed differences in power between themselves and others, and they do not exploit or mislead other people during or after professional relationships.

PRINCIPLE F: SOCIAL RESPONSIBILITY

Psychologists are aware of their professional and scientific responsibilities to the community and the society in which they work and live. They apply and make public their knowledge of psychology in order to contribute to human welfare. Psychologists are concerned about and work to mitigate the causes of human suffering. When undertaking research, they strive to advance human welfare and the science of psychology. Psychologists try to avoid misuse of their work. Psychologists comply with the law and encourage the development of law and social policy that serve the interests of their patients and clients and the public. They are encouraged to contribute a portion of their professional time for little or no personal advantage.

1. GENERAL STANDARDS

These General Standards are potentially applicable to the professional and scientific activities of all psychologists.

1.01   Applicability of the Ethics Code.

The activity of a psychologist subject to the Ethics Code may be reviewed under these Ethical Standards only if the activity is part of his or her work-related functions or the activity is psychological in nature. Personal activities having no connection to or effect on psychological roles are not subject to the Ethics Code.

1.02   Relationship of Ethics and Law.

If psychologists' ethical responsibilities conflict with law, psychologists make known their commitment to the Ethics Code and take steps to resolve the conflict in a responsible manner.

1.03   Professional and Scientific Relationship.

Psychologists provide diagnostic, therapeutic, teaching, research, supervisory, consultative, or other psychological services only in the context of a defined professional or scientific relationship or role. (See also Standards 2.01, Evaluation, Diagnosis, and Interventions in Professional Context, and 7.02, Forensic Assessments.)

1.04   Boundaries of Competence.

(a)   Psychologists provide services, teach, and conduct research only within the boundaries of their competence, based on their education, training, supervised experience, or appropriate professional experience.

(b)   Psychologists provide services, teach, or conduct research in new areas or involving new techniques only after first undertaking appropriate study, training, supervision, and/or consultation from persons who are competent in those areas or techniques.

(c)   In those emerging areas in which generally recognized standards for preparatory training do not yet exist, psychologists nevertheless take reasonable steps to ensure the competence of their work and to protect patients, clients, students, research participants, and others from harm.

1.05   Maintaining Expertise.

Psychologists who engage in assessment, therapy, teaching, research, organizational consulting, or other professional activities maintain a reasonable level of awareness of current scientific and professional information in their fields of activity, and undertake ongoing efforts to maintain competence in the skills they use.

1.06   Basis for Scientific and Professional Judgments.

Psychologists rely on scientifically and professionally derived knowledge when making scientific or professional judgments or when engaging in scholarly or professional endeavors.

1.07   Describing the Nature and Results of Psychological Services.

(a)   When psychologists provide assessment, evaluation, treatment, counseling, supervision, teaching, consultation, research, or other psychological services to an individual, a group, or an organization, they provide, using language that is reasonably understandable to the recipient of those services, appropriate in- formation beforehand about the nature of such services and appropriate information later about results and conclusions. (See also Standard 2.09, Explaining Assessment Results.)

(b)   If psychologists will be precluded by law or by organizational roles from providing such information to particular individuals or groups, they so inform those individuals or groups at the outset of the service.

1.08   Human Differences.

Where differences of age, gender, race, ethnicity, national origin, religion, sexual orientation, disability, language, or socioeconomic status significantly affect psychologists' work concerning particular individuals or groups, psychologists obtain the training, experience, consultation, or supervision necessary to ensure the competence of their services, or they make appropriate referrals.

1.09   Respecting Others.

In their work-related activities, psychologists respect the rights of others to hold values, attitudes, and opinions that differ from their own.

1.10   Nondiscrimination.

In their work-related activities, psychologists do not engage in unfair discrimination based on age, gender, race, ethnicity, national origin, religion, sexual orientation, disability, socioeconomic status, or any basis proscribed by law.

1.11 Sexual Harassment.

(a) Psychologists do not engage in sexual harassment. Sexual harassment is sexual solicitation, physical advances, or verbal or nonverbal conduct that is sexual in nature, that occurs in connection with the psychologist's activities or roles as a psychologist, and that either:(1) is unwelcome, is offensive, or creates a hostile workplace environment, and the psychologist knows or is told this; or (2) is sufficiently severe or intense to be abusive to a reasonable person in the context. Sexual harassment can consist of a single intense or severe act or of multiple persistent or pervasive acts.

(b) Psychologists accord sexual-harassment complainants and respondents dignity and respect. Psychologists do not participate in denying a person academic admittance or advancement, employment, tenure, or promotion, based solely upon their having made, or their being the subject of, sexual harassment charges. This does not preclude taking action based upon the outcome of such proceedings or consideration of other appropriate information.

1.12 Other Harassment.

Psychologists do not knowingly engage in behavior that is harassing or demeaning to persons with whom they interact in their work based on factors such as those persons' age, gender, race, ethnicity, national origin, religion, sexual orientation, disability, language, or socioeconomic status.

1.13 Personal Problems and Conflicts.

(a) Psychologists recognize that their personal problems and conflicts may interfere with their effectiveness. Accordingly, they refrain from undertaking an activity when they know or should know that their personal problems are likely to lead to harm to a patient, client, colleague, student, research participant, or other person to whom they may owe a professional or scientific obligation.

(b) In addition, psychologists have an obligation to be alert to signs of, and to obtain assistance for, their personal problems at an early stage, in order to prevent significantly impaired performance.

(c) When psychologists become aware of personal problems that may interfere with their performing work-related duties adequately, they take appropriate measures, such as obtaining professional consultation or assistance, and determine whether they should limit, suspend, or terminate their work-related duties.

1.14 Avoiding Harm.

Psychologists take reasonable steps to avoid harming their patients or clients, research participants, students, and others with whom they work, and to minimize harm where it is foreseeable and unavoidable.

1.15 Misuse of Psychologists' Influence.

Because psychologists' scientific and professional judgments and actions may affect the lives of others, they are alert to and guard against personal, financial, social, organizational, or political factors that might lead to misuse of their influence.

1.16 Misuse of Psychologists' Work.

(a) Psychologists do not participate in activities in which it appears likely that their skills or data will be misused by others, unless corrective mechanisms are available. (See also Standard 7.04, Truthfulness and Candor.)

(b) If psychologists learn of misuse or misrepresentation of their work, they take reasonable steps to correct or minimize the misuse or misrepresentation.

1.17 Multiple Relationships.

(a) In many communities and situations, it may not be feasible or reasonable for psychologists to avoid social or other nonprofessional contacts with persons such as patients, clients, students, supervisees, or research participants. Psychologists must always be sensitive to the potential harmful effects of other contacts on their work and on those persons with whom they deal. A psychologist refrains from entering into or promising another personal, scientific, professional, financial, or other relationship with such persons if it appears likely that such a relationship reasonably might impair the psychologist's objectivity or otherwise interfere with the psychologist's effectively performing his or her functions as a psychologist, or might harm or exploit the other party.

(b) Likewise, whenever feasible, a psychologist refrains from taking on professional or scientific obligations when pre-existing relationships would create a risk of such harm.

(c) If a psychologist finds that, due to unforeseen factors, a potentially harmful multiple relationship has arisen, the psychologist attempts to resolve it with due regard for the best interests of the affected person and maximal compliance with the Ethics Code.

1.18 Barter (With Patients or Clients).

Psychologists ordinarily refrain from accepting goods, services, or other nonmonetary remuneration from patients or clients in return for psychological services because such arrangements create inherent potential for conflicts, exploitation, and distortion of the professional relationship. A psychologist may participate in bartering only if (1) it is not clinically contraindicated, and (2) the relationship is not exploitative. (See also Standards 1.17, Multiple Relationships, and 1.25, Fees and Financial Arrangements.)

1.19 Exploitative Relationships.

(a) Psychologists do not exploit persons over whom they have supervisory, evaluative, or other authority such as students, supervisees, employees, research participants, and clients or patients. (See also Standards 4.05 - 4.07 regarding sexual involvement with clients or patients.)

(b) Psychologists do not engage in sexual relationships with students or supervisees in training over whom the psychologist has evalua-

tive or direct authority, because such relationships are so likely to impair judgment or be exploitative.

1.20 Consultations and Referrals.

(a) Psychologists arrange for appropriate consultations and referrals based principally on the best interests of their patients or clients, with appropriate consent, and subject to other relevant considerations, including applicable law and contractual obligations. (See also Standards 5.01, Discussing the Limits of Confidentiality, and 5.06, Consultations.)

(b) When indicated and professionally appropriate, psychologists cooperate with other professionals in order to serve their patients or clients effectively and appropriately.

(c) Psychologists' referral practices are consistent with law.

1.21 Third-Party Requests for Services.

(a) When a psychologist agrees to provide services to a person or entity at the request of a third party, the psychologist clarifies to the extent feasible, at the outset of the service, the nature of the relationship with each party. This clarification includes the role of the psychologist (such as therapist, organizational consultant, diagnostician, or expert witness), the probable uses of the services provided or the information obtained, and the fact that there may be limits to confidentiality.

(b) If there is a foreseeable risk of the psychologist's being called upon to perform conflicting roles because of the involvement of a third party, the psychologist clarifies the nature and direction of his or her responsibilities, keeps all parties appropriately informed as matters develop, and resolves the situation in accordance with this Ethics Code.

1.22 Delegation to and Supervision of Subordinates.

(a) Psychologists delegate to their employees, supervisees, and research assistants only those responsibilities that such persons can reasonably be expected to perform competently, on the basis of their education, training, or experience, either independently or with the level of supervision being provided.

(b) Psychologists provide proper training and supervision to their employees or supervisees and take reasonable steps to see that such persons perform services responsibly, competently, and ethically.

(c) If institutional policies, procedures, or practices prevent fulfillment of this obligation, psychologists attempt to modify their role or to correct the situation to the extent feasible.

1.23 Documentation of Professional and Scientific Work.

(a) Psychologists appropriately document their professional and scientific work in order to facilitate provision of services later by them or by other professionals, to ensure accountability, and to meet other requirements of institutions or the law.

(b) When psychologists have reason to believe that records of their professional services will be used in legal proceedings involving recipients of or participants in their work, they have a responsibility to create and maintain documentation in the kind of detail and quality that would be consistent with reasonable scrutiny in an adjudicative forum. (See also Standard 7.01, Professionalism, under Forensic Activities.)

1.24 Records and Data.

Psychologists create, maintain, disseminate, store, retain, and dispose of records and data relating to their research, practice, and other work in accordance with law and in a manner that permits compliance with the requirements of this Ethics Code. (See also Standard 5.04, Maintenance of Records.)

1.25 Fees and Financial Arrangements.

(a) As early as is feasible in a professional or scientific relationship, the psychologist and the patient, client, or other appropriate recipient of psychological services reach an agreement specifying the compensation and the billing arrangements.

(b) Psychologists do not exploit recipients of services or payors with respect to fees.

(c) Psychologists' fee practices are consistent with law.

(d) Psychologists do not misrepresent their fees.

(e) If limitations to services can be anticipated because of limitations in financing, this is discussed with the patient, client, or other appropriate recipient of services as early as is feasible. (See also Standard 4.08, Interruption of Services.)

(f) If the patient, client, or other recipient of services does not pay for services as agreed, and if the psychologist wishes to use collection agencies or legal measures to collect the fees, the psychologist first informs the person that such measures will be taken and provides that person an opportunity to make prompt payment. (See also Standard 5.11, Withholding Records for Nonpayment.)

1.26 Accuracy in Reports to Payors and Funding Sources.

In their reports to payors for services or sources of research funding, psychologists accurately state the nature of the research or service provided, the fees or charges, and where applicable, the identity of the provider, the findings, and the diagnosis. (See also Standard 5.05, Disclosures.)

1.27 Referrals and Fees.

When a psychologist pays, receives payment from, or divides fees with another professional other than in an employer - employee relationship, the payment to each is based on the services (clinical, consultative, administrative, or other) provided and is not based on the referral itself.

2. EVALUATION, ASSESSMENT, OR INTERVENTION

2.01 Evaluation, Diagnosis, and Interventions in Professional Context.

(a) Psychologists perform evaluations, diagnostic services, or interventions only within the context of a defined professional relationship. (See also Standards 1.03, Professional and Scientific Relationship.)

(b) Psychologists' assessments, recommendations, reports, and psychological diagnostic or evaluative statements are based on information and techniques (including personal interviews of the individual when appropriate) sufficient to provide appropriate substantiation for their findings. (See also Standard 7.02, Forensic Assessments.)

2.02 Competence and Appropriate Use of Assessments and Interventions.

(a) Psychologists who develop, administer, score, interpret, or use psychological assessment techniques, interviews, tests, or instruments do so in a manner and for purposes that are appropriate in light of the research on or evidence of the usefulness and proper application of the techniques.

(b) Psychologists refrain from misuse of assessment techniques, interventions, results, and interpretations and take reasonable steps to prevent others from misusing the information these techniques provide. This includes refraining from releasing raw test results or raw data to persons, other than to patients or clients as appropriate, who are not qualified to use such information. (See also Standards 1.02, Relationship of Ethics and Law, and 1.04, Boundaries of Competence.)

2.03 Test Construction.

Psychologists who develop and conduct research with tests and other assessment techniques use scientific procedures and current professional knowledge for test design, standardization, validation, reduction or elimination of bias, and recommendations for use.

2.04 Use of Assessment in General and With Special Populations.

(a) Psychologists who perform interventions or administer, score, interpret, or use assessment techniques are familiar with the reliability, validation, and related standardization or outcome studies of, and proper applications and uses of, the techniques they use.

(b) Psychologists recognize limits to the certainty with which diagnoses, judgments, or predictions can be made about individuals.

(c) Psychologists attempt to identify situations in which particular interventions or assessment techniques or norms may not be applicable or may require adjustment in administration or interpretation because of factors such as individuals' gender, age, race, ethnicity, national origin, religion, sexual orientation, disability, language, or socioeconomic status.

2.05 Interpreting Assessment Results.

When interpreting assessment results, including automated interpretations, psychologists take into account the various test factors and characteristics of the person being assessed that might affect psychologists' judgments or reduce the accuracy of their interpretations. They indicate any significant reservations they have about the accuracy or limitations of their interpretations.

2.06 Unqualified Persons.

Psychologists do not promote the use of psychological assessment techniques by unqualified persons. (See also Standard 1.22, Delegation to and Supervision of Subordinates.)

2.07 Obsolete Tests and Outdated Test Results.

(a) Psychologists do not base their assessment or intervention decisions or recommendations on data or test results that are outdated for the current purpose.

(b) Similarly, psychologists do not base such decisions or recommendations on tests and measures that are obsolete and not useful for the current purpose.

2.08 Test Scoring and Interpretation Services.

(a) Psychologists who offer assessment or scoring procedures to other professionals accurately describe the purpose, norms, validity, reliability, and applications of the procedures and any special qualifications applicable to their use.

(b) Psychologists select scoring and interpretation services (including automated services) on the basis of evidence of the validity of the program and procedures as well as on other appropriate considerations.

(c) Psychologists retain appropriate responsibility for the appropriate application, interpretation, and use of assessment instruments, whether they score and interpret such tests themselves or use automated or other services.

2.09 Explaining Assessment Results.

Unless the nature of the relationship is clearly explained to the person being assessed in advance and precludes provision of an explanation of results (such as in some organizational consulting, pre-employment or security screenings, and forensic evaluations), psychologists ensure that an explanation of the results is provided using language that is reasonably understandable to the person assessed or to another legally authorized person on behalf of the client. Regardless of whether the scoring and interpretation are done by the psychologist, by assistants, or by automated or other outside services, psychologists take reasonable steps to ensure that appropriate explanations of results are given.

2.10 Maintaining Test Security.

Psychologists make reasonable efforts to maintain the integrity and security of tests and other assessment techniques consistent with law, contractual obligations, and in a manner that permits compliance with the requirements of this Ethics Code. (See also Standard 1.02, Relationship of Ethics and Law.)

3. ADVERTISING AND OTHER PUBLIC STATEMENTS

3.01 Definition of Public Statements.

Psychologists comply with this Ethics Code in public statements relating to their professional services, products, or publications or to the field of psychology. Public statements include but are not limited to paid or unpaid advertising, brochures, printed matter, directory listings, personal resumes or curriculum vitae, interviews or comments for use in media, statements in legal proceedings, lectures and public oral presentations, and published materials.

3.02 Statements by Others.

(a) Psychologists who engage others to create or place public statements that promote their professional practice, products, or activities retain professional responsibility for such statements.

(b) In addition, psychologists make reasonable efforts to prevent others whom they do not control (such as employers, publishers, sponsors, organizational clients, and representatives of the print or broadcast media) from making deceptive statements concerning psychologists' practice or professional or scientific activities.

(c) If psychologists learn of deceptive statements about their work made by others, psychologists make reasonable efforts to correct such statements.

(d) Psychologists do not compensate employees of press, radio, television, or other communication media in return for publicity in a news item.

(e) A paid advertisement relating to the psychologist's activities must be identified as such, unless it is already apparent from the context.

3.03 Avoidance of False or Deceptive Statements.

(a) Psychologists do not make public statements that are false, deceptive, misleading, or fraudulent, either because of what they state, convey, or suggest or because of what they omit, concerning their research, practice, or other work activities or those of persons or organizations with which they are affiliated. As examples (and not in limitation) of this standard, psychologists do not make false or deceptive statements concerning (1) their training, experience, or competence; (2) their academic degrees; (3) their credentials; (4) their institutional or association affiliations; (5) their services; (6) the scientific or clinical basis for, or results or degree of success of, their services; (7) their fees; or (8) their publications or research findings. (See also Standards 6.15, Deception in Research, and 6.18, Providing Participants With Information About the Study.)

(b) Psychologists claim as credentials for their psychological work, only degrees that (1) were earned from a regionally accredited educational institution or (2) were the basis for psychology licensure by the state in which they practice.

3.04 Media Presentations.

When psychologists provide advice or comment by means of public lectures, demonstrations, radio or television programs, prerecorded tapes, printed articles, mailed material, or other media, they take reasonable precautions to ensure that (1) the statements are based on appropriate psychological literature and practice, (2) the statements are otherwise consistent with this Ethics Code, and (3) the recipients of the information are not encouraged to infer that a relationship has been established with them personally.

3.05 Testimonials.

Psychologists do not solicit testimonials from current psychotherapy clients or patients or other persons who because of their particular circumstances are vulnerable to undue influence.

3.06 In-Person Solicitation.

Psychologists do not engage, directly or through agents, in uninvited in-person solicitation of business from actual or potential psychotherapy patients or clients or other persons who because of their particular circumstances are vulnerable to undue influence. However, this does not preclude attempting to implement appropriate collateral contacts with significant others for the purpose of benefiting an already engaged therapy patient.

4. THERAPY

4.01 Structuring the Relationship.

(a) Psychologists discuss with clients or patients as early as is feasible in the therapeutic relationship appropriate issues, such as the nature and anticipated course of therapy, fees, and confidentiality. (See also Standards 1.25, Fees and Financial Arrangements, and 5.01, Discussing the Limits of Confidentiality.)

(b) When the psychologist's work with clients or patients will be supervised, the above discussion includes that fact, and the name of the supervisor, when the supervisor has legal responsibility for the case.

(c) When the therapist is a student intern, the client or patient is informed of that fact.

(d) Psychologists make reasonable efforts to answer patients' questions and to avoid apparent misunderstandings about therapy. Whenever possible, psychologists provide oral and/or written information, using language that is reasonably understandable to the patient or client.

4.02 Informed Consent to Therapy.

(a) Psychologists obtain appropriate informed consent to therapy or related procedures, using language that is reasonably understandable to participants. The content of informed consent will vary depending on many circumstances; however, informed consent generally implies that the person (1) has the capacity to consent, (2) has been informed of significant information concerning the procedure, (3) has freely and without undue influence expressed consent, and (4) consent has been appropriately documented.

ETHICS

(b) When persons are legally incapable of giving informed consent, psychologists obtain informed permission from a legally authorized person, if such substitute consent is permitted by law.

(c) In addition, psychologists (1) inform those persons who are legally incapable of giving informed consent about the proposed interventions in a manner commensurate with the persons' psychological capacities, (2) seek their assent to those interventions, and (3) consider such persons' preferences and best interests.

4.03 Couple and Family Relationships.

(a) When a psychologist agrees to provide services to several persons who have a relationship (such as husband and wife or parents and children), the psychologist attempts to clarify at the outset (1) which of the individuals are patients or clients and (2) the relationship the psychologist will have with each person. This clarification includes the role of the psychologist and the probable uses of the services provided or the information obtained. (See also Standard 5.01, Discussing the Limits of Confidentiality.)

(b) As soon as it becomes apparent that the psychologist may be called on to perform potentially conflicting roles (such as marital counselor to husband and wife, and then witness for one party in a divorce proceeding), the psychologist attempts to clarify and adjust, or withdraw from, roles appropriately. (See also Standard 7.03, Clarification of Role, under Forensic Activities.)

4.04 Providing Mental Health Services to Those Served by Others.

In deciding whether to offer or provide services to those already receiving mental health services elsewhere, psychologists carefully consider the treatment issues and the potential patient's or client's welfare. The psychologist discusses these issues with the patient or client, or another legally authorized person on behalf of the client, in order to minimize the risk of confusion and conflict, consults with the other service providers when appropriate, and proceeds with caution and sensitivity to the therapeutic issues.

4.05 Sexual Intimacies With Current Patients or Clients.

Psychologists do not engage in sexual intimacies with current patients or clients.

4.06 Therapy With Former Sexual Partners.

Psychologists do not accept as therapy patients or clients persons with whom they have engaged in sexual intimacies.

4.07 Sexual Intimacies With Former Therapy Patients.

(a) Psychologists do not engage in sexual intimacies with a former therapy patient or client for at least two years after cessation or termination of professional services.

(b) Because sexual intimacies with a former therapy patient or client are so frequently harmful to the patient or client, and because such intimacies undermine public confidence in the psychology profession and thereby deter the public's use of needed services, psychologists do not engage in sexual intimacies with former therapy patients and clients even after a two-year interval except in the most unusual circumstances. The psychologist who engages in such activity after the two years following cessation or termination of treatment bears the burden of demonstrating that there has been no exploitation, in light of all relevant factors, including (1) the amount of time that has passed since therapy terminated, (2) the nature and duration of the therapy, (3) the circumstances of termination, (4) the patient's or client's personal history, (5) the patient's or client's current mental status, (6) the likelihood of adverse impact on the patient or client and others, and (7) any statements or actions made by the therapist during the course of therapy suggesting or inviting the possibility of a post-termination sexual or romantic relationship with the patient or client. (See also Standard 1.17, Multiple Relationships.)

4.08 Interruption of Services.

(a) Psychologists make reasonable efforts to plan for facilitating care in the event that psychological services are interrupted by factors such as the psychologist's illness, death, unavailability, or relocation or by the client's relocation or financial limitations. (See also Standard 5.09, Preserving Records and Data.)

(b) When entering into employment or contractual relationships, psychologists provide for orderly and appropriate resolution of responsibility for patient or client care in the event that the employment or contractual relationship ends, with paramount consideration given to the welfare of the patient or client.

4.09 Terminating the Professional Relationship.

(a) Psychologists do not abandon patients or clients. (See also Standard 1.25e, under Fees and Financial Arrangements.)

(b) Psychologists terminate a professional relationship when it becomes reasonably clear that the patient or client no longer needs the service, is not benefiting, or is being harmed by continued service.

(c) Prior to termination for whatever reason, except where precluded by the patient's or client's conduct, the psychologist discusses the patient's or client's views and needs, provides appropriate pretermination counseling, suggests alternative service providers as appropriate, and takes other reasonable steps to facilitate transfer of responsibility to another provider if the patient or client needs one immediately.

5. PRIVACY AND CONFIDENTIALITY

These Standards are potentially applicable to the professional and scientific activities of all psychologists.

5.01 Discussing the Limits of Confidentiality.

(a) Psychologists discuss with persons and organizations with whom they establish a scientific or professional relationship (including, to the extent feasible, minors and their legal representatives) (1) the relevant limitations on confidentiality, including limitations where applicable in group, marital, and family therapy or in organizational consulting, and (2) the foreseeable uses of the information generated through their services.

(b) Unless it is not feasible or is contraindicated, the discussion of confidentiality occurs at the outset of the relationship and thereafter as new circumstances may warrant.

(c) Permission for electronic recording of interviews is secured from clients and patients.

5.02 Maintaining Confidentiality.

Psychologists have a primary obligation and take reasonable precautions to respect the confidentiality rights of those with whom they work or consult, recognizing that confidentiality may be established by law, institutional rules, or professional or scientific relationships. (See also Standard 6.26, Professional Reviewers.)

5.03 Minimizing Intrusions on Privacy.

(a) In order to minimize intrusions on privacy, psychologists include in written and oral reports, consultations, and the like, only information germane to the purpose for which the communication is made.

(b) Psychologists discuss confidential information obtained in clinical or consulting relationships, or evaluative data concerning patients, individual or organizational clients, students, research participants, supervisees, and employees, only for appropriate scientific or professional purposes and only with persons clearly concerned with such matters.

5.04 Maintenance of Records.

Psychologists maintain appropriate confidentiality in creating, storing, accessing, transferring, and disposing of records under their control, whether these are written, automated, or in any other medium. Psychologists maintain and dispose of records in accordance with law and in a manner that permits compliance with the requirements of this Ethics Code.

5.05 Disclosures.

(a) Psychologists disclose confidential information without the consent of the individual only as mandated by law, or where permitted by law for a valid purpose, such as (1) to provide needed professional services to the patient or the individual or organizational client, (2) to obtain appropriate professional consultations, (3) to protect the patient or client or others from harm, or (4) to obtain payment for services, in which instance disclosure is limited to the minimum that is necessary to achieve the purpose.

(b) Psychologists also may disclose confidential information with the appropriate consent of the patient or the individual or organizational client (or of another legally authorized person on behalf of the patient or client), unless prohibited by law.

5.06 Consultations.

When consulting with colleagues,

(1) psychologists do not share confidential information that reasonably could lead to the identification of a patient, client, research participant, or other person or organization with whom they have a confidential relationship unless they have obtained the prior consent of the person or organization or the disclosure cannot be avoided, and

(2) they share information only to the extent necessary to achieve the purposes of the consultation. (See also Standard 5.02, Maintaining Confidentiality.)

5.07 Confidential Information in Databases.

(a) If confidential information concerning recipients of psychological services is to be entered into databases or systems of records available to persons whose access has not been consented to by the recipient, then psychologists use coding or other techniques to avoid the inclusion of personal identifiers.

(b) If a research protocol approved by an institutional review board or similar body requires the inclusion of personal identifiers, such identifiers are deleted before the information is made accessible to persons other than those of whom the subject was advised.

(c) If such deletion is not feasible, then before psychologists transfer such data to others or review such data collected by others, they take reasonable steps to determine that appropriate consent of personally identifiable individuals has been obtained.

5.08 Use of Confidential Information for Didactic or Other Purposes.

(a) Psychologists do not disclose in their writings, lectures, or other public media, confidential, personally identifiable information concerning their patients, individual or organizational clients, students, research participants, or other recipients of their services that they obtained during the course of their work, unless the person or organization has consented in writing or unless there is other ethical or legal authorization for doing so.

(b) Ordinarily, in such scientific and professional presentations, psychologists disguise confidential information concerning such persons or organizations so that they are not individually identifiable to others and so that discussions do not cause harm to subjects who might identify themselves.

5.09 Preserving Records and Data.

A psychologist makes plans in advance so that confidentiality of records and data is protected in the event of the psychologist's death, incapacity, or withdrawal from the position or practice.

5.10 Ownership of Records and Data.

Recognizing that ownership of records and data is governed by legal principles, psychologists take reasonable and lawful steps so that records and

ETHICS

data remain available to the extent needed to serve the best interests of patients, individual or organizational clients, research participants, or appropriate others.

5.11   Withholding Records for Nonpayment.
Psychologists may not withhold records under their control that are requested and imminently needed for a patient's or client's treatment solely because payment has not been received, except as otherwise provided by law.

6.   TEACHING, TRAINING SUPERVISION, RESEARCH, AND PUBLISHING

6.01   Design of Education and Training Programs.
Psychologists who are responsible for education and training programs seek to ensure that the programs are competently designed, provide the proper experiences, and meet the requirements for licensure, certification, or other goals for which claims are made by the program.

6.02   Descriptions of Education and Training Programs.
(a)   Psychologists responsible for education and training programs seek to ensure that there is a current and accurate description of the program content, training goals and objectives, and requirements that must be met for satisfactory completion of the program. This information must be made readily available to all interested parties.

(b)   Psychologists seek to ensure that statements concerning their course outlines are accurate and not misleading, particularly regarding the subject matter to be covered, bases for evaluating progress, and the nature of course experiences. (See also Standard 3.03, Avoidance of False or Deceptive Statements.)

(c)   To the degree to which they exercise control, psychologists responsible for announcements, catalogs, brochures, or advertisements describing workshops, seminars, or other non-degree- granting educational programs ensure that they accurately describe the audience for which the program is intended, the educational objectives, the presenters, and the fees involved.

6.03   Accuracy and Objectivity in Teaching.
(a)   When engaged in teaching or training, psychologists present psychological information accurately and with a reasonable degree of objectivity.

(b)   When engaged in teaching or training, psychologists recognize the power they hold over students or supervisees and therefore make reasonable efforts to avoid engaging in conduct that is personally demeaning to students or supervisees. (See also Standards 1.09, Respecting Others, and 1.12, Other Harassment.)

6.04   Limitation on Teaching.
Psychologists do not teach the use of techniques or procedures that require specialized training, licensure, or expertise, including but not limited to hypnosis, biofeedback, and projective techniques, to individuals who lack the prerequisite training, legal scope of practice, or expertise.

6.05   Assessing Student and Supervisee Performance.
(a)   In academic and supervisory relationships, psychologists establish an appropriate process for providing feedback to students and supervisees.

(b)   Psychologists evaluate students and supervisees on the basis of their actual performance on relevant and established program requirements.

6.06   Planning Research.
(a)   Psychologists design, conduct, and report research in accordance with recognized standards of scientific competence and ethical research.

(b)   Psychologists plan their research so as to minimize the possibility that results will be misleading.

(c)   In planning research, psychologists consider its ethical acceptability under the Ethics Code. If an ethical issue is unclear, psychologists seek to resolve the issue through consultation with institutional review boards, animal care and use committees, peer consultations, or other proper mechanisms.

(d)   Psychologists take reasonable steps to implement appropriate protections for the rights and welfare of human participants, other persons affected by the research, and the welfare of animal subjects.

6.07   Responsibility.
(a)   Psychologists conduct research competently and with due concern for the dignity and welfare of the participants.

(b)   Psychologists are responsible for the ethical conduct of research conducted by them or by others under their supervision or control.

(c)   Researchers and assistants are permitted to perform only those tasks for which they are appropriately trained and prepared.

(d)   As part of the process of development and implementation of research projects, psychologists consult those with expertise concerning any special population under investigation or most likely to be affected.

6.08   Compliance With Law and Standards.
Psychologists plan and conduct research in a manner consistent with federal and state law and regulations, as well as professional standards governing the conduct of research, and particularly those standards governing research with human participants and animal subjects.

6.09   Institutional Approval.
Psychologists obtain from host institutions or organizations appropriate approval prior to conducting research, and they provide accurate information about their research proposals. They conduct the research in accordance with the approved research protocol.

6.10   Research Responsibilities.
Prior to conducting research (except research involving only anonymous surveys, naturalistic observations, or similar research), psychologists enter into an agreement with participants that clarifies the nature of the research and the responsibilities of each party.

6.11   Informed Consent to Research.
(a)   Psychologists use language that is reasonably understandable to research participants in obtaining their appropriate informed consent (except as provided in Standard 6.12, Dispensing with Informed Consent). Such informed consent is appropriately documented.

(b)   Using language that is reasonably understandable to participants, psychologists inform participants of the nature of the research; they inform participants that they are free to participate or to decline to participate or to withdraw from the research; they explain the foreseeable consequences of declining or withdrawing; they inform participants of significant factors that may be expected to influence their willingness to participate (such as risks, discomfort, adverse effects, or limitations on confidentiality, except as provided in Standard 6.15, Deception in Research); and they explain other aspects about which the prospective participants inquire.

(c)   When psychologists conduct research with individuals such as students or subordinates, psychologists take special care to protect the prospective participants from adverse consequences of declining or withdrawing from participation.

(d)   When research participation is a course requirement or opportunity for extra credit, the prospective participant is given the choice of equitable alternative activities.

(e)   For persons who are legally incapable of giving informed consent, psychologists nevertheless (1) provide an appropriate explanation, (2) obtain the participant's assent, and (3) obtain appropriate permission from a legally authorized person, if such substitute consent is permitted by law.

6.12   Dispensing With Informed Consent.
Before determining that planned research (such as research involving only anonymous questionnaires, naturalistic observations, or certain kinds of archival research) does not require the informed consent of research participants, psychologists consider applicable regulations and institutional review board requirements, and they consult with colleagues as appropriate.

6.13   Informed Consent in Research Filming or Recording.
Psychologists obtain informed consent from research participants prior to filming or recording them in any form, unless the research involves simply naturalistic observations in public places and it is not anticipated that the recording will be used in a manner that could cause personal identification or harm.

6.14   Offering Inducements for Research Participants.
(a)   In offering professional services as an inducement to obtain research participants, psychologists make clear the nature of the services, as well as the risks, obligations, and limitations. (See also Standard 1.18, Barter [With Patients or Clients].)

(b)   Psychologists do not offer excessive or inappropriate financial or other inducements to obtain research participants, particularly when it might tend to coerce participation.

6.15   Deception in Research.
(a)   Psychologists do not conduct a study involving deception unless they have determined that the use of deceptive techniques is justified by the study's prospective scientific, educational, or applied value and that equally effective alternative procedures that do not use deception are not feasible.

(b)   Psychologists never deceive research participants about significant aspects that would affect their willingness to participate, such as physical risks, discomfort, or unpleasant emotional experiences.

(c)   Any other deception that is an integral feature of the design and conduct of an experiment must be explained to participants as early as is feasible, preferably at the conclusion of their participation, but no later than at the conclusion of the research. (See also Standard 6.18, Providing Participants With Information About the Study.)

6.16   Sharing and Utilizing Data.
Psychologists inform research participants of their anticipated sharing or further use of personally identifiable research data and of the possibility of unanticipated future uses.

6.17   Minimizing Invasiveness.
In conducting research, psychologists interfere with the participants or milieu from which data are collected only in a manner that is warranted by an appropriate research design and that is consistent with psychologists' roles as scientific investigators.

6.18   Providing Participants With Information About the Study.
(a)   Psychologists provide a prompt opportunity for participants to obtain appropriate information about the nature, results, and conclusions of the research, and psychologists attempt to correct any misconceptions that participants may have.

(b)   If scientific or humane values justify delaying or withholding this information, psychologists take reasonable measures to reduce the risk of harm.

6.19   Honoring Commitments.
Psychologists take reasonable measures to honor all commitments they have made to research participants.

6.20   Care and Use of Animals Research.

ETHICAL PRINCIPLES OF PSYCHOLOGISTS   **549**

(a) Psychologists who conduct research involving animals treat them humanely.

(b) Psychologists acquire, care for, use, and dispose of animals in compliance with current federal, state, and local laws and regulations, and with professional standards.

(c) Psychologists trained in research methods and experienced in the care of laboratory animals supervise all procedures involving animals and are responsible for ensuring appropriate consideration of their comfort, health, and humane treatment.

(d) Psychologists ensure that all individuals using animals under their supervision have received instruction in research methods and in the care, maintenance, and handling of the species being used, to the extent appropriate to their role.

(e) Responsibilities and activities of individuals assisting in a research project are consistent with their respective competencies. (f) Psychologists make reasonable efforts to minimize the discomfort, infection, illness, and pain of animal subjects.

(g) A procedure subjecting animals to pain, stress, or privation is used only when an alternative procedure is unavailable and the goal is justified by its prospective scientific, educational, or applied value.

(h) Surgical procedures are performed under appropriate anesthesia; techniques to avoid infection and minimize pain are followed during and after surgery.

(i) When it is appropriate that the animal's life be terminated, it is done rapidly, with an effort to minimize pain, and in accordance with accepted procedures.

6.21 Reporting of Results.

(a) Psychologists do not fabricate data or falsify results in their publications.

(b) If psychologists discover significant errors in their published data, they take reasonable steps to correct such errors in a correction, retraction, erratum, or other appropriate publication means.

6.22 Plagiarism.

Psychologists do not present substantial portions or elements of another's work or data as their own, even if the other work or data source is cited occasionally.

6.23 Publication Credit.

(a) Psychologists take responsibility and credit, including authorship credit, only for work they have actually performed or to which they have contributed.

(b) Principal authorship and other publication credits accurately reflect the relative scientific or professional contributions of the individuals involved, regardless of their relative status. Mere possession of an institutional position, such as Department Chair, does not justify authorship credit. Minor contributions to the research or to the writing for publications are appropriately acknowledged, such as in footnotes or in an introductory statement.

(c) A student is usually listed as principal author on any multiple-authored article that is substantially based on the student's dissertation or thesis.

6.24 Duplicate Publication of Data.

Psychologists do not publish, as original data, data that have been previously published. This does not preclude republishing data when they are accompanied by proper acknowledgment.

6.25 Sharing Data.

After research results are published, psychologists do not withhold the data on which their conclusions are based from other competent professionals who seek to verify the substantive claims through reanalysis and who intend to use such data only for that purpose, provided that the confidentiality of the participants can be protected and unless legal rights concerning proprietary data preclude their release.

6.26 Professional Reviewers.

Psychologists who review material submitted for publication, grant, or other research proposal review respect the confidentiality of and the proprietary rights in such information of those who submitted it.

7. FORENSIC ACTIVITIES

7.01 Professionalism.

Psychologists who perform forensic functions, such as assessments, interviews, consultations, reports, or expert testimony, must comply with all other provisions of this Ethics Code to the extent that they apply to such activities. In addition, psychologists base their forensic work on appropriate knowledge of and competence in the areas underlying such work, including specialized knowledge concerning special populations. (See also Standards 1.06, Basis for Scientific and Professional Judgments;

1.08, Human Differences; 1.15, Misuse of Psychologists' Influence; and 1.23, Documentation of Professional and Scientific Work.)

7.02 Forensic Assessments.

(a) Psychologists' forensic assessments, recommendations, and reports are based on information and techniques (including personal interviews of the individual, when appropriate) sufficient to provide appropriate substantiation for their findings. (See also Standards 1.03, Professional and Scientific Relationship; 1.23, Documentation of Professional and Scientific

Work; 2.01, Evaluation, Diagnosis, and Interventions in Professional Context; and 2.05, Interpreting Assessment Results.)

(b) Except as noted in ©, below, psychologists provide written or oral forensic reports or testimony of the psychological characteristics of an individual only after they have conducted an examination of the individual adequate to support their statements or conclusions.

© When, despite reasonable efforts, such an examination is not feasible, psychologists clarify the impact of their limited information on the reliability and validity of their reports and testimony, and they appropriately limit the nature and extent of their conclusions or recommendations.

7.03 Clarification of Role.

In most circumstances, psychologists avoid performing multiple and potentially conflicting roles in forensic matters. When psychologists may be called on to serve in more than one role in a legal proceeding - for example, as consultant or expert for one party or for the court and as a fact witness - they clarify role expectations and the extent of confidentiality in advance to the extent feasible, and thereafter as changes occur, in order to avoid compromising their professional judgment and objectivity and in order to avoid misleading others regarding their role.

7.04 Truthfulness and Candor.

(a) In forensic testimony and reports, psychologists testify truthfully, honestly, and candidly and, consistent with applicable legal procedures, describe fairly the bases for their testimony and conclusions. (b) Whenever necessary to avoid misleading, psychologists acknowledge the limits of their data or conclusions.

7.05 Prior Relationships.

A prior professional relationship with a party does not preclude psychologists from testifying as fact witnesses or from testifying to their services to the extent permitted by applicable law. Psychologists appropriately take into account ways in which the prior relationship might affect their professional objectivity or opinions and disclose the potential conflict to the relevant parties.

7.06 Compliance With Law and Rules.

In performing forensic roles, psychologists are reasonably familiar with the rules governing their roles. Psychologists are aware of the occasionally competing demands placed upon them by these principles and the requirements of the court system, and attempt to resolve these conflicts by making known their commitment to this Ethics Code and taking steps to resolve the conflict in a responsible manner. (See also Standard 1.02, Relationship of Ethics and Law.)

8. RESOLVING ETHICAL ISSUES

8.01 Familiarity With Ethics Code.

Psychologists have an obligation to be familiar with this Ethics Code, other applicable ethics codes, and their application to psychologists' work. Lack of awareness or misunderstanding of an ethical standard is not itself a defense to a charge of unethical conduct.

8.02 Confronting Ethical Issues.

When a psychologist is uncertain whether a particular situation or course of action would violate this Ethics Code, the psychologist ordinarily consults with other psychologists knowledgeable about ethical issues, with state or national psychology ethics committees, or with other appropriate authorities in order to choose a proper response.

8.03 Conflicts Between Ethics and Organizational Demands.

If the demands of an organization with which psychologists are affiliated conflict with this Ethics Code, psychologists clarify the nature of the conflict, make known their commitment to the Ethics Code, and to the extent feasible, seek to resolve the conflict in a way that permits the fullest adherence to the Ethics Code.

8.04 Informal Resolution of Ethical Violations.

When psychologists believe that there may have been an ethical violation by another psychologist, they attempt to resolve the issue by bringing it to the attention of that individual if an in-formal resolution appears appropriate and the intervention does not violate any confidentiality rights that may be involved.

8.05 Reporting Ethical Violations.

If an apparent ethical violation is not appropriate for informal resolution under Standard 8.04 or is not resolved properly in that fashion, psychologists take further action appropriate to the situation, unless such action conflicts with confidentiality rights in ways that cannot be resolved. Such action might include referral to state or national committees on professional ethics or to state licensing boards.

8.06 Cooperating With Ethics Committees.

Psychologists cooperate in ethics investigations, proceedings, and resulting requirements of the APA or any affiliated state psychological association to which they belong. In doing so, they make reasonable efforts to resolve any issues as to confidentiality. Failure to cooperate is itself an ethics violation.

8.07 Improper Complaints.

Psychologists do not file or encourage the filing of ethics complaints that are frivolous and are intended to harm the respondent rather than to protect the public.

A

absolute threshold   the smallest amount of a particular stimulus that can be detected, **78**

accommodation   the process of adjusting existing ways of thinking to encompass new information, ideas, or objects, **241**

acculturation   the process of adapting to a new or different culture, **339**

achievement   knowledge and skills gained from experience and education, **206**

achievement motivation   the desire to persevere with work and to avoid distraction in order to reach personal goals, **308**

achievement test   test that measures the amount of knowledge one has in specific academic areas, **347**

active coping   a response to a stressor that reduces stress by changing the situation to eliminate or lessen the negative effects of the stressor, **403**

active listening   empathic listening in which the listener acknowledges, restates, and clarifies the speaker's thoughts and concerns, **444**

actor-observer bias   the tendency to attribute one's own behavior to situational factors but to attribute the behavior of others to dispositional factors, **470**

addiction   a compulsive need for and use of a habit-forming substance, **116**

adolescent growth spurt   a sudden, brief burst of physical growth during which adolescents typically make great gains in height and weight, **252**

affiliation   the desire to join with others and to be a part of something larger than oneself, **310**

afterimage   the visual sensation that occurs after the original stimulus has been removed, **84**

agoraphobia   a fear of crowded, public places, **416**

algorithm   a problem-solving strategy that eventually leads to a solution; usually involves trying random solutions to a problem in a systematic way, **179**

altered state of consciousness   a type of consciousness other than normal waking consciousness, **106**

altruism   unselfish regard for the welfare of others, **494**

Alzheimer's disease   an irreversible, progressive brain disorder characterized by the deterioration of memory, language, and eventually, physical functioning, **287**

amphetamine   a type of stimulant often used to stay awake or to reduce appetite, **118**

analogy   a likeness that exists between two or more things that are in other ways unlike, **184**

anchoring   the process of making decisions based on certain ideas or standards held by the decision maker, **193**

anorexia nervosa   an eating disorder characterized by extreme weight loss due to self-starvation, **265**

anterograde amnesia   the inability to form new memories because of brain trauma, **170**

antianxiety drug   a type of medication that relieves anxiety disorders and panic disorders by depressing the activity of the central nervous system, **451**

antidepressant drug   a type of medication used to treat major depression by increasing the amount of one or both of the neurotransmitters noradrenaline and serotonin, **452**

antipsychotic drug   a type of medication used to reduce agitation, delusions, and hallucinations by blocking the activity of dopamine in the brain; also called a major tranquilizer, **452**

anxiety   a psychological state characterized by tension and apprehension, foreboding, and dread, **415**

approach-approach conflict   a type of conflict involving a choice between two positive but mutually exclusive options, **388**

approach-avoidance conflict   a type of conflict involving a single goal that has both positive and negative aspects, **390**

aptitude test   a test that is designed to predict a person's future performance or capacity to learn, **348**

archetype   an original model from which later forms develop; in Jung's personality theory, an archetype is a primitive image or concept that resides in the collective unconscious, **330**

assimilation   the process by which new information is placed into preexisting categories, **241**

association areas   areas of the cerebral cortex that are involved in such mental operations as thinking, memory, learning, and problem solving, **63**

attachment   an active and intense emotional relationship between two people that endures over time, **234**

attitude   an enduring belief about people, places, or objects that evokes certain feelings and influences behavior, **460**

attraction   in social psychology, an attitude of liking (positive attraction) or disliking (negative attraction), **472**

attribution theory   the suggestion that there is a tendency to explain a person's behavior in terms of the situation or the person's personality, **468**

auditory nerve   the cranial nerve that carries sound from the cochlea of the inner ear to the brain, **86**

authoritarian   a leadership or parenting style that stresses unquestioning obedience, **237**

authoritarian leader   a leader who makes decisions for the group and tells other group members what to do, **484**

authoritative   a leadership or parenting style based on recognized authority or knowledge and characterized by mutual respect, **237**

GLOSSARY

GLOSSARY

autonomic nervous system   the subdivision of the peripheral nervous system that regulates body functions, such as respiration and digestion, **58**

availability   the tendency to make decisions on the basis of information that is available in one's immediate consciousness, **193**

aversive conditioning   a type of counterconditioning that links an unpleasant state with an unwanted behavior in an attempt to eliminate the behavior, **449**

avoidance-avoidance conflict   a type of conflict involving a choice between two negative or undesirable options, **390**

axon   a long tubelike structure attached to a neuron that transmits impulses away from the neuron cell body, **55**

axon terminal   small fibers branching out from an axon, **55**

B

balance theory   the view that people have a need to organize their perceptions, opinions, and beliefs in a manner that is in harmony with those of the people around them, **309**

basic research   research that is conducted for its own sake, that is, without seeking a solution to a specific problem, **10**

behavior   observable and measurable actions of people and animals, **4**

behaviorism   the school of psychology, founded by John Watson, that defines psychology as the scientific study of observable behavior, **14**

behavior-rating scales   systematic means of recording the frequency with which certain behaviors occur, **344**

bereaved   suffering from the death of a loved one, **293**

binocular cue   a visual cue for depth that requires the use of both eyes, **96**

biofeedback   a system for monitoring and feeding back information about certain biological processes, such as blood pressure, **112**

biological perspective   the psychological perspective that emphasizes the influence of biology on behavior, **18**

bipolar disorder   a disorder in which a person's mood inappropriately alternates between extremes of elation and depression, **423**

blind spot   the part of the retina that contains no photoreceptors, **83**

bulimia   an eating disorder in which enormous quantities of food are consumed and then purged by means of laxatives or self-induced vomiting, **266**

bystander effect   the tendency for a person to be less likely to give aid if other bystanders are present, **495**

C

case study   an in-depth study of a single person or group to reveal some universal principle, **35**

catatonic stupor   an immobile, expressionless, coma-like state associated with schizophrenia, **426**

catharsis   in psychology, the release of aggressive energy through action or fantasy, **491**

cell body   the part of a neuron that produces the energy needed for the activity of the cell, **55**

cellular damage theories   the view that aging occurs because body cells lose the capacity to reproduce and maintain themselves as a result of damage, **285**

central nervous system   the part of the nervous system that consists of the brain and spinal cord, **54**

central route   a method of persuasion that uses evidence and logical arguments to influence people, **463**

cerebellum   the area of the brain that is responsible for voluntary movement and balance, **60**

cerebral cortex   the bumpy, convoluted surface of the brain; the body's control and information-processing center, **61**

cerebrum   the large mass of the forebrain, consisting of two hemispheres, **61**

childhood   the stage of life that follows infancy and spans the period from the second birthday to the beginning of adolescence, **231**

chromosome   a microscopic threadlike structure in the nucleus of every living cell; it contains genes, the basic units of heredity, **70**

chunking   a mental process for organizing information into meaningful units, or "chunks," **162**

circadian rhythm   a regular sequence of biological processes, such as temperature and sleep, that occurs every 24 hours, **106**

classical conditioning   a type of learning in which a neutral stimulus comes to elicit an unconditioned response when that neutral stimulus is repeatedly paired with a stimulus that normally causes an unconditioned response, **128**

clique   a small, exclusive group of people within a larger group, **258**

closure   the tendency to perceive a complete or whole figure even when there are gaps in sensory information, **93**

cochlea   the fluid-filled structure of the inner ear that transmits sound impulses to the auditory nerve, **86**

cognitive activity   private, unobservable mental processes such as sensation, perception, thought, and problem solving, **4**

cognitive anchors   early attitudes and persistent beliefs that shape the ways in which people see and interpret the world, **461**

cognitive consistency   the state in which a person's thoughts and behaviors match his or her beliefs and the expectations of others, **309**

cognitive-dissonance theory   the theory that suggests that people make attitudinal changes to reduce the tension that occurs when their thoughts and attitudes are inconsistent with their actions, **310**

cognitive perspective   the viewpoint that emphasizes the role of thought processes in determining behavior, **18**

cognitive restructuring   a method of coping in which one changes the thoughts one has in a particular situation, **359**

collective unconscious   Jung's concept of a shared, inherited body of memory that all humans have, **330**

commitment   a pledge or promise, **475**

common fate   the tendency to perceive objects that are moving together as belonging together, **94**

complementary   the colors across from each other on the color circle, **84**

compulsion   an apparently irresistible urge to repeat an act or engage in ritualistic behavior, such as hand washing, **416**

concept   a mental structure used to categorize objects, people, or events that share similar characteristics, **178**

concrete-operational stage   according to Piaget, the stage of cognitive development during which children acquire the ability to think logically, **243**

conditional positive regard   an expression of esteem given only when an individual has exhibited suitable behavior, **240**

conditioned response   a learned response to a previously neutral stimulus, **130**

conditioned stimulus   a previously neutral stimulus that, because of pairing with an unconditioned stimulus, now causes a conditioned response, **130**

conditioning   a type of learning that involves stimulus-response connections, in which the response is conditional on the stimulus, **128**

conductive deafness   hearing loss caused by damage to the middle ear, thus interfering with the transmission of sound waves to the cochlea, **87**

confirmation bias   the tendency to look for information that confirms one's preconceived notions, **190**

conform   to change one's attitudes or behavior in accordance with generally accepted standards, **484**

congruence   agreement; in psychology, consistency between one's self-concept and one's experience, **335**

consciousness   awareness of oneself and one's environment, **103**

conservation   according to Piaget, the principle that the properties of substances remain the same despite changes in their shape or arrangement, **242**

construct   a theoretical entity, or concept, that enables one to discuss something that cannot be seen, touched, or measured directly, **104**

contact comfort   the satisfaction obtained from pleasant, soft stimulation, **234**

context-dependent memory   information that is more easily retrieved in the context in which it was encoded and stored, **159**

continuity   the perceptual tendency to group stimuli into continuous patterns, **94**

continuous reinforcement   the reinforcement of a desired response every time it occurs, **139**

control group   in an experiment, the group that does not receive the treatment, **41**

controlled experiment   an experiment that uses both a control group and an experimental group to determine whether the independent variable influences behavior and, if so, how it does so, **41**

conventional moral reasoning   the level of moral development at which a person makes judgments based on conventional standards of right and wrong, **246**

convergent thinking   thinking that is limited to available facts, **187**

corpus callosum   the nerve fibers that connect the left and right hemispheres of the cerebral cortex, **61**

correlation   the relationship between variables, **39**

counterconditioning   a therapy procedure based on classical conditioning that replaces a negative response to a stimulus with a positive response, **135**

creativity   the ability to invent new solutions to problems or to create original or ingenious materials, **216**

critical period   a stage or point in development during which a person or animal is best suited to learn a particular skill or behavior, **229**

cross-linking   a possible cause of aging in which proteins within a cell bind together, toughening body tissues and eventually leading to the breakdown of various bodily processes, **286**

cross-sectional method   a method of research that looks at different age groups at the same time in order to understand changes that occur during the life span, **36**

crowd   large groups of people who share attitudes and a group identity, **258**

culture-bound syndrome   clusters of symptoms that define or describe an illness in a particular culture, **411**

decay   disintegration; in psychology, the fading away of memory, **169**

deductive reasoning   a form of thinking in which conclusions are inferred from premises; the conclusions are true if the premises are true, **189**

defense mechanisms   psychological distortions used to remain psychologically stable or in balance, **326**

GLOSSARY

defensive coping   a response to a stressor that temporarily reduces stress but may be harmful in the long run because it neither changes the situation nor removes the stressor, **403**

delusion   an erroneous belief, as of persecution or grandeur, that may accompany certain psychotic disorders, **120**

dementia   a serious loss of cognitive function, **286**

democratic leader   a leader who encourages group members to express and discuss their ideas and to make their own decisions, **484**

dendrites   the branchlike extensions of a neuron that receive impulses and conduct them toward the cell body, **55**

denial   a defense mechanism in which the individual refuses to admit that a problem exists, **327**

dependent variable   in an experiment, the factor that is being measured and that may change in response to manipulations of the independent variable, **41**

depersonalization   a dissociative disorder characterized by persistent or recurrent feelings that one is unreal or is detached from one's own experiences or body, **421**

depressant   a drug that reduces neural activity and slows body functions, **117**

depression   a psychological disorder characterized by extreme sadness, an inability to concentrate, and feelings of helplessness and dejection, **423**

detoxification   the removal of a poisonous or otherwise harmful substance, such as alcohol or other drugs, from the body, **121**

developmental psychology   the branch of psychology that studies the physical, cognitive, and social changes that occur throughout the life cycle, **228**

difference reduction   a problem-solving method that involves reducing the difference between the present situation and the desired one, **182**

difference threshold   the minimum difference that an individual can detect between two stimuli, **78**

diffusion of responsibility   the sharing of responsibility for a decision or behavior among the members of a group, **480**

discrimination   (1) in classical conditioning, the ability to distinguish the conditioned stimulus from other stimuli that are similar, **133**; (2) unfair treatment of a person or group based on prejudice, **465**

displacement   the defense mechanism that shifts negative impulses toward a more acceptable object or person, **326**

dissociation   a split in consciousness, **420**

distress   stress that is damaging or negative, **386**

divergent thinking   a thought process that attempts to generate multiple solutions to a problem, **187**

double-blind study   an experiment in which neither the participant nor the researcher knows whether the participant has received the treatment or the placebo, **43**

dream analysis   a technique used by psychoanalysts to interpret the content of patients' dreams, **441**

drive   a condition of arousal or tension within an organism that motivates the organism; usually associated with a need, **300**

echoic memory   the sensory register in which traces of sounds are held and may be retrieved within several seconds, **161**

ego   in psychoanalytic theory, the personality component that is conscious and that controls behavior, **325**

egocentrism   in Piaget's theory, the inability of the preoperational child to understand another's point of view, **243**

ego integrity   according to Erikson, a strong sense of identity during late adulthood that is characterized by the wisdom to accept the fact that life is limited, **288**

eidetic imagery   the maintenance of a very detailed visual memory over several months, **161**

elaborative rehearsal   a memory device that creates a meaningful link between new information and the information already known, **157**

electroconvulsive therapy   a radical treatment for psychological disorders that involves passing an electric current through the brain of an anesthetized patient, **452**

emotion   a state of feeling that involves physical arousal, expressive behaviors, and conscious experience, **311**

emotional appeal   a type of persuasive communication that influences behavior on the basis of feelings rather than on an analysis of the issues, **463**

empty-nest syndrome   a sense of depression and a loss of purpose that some parents experience when the youngest child leaves home, **282**

encoding   the translation of information into a form that can be stored in memory, **156**

encounter group   a structured group that aims to foster self-awareness by focusing on how group members relate to one another in a setting that encourages frank expression of feelings, **440**

endocrine system   the glands that secrete hormones into the bloodstream, **67**

episodic memory   a memory of a specific experienced event, **154**

ethics   rules and standards for proper and responsible behavior, **44**

GLOSSARY

eustress   stress that is positive or motivating, **386**

euthanasia   the act of killing or enabling the death of a hopelessly sick or injured individual in a relatively painless way; also called mercy killing, **292**

evaluation apprehension   concern that others are judging one's performance, **480**

experiment   a controlled scientific procedure to determine whether certain variables manipulated by the researcher have an effect on other variables, **40**

experimental group   in a study, the participants who receive the treatment, **41**

explicit norms   spoken or written rules of social behavior, such as traffic rules, **485**

extinction   in classical conditioning, the disappearance of a conditioned response when an unconditioned stimulus no longer follows a conditioned stimulus, **131**

extrinsic reward   something external given in response to the attainment of a goal, such as good grades, **309**

extrovert   a person who tends to be active and self-expressive and to gain energy from interaction with others, **323**

F

first-shift scheme   situation in which one person changes his or her mind to break a deadlock, **481**

flashbulb memory   a clear memory of an emotionally significant moment or event, **154**

flooding   based on the principles of classical conditioning, a fear-reduction technique that involves exposing the individual to a harmless stimulus until fear responses to that stimulus are extinguished, **133**

foot-in-the-door effect   the tendency for people to comply with a large request after they have agreed to smaller requests, **489**

forced-choice format   a method of presenting test questions that requires a respondent to select one of several possible answers, **349**

formal-operational stage   according to Piaget, the stage of cognitive development during which people begin to think logically about abstract concepts, **244**

framing effect   the influence of wording, or the way in which information is presented, on decision making, **194**

free association   in psychoanalysis, the uncensored uttering of all thoughts that come to mind, **441**

free radical   an unstable molecule present in the human body that is thought by some scientists to be a cause of aging, **285**

functional fixedness   a barrier to problem solving that involves the tendency to think of objects only in terms of their common uses, **187**

functionalism   the school of psychology, founded by William James, that emphasizes the purposes of behavior and mental processes, **13**

fundamental attribution error   a bias in social perception characterized by the tendency to assume that others generally act on the basis of their dispositions, even when there is evidence suggesting the importance of their situations, **470**

G

gate theory   the suggestion that only a certain amount of information can be processed by the nervous system at a given time, **91**

gender   classifications of sex, based on mostly nonbiological traits such as physical structure and appearance, **364**

gender roles   the differing sets of behaviors that a culture considers appropriate for males or females, **364**

gender schema   the set of traits and behaviors by which a child learns to classify male and female gender roles and by which the child models and measures his or her own relation to those roles, **376**

gender stereotypes   oversimplified generalizations about the characteristics of males and females, **365**

gender typing   the process by which people learn to conform to gender roles, **372**

gene   the basic building block of heredity, **70**

general adaptation syndrome (GAS)   the three-stage sequence of behavior in response to stress, consisting of an alarm reaction, a resistance stage, and an exhaustion stage, **395**

generalization   the tendency to respond in the same way to stimuli that have similar characteristics, **132**

generativity   according to Erikson, the ability to create, originate, and produce throughout adulthood, **280**

generic memory   general knowledge and information that can be recalled, **154**

Gestalt psychology   the school of psychology that emphasizes the tendency to organize perceptions into meaningful wholes, **16**

gifted   a term used to describe children with IQ scores above 130 or children with outstanding talent for performing at much higher levels than others of the same age and background, **216**

H

hallucination   a false sensory perception that occurs in the absence of any actual stimulus, **120**

hallucinogen   a psychedelic drug, such as LSD, that distorts perceptions and evokes sensory images in the absence of actual sensory input, **120**

heredity   the genetic transmission of traits from one generation to the next, **69**

heritability the proportion of variation among individuals that can be attributed to genes, **219**

heuristic a strategy for making judgments and solving problems, **181**

homeostasis an internal balance or equilibrium that is achieved through adjustments of the nervous system, **301**

hormone one of several chemicals produced by the endocrine glands that regulates specific body functions, **67**

hospice a type of care for terminally ill patients; an organization that provides such care, **292**

humanistic perspective the psychological view that assumes the existence of the self and emphasizes the importance of self-awareness and the freedom to make choices, **19**

humanistic therapy a treatment method based on the assumption that most people are basically good and have a natural tendency to strive for self-actualization, **444**

hypnosis a condition in which people appear to be highly suggestible and to behave as if they are in a trance, **113**

hypothalamus the neural structure located below the thalamus that controls temperature, hunger, thirst, and various aspects of emotion, **61**

hypothesis a prediction or assumption about behavior that is tested through scientific research, **26**

i

iconic memory the sensory register that briefly holds mental images of visual stimuli, **161**

id in psychoanalytic theory, the reservoir of unconscious psychic energy that strives to satisfy basic sexual and aggressive drives, **325**

identification in psychoanalytic theory, the process by which children adopt the values of their parents, **327**

identity achievement a stage in identity development in which a person has committed to an occupational direction and made decisions about important life questions, **262**

identity crisis a period of inner conflict during which one examines one's values and makes decisions about one's life direction, **260**

identity diffusion the constant search for meaning and identity without committing oneself to a set of personal beliefs or an occupational path, **262**

identity foreclosure the act of making a commitment based on other's values in order to avoid an identity crisis, **262**

identity moratorium a period of time in the development of identity in which a person delays making a decision about important issues but actively explores various alternatives, **262**

identity status according to Marcia, one of four reaction patterns or processes in the development of identity during adolescence, **262**

imbalance a state in which people who have strong feelings about each other disagree on a major issue, **310**

implicit norms unspoken, unwritten standards of behavior for a group of people, **485**

imprinting the process by which animals form strong attachments during a critical period very early in life, **235**

incubation effect the tendency to arrive at a solution after a period of time away from the problem, **185**

independent variable the factor that is manipulated by the researcher to determine its effect on another variable, **41**

inductive reasoning a form of thinking that involves using individual cases or particular facts to reach a general conclusion, **190**

infancy in humans, the stage of life from birth to age two, **231**

infantile amnesia the inability to remember events that occurred during one's early years (before age three), **169**

inferiority complex according to Adler, feelings of inadequacy and insecurity that serve as a central source of motivation, **330**

informed consent an agreement by an individual to participate in research after receiving information about the purpose of the study and the nature of the treatment, **46**

insight a sudden flash of understanding about the solution to a problem, **185**

insomnia a sleep disorder characterized by recurring problems in falling asleep or staying asleep, **110**

instinct a complex, unlearned behavior that is present throughout a species, **300**

intelligence the capacity to learn from experience, solve problems, and adapt to a changing environment, **206**

intelligence quotient the ratio of mental age to chronological age multiplied by 100; the average performance for a given age is assigned a score of 100, **212**

interference the process that occurs when new information appears in short-term memory and replaces what was already there, **163**

intimacy feelings of closeness and concern for another person, **475**

intoxication a state of drunkenness characterized by impaired coordination and judgment, **117**

intrinsic reward an internal reward, such as self-satisfaction, that is given in response to the attainment of a goal, **309**

GLOSSARY

introspection   an examination of one's own thoughts and feelings, **12**

introvert   a person who tends to be more interested in his or her own thoughts and feelings than in what is going on around him or her, **323**

J

juvenile delinquency   a violation of the law committed by a child or adolescent, **268**

K

kinesthesis   the sense that provides information about the position and movement of individual body parts, **92**

L

laboratory observation   the study of behavior in a controlled situation, **37**

laissez-faire leader   a leader who stands back from decision making and allows group members to explore and express their own ideas, **484**

language   the communication of ideas through sounds and symbols that are arranged according to the rules of grammar, **195**

language acquisition device   according to Chomsky, the inborn ability of humans to acquire language, **199**

latent content   according to Freud, the hidden meaning of a dream, **441**

latent learning   learning that occurs but remains hidden until there is a need to use it, **145**

lateralization   the development, prior to birth, of the tendencies of the brain's left and right hemispheres to specialize in certain functions, **372**

learning goal   achievement that is motivated by the desire to enhance one's knowledge and skills, **309**

learning perspective   the psychological point of view that emphasizes the effects of experience on behavior, **20**

lens   the transparent structure of the eye that focuses light on the retina, **81**

limbic system   a group of neural structures at the base of the cerebral hemispheres that is associated with emotion and motivation, **61**

lithium   a chemical used to treat the mood swings of bipolar disorder, **452**

living will   a legal document in which the signer requests to be allowed to die rather than be kept alive by artificial means if disabled beyond a reasonable expectation of recovery, **293**

longitudinal method   a type of research in which the same people are studied over a long time period, **36**

long-term memory   the type or stage of memory capable of large and relatively permanent storage, **163**

M

maintenance rehearsal   the repetition of new information in an attempt to keep from forgetting it, **157**

majority-wins scheme   in group decision making, an agreement initially supported by a majority of the group members and then agreed to by all, **481**

mania   a mood characterized by extreme elation and hyperactivity, **424**

manifest content   according to Freud, the apparent and remembered content of a dream, **441**

matching hypothesis   the view that people tend to choose other people similar to themselves in attractiveness and attitudes in the formation of interpersonal relationships, **473**

maturation   developmental changes that occur as a result of automatic, genetically determined signals, **229**

means-end analysis   a heuristic device in which a solution to a problem is found by evaluating the difference between the current situation and the goal, **183**

meditation   a systematic narrowing of attention that slows the metabolism and helps produce feelings of relaxation, **112**

medulla   a structure at the base of the brain stem that controls vital functions such as heartbeat and breathing, **59**

memory   the processes by which information is encoded, stored, and retrieved, **154**

menarche   a female's first menstrual period, **254**

menopause   the cessation of menstruation; also, the biological changes that a woman experiences during the years of her declining ability to reproduce, **283**

mental age   the level of intellectual functioning, which is compared to chronological age to give an IQ, **211**

mental retardation   intellectual functioning that is below average, as indicated by an intelligence score at or below 70, **215**

mental set   the tendency to approach a new problem in a way that has been successful in the past, **186**

midlife crisis   a turning point experienced by many people between ages 45 to 65, when they realize that life may be half over and they feel trapped in meaningless life roles, **281**

midlife transition   a period in middle adulthood when a person's perspective on his or her life may change significantly, **280**

modeling   the process of learning behavior through the observation and imitation of others, **374**

monocular cue   a cue for distance that may be available to either eye alone, **95**

morpheme   the smallest meaningful unit of language, such as a prefix or suffix, **195**

motive   a need or desire that energizes and directs behavior, **300**

multiple approach-avoidance conflict   a conflict involving a choice between two or more options, each of which has both positive and negative aspects, **390**

myelin   a white, fatty substance that insulates axons and enables rapid transmission of neural impulses, **55**

narcolepsy   an uncommon sleep disorder characterized by brief attacks of REM sleep, often at inopportune moments, **112**

narcotic   a type of drug that dulls the senses, relieves pain, and induces sleep; the term is usually reserved for those drugs derived from the opium poppy plant, **117**

naturalistic observation   the study of behavior in naturally occurring situations without manipulation or control on the part of the observer, **36**

need   the biological or psychological requirements for the well-being of an organism, **300**

negative correlation   an unpleasant stimulus between two variables in which one variable increases as the other variable decreases, **39**

negative reinforcer   an unpleasant stimulus that increases the frequency of behavior when it is removed, **137**

neuron   a nerve cell; the basic building block of the nervous system, **54**

neurotransmitter   a chemical messenger that carries impulses across the synaptic gaps between neurons, **56**

night terror   a sleep disorder characterized by high arousal and apparent terror; unlike nightmares, night terrors are seldom remembered, **111**

nonbalance   in balance theory, a condition in which people who dislike each other or have no feeling for each other feel indifferent if they disagree, **310**

nonconscious   descriptive of bodily processes, such as the growing of hair, of which we are not aware, **105**

nondirective therapy   a type of therapy in which the client rather than the therapist is encouraged to take the lead, **444**

norm   an established standard of performance or behavior, **347**

norm group   a group of test takers whose scores establish the norm for a particular test, **347**

nurturance   loving care and attention, **368**

obesity   a condition characterized by excessive body fat, **304**

objective test   a test that has a group of standardized test items and specific answers that are considered to be correct, **350**

object permanence   the awareness that people and objects continue to exist even when they cannot be perceived, **242**

observational learning   learning by observing and imitating the behavior of others, **146**

obsession   a recurring thought or image that seems to be beyond control, **416**

olfactory nerve   the nerve that transmits information about odors from olfactory receptors to the brain, **89**

operant conditioning   learning that is strengthened when behavior is followed by positive reinforcement, **135**

opponent-process theory   according to Solomon, the idea that an intense emotion often is followed by its opposite, **314**

overextension   in the acquisition of language, the tendency for children to extend the meaning of words to objects for which they do not have words, **198**

overregularization   the formation of plurals and the past tense of irregular nouns and verbs according to rules of grammar that apply to regular nouns and verbs; characteristic of the speech of young children, **199**

panic attack   an episode of intense dread in which a person experiences terror and other frightening sensations, such as chest pain, rapid heartbeat, or choking, **416**

partial reinforcement   a type of conditioned learning in which only some of the responses are reinforced, **140**

passion   an aroused state of intense desire for another person, **475**

patriarchy   a social organization marked by the supremacy of males in the clan or family, **276**

perception   the process of organizing and interpreting sensory information, **78**

performance goal   an achievement motivated by a concrete, external reward, **308**

peripheral nervous system   the neurons that connect the central nervous system to the rest of the body, including the muscles and glands, **54**

peripheral route   a method of persuasion characterized by an emphasis on factors other than the message itself, **463**

personality   the pattern of feelings, thoughts, and behavior that sets people apart from one another, **321**

person-centered therapy   a humanistic therapy, developed by Carl Rogers, in which the therapist creates an accepting, empathic environment to facilitate the client's growth, **444**

persuasion   the attempt to influence people's attitudes and choices through argument, entreaty, or explanation, **462**

GLOSSARY

phobia   an excessive, irrational fear out of proportion to the actual danger, **415**

phoneme   the basic sound unit in a spoken language, **195**

photoreceptor   a neuron that responds to light, **83**

placebo   an inert substance used in controlled experiments to test the effectiveness of another substance, **42**

polarization   the strengthening of a group's shared attitudes over time, **482**

pons   a brain structure located at the top of the brain stem that is involved in respiration, movement, and sleep, **59**

positive correlation   a relationship between variables in which one variable increases as the other variable also increases, **39**

positive reinforcer   an encouraging stimulus that increases the frequency of a behavior when it is presented, **137**

postconventional moral reasoning   according to Kohlberg, a level of moral development during which moral judgments are derived from a person's own moral standards, **246**

posthypnotic suggestion   instructions given toa person under hypnosis that are supposed to be carried out after the hypnosis session has ended, **116**

post-traumatic stress disorder   a disorder that follows a distressing event outside the range of normal human experience and is characterized by intense fear, avoidance of stimuli associated with the event, and reliving of the event, **417**

preconscious   descriptive of information that is not conscious but is retrievable into conscious awareness, **105**

preconventional moral reasoning   according to Kohlberg, a level of moral development in which moral judgments are based on fear of punishment or desire for pleasure, **246**

prefrontal lobotomy   a radical form of psychosurgery in which a section of the frontal lobe of the brain is severed or destroyed, **453**

prejudice   an unjustifiable, and usually negative, attitude toward a person or group, **465**

premise   a statement or assertion that serves as the basis for an argument, **189**

preoperational stage   in Piaget's theory, the stage during which a child learns to use language but does not yet think logically, **242**

primacy effect   (1) the tendency to recall the initial item or items in a series, **162**; (2) the tendency to form opinions of others based on first impressions, **468**

primary reinforcer   a stimulus, such as food or warmth, that has reinforcement value without learning, **137**

primary sex characteristic   the organs that make sexual reproduction possible, such as the ovaries and testes, **253**

procedural memory   memory that consists of the skills and procedures one has learned, **155**

programmed theories   the view that aging is the result of genetics, **285**

projection   in psychoanalytic theory, the defense mechanism by which people attribute their own unacceptable impulses to others, **327**

projective test   a psychological test that presents ambiguous stimuli designed to elicit a response that reflects the test taker's feelings, interests, and biases, **352**

prototype   an original model on which others in the same category are patterned, **179**

proximity   the perceptual tendency to group together visual and auditory events that are near each other, **93**

psychoanalysis   the school of psychology, founded by Sigmund Freud, that emphasizes the importance of unconscious motives and conflicts as determinants of human behavior, **17**

psychoanalytic perspective   the perspective that stresses the influences of unconscious forces on human behavior, **19**

psychological disorder   a pattern of behavior or a mental process that causes serious personal suffering or interferes with a person's ability to cope with everyday life, **410**

psychology   the scientific study of behavior and mental processes, **4**

psychosurgery   biological treatments in which specific areas or structures of the brain are removed or destroyed to change behavior, **453**

psychotherapy   the application of psychological principles and techniques to influence a person's thoughts, feelings, or behaviors in an attempt to help that person overcome psychological disorders or adjust to problems in living, **436**

puberty   the period of sexual maturation; the onset of one's ability to reproduce, **253**

pupil   the opening in the center of the eye that adjusts to allow light to enter, **81**

random sample   a survey population, selected by chance, which fairly represents the general population, **31**

rapid-eye-movement sleep   a stage of sleep characterized by rapid eye movements and linked to dreaming; also called REM sleep, **108**

rational-emotive therapy   a confrontational cognitive therapy, developed by Albert Ellis, that encourages people to challenge illogical, self-defeating thoughts and attitudes, **447**

rationalization   in psychoanalytic theory, the defense mechanism by which an individual finds justifications for unacceptable thoughts, impulses, or behaviors, **326**

reaction formation   in psychoanalytic theory, a defense mechanism by which the ego unconsciously switches unacceptable impulses into their opposites, **327**

reasoning   the process of drawing logical conclusions from facts and arguments, **189**

recall   retrieval of learned information, **168**

recency effect   (1) the tendency to recall the last item in a series, **162**; (2) the tendency for people to change their opinions of others based on recent interactions, **468**

reciprocity   in interpersonal relationships, the tendency to return feelings and attitudes that are expressed about us, **474**

recognition   a memory process in which one identifies objects or events that have previously been encountered, **167**

reflex   an automatic, unlearned response to a sensory stimulus, **230**

regression   in psychoanalytic theory, a defense mechanism by which an individual retreats to an earlier stage of development when faced with anxiety, **327**

reinforcement   a stimulus or event that follows a response and increases the frequency of that response, **136**

relearning   learning material a second time, usually in less time than it was originally learned, **169**

reliability   the extent to which a test yields consistent results, **214**

replicate   to repeat a research study, usually with different participants and in different situations, to confirm the results of the original study, **28**

representativeness   the process of making decisions about a sample according to the population that the sample appears to represent, **192**

repression   in psychoanalytic theory, the defense mechanism that removes anxiety-arousing thoughts, feelings, and memories from one's consciousness, **326**

resistance   in psychoanalysis, a blocking from consciousness of issues that might cause anxiety, **441**

response   an observable reaction to a stimulus, **128**

reticular activating system   the part of the brain that is involved in attention, sleep, and arousal, **60**

retina   the light-sensitive inner surface of the eye that contains the rods, cones, and neurons that process visual stimuli, **81**

retinal disparity   a binocular cue for perceiving depth based on the difference between the two images of an object that the retina receives as the object moves closer or farther away, **96**

retrieval   the process of recalling information from memory storage, **158**

retrograde amnesia   the failure to remember events that occurred prior to physical trauma because of the effects of the trauma, **170**

risky shift   the tendency to make riskier decisions as a member of a group than as an individual acting alone, **481**

sales resistance   the ability to refuse a request or sales pitch, **464**

sample   a representative segment of a target population, **31**

scapegoat   a person or group unfairly blamed for the problems of others; to blame a person or group unfairly, **466**

schedule of reinforcement   a timetable for when and how often reinforcement for a particular behavior occurs, **139**

schema   an idea or mental framework that helps one organize and interpret information, **164**

schizophrenia   a group of severe psychotic disorders characterized by distortions in thinking, perception, emotion, and behavior, **426**

secondary reinforcer   a stimulus that increases the probability of a response because of its association with a primary reinforcer, **137**

secondary sex characteristic   sexual characteristics that are not involved in reproduction, such as the growth of facial hair in males and the rounding of hips and breasts in females, **253**

self-actualization   according to Maslow, the self-motivated striving to reach one's potential, **302**

self-concept   one's view of oneself as an individual, **335**

self-efficacy expectation   a person's beliefs that he or she can bring about desired changes or goals through his or her own efforts, **393**

self-esteem   the value or worth that people attach to themselves, **240**

self-help group   a type of therapy group in which members share a common problem, such as alcoholism, **440**

self-report   an interview or questionnaire in which a person reports his or her attitudes, feelings, and behaviors, **344**

self-serving bias   the tendency to view one's successes as stemming from internal factors and one's failures as stemming from external factors, **470**

semantics   the study of meaning in language; the relationship between language and the objects depicted by the language, **196**

senile dementia a decrease in mental ability that sometimes occurs after the age of 65, **286**

sensation the stimulation of sensory receptors and the transmission of sensory information to the brain, **78**

sensorimotor stage according to Piaget, the stage during which infants know the world mostly in terms of their sensory impressions and motor activities, **242**

sensorineural deafness deafness that results from damage to the auditory nerve, **87**

sensory adaptation the process by which an organism becomes more sensitive to stimuli that are low in magnitude and less sensitive to stimuli that are constant, **80**

sensory deprivation a state in which there is little or no sensory stimulation, **307**

sensory memory the immediate, initial recording of sensory information in the memory system, **160**

separation anxiety distress that is sometimes experienced by infants when they are separated from their primary caregivers, **234**

shaping in operant conditioning, a procedure in which reinforcement guides behavior toward closer approximations of the desired goal, **142**

short-term memory memory that holds information briefly before it is stored or forgotten, **161**

signal-detection theory the idea that distinguishing sensory stimuli takes into account not only the strength of the stimuli but also such elements as setting and one's physical state, mood, and attitudes, **79**

similarity the perceptual tendency to group together elements that seem alike, **94**

simple phobia an anxiety disorder characterized by a persistent, irrational fear of a specific object or situation, **415**

single-blind study a study in which the participants are unaware of whether they are in the control group or the experimental group, **43**

sleep apnea a sleep disorder in which breathing is interrupted, **111**

social decision scheme rules for predicting the final outcome of group decision making, **481**

social facilitation improved performance of tasks because of the presence of others, **480**

socialization the guidance of people, especially children, into socially desirable behavior by means of verbal messages, the systematic use of rewards and punishments, and other teaching methods, **333**

social-learning theory the theory that suggests that people have the ability to change their environments or to create new ones, **20**

social loafing the tendency for people to exert less effort toward completing a task when they are part of a group than when they are performing the task alone, **480**

social norm explicit and implicit rules that reflect social expectations and influence the ways in which people behave in social situations, **485**

social perception the ways in which people form and modify their impressions of others, **468**

social phobia an irrational fear of social situations in which one might be exposed to the close scrutiny of others, **416**

sociobiology the subfield of biology that studies the genetic basis of social organization and behavior in humans and other animals, **490**

sociocultural perspective in psychology, the perspective that focuses on the roles of ethnicity, gender, culture, and socioeconomic status in personality formation, behavior, and mental processes, **21**

somatic nervous system the division of the peripheral nervous system that connects the central nervous system with sensory receptors, muscles, and the skin, **57**

somatization the expression of psychological distress through physical symptoms, **421**

source trait according to Cattell, an underlying trait from which surface traits are derived, **323**

spinal cord a column of nerves within the spine that transmit messages to and from the brain, **57**

spontaneous recovery the reappearance of an extinguished conditioned response after some time has passed, **132**

standardized tests tests for which norms are based on the performance of a range of individuals, **344**

state-dependent memory memory in which information is more easily retrieved when one is in the same physiological or emotional state as when the memory was originally encoded or learned, **160**

status offense an action that is illegal when committed by a minor, such as consuming alcohol, **269**

stimulant a drug that increases neural activity and speeds up body functions, **118**

stimulus a feature in the environment that is detected by an organism or that leads to a change in behavior, **128**

stimulus motive a desire for increased stimulation, **306**

storage the maintenance of encoded information over time, **157**

stranger anxiety the fear of strangers that infants commonly display, **234**

stratified sample a sample drawn in such a way that known subgroups within a population are represented in proportion to their numbers in the general population, **31**

stress the physical and mental strain a person experiences in association with demands to adapt to a challenging situation, **386**

GLOSSARY

stressor an event or circumstance that produces stress, 386

stroboscopic motion a visual illusion in which the perception of motion is generated by the presentation of a series of stationary images in rapid succession, 45

structuralism the school of psychology, founded by Wilhelm Wundt, that maintains that conscious experience breaks down into objective sensations and subjective feelings, 13

sublimation in psychoanalytic theory, the defense mechanism by which people channel their socially unacceptable impulses into more acceptable activities, 327

successive approximations in operant conditioning, a series of behaviors that gradually become more similar to a desired behavior, 450

superego according to Freud, the part of personality that represents the individual's internalized ideals and provides standards for judgment, 326

surface trait according to Cattell, a characteristic and observable way of behaving, 323

survey a research technique for acquiring data about the attitudes or behaviors of a group of people, usually by asking questions of a representative, random sample, 29

symbol an object or an act that stands for something else, 178

synapse the junction between the axon terminals of the sending neuron and the dendrites of the receiving neuron, 55

syntax the ways in which words and phrases are arranged into grammatical sentences, 195

systematic desensitization a type of counterconditioning, used to treat phobias, in which a pleasant, relaxed state is associated with gradually increasing anxiety-triggering stimuli, 135

𝒯

target population the total group to be studied or described and from whom samples may be drawn, 31

taste aversion a type of classical conditioning in which a previously desirable or neutral food comes to be perceived as repugnant because it is associated with negative stimulation, 130

test-retest reliability a method for determining the reliability of a test by comparing a test taker's scores on the same test taken on separate occasions, 214

thalamus the structure of the brain that relays messages from the sense organs to the cerebral cortex, 61

theory a set of assumptions about why something is the way it is and happens the way it does, 6

thinking mental activity that involves understanding, manipulating, and communicating information, 178

tip-of-the-tongue phenomenon the belief that a piece of information is stored in our memory although we cannot retrieve it easily, 160

token economy a controlled environment in which people's desired behaviors are reinforced with tokens that may be exchanged for privileges or other rewards, 450

trait an aspect of personality that is considered to be reasonably consistent, 322

transference in psychoanalysis, the patient's transfer of emotions associated with other relationships to the therapist, 442

triangular model of love according to Sternberg, the components of love, which include passion, intimacy, and commitment, 474

truth-wins scheme in group decision making, an agreement reached when members realize that one option is clearly better than the others, 481

two-sided argument a method of discrediting an opponent by presenting his or her argument and then refuting it, 463

two-thirds–majority scheme in group decision making, an agreement that is supported by two thirds of the members, 481

𝒰

unconditional positive regard a consistent expression of esteem for the basic value of a person, 240

unconditioned response in classical conditioning, an unlearned response, 130

unconditioned stimulus in classical conditioning, a stimulus that elicits an unlearned, naturally occurring response, 130

unconscious according to Freud, a reservoir of mostly unacceptable thoughts, wishes, feelings, and memories of which we are unaware but which influences our behavior, 105

𝒱

validity the extent to which a test measures what it is suppose to measure, 214

validity scale a group of test items that suggest whether or not the test taker is answering honestly, 345

variable a factor that is measured or controlled in a scientific study, 41

vestibular sense the sense that provides information about the position of the body, 92

visual acuity keenness or sharpness of vision, 83

vocational interest inventories tests that are used to help people make decisions about career options, 348

volunteer bias the concept that people who volunteer to participate in research studies often differ from those who do not volunteer, 33

INDEX

INDEX

INDEX

INDEX

INDEX

INDEX

INDEX

INDEX

ACKNOWLEDGEMENTS

For permission to reprint copyrighted material, grateful acknowledgment is made to the following sources:

American Psychological Association: "Ethical Principles of Psychologists and Code of Conduct" from *American Psychologist, vol. 47; pp. 1597–1611.* Copyright © 1982 by the American Psychological Association.

Thomas J. Bouchard, Jr. and American Association for the Advancement of Science: From "Sources of Human Psychological Differences: The Minnesota Study of Twins Reared Apart" by Thomas J. Bouchard, Jr., David T. Lykken, Matthew McGue, Nancy L. Segal, and Auke Tellegen from *Science, vol. 250, October 1990.* Copyright © 1990 by American Association for the Advancement of Science.

Cambridge University Press: From "Love Stories" by Robert J. Sternberg from *Personal Relationships, vol. 3, 1996.* Copyright © 1996 by Cambridge University Press.

Elsevier Science, Inc.: Adapted from "The Social Readjustment Rating Scale" by Thomas H. Holmes and Richard H. Rahe from *Journal of Psychosomatic Research, vol. 11, 1967, pp. 213-218.* Copyright © 1967 by T. H. Holmes and R. H. Rahe.

Laurence Erlbaum Associates: From "Beyond Insight: An additional necessary step in redressing intraspychic conflict" by Lloyd H. Silverman from *Psychoanalytical Psychology, vol. 1(3), Summer 1994.* Copyright ©1994 by Psychoanalytic Psychology.

HarperCollins Publishers, Inc.: From *Ordinary Men: Reserve Police Battalion 101 and the Final Solution in Poland* by Christopher R. Browning. Copyright © 1992 by Christopher R. Browning.

Alfred A. Knopf, Inc.: From *Beyond Freedom and Dignity* by B. F. Skinner. Copyright © 1971 by B. F. Skinner.

The Psychological Corporation, a subsidiary of Harcourt Brace & Company: Simulated items from the *Wechsler Adult Intelligence Scale-Revised.* Copyright © 1981, 1955 by The Psychological Corporation.

B. F. Skinner Foundation: From *Walden Two* by B. F. Skinner. Copyright © 1948, 1976 by B. F. Skinner.

University of Nebraska Press: From "The Actualizing Tendency in Relation to 'Motives' and to Consciousness" by Carl R. Rogers. Copyright © 1963 by the University of Nebraska Press.

ILLUSTRATIONS

All art, unless otherwise noted, by Holt, Rinehart and Winston.

Abbreviated as follows:
(t) top; (b) bottom; (l) left; (r) right; (c) center.

Unit 1: Chapter 1: Page 8 (b), Doug Walston; 17 (t), Doug Walston; **Chapter 2:** Page 31 (b), Doug Walston; **Unit 2: Chapter 3:** Page 57 (r), Jean E. Calder; 68 (l), Jean E.Calder; **Chapter 4:** Page 86 (b), Digital Art; 89 (b), Jean E. Calder; 93 (b), Doug Walston; **Chapter 5:** Page 106 (t), Stephen Durke / Washington-Artists' Represents, Inc.; 113 (t), Stephen Durke / Washington-Artists' Represents, Inc.; **Unit 3: Chapter 6:** Page 129 (t), Blake Thornton / Rita Marie and Friends; 130 (b), Blake Thornton / Rita Marie and Friends; **Chapter 8:** Page 180, Blake Thornton / Rita Marie and Friends; 184 (l), Stephen Durke / Washington-Artists' Represents, Inc.; 187 (r), Blake Thornton / Rita Marie and Friends; **Unit 4: Chapter 10:** Page 231 (r), Blake Thornton / Rita Marie and Friends; 237 (t), Digital Art; **Unit 5: Chapter 14:** Page 338 (t), Blake Thornton / Rita Marie and Friends; **Chapter 18:** Page 396 (t), Blake Thornton / Rita Marie and Friends.

PHOTOGRAPHY

All photos, unless otherwise noted, by Holt, Rinehart and Winston.

Abbreviated as follows: (t) top; (b) bottom; (l) left; (r) right; (c) center, (bckgd) background, (bdr) border.

Front Cover: Private collection/Diana Ong/Super Stock

Back Cover, Title Page, Copyright Page (detail of front-cover image)

Table Of Contents: Page iv(cl), Archive Photos; iv(bl), Jeff Greenberg/Photo Edit; v(cl), Diane Schuimo/Fundamental Photographs; v(bl), Mehmet Biber/Photo Researchers, Inc.; vi(tl), Mitch Kezar/Tony Stone Images; vi(cl), Ian Shaw/Tony Stone Images; vi(bl), H.S. Terrace/Animals Animals/ Eartyh Scenes; vii(tl), L. Kesterson/Sygma; vii(cl), Super Stock; vii(bl), Richard Hutching/ Photo Edit; viii(tl), Zigy Kalunzy/Tony Stone Images; viii(c), John Henley/The Stock Market; viii(bl), Super Stock; ix(tl), Giraudon/Art Resource; ix(cl), Bob Daemmrich/Bob Daemmrich Photography; ix(bl), Elizabeth Zuckerman/Photo Edit.; x(tl), Michael Newman/Photo Edit, x(cl), Derek Bayes/Tony Stone; x(bl), Bruce Ayres/Tony Stone; xi(tl), Michael Newman/Photo Edit; xi(c), Archive Photo; xi(bl), Frank Siteman/Tone Stone;

Skills Handbook: Page xvii(b), Warren Anatomical Museum, Harvard Medical School;

Unit One: Page 1(br), Jim Pickerell/Tony Stone Images; **Chapter One:** Page 5(t), Bob Daemmrich/Bob Daemmrich Photography; 6(b), Yoav Levy/PhotoTake; 9(t), Paul Meredeth/Tony Stone Images; 11(t), Bob Daemmrich/Bob Daemmrich Photography; 12(b), Archive Photos; 13(t), Corbis-The Bettmann Archive; 13(b), Corbis- The Bettmann Archive; 14(c), Archive Photos; 15(c), AP/Wide World Photos; 16(t), Corbis-The Bettmann Archive; 16(b), L.L.T. Rhodes/Animals Animals/Earth Scenes; 17(b), NY Public Library Prints Division; 19(t), Yoav Levy/PhotoTake; 21(t), Bob Daemmrich/Bob Daemmrich Photography; **Chapter Two:** Page 28(t), SuperStock; 30(b), Jeff Greeenberg/Photo Edit; 32(c), Mark Scott/FPG International; 35(t), Jim Pickerell/Tony Stone Images; 37(t), David Macdonald/Animals Animals/Earth Scenes; 39(bckgd),Russell Dian/ HRW; 42(b), Michael Newman/PhotoEdit; 47(t), Michael Schwarz/The Image Works;

Unit Two: Page 51(bl), Chris Cheadle/Tony Stone Images; Chapter Three: Page 56(t), Brad Mangin/Duomo; 56(b), SuperStock; 58(t), Richard Hutchings/PhotoEdit; 64(tl), Roon Chapple/FPG International; 64(tr), SuperStock; 65(c), Warren Anatomical Museum, Harvard Medical School; 66(bl), Jim Pickerell/Tony Stone Images; 66(br), Charles Thatcher/Tony Stone Images; 67(t), Jan Halaska/Tony Stone Images; 69(t), Charles Thatcher/Tony Stone Images; 70(b), Mugshots/The Stock Market; 72(t), Cosmo Condina/Tony Stone Images; Chapter Four: Page 80(t), Peter A. Simon/PhotoTake; 82(c), ©1995 Louis Psihoyos/Matrix International; 85(t), Diane Schuimo/ Fundamental Photographs; 87(b), Kurt Viavant/Sipa Press; 88(t), Bob Daemmrich/Bob Daemmrich Photography; 92(t), William R. Sallaz/Duomo; 95(t), Kim Taylor/Bruce Coleman, Inc.; Chapter Five: Page 105(t), Bob Daemmrich/The Image Works; 107(t), Richard Haynes/ HRW109(t), © 1996 Michael Parkes/Steltman Galleries New York. Desert Dream oil painting on wood, 110 x 90cm.; 111(t), Jane Meddaugh/David Frazier Photolibrary; 112(b), Bill Wassman/The Stock Market; 115(t), The Bettmann Archive; 117(t), Culver Pictures, Inc.; 119(c), Mehmet Biber/Photo Researchers, Inc.; 120(t), Bob Daemmrich/Bob Daemmrich Photography; 121(t), M. Siluk/The Image Works;

Unit Three: Page 125(br), Robert A. Propper/Leo de Wys, Inc.; Chapter Six: Page 128(b), ©1992 Molkenthin/The Stock Marke; 131(b), Ed Degginger/Animals Animals/Earth Scenes; 133(t), James Hackett/Leo de Wys, Inc.; 134(c), Tom McCarthy/The Stock Market; 139(b), Michael Newman/PhotoEdit/; 141(t), SuperStock; 144(t), Mitch Kezar/Tony Stone Images, Inc.; 145(b), Will & Deni McIntyre/Photo Researchers, Inc.; 146(b), Dion Ogust/The Image Works; 149(t), Jose L. Pelaez/The Stock Market; 149(t), Jose L. Pelaez/The Stock Market; Chapter Seven: Page 155(t), NASA/The Image Works; 156(t), Ian Shaw/Tony Stone Images; 158(t), H. Kaiser/Leo de Wys, Inc.; 161(b), Micahel Krasowitz/FPG International; 165(c), John Neubauer/PhotoEdit; Chapter Eight: Page 178(t), Copyright © 1996 by the American Psychological Association. Reprinted with permission.; 179(t), Charles Gupton/Tony Stone Images; 182(b), Amy Etra/PhotoEdit; 183(t), Bob Daemmrich/The Image Works; 185(tl), SuperStock; 185(tc), SuperStock; 185(tr), SuperStock; 188(b), Bruce Ayres/Tony Stone Images; 192(b), SuperStock; 193(t), Richard Kaylin/Tony Stone Images; 194(b), Jon Riley/Tony Stone Images; 196(b), Joe Carini/The Image Works; 197(b), Universal Press; 198(b), Chip Henderson/Tony Stone Images; 199(b), Craig Newbauer/Peter Arnold; 200(c), H.S. Terrace/Animals Animals/ Earth Scenes; 207(t), Bob Daemmrich/Bob Daemmrich Photography; 207(b), AP/Wide World Photos; 209(c), L. Kesterson/Sygma; 210(t), David Frazier/David R. Frazier Photolibrary; 212(t), Laura Dwight/PhotoEdit; 216(t), Bob Daemmrich/Bob Daemmrich Photography; 216(b), Dick Luria/FPG International; 217(c), Corbis-The Bettmann Archive; 218(t), Scala/Art Resource, NY; 219(b), David Young Wolff/Tony Stone Images; 220(b), N. Rowan/The Image Works; 221(b), Bob Daemmrich/Bob Daemmrich Photography;

Unit Four: Page 225(b), Dan Bosler/Tony Stone Images; Chapter Ten: Page 228(b), SuperStock; 230(b), Laura Dwight/Peter Arnold, Inc.; 232(t), Super Stock; 233(t), Mark Richards/PhotoEdit; 234(b), Tim Brown/Tony Stone Images; 235(t), Martin Rogers/Tony Stone Images; 235(b), Nina Leen, Life Magazine © Time, Inc.; 238(c), Chuck Savage/The Stock Market; 240(t), Ariel Skelley/The Stock Market; 241(c), Archive PhotosLine: Archive Photos/A.F.P.; 242(t), Michael Newman/PhotoEdit; Chapter Eleven: Page 254(t), Richard Hutchings/PhotoEdit; 255(c), Mark Richards/PhotoEdit; 258(t), David Frazier Photolibrary; 259(t), Bob Daemmrich/Bob Daemmrich Photography; 260(b), Bob Daemmrich/Tony Stone Images; 264(t), Robert Sorbo/AP/Wide World Photos; 266(t), Bob Daemmrich/Bob Daemmrich Photography; 267(t), Tom McCarthy/PhotoEdit; 268(t), Rhoda Sidney/PhotoEdit; 255(c), Mark Richards/PhotoEdit; 258(t), David Frazier/ David Frazier Photolibrary; 259(t), Bob Daemmrich/Bob Daemmrich Photography; 260(b), Bob Daemmrich/Tony Stone Images; 264(t), Robert Sorbo/AP/Wide World Photos; 266(t), Bob Daemmrich/Bob Daemmrich Photography; 267(t), Tom McCarthy/PhotoEdit; 268(t), Rhoda Sidney/PhotoEdit; Chapter Twelve: Page 275(t), SuperStock; 276(t), Paul Rees/Tony Stone Images; 278(t), M. Greenlar/The Image Works; 279(b), Michael Newman/PhotoEdit; 281(t), SuperStock; 282(t), United Media; 282(b), Michael Newman/PhotoEdit; 284(bckgd), HRW; 285(t), Zigy Kaluzny/Tony Stone Images; 286(t), Michael Newman/PhotoEdit; 288(t), SuperStock; 290(t), Tom McCarthy/ Photo Edit; 292(t), SuperStock; 293(t), Leslye Borden/PhotoEdit;

Unit Five: Page 297(b), Super Stock; Chapter Thirteen: Page 298(r) HRW/Michelle Bridwell; 301(t), SuperStock; 303(t), Eric R. Berndt/Unicorn Stock Photos; 304(t), Picture taken by J.A.F. Stevenson, a collaborator on the original study, but first published by Neal E. Miller in an article summarizing a number of studies from his laboratory.; 306(b), Bob Daemmrich/The Image Works; 307(b), Super Stock; 308(tl), Harlow Primate Laboratory, University of Wisconsin (Madison); 308(tr), James McLoughlin/FPG; 309(b), John Henley/The Stock Market; 311(b), Bob Daemmrich/Bob Daemmrich Photography; 314(t), SuperStock; 315(bl), M. Eastcott/The Image Works; 315(br), Michael Goldman/FPG; 315(bcl), David Frazier/David Frazier Photolibrary; 315(bcr), Comstock; Chapter Fourteen: Page 325(t),Reuters/Corbis-Bettmann; 327(b), Lawrence Migdale/Tony Stone Images; 329(t), Giraudon/Art Resource, NY; 330(tl), John Neubauer/PhotoEdit; 330(tr), Ben Simmons/The Stock Market; 334(t), SuperStock; 335(b), Rhoda Sidney/The Image Works; 337(b), Charles Gupton/The Stock Market; Chapter Fifteen: Page 345(t), Bonnie Kamin/PhotoEdit; 346(c), Super Stock; 347(t), Martha M Bride/Unicorn Stock Photos; 348(t), Laura Elliott/Comstock; 349(cl), SuperStock; 349(cr), Thomas Ives/The Stock Market; 349(bl), Bob Daemmrich/Bob Daemmrich Photography; 349(br), Ted Horowitz/The Stock Market; 350(t), SuperStock; 352(b), Bob Daemmrich/Bob Daemmrich Photography; 354(b), Reprinted by permission of the publishers from Henry A. Murray, THEMATIC APPERCEPTION TEST, Cambridge, Mass.: Harvard University Press, Copyright 1943 by the President and Fellows of Harvard College. Copyright ©1971 by Henry A. Murray. 355(t), Robert Brenner/PhotoEdit; 357(t), Comstock; 358(b), Bob Daemmrich/Bob Daemmrich Photography; 359(t), SuperStock; Chapter Sixteen: Page 365(tl), SuperStock; 365(tc), SuperStock; 365(tr), Tony Freeman/PhotoEdit; 366(b), Tony Freeman/PhotoEdit; 368(t), Tony Freeman/PhotoEdit; 370(tl), John Giffin/Image Works; 370(tcl), Fujifotos/The Image Works; 370/371(tcr), Super Stock; 371(tr), SuperStock; 374(t), Tony Freeman/Photo Edit; 376(b),

Elizabeth Zuckerman/PhotoEdit; 378(t), SuperStock; 378(b), D. Young-Wolff/Photo Edit; 379(t), Margret Mead Papers, Manuscript Divion, Library of Congress;

Unit Six: Page 383(br), Super Stock;
Chapter Seventeen: Page 387(b), Joes Pelaez/The Stock Market; 388(t), Michael Newman/PhotoEdit; 392(t), Jose L. Pelaez/The Stock Market; 392(b), The Stock Market; 393(t), Bob Daemmrich; 394(t), David Young-Wolff/PhotoEdit; 395(t), SuperStock; 397(t), Tony Freeman/PhotoEdit; 398(b), SuperStock; 400(c), Christian Michaels/FPG; 403(b), David Young-Wolff/PhotoEdit; 405(t), Michael Newman/PhotoEdit;
Chapter Eighteen: Page 410(t), Art Montes DeOcal/FPG; 412(c), UPI/Corbis-Bettmann; 416(t), Luis Rosendo/FPG; 417(b), Bob Dammrich/Image Works; 426(b), Derek Bayes/Tony Stone; 428(t), Monkmeyer/Grunnitus; 431(t), Ron Chapple/FPG;
Chapter Nineteen: Page 436(t), Zigy Kaluzny/Tony Stone; 439(t), David Harry Stewart/Tony Stone; 440(t), F. Pedrick/The Image Works; 442(t), Bruce Ayres/Tony Stone; 445(c) HRW/Michelle Bridwell; 448(t), Peter Steiner/The Stock Market; 449(t), Michael Newman/Photo Edit; 449(c), Michael Newman/Photo Edit; 449(b), Michael New man/Photo Edit; 453(t), Will & Deni McIntyre/Tony Stone;

Unit Seven: Page 457(br), composite, David Young- Wolff/ Photo Edit, © 1996 Daivd Eisenberg/ Development Center for Appropriate Technology/ Habitat for Humanity;
Chapter Twenty: Page 460(b), Myrleen Ferguson/Photo Edit; 461(t), Michael Newman/Photo Edit; 462(b), Paul Conklin/Photo Edit; 463(b), Stock Market; 464(t),Courtesy of Save The Children; 465(t), Reuters/Bettmann; 466(b), Michael Newman/Photo Edit; 467(c), Archive Photos; 473(bl), Art Wolfe/Tony Stone; 473(br), Bob Daemmrich/HRW; 473(bcl), Bill Wassman/The Stock Market; 473(bcr),Zviki- Eshet/The Stock Market; 474(t), Tony Freeman/Photo Edit; **Chapter Twenty-One:** Page 480(t),Chuck Savage/The Stock Market; 483(c), Archive Photos; 485(tl), Eastcott/The Image Bank; 485(tc), Stock Market ©1994 Latin Stock/Carlos Goldin/ Stock Market; 485(tr), David Young Wolff/Tony Stone Images; 487(t), Anthony Edgeworth/Stock Market; 488(t)(c)(b), From the film OBEDIENCE,© 1965 by Stanley Milgram, and distributed by PennState Media Sales. Permission granted by Alexandra Milgram; 489(b), R Hutchings/ Photo Edit; 490(b), Leanna Rathkelly/Tony Stone Images; 491(t), Glyn Kirk/Tony Stone; 494(t), Frank Siteman/Tony Stone; 495(b), Michael Newman/Photo Edit;

Careers: Page 508(t), SuperStock; 509(b), Michael Newman/Photo Edit; 510(b), Martha M. Bride/Unicorn Stock Photos; 511(t), Comstock; 512(t), Ariel Skelley/The Stock Market; 512(t), Glyn Kirk/Tony Stone; 513(t), Michael Schwarz/The Image Works; 514(b), SuperStock;